Managing NFS and NIS

Managing NFS and NIS

Second Edition

Hal Stern, Mike Eisler, and Ricardo Labiaga

O'REILLY®

Beijing · Cambridge · Farnham · Köln · Paris · Sebastopol · Taipei · Tokyo

Managing NFS and NIS, Second Edition
by Hal Stern, Mike Eisler, and Ricardo Labiaga

Copyright © 2001, 1991 O'Reilly & Associates, Inc. All rights reserved.
Printed in the United States of America.

Published by O'Reilly & Associates, Inc., 101 Morris Street, Sebastopol, CA 95472.

Editor: Mike Loukides

Production Editor: Nicole Arigo

Cover Designer: Edie Freedman

Printing History:

June 1991:	First Edition.
April 1992:	Minor corrections.
June 2001:	Second Edition.

Library of Congress Cataloging-in-Publication Data

Stern, Hal.
    NFS & NIS / Hal Stern, Mike Eisler & Ricardo Labiaga. -- 2nd ed.
      p. cm.
    Rev. ed. of: Managing NFS and NIS / Hal Stern. c1991.
    Includes index.
    ISBN 1-56592-510-6
    1. Network File System (Computer network protocol) 2. Computer networks. 3. UNIX
      (Computer file) I. Eisler, Mike. II. Labiaga, Ricardo. III. Stern, Hal. Managing NFS and
      NIS. IV. Title. V. Title: NFS and NIS.

TK5105.574.S74 2001
005.7'13--dc21   2001033094

ISBN: 1-56592-510-6
[DS]

Table of Contents

Preface

Twenty years ago, most computer centers had a few large computers shared by several hundred users. The "computing environment" was usually a room containing dozens of terminals. All users worked in the same place, with one set of disks, one user account information file, and one view of all resources. Today, local area networks have made terminal rooms much less common. Now, a "computing environment" almost always refers to distributed computing, where users have personal desktop machines, and shared resources are provided by special-purpose systems such as file, computer, and print servers. Each desktop requires redundant configuration files, including user information, network host addresses, and local and shared remote filesystem information.

A mechanism to provide consistent access to all files and configuration information ensures that all users have access to the "right" machines, and that once they have logged in they will see a set of files that is both familiar and complete. This consistency must be provided in a way that is transparent to the users; that is, a user should not know that a filesystem is located on a remote fileserver. The transparent view of resources must be consistent across all machines and also consistent with the way things work in a non-networked environment. In a networked computing environment, it's usually up to the system administrator to manage the machines on the network (including centralized servers) as well as the network itself. Managing the network means ensuring that the network is transparent to users rather than an impediment to their work.

The Network File System (NFS) and the Network Information Service (NIS)* provide mechanisms for solving "consistent and transparent" access problems. The

---

* NIS was formerly called the "Yellow Pages." While many commands and directory names retain the *yp* prefix, the formal name of the set of services has been changed to avoid conflicting with registered trademarks.

NFS and NIS protocols were developed by Sun Microsystems and are now licensed to hundreds of vendors and universities, not to mention dozens of implementations from the published NFS and NFS specifications. NIS centralizes commonly replicated configuration files, such as the password file, on a single host. It eliminates duplicate copies of user and system information and allows the system administrator to make changes from one place. NFS makes remote filesystems appear to be local, as if they were on disks attached to the local host. With NFS, all machines can share a single set of files, eliminating duplicate copies of files on different machines in the network. Using NFS and NIS together greatly simplifies the management of various combinations of machines, users, and filesystems.

NFS provides network and filesystem transparency because it hides the actual, physical location of the filesystem. A user's files could be on a local disk, on a shared disk on a fileserver, or even on a machine located across a wide-area network. As a user, you're most content when you see the same files on all machines. Just having the files available, though, doesn't mean that you can access them if your user information isn't correct. Missing or inconsistent user and group information will break Unix file permission checking. This is where NIS complements NFS, by adding consistency to the information used to build and describe the shared filesystems. A user can sit down in front of any workstation in his or her group that is running NIS and be reasonably assured that he or she can log in, find his or her home directory, and access tools such as compilers, window systems, and publishing packages. In addition to making life easier for the users, NFS and NIS simplify the tasks of system administrators, by centralizing the management of both configuration information and disk resources.

NFS can be used to create very complex filesystems, taking components from many different servers on the network. It is possible to overwhelm users by providing "everything everywhere," so simplicity should rule network design. Just as a database programmer constructs views of a database to present only the relevant fields to an application, the user community should see a logical collection of files, user account information, and system services from each viewpoint in the computing environment. Simplicity often satisfies the largest number of users, and it makes the system administrator's job easier.

Who this book is for

This book is of interest to system administrators and network managers who are installing or planning new NFS and NIS networks, or debugging and tuning existing networks and servers. It is also aimed at the network user who is interested in the mechanics that hold the network together.

We'll assume that you are familiar with the basics of Unix system administration and TCP/IP networking. Terms that are commonly misused or particular to a discussion will be defined as needed. Where appropriate, an explanation of a low-level phenomenon, such as Ethernet congestion will be provided if it is important to a more general discussion such as NFS performance on a congested network. Models for these phenomena will be drawn from everyday examples rather than their more rigorous mathematical and statistical roots.

This book focuses on the way NFS and NIS work, and how to use them to solve common problems in a distributed computing environment. Because Sun Microsystems developed and continues to innovate NFS and NIS, this book uses Sun's Solaris operating system as the frame of reference. Thus if you are administering NFS on non-Solaris systems, you should use this book in conjunction with your vendor's documentation, since utilities and their options will vary by implementation and release. This book explains what the configuration files and utilities do, and how their options affect performance and system administration issues. By walking through the steps comprising a complex operation or by detailing each step in the debugging process, we hope to shed light on techniques for effective management of distributed computing environments. There are very few absolute constraints or thresholds that are universally applicable, so we refrain from stating them. This book should help you to determine the fair utilization and performance constraints for your network.

Versions

This book is based on the Solaris 8 implementations of NFS and NIS. When used without a version number, "Solaris" refers to the Solaris 2.x, Solaris 7, and Solaris 8 operating systems and their derivatives (note that the next version of Solaris after Solaris 2.6 was Solaris 7; in the middle of the development process, Sun renamed Solaris 2.7 to Solaris 7). NFS- and NIS-related tools have changed significantly between Solaris 2.0 and Solaris 8, so while it is usually the case that an earlier version of Solaris supports a function we discuss, it is not infrequent that it will not. For example, early releases of Solaris 2.x did not even have true NIS support. For another, Sun has made profound enhancements to NFS with nearly every release of Solaris.

The Linux examples presented throughout the book were run on the Linux 2.2.14-5 kernel. Linux kernels currently implement NFS Version 2, although a patch is available that provides Version 3 support.

Organization

This book is divided into two sections. The first twelve chapters contain explanations of the implementation and operation of NFS and NIS. Chapters 13 through 18 cover advanced administrative and debugging techniques, performance analysis, and tuning. Building on the introductory material, the second section of the book delves into low-level details such as the effects of network partitioning hardware and the various steps in a remote procedure call. The material in this section is directly applicable to the ongoing maintenance and debugging of a network.

Here's the chapter-by-chapter breakdown:

- Chapter 1, *Networking Fundamentals*, provides an introduction to the underlying network protocols and services used by NFS and NIS.

- Chapter 2, *Introduction to Directory Services*, provides a survey of the popular directory services.

- Chapter 3, *Network Information Service Operation*, discusses the architecture of NIS and its operation on both NIS servers and NIS clients. The focus is on how to set up NIS and its implementation features that affect network planning and initial configuration.

- Chapter 4, *System Management Using NIS*, discusses operational aspects of NIS that are important to network administrators. This chapter explores common NIS administration techniques, including map management, setting up multiple NIS domains, and using NIS with domain name services.

- Chapter 5, *Living with Multiple Directory Servers*, explains the issues around using both NIS and the Directory Name Service (DNS) on the same network.

- Chapter 6, *System Administration Using the Network File System*, covers basic NFS operations, such as mounting and exporting filesystems.

- Chapter 7, *Network File System Design and Operation*, explains the architecture of NFS and the underlying virtual filesystem. It also discusses the implementation details that affect performance, such as file attributes and data caching.

- Chapter 8, *Diskless Clients*, is all about diskless clients. It also presents debugging techniques for clients that fail to boot successfully.

- Chapter 9, *The Automounter*, discusses the automounter, a powerful but sometimes confusing tool that integrates NIS administrative techniques and NFS filesystem management.

- Chapter 10, *PC/NFS Clients*, covers PC/NFS, a client-side implementation of NFS for Microsoft Windows machines.

- Chapter 11, *File Locking*, focuses on file locking and how it relates to NFS.

- Chapter 12, *Network Security*, explores network security. Issues such as restricting access to hosts and filesystems form the basis for this chapter. We'll also go into how to make NFS more secure, including a discussion of setting up NFS security that leverages encryption for stronger protection.

- Chapter 13, *Network Diagnostic and Administrative Tools*, describes the administrative and diagnostic tools that are applied to the network and its systems as a whole. This chapter concentrates on the network and on interactions between hosts on the network, instead of the per-machine issues presented in earlier chapters. Tools and techniques are described for analyzing each layer in the protocol stack, from the Ethernet to the NFS and NIS applications.

- Chapter 14, *NFS Diagnostic Tools*, focuses on tools used to diagnose NFS problems.

- Chapter 15, *Debugging Network Problems*, describes how to debug common network problems.

- Chapter 16, *Server-Side Performance Tuning*, discusses how to tune your NFS and, to a lesser extent, NIS servers.

- Chapter 17, *Network Performance Analysis*, covers performance tuning and analysis of machines and the network.

- Chapter 18, *Client-Side Performance Tuning*, explores NFS client tuning, including NFS mount parameter adjustments.

- Appendix A, *IP Packet Routing*, explains how IP packets are forwarded to other networks. It is additional background information for discussions of performance and network configuration.

- Appendix B, *NFS Problem Diagnosis*, summarizes NFS problem diagnosis using the NFS statistics utility and the error messages printed by clients experiencing NFS failures.

- Appendix C, *Tunable Parameters*, summarizes parameters for tuning NFS performance and other attributes.

Conventions used in this book

Font and format conventions for Unix commands, utilities, and system calls are:

- Excerpts from script or configuration files will be shown in a constant-width font:

  ```
  192.9.200.1   bitatron
  ```

- Sample interactive sessions, showing command-line input and corresponding output, will be shown in a constant-width font, with user-supplied input in bold:

  ```
  % ls
  foobar
  ```

- If the command can be typed by any user, the percent sign (%) will be shown as the prompt. If the command must be executed by the superuser, then the pound sign (#) will be shown as the prompt:

  ```
  # /usr/sbin/ypinint -m
  ```

- If a particular command must be typed on a particular machine, the prompt will include a hostname:

  ```
  bitatron# mount wahoo:/export /mnt
  ```

- Inside of an excerpt from a script, configuration file, or other ASCII file, the pound sign will be used to indicate the beginning of a comment (unless the configuration file requires a different comment character, such as an asterisk (*)):

  ```
  #
  #Hal's machine
  192.9.200.1   bitatron
  ```

- Unix commands and command lines are printed in italics when they appear in the body of a paragraph. For example, the *ls* command lists files in a directory.

- Hostnames are printed in italics. For example, server *wahoo* contains home directories.

- Filenames are printed in italics, for example, the */etc/passwd* file.

- NIS map names and mount options are printed in italics. The *passwd* map is used with the */etc/passwd* file, and the *timeo* mount option changes NFS client behavior.

- System and library calls are printed in italics, with parentheses to indicate that they are C routines. For example, the *gethostent( )* library call locates a hostname in an NIS map.

- Control characters will be shown with a CTRL prefix, for example, CTRL-Z.

Differences between the first edition and second edition

The first edition was based on SunOS 4.1, whereas this edition is based on Solaris 8. The second edition covers much more material, mostly due to the enhancements made to NFS, including a new version of NFS (Version 3), a new transport protocol for NFS (TCP/IP), new security options (IPsec and Kerberos V5), and also more tools to analyze your systems and network.

The second edition also drops or sharply reduces the following material from the first edition (all chapter numbers and titles are from the first edition):

- Chapter 4, *Building Applications with NIS*. Systems and networks are now bigger, faster, and more complicated. We believe the target reader will be more interested in administering NIS and NFS, rather than writing applications based on NIS.

- Chapter 9, *Centralizing Mail Services with NFS and NIS*. At the time the second edition was written, most people were accessing their electronic mail boxes using the POP or IMAP protocols. A chapter focused on using NFS to access mail would appeal but to a small minority.

- Chapter 14, *PC/NFS*. This chapter survives in the second edition, but it is much smaller. This is because there are more competing PC/NFS products available than before, and also because many people who want to share files between PCs and Unix servers run the open source *Samba* package on their Unix servers. Still, there are some edge conditions that justify PC/NFS, so we discuss those, as well as general PC/NFS issues.

- Appendix A, *Transmission Line Theory*. When this appendix was written, local area networks were much less reliable than they are today. The shift to better and standard technology, even low technology like Category 5 connector cables, has made a big difference. Thus, given the focus on software administration, there's not much practical use for presenting such material in this edition.

- Appendix D, *NFS Benchmarks*. The NFS Benchmark appendix in the first edition explained how to use the *nhfsstone* benchmark, and was relevant in the period of NFS history when there was no standard, industry-recognized benchmark. Since the first edition, the Standard Performance Evaluation Corporation (SPEC) has addressed the void with its SFS benchmark (sometimes referred to as LADDIS). The SFS benchmark provides a way for prospective buyers of an NFS server to compare it to others. Unfortunately, it's not practical for the target reader to build the complex test beds necessary to get good SFS benchmark numbers. A better alternative is to take advantage of the fact that SPEC lets anyone browse reported SFS results from its web site (*http://www.spec.org*).

Comments and questions

We have tested and verified all the information in this book to the best of our abilities, but you may find that features have changed or that we have let errors slip through the production of the book. Please let us know of any errors that you find, as well as suggestions for future editions, by writing to:

O'Reilly & Associates, Inc.
101 Morris St.
Sebastopol, CA 95472
(800) 998-9938 (in the U.S. or Canada)
(707) 829-0515 (international/local)
(707) 829-0104 (fax)

You can also send messages electronically. To be put on our mailing list or to request a catalog, send email to:

> *info@oreilly.com*

To ask technical questions or to comment on the book, send email to:

> *bookquestions@oreilly.com*

We have a web site for the book, where we'll list examples, errata, and any plans for future editions. You can access this page at:

> *http://www.oreilly.com/catalog/nfs2/*

For more information about this book and others, see the O'Reilly web site:

> *http://www.oreilly.com*

Hal's acknowledgments from the first edition

This book would not have been completed without the help of many people. I'd like to thank Brent Callaghan, Chuck Kollars, Neal Nuckolls, and Janice McLaughlin (all of Sun Microsystems); Kevin Sheehan (Kalli Consulting); Vicki Lewolt Schulman (Auspex Systems); and Dave Hitz (H&L Software) for their never-ending stream of answers to questions about issues large and small. Bill Melohn (Sun) provided the foundation for the discussion of computer viruses. The discussion of NFS performance tuning and network configuration is based on work done with Peter Galvin and Rick Sabourin at Brown University. Several of the examples of NIS and NFS configuration were taken from a system administrator's guide to NFS and NIS written by Mike Loukides for Multiflow Computer Company.

The finished manuscript was reviewed by: Chuck Kollars, Mike Marotta, Ed Milstein, and Brent Callaghan (Sun); Dave Hitz (H&L Software); Larry Rogers (Princeton University); Vicky Lewold Schulman (Auspex); Simson Garfinkel (NeXTWorld); and Mike Loukides and Tim O'Reilly (O'Reilly & Associates, Inc.). This book has benefited in many ways from their insights, comments, and corrections. The production group of O'Reilly & Associates also deserves my gratitude for applying the finishing touches to this book. I owe a tremendous thanks to Mike Loukides of O'Reilly & Associates who helped undo four years of liberal arts education and associated writing habits. It is much to Mike's credit that this book does not read like a treatise on Dostoevsky's *Crime and Punishment.**

---

* I think I will cause my freshman composition lecturer pain equal to the credit given to Mike, since she assured me that reading and writing about *Crime and Punishment* would prepare me for writing assignments the rest of my life. I have yet to see how, except possibly when I was exploring performance issues.

Acknowledgments for the second edition

Thanks to Pat Parseghian (Transmeta), Marc Staveley (Sun), and Mike Loukides (O'Reilly & Associates, Inc.) for their input to the outline of the second edition.

All the authors thank John Corbin, Evan Layton, Lin Ling, Dan McDonald, Shantanu Mehendale, Anay S. Panvalkar, Mohan Parthasarathy, Peter Staubach, and Marc Staveley (all of Sun); Carl Beame and Fred Whiteside (both of Hummingbird); Jeanette Arnhart; and Katherine A. Olsen, all for reviewing specific chapters and correcting many of our mistakes.

After we thought we were done writing, it fell to Brent Callaghan, David Robinson, and Spencer Shepler of Sun to apply their formidable expertise in NFS and NIS to make numerous corrections to the manuscript and many valuable suggestions on organization and content. Thank you gentlemen, and we hope you recognize that we have taken your input to heart.

Thanks to our editor, Mike Loukides, for giving us quick feedback on our chapters, as well as riding herd when we weren't on schedule.

Hal Stern's acknowledgments

More than a decade has gone by since the first edition of this book, during which I've moved three times and started a family. It was pretty clear to me that the state of networking in general, and NFS and NIS in particular, was moving much faster than I was, and the only way this second edition became possible was to hand over the reins. Mike Eisler and Ricardo Labiaga have done a superb job of bridging the technical eon since the first edition, and I thank them deeply for their patience and volumes of high-quality work. I also owe Mike Loukides the same kudos for his ability to guide this book into its current form. Finally, a huge hug, with ten years of interest, to my wife, Toby, who has been reminding me (at least weekly) that I left all mention of her out of the first edition. None of this would have been possible without her encouragement and support.

Mike Eisler's acknowledgments

First and foremost, I'm grateful for the opportunity Hal and Mike L. gave me to contribute to this edition.

I give thanks to my wife, Ruth, daughter, Kristin, and son, Kevin, for giving their husband and father the encouragement and space needed to complete this book.

I started on the second edition while working for Sun. Special thanks to my manager at the time, Cindy Vinores, for encouraging me to take on the responsibility for co-authoring this book. Thanks also to my successive managers at Sun, Karen

Spackman, David Brittle, and Cindy again, and to Emily Watts, my manager at Zambeel, Inc., for giving me the equipment, software, and most of all, time to write.

Ricardo Labiaga readily agreed to sign on to help write this book when several members of the second edition writing team had to back out, and thus took a big load off my shoulders.

This book was written using Adobe's Framemaker document editor. During the year 2000, Adobe made available to the world a free beta that ran on Linux. I thank Adobe for doing so, as it allowed me to make lots of progress while traveling on airliners.

Ricardo Labiaga's acknowledgments

Hal, Mike E., and Mike L., I have truly enjoyed working with you on this edition. Thank you; it's been an honor and a great experience.

I did most of the work on the second edition while working for the Solaris File Sharing Group at Sun Microsystems, Inc. I thank my manager at the time, Bev Crair, who enthusiastically encouraged me to sign up for the project and provided the resources to coauthor this edition. I also thank my successive managers at Sun, David Brittle and Penny Solin, for providing the necessary resources to complete the endeavor.

Words are not enough to thank my friends and colleagues at Sun and elsewhere, who answered many questions and provided much insight into the technologies. Special thanks to David Robinson for his technical and professional guidance throughout the years, as well as his invaluable feedback on the material presented in this book. Many thanks to Peter Staubach and Brent Callaghan for the time spent discussing what NFS should and should not do. Thanks to Mohan Parthasarathy and David Comay of Solaris Internet Engineering for answering my many questions about routing concepts. Thanks to Carl Williams and Sebastien Roy for their explanations of the IPv6 protocol. Thanks to Jim Mauro and Richard McDougall for providing the original Solaris priority paging information presented in Chapter 17. Thanks to Jeff Mogul of Compaq for his review of the NFSWATCH material, and Narendra Chaparala for introducing me to *ethereal*.

I wish to thank Dr. David H. Williams of The University of Texas at El Paso, for providing me the opportunity to work as a system administrator in the Unix lab, where I had my first encounter with Unix and networking twelve years ago. I thank my parents from the bottom of my heart, for their encouragement throughout the years, and for their many sacrifices that made my education possible.

My deepest gratitude goes to my wife, Kara, for her encouragement, understanding, and awesome support throughout the writing of this book. Thank you for putting up with my late hours, work weekends, and late dinner dates.

1

Networking
Fundamentals

The Network Information Service (NIS) and Network File System (NFS) are services that allow you to build distributed computing systems that are both consistent in their appearance and transparent in the way files and data are shared.

NIS provides a distributed database system for common configuration files. NIS servers manage copies of the database files, and NIS clients request information from the servers instead of using their own, local copies of these files. For example, the */etc/hosts* file is managed by NIS. A few NIS servers manage copies of the information in the *hosts* file, and all NIS clients ask these servers for host address information instead of looking in their own */etc/hosts* file. Once NIS is running, it is no longer necessary to manage every */etc/hosts* file on every machine in the network—simply updating the NIS servers ensures that all machines will be able to retrieve the new configuraton file information.

NFS is a distributed filesystem. An NFS server has one or more filesystems that are mounted by NFS clients; to the NFS clients, the remote disks look like local disks. NFS filesystems are mounted using the standard Unix *mount* command, and all Unix utilities work just as well with NFS-mounted files as they do with files on local disks. NFS makes system administration easier because it eliminates the need to maintain multiple copies of files on several machines: all NFS clients share a single copy of the file on the NFS server. NFS also makes life easier for users: instead of logging on to many different systems and moving files from one system to another, a user can stay on one system and access all the files that he or she needs within one consistent file tree.

This book contains detailed descriptions of these services, including configuration information, network design and planning considerations, and debugging, tuning, and analysis tips. If you are going to be installing a new network, expanding or fixing an existing network, or looking for mechanisms to manage data in a distributed environment, you should find this book helpful.

Many people consider NFS to be the heart of a distributed computing environment, because it manages the resource users are most concerned about: their files. However, a distributed filesystem such as NFS will not function properly if hosts cannot agree on configuration information such as usernames and host addresses. The primary function of NIS is managing configuration information and making it consistent on all machines in the network. NIS provides the framework in which to use NFS. Once the framework is in place, you add users and their files into it, knowing that essential configuration information is available to every host. Therefore, we will look at directory services and NIS first (in Chapters 2 through 4); we'll follow that with a discussion of NFS in Chapters 5 through 13.

Networking overview

Before discussing either NFS, or NIS, we'll provide a brief overview of network services.

NFS and NIS are high-level networking protocols, built on several lower-level protocols. In order to understand the way the high-level protocols function, you need to know how the underlying services work. The lower-level network protocols are quite complex, and several books have been written about them without even touching on NFS and NIS services. Therefore, this chapter contains only a brief outline of the network services used by NFS and NIS.

Network protocols are typically described in terms of a layered model, in which the protocols are "stacked" on top of each other. Data coming into a machine is passed from the lowest-level protocol up to the highest, and data sent to other hosts moves down the protocol stack. The layered model is a useful description because it allows network services to be defined in terms of their functions, rather than their specific implementations. New protocols can be substituted at lower levels without affecting the higher-level protocols, as long as these new protocols behave in the same manner as those that were replaced.

The standard model for networking protocols and distributed applications is the International Organization for Standardization (ISO) seven-layer model shown in Table 1-1.

Table 1-1. The ISO seven-layer model

Layer	Name	Physical Layer
7	Application	NFS and NIS
6	Presentation	XDR

Table 1-1. The ISO seven-layer model (continued)

Layer	Name	Physical Layer
5	Session	RPC
4	Transport	TCP or UDP
3	Network	IP
2	Data Link	Ethernet
1	Physical	CAT-5

Purists will note that the TCP/IP protocols do not precisely fit the specifications for the services in the ISO model. The functions performed by each layer, however, correspond very closely to the functions of each part of the TCP/IP protocol suite, and provide a good framework for visualizing how the various protocols fit together.

The lower levels have a well-defined job to do, and the higher levels rely on them to perform it independently of the particular medium or implementation. While TCP/IP most frequently is run over Ethernet, it can also be used with a synchronous serial line or fiber optic network. Different implementations of the first two network layers are used, but the higher-level protocols are unchanged. Consider an NFS server that uses all six lower protocol layers: it has no knowledge of the physical cabling connecting it to its clients. The server just worries about its NFS protocols and counts on the lower layers to do their job as well.

Throughout this book, the *network stack* or *protocol stack* refers to this layering of services. *Layer* or *level* will refer to one specific part of the stack and its relationship to its upper and lower neighbors. Understanding the basic structure of the network services on which NFS and NIS are built is essential for designing and configuring large networks, as well as debugging problems. A failure or overly tight constraint in a lower-level protocol affects the operation of all protocols above it. If the physical network cannot handle the load placed on it by all of the desktop workstations and servers, then NFS and NIS will not function properly. Even though NFS or NIS will appear "broken," the real issue is with a lower level in the network stack.

The following sections briefly describe the function of each layer and the mapping of NFS and NIS into them. Many books have been written about the ISO seven-layer model, TCP/IP, and Ethernet, so their treatment here is intentionally light. If you find this discussion of networking fundamentals too basic, feel free to skip over this chapter.

Physical and data link layers

The physical and data link layers of the network protocol stack together define a machine's *network interface*. From a software perspective, the network interface defines how the Ethernet device driver gets packets from or to the network. The physical layer describes the way data is actually transmitted on the network medium. The data link layer defines how these streams of bits are put together into manageable chunks of data.

Ethernet is the best known implementation of the physical and data link layers. The Ethernet specification describes how bits are encoded on the cable and also how stations on the network detect the beginning and end of a transmission. We'll stick to Ethernet topics throughout this discussion, since it is the most popular network medium in networks using NFS and NIS.

Ethernet can be run over a variety of media, including thinnet, thicknet, unshielded twisted-pair (UTP) cables, and fiber optics. All Ethernet media are functionally equivalent—they differ only in terms of their convenience, cost of installation, and maintenance. Converters from one media to another operate at the physical layer, making a clean electrical connection between two different kinds of cable. Unless you have access to high-speed test equipment, the physical and data link layers are not that interesting when they are functioning normally. However, failures in them can have strange, intermittent effects on NFS and NIS operation. Some examples of these spectacular failures are given in Chapter 15.

Frames and network interfaces

The data link layer defines the format of data on the network. A series of bits, with a definite beginning and end, constitutes a network *frame*, commonly called a *packet*. A proper data link layer packet has checksum and network-specific addressing information in it so that each host on the network can recognize it as a valid (or invalid) frame and determine if the packet is addressed to it. The largest packet that can be sent through the data link layer defines the *Maximum Transmission Unit*, or MTU, of the network.

All hosts have at least one network interface, although any host connected to an Ethernet has at least two: the *Ethernet interface* and the *loopback interface*. The Ethernet interface handles the physical and logical connection to the outside world, while the loopback interface allows a host to send packets to itself. If a packet's destination is the local host, the data link layer chooses to "send" it via the loopback, rather than Ethernet, interface. The loopback device simply turns the packet around and queues it at the bottom of the protocol stack as if it were just received from the Ethernet.

You may find it helpful to think of the protocol layers as passing packets upstream and downstream in envelopes, where the packet envelope contains some pro- tocol-specific header information but hides the remainder of the packet contents. As data messages are passed from the top most protocol layer down to the phys- ical layer, the messages are put into envelopes of increasing size. Each layer takes the entire message and envelope from the layer above and adds its own informa- tion, creating a new message that is slightly larger than the original. When a packet is received, the data link layer strips off its envelope and passes the result up to the network layer, which similarly removes its header information from the packet and passes it up the stack again.

Ethernet addresses

Associated with the data link layer is a method for addressing hosts on the net- work. Every machine on an Ethernet has a unique, 48-bit address called its *Ethernet* or *Media Access Control (MAC) address*. Vendors making network-ready equipment ensure that every machine in the world has a unique MAC address. 24- bit prefixes for MAC addresses are assigned to hardware vendors, and each vendor is responsible for the uniqueness of the lower 24 bits. MAC addresses are usually represented as colon-separated pairs of hex digits:

        8:0:20:ae:6:1f

Note that MAC addresses identify a *host*, and a host with multiple network inter- faces may use the same MAC address on each.

Part of the data link layer's protocol-specific header are the packet's source and destination MAC addresses. Each protocol layer supports the notion of a *broad- cast*, which is a packet or set of packets that must be sent to all hosts on the net- work. The broadcast MAC address is:

        ff:ff:ff:ff:ff:ff

All network interfaces recognize this wildcard MAC address as a broadcast address, and pass the packet up to a higher-level protocol handler.

Network layer

At the data link layer, things are fairly simple. Machines agree on the format of packets and a standard 48-bit host addressing scheme. However, the packet format and encoding vary with different physical layers: Ethernet has one set of character- istics, while an X.25-based satellite network has another. Because there are many physical networks, there should ideally be a standard interface scheme so that it isn't necessary to re-implement protocols on top of each physical network and its peculiar interfaces. This is where the network layer fits in. The higher-level proto- cols, such as TCP (at the transport layer), don't need to know any details about the physical network that is in use. As mentioned before, TCP runs over Ethernet, fiber optic network, or other media; the TCP protocols don't care about the physical connection because it is represented by a well-defined network layer interface.

The network layer protocol of primary interest to NFS and NIS is the Internet Protocol, or IP. As its name implies, IP is responsible for getting packets between hosts on one or more networks. Its job is to make a best effort to get the data from point A to point B. IP makes no guarantees about getting all of the data to the destination, or the order in which the data arrives—these details are left for higher-level protocols to worry about.

On a local area network, IP has a fairly simple job, since it just moves packets from a higher-level protocol down to the data link layer. In a set of connected networks, however, IP is responsible for determining how to get data from its source to the correct destination network. The process of directing datagrams to another network is called *routing*; it is one of the primary functions of the IP protocol. Appendix A contains a detailed description of how IP performs routing.

Datagrams and packets

IP deals with data in chunks called *datagrams*. The terms packet and datagram are often used interchangeably, although a packet is a data link-layer object and a datagram is network layer object. In many cases, particularly when using IP on Ethernet, a datagram and packet refer to the same chunk of data. There's no guarantee that the physical link layer can handle a packet of the network layer's size. As previously mentioned, the largest packet that can be handled by the physical link layer is called the Maximum Transmission Unit, or MTU, of the network media. If the medium's MTU is smaller than the network's packet size, then the network layer has to break large datagrams down into packet-sized chunks that the data link and physical layers can digest. This process is called *fragmentation*. The host receiving a fragmented datagram reassembles the pieces in the correct order. For example, an X.25 network may have an MTU as small as 128 bytes, so a 1518-byte IP datagram would have to be fragmented into many smaller network packets to be sent over the X.25 link. For the scope of this book, we'll use packet to describe both the IP and the data link-layer objects, since NFS is most commonly run on Ethernet rather than over wide-area networks with smaller MTUs. However, the distinction will be made when necessary, such as when discussing NFS traffic over a wide area point-to-point link.

IP host addresses

The internet protocol identifies hosts with a number called an *IP address* or a *host address*. To avoid confusion with MAC addresses (which are machine or *station* addresses), the term IP address will be used to designate this kind of address. IP addresses come in two flavors: 32-bit IP Version 4 (IPv4) or 128 bit IPv6 address. We will talk about IPv6 addresses later in this chapter. For now, we will focus on IPv4 addresses. IPv4 addresses are written as four dot-separated decimal numbers between 0–255 (a dotted quad):

```
192.9.200.1
```

IP addresses must be unique among all connected machines. Connected machines in this case are any hosts that you can get to over a network or connected set of networks, including your local area network, remote offices joined by the company's wide-area network, or even the entire Internet community. For a standalone system or a small office that is not connected (via an IP network) to the outside world, you can use the standard, private network addresses assigned such purposes. See the section "IPv4 address classes" later in this chapter. If your network is connected to the Internet, you have to get a range of IP addresses assigned to your machines through a central network administration authority, via your Internet Service Provider. If you are planning on joining the Internet in the future, you will need to obtain an address from your network service provider. This may be either an actual provider of Internet service, or your own organization, if it has addresses to hand out. We won't go into this further in this book.

The IP address uniqueness requirement differs from that for MAC addresses. IP addresses are unique only on connected networks, but machine MAC addresses are unique in the world, independent of any connectivity. Part of the reason for the difference in the uniqueness requirement is that IPv4 addresses are 32 bits, while MAC addresses are 48 bits, so mapping every possible MAC address into an IPv4 address requires some overlap. There are a variety of reasons why the IPv4 address is only 32 bits, while the MAC address is 48 bits, most of which are historical.

Since the network and data link layers use different addressing schemes, some system is needed to convert or map the IP addresses to MAC addresses. Transport-layer services and user processes use IP addresses to identify hosts, but packets that go out on the network need MAC addresses. The Address Resolution Protocol (ARP) is used to convert the 32-bit IPv4 address of a host into its 48-bit MAC address. When a host wants to map an IP address to a MAC address, it broadcasts an ARP request on the network, asking for the host using the IP address to respond. The host that sees its own IP address in the request returns its MAC address to the sender. With a MAC address, the sending host can transmit a packet on the Ethernet and know that the receiving host will recognize it.

A host can have more than one IP address. Usually this is because the host is connected to multiple physical network segments (requiring one network interface, such as an Ethernet controller, per segment), or because the host has multiple interfaces to the same physical network segment.

IPv4 address classes

Each IPv4 address has a *network number* and a *host number*. The host number identifies a particular machine on an organization's network. IP addresses are divided into *classes* that determine which parts of the address make up the network and host numbers, as demonstrated in Table 1-2.

Table 1-2. IPv4 address classes

Address Class and First Octet Value	Network Number Octets	Host Number Octets	Address Form	Number of Networks	Number of Hosts per Network	Maximum Number of Hosts per Class
Class A: 1-126	1	3	N.H.H.H	126	$256^3 - 2$	2,113,928,964
Class B: 128-191	2	2	N.N.H.H	16,384	$256^2 - 2$	1,073,709,056
Class C: 192-223	3	1	N.N.N.H	2,097,152	254	532,676,608
Class D: 224-239	N/A	N/A	M.M.M.M	N/A	N/A	N/A
Class E: 240-255	N/A	N/A	R.R.R.R	N/A	N/A	N/A

Each *N* represents part of the network number and each *H* is part of the address's host number. The 8-bit octet has 256 possible values, but 0 and 255 in the last host octet are reserved for forming broadcast addresses.

Network numbers with first octet values of 240–254 are reserved for future use. The network numbers 0, 127, 255, 10, 172.16–172.31, and 192.168.0–192.168.255 are also reserved:

- 0 is used as a place holder in forming a network number, and in some cases, for IP broadcast addresses.

- 127 is for a host's loopback interface.

- 255 is used for IPv4 broadcast addresses.

- 10, 172.16–172.31, and 192.168.0–192.168.255 are used for private networks that will never be connected to the global Internet.

Note that there are only 126 class A network numbers, but well over two million class C network numbers. When the Internet was founded, it was almost impossible to get a class A network number, and few organizations (aside from entire networks or countries) had enough hosts to justify a class A address. Most companies and universities requested class B or class C addresses. A medium-sized company, with several hundred machines, could request several class C network numbers, putting up to 254 hosts on each network. Now that the Internet is much bigger, the rules for class A, B, and C network number assignment have changed, as explained in the section "Classless IP addressing."

Class D addresses look similar to the other classes in that each address consists of 4 octets with a value no higher than 255 per octet. Unlike classes A, B, and C, a class D address does not have a network number and host number. Class D addresses are multicast addresses, which are used to send messages to more than one recipient host, whereas IP addresses in classes A, B, and C are unicast addresses destined for one recipient. Multicast on the Internet offers plenty of potential for efficient broadcast of information, such as bulk file transfers, audio and video, and stock pricing information, but has achieved limited deployment. There is an ongoing experiment known as the "MBONE" (Multicast backBONE) on the Internet to exploit this technology.

Class E addresses are reserved for future assignment.

Classless IP addressing

In the early 1990s, due to the advent of the World Wide Web, the Internet's growth exploded. In theory, if you sum the maximum number of hosts per classes A, B, and C (refer back to Table 1-2), the Internet can have a potential for over 3.7 billion hosts. In reality, the Internet was running out of address capacity for two reasons.

The first had to do with the inefficiencies built into the class partitioning. About 3.2 billion of the theoretical number of hosts were class A and class B, leaving about 500 million class C addresses. Most organizations did not need class A or class B addresses, and of those that did, a significant fraction of their assigned address space was not needed. Most users could get by with a class C network number, but the typical small business or home user did not need 254 hosts. Thus, the number of class C addresses was bounded by the maximum number of class C networks, about two million, which is far less than the number of users on the Internet.

The problem of only two million class C networks was mitigated by the introduction of dynamically assigned IP addresses, and by the introduction of policies that tended to assign IP network numbers only to Internet Service Providers (ISPs), or to organizations that effectively acted as their own ISP, which would then use the free market to efficiently reallocate the IP addresses dynamically or statically to their customers. Thus most Intenet users get assigned a single IP address, and the ISP is assigned the corresponding network number.

The second reason was routing scalability. When the Internet was orders of magnitude smaller then it is today, most address assignments were for class A or B and so routing between networks was straightforward. The routers simply looked at the network number, and sent it to a router responsible for that route. With the explosion of the Internet, and with most of that growth in class C network numbers, each network's router might have to maintain tables of hundreds of thousands of routes. As the Internet grew rapidly, keeping these tables up to date was difficult.

This situation was not sustainable, and so the concept of "classless addressing" was introduced. With the exception of grandfathered address assignments, each IP address, regardless of whether it's class A, B, or C, would not have an implicit network number part and host number part. Instead the network part would be designated explicitly via a suffix of the form: "/XX", where XX is the number of bits of the IP address that refer to the network. Those organizations that needed more than the 254 hosts that a class C address would provide, would instead be assigned consecutive class C addresses. For example, an ISP that was assigned 192.1.2 and 192.1.3 could have a classless network number of 192.1.3.0/23. Any router on a network other than 192.1.2 or 192.1.3 that wanted to send to either network number would instead route to a single router associated with the classless network number 192.1.3.0/23 (i.e., any IP address that had its first 23 bits equal to 1100 0000 0000 0001 0000 001).

With this new scheme, larger organizations get more consecutive class C network numbers. Within their local networks ("Intranets"), they can either use traditional class-based routing or classless routing that further subdivides the local network address space that can be used. The largest organizations may find that class-based routing doesn't scale, and so classless routing is the best approach.

Virtual interfaces

In the section "IP host addresses," we noted that a host could have multiple IP addresses assigned to it if it had multiple physical network interfaces. It is possible for a physical network segment to support more than one IP network number. For example, a segment might have 128.0.0.0/16 and 192.4.5.6/24. Some hosts on that segment might want to directly address hosts with either network number. Some operating systems, such as Solaris, will let you define multiple virtual or logical interfaces for a physical network interface. On most Unix systems, the *ifconfig* command is used to set up interfaces. See your vendor's *ifconfig* manual page for more details.

IP Version 6

Until now we have been discussing IPv4 addresses that are four octets long. The discussion in the "Classless IP addressing" section showed a clever way to extend the life of the 32 bit IPv4 address space. However, it was recognized long ago, even before the introduction of the World Wide Web, that the IPv4 address space was under pressure. IP Version 6 (IPv6) has been defined to solve the address space limitations by increasing the address length to 128 bit addresses. At the time of this writing, while most installed systems either do not support it or do not use it, most marketed systems support IPv6. Since it seems inevitable that you'll encounter some IPv6 networks in the next few years, we will explain some of the basics of IPv6. Note that IPv6 is sometimes referred to as IPng: IP Next Generation.

Instead of dotted quads, IPv6 addresses are usually expressed as:

```
x:x:x:x:x:x:x:x
```

where each *x* is a 16 bit hexadecimal value. In environments where a network is transitioning from IP Version 4 to Version 6, you might want to use a form like:

```
x:x:x:x:x:x:d.d.d.d
```

where d.d.d.d represents an IP Version 4 dotted quad.

When there are one or more consecutive sequences of *x's* such that each *x* is all zeroes, the sequence can be replaced with "::", but there can be only one such "::" abbreviation in an IPv6 address. Thus:

```
1234:0000:5678:9ABC:DEF0:1234:5678:9ABC
3:0:0:0:0:0:3333:4444
```

can be abbreviated as:

```
1234::5678:9ABC:DEF0:1234:5678:9ABC
3::3333:4444
```

As you might expect, IPv6 dispenses with address classes for unicast addresses. You specify classless network numbers (address prefixes), using the same classless addressing notation that IP Version 4 uses.

IP Version 6 address pools

While the designation of the network number in IPv6 is classless, the 128-bit address is still carved up into various pools. Portions of the address space are allocated for:

- Reserved or unassigned for future purposes
- Open Systems Interconnection (OSI) network protocols
- Novell IPX protocols
- Unicast addresses, including:
  - global unicast addresses that can be used to send packets to hosts outside the local site

- — site local unicast addresses than can be used to send packets only to hosts within a site

- — link local unicast addresses that can used to send packets only to hosts within a physical network segment

- Multicast addresses, which start with FF

- Addresses of nodes that support just IP Version 4. These are denoted as:

      ::FFFF:d.d.d.d

- Addresses of nodes that support IPv6, but want to use existing IP Version 4 infrastructure to encapsulate IPv6 packets within IPv4 packets for transport between networks. The last 32 bits of these addresses correspond to IPv4 addresses. These addresses are denoted as:

      ::d.d.d.d

  While this scheme does not let you benefit from IPv6's extended addressing, it does let you take advantage of IPv6's other features (such as a richer set of protocol options) while transitioning from IPv4.

IP Version 6 loopback address

Instead of dedicating about 16 million addresses for loopback interfaces as IPv4 does, IPv6 uses just one address for that purpose:

    ::1

IP Version 6 unspecified address

IPv6 introduces the concept of an "unspecified" address, which is all zeroes:

    ::0

This address can be used by hosts that don't know their own address, but need to generate queries to determine their address assignment. Such hosts would use "::0" as the source address in an IPv6 packet.

Transport layer

The transport layer has two major jobs: it must subdivide user-sized data buffers into network layer-sized datagrams, and it must enforce any desired transmission control such as reliable delivery. Two transport protocols that sit on top of IP are the Transmission Control Protocol (TCP) and the User Datagram Protocol (UDP), which offer different delivery guarantees.

TCP and UDP

TCP is best known as the first half of TCP/IP; as discussed in this and the preceding sections, the acronyms refer to two distinct services. TCP provides reliable, sequenced delivery of packets. It is ideally suited for connection-oriented communication, such as a remote login or a file transfer. Missing packets during a login session is both frustrating and dangerous—what happens if *rm *.o* gets truncated to *rm **? TCP-based services are generally geared toward long-lived network connections, and TCP is used in any case when ordered datagram delivery is a requirement. There is overhead in TCP for keeping track of packet delivery order and the parts of the data stream that must be resent. This is *state* information. It's not part of the data stream, but rather describes the state of the connection and the data transfer. Maintaining this information for each connection makes TCP an inherently *stateful* protocol. Because there is state, TCP can adapt its data flow rate when the network is congested.

UDP is a no-frills transport protocol: it sends large datagrams to a remote host, but it makes no assurances about their delivery or the order in which they are delivered. UDP is best for connectionless communication on local area networks in which no context is needed to send packets to a remote host and there is no concern about congestion. Broadcast oriented services use UDP, as do those in which repeated, out of sequence, or missed requests have no harmful side effects.

Reliable and unreliable delivery is the primary distinction between TCP and UDP. TCP will always try to replace a packet that gets lost on the network, but UDP does not. UDP packets can arrive in any order. If there is a network bottleneck that drops packets, UDP packets may not arrive at all. It's up to the application built on UDP to determine that a packet was lost, and to resend it if necessary. The state maintained by TCP has a fixed cost associated with it, making UDP a faster protocol on low-latency, high-bandwidth links. The price paid for speed (in UDP) is unreliability and added complexity to the higher level applications that must handle lost packets.

Port numbers

A host may have many TCP and UDP connections at any time. Connections to a host are distinguished by a *port number*, which serves as a sort of mailbox number for incoming datagrams. There may be many processes using TCP and UDP on a single machine, and the port numbers distinguish these processes for incoming packets. When a user program opens a TCP or UDP socket, it gets connected to a port on the local host. The application may specify the port, usually when trying to reach some service with a well-defined port number, or it may allow the operating system to fill in the port number with the next available free port number.

When a packet is received and passed to the TCP or UDP handler, it gets directed to the interested user process on the basis of the destination port number in the packet. The quadruple of:

```
source IP address, source port, destination IP address, destination port
```

uniquely identifies every interhost connection in the network. While many processes may be talking to the process that handles remote login requests (therefore their packets have the same destination IP addresses and port numbers), they will have unique pairs of source IP addresses and port numbers. The destination port number determines which of the many processes using TCP or UDP gets the data.

On most Unix systems port numbers below 1024 are reserved for the processes executing with superuser privileges, while ports 1024 and above may be used by any user. This enforces some measure of security by preventing random user applications from accessing ports used by servers. However, given that most nodes on the network don't run Unix, this measure of security is very questionable.

The session and presentation layers

The session and presentation layers define the creation and lifetime of network connections and the format of data sent over these connections. Sessions may be built on top of any supported transport protocol—login sessions use TCP, while services that broadcast information about the local host use UDP. The session protocol used by NFS and NIS is the Remote Procedure Call (RPC).

The client-server model

RPC provides a mechanism for one host to make a procedure call that appears to be part of the local process but is really executed on another machine on the network. Typically, the host on which the procedure call is executed has resources that are not available on the calling host. This distribution of computing services imposes a client/server relationship on the two hosts: the host owning the resource is a server for that resource, and the calling host becomes a client of the server when it needs access to the resource. The resource might be a centralized configuration file (NIS) or a shared filesystem (NFS).

Instead of executing the procedure on the local host, the RPC system bundles up the arguments passed to the procedure into a network datagram. The exact bundling method is determined by the presentation layer, described in the next section. The RPC client creates a session by locating the appropriate server and sending the datagram to a process on the server that can execute the RPC; see Figure 1-1. On the server, the arguments are unpacked, the server executes the result, packages the result (if any), and sends it back to the client. Back on the client side, the reply is converted into a return value for the procedure call, and the user application is re-entered as if a local procedure call had completed. This is the end of the "session," as defined in the ISO model.

RPC services may be built on either TCP or UDP transports, although most are UDP-oriented because they are centered around short-lived requests. Using UDP

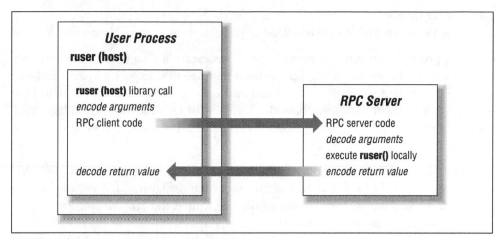

Figure 1-1. Remote procedure call execution

also forces the RPC call to contain enough context information for its execution independent of any other RPC requests, since UDP packets may arrive in any order, if at all.

When an RPC call is made, the client may specify a timeout period in which the call must complete. If the server is overloaded or has crashed, or if the request is lost in transit to the server, the remote call may not be executed before the timeout period expires. The action taken upon an RPC timeout varies by application; some resend the RPC call, while others may look for another server. Detailed mechanics of making an RPC call can be found in Chapter 13.

External data representation

At first look, the data presentation layer seems like overkill. Data is data, and if the client and server processes were written to the same specification, they should agree on the format of the data—so why bother with a presentation protocol? While a presentation layer may not be needed in a purely homogeneous network, it is required in a heterogeneous network to unify differences in data representation. These differences are outlined in the following list:

Data byte ordering
Does the most significant byte of an integer go in the odd- or even-numbered byte?

Compiler behavior
Do odd-sized quantities get padded out to even-byte boundaries? How are unions handled?

Floating point numbers
What standard is used for encoding floating point numbers?

Arrays and strings

How do you transmit variable-sized objects, such as arrays and strings?

Again, a presentation protocol would not be necessary if datagrams consisted only of byte-oriented data. However, applications that use RPC expect a system call-like interface, including support for structures and data types more complex than byte streams. The presentation layer provides services for encoding and decoding argument buffers that may then be passed down to RPC for transmission to the client or server.

The External Data Representation (XDR) protocol was developed by Sun Microsystems and is used by NIS and NFS at the presentation layer. XDR is built on the notion of an immutable network byte ordering, called the *canonical form*. It isn't really important what the canonical form is—your system may or may not use the same byte ordering and structure packing conventions. The canonical form simply allows network hosts to exchange structured data (as opposed to streams of bytes) independently of any peculiarities of a particular machine. All data structures are converted into the network byte ordering and padded appropriately.

The rule of XDR is "sender makes local canonical; receiver makes canonical local." Any data that goes over the network is in canonical form.* A host sending data on the network converts it to canonical form, and the host that receives the data converts it back into its local representation. A different way to implement the presentation layer might be "receiver makes local." In this case, the sender does nothing to the local data, and the receiver must deduce the packing and encoding technique and convert it into the local equivalent. While this scheme may send less data over the network—since it is not subject to additional padding—it places the burden of incorporating a new hardware architecture on the receiving side, rather than on the new machine. This doesn't seem like a major distinction, but consider having to change all existing, fielded software to handle the new machine's structure-packing conventions. It's usually worth the overhead of converting to and from canonical form to ensure that all new machines will be able to "plug in" to the network without any software changes.

The XDR and RPC layers complete the foundation necessary for a client/server distributed computing relationship. NFS and NIS are client/server applications, which means they sit at the top layer of the protocol stack and use the XDR and RPC services. To complete this introduction to network services, we'll take a look at the two mechanisms used to start and maintain servers for various network services.

---

* The canonical form matches the byte ordering of the Motorola and SPARC family of microprocessors, so these processors do not have to perform any byte swapping to translate to or from canonical form. This byte ordering is called Big Endian. Big Endian ordering is used for many Internet protocols.

Internet and RPC server configuration

The XDR and RPC services are useful for applications that need to exchange data structures over the network. Each new RPC request contains all required information in its XDR-encoded arguments, just as a local procedure call gets its inputs from passed-in arguments. RPC services are usually *connectionless* services because RPC requests do not require the creation of a long-lived network connection between the client and server. The client communicates with the server to send its request and receive a reply, but there is no connection or environment for the communication.

There are many other network services, such as *telnet* and *ftp*, that are commonly referred to as the Internet or ARPA services. They are part of the original suite of utilities designed for use on the Internet. Internet services are generally based on the TCP protocol and are *connection-oriented*—the service client establishes a connection to a server, and data is then exchanged in the form of a well-ordered byte stream. There is no need for RPC or XDR services, since the data is byte-oriented, and the service defines its own protocols for handling the data stream. The *telnet* service, for example, has its own protocol for querying the server about end-of-line, terminal type, and flow control conventions.

Note that RPC services are not required to be connectionless. RPC can be run over TCP, in a connection-oriented fashion. The TCP transport protocol may be used with RPC services whenever a large amount of data needs to be transferred. NIS, for example, uses UDP (in connectionless mode) for most of its operations, but switches to TCP whenever it needs to transfer an entire database from one machine to another. NFS supports either TCP or UDP for all its operations.

Most Internet services are managed by a super-daemon called *inetd* that accepts requests for connections to servers and starts instances of those servers on an as-needed basis. Rather than having many server processes, or *daemons*, running on each host, *inetd* starts them as requests arrive. Clients contact the *inetd* daemon on well-known port numbers for each service. These port numbers are published in the */etc/services* file.

inetd sets up a one-to-one relationship between service clients and server-side daemons. Every *rlogin* shell, for example, has a client side *rlogin* process (that calls *inetd* upon invocation) and a server-side *in.rlogind* daemon that was started by *inetd*. In this regard, *inetd* and the services it supports are *multi-threaded*: they can service multiple clients at the same time, creating a new separate connection (and state information) for each client. A new server instance, or thread, is initiated by each request for that service, but a single daemon handles all incoming requests at once.

Only traffic specific to a single session moves over the connection between a client and its server. When the client is done with the service, it asks the server to terminate its connection, and the server daemon cleans up and exits. If the server prematurely ends the connection due to a crash, for example, the client drops its end of the connection as well.

Some RPC services can't afford the overhead of using *inetd*. The standard *inetd*-based services, like *telnet*, tend to be used for a long time, so the cost of talking to *inetd* and having it start a new server process is spread out over the lifetime of the connection. Many RPC calls are short in duration, lasting at most the time required to perform a disk operation.

RPC servers are generally started during the boot process and run as long as the machine is up. While the time required to start a new server process may be small compared to the time a remote login or *rsh* session exists, this overhead is simply too large for efficient RPC operation. As a result, RPC servers typically have one server process for the RPC service, and it executes remote requests for all clients in the same process. Some RPC servers are single-threaded: they execute requests one at a time. To achieve better performance, some RPC servers are multi-threaded: they have multiple threads of execution within the same process, sharing the same address space. There may be many clients of the RPC server, but their requests intermingle in the RPC server queue and are processed in the order in which server threads are dispatched to deal with the requests.

Instead of using pre-assigned ports and a super-server, RPC servers are designated by service number. The file */etc/rpc* contains a list of RPC servers and their program numbers. Each program may contain many procedures. The NFS program, for example, contains more than a dozen procedures, one for each filesystem operation such as "read block," "write block," "create file," "make symbolic link," and so on. RPC services still must use TCP/UDP port numbers to fit the underlying protocols, so the mapping of RPC program numbers to port numbers is handled by the portmapper daemon (*portmap* on some systems, *rpcbind* on others).

When an RPC server initializes, it usually registers its service with the portmapper. The RPC server tells the portmapper which ports it will listen on for incoming requests, rather than having the portmapper listen for it, in *inetd* fashion. An RPC client contacts the portmapper daemon on the server to determine the port number used by the RPC server, or it may ask the portmapper to call the server indirectly on its behalf. In either case, the first RPC call from a client to a server must be made with the portmapper running. If the portmapper dies, clients will be unable to locate RPC daemons services on the server. A server without a running portmapper effectively stops serving NIS, NFS, and other RPC-based applications.

We'll come back to RPC mechanics and debugging techniques in later chapters. For now, this introduction to the configuration and use of RPC services suffices as a foundation for explaining the NFS and NIS applications built on top of them.

Socket RPC and Transport Independent RPC

RPC was originally designed to work over sockets, a programing interface for network communication introduced in the 1980s by the University of California in its 4.1c BSD version of Unix. Solaris 2.0 introduced Transport Independent RPC (TI-RPC). The motivation for TI-RPC was that it appeared that OSI networking would eventually supplant TCP/IP-based networking, and so a transport independent interface would make it easier to transition RPC applications was needed. While OSI networking did not take over, TI-RPC is still used in Solaris. TI-RPC introduces an additional configuration file, */etc/netconfig*, which defines each transport that RPC services can listen for requests over. In addition to TCP and UDP, the */etc/netconfig* file lists connectionless and connection-oriented loopback transports for RPC services that don't need to provide service outside the host. In Solaris 8, the */etc/netconfig* file will also let you specify services over TCP and UDP on IPv6 network interfaces.

2

Introduction to Directory Services

In this chapter:
- *Purpose of directory services*
- *Brief survey of common directory services*
- *Name service switch*
- *Which directory service to use*

The previous chapter gave an overview of the ISO seven-layer model, describing in some detail the lower layers. In this chapter, we will discuss a class of layer 7—application protocols known as *directory services*. NIS is an example of such a directory service.

Purpose of directory services

The purpose of a directory service is to map names of one form to names of another form. Often the names of the first form are alphanumeric strings, and the second form are numbers. Or the names of the first form are simple, whereas the names of second form are complex. In the days before computing, we used directories, but they were published on paper. The most obvious one, and perhaps the inspiration for network directory services, is the telephone book. A typical telephone book for a city in the United States consists of three directories:

- The white pages of residence listings
- The white pages of business listings
- The yellow pages of business listings

The residence white page listings contains a list of names, last name first, and for each entry, the telephone number. In many cases, each entry contains the street address of the residence. Thus you can think of the residence white pages in a telephone book, as a way to *direct* you from a person's name to his telephone number and address. Hence, a telephone book's formal name is a telephone *directory*.

The white pages of residence listings can be thought of as a "structured set of data." If this data were stored on a computer, a lexicographer would call it a *database*; a "structured set of data" is the definition of *database* in the Concise Oxford Dictionary. Sometimes, when you are in a hurry or don't have a telephone number, you dial a special telephone number (411 or 555-1212 in the United States) to ask an operator ("directory assistance") for the telephone number of the person you want to call. This directory assistance can be thought of as directory service. You, the caller, are a customer or client of the directory service, and the particular operator, is a server of the directory service. In the world of computer networking, the human server is replaced with a directory server of databases. Since there is a server, there has to be a client. The client-side of a directory service is typically a programming library which allows other applications to look up entries in the database.

The hosts database

We've so far described a lot of theory, but a concrete example of a database in directory services should crystallize the concept.

The metaphor of a telephone directory was useful in explaining the concepts of directory service, client, and server. It turns out that the concept of names of people and their telephone numbers is also a metaphor for a similar database in computer networking. Recall from the section "IP host addresses" in Chapter 1, that hosts have unique numbers or addresses, just as every telephone number in the world is unique. Just as we associate names of people with their telephone numbers, in computer networking we often want to give individual hosts a name in addition to a host address. The reasons are that it is easier to remember a name than a number, and just as people move geographically, requiring new telephone number assignments, hosts can move physically (requiring a new address assignment for the host) or conversely, the function the host was serving can move from one physical host to another (requiring a new name assignment for the host).

The hostname and address entries are stored in a hosts database that the directory server can use to respond to requests from clients. As was noted earlier, the client-side of the directory service is typically a programming library. This is the case for the hosts database. There is a subroutine, known as *gethostbyname( )* that takes a string name of a host and returns the address of the host. See your system's manual page for *gethostbyname* for the precise calling conventions. Solaris comes with a utility called *getent* for looking up database entries via the command line. For example:

```
% getent hosts frostback
128.0.0.1      frostback
```

getent can be thought of as one of the most primitive directory service clients, but nearly every application that deals with the network will be a client that needs to access the hosts database via the directory service. A more advanced client of the hosts database is a web browser such as Netscape Navigator or Internet Explorer. Browsers will link to *gethostbyname* or a similar interface to find the host addresses corresponding to Universal Resource Locators (URLs, those things that start with *http://*).

Going back to the telephone concept, sometimes we would like to know the name of the caller corresponding to a telephone number. In the United States, when you call a toll free number, the merchant receiving the call has the capability to display your phone number and can map it to your name (considering that the merchant is paying for your long distance call, some might reason that this is fair). In the computer networking world, it is sometimes useful to know the hostname of the client accessing the server. For example, suppose the server side of a web browser is a web server. Web servers often keep logs of the "hits" made to the server, for the purposes of understanding how popular a web site is, what is popular, and what hosts find it popular. The web server will always be able to find the host address of the client that made the hit. To figure out the name of the host, there is a programming interface called *gethostbyaddr()*, which takes a host address, and returns the name of the host. The information can be obtained from the hosts database, via the directory service. In other words, both servers and client of different services, in this case, web services, can be clients of directory services.

Brief survey of common directory services

There are numerous different directory services. Here we will discuss some of the commonly used ones.

Directory Name Service (DNS)

The roots of DNS are in the early (pre-Web) days of the Internet. DNS was developed to provide hostname and address resolution. Before DNS existed, the authorities for the Internet maintained a global flat text file of the mappings from hostname to IP address in a file called *hosts.txt*, which was then made available for all the nodes on the Internet to download via a program called *gettable*. This is analogous to the telephone company giving you an updated telephone book periodically. Systems like Unix would convert the file into */etc/hosts*.

This *hosts.txt* system worked fine for the Internet when it had only thousands of hosts. But when it reached tens of thousands of hosts, it wasn't practical, especially over the slow links available in the late 1980s. What was needed was a way to decentralize the process of looking up hostnames and addresses. The Internet was separated into domains, and each domain was left to identify its own authoritative server for hostnames and addresses within its domain. The only thing that needed to be maintained in a global database was the list of domain names, and the servers for that domain. Returning to the telephone directory analogy, when you live in one area code of the United States, and want to get directory information for another area code, you can prefix the area code to the number 555-1212 to get the appropriate directory service operator.

By assigning authority for a domain's directory information to each domain, DNS can be described as being hierarchical. Similarly, the United States telephone system assigns authority for a given area code's directory information to one pool of directory service operators that answer the 555-1212 number. DNS also lets domains within subdomains further delegate authority, and subdomains in turn. For example, in DNS there is a top-level domain called ".com" that assigns authority for administering *sun.com* and *oreilly.com* to DNS servers that the owners of *sun.com* and *oreilly.com* each designate. Within *sun.com*, there are several subdomains, such as *eng.sun.com*, and *east.sun.com*. Within *eng.sun.com*, there might be a *compiler.eng.sun.com*, *sunos.eng.sun.com*, *cde.eng.sun.com*. Thus DNS is a multilevel hierarchy, whereas the United States telephone directory service has but two levels of hierarchy.

DNS has stood the test of time. In 1993, a memorandum (RFC 1401) was written by the chair of the Internet Architecture Board that noted that the transition from *hosts.txt* to DNS was largely complete. This is fortuitous, as the World Wide Web was about to explode from tens of thousands of hosts to millions. DNS proved capable of handling that explosion.

Network Information Service (NIS)

NIS was developed by Sun Microsystems in the mid-1980s to solve a problem that until then had no solution in the Unix world. Let's return to the telephone directory service concept. One nice thing about calling your telephone company's directory service is that the operator (the server) is more apt to have up-to-date information than you would. Your telephone book is replaced once a year, whereas the server's information is updated more frequently, perhaps instantly with each new telephone number assignment and de-assignment. When networking was added to Unix systems, system administrators very quickly ran into difficulties keeping files like */etc/hosts* (holds hostname to host address mappings) and */etc/passwd* (holds username, user identifier, password). If a system administrator had 100 systems, then adding a host to a network or a user to the organization meant the tedium of updating the */etc/hosts* or */etc/passwd* files on all 100 systems. NIS, originally called the Yellow Pages or YP, was invented to simplify management of these files by changing the underlying programming interfaces, such as *gethostbyname( )* and *getpwnam( )*, to use NIS client libraries.

While DNS was being developed around the time NIS was, DNS was mostly concerned with the directory of hostnames and addresses, whereas NIS went beyond that. In addition, DNS was designed so that a host in one domain could access information from other domains, whereas NIS shared the limitations of the early Internet's *hosts.txt* file: flat and not very dynamic.

We will go into much more detail on how NIS operates in Chapter 3.

NIS+

In 1992, Sun Microsystems released NIS+ with Solaris 2.0. Despite its name, NIS+ was more different than it was similar to NIS. NIS+ was developed to address several deficiencies in NIS:

Hierarchical operation
> While NIS was designed to be split into unique domains, there was no simple way for a client in one domain to get directory information from another domain. NIS+ addressed this by supporting a multilevel hierarchy in a manner similar to DNS.

Security
> There are really two issues here. First is that some kinds of directory information need to be kept more secure than others, such as a directory containing credit card numbers. The directory server needs to know who is accessing the data, and properly authenticate the client. Second, the client needs to be certain that the server is the true authority for the service. An attacker in the middle between the client and real server could masquerade as the server and return bogus information. NIS+ deals with both these issues by supporting mutual authentication: the client and server authenticate each other, via a secure form of RPC known as *RPC/dh*, which is described in Chapter 12.

Updates
> Updating a NIS database and propagating the changes is a cumbersome process. Only the system administrator can make updates (with few exceptions), and the changes must be pushed to each replica server by pushing the entire database, even if only one record changes. NIS+ supports the ability to allow users to update directory entries they have access rights to. For example, a user changes the name that appears in the password database, which might be necessary upon a status change like a new job title, or a new surname as a result of a marriage or divorce. NIS+ servers have the capability to accept incremental updates, which allows the updates to be more efficiently distributed.

X.500

Around the same time DNS and NIS were being designed and deployed, the International Standards Organization (ISO) started meeting to define an ISO standard directory, called X.500. X.500 shares DNS's and NIS+'s attributes for hierarchical operation, and NIS+'s attributes for security and simple update. X.500 differs from DNS, NIS, and NIS+ in the following ways:

- X.500 is very explicit about what each level of the hierarchy of a domain name looks like. If you see a domain name like:

    ```
    chicago.manufacturing.widget.com
    ```

  it could easily be a DNS, NIS, or NIS+ name, and it could very well be for a host or a domain. Moreover, while it might seem like *chicago.manufacturing. widget.com* refers to a subdomain of hosts located in the city of Chicago, assigned to Widget, Inc.'s manufacturing division, it could just as easily refer to a hand held computer on space station Alpha. This ambiguity is a concern to some folks. Hence, X.500 explicitly identifies what each level of hierarchy means. For example, the X.500 distinguished name corresponding to DNS style *chicago.manufacturing.widget.com* name would be:

    ```
    { Country = US, Orglanization = Widget, Inc., Organizational Unit =
    Manufacturing, Location = Chicago }
    ```

- X.500 supports the notion of *schema*. A schema is a set of rules for what can be stored in a database. Defining a directory schema is useful when performing search operations on a directory. Say a database includes the hire dates of employees, and you want to search for all employees hired between a particular range of dates. Because the X.500 directory is "aware" that the field being searched is a date, it is possible to let the directory server do all the work of finding the matches. With DNS, NIS, and NIS+, you would be compelled to read every directory entry from the server, and perform the operation on the client, because the server treats the information opaquely. The X.500 way saves network bandwidth.

  For many common databases, X.500 is overkill, but there are situations where having an X.500 schema is handy. Say you want to find all the hosts that are in the 192.1.1 network. If you defined X.500's equivalent to the hosts database with a schema that had substring matching rules, this would be easy and efficient.

Lightweight Directory Access Protocol (LDAP)

X.500 has a protocol called the Directory Access Protocol (DAP) to allow clients to access X.500 servers. DAP was designed to operate over ISO's Open Systems Interconnect (OSI) transport and network protocols. Once upon a time, people believed that TCP/IP would wither away and be replaced by OSI. As it turned out, too many people had deployed TCP/IP-based networks, and they saw no compelling reason to switch to OSI. Despite OSI mandates by most governments in the developed world, the Internet transport and network protocols persisted, and it was obvious by 1994, if not earlier, that the OSI transport and network was dead. However, as discussed earlier, X.500 has some extremely attractive properties for a directory, but it comes with the baggage of OSI transport and complex ASN.1 encoding. The Lightweight Directory Access Protocol (LDAP) was invented to allow clients using TCP/IP and simpler encoding schemes, to take advantage of the richness of X.500 directory service.

Another difference between LDAP and DAP is that LDAP is under the control of the Internet Engineering Task Force (IETF), the same organization that produced the standards behind the Internet. Whether intended or not, the effect is to get IETF to buy into X.500, whereas previously IETF had no control over OSI transport and network, and so it was much harder (and eventually impossible) to get IETF to accept OSI transport and network.

LDAP specifies lots of different security flavors, including ones based on public key certificates and Kerberos V5.

At the time this book was written, LDAP was only starting to be integrated with operating systems. Windows 2000 is the first such offering from Microsoft. Solaris 8 includes a fully integrated LDAP client, but no server.

NT Domain

NT Domain is the directory service used in Windows NT. It was introduced by Microsoft in 1987 and was called Lan Manager at the time. NT Domain is intended to administer users, groups, printers, and hosts in a Windows environment. NT Domain now supports multilevel hierarchies, but requires a bilateral trust relationship between each domain. So if there are N domains in an organization, N * (N - 1) relationships need to be set up. NT Domain supports slightly better security than NIS. Perhaps the biggest issue with NT Domain is that it is an undocumented proprietary protocol, making it difficult for Windows and non-Windows systems to share NT Domain directory information.

Microsoft is moving away from NT Domain in favor of Active Directory, which is a derivation of the LDAP protocol and X.500.

While NT Domain is not supported on Solaris and most other Unix systems, if you have a mixed environment, you'll probably run into it.

Name service switch

With multiple directory services available, having the ability to access different ones is handy. Solaris has an */etc/nsswitch.conf* file that for each database, which lets you decide what directory you want to get the database contents from. You can even specify multiple directories. For example, *nsswitch.conf* might have this entry:

```
hosts:      files nis dns
```

This entry says that when *gethostbyname( )* and *gethostbyaddr( )* are called to look up hostnames and addresses, the interfaces will first try to find the information in the local */etc/hosts* file, then check with NIS, then check with DNS. Be aware that some directory services can't be combined in *nsswitch.conf.* For example, you cannot have both NIS and NIS+ listed in *nsswitch.conf,* even for different databases.

Which directory service to use

Clearly, LDAP is the future for directory services on all operating systems, including Solaris. However, at the time this book was written, LDAP was only starting to be integrated with operating systems. Windows 2000 is the first such offering from Microsoft. Solaris 8 includes a fully integrated LDAP client, but no server. Moreover, LDAP is more complex to administer than other directory services.

NIS is perhaps the easiest to administer, but it is also the most limited. It is, however, the universal directory for Unix systems.

DNS is the standard for hostnames and addresses, and you'll find it handy for accessing hosts outside your domain.

NIS+ has gained some acceptance among other non-Solaris Unix operating systems, including HP's HP-UX, IBM, AIX, and Linux. NIS+ is much more secure than NIS.

This rest of this book ignores NIS+ and LDAP, and focuses on NIS and to some degree DNS, since those are what you are most likely to encounter. If you are concerned about security, you'll need to seriously consider deploying NIS+ until LDAP catches up. If security is not a concern, then NIS is fine.

3

Network Information Service Operation

A major problem in running a distributed computing environment is maintaining separate copies of common configuration files such as the password, group, and hosts files. Ideally, the network should be consistent in its configuration, so that users don't have to worry about where they have accounts or if they'll be able to find a new machine on the network. Preserving consistency, however, means that every change to one of these common files must be propagated to every host on the network. In a small network, this might not be a major chore, but in a computing environment with hundreds or thousands of systems, simple administrative tasks can turn into all-day projects. Furthermore, without an automated tool for making changes, the probability of making mistakes grows with the size of the network and the number of places where changes must be made.

The Network Information System (NIS) addresses these problems. It is a distributed database system that replaces copies of commonly replicated configuration files with a centralized management facility. Instead of having to manage each host's files (like */etc/hosts*, */etc/passwd*, */etc/group*, */etc/ethers*, and so on), you maintain one database for each file on one central server. Machines that are using NIS retrieve information as needed from these databases. If you add a new system to the network, you can modify one file on a central server and propagate this change to the rest of the network, rather than changing the *hosts* file for each individual host on the network. For a network of two or three systems, the difference may not be crucial; but for a large network with hundreds of systems, NIS is life-saving.

Because NIS enforces consistent views of files on the network, it is suited for files that have no host-specific information in them. The */etc/vfstab* file of filesystems and mount points, for example, is a terrible candidate for management by NIS because it's different on just about every machine. Files that are generally the same on all hosts in a network, such as */etc/passwd* and */etc/hosts*, fit the NIS model of a distributed database nicely.

In addition to managing configuration files, NIS can be used for any general data file that is accessed on one or more key fields. In a later chapter, we will discuss how to use NIS to manage your own site-specific databases.

This discussion of networking services starts with NIS because it provides the consistency that is a prerequisite for the successful administration of a distributed filesystem. Imagine a network in which you share files from a common server, but you have a different home directory and user ID value on every host. The advantages of the shared filesystem are lost in such a loosely run network: you can't always read or write your files due to permission problems, and you don't get a consistent view of your files between machines because you don't always end up in the same home directory. We'll start with a brief description of the different roles systems play under NIS, and then look at how to install NIS on each type of machine.

Masters, slaves, and clients

NIS is built on the client-server model. An NIS server is a host that contains NIS data files, called *maps*. Clients are hosts that request information from these maps. Servers are further divided into master and slave servers: the master server is the true single owner of the map data. Slave NIS servers handle client requests, but they do not modify the NIS maps. The master server is responsible for all map maintenance and distribution to its slave servers. Once an NIS map is built on the master to include a change, the new map file is distributed to all slave servers. NIS clients "see" these changes when they perform queries on the map file—it doesn't matter whether the clients are talking to a master or a slave server, because once the map data is distributed, all NIS servers have the same information.

Before going any further, let's take a quick and simple look at how this works. Figure 3-1 shows the relationship between masters, slaves, and clients.

Consider the *hosts* NIS map, which replaces the */etc/hosts* files on individual systems. If you're familiar with Unix adminstration, you know that this file tells the system how to convert hostnames into IP (internet) addresses. When a client needs to look up the internet address of some system, it would normally read the *hosts* file. If NIS is running, however, the client bypasses its *hosts* file, and instead asks an NIS server (either a master or a slave server—it doesn't make any difference) for the information it needs.

Now the other side of the coin: you've added a system, and need to modify the *hosts* NIS map. You only modify the *hosts* file on the "master server"—remember,

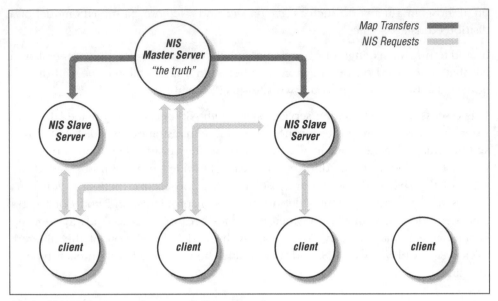

Figure 3-1. NIS masters, slaves, and clients

the master server knows the "truth" about the network.* Once you've made your changes, you can rebuild the NIS database (i.e., the NIS maps) on the master server. The master server then distributes new versions of the NIS maps to the slave servers, which now provide the updated information to the NIS clients.

With the distinction between NIS servers and clients firmly established, we can see that each system fits into the NIS scheme in one of three ways:

Client only
> This is typical of desktop workstations, where the system administrator tries to minimize the amount of host-specific tailoring required to bring a system onto the network. As an NIS client, the host gets all of its common configuration information from an extant server.

Server only
> While the host services client requests for map information, it does not use NIS for its own operation. Server-only configuration may be useful when a server must provide global host and password information for the NIS clients, but security concerns prohibit the server from using these same files. However, bypassing the central configuration scheme opens some of the same loopholes that NIS was intended to close. Although it is possible to configure a system to be an NIS server only, we don't recommend it and don't cover it in this book.

---

* Remember: when you want to make a global change to the network, you *must* modify the file on the master server. Global changes made to slave servers or clients will, at best, be ignored.

Client and server

In most cases, an NIS server also functions as an NIS client so that its management is streamlined with that of other client-only hosts.

It is possible to limit the scope of NIS to a few files that are changed infrequently, such as the */etc/protocols* file, but doing so defeats the purpose of using NIS and greatly increases the cost of network management. Once NIS is running, it will be used by all system library functions that refer to maps (files) under NIS control. As mentioned in the section "Name service switch" in Chapter 2, it is possible to configure a client to get map or file information for a particular database from either NIS, files, or both.

Now that we have this client-server model for the major administrative files, we need a way to discuss where and when a particular set of files applies to a given host. It is much too simple-minded for a single set of files to apply to every host on a network; a reasonable system must support different clusters of systems with different administrative requirements. For example, a group of administrative systems and a group of research systems might share the same network. In most cases, these two clusters of systems don't need to share the same administrative information. In some cases, sharing the same administrative files might be harmful.

To allow an administrator to set different policies for different systems, NIS provides the concept of a *domain*. Most precisely, a domain is a set of NIS maps. A client can refer to a map (for example, the *hosts* map) from any of several different domains. Most of the time, however, any given host will only look up data from one set of NIS maps. Therefore, it's common (although not precisely correct) to use the term "domain" to mean "the group of systems that share a set of NIS maps." All systems that need to share common configuration information are put into an NIS domain. Although each system can potentially look up information in any NIS domain, each system is assigned to a "default domain," meaning that the system, by default, looks up information from a particular set of NIS maps. In our example, the research systems would, by default, look at the maps in the *research* domain, rather than the maps from the *accounting* domain; and so on.

It is up to the administrator (or administrators) to decide how many different domains are needed. In Chapter 4, we will give some rules-of-thumb for deciding how many domains are needed. Lest you think this is terribly complex, we'll tell you now: many networks, possibly even most small networks, can get by with a single domain. We will also take a closer look at the precise definition of an NIS domain.

Basics of NIS management

Now that we have laid a conceptual foundation, let's look at how to set the machinery in motion. Basic NIS management involves setting up NIS servers and enabling NIS on client hosts. Server management includes three tasks:

- Installing a new NIS environment, building both master and slave servers.

- Starting the *ypserv* daemon, which enables the system to act as an NIS server.

- Adding new slave servers when growth of your network or NIS performance requires more server bandwidth.

Enabling NIS on a client requires two tasks:

- Modifying the client's administrative files so that the client can take advantage of NIS.

- Starting the *ypbind* daemon, which allows the client to make NIS requests.

In this section, we'll review the procedures required to initialize NIS, set up slave servers, and configure NIS clients.

Choosing NIS servers

First, a few words on how to plan your network. One of the most important decisions you will make is which systems will be your NIS servers. Because a client gets almost all of its configuration information from NIS, servers must be highly available in measures of both uptime and request handling bandwidth. If an NIS server stops responding or replies too slowly, the client tries to find another, less-loaded server. While this is an argument for at least one slave server for each master server, it supports an equally strong case for building NIS on reliable hosts. An interruption in NIS service affects all NIS clients if no other servers are available. Even if another server is available, clients will suffer periodic slowdowns as they recognize the current server is down and hunt for a new one.

Use your judgement in defining "highly available." You know what machines have troublesome hardware or are likely to be commandeered for a trade show, and would therefore make poor NIS servers. Request handling bandwidth is much harder to measure, because it is a product of network loading, CPU utilization, and disk activity. In later chapters, we'll come back to choosing the number of NIS servers and identifying signs that you have too few servers.

A second imperative for NIS servers is synchronization. Clients may get their NIS information from any server, so all servers must have copies of every map file to ensure proper NIS operation. Furthermore, the data in each map on the slave servers must agree with that on the master server, so that NIS clients cannot get out-of-date or stale data. NIS contains several mechanisms for making changes to map files and distributing these changes to all NIS servers on a regular basis.

Installing the NIS master server

We'll assume that you've already done your planning and decided that you need a single NIS domain, which will be called *bedrock*.* Before going any further, make sure you've set the NIS domain name on the master server using *domainname*. We'll install a server for an NIS domain named *bedrock*:

```
newmaster# domainname bedrock
```

A line like this will usually appear in the */etc/rc2.d/S69inet* file for every host (server and client) in the domain. Setting the domain name if you aren't using NIS is harmless. Reminder: you are setting the NIS domain name here, not the DNS domain. See "Internet domains versus NIS domains" later in this chapter.

Note that on Solaris, the domain name setting will not survive a server reboot unless it is stored in the */etc/defaultdomain* file. So, you need to do:

```
newmaster# domainname > /etc/defaultdomain
```

After establishing the domain's name, you should go over all the system's administrative files with a fine-toothed comb: make sure they contain only the entries you want, no more, and no less. It is important for your network to start with correct map information. Which administrative files NIS cares about varies, but generally includes the information shown in Table 3-1.

Table 3-1. Files managed by NIS

File	Contains
/etc/auto_*	Automounter maps
/etc/bootparams	Information about diskless nodes
/etc/ethers	Ethernet numbers (MAC addresses)
/etc/group	User groups
/etc/hosts	Hostnames and IP addresses
/etc/inet/ipnodes	Hostnames, IPv4, and IPv6 addresses
/etc/mail/aliases	Aliases and mailing lists for the mail system
/etc/netgroup	Netgroup definitions (used by NIS)
/etc/netid	Netname database for RPC/dh (RPC/dh is discussed in "AUTH_DH: Diffie-Hellman authentication" in Chapter 12)
/etc/netmasks	Network "masks"

---

* The multiple-domain case is really no different than this; you just have to remember which systems belong to which domain.

Table 3-1. Files managed by NIS (continued)

File	Contains
/etc/networks	Network addresses
/etc/passwd	Usernames and user IDs
/etc/protocols	Network protocol names and numbers
/etc/publickey	Public key database for RPC/dh
/etc/rpc	Remote procedure call program numbers
/etc/services	Network port numbers and service names
/etc/shadow	User passwords

With the exception of *netgroup*, these are all standard Solaris administrative files. Once NIS is running, it will replace or supplement all of these files, depending on how */etc/nsswitch.conf* is configured. */etc/netgroup* is an administrative file that is only consulted via the NIS database. Before creating it, see the section "Net-groups" later in this chapter.

Make sure that your */etc/passwd* file on the master server does *not* include the entry:

```
+::0:0::
```

This entry is used by NIS client hosts to indicate that they want to include NIS map information in their password files. On the NIS master server, all entries in the */etc/passwd* file get put into the *passwd* NIS map. If you leave this NIS "marker" in the master server's */etc/passwd* file, your NIS password file map will contain an entry for a user named +. If you do leave the entry in the password file, be sure to put an asterisk (*) in the password field so that this "user" will not have a valid password:

```
+:*:0:0::
```

Note that this will not work under all operating systems; in particular you must not use an asterisk in SunOS 4.0 or later. If you cannot fill the password field of the NIS "marker" entry, make sure you remove this entry if you decide not to run NIS at some future point. Also, in Solaris, the plus sign entry has been deprecated in favor of the use of the Name Service Switch, via the *nsswitch.conf* file.

If you are using NIS to manage any local files (company phone lists, etc.), you must also make sure that your local source files are up-to-date. Once you have established the domain's name and "purified" the master server's source files, you're ready to initialize a master server. To do so, you will use the *ypinit* utility. You will first need to ensure that *ypinit* gets its naming information from files:

```
newmaster# cp /etc/nsswitch.files /etc/nsswitch.conf
```

At this point, you are quite close to creating the NIS maps via the *ypinit* utility. However, there is one security issue you need to be aware of. The *ypinit* utility will generate maps from the set of files listed in Table 3-1. One of these files is */etc/shadow*, which contains a one-way hash of the password for every account name listed in */etc/passwd*. If you look at */etc/shadow*, you should see something like:

```
root:eOUqsdfpdIaiA:6445::::::
daemon:NP:6445::::::
bin:NP:6445::::::
sys:NP:6445::::::
adm:NP:6445::::::
lp:NP:6445::::::
uucp:NP:6445::::::
nuucp:NP:6445::::::
listen:*LK*:::::::
nobody:NP:6445::::::
noaccess:NP:6445::::::
nobody4:NP:6445::::::
stern:aSuxcvmyerjDM:6445::::::
mre:96wqktpdmrkjsE:6445::::::
```

The fields are separated by colons (:). The first field is the name of the account or login. The second field is the one-way hash. Note that the "system" accounts, except for *root*, have a password hash of NP or *LK*. These are not valid hashes, so the accounts are effectively locked. The nonprivileged accounts, such as *stern* and *mre*, have a valid password hash. It is safe to put the locked accounts in the NIS *passwd* map, because the password hash is of no use to an attacker. It is safe to put the nonprivileged accounts in the map because they don't have privileges. However, it is not safe for the root account to be put into NIS. The reason is that if an attacker obtains the hash for root, he can perform an off-line brute force attack to determine the root password of the master NIS server. With that password, the attacker could render havoc on your network.

Thus, you must take steps to ensure that the *passwd* map does not have a root entry. The *ypinit* utility will invoke the *make* utility on */var/yp/Makefile*. Then *Makefile* will by default get the *passwd* map contents from */etc/passwd* and */etc/shadow*, but by setting the *PWDIR Makefile* variable to something else, you can ensure that *ypinit* will create the *passwd* map without root in it. So do the following:

```
newmaster# mkdir /etc/nispw
newmaster# chmod 0700 /etc/nispw
newmaster# grep -v '^root:' /etc/passwd > /etc/nispw/passwd
newmaster# grep -v '^root:' /etc/shadow > /etc/nispw/shadow
newmaster# vi /etc/passwd /etc/shadow    # delete the nonprivileged entries,
                                         # e.g., stern and mre
newmaster# cp /var/yp/Makefile /var/yp/Makefile.save
newmaster# vi /var/yp/Makefile           # change the PWDIR variable to /etc/nispw
```

Before you create the new master server, you must decide how many slave servers you will have. For availability, it is a good idea to have at minimum one slave. Once NIS is installed, if it ever becomes unavailable, your network will become unusable. The first time your master server becomes unavailable, your users and you will appreciate being able to use the network. If you need additional server horsepower, then set up more than one NIS slave server. Once you know what the names of the slaves are, make sure that the master's */etc/hosts* file has entries for each slave.

To create a new master server, become the superuser on the host and invoke *ypinit* with the *-m* flag:

> *Edit /etc/hosts to add entries for each slave*
> newmaster# **/usr/sbin/ypinit -m**

ypinit builds the domain subdirectory of */var/yp* for the current default domain. Note that the *ypinit* utility lives in */usr/sbin*, so you should use its full pathname if you don't have this directory in your search path. In this example, *ypinit* creates */var/yp/bedrock*.

After building the domain subdirectory, *ypinit* builds a complete set of administrative maps for your system and places them in this directory. The first map created by *ypinit -m* is the *ypservers* map. *ypinit* will ask you for a list of hosts that will be running NIS. The hosts named in the *ypservers* map do not have to be running NIS at that time, but they should become NIS servers before the first modifications are made to NIS maps.

You must have one and only one master server per NIS domain. There is nothing in *ypinit* that checks for the existence of another master server, so it's possible to create two masters accidentally in the same domain. Having more than one master may lead to NIS map corruption; at best it confuses procedures that contact the NIS master, such as map transfers and NIS password file updates.

Now enable NIS in *nsswitch.conf* so that processes on your NIS master host can use NIS for all of its name service accesses:

> newmaster# **cp /etc/nsswitch.nis /etc/nsswitch.conf**

If you are running Solaris 8 and if you think you will ever use the *sec=dh* option with NFS, then it would be an excellent idea to change the entry for *publickey* in *nsswitch.conf* to:

> **publickey: nis**

The reason for this step is that the Solaris 8 utilities that manipulate the *publickey* map get confused if there are multiple database sources in the *publickey* entry of *nsswitch.conf*. You should do this on NIS slaves and NIS clients as well.

Once *ypinit* finishes and *nsswitch.conf* is set up to use NIS, you should start the NIS service manually via the *ypstart script* or by rebooting the server host. In Solaris, the relevant part of the boot script */etc/rc2.d//S71rpc* normally looks like this:

```
# Start NIS (YP) services. The ypstart script handles both client
# and server startup, whichever is appropriate.

if [ -x /usr/lib/netsvc/yp/ypstart ]; then
        /usr/lib/netsvc/yp/ypstart rpcstart
fi
```

Assuming you opt to start the NIS service manually, you would do:

```
newmaster# /usr/lib/netsvc/yp/ypstart
```

As the comment in *S71rpc* says, the *ypstart* script handles the case when the host is an NIS server or NIS client or both. Both *S71rpc* and *ypstart* came with the system when it was installed, and normally won't need modifications. The logic in *ypstart* may require modifications if a server is a client of one domain but serves another; this situation sometimes occurs when a host is on multiple networks. Issues surrounding multiple domains are left for the next chapter.

Test that your NIS server is working:

```
newmaster# ypcat passwd
noaccess:NP:60002:60002:No Access User:/:
nobody4:NP:65534:65534:SunOS 4.x Nobody:/:
nobody:NP:60001:60001:Nobody:/:
listen:*LK*:37:4:Network Admin:/usr/net/nls:
daemon:NP:1:1::/:
nuucp:NP:9:9:uucp Admin:/var/spool/uucppublic:/usr/lib/uucp/uucico
uucp:NP:5:5:uucp Admin:/usr/lib/uucp:
sys:NP:3:3::/:
bin:NP:2:2::/usr/bin:
adm:NP:4:4:Admin:/var/adm:
lp:NP:71:8:Line Printer Admin:/usr/spool/lp:
stern:aSuxcvmyerjDM:6445::::::
mre:96wqktpdmrkjsE:6445::::::
```

You are now ready to add new slave servers or to set up NIS clients. Note that NIS *must* be running on a master server before you can proceed.

Installing NIS slave servers

As with a master server, you must establish the domain name and the */etc/hosts* file with the IP addresses of all the slaves and the master:

```
newslave# domainname bedrock
newslave# domainname > /etc/defaultdomain
```
Edit /etc/hosts to add master and slaves

When you initialize a new slave server, it transfers the data from the master
server's map files and builds its own copies of the maps. No ASCII source files are
used to build the NIS maps on a slave server—only the information already in the
master server's maps. If the slave has information in ASCII configuration files that
belongs in the NIS maps, make sure the master NIS server has a copy of this data
before beginning the NIS installation. For example, having password file entries
only on an NIS slave server will not add them to the NIS *passwd* map. The map
source files on the master server must contain *all* map information, since it is the
only host that constructs map files from their sources.

The slave will need to act as an NIS client in order get initial copies of the maps
from the server. Thus you must first set up the slave as a client:

```
newslave# /usr/sbin/ypinit -c
```

You will be prompted for a list of NIS servers. You should start with the name of
the local host (in this example, *newslave*), followed by the name of the master (in
this example, *newmaster*), followed by the remaining slave servers, in order of
physical proximity.

Now check to see if your slave was already acting as an NIS client already. If so,
use *ypstop* to terminate it:

```
newslave# ps -ef | grep ypbind
newslave# /usr/lib/netsvc/yp/ypstop
```

Now start *ypbind*:

```
newslave# /usr/lib/netsvc/yp/ypstart
```

Slave servers are also initialized using *ypinit*. Instead of specifying the *-m* option,
use *-s* and the name of the NIS master server:

```
newslave# /usr/sbin/ypinit -s newmaster
```

Now you need to start the *ypserv* daemon:

```
newslave# /usr/lib/netsvc/yp/ypstop
newslave# /usr/lib/netsvc/yp/ypstart
```

Finally, set up *nsswitch.conf* to use NIS:

```
newslave# cp /etc/nsswitch.nis /etc/nsswitch.conf
```

Adding slave servers later

In general, it is a good idea to initialize your NIS slave servers as soon as possible
after building the master server, so that there are no inconsistencies between the
ypservers map and the hosts that are really running NIS. Once the initial installation is complete, though, you can add slave servers at any time. If you add an NIS
slave server that was not listed in the *ypservers* map, you must add its hostname to
this map so that it receives NIS map updates.

To edit *ypservers*, dump out its old contents with *ypcat*, add the new slave server name, and rebuild the map using *makedbm*. This procedure must be done on the NIS master server:

```
master# ypcat -k ypservers > /tmp/ypservers
Edit /tmp/ypservers to add new server name
master# cd /var/yp
master# cat /tmp/ypservers | makedbm - /var/yp/`domainname`/ypservers
```

Once you've changed the master *ypservers* map on the new slave, you must follow the steps described in the "Installing NIS slave servers" section in this chapter.

Enabling NIS on client hosts

Once you have one or more NIS servers running *ypserv*, you can set up NIS clients that query them. Make sure you do not enable NIS on any clients until you have at least one NIS server up and running. If no servers are available, the host that attempts to run as an NIS client will hang.

To enable NIS on a client host, first set up the *nsswitch.conf* file:

```
newclient# cp /etc/nsswitch.nis /etc/nsswitch.conf
```

Set up the domain name:

```
newclient# domainname bedrock
newclient# domainname > /etc/defaultdomain
```

Run *ypinit*:

```
newclient# /usr/sbin/ypinit -c
```

You will be prompted for a list of NIS servers. Enter the servers in order of proximity to the client.

Kill (if necessary) *ypbind*, and restart it:

```
newclient# ps -ef | grep ypbind
newclient# /usr/lib/netsvc/yp/ypstop
newclient# /usr/lib/netsvc/yp/ypstart
```

Once NIS is running, references to the basic administrative files are handled in two fundamentally different ways, depending on how *nsswitch.conf* is configured:

- The NIS database *replaces* some files. Local copies of replaced files (*ethers*, *hosts*, *netmasks*, *netgroups*,* *networks*, *protocols*, *rpc*, and *services*) are ignored as soon as the *ypbind* daemon is started (to enable NIS).

---

* The *netgroups* file is a special case. Netgroups are only meaningful when NIS is running, in which case the *netgroups* map (rather than the file) is consulted. The *netgroups* file is therefore only used to build the *netgroups* map; it is never "consulted" in its own right.

- Some files are *augmented,* or *appended* to, by NIS. Files that are appended, or augmented, by NIS are consulted before the NIS maps are queried. The default */etc/nsswitch.conf* file for NIS has these appended files: *aliases, auto_*, group, passwd, services,* and *shadow.* These files are read first, and if an appropriate entry isn't found in the local file, the corresponding NIS map is consulted. For example, when a user logs in, an NIS client will first look up the user's login name in the local *passwd* file; if it does not find anything that matches, it will refer to the NIS *passwd* map.

Although the replaced files aren't consulted once NIS is running, they shouldn't be deleted. In particular, the */etc/hosts* file is used by an NIS client during the boot process, before it starts NIS, but is ignored as soon as NIS is running. The NIS client needs a "runt" *hosts* file during the boot process so that it can configure itself and get NIS running. Administrators usually truncate *hosts* to the absolute minimum: entries for the host itself and the "loopback" address. Diskless nodes need additional entries for the node's boot server and the server for the diskless node's */usr* filesystem. Trimming the *hosts* file to these minimal entries is a good idea because, for historical reasons, many systems have extremely long host tables. Other files, like *rpc, services,* and *protocols,* could probably be eliminated, but it's safest to leave the files distributed with your system untouched; these will certainly have enough information to get your system booted safely, particularly if NIS stops running for some reason. However, you should make any local additions to these files on the master server alone. You don't need to bother keeping the slaves and clients up to date.

We'll take a much closer look at the files managed by NIS and the mechanisms used to manage appended files in the section "Files managed under NIS." Meanwhile, we'll assume that you have modified these files correctly and proceed with NIS setup.

Files managed under NIS

Now that we've walked through the setup procedure, we will discuss how the NIS maps relate to the files that they replace. In particular, we'll discuss how to modify the files that are appended by NIS so they can take advantage of NIS features. We will also pay special attention to the *netgroups* NIS map, a confusing but nevertheless important part of the overall picture.

Table 3-2 lists the most common files managed by NIS. Not all vendors use NIS for all of these files, so it is best to check your documentation for a list of NIS-supported files.

Table 3-2. Summary of NIS maps

Map Name	Nickname	Access By	Contains	Default Integration
auto.*		Map key	/etc/auto_*	Append
bootparams		Hostname	/etc/bootparams	Append
ethers.byname	ethers	Hostname	/etc/ethers	Replace
ethers.byaddr		MAC address	/etc/ethers	Replace
group.byname	group	Group name	/etc/group	Append
group.bygid		Group ID	/etc/group	Append
hosts.byname	hosts	Hostname	/etc/hosts	Replace
hosts.byaddr		IP address	/etc/hosts	Replace
ipnodes.byname	ipnodes	Hostname	/etc/inet/ipnodes	None; only integrated if IPv6 enabled
ipnodes.byaddr		IP address	/etc/inet/ipnodes	None; only integrated if IPv6 enabled
mail.aliases	aliases	Alias name	/etc/aliases	Append
mail.byaddr		Expanded alias	/etc/aliases	Append
netgroup.byhost		Hostname	/etc/netgroup	Replace
netgroup.byuser		Username	/etc/netgroup	Replace
netid.byname		Username	UID & GID info	Replace
netmasks.byaddr		IP address	/etc/netmasks	Replace
networks.byname		Network name	/etc/networks	Replace
networks.byaddr		IP address	/etc/networks	Replace
passwd.byname	passwd	Username	/etc/passwd /etc/shadow	Append
passwd.byuid		User ID	/etc/passwd /etc/shadow	Append
publickey.byname		Principal name	/etc/publickey	Replace
protocols.bynumber	protocols	Port number	/etc/protocols	Replace
protocols.byname		Protocol name	/etc/protocols	Replace
rpc.bynumber		RPC number	/etc/rpc	Replace
services.byname	services	Service name	/etc/services	Replace
ypservers		Hostname	NIS server names	Replace

It's now time to face up to some distortions we've been making for the sake of simplicity. We've assumed that there's a one-to-one correspondence between files and maps. In fact, there are usually several maps for each file. A map really corresponds to a particular way of accessing a file: for example, the *passwd. byname* map looks up data in the password database by username. There's also a *passwd.byuid* that looks up users according to their user ID number. There could be (but there aren't) additional maps that looked up users on the basis of their group ID number, home directory, or even their choice of login shell. To make things a bit easier, the most commonly used maps have "nicknames," which correspond directly to the name of the original file: for example, the nickname for *passwd.byname* is simply *passwd*. Using nicknames as if they were map names rarely causes problems—but it's important to realize that there is a distinction. It's also important to realize that nicknames are recognized by only two NIS utilities: *ypmatch* and *ypcat*.

Another distortion: this is the first time we've seen the *netid.byname* map. On the master NIS server, this map is not based on any single source file, but instead is derived from information in the group, password, and hosts files, via */var/yp/ Makefile*. It contains one entry for each user in the password file. The data associated with the username is a list of every group to which the user belongs. The *netid* is used to determine group memberships quickly when a user logs in. Instead of reading the entire *group* map, searching for the user's name, the *login* process performs a single map lookup on the *netid* map. You usually don't have to worry about this map—it will be built for you as needed—but you should be aware that it exists. If NIS is not running, and if an NIS client has an */etc/netid* file, then the information will be read from */etc/netid*.

Working with the maps

Earlier, we introduced the concept of replaced files and appended files. Now, we'll discuss how to work with these files. First, let's review: these are important concepts, so repetition is helpful. If a map *replaces* the local file, the file is ignored once NIS is running. Aside from making sure that misplaced optimism doesn't lead you to delete the files that were distributed with your system, there's nothing interesting that you can do with these replaced files. We won't have anything further to say about them.

Conversely, local files that are *appended* to by NIS maps are always consulted first, even if NIS is running. The password file is a good example of a file augmented by NIS. You may want to give some users access to one or two machines, and not include them in the NIS password map. The solution to this problem is to put these users into the local *passwd* file, but not into the master *passwd* file on the master server. The local password file is always read before *getpwuid( )* goes to an NIS server. Password-file reading routines find locally defined users as well as those in the NIS map, and the search order of "local, then NIS" allows local password file entries to override values in the NIS map. Similarly, the local aliases file can be used to override entries in the NIS mail aliases map, setting up machine-specific expansion of one or more aliases.

There is yet another group of files that can be augmented with data from NIS. These files are not managed by NIS directly, but you can add special entries referring to the NIS database (in particular, the *netgroups* map). Such files include *hosts.equiv* and *.rhosts*. We won't discuss these files in this chapter; we will treat them as the need arises. For example, we will discuss *hosts.equiv* in Chapter 12.

Now we're going to discuss the special *netgroups* map. This new database is the basis for the most useful extensions to the standard administrative files; it is what prevents NIS from becoming a rigid, inflexible system. After our discussion of netgroups, we will pay special attention to the appended files.

Netgroups

In addition to the standard password, group, and host file databases, NIS introduces a new database for creating sets of users and hosts called the *netgroups* map. The user and hostname fields are used to define groups (of hosts or users) for administrative purposes. For example, to define a subset of the users in the *passwd* map that should be given access to a specific machine, you can create a netgroup for those users.

A netgroup is a set of triples of the form:

```
(hostname, username, domain name)
```

A single netgroup contains one or more of these triples. Host and usernames have their usual meanings, but a domain name in this instance refers to the NIS domain in which the netgroup is valid. If an entry in the triple is left blank, that field becomes a wildcard. If the entry is specified as a dash (-), the field can take no value.

Netgroups are typically used to augment other maps and files; for example, adding a selected group of users to the password file. The definitions and behavior of netgroups are confusing because their syntax doesn't exactly match the way the netgroup information is used. Even though the netgroup syntax allows you to specify user and hostnames in the same triple, user and hostnames are rarely used *together*. For example, when a netgroup is used to add users to an NIS-managed password file, only the usernames are taken from the netgroup. The hostnames are ignored, because hostnames have no place in the password file. Similarly, when using a netgroup to grant filesystem access permissions to a set of NFS clients, only the hostname fields in the netgroup are used. Usernames are ignored in this case, which means a hostname will be included in the list even if - is used as the username in its triple.

Some examples are helpful:

```
source (-,stern,nesales), (-,julie,nesales), (-,peter,nesales)
trusted-hosts (bitatron,,), (corvette,,)
```

```
trusted-users (bitatron,stern,), (corvette,johnc,)
dangerous-users (,jimc,), (,dave,)
```

In the first example, *source* is a group of three users; in this respect, the netgroup is similar to an entry in */etc/group*. The *source* netgroup in this case grants no specific permissions, although it could be included in the password file for the source archive machine, granting selected users access to that host. The second example shows a definition for a set of hosts, and would be of no use in a password file. In the third example, *stern* and *johnc* are members of the *trusted-users* group when it is parsed for usernames. Hosts *bitatron* and *corvette* are members of *trusted-users* when it is parsed for hostnames. Note that there is no interpretation of the netgroup that associates user *stern* with host *bitatron*. In the fourth example, *dave* and *jimc* are members of *dangerous-users*, but no hosts are included in this group. The domain name field is used when multiple NIS domains exist on the same network and it is necessary to create a group that is valid in only one or the other domain.

These groups are very different from those in */etc/group*. The group file (or equivalent NIS map) explicitly grants permissions to users while the netgroup mechanism simply creates shorthand notations or nicknames. A netgroup can be used in many places where a user or hostname would appear, such as the password file or in the list of hosts that can access an NFS filesystem.

You can also build netgroups from other netgroups. For example, you could create the netgroup *hosts-n-users* from the following entry:

```
hosts-n-users trusted-hosts, trusted-users
```

This netgroup contains all the members of both *trusted-hosts* and *trusted-users*.

By using netgroups carefully, you can create special-purpose groups that can be managed separately. For example, you could create a group of "administrators" that can easily be added to the password list of every machine, or a group of "visitors" who are only added to the password files of certain machines.

A final note about netgroups: they are accessible *only* through NIS. The library routines that have been modified to use NIS maps have also been educated about the uses of the netgroup map, and use the *netgroup*, *password*, and *host* maps together. If NIS is not running, netgroups are not defined. This implies that any *netgroup* file on an NIS client is ignored, because the NIS *netgroup* map replaces the local file. A local *netgroup* file does nothing at all. The uses of netgroups will be revisited as a security mechanism.

Hostname formats in netgroups

The previous section used nonfully qualified hostnames, which are hostnames without a domain name suffix. This is the norm when using the *hosts* map in NIS to store hostnames. If you have hostnames that are available only in DNS, then you can and must use fully qualified hostnames in the *netgroup* map if you want those hosts to be members of a particular netgroup. See Chapter 5 for more details on running NIS and DNS on the same network.

Integrating NIS maps with local files

For files that are augmented by NIS maps, you typically strip the local file to the minimum number of entries needed for bootstrap or single-user operation. You then add in entries that are valid only on the local host—for example, a user with an account on only one machine—and then integrate NIS services by adding special entries that refer to the NIS map files.

The */etc/nsswitch.conf* file is used to control how NIS maps and local files are integrated. Normally if the two are integrated, the file is interpreted first, followed by the NIS map. For example, look at the *passwd* entry in the default *nsswitch.conf* for NIS clients:

```
passwd:     files nis
```

The keyword *files* tells the system to read */etc/passwd* first, and if the desired entry is not found, search *passwd.byname* or *passwd.byuid*, depending on whether the system is searching by account name or user identifier number. The reason why the *passwd* file is examined before the NIS map is that some accounts, such as *root*, are not placed in NIS, for security reasons (see "Installing the NIS master server" in this chapter). If NIS were searched before the local *passwd* file, and if *root* were in NIS, then there would effectively be one global password for *root*. This is not desirable, because once an attacker figured out the *root* password for one system, he'd know the *root* password for all systems. Or, even if *root* were not in NIS, if clients were configured to read NIS before files for *passwd* information, the attacker that successfully compromised a NIS server, would be able to insert a root entry in the *passwd* map and gain access to every client.

 The default files and NIS integration will have your clients getting hostname and address information from NIS. Since you will likely have DNS running, you will find it better to get host informaton from DNS. See Chapter 5.

At this point, we've run through most of what you need to know to get NIS running. With this background out of the way, we'll look at how NIS works. Along the way, we will give more precise definitions of terms that, until now, we have been using fairly loosely. Understanding how NIS works is essential to successful debugging. It is also crucial to planning your NIS network.

NIS is built on the RPC protocol, and uses the UDP transport to move requests from the client host to the server. NIS services are integrated into the standard Unix library calls so that they remain transparent to processes that reference NIS-managed files. If you have a process that reads */etc/passwd*, most of the queries about that file will be handled by NIS RPC calls to an NIS server. The library calling interface used by the application does not change at all, but the implementations of library routines such as *getpwuid( )* that read the */etc/passwd* file are modified to refer to NIS or to NIS and local files. The application using *getpwuid( )* is oblivious to the change in its implementation.

Therefore, when you enable NIS, you don't have to change any existing software. A vendor that supports NIS has already modified all of the relevant library calls to have them make NIS RPC calls in addition to looking at local files where relevant. Any process that used to do lookups in the host table still works; it just does something different in the depths of the library calls.

Map files

Configuration files managed by NIS are converted into keyword and value pair tables called *maps*. We've been using the term "map" all along, as if a map were equivalent to the ASCII files that it replaces or augments. For example, we have said that the *passwd* NIS map is appended to the NIS client's */etc/passwd* file. Now it's time to understand what a map file really is.

NIS maps are constructed from DBM database files. DBM is the database system that is built into BSD Unix implementations; if it is not normally shipped as part of your Unix system, your vendor will supply it as part of the NIS implementation. Under DBM, a database consists of a set of keys and associated values organized in a table with fast lookup capabilities. Every key and value pair may be located using at most two filesystem accesses, making DBM an efficient storage mechanism for NIS maps. A common way to use the password file, for example, is to locate an entry by user ID number, or UID. Using the flat */etc/passwd* file, a linear search is required, while the same value can be retrieved from a DBM file with a single lookup. This performance improvement in data location offsets the overhead of performing a remote procedure call over the network.

Each DBM database, and therefore each NIS map, comprises two files: a hash-table accessed bitmap of indices and a data file. The index file has the *.dir* extension and the data file uses *.pag*. A database called *addresses* would be stored in:

```
addresses.dir        index file
addresses.pag        data file
```

A complete map contains both files.

Consecutive records are not packed in the data file; they are arranged in hashed order and may have empty blocks between them. As a result, the DBM data file may appear to be up to four times as large as the data that it contains. The Unix operating system allows a file to have holes in it that are created when the file's write pointer is advanced beyond the end of the file using *lseek()*. Filesystem data blocks are allocated only for those parts of the file containing data. The empty blocks are not allocated, and the file is only as large as the total number of used filesystem blocks and fragments.

The holes in DBM files make them difficult to manipulate using standard Unix utilities. If you try to copy an NIS map using *cp*, or move it across a filesystem boundary with *mv*, the new file will have the holes expanded into zero-filled disk blocks. When *cp* reads the file, it doesn't expect to find holes, so it reads sequentially from the first byte until the end-of-file is found. Blocks that are not allocated are read back as zeros, and written to the new file as all zeros as well. This has the unfortunate side effect of making the copied DBM files consume much more disk space than the hole-filled files. Furthermore, NIS maps will not be usable on a machine of another architecture: if you build your maps on a SPARC machine, you can't copy them to an Intel-based machine. Map files are not ASCII files. For the administrator, the practical consequence is that you must always use NIS tools (like *ypxfr* and *yppush*, discussed in "Map distribution" in Chapter 4) to move maps from one machine to another.

Map naming

ASCII files are converted into DBM files by selecting the key field and separating it from the value field by spaces or a tab. The *makedbm* utility builds the *.dir* and *.pag* files from ASCII input files. A limitation of the DBM system is that it supports only one key per value, so files that are accessed by more than one field value require an NIS map for each key field. With a flat ASCII file, you can read the records sequentially and perform comparisons on any field in the record. However, DBM files are indexed databases, so only one field—the key—is used for comparisons. If you need to search the database in two different ways, using two fields, then you must use two NIS maps or must implement one of the searches as a linear walk through all of the records in the NIS map.

The password file is a good example of an ASCII file that is searched on multiple fields. The *getpwnam()* library call opens the password file and looks for the entry for a specific username. Equal in popularity is the *getpwuid()* library routine, which searches the database looking for the given user ID value. While *getpwnam()* is used by *login* and *chown*, *getpwuid()* is used by processes that need to match numeric user ID values to names, such as *ls -l*. To accommodate both access methods, the standard set of NIS maps includes two maps derived from the password file: one that uses the username as a key and one that uses the user ID field as a key.

The map names used by NIS indicate the source of the data and the key field. The convention for map naming is:

```
filename.bykeyname
```

The two NIS maps generated from the password file, for example, are *passwd. byname* (used by *getpwnam( )*) and *passwd.byuid* (used by *getpwuid( )*). These two maps are stored on disk as four files:

```
passwd.byname.dir
passwd.byname.pag
passwd.byuid.dir
passwd.byuid.pag
```

The order of the records in the maps will be different because they have different key fields driving the hash algorithm, but they contain exactly the same sets of entries.

Map structure

Two extra entries are added to each NIS map by *makedbm*. The master server name for the map is embedded in one entry and the map's *order*, or modification timestamp, is put in the other. These additional entries allow the map to describe itself fully, without requiring NIS to keep map management data. Again, NIS is ignorant of the content of the maps and merely provides an access mechanism. The maps themselves must contain timestamp and ownership information to coordinate updates with the master NIS server.

Some maps are given nicknames based on the original file from which they are derived. Map nicknames exist only within the *ypwhich* and *ypmatch* utilities (see "NIS tools" in Chapter 13) that retrieve information from NIS maps. Nicknames are neither part of the NIS service nor embedded in the maps themselves. They do provide convenient shorthands for referring to popular maps such as the password or hosts files. For example, the map nickname *passwd* refers to the *passwd.byname* map, and the *hosts* nickname refers to the *hosts.byname* map. To locate the password file entry for user *stern* in the *passwd.byname* map, use *ypmatch* with the map nickname:

```
% ypmatch stern passwd
stern:passwd:1461:10:Hal Stern:/home/thud/stern:/bin/csh
```

In this example, *ypmatch* expands the nickname *passwd* to the map name *passwd.byname*, locates the key *stern* in that map, and prints the data value associated with the key.

The library routines that use NIS don't retain any information from the maps. Once a routine looks up a hostname, for example, it passes the data back to the caller and "forgets" about the transaction. On Solaris, if the name service cache daemon (nscd) is running, then the results of queries from the *passwd*, group, and hosts maps are cached in the *nscd* daemon. Subsequent queries for the same entry will be satisfied out of the cache. The cache will keep the result of an NIS query until the entry reaches its time to live (ttl) threshold. Each cached NIS map has different time to live values. You can invoke *nscd* with the -g option to see what the time to live values are.

NIS domains

"Domain" is another term that we have used loosely; now we'll define domains more precisely. Groups of hosts that use the same set of maps form an NIS *domain*. All of the machines in an NIS domain will share the same password, hosts, and group file information. Technically, the maps themselves are grouped together to form a domain, and hosts join one or more of these NIS domains. For all practical purposes, though, an NIS domain includes both a set of maps and the machines using information in those map files.

NIS domains define spheres of system management. A domain is a name applied to a group of NIS maps. The hosts that need to look up information in the maps *bind* themselves to the domain, which involves finding an NIS server that has the maps comprising the domain. It's easy to refer to the hosts that share a set of maps and the set of maps themselves interchangeably as a domain. The important point is that NIS domains are *not* just defined as a group of hosts; NIS domains are defined around a set of maps and the hosts that use these map files. Think of setting up NIS domains as building a set of database definitions. You need to define both the contents of the database and the users or hosts that can access the data in it. When defining NIS domains, you must decide if the data in the NIS maps applies to all hosts in the domain. If not, you may need to define multiple domains. This is equivalent to deciding that you really need two or more groups of databases to meet the requirements of different groups of users and hosts.

As we've seen, the default domain name for a host is set using the *domainname* command:

```
nisclient# domainname nesales
```

This usually appears in the boot scripts as:

```
/usr/bin/domainname `cat /etc/defaultdomain`
```

Only the superuser can set or change the default domain. Without an argument, *domainname* prints the currently set domain name. Library calls that use NIS always request maps from the default domain, so setting the domain name must be the first step in NIS startup. It is possible for an application to request map information from more than one domain, but assume for now that all requests refer to maps in the current default domain.

Despite the long introduction, a domain is implemented as nothing more than a subdirectory of the top-level NIS directory, */var/yp*. Nothing special is required to create a new domain—you simply assign it a name and then put maps into it using the server initialization procedures described later. The map files for a domain are placed in its subdirectory:

    /var/yp/*domainname*/*mapname*

You can create multiple domains by repeating the initialization using different NIS domain names. Each new domain initialization creates a new subdirectory in the NIS map directory */var/yp*. An NIS server provides service for every domain represented by a subdirectory in */var/yp*. If multiple subdirectories exist, the NIS server answers binding requests for all of them. You do not have to tell NIS which domains to serve explicitly—it figures this out by looking at the structure of its map directory.

It's possible to treat NIS as another administrative tool. However, it's more flexible than a simple configuration file management system. NIS resembles a database management system with multiple tables. As long as the NIS server can locate map information with well-known file naming and key lookup conventions, the contents of the map files are immaterial to the server. A relational database system such as Oracle provides the framework of schemas and views, but it doesn't care what the schemas look like or what data is in the tables. Similarly, the NIS system provides a framework for locating information in map files, but the information in the files and the existence or lack of map files themselves is not of consequence to the NIS server. There is no minimal set of map files necessary to define a domain. While this places the responsibility for map synchronization on the system manager, it also affords the flexibility of adding locally defined maps to the system that are managed and accessed in a well-known manner.

Internet domains versus NIS domains

The term "domain" is used in different ways by different services. In the Internet community, a domain refers to a group of hosts that are managed by an Internet Domain Name Service. These domains are defined strictly in terms of a group of hosts under common management, and are tied to organizations and their hierarchies. These domains include entire corporations or divisions, and may encompass several logical TCP/IP networks. The Internet domain *east.sun.com*, for example, spans six organizations spread over at least 15 states.

Domains in the NIS world differ from Internet name service domains in several ways. NIS domains exist only in the scheme of local network management and are usually driven by physical limits or political "machine ownership" issues. There may be several NIS domains on one network, all managed by the same system administrator. Again, it is the set of maps and the hosts that use the maps that define an NIS domain, rather than a particular network partitioning. In general, you may find many NIS domains in an Internet name service domain; the name service's hostname database is built from the hostname maps in the individual NIS domains. Integration of NIS and name services is covered in "Domain name servers" in Chapter 5. From here on, "domain" refers to an NIS domain unless explicitly noted.

The ypserv daemon

NIS service is provided by a single daemon, *ypserv*, that handles all client requests. It's simple to tell whether a system is an NIS server: just look to see whether *ypserv* is running. In this section we'll look at the RPC procedures implemented as part of the NIS protocol and the facilities used to transfer maps from master to slave servers.

Three sets of procedure calls make up the NIS protocol: client lookups, map main tenance calls, and NIS internal calls. Lookup requests are key-driven, and return one record from the DBM file per call. There are four kinds of lookups: match (single key), get-first, get-next, and get-all records. The get-first and get-next requests are used to scan the NIS map linearly, although keys are returned in a random order. "First" refers to the first key encountered in the data file based on hash table ordering, not the first key from the ASCII source file placed into the map.

Map maintenance calls are used when negotiating a map transfer between master and slave servers, although they may be made by user applications as well. The get-master function returns the master server for a map and the get-order request returns the timestamp from the last generation of the map file. Both values are available as records in the NIS maps. Finally, the NIS internal calls are used to effect a map transfer and answer requests for service to a domain. An NIS server replies only positively to a service request; if it cannot serve the named domain it will not send a reply.

The server daemon does not have any intrinsic knowledge of what domains it serves or which maps are available in those domains. It answers a request for service if the domain has a subdirectory in the NIS server directory. That is, a request for service to domain *polygon* will be answered if the */var/yp/polygon* directory exists. This directory may be empty, or may not contain a full complement of maps, but the server still answers a service request if the map directory exists.

There is no NIS RPC procedure to inquire about the existence of a map on a server; a "no such map" error is returned on a failed lookup request for the missing map. This underscores the need for every NIS server to have a full set of map files—the NIS mechanism itself can't tell when a map is missing until an NIS client asks for information from it.

If the log file */var/yp/ypserv.log* exists when *ypserv* is started, error and warning messages will be written to this file. If an NIS server receives a service request for a domain it cannot serve, it logs messages such as:

```
ypserv: Domain financials not supported (broadcast)
```

indicating that it ignored a broadcast request for an unknown domain. If each server handles only its default domain, binding attempts overheard from other domains generate large numbers of these log messages. Running multiple NIS domains on a single IP network is best done if every server can handle every domain, or if you turn off logging. If not, you will be overwhelmed with these informational error messages that do nothing but grow the log file.

ypserv keeps the file open while it is running, so a large log file must be cleaned up by truncating it:

```
# cat /dev/null > /var/yp/ypserv.log
```

Removing the file with *rm* clears the directory entry, but does not free the disk space because the *ypserv* process still has the file open. If you have multiple domains with distinct servers on a single network, you probably shouldn't enable NIS logging.

The ypbind daemon

The *ypbind* daemon is central to NIS client operation. Whenever any system is running *ypbind*, it is an NIS client—no matter what else it is doing. Therefore, it will be worth our effort to spend some time thinking about *ypbind*.

When *ypbind* first starts, it finds a server for the host's default domain. The process of locating a server is called *binding* the domain. If processes request service from other domains, *ypbind* attempts to locate servers for them as needed. *ypbind* reads a file like */var/yp/binding/bedrock/ypservers* to get the name of an NIS server to bind to. If the NIS server chosen for a domain crashes or begins to respond slowly due to a high load, *ypbind* selects the next NIS server in the *ypservers* file to re-bind. The NIS timeout period varies by implementation, but is usually between two and three minutes. Each client can be bound to several domains at once; *ypbind* manages these bindings and locates servers on demand for each newly referenced NIS domain.

A client in the NIS server-client relationship is not just a host, but a process on that host that needs NIS map information. Every client process must be bound to a server, and they do so by asking *ypbind* to locate a server on their behalf. *ypbind* keeps track of the server to which it is currently directing requests, so new client binding requests can be answered without having to contact an NIS server. *ypbind* continues to use its current server until it is explicitly told, as the result of an NIS RPC timeout, that the current server is not providing prompt service. After an RPC timeout, *ypbind* will try the next server in the *ypservers* file in an attempt to locate a faster NIS server. Because all client processes go through *ypbind*, we usually don't make a distinction between the client processes and the host on which they are running—the host itself is called the NIS client.

Once *ypbind* has created a binding between a client and a server, it never talks to the server again. When a client process requests a binding, *ypbind* simply hands back the name of the server to which the queries should be directed. Once a process has bound to a server, it can use that binding until an error occurs (such as a server crash or failure to respond). A process does *not* bind its domain before each NIS RPC call.

Domain bindings are shown by *ypwhich*:

```
% domainname
nesales
% ypwhich
wahoo
```

Here, *ypwhich* reports the currently bound server for the named domain. If the default or the named domain is not bound, *ypwhich* reports an error:

```
gonzo% ypwhich -d financials
Domain financials not bound on gonzo
```

An NIS client can be put back in standalone operation by modifying */etc/nsswitch. conf*:

```
client# cp /etc/nsswitch.files /etc/nsswitch.conf
```

NIS server as an NIS client

Previously, we recommended that NIS servers also be NIS clients. This has a number of important effects on the network's behavior. When NIS servers are booted, they may bind to each other instead of to themselves. A server that is booting executes a sequence of commands that keep it fairly busy; so the local *ypbind* process may timeout trying to bind to the local NIS server, and bind successfully with another host. Thus multiple NIS servers usually end up cross-binding—they bind to each other instead of themselves.

If servers are also NIS clients, then having only one master and one slave server creates a window in which the entire network pauses if either server goes down. If the servers have bound to each other, and one crashes, the other server rebinds to itself after a short timeout. In the interim, however, the "live" server is probably not doing useful work because it's waiting for an NIS server to respond. Increasing the number of slave servers decreases the probability that a single server crash hangs other NIS servers and consequently hangs their bound clients. In addition, running more than two NIS servers prevents all NIS clients from rebinding to the same server when an NIS server becomes unavailable.

Trace of a key match

Now we've seen how all of the pieces of NIS work by themselves. In reality, of course, the clients and servers must work together with a well-defined sequence of events. To fit all of the client- and server-side functionality into a time-sequenced picture, here is a walk-through the *getpwuid()* library call. The interaction of library routines and NIS daemons is shown in Figure 3-2.

1. A user runs *ls -l*, and the *ls* process needs to find the username corresponding to the UID of each file's owner. In this case, *ls -l* calls *getpwuid(11461)* to find the password file entry—and therefore username—for UID 11461.

2. The local password file looks like this:

    ```
    root:passwd:0:1:Operator:/:/bin/csh
    daemon:*:1:1::/:
    sys:*:2:2::/:/bin/csh
    bin:*:3:3::/bin:
    uucp:*:4:8::/var/spool/uucppublic:
    ```

    The local file is checked first, but there is no UID 11461 in it. However, */etc/nsswitch.conf* has this entry:

    ```
    passwd:      files nis
    ```

    which effectively appends the entire NIS password map. *getpwuid()* decides it needs to go to NIS for the password file entry.

3. *getpwuid()* grabs the default domain name, and binds the current process to a server for this domain. The bind can be done explicitly by calling an NIS library routine, or it may be done implicitly when the first NIS lookup request is issued. In either case, *ypbind* provides a server binding for the named domain. If the default domain is used, *ypbind* returns the current binding after pinging the bound server. However, the calling process may have specified another domain, forcing *ypbind* to locate a server for it. The client may have bindings to several domains at any time, all of which are managed by the single *ypbind* process.

4. The client process calls the NIS lookup RPC with *key=11461* and *map=passwd.byuid*. The request is bundled up and sent to the *ypserv* process on the bound server.

5. The server does a DBM key lookup and returns a password file entry, if one is found. The record is passed back to the *getpwuid()* routine, where it is returned to the calling application.

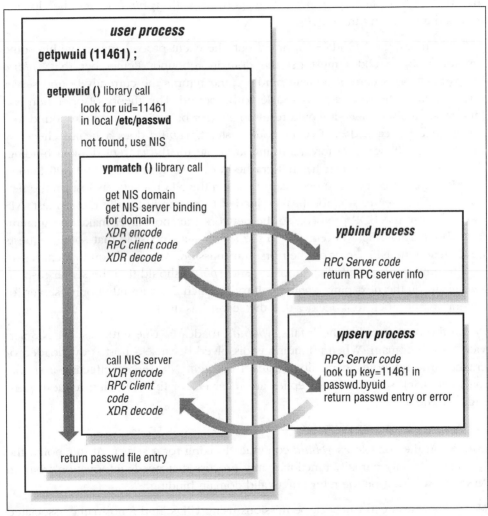

Figure 3-2. Trace of the getpwuid() library call

The server can return a number of errors on a lookup request. Obviously, the specified key might not exist in the DBM file, or the map file itself might not be present on the server. At a lower level, the RPC might generate an error if it times out before the server responds with an error or data; this would indicate that the server did not receive the request or could not process it quickly enough.

Whenever an RPC call returns a timeout error, the low-level NIS RPC routine instructs *ypbind* to dissolve the process's binding for the domain.

NIS RPC calls continue trying the remote server after a timeout error. This happens transparently to the user-level application calling the NIS RPC routine; for example, *ls* has no idea that one of its calls to *getpwuid()* resulted in an RPC timeout. The *ls* command just patiently waits for the *getpwuid()* call to return, and the RPC code called by *getpwuid()* negotiates with *ypbind* to get the domain rebound and to retry the request.

Before retrying the NIS RPC that timed out, the client process (again, within some low-level library code) must get the domain rebound. Remember that *ypbind* keeps track of its current domain binding, and returns the currently bound server for a domain whenever a process asks to be bound. This theory of operation is a little too simplistic, since it would result in a client being immediately rebound to a server that just caused an RPC timeout. Instead, *ypbind* does a health check by pinging the NIS server before returning its name for the current domain binding. This ensures that the server has not crashed or is not the cause of the RPC failure. An RPC timeout could have been caused when the NIS packet was lost on the network or if the server was too heavily loaded to promptly handle the request. NIS RPC calls use the UDP protocol, so the network transport layer makes no guarantees about delivering NIS requests to the server—it's possible that some requests never reach the NIS server on their first transmission. Any condition that causes an RPC to time out is hopefully temporary, and *ypbind* should find the server responsive again on the next ping. *ypbind* will try to reach the currently bound server for several minutes before it decides that the server has died.

When the server health check fails, *ypbind* broadcasts a new request for NIS service for the domain. When a binding is dissolved because a host is overloaded or crashes, the rebinding generally locates a different NIS server, effecting a simple load balancing scheme. If no replies are received for the rebinding request, messages of the form:

```
NIS server not responding for domain "nesales"; still trying
```

appear on the console as *ypbind* continues looking for a server. At this point, the NIS client is only partially functional; any process that needs information from an NIS map will wait on the return of a valid domain binding.

Most processes need to check permissions using UIDs, find a hostname associated with an IP address, or make some other reference to NIS-managed data if they are doing anything other than purely CPU-bound work. A machine using NIS will not run for long once it loses its binding to an NIS server. It remains partially dead until a server appears on the network and answers *ypbind*'s broadcast requests for service. The need for reliable NIS service cannot be stressed enough. In the next chapter, we'll look at ways of using and configuring the service efficiently.

In this chapter:
- *NIS network design*
- *Managing map files*
- *Advanced NIS server administration*
- *Managing multiple domains*

4

System Management Using NIS

We've seen how NIS operates on master servers, slave servers, and clients, and how clients get map information from the servers. Just knowing how NIS works, however, does not lead to its efficient use. NIS servers must be configured so that map information remains consistent on all servers, and the number of servers and the load on each server should be evaluated so that there is not a user-noticeable penalty for referring to the NIS maps.

Ideally, NIS streamlines system administration tasks by allowing you to update configuration files on many machines by making changes on a single host. When designing a network to use NIS, you must ensure that its performance cost, measured by all users doing "normal" activities, does not exceed its advantages. This chapter explains how to design an NIS network, update and distribute NIS map data, manage multiple NIS domains, and integrate NIS hostname services with the Domain Name Service.

NIS network design

At this point, you should be able to set up NIS on master and slave servers and have a good understanding of how map changes are propagated from master to slave servers. Before creating a new NIS network, you should think about the number of domains and servers you will need. NIS network design entails deciding the number of domains, the number of servers for each domain, and the domain names. Once the framework has been established, installation and ongoing maintenance of the NIS servers is fairly straightforward.

Dividing a network into domains

The number of NIS domains that you need depends upon the division of your computing resources. Use a separate NIS domain for each group of systems that has its own system administrator. The job of maintaining a system also includes maintaining its configuration information, wherever it may exist.

Large groups of users sharing network resources may warrant a separate NIS domain if the users may be cleanly separated into two or more groups. The degree to which users in the groups share information should determine whether you should split them into different NIS domains. These large groups of users usually correspond very closely to the organizational groups within your company, and the level of information sharing within the group and between groups is fairly well defined.

A good example is that of a large university, where the physics and chemistry departments have their own networked computing environments. Information sharing within each department will be common, but interdepartment sharing is minimal. The physics department isn't that interested in the machine names used by the chemistry department. The two departments will almost definitely be in two distinct NIS domains if they do not have the same system administrator (each probably gets one of its graduate students to assume this job). Assume, though, that they share an administrator—why create two NIS domains? The real motivation is to clearly mark the lines along which information is commonly shared. Setting up different NIS domains also keeps users in one department from using machines in another department.

Conversely, the need to create splinter groups of a few users for access to some machines should not warrant an independent NIS domain. Netgroups are better suited to handle this problem, because they create subsets of a domain, rather than an entirely new domain. A good example of a splinter group is the system administration staff—they may be given logins on central servers, while the bulk of the user community is not. Putting the system administrators in another domain generally creates more problems than the new domain was intended to solve.

Domain names

Choosing domain names is not nearly as difficult as gauging the number of domains needed. Just about any naming convention can be used provided that domain names are unique. You can choose to apply the name of the group as the NIS domain name; for example, you could use *history*, *politics*, and *comp-sci* to name the departments in a university.

If you are setting up multiple NIS domains that are based on hierarchical divisions, you may want to use a multilevel naming scheme with dot-separated name components:

> *cslab.comp-sci*
> *staff.comp-sci*

profs.history
grad.history

The first two domain names would apply to the "lab" machines and the depart-mental staff machines in the computer science department, while the two *.history* domain names separate the professors and graduate students in that department.

Multilevel domain names are useful if you will be using an Internet Domain Name Service. You can assign NIS domain names based on the name service domain names, so that every domain name is unique and also identifies how the addi-tional name service is related to NIS. Integration of Internet name services and NIS is covered at the end of this chapter.

Number of NIS servers per domain

The number of servers per NIS domain is determined by the size of the domain and the aggregate service requirements for it, the level of failure protection required, and any physical network constraints that might affect client binding pat-terns. As a general rule, there should be at least two servers per domain: one master and one slave. The dual-server model offers basic protection if one server crashes, since clients of that server will rebind to the second server. With a soli-tary server, the operation of the network hinges on the health of the NIS server, creating both a performance bottleneck and a single point of failure in the net-work.

Increasing the number of NIS servers per domain reduces the impact of any one server crashing. With more servers, each one is likely to have fewer clients binding to it, assuming that the clients are equally likely to bind to any server. When a server crashes, fewer clients will be affected. Spreading the load out over several hosts may also reduce the number of domain rebindings that occur during unusu-ally long server response times. If the load is divided evenly, this should level out variations in the NIS server response time due to server crashes and reboots.

There is no golden rule for allocating a certain number of servers for every *n* NIS clients. The total NIS service load depends on the type of work done on each machine and the relative speeds of client and server. A faster machine generates more NIS requests in a given time window than a slower one, if both machines are doing work that makes equal use of NIS. Some interactive usage patterns gen-erate more NIS traffic than work that is CPU-intensive. A user who is continually listing files, compiling source code, and reading mail will make more use of pass-word file entries and mail aliases than one who runs a text editor most of the time.

The bottom line is that very few types of work generate endless streams of NIS requests; most work makes casual references to the NIS maps separated by at most several seconds (compare this to disk accesses, which are usually separated by milliseconds). Generally, 30–40 NIS clients per server is an upper limit if the clients and servers are roughly the same speed. Faster clients need a lower client/server ratio, while a server that is faster than its clients might support 50 or more NIS clients. The best way to gauge server usage is to watch for *ypbind* requests for domain bindings, indicating that clients are timing out waiting for NIS service. Methods for observing binding requests are discussed in "Displaying and analyzing client bindings" in Chapter 13.

Finally, the number of servers required may depend on the physical structure of the network. If you have decided to use four NIS servers, for example, and have two network segments with equal numbers of clients, joined by a bridge or router, make sure you divide the NIS servers equally on both sides of the network-partitioning hardware. If you put only one NIS server on one side of a bridge or router, then clients on that side will almost always bind to this server. The delay experienced by NIS requests in traversing the bridge approaches any server-related delay, so that the NIS server on the same side of the bridge will answer a client's request before a server on the opposite side of the bridge, even if the closer server is more heavily loaded than the one across the bridge. With this configuration, you have undone the benefits of multiple NIS servers, since clients on the one-server side of the bridge bind to the same server in most cases. Locating lopsided NIS server bindings is discussed in "Displaying and analyzing client bindings" in Chapter 13.

Managing map files

Keeping map files updated on all servers is essential to the proper operation of NIS. There are two mechanisms for updating map files: using *make* and the NIS *Makefile*, which pushes maps from the master server to the slave servers, and the *ypxfr* utility, which pulls maps from the master server. This section starts with a look at how map file updates are made and how they get distributed to slave servers.

Having a single point of administration makes it easier to propagate configuration changes through the network, but it also means that you may have more than one person changing the same file. If there are several system administrators maintaining the NIS maps, they need to coordinate their efforts, or you will find that one person removes NIS map entries added by another. Using a source code control system, such as SCCS or RCS, in conjunction with NIS often solves this problem. In the second part of this section, we'll see how to use alternate map source files and source code control systems with NIS.

Map distribution

Master and slave servers are distinguished by their ability to effect permanent changes to NIS maps. Changes may be made to an NIS map on a slave server, but the next map transfer from the master will overlay this change. Modify maps *only* on the master server, and push them from the master server to its slave servers. On the NIS master server, edit the source file for the map using your favorite text editor. Source files for NIS maps are listed in Table 3-1. Then go to the NIS map directory and build the new map using *make*, as shown here:

```
# vi /etc/hosts
# cd /var/yp
# make
   ...New hosts map is built and distributed...
```

Without any arguments, *make* builds all maps that are out-of-date with respect to their ASCII source files. When more than one map is built from the same ASCII file, for example the *passwd.byname* and *passwd.byuid* maps built from */etc/ passwd*, they are all built when *make* is invoked.

When a map is rebuilt, the *yppush* utility is used to check the order number of the same map on each NIS server. If the maps are out-of-date, *yppush* transfers the map to the slave servers, using the server names in the *ypservers* map. Scripts to rebuild maps and push them to slave servers are part of the NIS *Makefile*, which is covered in an upcoming section, ""Map file dependencies."

Map transfers done on demand after source file modifications may not always complete successfully. The NIS slave server may be down, or the transfer may timeout due to severe congestion or server host loading. To ensure that maps do not remain out-of-date for a long time (until the next NIS map update), NIS uses the *ypxfr* utility to transfer a map to a slave server. The slave transfers the map after checking the timestamp on its copy; if the master's copy has been modified more recently, the slave server will replace its copy of the map with the one it transfers from the server. It is possible to force a map transfer to a slave server, ignoring the slave's timestamp, which is useful if a map gets corrupted and must be replaced. Under Solaris, an additional master server daemon called *ypxfrd* is used to speed up map transfer operations, but the map distribution utilities resort to the old method if they cannot reach *ypxfrd* on the master server.

The map transfer—both in *yppush* and in *ypxfr*—is performed by requesting that the slave server walk through all keys in the modified map and build a map containing these keys. This seems quite counterintuitive, since you would hope that a map transfer amounts to nothing more than the master server sending the map to the slave server. However, NIS was designed to be used in a heterogeneous environment, so the master server's DBM file format may not correspond to that used by the slave server. DBM files are tightly tied to the byte ordering and file block allocation rules of the server system, and a DBM file must be created on the system that indexes it. Slave servers, therefore, have to enumerate the entries in an NIS map and rebuild the map from them, using their own local conventions for

DBM file construction. Indeed, it is theoretically possible to have NIS server implementation that does not use DBM. When the slave server has rebuilt the map, it replaces its existing copy of the map with the new one. Schedules for transferring maps to slave servers and scripts to be run out of *cron* are provided in the next section.

Regular map transfers

Relying on demand-driven updates is overly optimistic, since a server may be down when the master is updated. NIS includes the *ypxfr* tool to perform periodic transfers of maps to slave servers, keeping them synchronized with the master server even if they miss an occasional *yppush*. The *ypxfr* utility will transfer a map only if the slave's copy is out-of-date with respect to the master's map.

Unlike *yppush*, *ypxfr* runs on the slave. *ypxfr* contacts the master server for a map, enumerates the entries in the map, and rebuilds a private copy of the map. If the map is built successfully, *ypxfr* replaces the slave server's copy of the map with the newly created one. Note that doing a *yppush* from the NIS master essentially involves asking each slave server to perform a *ypxfr* operation if the slave's copy of the map is out-of-date. The difference between *yppush* and *ypxfr* (besides the servers on which they are run) is that *ypxfr* retrieves a map even if the slave server does not have a copy of it, while *yppush* requires that the slave server have the map in order to check its modification time.

ypxfr map updates should be scheduled out of *cron* based on how often the maps change. The *passwd* and *aliases* maps change most frequently, and could be transferred once an hour. Other maps, like the *services* and *rpc* maps, tend to be static and can be updated once a day. The standard mechanism for invoking *ypxfr* out of *cron* is to create two or more scripts based on transfer frequency, and to call *ypxfr* from the scripts. The maps included in the *ypxfr_1perhour* script are those that are likely to be modified several times during the day, while those in *ypxfr_2perday*, and *ypxfr_1perday* may change once every few days:

```
ypxfr_1perhour script:
/usr/lib/netsvc/yp/ypxfr passwd.byuid
/usr/lib/netsvc/yp/ypxfr passwd.byname

ypxfr_2perday script:
/usr/lib/netsvc/yp/ypxfr hosts.byname
/usr/lib/netsvc/yp/ypxfr hosts.byaddr
/usr/lib/netsvc/yp/ypxfr ethers.byaddr
/usr/lib/netsvc/yp/ypxfr ethers.byname
/usr/lib/netsvc/yp/ypxfr netgroup
/usr/lib/netsvc/yp/ypxfr netgroup.byuser
/usr/lib/netsvc/yp/ypxfr netgroup.byhost
/usr/lib/netsvc/yp/ypxfr mail.aliases
```

ypxfr_1perday script:
```
/usr/lib/netsvc/yp/ypxfr group.byname
/usr/lib/netsvc/yp/ypxfr group.bygid
/usr/lib/netsvc/yp/ypxfr protocols.byname
/usr/lib/netsvc/yp/ypxfr protocols.bynumber
/usr/lib/netsvc/yp/ypxfr networks.byname
/usr/lib/netsvc/yp/ypxfr networks.byaddr
/usr/lib/netsvc/yp/ypxfr services.byname
/usr/lib/netsvc/yp/ypxfr ypservers
```

crontab entry:
```
0 *     * * * /usr/lib/netsvc/yp/ypxfr_1perhour
0 0,12 * * * /usr/lib/netsvc/yp/ypxfr_2perday
0 0     * * * /usr/lib/netsvc/yp/ypxfr_1perday
```

ypxfr logs its activity on the slave servers if the log file */var/yp/ypxfr.log* exists when *ypxfr* starts.

Map file dependencies

Dependencies of NIS maps on ASCII source files are maintained by the NIS *Makefile*, located in the NIS directory */var/yp* on the master server. The *Makefile* dependencies are built around timestamp files named after their respective source files. For example, the timestamp file for the NIS maps built from the password file is *passwd.time*, and the timestamp for the hosts maps is kept in *hosts.time*.

The timestamp files are empty because only their modification dates are of interest. The *make* utility is used to build maps according to the rules in the *Makefile*, and *make* compares file modification times to determine which targets need to be rebuilt. For example, *make* compares the timestamp on the *passwd.time* file and that of the ASCII */etc/passwd* file, and rebuilds the NIS *passwd* map if the ASCII source file was modified since the last time the NIS *passwd* map was built.

After editing a map source file, building the map (and any other maps that may depend on it) is done with *make*:
```
# cd /var/yp
# make passwd    Rebuilds only password map.
# make           Rebuilds all maps that are out-of-date.
```

If the source file has been modified more recently than the timestamp file, *make* notes that the dependency in the *Makefile* is not met and executes the commands to regenerate the NIS map. In most cases, map regeneration requires that the ASCII file be stripped of comments, fed to *makedbm* for conversion to DBM format, and then pushed to all slave servers using *yppush*.

Be careful when building a few selected maps; if other maps depend on the modified map, then you may distribute incomplete map information. For example, Solaris uses the *netid* map to combine password and group information. The *netid* map is used by login shells to determine user credentials: for every user, it lists all of the groups that user is a member of. The *netid* map depends on both the */etc/passwd* and */etc/group* files, so when either one is changed, the *netid* map should be rebuilt.

But let's say you make a change to the */etc/groups* file, and decide to just rebuild and distribute the *group* map:

```
nismaster# cd /var/yp
nismaster# make group
```

The commands in this example do not update the *netid* map, because the *netid* map doesn't depend on the *group* map at all. The *netid* map depends on the */etc/group* file—as does the *group* map—but in the previous example, you would have instructed *make* to build only the *group* map. If you build the *group* map without updating the *netid* map, users will become very confused about their group memberships: their login shells will read *netid* and get old group information, even though the NIS map source files *appear* correct.

The best solution to this problem is to build all maps that are out-of-date by using *make* with no arguments:

```
nismaster# cd /var/yp
nismaster# make
```

Once the map is built, the NIS *Makefile* distributes it, using *yppush*, to the slave servers named in the *ypservers* map. *yppush* walks through the list of NIS servers and performs an RPC call to each slave server to check the timestamp on the map to be transferred. If the map is out-of-date, *yppush* uses another RPC call to the slave server to initiate a transfer of the map.

A map that is corrupted or was not successfully transferred to all slave servers can be explicitly rebuilt and repushed by removing its timestamp file on the master server:

```
master# cd /var/yp
master# rm hosts.time
master# make hosts
```

This procedure should be used if a map was built when the NIS master server's time was set incorrectly, creating a map that becomes out-of-date when the time is reset. If you need to perform a complete reconstruction of all NIS maps, for any reason, remove all of the timestamp files and run *make*:

```
master# cd /var/yp
master# rm *.time
master# make
```

This extreme step is best reserved for testing the map distribution mechanism, or recovering from corruption of the NIS map directory.

Password file updates

One exception to the *yppush* push-on-demand strategy is the *passwd* map. Users need to be able to change their passwords without system manager intervention. The hosts file, for example, is changed by the superuser and then pushed to other servers when it is rebuilt. In contrast, when you change your password, you (as a nonprivileged user) modify the local password file. To change a password in an NIS map, the change must be made on the master server and distributed to all slave servers in order to be seen back on the client host where you made the change.

yppasswd is a user utility that is similar to the *passwd* program, but it changes the user's password in the original source file on the NIS master server. *yppasswd* usually forces the password map to be rebuilt, although at sites choosing not to rebuild the map on demand, the new password will not be distributed until the next map transfer. *yppasswd* is used like *passwd*, but it reports the server name on which the modifications are made. Here is an example:

```
[wahoo]% yppasswd
Changing NIS password for stern on mahimahi.
Old password:
New password:
Retype new password:
NIS entry changed on mahimahi
```

Some versions of *passwd* (such as Solaris 2.6 and higher) check to see if the password file is managed by NIS, and invoke *yppasswd* if this is the case. Check your vendor's documentation for procedures particular to your system.

NIS provides read-only access to its maps. There is nothing in the NIS protocol that allows a client to rewrite the data for a key. To accept changes to maps, a server distinct from the NIS server is required that modifies the source file for the map and then rebuilds the NIS map from the modified ASCII file. To handle incoming *yppasswd* change requests, the master server must run the *yppasswdd* daemon (note the second "d" in the daemon's name). This RPC daemon gets started in the */usr/lib/netsvc/yp/ypstart* boot script on the master NIS server only:

```
if [ "$master" = "$hostname" -a X$YP_SERVER = "XTRUE" ]; then
        ...
        if [ -x $YPDIR/rpc.yppasswdd ]; then
                PWDIR=`grep "^PWDIR" /var/yp/Makefile 2> /dev/null` \
                && PWDIR=`expr "$PWDIR" : `.*=[          ]*<[^   ]*>``
                if [ "$PWDIR" ]; then
                        if [ "$PWDIR" = "/etc" ]; then
                                unset PWDIR
                        else
                                PWDIR="-D $PWDIR"
                        fi
        fi
```

```
            $YPDIR/rpc.yppasswdd $PWDIR -m \
                  && echo ` rpc.yppasswdd\c`
         fi
         ...
   fi
```

The host making a password map change locates the master server by asking for
the master of the NIS *passwd* map, and the *yppasswdd* daemon acts as a gateway
between the user's host and a *passwd*-like utility on the master server. The location of the master server's password file and options to build a new map after
each update are given as command-line arguments to *yppasswdd*, as shown in the
previous example.

The *-D* argument specifies the name of the master server's source for the password map; it may be the default */etc/passwd* or it may point to an alternative password file.* The *-m* option specifies that *make* is to be performed in the NIS
directory on the master server. You can optionally specify arguments after *-m* that
are passed to make. With a default set up, the fragment in *ypstart* would cause
yppasswdd to invoke *make* as:

 # (cd /var/yp; make)

after each change to the master's password source file. Since it is likely only the
password file will have changed, only the password maps get rebuilt and pushed.
You can ensure that only the password maps get pushed changing the *yppaswdd*
line in *ypstart* to:

```
$YPDIR/rpc.yppasswdd $PWDIR -m passwd \
                  && echo ` rpc.yppasswdd\c`
```

Source code control for map files

With multiple system administrators and a single point of administration, it is possible for conflicting or unexplained changes to NIS maps to wreak havoc with the
network. The best way to control modifications to maps and to track the change
history of map source files is to put them under a source code control system such
as SCCS.

Source code files usually contain the SCCS headers in a comment or in a global
string that gets compiled into an executable. Putting SCCS keywords into comments in the */etc/hosts* and */etc/aliases* files allows you to track the last version and
date of edit:

```
header to be added to file:
#       /etc/hosts header
#       %M%      %I%          %H% %T%
#       %W%
```

---

* Recall from "Installing the NIS master server" in Chapter 3 that we changed PWDR to */etc/nispw*.

keywords filled in after getting file from SCCS:

```
#        /etc/hosts header
#        hosts        1.32        12/29/90 16:37:52
#        @(#)hosts        1.32
```

Once the headers have been added to the map source files, put them under SCCS administration:

```
nismaster# cd /etc
nismaster# mkdir SCCS
nismaster# /usr/ccs/bin/sccs admin -ialiases aliases
nismaster# /usr/ccs/bin/sccs admin -ihosts hosts
nismaster# /usr/ccs/bin/sccs get aliases hosts
```

The copies of the files that are checked out of SCCS control are read-only. Someone making a casual change to a map is forced to go and check it out of SCCS properly before doing so. Using SCCS, each change to a file is documented before the file gets put back under SCCS control. If you always return a file to SCCS before it is converted into an NIS map, the SCCS control file forms an audit trail for configuration changes:

```
nismaster# cd /etc
nismaster# sccs prs hosts
D 1.31 00/05/22 08:52:35 root 31 30        00001/00001/00117
MRs:
COMMENTS:
added new host for info-center group
D 1.30 00/06/04 07:19:04 root 30 29        00001/00001/00117
MRs:
COMMENTS:
changed bosox-fddi to jetstar-fddi
D 1.29 90/11/08 11:03:47 root 29 28        00011/00011/00107
MRs:
COMMENTS:
commented out the porting lab systems.
```

If any change to the hosts or aliases file breaks, SCCS can be used to find the exact lines that were changed and the time the change was made (for confirmation that the modification caused the network problems).

The two disadvantages to using SCCS for NIS maps are that all changes must be made as *root* and that it won't work for the password file. The superuser must perform all file checkouts and modifications, unless the underlying file permissions are changed to make the files writable by nonprivileged users. If all changes are made by *root*, then the SCCS logs do not contain information about the user making the change. The password file falls outside of SCCS control because its contents will be modified by users changing their passwords, without being able to check the file out of SCCS first. Also, some files, such as */etc/group*, have no comment lines, so you cannot use SCCS keywords in them.

Using alternate map source files

You may decide to use nonstandard source files for various NIS maps on the master server, especially if the master server is not going to be an NIS client. Alternatively, you may need to modify the standard NIS *Makefile* to build your own NIS maps. Approaches to both of these problems are discussed in this section.

Some system administrators prefer to build the NIS password map from a file other than */etc/passwd*, giving them finer control over access to the server. Separating the host's and the NIS password files is also advantageous if there are password file entries on the server (such as those for dial-in UUCP) that shouldn't be made available on all NIS clients. To avoid distributing UUCP password file entries to all NIS clients, the NIS password file should be kept separately from */etc/passwd* on the master server. The master can include private UUCP password file entries and can embed the entire NIS map file via *nsswitch.conf*.

If you de-couple the NIS password map from the master server's password file, then the NIS *Makefile* should be modified to reflect the new dependency. Refer back to the procedure described in "Installing the NIS master server" in Chapter 3.

Advanced NIS server administration

Once NIS is installed and running, you may find that you need to remove or rearrange your NIS servers to accommodate an increased load on one server. For example, if you attach several printers to an NIS server and use it as a print server, it may no longer make a good NIS server if most of its bandwidth is used for driving the printers. If this server is your master NIS server, you may want to assign NIS master duties to another host. We'll look at these advanced administration problems in this section.

Removing an NIS slave server

If you decommission an NIS slave server, or decide to stop running NIS on it because the machine is loaded by other functions, you need to remove it from the *ypserver* map and turn off NIS. If a host is listed in the *ypservers* map but is not running *ypserv*, then attempts to push maps to this host will fail. This will not cause any data corruption or NIS service failures. It will, however, significantly increase the time required to push the NIS maps because *yppush* times out waiting for the former server to respond before trying the next server.

There is no explicit "remove" procedure in the NIS maintenance tools, so you have to do this manually. Start by rebuilding the *ypservers* map on the NIS master server:

```
master# cd /var/yp
master# ypcat -k ypservers | grep -v servername\
     | makedbm - /var/yp/`domainname`/ypservers
```

The *ypcat* command line prints the entries in the current *ypservers* map, then removes the entry for the desired server using *grep -v*. This shortened list of servers is given to *makedbm*, which rebuilds the *ypservers* map. If the decommissioned server is not being shut down permanently, make sure you remove the NIS maps in */var/yp* on the former server so that the machine doesn't start *ypserv* on its next boot and provide out-of-date map information to the network. Many strange problems result if an NIS server is left running with old maps: the server will respond to requests, but may provide incorrect information to the client. After removing the maps and rebuilding *ypservers*, reboot the former NIS server and check to make sure that *ypserv* is not running. You may also want to force a map distribution at this point to test the new *ypservers* map. The *yppush* commands used in the map distribution should not include the former NIS server.

Changing NIS master servers

The procedure described in the previous section works only for slave servers. There are some additional dependencies on the master server that must be removed before an NIS master can be removed. To switch NIS master service to another host, you must rebuild all NIS maps to reflect the name of the new master host, update the *ypservers* map if the old master is being taken out of service, and distribute the new maps (with the new master server record) to all slave servers.

Here are the steps used to change master NIS servers:

1. Build the new master host as a slave server, initializing its domain directory and filling it with copies of the current maps. Each map must be rebuilt on the new master, which requires the NIS *Makefile* and map source files from the old master. Copy the source files and the NIS *Makefile* to the new master, and then rebuild all of the maps—but do not attempt to push them to other slave servers:

   ```
   newmaster# cd /var/yp
   newmaster# rm *.time
   newmaster# make NOPUSH=1
   ```

   Removing all of the timestamp files forces every map to be rebuilt; passing NOPUSH=1 to *make* prevents the maps from being pushed to other servers. At this point, you have NIS maps that contain master host records pointing to the new NIS master host.

2. Install copies of the new master server's maps on the old master server. Transferring the new maps to existing NIS servers is made more difficult because of the process used by *yppush*: when a map is pushed to a slave server via the

transfer-map NIS RPC call, the slave server consults *its own* copy of the map to determine the master server from which it should load a new copy. This is an NIS security feature: it prevents someone from creating an NIS master server and forcing maps onto the valid slave servers using *yppush*. The slave servers will look to their current NIS master server for map data, rather than accepting it from the renegade NIS master server.

In the process of changing master servers, the slave servers' maps will point to the old master server. To work around *yppush*, first move the new maps to the old master server using *ypxfr*:

```
oldmaster# /usr/lib/netsvc/yp/ypxfr -h newmaster -f passwd.byuid
oldmaster# /usr/lib/netsvc/yp/ypxfr -h newmaster -f passwd.byname
oldmaster# /usr/lib/netsvc/yp/ypxfr -h newmaster -f hosts.byname
...include all NIS maps...
```

The *-h newmaster* option tells the old master server to grab the map from the new master server, and the *-f* flag forces a transfer even if the local version is not out of order with the new map. Every NIS map must be transferred to the old master server. When this step is complete, the old master server's maps all point to the new master server.

3. On the old master server, distribute copies of the new maps to all NIS slave servers using *yppush*:

```
oldmaster# /usr/lib/netsvc/yp/yppush passwd.byuid
oldmaster# /usr/lib/netsvc/yp/yppush passwd.byname
oldmaster# /usr/lib/netsvc/yp/yppush hosts.byname
...include all NIS maps...
```

yppush forces the slave servers to look at their old maps, find the master server (still the old master), and copy the current map from the master server. Because the map itself contains the pointer record to the master server, transferring the entire map automatically updates the slave servers' maps to point to the new master server.

4. If the old master server is being removed from NIS service, rebuild the *ypservers* map.

Many of these steps can be automated using shell scripts or simple rule additions to the NIS *Makefile*, requiring less effort than it might seem. For example, you can merge steps 2 and 3 in a single shell script that transfers maps from the new master to the old master, and then pushes each map to all of the slave servers. Run this script on the old master server:

```
#! /bin/sh
MAPS="passwd.byuid passwd.byname hosts.byname ..."
NEWMASTER=newmaster
for map in $MAPS
do
        echo moving $map
```

```
          /usr/lib/netsvc/yp/ypxfr -h $NEWMASTER -f $map
          /usr/lib/netsvc/yp/yppush $map
done
```

The alternative to this method is to rebuild the entire NIS system from scratch, starting with the master server. In the process of building the system, NIS service on the network will be interrupted as slave servers are torn down and rebuilt with new maps.

Managing multiple domains

A single NIS server may be a slave of more than one master server, if it is providing service to multiple domains. In addition, a server may be a master for one domain and a slave of another. Multimaster relationships are set up when NIS is installed on each of the master servers. In the course of building the *ypservers* map, the slave servers handling multiple domains are named in the *ypservers* map for each domain.

When multiple domains are used with independent NIS servers (each serving only one domain), it is sometimes necessary to keep one or more of the maps in these domains in perfect synchronization. Domains with different password and group files, for example, might still want to share global alias and host maps to simplify administration. Adding a new user to either domain would make the user's mail aliases appear in the global alias file, to be shared by both domains. Figure 4-1 shows three NIS domains that share some maps and keep private copies of others.

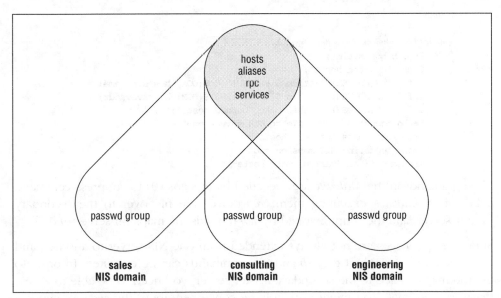

Figure 4-1. Map sharing in multiple domains

The *hosts* and *aliases* maps are shared between the NIS domains so that any changes to them are reflected on all NIS clients in all domains. The *passwd* and *group* files are managed on a per-domain basis so that new users or groups in one domain do not automatically appear in the other domains. This gives the system administrators fine control over user access to machines and files in each NIS domain.

A much simpler case is the argument for having a single */etc/rpc* file and an */etc/services* file across all domains in an organization. As locally developed or third-party software that relies on these additional services is distributed to new networks, the required configuration changes will be in place. This scenario is most common when multiple NIS domains are run on a single network with less than one system administrator per domain.

Sharing maps across domains involves setting up a master/slave relationship between the two NIS master servers. The map transfer can be done periodically out of *cron* on the "slave" master server, or the true master server for the map can push the modified source file to the secondary master after each modification. The latter method offers the advantages of keeping the map source files synchronized and keeping the NIS maps current as soon as changes are made, but it requires that the superuser have remote execution permissions on the secondary NIS master server.

To force a source file to be pushed to another domain, modify the NIS *Makefile* to copy the source file to the secondary master server, and rebuild the map there:

```
hosts.time:
    ....
    rebuild hosts.byname and hosts.byaddr
        @touch hosts.time;
        @echo "updated hosts";
        @if [ ! $(NOPUSH) ]; then $(YPPUSH) -d $(DOM) hosts.byname; fi
        @if [ ! $(NOPUSH) ]; then $(YPPUSH) -d $(DOM) hosts.byaddr; fi
        @if [ ! $(NOPUSH) ]; then echo "pushed hosts"; fi
        @echo "copying hosts file to NIS server ono"
        @rcp /etc/hosts ono:/etc/hosts
        @echo "updating NIS maps on ono"
        @rsh ono "( cd /var/yp; make hosts )"
```

The commands in the *Makefile* are preceded by at signs (@) to suppress command echo when *make* is executing them. *rcp* moves the file over to the secondary master server, and the script invoked by *rsh* rebuilds the maps on server *ono*.

Superuser privileges are not always extended from one NIS server to another, and this scheme works only if the *rsh* and *rcp* commands can be executed. In order to get the maps copied to the secondary master server, you need to be able to access that server as *root*. You might justifiably be concerned about the security implications, since the *rcp* and *rsh* commands work without password prompts. One alternative is to leave the source files out-of-date and simply move the map file to the secondary master and have it distributed to slave servers in the second domain. Another alternative is to use Kerberos V5 versions of *rcp* and *rsh* or to use the secure shell (*ssh*). Kerberos V5 and *ssh* are available as free software or in commercial form. Your vendor might even provide one or both. For Solaris 2.6 and upward, you can get the Sun Enterprise Authentication Mechanism (SEAM) product from Sun, which has Kerberos V5, including *rcp* and *rsh* using Kerberos V5 security (see "SEAM: Kerberos V5 for Solaris" in Chapter 12). If you use SEAM, you'll want to prefix *rcp* and *rsh* in the *Makefile* with */usr/krb5/bin/*.

The following script can be run out of *cron* on the secondary master server to pick up the host maps from NIS server *mahimahi*, the master server for domain *nesales*:

```
#! /bin/sh
/usr/lib/netsvc/yp/ypxfr -h mahimahi -s nesales hosts.byname
/usr/lib/netsvc/yp/ypxfr -h mahimahi -s nesales hosts.byaddr
/usr/lib/netsvc/yp/yppush -d `domainname` hosts.byname
/usr/lib/netsvc/yp/yppush -d `domainname` hosts.byaddr
```

The *ypxfr* commands get the maps from the primary master server, and then the *yppush* commands distribute them in the local, secondary NIS domain. The *-h* option to *ypxfr* specifies the hostname from which to initiate the transfer, and overrides the map's master record. The *-s* option indicates the domain from which the map is to be taken. Note that in this approach, the hosts map points to *mahimahi* as the master in *both* domains. If the *rcp*-based transfer is used, then the hosts map in each domain points to the master server in that domain. The master server record in the map always indicates the host containing a source file from which the map can be rebuilt.

5

In this chapter:
• Domain name
  servers
• Implementation
• Fully qualified and
  unqualified
  hostnames
• Centralized versus
  distributed
  management
• Migrating from NIS
  to DNS for host
  naming
• What next?

Living with Multiple
Directory Servers

Domain name servers

The hostname management provided by NIS can be integrated with an Internet
Domain Name Service (DNS), or the DNS facilities can be used to replace the NIS
host map in its entirety. We'll avoid a full-length discussion of setting up a name
server. That process depends on the type of name server supported by your
vendor, and it is best described by your vendor's documentation. Instead, this section concentrates on differences between the scope of the two hostname services,
and support for DNS with and without NIS. Note that the implementation of
Domain name services provided by your vendor may not be called DNS. If the
Berkeley Internet Name Domain name service or one of its derivatives is used, the
service is often called BIND.

DNS versus NIS

DNS provides a hierarchical hostname management system that spans the entire
Internet. Each level in the hierarchy designates authoritative name servers that contain maps of hostnames and IP addresses, similar to the NIS *hosts* map but on a
larger scale. The DNS server for a large name service domain would have host
information merged from dozens of NIS domains. First among the advantages of
DNS is its ability to decentralize responsibility for the maintenance of hostname-to-
IP address mappings and the resulting domain name qualification that is used to
differentiate identically named hosts.

Decentralized name management means that each organization running a name
service domain—whether it is a subdivision of a corporation or an entire
company—can maintain its own host information without having to notify some
central authority of changes in its local configuration. Host information is
published through the authoritative name server for that domain, and hosts in

other name service domains retrieve information from the name server when needed. Every domain knows how to reach the next highest level in the name space hierarchy, and it can generally find most of its peer name servers within the same organization. If a name server does not know how to reach the name server for another domain, it can ask the next higher level domain name server for assistance.

For example, Princeton University is part of the educational, or *.edu*, domain. The domain name for the entire university is *princeton.edu*, and it is further divided by department:

> *cs.princeton.edu*
> *politics.princeton.edu*
> *history.princeton.edu*

and so on. Each of the name servers for the departmental name service domains knows how to reach most of the others; therefore each department can run its own systems without having to notify a campus-wide network manager of any changes to host information. There is also a name server for the entire *princeton.edu* domain that points to lower-level name servers for incoming queries and locates other domains in *.edu*, *.com*, or *.gov* for outbound requests.

In a world in which every machine name must be unique, all of the good names are taken very quickly. DNS allows each domain to have a distinct name space, so that two domains may have hosts with the same name: the name service domain suffix distinguishes them on a higher level in the hierarchy. This is a job that cannot be performed by NIS, since the concatenation of */etc/hosts* files from several different domains would result in hostname clashes. If the NIS domains are left independent, there is no global naming authority, because NIS lacks a mechanism for cross-domain hostname queries.

DNS integration with NIS

Hostnames are managed in a hierarchy. Each host manages its own name, so the hosts are the "leaf nodes" in this management tree. Hosts are grouped together into NIS or DNS domains, creating a two-level tree. DNS domains may be further grouped together by company, department, or physical location, adding more levels to the management hierarchy. NIS fits into the DNS management scheme at the lowest level in this hierarchy.

Within a single DNS domain, there may be many physical networks with several system administrators. NIS provides a system for the independent management of these small networks; NIS host map information can be combined to form the DNS host file. The approaches for doing this are described the section "Implementation" later in this chapter.

NIS and DNS domain names

If an Internet DNS is used in conjunction with NIS, it is helpful to tie the NIS domain names to the DNS domain name. Deriving NIS domain names from the DNS domain name links the two management schemes: the DNS-derived portion of the NIS domain name indicates where the NIS domain looks for its hostname information. Joining NIS and DNS domain names also makes sense if you have a single DNS domain that spans several physical locations. Each office will have its own networks, and its own NIS domains, so using the DNS domain name in the NIS domain name indicates how these locations fit into the "big picture."

For example, the Polygon Company uses the DNS domain name *polygon.com*. It has four NIS domains in its main office, which uses the *polygon.com* DNS domain name. The NIS domain names use the DNS domain name as a suffix:

> *bos-engin.polygon.com*
> *philly-engin.polygon.com*
> *finance.polygon.com*
> *sales.polygon.com*

If NIS is set up as the primary directory service, then Solaris versions of *sendmail* assume that an NIS domain name was derived from a DNS domain name, and they will strip the first component to derive the mail domain name. That is, if your NIS domain name is *bos-engin.polygon.com*, then *sendmail* uses *polygon.com* as your mail domain name by default. There may be many NIS domains in this DNS domain; *sendmail* strips off the leading component to form the DNS domain name.

However, if there are multiple NIS domains within the DNS domain—several sales offices in different cities, for example—then the NIS domain names should reflect the subdivision of the DNS domain, as shown in Table 5-1.

Table 5-1. Subdividing a DNS domain into NIS domains

NIS Domain	DNS Domain
boston.sales.polygon.com	*.sales.polygon.com*
philly.sales.polygon.com	*.sales.polygon.com*
rahway.sales.polygon.com	*.sales.polygon.com*
waltham.engin.polygon.com	*.engin.polygon.com*
alameda.engin.polygon.com	*.engin.polygon.com*

Because the NIS domain name contains four dot-separated components, *sendmail* drops the first component and uses the remainder as a DNS domain name. This allows all of the sales offices to be treated as a single administrative unit for mail and hostname management, even though they require distinct NIS domains.

It is important to note that each single administrative unit, whether it is implemented with one NIS domain or multiple NIS domains must share the same map entries. Thus, all the hosts listed in the *hosts* map of *waltham.engin.polygon.com* must be listed in the *hosts* map of *alameda.engin.polygon.com*. The converse must be true as well. Getting all hosts to agree on usernames, *uid/gid* values, and host addresses is a prerequisite for adding other distributed services such as the Network File System.

Domain aliases

Some systems impose a fairly small limit on the length of a domain name. If you've chosen a long NIS domain name, say *nesales.East.Sun.COM*, then implementations of NIS that restrict the length of a domain name will not be able to bind to a server.

You could build a second NIS domain with a shorter name and duplicate the maps from the first domain, but this leaves you with twice the administrative work. An easier solution to this problem is to create a domain name alias for the longer name by making a symbolic link in the NIS server directory */var/yp* on each server host:

```
master# cd /var/yp
master# ln -s nesales.East.Sun.COM nesales
```

NIS servers in the fully qualified domain respond to requests for service for the truncated domain name because they believe they have a set of maps for the specified domain. It is of no consequence that the "directory" is really a link to another domain's directory. This trick can also be used to force two distinct NIS domains to share exactly the same set of maps.

In a simple network, your domain names are likely to be short and easily managed. However, if you integrate DNS with NIS, and choose NIS domain names based on name service domains, you may end up with long, multicomponent names such as *grad.history.princeton.edu*. Using symbolic links to create aliases for long names may be necessary to make all of your NIS clients find NIS servers.

Implementation

There are four ways to integrate NIS with DNS, each of which is described in more detail in the following subsections.

Run NIS without DNS on client and server

This is the default for many systems, including Solaris. In this approach, the name services switch file, *nsswitch.conf*, is set up so that *nis* and *files* are the only

directory services listed in the *hosts* entry of the *nsswitch.conf* file. The NIS server
is configured (by default) to not use DNS to resolve hostnames not found in the
hosts map.

Run NIS on client, enable DNS on NIS server

Use the NIS maps first, then go to DNS for hostnames that aren't managed by NIS.
This is done using a special flag in the NIS *hosts* map.

NIS is forced to query DNS for hostnames not found in the *hosts* map if the map is
built with the "Inter-Domain" key. The NIS-then-DNS algorithm is embedded in
the implementation of *ypserv*. This means that individual NIS clients don't need to
know about the DNS; only the NIS servers will be calling DNS for non-local hostnames.

In the NIS *Makefile*, add the *-b* flag to the *makedbm* script for the *hosts.byname*
and *hosts.byaddr* maps, which will cause the *YP_INTERDOMAIN* key to be added
to the *hosts* maps. In Solaris, this is done by changing the following lines in */var/
yp/Makefile* from:

```
#B=-b
B=
```

to:

```
B=-b
#B=
```

If a hostname is not found in the NIS map, the *YP_INTERDOMAIN* key instructs
NIS to look up the name with the domain name server. Instead of immediately
returning an error indicating that the hostname key was not found, *ypserv* asks the
DNS server to look up the hostname. If DNS cannot find the name, then *ypserv*
returns an error to the client. However, if the DNS server locates the hostname, it
returns the IP address information to *ypserv*, and *ypserv* returns it to the client.
Integration of NIS and DNS is completely invisible to the client in terms of calling
interfaces: all of the work is done by *ypserv* on the NIS server.

NIS servers locate DNS servers through the *resolver* interface, which relies on information in the */etc/resolv.conf* configuration file. The resolver configuration file
should point to at least two DNS servers to provide redundancy in case one DNS
server becomes unavailable:

```
nameserver 130.1.52.28
nameserver 130.1.1.15
```

The *nameserver* keyword is used to identify the IP address of a DNS server. The
servers are listed by IP address, since hostnames are dependent on the very mechanism being configured by this file. Set up a *resolv.conf* file on every NIS server.

Run DNS on NIS clients and servers

In this approach, NIS clients and servers ignore NIS for hostnames and use only DNS.

Given that DNS is a full-service hostname management system, some network managers choose to eliminate the NIS *hosts* map file and use pure DNS service for hostnames and IP addresses. On some systems, a new version of *gethostent()* is required that skips the NIS query and directly calls the DNS *resolver* routines for hostname lookups. Check with your vendor for instructions on how to do this. In Solaris, the name services switch can be used to set the hosts lookups to just DNS. If you disable NIS hostname management and use DNS alone, you'll need to set up a *resolv.conf* file on *every* host in the network, so that they can find DNS servers.

The main argument for using DNS only is that it consolidates hostname management under one distributed service, instead of having it split across two services. The drawbacks to this approach are that each host is then dependent upon both an NIS and a DNS server for normal operation (if NIS is running), and a reliable DNS server or sufficient resolver information is required to make each small network self-supporting. Widespread use of DNS to replace NIS host maps suffers from the same server availability problems that NIS does—the entire network is dependent upon reliable and well-behaved servers.

Run NIS on client, enable DNS on NIS client

In this approach, the name services switch file, *nsswitch.conf,* is set up so that both *nis* and *dns* appear in the *hosts* entry of the *nsswitch.conf* file. The host maps should not have the "Inter-Domain" key enabled since all that will do is result in hostname resolutions via DNS occurring twice: once in the NIS client and once in the NIS server.

Fully qualified and unqualified hostnames

DNS and NIS have different semantics when it comes to dealing with qualified and unqualified hostnames. A fully qualified hostname is one that includes the DNS domain name as the suffix, whereas the unqualified hostname does not have a domain suffix. So for example, *gonzo.sales.polygon.com* is a fully qualified DNS name, but *gonzo* is an unqualified name. With both DNS and NIS, there is associated with the name service configuration a default domain name. If an unqualified hostname is passed to *gethostbyname()* to be resolved, then both DNS and NIS will associate the query with the default domain name. When doing an address to name query, such as via *gethostbyaddr( )*, DNS and NIS behave differently. DNS will always return the fully qualified hostname, whereas NIS may return the unqualified hostname. You can do one of two things to address this issue:

- Set up the *hosts* map to contain only fully qualified names. The problem is that attempts to look up an unqualified hostname would then fail with NIS, whereas such attempts would succeed with DNS.

- Include both the fully qualified and unqualified names in the *hosts* map. A caveat is that it is not defined as to which hostname, qualified or unqualified, is returned first in the list of hostnames returned by *gethostbyaddr( )*. In other words, NIS has no concept of a canonical form for hostnames, unlike DNS. You can mitigate this by ensuring that for a given IP address there is just one entry in the *hosts* file used to build the *hosts* maps and ensuring that the fully qualified hostname is listed first in the *hosts* entry for a given IP address. If you take this route, it is a good idea to use fully qualified hostnames in netgroups.

The fully qualified versus unqualified hostname issue can produce practical problems on the server side of services like NFS and *rlogin*, which have lists of hostnames to control access. If the server has both NIS and DNS enabled, then it is possible that sometimes clients will have hostnames that appear as unqualified, and sometimes as fully qualified. Unless the hostnames that appear in files such as */etc/dfs/dfstab* or */etc/hosts.equiv* correspond with what the directory service uses, access will be mistakenly denied. For example, while we have not covered NFS operation yet, this is as good as place as any to explain a common NFS access problem when DNS is being used to resolve hostnames to IP addresses. Suppose you have the following entry in */etc/dfs/dfstab:*

```
share -o rw=gonzo /export
```

If DNS is being used, NFS client *gonzo* will be denied access. This is because if DNS is being used to resolve hostnames to IP addresses, it is also being used to resolve IP addresses to hostnames, and DNS always generates fully qualified hostnames. Thus if *gonzo* is in the *sales.polygon.com* domain, then the following gives *gonzo* access:

```
share -o rw=gonzo.sales.polygon.com /export
```

The qualified versus unqualified hostname issue is one that has the potential for causing you major grief, and at the end of the day, you may decide that it is far simpler to use DNS across the board. If you do opt to use both NIS and DNS, for consistent results, the following is recommended:

- Place in the *hosts* map only unqualified hostnames and only hosts that belong to the same DNS domain that the NIS domain is based upon.

- Place *nis* before *dns* in the *hosts* entry of *nsswitch.conf.* This way, if a host is in NIS, then you will consistently use its unqualified form. If you had DNS before NIS, then there would be no point in having NIS, except as a fallback in case DNS became unavailable. In that case, you would find that when DNS failed, access control lists set up to use the qualified hostname form would not suddenly result in access failures.

- Configure *nsswitch.conf* to return an error if NIS is down:

      hosts: files nis [UNAVAIL=return] dns

    This seems nonintuitive, since it means that if NIS is down, you won't be able to resolve hostnames and addresses. Let's suppose that you had the following in *nsswitch.conf*:

      hosts: files nis dns

    Now suppose *gonzo* is in NIS, and *gonzo.sales.polygon.com* is in DNS. Assume */etc/hosts.equiv* contains an entry for *gonzo.* If you use *rlogin* to log in from *gonzo* to another machine, while NIS is up, then you will be able to log in without a password prompt. This is because when NIS is up, the IP address of *gonzo* is resolved by *gethostbyaddr( )* to *gonzo.* When NIS is down, you will get a password prompt, because the IP address is resolved in DNS to *gonzo.sales.polygon.com.* A workaround would be to place both *gonzo* and *gonzo.sales.polygon.com* in the */etc/hosts.equiv* file, but this is prone to error.

    Of course, if you do configure *nsswitch.conf* to return an error if NIS is down, then when NIS is down, you will not be able to access hostnames that are in a different DNS domain. For example:

      % telnet quote.triangle.com

    Not to belabor the point, but if NIS availability is a concern for you, and you are running DNS, then you will want to give serious consideration to not using the *hosts* map in *nsswitch.conf*:

      hosts: dns

Centralized versus distributed management

This section applies to those organizations that have multiple system administration groups, each responsible for different departments within the organizations. If your organization has centralized remote control of all soft administration, then these issues will be of less interest to you.[*]

---

[*] Soft administraton includes everything that does not require onsite personnel. An example of something that is not soft administration would be replacing a disk drive.

NIS lends itself to allowing you to give system administration groups for a given department within your organization responsibility for maintaining the department's NIS maps without the need for centralized control. However, the nature of hostnames, host addresses, and domain name management is that some central controls or rules are necessary in order to prevent mistakes in one department from affecting other departments and beyond.

There are at least three basic approaches to consider for managing hosts and domains.

Complete centralization

In this model, if someone wants an IP address, he or she contacts a single central committee to get one; the chances of errors are as low as possible, but the latency in getting requests honored is the longest. Adding new subdomains is also centralized. In this model, as there are specific system management groups managing the non-hosts NIS maps for a given department, it is not practical to manage hosts via NIS; you would use DNS exclusively.

Federation

In this model, the central committee has delegated responsibility for portions of the IP address space to individual groups responsible for a DNS subdomain. In this model, either a DNS or a hybrid NIS/DNS model for managing hosts works (such as via the technical rules listed in "Fully qualified and unqualified hostnames" earlier in this chapter). If the individual groups are using DNS to the exclusion of the NIS *hosts* map, then there is little work for the central committee other than to maintain the mapping of subdomains to subdomain name servers. The central committee, of course, is responsible for adding or deleting subdomains. If the individual groups use NIS for local host-name information, then the central committee would maintain the entire DNS infrastructure by periodically gathering host map information from each group. This could be done automatically.

Complete decentralization

Each system administration group has the autonomy to modify its NIS host maps as well as the authority to modify the common DNS database. Such a system will not scale as the number of subdomains and system administration groups rises. With too many authorized players, it will be hard to track down problems caused by mistakes, not to mention avoiding duplicate efforts.

Migrating from NIS to DNS for host naming

By now you should have a good handle on the differences between NIS and DNS as they impact host naming. If you are considering migrating from NIS to DNS, you need to decide what you want to do about unqualified versus qualified host-names. By going from NIS to DNS, you are exposing your users to a hierarchical (qualified) naming scheme versus the flat (unqualified) one they knew under NIS. While you don't want to continue a flat naming scheme for accessing hosts outside the user's subdomain, you may want to temporarily or permanently support a flat naming scheme for hosts within each user's subdomain, using techniques described earlier. Such an approach also gives you more time to find all references to unqualified hostnames in configuration files and in software packages and correct them to be qualified.

What next?

The Network Information Service provides an easy-to-manage general purpose distributed database system. When used in conjunction with a source code control system and local tools, it solves many problems with configuration file management by providing audit trails and a single point of administration. The single biggest advantage of NIS is that it adds consistency to a network. Getting all hosts to agree on usernames, *uid* and *gid* values, and hostnames and host addresses is a prerequisite for adding other distributed services such as NFS.

6

In this chapter:
- *Setting up NFS*
- *Exporting filesystems*
- *Mounting filesystems*
- *Symbolic links*
- *Replication*
- *Naming schemes*

System Administration Using the Network File System

The Network File System (NFS) is a distributed filesystem that provides transparent access to remote disks. Just as NIS allows you to centralize administration of user and host information, NFS allows you to centralize administration of disks. Instead of duplicating common directories such as */usr/local* on every system, NFS provides a single copy of the directory that is shared by all systems on the network. To a host running NFS, remote filesystems are indistinguishable from local ones. For the user, NFS means that he or she doesn't have to log into other systems to access files. There is no need to use *rcp* or tapes to move files onto the local system. Once NFS has been set up properly, users should be able to do all their work on their local system; remote files (data and executables) will appear to be local to their own system. NFS and NIS are frequently used together: NIS makes sure that configuration information is propagated to all hosts, and NFS ensures that the files a user needs are accessible from these hosts.

NFS is also built on the RPC protocol and imposes a client-server relationship on the hosts that use it. An NFS server is a host that owns one or more filesystems and makes them available on the network; NFS clients mount filesystems from one or more servers. This follows the normal client-server model where the server owns a resource that is used by the client. In the case of NFS, the resource is a physical disk drive that is shared by all clients of the server.

There are two aspects to system administration using NFS: choosing a filesystem naming and mounting scheme, and then configuring the servers and clients to adhere to this scheme. The goal of any naming scheme should be to use network transparency wisely. Being able to mount filesystems from any server is useful only if the files are presented in a manner that is consistent with the users' expectations.

If NFS has been set up correctly, it should be transparent to the user. For example, if locally developed applications were found in */usr/local/bin* before NFS was installed, they should continue to be found there when NFS is running, whether */usr/local/bin* is on a local filesystem or a remote one. To the user, the actual disk holding */usr/local/bin* isn't important as long as the executables are accessible and built for the right machine architecture. If users must change their environments to locate files accessed through NFS, they will probably dislike the new network architecture because it changes the way things work.

An environment with many NFS servers and hundreds of clients can quickly become overwhelming in terms of management complexity. Successful system administration of a large NFS network requires adding some intelligence to the standard procedures. The cost of consistency on the network should not be a large administrative overhead. One tool that greatly eases the task of running an NFS network is the *automounter*, which applies NIS management to NFS configuration. This chapter starts with a quick look at how to get NFS up and running on clients and servers, and then explores NFS naming schemes and common filesystem planning problems. We'll cover the automounter in detail in Chapter 9.

Setting up NFS

Setting up NFS on clients and servers involves starting the daemons that handle the NFS RPC protocol, starting additional daemons for auxiliary services such as file locking, and then simply exporting filesystems from the NFS servers and mounting them on the clients.

On an NFS client, you need to have the *lockd* and *statd* daemons running in order to use NFS. These daemons are generally started in a boot script (Solaris uses */etc/init.d/nfs.client*):

```
if [ -x /usr/lib/nfs/statd -a -x /usr/lib/nfs/lockd ]
then
    /usr/lib/nfs/statd > /dev/console 2>&1
    /usr/lib/nfs/lockd > /dev/console 2>&1
fi
```

On some non-Solaris systems, there may also be *biod* daemons that get started. The *biod* daemons perform block I/O operations for NFS clients, performing some simple read-ahead and write-behind performance optimizations. You run multiple instances of *biod* so that each client process can have multiple NFS requests outstanding at any time. Check your vendor's documentation for the proper invocation of the *biod* daemons. Solaris does not have *biod* daemons because the read-ahead and write-behind function is handled by a tunable number of asynchronous I/O threads that reside in the system kernel.

The *lockd* and *statd* daemons handle file locking and lock recovery on the client. These locking daemons also run on an NFS server, and the client-side daemons coordinate file locking on the NFS server through their server-side counterparts. We'll come back to file locking later when we discuss how NFS handles state information.

On an NFS server, NFS services are started with the *nfsd* and *mountd* daemons, as well as the file locking daemons used on the client. You should see the NFS server daemons started in a boot script (Solaris uses */etc/init.d/nfs.server*):

```
if grep -s nfs /etc/dfs/sharetab >/dev/null ; then
    /usr/lib/nfs/mountd
    /usr/lib/nfs/nfsd -a 16
fi
```

On most NFS servers, there is a file that contains the list of filesystems the server will allow clients to mount via NFS. Many servers store this list in */etc/exports* file. Solaris stores the list in */etc/dfs/dfstab*. In the previous script file excerpt, the NFS server daemons are not started unless the host shares (exports) NFS filesystems in the */etc/dfs/dfstab* file. (The reference to */etc/dfs/sharetab* in the script excerpt is not a misprint; see the following section, "Exporting filesystems.") If there are filesystems to be made available for NFS service, the machine initializes the export list and starts the NFS daemons. As with the client-side, check your vendor's documentation or the boot scripts themselves for details on how the various server daemons are started.

The *nfsd* daemon accepts NFS RPC requests and executes them on the server. Some servers run multiple copies of the daemon so that they can handle several RPC requests at once. In Solaris, a single copy of the daemon is run, but multiple threads run in the kernel to provide parallel NFS service. Varying the number of daemons or threads on a server is a performance tuning issue that we will discuss in Chapter 17. By default, *nfsd* listens over both the TCP and UDP transport protocols. There are several options to modify this behavior and also to tune the TCP connection management. These options will be discussed in Chapter 17 as well.

The *mountd* daemon handles client mount requests. The *mount* protocol is not part of NFS. The *mount* protocol is used by an NFS server to tell a client what filesystems are available (exported) for mounting. The NFS client uses the *mount* protocol to get a filehandle for the exported filehandle.

Exporting filesystems

Usually, a host decides to become an NFS server if it has filesystems to export to the network. A server does not explicitly advertise these filesystems; instead, it keeps a list of currently exported filesystems and associated access restrictions in a file and compares incoming NFS mount requests to entries in this table. It is up to the server to decide if a filesystem can be mounted by a client. You may change the rules at any time by rebuilding its exported filesystem table.

This section uses filenames and command names that are specific to Solaris. On non-Solaris systems, you will find the rough equivalents shown in Table 6-1.

Table 6-1. Correspondence of Solaris and non-Solaris export components

Description	Solaris	Non-Solaris
Initial list of filesystems to export	*/etc/dfs/dfstab*	*/etc/exports*
Command to export initial list	*shareall*	*exportfs*
List of currently exported filesystems	*/etc/dfs/sharetab*	*/etc/xtab*
Command to export one filesystem	*share*	*exportfs*
List of local filesystems on server	*/etc/vfstab*	*/etc/fstab*

The exported filesystem table is initialized from the */etc/dfs/dfstab* file. The super-user may export other filesystems once the server is up and running, so the */etc/dfs/dfstab* file and the actual list of currently exported filesystems, */etc/dfs/sharetab*, are maintained separately. When a fileserver boots, it checks for the existence of */etc/dfs/dfstab* and runs *shareall(1M)* on it to make filesystems available for client use. If, after *shareall* runs, */etc/dfs/sharetab* has entries, the *nfsd* and *mountd* daemons are run.

After the system is up, the superuser can export additional filesystems via the *share* command.

 A common usage error is invoking the *share* command manually on a system that booted without entries in */etc/dfs/dfstab*. If the *nfsd* and *mountd* daemons are not running, then invoking the *share* command manually does not enable NFS service. Before running the *share* command manually, you should verify that *nfsd* and *mountd* are running. If they are not, then start them. On Solaris, you would use the */etc/init.d/nfs.server* script, invoked as */etc/init.d/nfs.server start*. However, if there is no entry in */etc/dfs/dfstab*, you must add one before the */etc/init.d/nfs.server* script will have an effect.

Rules for exporting filesystems

There are four rules for making a server's filesystem available to NFS:

1. Any filesystem, or proper subset of a filesystem, can be exported from a server. A proper subset of a filesystem is a file or directory tree that starts

below the mount point of the filesystem. For example, if */usr* is a filesystem, and the */usr/local* directory is part of that filesystem, then */usr/local* is a proper subset of */usr*.

2. You cannot export any subdirectory of an exported filesystem unless the subdirectory is on a different physical device.

3. You cannot export any parent directory of an exported filesystem unless the parent is on a different physical device.

4. You can export only local filesystems.

The first rule allows you to export selected portions of a large filesystem. You can export and mount a single file, a feature that is used by diskless clients. The second and third rules seem both redundant and confusing, but are in place to enforce the selective views imposed by exporting a subdirectory of a filesystem.

The second rule allows you to export */usr/local/bin* when */usr/local* is already exported from the same server only if */usr/local/bin* is on a different disk. For example, if your server mounts these filesystems using */etc/vfstab* entries like:

```
/dev/dsk/c0t0d0s5    /dev/rdsk/c0t0d0s5    /usr/local       ufs    2    no    rw
/dev/dsk/c0t3d0s0    /dev/rdsk/c0t3d0s0    /usr/local/bin   ufs    2    no    rw
```

then exporting both of them is allowed, since the exported directories reside on different filesystems. If, however, *bin* was a subdirectory of */usr/local*, then it could not be exported in conjunction with its parent.

The third rule is the converse of the second. If you have a subdirectory exported, you cannot also export its parent unless they are on different filesystems. In the previous example, if */usr/local/bin* is already exported, then */usr/local* can be exported only if it is on a different filesystem. This rule prevents entire filesystems from being exported on the fly when the system administrator has carefully chosen to export a selected set of subdirectories.

Together, the second and third rules say that you can export a local filesystem only one way. Once you export a subdirectory of it, you can't go and export the whole thing; and once you've made the whole thing public, you can't go and restrict the export list to a subdirectory or two.

One way to check the validity of subdirectory exports is to use the *df* command to determine on which local filesystem the current directory resides. If you find that the parent directory and its subdirectory appear in the output of *df*, then they are on separate filesystems, and it is safe to export them both.

Exporting subdirectories is similar to creating views on a relational database. You choose the portions of the database that a user needs to see, hiding information that is extraneous or sensitive. In NFS, exporting a subdirectory of a filesystem is useful if the entire filesystem contains subdirectories with names that might confuse users, or if the filesystem contains several parallel directory trees of which only one is useful to the user.

Exporting options

The */etc/dfs/dfstab* file contains a list of filesystems that a server exports and any restrictions or export options for each. The */etc/dfs/dfstab* file is really just a list of individual *share* commands, and so the entries in the file follow the command-line syntax of the *share* command:

```
share [ -d description ] [ -F nfs ] [ -o suboptions ] pathname
```

Before we discuss the options, *pathname* is the filesystem or subdirectory of the filesystem being exported.

The *-d* option allows you to insert a comment describing what the exported filesystem contains. This option is of little use since there are no utilities to let an NFS client see this information.

The *-F* option allows you to specify the type of fileserver to use. Since the *share* command supports just one fileserver—NFS—this option is currently redundant. Early releases of Solaris supported a distributed file-sharing system known as RFS, hence the historical reason for this option. It is conceivable that another file sharing system would be added to Solaris in the future. For clarity, you should specify *-F nfs* to ensure that the NFS service is used.

The *-o* option allows you to specify a list of suboptions. (Multiple suboptions would be separated by commas.) For example:

```
# share -F nfs /export/home
# share -F nfs -o rw=corvette /usr/local
```

Several options modify the way a filesystem is exported to the network:

rw

Permits NFS clients to read from or write to the filesystem. This option is the default; i.e., if none of *rw*, *ro*, *ro=client_list*, or *rw=client_list* are specified, then read/write access to the world is granted.

ro

Prevents NFS clients from writing to the filesystem. Read-only restrictions are enforced when a client performs an operation on an NFS filesystem: if the client has mounted the filesystem with read and write permissions, but the server specified *ro* when exporting it, any attempt by the client to write to the filesystem will fail, with "Read-only filesystem" or "Permission denied" messages.

rw=client_list

> Limits the set of hosts that may write to the filesystem to the NFS clients identi-
> fied in *client_list*.

A *client_list* has the form of a colon-separated list of components, such that a
component is one of the following:

hostname

> The hostname of the NFS client.

netgroup

> The NIS directory services support the concept of a set of hostnames
> named collectively as a *netgroup*. See Chapter 7 for a description on how
> to set up netgroups under NIS.

DNS domain

> An Internet Domain Name Service domain is indicated by a preceding dot.
> For example:

```
# share -o rw=.widget.com /export2
```

> grants access to any host in the *widget.com* domain. In order for this to
> work, the NFS server must be using DNS as its primary directory service
> ahead of NIS (see Chapter 4).

netmask

> A netmask is indicated by a preceding at-sign (@) and possibly by a suffix
> with a slash and length to indicate the number of bits in the netmask.
> Examples will help here:

```
# share -o rw=@129.100.0.0 /export
# share -o rw=@193.150.145.63/27 /export2
```

> The notation of four decimal values separated by periods is known as a
> *dotted quad*.

> In the first example, any client with an Internet Protocol (IP) address such
> that its first two octets are 129 and 100 (in decimal), will get read/write
> access to */export*.

> In the second example, a client with an address such that the first 27 bits
> match the first 27 bits of *193.150.145.63* will get read/write access. The
> notation *193.150.145.63/27* is an example of *classless addressing*, which
> was previously discussed in "IPv4 address classes" in Chapter 1.

> So in the second example, a client with an address of *193.150.145.33*
> would get access, but another client with the address *193.150.145.128*
> would not. Table 6-2 clarifies this.

Table 6-2. Netmask matching

Client Address		Netmask		Access?
dotted quad	hexadecimal	dotted quad	hexadecimal	
193.150.145.33	0xc1969121	193.150.145.63/27	0xc1969120	Yes
193.150.145.128	0xc1969180	193.150.145.63/27	0xc1969120	No

-component

Each component in the *client_list* can be prefixed with a minus sign (-) to offer negative matching. This indicates that the component should not get access, even if it is included in another component in the *client_list*. For example:

```
# share -o rw=-wrench.widget.com:.widget.com /dir
```

would exclude the host *wrench* in the domain *widget.com*, but would give access to all other hosts in the domain *widget.com*. Note that order matters. If you did this:

```
# share -o rw=.widget.com:-wrench.widget.com /dir
```

host *wrench* would *not* be denied access. In other words, the NFS server will stop processing the *client_list* once it gets a positive or negative match.

ro=client_list

Limits the set of hosts that may read (but not write to) the filesystem to the NFS clients identified in *client_list*. The form of *client_list* is the same as that described for the *rw=client_list* option.

anon=uid

Maps anonymous, or unknown, users to the user identifier *uid*. Anonymous users are those that do not present valid credentials in their NFS requests. Note that an anonymous user is *not* one that does not appear in the server's password file or NIS *passwd* map. If no credentials are included with the NFS request, it is treated as an anonymous request. NFS clients can submit requests from unknown users if the proper user validation is not completed; we'll look at both of these problems in later chapters. The section "NFS security" in Chapter 12 discusses the *anon* option in more detail.

root=client_list

Grants superuser access to the NFS clients identified in *client_list*. The form of *client_list* is the same as that described for the *rw=client_list* option. To enforce basic network security, by default, superuser privileges are not extended over the network. The *root* option allows you to selectively grant root access to a filesystem. This security feature will be covered in "Superuser mapping" in Chapter 12.

sec=mode[:mode ...]

Requires that NFS clients use the security mode(s) specified. Security modes can be:

sys

This is the default form of security, which assumes a trusted relationship between NFS clients and servers.

dh

This is a stronger form of security based on a cryptographic algorithm known as Diffie-Hellman Key Exchange.

krb5
krb5i
krb5p

This is a trio of stronger forms of security based on a key management system called Kerberos Version 5.

none

This is the weakest form of security. All users are treated as unknown and are mapped to the anonymous user.

The *sec=* option can be combined with *rw, ro, rw=, ro=,* and *root=* in interesting ways. We will look at that and other security modes in more detail in Chapter 12.

aclok

ACL stands for Access Control List. The *aclok* option can sometimes prevent interoperability problems involving NFS Version 2 clients that do not understand Access Control Lists. We will explore ACLs and the *aclok* option in "Access control lists" in Chapter 12.

nosub
nosuid

Under some situations, the *nosub* and *nosuid* options prevent security exposures. We will go into more detail in Chapter 12.

public

This option is useful for environments that have to cope with firewalls. We will discuss it in more detail also in Chapter 12.

Your system may support additional options, so check your vendor's relevant manual pages.

Mounting filesystems

This section uses filenames and command names specific to Solaris. Note that you are better off using the *automounter* (see Chapter 9) to mount filesystems, rather than using the *mount* utility described in this section. However, understanding the automounter, and why it is better than *mount*, requires understanding *mount*. Thus, we will discuss the concept of NFS filesystem mounting in the context of *mount*.

Solaris has different component names from non-Solaris systems. Table 6-3 shows the rough equivalents to non-Solaris systems.

Table 6-3. Correspondence of Solaris and non-Solaris mount components

Description	Solaris	Non-Solaris
List of filesystems	*/etc/vfstab*	*/etc/fstab*
List of mounted filesystems	*/etc/mnttab*	*/etc/mtab*
RPC program number to network address mapper (portmapper)	*rpcbind*	*portmap*
MOUNT daemon	*mountd*	*rpc.mountd*

NFS clients can mount any filesystem, or part of a filesystem, that has been exported from an NFS server. The filesystem can be listed in the client's */etc/vfstab* file, or it can be mounted explicitly using the *mount(1M)* command. (Also, in Solaris, see the *mount_nfs(1M)* manpage, which explains NFS-specific details of filesystem mounting.)

NFS filesystems appear to be "normal" filesystems on the client, which means that they can be mounted on any directory on the client. It's possible to mount an NFS filesystem over all or part of another filesystem, since the directories used as mount points appear the same no matter where they actually reside. When you mount a filesystem on top of another one, you obscure whatever is "under" the mount point. NFS clients see the most recent view of the filesystem. These potentially confusing issues will be the foundation for the discussion of NFS naming schemes later in this chapter.

Using /etc/vfstab

Adding entries to */etc/vfstab* is one way to mount NFS filesystems. Once the entry has been added to the *vfstab* file, the client mounts it on every reboot. There are several features that distinguish NFS filesystems in the *vfstab* file:

- The "device name" field is replaced with a *server:filesystem* specification, where the filesystem name is a pathname (not a device name) on the server.

- The "raw device name" field that is checked with *fsck*, is replaced with a –.

- The filesystem type is *nfs*, not *ufs* as for local filesystems.

- The *fsck* pass is set to –.

- The options field can contain a variety of NFS-specific mount options, covered in the next section, "Using mount."

Some typical *vfstab* entries for NFS filesystems are:

```
ono:/export/ono        -    /hosts/ono      nfs   -   yes   rw,bg,hard
onaga:/export/onaga    -    /hosts/onaga    nfs   -   yes   rw,bg,hard
wahoo:/var/mail        -    /var/mail       nfs   -   yes   rw,bg,hard
```

The *yes* in the above entries says to mount the filesystems whenever the system boots up. This field can be *yes* or *no*, and has the same effect for NFS and non-NFS filesystems.

Of course, each vendor is free to vary the server and filesystem name syntax, and your manual set should provide the best sample *vfstab* entries.

Using mount

While entries in the v*fstab* file are useful for creating a long-lived NFS environment, sometimes you need to mount a filesystem right away or mount it temporarily while you copy files from it. The *mount* command allows you to perform an NFS filesystem mount that remains active until you explicitly unmount the filesystem using *umount*, or until the client is rebooted.

As an example of using *mount*, consider building and testing a new */usr/local* directory. On an NFS client, you already have the "old" */usr/local*, either on a local or NFS-mounted filesystem. Let's say you have built a new version of */usr/local* on the NFS server *wahoo* and want to test it on this NFS client. Mount the new filesystem on top of the existing */usr/local*:

```
# mount wahoo:/usr/local /usr/local
```

Anything in the old */usr/local* is hidden by the new mount point, so you can debug your new */usr/local* as if it were mounted at boot time.

From the command line, *mount* uses a server name and filesystem name syntax similar to that of the *vfstab* file. The *mount* command assumes that the type is *nfs* if a hostname appears in the device specification. The server filesystem name must be an absolute pathname (usually starting with a leading /), but it need not exactly match the name of a filesystem exported from the server. Barring the use of the *nosub* option on the server (see the section "Exporting options" earlier in this chapter), the only restriction on server filesystem names is that they must contain a valid, exported server filesystem name as a prefix. This means that you can mount a subdirectory of an exported filesystem, as long as you specify the entire pathname to the subdirectory in either the *vfstab* file or on the *mount* command line.

Note that the *rw* and *hard* suboptions are redundant since they are the defaults (in Solaris at least). This book often specifies them in examples to make it clear what semantics will be.

For example, to mount a particular home directory from */export/home of server ono*, you do not have to mount the entire filesystem. Picking up only the subdirectory that's needed may make the local filesystem hierarchy simpler and less cluttered. To mount a subdirectory of a server's exported filesystem, just specify the pathname to that directory in the *vfstab* file:

```
ono:/export/home/stern  -  /users/stern nfs  -  yes  rw,bg,hard
```

Even though server *ono* exports all of */export/home*, you can choose to handle some smaller portion of the entire filesystem.

Mount options

NFS mount options are as varied as the vendors themselves. There are a few well-known and widely supported options, and others that are added to support additional NFS features or to integrate secure remote procedure call systems. As with everything else that is vendor-specific, your system's manual set provides a complete list of supported mount options. Check the manual pages for *mount(1M)*, *mount_nfs(1M)*, and *vfstab(4)*.

For the most part, the default set of mount options will serve you fine. However, pay particular attention to the *nosuid* suboption, which is described in Chapter 12. The *nosuid* suboption is not the default in Solaris, but perhaps it ought to be.

The Solaris *mount* command syntax for mounting NFS filesystems is:

```
mount [ -F nfs ] [-mrO] [ -o suboptions ] server:pathname
mount [ -F nfs ] [-mrO] [ -o suboptions ] mount_point
mount [ -F nfs ] [-mrO] [ -o suboptions ] server:pathname mount_point
mount [ -F nfs ] [-mrO] [ -o suboptions ]
        server1:pathname1,server2:pathname2,...serverN:pathnameN mount_point
mount [ -F nfs ] [-mrO] [ -o suboptions ]
        server1,server2,...serverN:pathname mount_point
```

The first two forms are used when mounting a filesystem listed in the *vfstab* file. Note that *server* is the hostname of the NFS server. The last two forms are used when mounting replicas. See the section "Naming schemes" later in this chapter.

The *-F nfs* option is used to specify that the filesystem being mounted is of type NFS. The option is not necessary because the filesystem type can be discerned from the presence of *host:pathname* on the command line.

The *-r* option says to mount the filesystem as read-only. The preferred way to specify read-only is the *ro* suboption to the *-o* option.

The *-m* option says to not record the entry in the */etc/mnttab* file.

The *-O* option says to permit the filesystem to be mounted over an existing mount point. Normally if *mount_point* already has a filesystem mounted on it, the *mount* command will fail with a filesystem busy error.

In addition, you can use *-o* to specify suboptions. Suboptions can also be specified (without *-o*) in the mount options field in */etc/vfstab*. The common NFS mount suboptions are:

rw/ro

> *rw* mounts a filesystem as read-write; this is the default. If *ro* is specified, the filesystem is mounted as read-only. Use the *ro* option if the server enforces write protection for various filesystems.

bg/fg

> The *bg* option tells *mount* to retry a failed mount attempt in the background, allowing the foreground *mount* process to continue. By default, NFS mounts are not performed in the background, so *fg* is the default. We'll discuss the *bg* option further in the next section. Note that the *bg* option does not apply to the automounter (see Chapter 9).

grpid

> Since Solaris is a derivative of Unix System V, it will by default obey System V semantics. One area in which System V differs from 4.x BSD systems is in the group identifier of newly created files. System V will set the group identifier to the effective group identifier of the calling process. If the *grpid* option is set, BSD semantics are used, and so the group identifier is always inherited from the file's directory. You can control this behavior on a per-directory basis by not specifying *grpid*, and instead setting the set group id bit on the directory with the *chmod* command:

```
% chmod g+s /export/home/dir
```

If the set group id bit is set, then even if *grpid* is absent, the group identifier of a created file is inherited from the group identifier of the file's directory. So for example:

```
% chmod g+s /export/home/dir
% ls -ld /export/home/dir
drwxr-sr-x   6 mre      writers 3584 May 24 09:17 /export/home/dir/
% touch /export/home/dir/test
% ls -l /export/home/dir/test
-rw-r--r--   1 mre      writers 0    May 27 06:07 /export/home/dir/test
```

quota/noquota

Enables/prevents the quota command to check for quotas on the filesystem.

port=n

Specify the port number of the NFS server. The default is to use the port number as returned by the *rpcbind*. This option is typically used to support pseudo NFS servers that run on the same machine as the NFS client. The Solaris removable media (CD-ROMs and floppy disks) manager (*vold*) is an example of such a server.

public

This option is useful for environments that have to cope with firewalls. We will discuss it in more detail in Chapter 12.

suid/nosuid

Under some situations, the *nosuid* option prevents security exposures. The default is *suid*. We will go into more detail in Chapter 12.

sec=mode

This option lets you set the security *mode* used on the filesystem. Valid security modes are as specified in the section "Exporting options" earlier in this chapter. If you're using NFS Version 3, normally you need not be concerned with security modes in *vfstab* or the *mount* command, because Version 3 has a way to negotiate the security mode. We will go into more detail in Chapter 12.

hard/soft

By default, NFS filesystems are *hard* mounted, and operations on them are retried until they are acknowledged by the server. If the *soft* option is specified, an NFS RPC call returns a timeout error if it fails the number of times specified by the *retrans* option.

vers=version

The NFS protocol supports two versions: 2 and 3. By default, the *mount* command will attempt to use Version 3 if the server also supports Version 3; otherwise, the *mount* will use Version 2. Once the protocol version is negotiated, the version is bound to the filesystem until it is unmounted and remounted. If you are mounting multiple filesystems from the same server, you can use different versions of NFS. The binding of the NFS protocol versions is per mount point and not per NFS client/server pair. Note the NFS protocol version is independent of the transport protocol used. See the discussion of the *proto* option later in this section.

proto=protocol

The NFS protocol supports arbitrary transport protocols, both connection-oriented and connectionless. TCP is the commonly used connection-oriented protocol for NFS, and UDP is the commonly used connectionless protocol. The *protocol* specified in the *proto* option is the *netid* field (the first field) in the */etc/netconfig* file. While the */etc/netconfig* file supports several different netids, practically speaking, the only ones NFS supports today are *tcp* and *udp*. By default, the *mount* command will select TCP over UDP if the server supports TCP. Otherwise UDP will be used.

It is a popular misconception that NFS Version 3 and NFS over TCP are synonymous. As noted previously, the NFS protocol version is independent of the transport protocol used. You can have NFS Version 2 clients and servers that support TCP and UDP (or just TCP, or just UDP). Similarly, you can have NFS Version 3 clients that support TCP and UDP (or just TCP, or just UDP). This misconception arose because Solaris 2.5 introduced both NFS Version 3 and NFS over TCP at the same time, and so NFS mounts that previously used NFS Version 2 over UDP now use NFS Version 3 over TCP.

---

retrans/timeo

The *retrans* option specifies the number of times to repeat an RPC request before returning a timeout error on a soft-mounted filesystem. The *retrans* option is ignored if the filesystem is using TCP. This is because it is assumed that the system's TCP protocol driver will do a better of job than the user of the *mount* command of judging the necessary TCP level retransmissions. Thus when using TCP, the RPC is sent just once before returning an error on a *soft* mounted filesystem. The *timeo* parameter varies the RPC timeout period and is given in tenths of a second. For example, in */etc/vfstab, you* could have:

```
onaga:/export/home/mre  -  /users/mre nfs  -  yes  rw,proto=udp,retrans=6,timeo=11
```

retry=n

This option specifies the number of times to retry the mount attempt. The default is 10000. (The default is only 1 when using the automounter. See Chapter 9.) See the section "Backgrounding mounts" later in this chapter.

rsize=n/wsize=n

This option controls the maximum transfer size of read (*rsize*) and write (*wsize*) operations. For NFS Version 2, the maximum transfer size is 8192 bytes, which is the default. For NFS Version 3, the client and server negotiate the maximum. Solaris systems will by default negotiate a maximum transfer size of 32768 bytes.

intr/nointr

Normally, an NFS operation will continue until an RPC error occurs (and if mounted *hard*, most RPC errors will not prevent the operation from continuing) or until it has completed successfully. If a server is down and a client is waiting for an RPC call to complete, the process making the RPC call hangs until the server responds (unless mounted *soft*). With the *intr* option, the user can use Unix signals (see the manpage for *kill(1)*) to interrupt NFS RPC calls and force the RPC layer to return an error. The *intr* option is the default. The *nointr* option will cause the NFS client to ignore Unix signals.

noac

This option suppresses attribute caching and forces writes to be synchronously written to the NFS server. The purpose behind this option to is let each client that mounts with *noac* be guaranteed that when it reads a file from the server it will always have the most recent copy of the data at the time of the read. We will discuss attribute caching and asynchronous/synchronous NFS input/output in more detail in Chapter 7.

actimeo=n

The options that have the prefix *ac* (collectively referred to as the *ac** options) affect the length of time that attributes are cached on NFS clients before the client will get new attributes from the server. The quantity *n* is specified in seconds. The two options prefixed with *acdir* affect the cache times of directory attributes. The two options prefixed with *acreg* affect the cache times of regular file attributes. The *actimeo* option simply sets the minimum and maximum cache times of regular files and directory files to be the same. We will discuss attribute caching in more detail in Chapter 7.

It is a popular misconception that if the minimum attribute timeout is set to 30 seconds, that the NFS client will issue a request to get new attributes for each open file every 30 seconds. Marketing managers for products that compete with NFS use this misconception to claim that NFS is therefore a network bandwidth hog because of all the attribute requests that are sent around. The reality is that the attribute timeouts are checked only whenever a process on the NFS client tries to access the file. If the attribute timeout is 30 seconds and the client has not accessed the file in five hours, then during that five-hour period, there will be no NFS requests to get new attributes. Indeed, there will be no NFS requests at all. For files that are being continuously accessed, with an attribute timeout of 30 seconds, you can expect to get new attribute requests to occur no more often than every 30 seconds. Given that in NFS Version 2, and to an even higher degree in NFS Version 3, attributes are piggy-backed onto the NFS responses, attribute requests would tend to be seen far less often than every 30 seconds. For the most part, attribute requests will be seen most often when the NFS client opens a file. This is to guarantee cache consistency. See "File attribute caching" in Chapter 7 for more details.

acdirmax=n

> This option is like *actimeo*, but it affects the maximum attribute timeout on directories; it defaults to 60 seconds. It can't be higher than 10 hours (36000 seconds).

acdirmin=n

> This option is like *actimeo*, but it affects the minimum attribute timeout on directories; it defaults to 30 seconds. It can't be higher than one hour (3600 seconds).

acregmax=n

> This option is like *actimeo*, but it affects the maximum attribute timeout on regular files; it defaults to 60 seconds. It can't be higher than 10 hours (36000 seconds).

acregmin=n

> This option is like *actimeo*, but it affects the minimum attribute timeout on regular files; it defaults to three seconds. It can't be higher than one hour (3600 seconds).

The *nointr, intr, retrans, rsize, wsize, timeo, hard, soft, and ac** options will be discussed in more detail in the Chapter 18, since they are directly responsible for altering clients' performance in periods of peak server loading.

Backgrounding mounts

The mount protocol used by clients is subject to the same RPC timeouts as individual NFS RPC calls. When a client cannot mount an NFS filesystem during the allotted RPC execution time, it retries the RPC operation up to the count specified by the *retry* mount option. If the *bg* mount option is used, *mount* starts another process that continues trying to mount the filesystem in the background, allowing the *mount* command to consider that request complete and to attempt the next mount operation. If *bg* is not specified, *mount* blocks waiting for the remote fileserver to recover, or until the mount retry count has been reached. The default value of 10,000 may cause a single mount to hang for several hours before *mount* gives up on the fileserver.

You cannot put a mount in the background of any system-critical filesystem such as the root (/) or */usr* filesystem on a diskless client. If you need the filesystem to run the system, you must allow the mount to complete in the foreground. Similarly, if you require some applications from an NFS-mounted partition during the boot process—let's say you start up a license server via a script in */etc/rc2.d*—you should hard-mount the filesystem with these executables so that you are not left with a half-functioning machine. Any filesystem that is not critical to the system's operation can be mounted with the *bg* option. Use of background mounts allows your network to recover more gracefully from widespread problems such as power failures.

When two servers are clients of each other, the *bg* option must be used in at least one of the server's */etc/vfstab* files. When both servers boot at the same time, for example as the result of a power failure, one usually tries to mount the other's filesystems before they have been exported and before NFS is started. If both servers use foreground mounts only, then a deadlock is possible when they wait on each other to recover as NFS servers. Using *bg* allows the first mount attempt to fail and be put into the background. When both servers finally complete booting, the backgrounded mounts complete successfully. So what if you have critical mounts on each client, such that backgrounding one is not appropriate? To cope, you will need to use the automounter (see Chapter 9) instead of *vfstab* to mount NFS filesystems.

The default value of the *retry* option was chosen to be large enough to guarantee that a client makes a sufficiently good effort to mount a filesystem from a crashed or hung server. However, if some event causes the client and the server to reboot at the same time, and the client cannot complete the mount before the retry count is exhausted, the client will not mount the filesystem even when the remote server comes back online. If you have a power failure early in the weekend, and all the clients come up but a server is down, you may have to manually remount filesystems on clients that have reached their limit of mount retries.

Hard and soft mounts

The *hard* and *soft* mount options determine how a client behaves when the server is excessively loaded for a long period or when it crashes. By default, all NFS filesystems are mounted *hard*, which means that an RPC call that times out will be retried indefinitely until a response is received from the server. This makes the NFS server look as much like a local disk as possible—the request that needs to go to disk completes at some point in the future. An NFS server that crashes looks like a disk that is very, very slow.

A side effect of hard-mounting NFS filesystems is that processes block (or "hang") in a high-priority disk wait state until their NFS RPC calls complete. If an NFS server goes down, the clients using its filesystems hang if they reference these filesystems before the server recovers. Using *intr* in conjunction with the *hard* mount option allows users to interrupt system calls that are blocked waiting on a crashed server. The system call is interrupted when the process making the call receives a signal, usually sent by the user typing CTRL-C (interrupt) or using the *kill* command. CTRL-\ (quit) is another way to generate a signal, as is logging out of the NFS client host. When using *kill*, only *SIGINT*, *SIGQUIT*, and *SIGHUP* will interrupt NFS operations.

When an NFS filesystem is *soft*-mounted, repeated RPC call failures eventually cause the NFS operation to fail as well. Instead of emulating a painfully slow disk, a server exporting a soft-mounted filesystem looks like a failing disk when it crashes: system calls referencing the soft-mounted NFS filesystem return errors. Sometimes the errors can be ignored or are preferable to blocking at high priority; for example, if you were doing an *ls -l* when the NFS server crashed, you wouldn't really care if the *ls* command returned an error as long as your system didn't hang.

The other side to this "failing disk" analogy is that you *never* want to write data to an unreliable device, nor do you want to try to load executables from it. You should not use the *soft* option on any filesystem that is writable, nor on any filesystem from which you load executables. Furthermore, because many applications do not check return value of the *read(2)* system call when reading regular files (because those programs were written in the days before networking was ubiquitous, and disks were reliable enough that reads from disks virtually never failed), you should not use the *soft* option on any filesystem that is supplying input to applications that are in turn using the data for a mission-critical purpose. NFS only guarantees the consistency of data after a server crash if the NFS filesystem was hard-mounted by the client. Unless you really know what you are doing, *never* use the *soft* option.

We'll come back to *hard-* and *soft*-mount issues in when we discuss modifying client behavior in the face of slow NFS servers in Chapter 18.

Resolving mount problems

There are several things that can go wrong when attempting to mount an NFS filesystem. The most obvious failure of *mount* is when it cannot find the server, remote filesystem, or local mount point. You get the usual assortment of errors such as "No such host" and "No such file or directory." However, you may also get more cryptic messages like:

```
client# mount orion:/export/orion /hosts/orion
mount: orion:/export/orion on /hosts/orion: No such device.
```

If either the local or remote filesystem was specified incorrectly, you would expect a message about a nonexistent file or directory. The *device* hint in this error indicates that NFS is not configured into the client's kernel. The *device* in question is more of a pseudo-device—it's the interface to the NFS vnode operations. If the NFS client code is not in the kernel, this interface does not exist and any attempts to use it return invalid device messages. We won't discuss how to build a kernel; check your documentation for the proper procedures and options that need to be included to support NFS.

Another cryptic message is "Permission denied." Often this is because the filesystem has been exported with the options *rw=client_list* or *ro=client_list* and your client is not in *client_list*. But sometimes it means that the filesystem on the server is not exported at all.

Probably the most common message on NFS clients is "NFS server not responding. " An NFS client will attempt to complete an RPC call up to the number of times specified by the *retrans* option. Once the retransmission limit has been reached, the "not responding" message appears on the system's console (or in the console window):

```
NFS server bitatron not responding, still trying
```

followed by a message indicating that the server has responded to the client's RPC requests:

```
NFS server bitatron OK
```

These "not responding" messages may mean that the server is heavily loaded and cannot respond to NFS requests before the client has had numerous RPC timeouts, or they may indicate that the server has crashed. The NFS client cannot tell the difference between the two, because it has no knowledge of why its NFS RPC calls are not being handled. If NFS clients begin printing "not responding" messages, a server have may have crashed, or you may be experiencing a burst of activity causing poor server performance.

A less common but more confusing error message is "stale filehandle." Because NFS allows multiple clients to share the same directory, it opens up a window in which one client can delete files or directories that are being referenced by another NFS client of the same server. When the second client goes to reference the deleted directory, the NFS server can no longer find it on disk, and marks the handle, or pointer, to this directory "invalid." The exact causes of stale filehandles and suggestions for avoiding them are described in "Stale filehandles" in Chapter 18.

If there is a problem with the server's NFS configuration, your attempt to mount filesystems from it will result in RPC errors when *mount* cannot reach the portmapper (*rpcbind*) on the server. If you get RPC timeouts, then the remote host may have lost its portmapper service or the *mountd* daemon may have exited prematurely. Use *ps* to locate these processes:

```
server% ps -e | grep -w mountd
274 ?       0:00 mountd
server% ps -e | grep -w rpcbind
106 ?       0:00 rpcbind
```

You should see both the *mountd* and the *rpcbind* processes running on the NFS server.

If *mount* promptly reports "Program not registered," this means that the *mountd* daemon never started up and registered itself. In this case, make sure that *mountd* is getting started at boot time on the NFS server, by checking the */etc/dfs/dfstab* file. See the section "Setting up NFS" earlier in this chapter.

Another *mountd*-related problem is two *mountd* daemons competing for the same RPC service number. On some systems (not Solaris), there might be a situation when one mount daemon can be started in the boot script and one configured into */etc/inet/inetd.conf*, the second instance of the server daemon will not be able to register its RPC service number with the portmapper. Since the *inetd*-spawned process is usually the second to appear, it repeatedly exits and restarts until *inetd* realizes that the server cannot be started and disables the service. The NFS RPC daemons should be started from the boot scripts and not from *inetd*, due to the overhead of spawning processes from the *inetd* server (see "Internet and RPC server configuration" in Chapter 1).

There is also a detection mechanism for attempts to make "transitive," or multihop, NFS mounts. You can only use NFS to mount another system's local filesystem as one of your NFS filesystems. You can't mount another system's NFS-mounted filesystems. That is, if */export/home/bob* is local on *serverb*, then all machines on the network must mount */export/home/bob* from *serverb*. If a client attempts to mount a remotely mounted directory on the server, the mount fails with a multihop error message. Let's say NFS client marble has done:

```
# mount serverb:/export/home/bob /export/home/bob
```

and *marble* is also an NFS server that exports */export/home*. If a third system tries to mount *marble:/export/home/bob*, then the mount fails with the error:

```
mount: marble:/export/home/bob on /users/bob: Too many levels of remote in path
```

"Too many levels" means more than one—the filesystem on the server is itself NFS-mounted. You cannot nest NFS mounts by mounting through an intermediate fileserver. There are two practical sides to this restriction:

- Allowing multihop mounts would defeat the host-based permission checking used by NFS. If a *server* limits access to a filesystem to a few clients, then one of these client should not be allowed to NFS-mount the filesystem and make it available to other, non-trusted systems. Preventing multihop mounts makes the server owning the filesystem the single authority governing its use—no other machine can circumvent the access policies set by the NFS server owning a filesystem.

- Any machine used as an intermediate server in a multihop mount becomes a very inefficient "gateway" between the NFS client and the server owning the filesystem.

We've seen how to export NFS filesystems on a network and how NFS clients mount them. With this basic explanation of NFS usage, we'll look at how NFS mounts are combined with symbolic links to create more complex—and sometimes confusing—client filesystem structures.

Symbolic links

Symbolic links are both useful and confusing when used with NFS-mounted filesystems. They can be used to "shape" a filesystem arbitrarily, giving the system administrator freedom to organize filesystems and pathnames in convenient ways. When used badly, symbolic links have unexpected and unwanted side effects, including poor performance and "missing" files or directories. In this section, we'll discuss the many effects that symbolic links can have on NFS.

Symbolic links differ from hard links in several ways, but the salient distinction is that hard links duplicate directory entries, while symbolic links are new directory entries of a special type. Using a hard link to a file is no different from using the original file, but referencing a symbolic link requires reading the link to find out where it points and then referencing that file or directory. It is possible to create a loop of symbolic links, but the kernel routines that read the links and build up pathnames eventually return an error when too many links have been traversed in a single pathname.

Resolving symbolic links in NFS

When an NFS client does a *stat()* of a directory entry and finds it is a symbolic link, it issues an RPC call to read the link (on the server) and determine where the link points. This is the equivalent of doing a local *readlink()* system call to examine the contents of a symbolic link. The server returns a pathname that is interpreted on the client, not on the server.

The pathname may point to a directory that the client has mounted, or it may not make sense on the client. If you uncover a link that was made on the server that points to a filesystem not exported from the server, you will have either trouble or confusion if you resolve the link. If the link accidentally points to a valid file or directory on the client, the results are often unpredictable and sometimes unwanted. If the link points to something nonexistent on the client, an attempt to use it produces an error.

An example here helps explain how links can point in unwanted directions. Let's say that you install a new publishing package, *marker*, in the *tools* filesystem on an NFS server. Once it's loaded, you realize that you need to free some space on the */tools* filesystem, so you move the font directory used by *marker* to the */usr* filesystem, and make a symbolic link to redirect the *fonts* subdirectory to its new location:

```
# mkdir /usr/marker
# cd /tools/marker
# tar cf - fonts | ( cd /usr/marker; tar xbBfp 20 - )
# rm -rf fonts
# ln -s /usr/marker/fonts fonts
```

The *tar* command copies the entire directory tree from the current directory to */usr/marker* (see the manpage for *tar(1)* for a more detailed explanation).

On the server, the redirection imposed by the symbolic link is invisible to users. However, an NFS client that mounts */tools/marker* and tries to use it will be in for a surprise when the client tries to find the *fonts* subdirectory. The client looks at */tools/marker/fonts*, realizes that it's a symbolic link, and asks the NFS server to read the link. The NFS server returns the link's target—*/usr/marker/fonts*—and the client tries to open this directory instead. On the client, however, this directory *does not exist*. It was created for convenience on the server, but breaks the NFS clients that use it. To fix this problem, you must create the same symbolic link on all of the clients, and ensure that the clients can locate the target of the link.

Think of symbolic links as you would files on an NFS server. The server does not interpret the contents of files, nor does it do anything with the contents of a link except pass it back to the user process that issued the *readlink* RPC. Symbolic links are treated as if they existed on the local host, and they are interpreted relative to the client's filesystem hierarchy.

Absolute and relative pathnames

Symbolic links can point to an absolute pathname (one beginning with */*) or a pathname relative to the link's path. Relative symbolic link targets are resolved relative to the place at which the link appears in the client's filesystem, not the server's, so it is possible for a relative link to point at a nonexistent file or directory on the client. Consider this server for */usr/local*:

```
% cd /usr/local/bin
% ls -l
total 1
lrwxrwxrwx  1 root        bin         16 Jun  8  1990 a2ps -> ../bin.mips/a2ps
lrwxrwxrwx  1 root        bin         12 Jun  8  1990 mp -> ../bin.mips/mp
```

If you mount just */usr/local/bin* from this server, you will not be able to use any of the executables in it unless you have them in the directory */usr/local/bin.mips*.

Using symbolic links to reduce the number of directories in a pathname is beneficial only if users are not tempted to *cd* from one link to another:

```
# ln -s /minnow/fred /u/fred
# ln -s /alewife/lucy /u/lucy
```

The unsuspecting user tries to use the path-compressed names, but finds that relative pathnames aren't relative to the link directory:

```
% cd /u/fred
% cd ../lucy
../lucy: No such file or directory
```

A user may be bewildered by this behavior. According to the */u* directory, *fred* and *lucy* are subdirectories of a common parent. In reality, they aren't. The symbolic links hide the real locations of the *fred* and *lucy* directories, which do not have a common parent. Using symbolic links to shorten pathnames in this fashion is not always the most efficient solution to the problem; NFS mounts can often be used to produce the same filesystem naming conventions.

Mount points, exports, and links

Symbolic links have strange effects on mounting and exporting filesystems. A good general rule to remember is that filesystem operations apply to the target of a link, not to the link itself. The symbolic link is just a pointer to the real operand.

If you mount a filesystem on a symbolic link, the actual mount occurs on the directory pointed to by the link. The following sequence of operations produces the same net result:

```
# mkdir -p /users/hal
# ln -s /users/hal /usr/hal
# mount bitatron:/export/home/hal /usr/hal
```

as this sequence does:

```
# mkdir -p /users/hal
# mount bitatron:/export/home/hal /users/hal
# ln -s /users/hal /usr/hal
```

The filesystem is mounted on the directory */users/hal* and the symbolic link */usr/hal* has the mount point as its target. You should make sure that the directory pointed to by the link is on a filesystem that is mounted read/write and that performing the mount will not obscure any required filesystem underneath the symbolic link target.

Exporting a symbolic link from a server follows similar rules. The filesystem or subtree of a filesystem that is really exported is the one pointed to by the symbolic link. If the parent of the link's target has already been exported, or a subtree of it is exported, the attempt to export the link fails.

More interesting than exporting a symbolic link is mounting one from the server. Mounting a link from a server is not the same thing as mounting a filesystem containing a symbolic link. The latter means that there is a symbolic link somewhere

in the filesystem mounted using NFS. The former case implies that the server pathname used to locate the remote filesystem is a link and directs the mount somewhere else. The client mounts the directory pointed to by the link. As shown in
Figure 6-1, if */usr/man* is a symbolic link to */usr/share/man,* then this *mount*
command:

```
# mount bitatron:/usr/share/man /mnt
```

does the same thing as this mount command:

```
# mount bitatron:/usr/man  /mnt
```

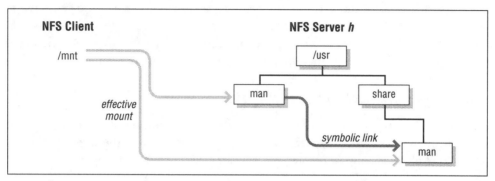

Figure 6-1. Mounting a server's symbolic link

A potential problem arises if the symbolic link and the directory it points to are
on different filesystems: it's possible that the server has exported the link's filesystem but not the filesystem containing the link's target. In this example, */usr/
man* and */usr/share/man* could be in two distinct filesystems, which would
require two entries in the server's *dfstab* file.

Replication

Solaris 2.6 introduced the concept of replication to NFS clients. This feature is
known as *client-side failover.* Client-side failover is useful whenever you have
read-only data that you need to be highly available. An example will illustrate this.

Suppose your user community needs to access a collection of historical data on
the last 200 national budgets of the United States. This is a lot of data, and so is a
good candidate to store on a central NFS server. However, because your users'
jobs depend on it, you do not want to have a single point of failure, and so you
keep the data on several NFS servers. (Keeping the data on several NFS servers
also gives one the opportunity to load balance). Suppose you have three NFS
servers, named *hamilton, wolcott,* and *dexter,* each exporting a copy of data. Then
each server might have an entry like this in its *dfstab* file:

```
share -o ro /export/budget_stats
```

Now, without client-side failover, each NFS client might have one of the following *vfstab* entries:

```
hamilton:/export/budget_stats    -    /stats/budget    nfs    -    yes    ro
wolcott:/export/budget_stats     -    /stats/budget    nfs    -    yes    ro
dexter:/export/budget_stats      -    /stats/budget    nfs    -    yes    ro
```

Suppose an NFS client is mounting */stats/budget* from NFS server *hamilton*, and *hamilton* stops responding. The user on that client will want to mount a different server. In order to do this, he'll have to do all of the following:

1. Terminate any applications that are currently accessing files under the */budget_stats* mount point.

2. Unmount */stats/budget*.

3. Edit the *vfstab* file to point at a different server.

4. Mount */stats/budget*.

The user might have a problem with the first step, especially if the application has buffered some unsaved critical information. And the other three steps are tedious.

With client side failover, each NFS client can have a single entry in the *vfstab* file such as:

```
hamilton,wolcott,dexter:/export/budget_stat    -    /budget_stats    nfs    -    yes    ro
```

This *vfstab* entry defines a *replicated* NFS filesystem. When this *vfstab* entry is mounted, the NFS client will:

1. Contact each server to verify that each is responding and exporting */export/budget_stats*.

2. Generate a list of the NFS servers that are responding and exporting */export/budget_stats* and associate that list with the mount point.

3. Pick one of the servers to get NFS service from. In other words, the NFS traffic for the mount point is bound to one server at a time.

As long as the server selected to provide NFS service is responding, the NFS mount operates as a normal non-client-side failover mount. Assuming the NFS client selected server *hamilton*, if *hamilton* stops responding, the NFS client will automatically select the next server, in this case *wolcott*, without requiring that one manually unmount *hamilton*, and mount *wolcott*. And if *wolcott* later stops responding, the NFS client would then select *dexter*. As you might expect, if later on *dexter* stops responding, the NFS client will bind the NFS traffic back to *hamilton*. Thus, client-side failover uses a round-robin scheme.

You can tell which server a replicated mount is using via the *nfsstat* command:

```
% nfsstat -m
...
/budget_stats from hamilton,wolcott,dexter:/export/budget_stats
```

```
Flags:
vers=3,proto=tcp,sec=sys,hard,intr,llock,link,symlink,acl,rsize=32768,wsize=32768,
retrans-5
Failover:noresponse=1, failover=1, remap=1, currserver=wolcott
```

The *currserver* value tells us that NFS traffic for the */budget_stats* mount point is bound to server *wolcott*. Apparently *hamilton* stopped responding at one point, because we see non-zero values for the counters *noresponse, failover* and *remap*. The counter *noresponse* counts the number of times a remote procedure call to the currently bound NFS server timed out. The counter *failover* counts the number of times the NFS client has "failed over" or switched to another NFS server due to a timed out remote procedure call. The counter *remap* counts the number of files that were "mapped" to another NFS server after a failover. For example, if an application on the NFS client had */budget_stats/1994/deficit* open, and then the client failed over to another server, the next time the application went to read data from */budget_stats/1944/deficit*, the open file reference would be re-mapped to the corresponding *1944/deficit* file on the newly bound NFS server.

Solaris will also notify you when a failover happens. Expect a message like:

```
NOTICE: NFS: failing over from hamilton to wolcott
```

on both the NFS client's system console and in its */var/adm/messages* file.

By the way, it is not required that each server have the same pathname mounted. The *mount* command will let you mount replica servers with different directories. For example:

```
# mount -o ro serverX:/q,serverY:/m /mnt
```

As long as the contents of *serverX:/q* and *serverY:/m* are the same, the top level directory name does not have to be. The next section discusses rules for content of replicas.

Properties of replicas

Replicas on each server in the replicated filesystem have to be the same in content. For example, if on an NFS client we have done:

```
# mount -o ro serverX,serverY:/export /mnt
```

then */export* on both servers needs to be an exact copy. One way to generate such a copy would be:

```
# rlogin serverY
serverY # cd /export
serverY # rm -rf ../export
serverY # mount serverX:/export /mnt
serverY # cd /mnt
serverY # find . -print | cpio -dmp /export
```

```
serverY # umount /mnt
serverY # exit
#
```

The third command invoked here, *rm -rf ./export* is somewhat curious. What we want to do is remove the contents of */export* in a manner that is as fast and secure as possible. We could do *rm -rf /export* but that has the side of effect of removing */export* as well as its contents. Since */export* is exported, any NFS client that is currently mounting *serverY:/export* will experience stale filehandles (see the section "Stale filehandles" in Chapter 18). Recreating */export* immediately with the *mkdir* command does not suffice because of the way NFS servers generate filehandles for clients. The filehandle contains among other things the inode number (a file's or directory's unique identification number) and this is almost guaranteed to be different. So we want to remove just what is under */export*. A commonly used method for doing that is:

```
# cd /export ; find . -print | xargs rm -rf
```

but the problem there is that if someone has placed a filename like *foo /etc/passwd* (i.e., a file with an embedded space character) in */export*, then the *xargs rm -rf* command will remove a file called *foo* and a file called */etc/passwd,* which on Solaris may prevent one from logging into the system. Doing *rm -rf ./export* will prevent */export* from being removed because *rm* will not remove the current working directory. Note that this behavior may vary with other systems, so test it on something unimportant to be sure.

At any rate, the aforementioned sequence of commands will create a replica that has the following properties:

- Each regular file, directory, named pipe, symbolic link, socket, and device node in the original has a corresponding object with the same name in the copy.

- The file type of each regular file, directory, named pipe, symbolic link, socket, and device node in the original is the same in the corresponding object with same name in the copy.

- The contents of each regular file, directory, symbolic link and device node in the original are the equal to the contents of each corresponding object with same name in the copy.

- The user identifier, group identifier, and file permissions of each regular file, directory, name pipe, symbolic link, socket, and device node in the original are to equal the user identifier, group identifier, and file permissions of each corresponding object with the same name in the copy. Strictly speaking this last property is not mandatory for client-side failover to work, but if after a failover, the user on the NFS client no longer has access to the file his application was reading, then the user's application will stop working.

Rules for mounting replicas

In order to use client-side failover, the filesystem must be mounted with the sub-options *ro* (read-only) and *hard*.

The reason why it has to be mounted read-only is that if NFS clients could write to the replica filesystem, then the replicas would be no longer synchronized, producing the following undesirable effects:

- If another NFS client failed over from one server to the server with the modified file, it would encounter an unexpected inconsistency.

- Likewise, if the NFS client or application that modified the file failed over to another server, it would find that its changes were no longer present.

The filesystem has to be mounted *hard* because it is not clear what it would mean to mount a replicated filesystem *soft*. When a filesystem is mounted *soft*, it is supposed to return an error from a timed-out remote procedure call. When a replicated filesystem is mounted, after a remote procedure call times out, the NFS filesystem is supposed to try the next server in the list associated with the mount point. These two semantics are at odds, so replicated filesystems must be mounted *hard*.

The NFS servers in the replica list must support a common NFS version. When specifying a replicated filesystem that has some servers that support NFS Version 3, and some that support just NFS Version 2, the *mount* command will fail with the error "replicas must have the same version." Usually, though, the NFS servers that support Version 3 will also support Version 2. Thus, if you are happy with using NFS Version 2 for your replicated filesystem, then you can force the mount to succeed by specifying the *vers=2* suboption. For example:

```
# mount -o vers=2 serverA,serverB,serverC:/export /mnt
```

Note that it is not a requirement that all the NFS servers in the replicated filesystem support the same transport protocol (TCP or UDP).

Managing replicas

In Solaris, the onus for creating, distributing, and maintaining replica filesystems is on the system administrator; there are no tools to manage replication. The techniques used in the example given in the earlier subsection, "Properties of replicas," can be used, although the example script given in that subsection for generating a replica may cause stale filehandle problems when using it to update a replica; we will address this in the section, "Stale filehandles" in Chapter 18. You will want to automate the replica distribution procedure. In the example, you would alter the aforementioned example to:

- Prevent stale filehandles.

- Use the *rsh* command instead of the *rlogin* command.

Other methods of distribution to consider are ones that use tools like the *rdist* and *filesync* commands.

Replicas and the automounter

Replication is best combined with use of the automounter. The integration of the two is described in "Replicated servers" in Chapter 9.

Naming schemes

Simple, efficient naming schemes make the difference between a filesystem that is well organized and a pleasure to use, and a filesystem that you are constantly fighting against. In this section, we'll look at ways of using mount points and symbolic links to create simple, consistent naming schemes on all NFS clients. NFS provides the mechanism for making distributed filesystems transparent to the user, but it has no inherent guidelines for creating easy to use and easier to manage filesystem hierarchies. There are few global rules, and each network will adopt conventions based on the number of servers, the kinds of files handled by those servers, and any peculiar naming requirements of locally developed or third-party software.

Note that this section assumes that you will not be using the automounter (see Chapter 9). It is strongly advised that you *do* use the automounter, because every issue mentioned and solved here is much more easily solved with the automounter.

As a system administrator, you should first decide how the various NFS fileservers fit together on a client before assigning filesystem names and filling them with software or users. Here are some ideas and suggestions for choosing NFS naming schemes:

- Avoid having NFS mounts on directories directly under the root (/) directory of each NFS client. The reason is that if an NFS server crashes, then any attempts to access the mounted directory will hang the application even if it is not interested in the NFS mount point. This can happen if an application invokes the library equivalent of the *pwd* command: *getcwd()*. *

---

* The *getcwd()* routine builds its pathname of the current working directory by searching upward via the ".." directory, and then reading each directory to find the directory with the same file ID number as the current working directory. To get the file ID requires invoking the *stat()* system call on the directory. If the directory is served by an NFS server, and the server is unavailable, then *stat()*, hence *getcwd()*, and the application will hang indefinitely.

- Pick a common directory on each client under which you will mount each user's home directory. For example, if you pick */users*, then each user's home directory is accessed via the */users/username* naming scheme.*

  This makes it easier to deal with servers that have several filesystems of home directories. The disadvantage to this approach is that it requires a larger */etc/vfstab* file, with one entry for each user's home directory. If you use the NFS automounter, this naming scheme is more easily managed than the hostname-oriented one (and the automounter has a */home/username* scheme preconfigured). Directories that follow any regular naming scheme are easily managed by the automounter, as discussed in Chapter 9.

- Do not allow the physical location of the files on the server to dictate the pathnames to be used on the client. For example, if the software tools directory is on *wahoo:/export/home/toolbox*, then instead of mounting *wahoo:/export/home/toolbox* onto each client's */export/home/toolbox* directory, use something more user friendly, like */software/toolbox*:

  ```
  mount wahoo:/export/home/toolbox /software/toolbox
  ```

  Normally you don't want people running applications on hosts that are also NFS servers. However, if you allow this, and if you want users on the NFS server to be able to access the toolbox as */software/toolbox*, then you can either create a symbolic link from */software/toolbox* to */export/home/toolbox*, or use the loopback filesystem in Solaris to accomplish the same thing without the overhead of a symbolic link:

  ```
  mount -F lofs /export/home/toolbox /software/toolbox
  ```

- Keep growth in mind. Having a single third-party software filesystem may be the most effective (or only) solution immediately, but over the next year you may need to add a second or third filesystem to make room for more tools. To provide adequate performance, you may want to put each filesystem on a different server, distributing the load. If you choose a naming scheme that cannot be extended, you will end up renaming things later on and having to support the "old style" names.

In the third-party tools directory example, you could separate tools into subdirectories grouped by function: */software/tools/epubs* for page composition and publishing software, and */software/tools/cae* for engineering tools. If either directory grows enough to warrant its own filesystem, you can move the subdirectory to a

---

* The example uses */users* and not */home*. This is because the automounter in Solaris reserves */home*. While you can modify each Solaris client to remove the reservation, that is tedious. A common error is for people to use *vfstab* or the *mount* command to mount onto */home*, and if the automounter has reserved */home*, things will fail in odd ways.

new server and preserve the existing naming scheme by simply mounting both subdirectories on clients:

Before: single tools depository
```
# mount toolbox:/export/home/tools  /software/tools
```

After: multiple filesystems
```
# mount toolbox:/export/home/epubs /software/tools/epubs
# mount backpack:/export/home/case /software/tools/cae
```

Solving the /usr/local puzzle

Let's assume you have a network with many different kinds of workstations: SPARC workstations, PowerPC-based workstations, Unix PCs, and so on. Of course, each kind of workstation has its own set of executables. The executables may be built from the same source files, but you need a different binary for each machine architecture. How do you arrange the filesystem so that each system has a */usr/local/bin* directory (and, by extension, other executable directories) that contains only the executables that are appropriate for its architecture? How do you "hide" the executables that aren't appropriate, so there's no chance that a user will mistakenly try to execute them? This is the */usr/local* puzzle: creating an "architecture neutral" executable directory.

Implementing an architecture-neutral */usr/local/bin* is probably one of the first challenges posed to the system administrator of a heterogeneous network. Everybody wants the standard set of tools, such as emacs, PostScript filters, mail-pretty printers, and the requisite telephone list utility. Ideally, there should be one *bin* directory for each architecture, and when a user looks in */usr/local/bin* on any machine, he or she should find the proper executables. Hiding the machine architecture is a good job for symbolic links.

One solution is to name the individual binary directories with the machine type as a suffix and then mount the proper one on */usr/local/bin*:

On server toolbox:
```
# cd /export/home/local
# ls
bin.mips bin.sun3 bin.sun4 bin.vax
```

On client:
```
# mount toolbox:/export/home/local/bin.`arch` /usr/local/bin
```

The *mount* command determines the architecture of the local host and grabs the correct binary directory from the server.

This scheme is sufficient if you only have binaries in your local depository, but most sites add manual pages, source code, and other ASCII files that are shared across client architectures. There is no need to maintain multiple copies of these files. To accommodate a mixture of shared ASCII and binary files, use two mounts of the same filesystem: the first mount sets up the framework of directories, and puts the shared file directories in their proper place. The second mount deposits the proper binary directory on top of */usr/local/bin*:

```
On server toolbox:
# cd /export/home/local
# ls bin
bin.mips bin.sun3 bin.sun4 bin.vax mansharesrc

On client:
# mount toolbox:/export/home/local /usr/local
# mount toolbox:/export/home/local/bin.`arch` /usr/local/bin
```

At first glance, the previous example appears to violate the NFS rules prohibiting the export of a directory and any of its subdirectories. However, there is only one exported filesystem on server *toolbox*, namely, */export/home*. The clients mount different parts of this exported filesystem on top of one another. NFS allows a client to mount any part of an exported filesystem, on any directory.

To save disk space with the two-mount approach, populate */export/home/bin* on the server with the proper executables, and make the *bin.arch* directory a symbolic link to *bin*. This allows clients of the same architecture as the server to get by with only one mount.

If you keep *all* executables—scripts and compiled applications—in the *bin* directories, you still have a problem with duplication. At some sites, scripts may account for more than half of the tools in */usr/local/bin*, and having to copy them into each architecture-specific *bin* directory makes this solution less pleasing.

A more robust solution to the problem is to divide shell scripts and executables into two directories: scripts go in */usr/local/share* while compiled executables live in the familiar */usr/local/bin*. This makes *share* a peer of the */usr/local/man* and *src* directories, both of which contain architecture-neutral ASCII files. To adapt to the fully architecture-neutral */usr/local/bin*, users need to put both */usr/local/bin* and */usr/local/share* in their search paths, although this is a small price to pay for the guarantee that all tools are accessible from all systems.

There is one problem with mounting one filesystem on top of another: if the server for these filesystems goes down, you will not be able to unmount them until the server recovers. When you unmount a filesystem, it gets information about all of the directories above it. If the filesystem is not mounted on top of another NFS filesystem, this isn't a problem: all of the directory information is on the NFS client. However, the hierarchy of mounts used in the */usr/local/bin* example presents a problem. One of the directories that an unmount operation would need to check is located on the server that crashed. An attempt to unmount the */usr/local/bin* directory will hang because it tries to get information about the */usr/local* mount point—and the server for that mount point is the one that crashed. Similarly, if you try to unmount the */usr/local* filesystem, this attempt will fail because the */usr/local/bin* directory is in use: it has a filesystem mounted on it.

7

In this chapter:
- *Virtual filesystems and virtual nodes*
- *NFS protocol and implementation*
- *NFS components*
- *Caching*
- *File locking*
- *NFS futures*

Network File System Design and Operation

It's possible to configure and use the Network File System without too much knowledge of how it is implemented or why various design decisions were made. But if you need to debug problems, or analyze patterns of NFS usage to suggest performance optimizations, you will need to know more about the inside workings of the NFS protocol and the daemons that implement it. With an understanding of how and why NFS does the things it does, you can more readily determine why it is broken or slow—probably the two most common complaints in any large NFS network.

Like NIS, NFS is implemented as a set of RPC procedures that use eXternal Data Representation (XDR) encoding to pass arguments between client and server. A filesystem mounted using NFS provides two levels of transparency:

- The filesystem appears to be resident on a disk attached to the local system, and all of the filesystem entries—files and directories—are viewed the same way, whether local or remote. NFS hides the location of the file on the network.

- NFS-mounted filesystems contain no information about the file server from which they are mounted. The NFS file server may be of a different architecture or running an entirely different operating system with a radically different filesystem structure. For example, a Sun machine running Solaris can mount an NFS filesystem from a Windows NT system or an IBM MVS mainframe, using NFS server implementations for each of these systems. NFS hides differences in the underlying remote filesystem structure and makes the remote filesystem appear to be of the exact same structure as that of the client.

NFS achieves the first level of transparency by defining a generic set of filesystem operations that are performed on a *Virtual File System* (VFS). The second level comes from the definition of *virtual nodes*, which are related to the more familiar Unix filesystem *inode* structures but hide the actual structure of the physical filesystem beneath them. The set of all procedures that can be performed on files is the vnode interface definition. The vnode and VFS specifications together define the NFS protocol.

Virtual filesystems and virtual nodes

The Virtual File System allows a client system to access many different types of filesystems as if they were all attached locally. VFS hides the differences in implementations under a consistent interface. On a Unix NFS client, the VFS interface makes all NFS filesystems look like Unix filesystems, even if they are exported from IBM MVS or Windows NT servers. The VFS interface is really nothing more than a switchboard for filesystem- and file-oriented operations, as shown in Figure 7-1.

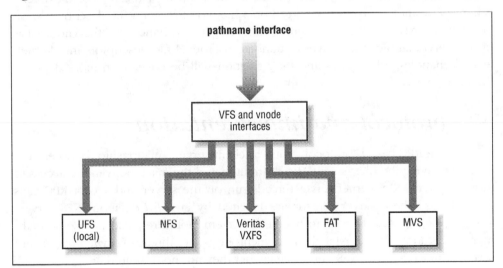

Figure 7-1. Virtual File System interfaces

Actions that operate on entire filesystems, such as getting the amount of free space left in the filesystem, are called *VFS operations*; calls that operate on files or directories are *vnode operations*. On the server side, implementing a VFS entails taking the generic VFS and vnode operations and converting them into the appropriate actions on the real, underlying filesystem. This conversion happens invisibly to the NFS client process. It made a straightforward system call, which the client-side VFS turned into a vnode operation, and the server then converted into an equivalent operation on its filesystem.

For example, the *chown()* system call has an analogous operator in the vnode interface that sets the attributes of a file, as does the *stat()* system call that retrieves these attributes. There is not a strict one-to-one relationship of Unix system calls to vnode operations. The *write()* system call uses several filesystem calls to get a file's attributes, and append or modify blocks in the file. Some vnode operations are not defined on certain types of filesystems. The FAT filesystem, for example, doesn't have an equivalent of symbolic links, so an NFS file server running on an Windows NT machine rejects any attempts to use the vnode operation to create a symbolic link.

So far we have defined an interface to some filesystem objects, but not the mechanism used to "name" objects in the system. In a local Unix system call, these object names are file descriptors, which uniquely identify a file within the scope of a process. The counterparts of file descriptors in NFS are filehandle*s*, which are opaque "pointers" to files on the remote system. An opaque handle is of no value to the client because it can only be interpreted in the context of the remote filesystem. When you want to make a system call on a file, you first get a file descriptor for it. To make an NFS call (in the kernel) you must get a filehandle for the vnode. It is up to the virtual filesystem layer to translate user-level file descriptors into kernel-level filehandles. Filehandles and their creation will be covered in more depth in the next section.

NFS protocol and implementation

NFS is an RPC-based protocol, with a client-server relationship between the machine having the filesystem to be distributed and the machine wanting access to that filesystem. NFS kernel server threads run on the server and accept RPC calls from clients. These server threads are initiated by an *nfsd* daemon. NFS servers also run the *mountd* daemon to handle filesystem mount requests and some pathname translation. On an NFS client, asynchronous I/O threads (*async threads*) are usually run to improve NFS performance, but they are not required.

On the client, each process using NFS files is a client of the server. The client's system calls that access NFS-mounted files make RPC calls to the NFS servers from which these files were mounted. The virtual filesystem really just extends the operation of basic system calls like *read()* and *write()*, similar to the way that NIS extends the operation of library calls like *getpwuid()*. In NIS, the *getpwuid()* routine knows how to use the NIS RPC protocol to locate user information that isn't in the local */etc/passwd* file. Within the virtual filesystem, the basic file- and filesystem-oriented system calls were modified to "know" how to operate on non-local filesystems.

Let's look at this with an example. On an NFS client, a user process executes a *chmod()* system call on an NFS-mounted file. The virtual filesystem passes this system call to NFS, which then executes a remote procedure call to set the permissions on the file, as specified in the process's system call. When the RPC completes, the system call returns to the user process. This example is fairly simple, because it doesn't involve any block I/O to get file data to or from the NFS server. When blocks of files are moved around, the async threads get involved to improve NFS performance. This section covers the protocols used by NFS and features of its implementation that were driven by performance or transparency goals.

NFS RPC procedures

Each version of the NFS RPC protocol contains several procedures, each of which operates on either a file or a filesystem object. The basic procedures performed on an NFS server can be grouped into directory operations, file operations, link operations, and filesystem operations. Directory operations include *mkdir* and *rmdir*, which create and destroy directories like their Unix system call equivalents. *readdir* reads a directory, using an opaque directory pointer to perform sequential reads of the same directory. Other directory oriented procedures are *rename* and *remove*, which operate on entries in a directory the same way the *mv* and *rm* commands do. *create* makes a new directory entry for a file.

The *lookup* operation is the heart of the pathname-to-filehandle translation mechanism. *lookup* finds a named directory entry and returns a filehandle pointing to it. The *open()* system call uses *lookup()* extensively: it breaks a pathname down into its components and locates each component in its parent directory. For example, *open()* would handle the pathname */home/thud/stern* by performing three operations:

- Look up *home* in the root directory (/).
- Look up *thud* in */home*.
- Look up *stern* in */home/thud*.

File operations are very closely associated with Unix system calls: *read* and *write* move data to and from the NFS client, and *getattr* and *setattr* get or modify the file's attributes. In a local filesystem, such as UFS, these attributes are stored in the file's inode, but file attributes are mapped to whatever system is used by the NFS server. Link operations include *link*, which creates a hard link on the server, and *symlink* and *readlink* which create and read the values of symbolic links, respectively. Finally, *statfs* is a filesystem operation that returns information about the mounted filesystem that might be needed by *df*, for example.

Other filesystem operations include mounting and unmounting a filesystem, but these are handled through the NFS *mountd* server rather than the server threads. Mount operations are separated from the NFS protocol because mount points revolve around pathnames, and pathname syntax is peculiar to each operating system. Unix and VMS, for example, do not use the same syntax to specify the path to a file. The mount protocol is responsible for turning the server's file pathname into information that NFS can use to locate the file in future operations.

From the preceding descriptions, it is fairly clear how the basic Unix system calls map into NFS RPC calls. It is important to note that the NFS RPC protocol and the vnode interface are two different things. The vnode interface defines a set of operating system services that are used to access all filesystems, NFS or local. Vnodes simply generalize the interface to file objects. There are many routines in the vnode interface that correspond directly to procedures in the NFS protocol, but the vnode interface also contains implementations of operating system services such as mapping file blocks and buffer cache management.

The NFS RPC protocol is a specific realization of one of these vnode interfaces. It is used to perform specific vnode operations on remote files. Using the vnode interface, new filesystem types may be plugged into the operating system by adding kernel routines that perform the necessary vnode operations on objects in that filesystem.

Statelessness and crash recovery

The NFS protocol is stateless, meaning that there is no need to maintain information about the protocol on the server. The client keeps track of all information required to send requests to the server, but the server has no information about previous NFS requests, or how various NFS requests relate to each other. Remember the differences between the TCP and UDP protocols: UDP is a stateless protocol that can lose packets or deliver them out of order; TCP is a stateful protocol that guarantees that packets arrive and are delivered in order. The hosts using TCP must remember connection state information to recognize when part of a transmission was lost.

The choice of a stateless protocol has two implications for the design and implementation of NFS:

- NFS RPC requests must completely describe the operation to be performed. When writing a file block, for example, the write operation must contain a filehandle, the offset into the file, and the length of the write operation. This is distinctly different from the Unix *write()* system call, which writes a buffer to wherever the current file descriptor's write pointer directs it. The state contained in the file descriptor does not exist on the NFS server.

- Most NFS requests are *idempotent*, which means that an NFS client may send the same request one or more times without any harmful side effects. The net result of these duplicate requests is the same. For example, reading a specific block from a file is idempotent: the same data is returned from each operation.

  Obviously, some operations are not idempotent: removing a file can't be repeated without side effects, because a second attempt to remove the file will fail if the first one succeeded. Most NFS servers make all requests idempotent by recording recently performed operations. A duplicate request that matches one of the recently performed requests is thrown away by the NFS server.*

The primary motivation for choosing a stateless protocol was to minimize the burden of crash recovery. Unlike a database system, which must verify transaction logs and look for incomplete operations, NFS has no explicit crash recovery mechanism. Because no state is maintained, the server may reboot and begin accepting client NFS requests again as if nothing had happened. Similarly, when clients reboot, the server does not need to know anything about them. Each NFS request contains enough information to be completed without any reference to state on the client or server.

Request retransmission

NFS RPC requests are sent from a client to the server one at a time. A single client process will not issue another RPC call until the call in progress completes and has been acknowledged by the NFS server. In this respect NFS RPC calls are like system calls—a process cannot continue with the next system call until the current one completes. A single client host may have several RPC calls in progress at any time, coming from several processes, but each process ensures that its file operations are well ordered by waiting for their acknowledgements. Using the NFS async threads makes this a little more complicated, but for now it's helpful to think of each process sending a stream of NFS requests, one at a time.

When a client makes an RPC request, it sets a timeout period during which the server must service and acknowledge it. If the server doesn't get the request because it was lost along the way, or because the server is too overloaded to complete the request within the timeout period, the client *retransmits* the request. Requests are idempotent (if the server has a duplicate request cache), so no harm

---

* Not all implementations of NFS have this duplicate request cache. Current releases of Solaris, Compaq's Tru64 Unix, and other current operating systems implement the cache to improve the performance and "correctness" of NFS. A few, older implementations of NFS do not reject nonidempotent, duplicate requests. This produces some strange and often incorrect results when requests are retransmitted. An NFS client that sends the same *remove* operation to such a server may find that the designated file was removed, but the RPC call returns the "No such file or directory" error.

is done if the server executes the same request twice—when the NFS client gets a second confirmation from the RPC request, the client discards it.

NFS clients continue to retransmit requests until the request completes, either with an acknowledgement from the server or an error from the RPC layer. If an NFS server crashes, clients continue to repeat the call to the RPC layer (if the NFS filesystem is hard-mounted, otherwise the RPC timeout error is returned to the application) until the server reboots and can service them again. When the server is up again, NFS clients continue as if nothing happened. NFS clients cannot tell the difference between a server that has crashed and one that is very slow. This raises some important issues for tuning NFS servers and networks, which will be visited in "Slow server compensation" in Chapter 18.

The duplicate request cache on NFS servers usually contains a few hundred entries—the last few seconds (at most) of NFS requests on a busy server. This cache is limited in size to establish a "window" in which non-idempotent NFS requests are considered duplicates caused by retransmission rather than distinct requests. For example, if you execute:

```
% rm foo
```

on an NFS client, the client may need to send two or more *remove* requests to the NFS server before it receives an acknowledgment. It's up to the NFS server to weed out the duplicate *remove* requests, even if they are a second or so apart. However, if you execute *rm foo* on Monday, and then on Tuesday you execute the same command in the same directory (where the file has already been removed), you would be very surprised if *rm* did not return an error. Executing this "duplicate request" a day later should produce this familiar error:

```
% rm foo
rm: foo: No such file or directory
```

To distinguish between duplicates generated due to an RPC timeout and retry and duplicates due to you repeating a command (whether it be a day later or a second later), NFS servers record a 32-bit RPC transaction identifier (*xid*) with each entry in the duplicate request cache. The *xid* is part of every RPC request's header, and it is expected that the NFS client will generate unique *xid*s.

Preserving Unix filesystem semantics

The VFS makes all filesystems appear homogeneous to user processes. There is a single Unix system call interface that operates on files, and the VFS and underlying vnode interface translate semantics of these system calls into actions appropriate for each type of underlying filesystem. It's important to stress the difference between *syntax* and *semantics* of system calls. Consistent syntax means that the system calls take the same arguments independent of the underlying filesystem.

Semantics refers to what the system calls actually do: preserving semantics across different filesystem types means that a system call will have the same net effect on the files in each filesystem type. *Unix filesystem semantics* collectively refers to the way in which Unix files behave when various sequences of system calls are made. For example, opening a file and then unlinking it doesn't cause the file's data blocks to be released until the *close()* system call is made. A new filesystem that wants to maintain Unix filesystem semantics must support this behavior.

The VFS definition makes it possible to ensure that semantics are preserved for all filesystems, so they all behave in the same manner when Unix system calls are made on their files. It is easy to use VFS to implement a filesystem with non-Unix semantics. It's also possible to integrate a filesystem into the VFS interface without supporting all of the Unix semantics; for example, you can put FAT (a filesystem used in MS-DOS, Windows, and NT operating systems) filesystems under VFS, but you can't create Unix-like symbolic links on them because the native FAT filesystem doesn't support symbolic links.

In this section, we'll look at how NFS deals with Unix filesystem semantics, including some of the operations that aren't exactly the same under NFS. NFS has slightly different semantics than the local Unix filesystem, but it tries to preserve the Unix semantics. An application that works with a local filesystem works equally well with an NFS-mounted filesystem and will not be able to distinguish between the two.

Consistency at the vnode interface level makes NFS a powerful tool for creating filesystem hierarchies using many different NFS servers. The *mount* command requires that a filesystem be mounted on a directory; but directories are vnodes themselves. An NFS filesystem can be mounted on any vnode, which means that NFS filesystems can be mounted on top of other NFS filesystems or local filesystems. This is completely consistent with the way in which local disks are mounted on local filesystems. */net* may be on the root filesystem, and */net/host* is mounted on top of it. A workstation configured using NFS can create a view of the filesystems on the network that best meets its requirements by mounting these filesystems with a directory naming scheme of its choice.

Maintaining other Unix filesystem semantics is not quite as easy. Locking operations, for example, introduce state into a system that was meant to be stateless. This problem is addressed by a separate lock manager daemon. Another bit of Unix lore that had be preserved was the retention of an open file's data blocks, even when the file's directory entry was removed. Many Unix utilities including shells and mailers, use this "delayed unlink" feature to create temporary files that have no name in the filesystem, and are therefore invisible to probing users.

A complete solution to the problem would require that the server keep open file reference counts for each file and not free the file's data blocks until the reference count decreased to zero. However, this is precisely the kind of state information that makes crash recovery difficult, so NFS was implemented with a client-side solution that handles the common applications of this feature. When a *remove* operation is performed on an open file, the client issues a *rename* NFS RPC instead. The file is renamed to *.nfsXXXX*, where *XXXX* is a suffix to make the filename unique. When the file is eventually closed, the client issues the *remove* operation on the previously unlinked file. Note that there is no need for an "open" or "close" NFS RPC procedure, since "opened" and "closed" are states that are maintained on the client. It is still possible to confuse two clients that attempt to unlink a shared, open NFS-mounted file, since one client will not know that the other has the file open, but it emulates the behavior of a local filesystem sufficiently to eliminate the need to change utilities that rely on it.

Pathnames and filehandles

All NFS operations use filehandles to designate the files or directories on which they will be performed. Filehandles are created on the server and contain information that uniquely identifies the file or directory on the server. The client's NFS *mount* and *lookup* requests retrieve these filehandles for existing files. A side effect of making all vnodes homogeneous is that file pathname lookup must be done one component at a time. Each directory in the pathname might be a mount point for another filesystem, so each name look-up request cannot include multiple components. For example, let's look at *Client A* that NFS-mounts the */usr/local* filesystem and also NFS-mounts a filesystem on */usr/local/bin*:

```
clientA# mount server1:/usr/local /usr/local
clientA# mount server2:/usr/local/bin.mips /usr/local/bin
```

When the NFS client reaches the *bin* component in the pathname, it realizes that there is an NFS filesystem mounted on this directory, and it sends its lookup requests to *server2* instead of *server1*. If the NFS client passed the whole pathname to *server1*, it might get the wrong answer on its lookup: *server1* has its own */usr/local/bin* directory that may or may not be the same directory that *Client A* has mounted. While this may seem to be a very expensive series of operations, the kernel keeps a directory name lookup cache (DNLC) that prevents every look-up request from going to an NFS server.

The *lookup* operation takes a filename and a filehandle for a directory, and returns a filehandle pointing to the named file on the server. How then does the pathname traversal get started, if every *lookup* requires a filehandle from a previous pathname resolution? The *mount* operation seeds the lookup process by providing a filehandle for the root of the mounted filesystem. Within NFS, the only procedure that accepts full pathnames is the *mount* RPC, which turns the pathname into a filehandle for the mounted filesystem.

Let's look at how NFS turns the pathname */usr/local/bin/emacs* into an NFS filehandle, assuming that it's on a filesystem mounted on */usr/local* from server *wahoo*:

- The NFS client asks the *mountd* daemon on *wahoo* for a filehandle for the filesystem the client has mounted on */usr/local*, using the server's pathname that was supplied in the */etc/vfstab* file or *mount* command. That is, if the client has mounted */usr/local* with the */etc/vfstab* entry:

    ```
    wahoo:/tools/local   - /usr/local    nfs - yes ro,hard
    ```

    then the client will ask *wahoo* for a filehandle for the */tools/local* directory.*

- Using the mount point filehandle, the client performs a lookup operation on the next component in the pathname: *bin*. It sends a *lookup* to *wahoo*, supplying the filehandle for the */usr/local* directory and the name "bin." Server *wahoo* returns another filehandle for this directory.

- The client goes to work on the next component in the path, *emacs*. Again, it sends a *lookup* using the filehandle for the directory containing *emacs* and the name it is looking for. The filehandle returned by the server is used by the client as a "pointer" (on the server) to */usr/local/bin/emacs* (in the filesystem seen by client) for all future operations on that file.

Filehandles are opaque to the client. In most NFS implementations on Unix machines, they are an encoding of the file's inode number, disk device number, and inode generation number. Other implementations, particularly non-Unix NFS servers that do not have inodes, encode their own native filesystem information in the filehandle. In any system, the filehandle is in a form that can be disassembled only on the NFS server. The structures contained in the filehandle are kept hidden from the client, the same way the structures in an object-oriented system are hidden in the object's implementation routines. In the case of NFS filehandles, the data described by the structure doesn't even exist on the client—it's all on the server, where the filehandle can be converted into a pointer to local file.

Filehandles become invalid, or stale, when the inodes to which they point (on the server) are freed or re-used. NFS clients have no way of knowing what other operations may be affecting objects pointed to by their filehandles, so there is no way to warn a client in advance that a filehandle is invalid. If an RPC call is made with a filehandle that is stale, the NFS server returns a *stale filehandle* error to the

---

* Asking the *mountd* daemon isn't the only way to get the filehandle for a filesystem. Recall that Chapter 6 briefly mentioned the *public* option to the *mount* command. We will discuss this in more detail in Chapter 12.

caller. Say that a user on one client removes an NFS-mounted directory and its contents using *rm -rf test*, while another client has a process using *test* as its current working directory. The next time the other process tries to read its working directory, it gets a stale filehandle error back from the NFS server:

Client A	Client B
`cd /mnt/test`	`cd /mnt`
	`rm -rf test`
`stat(.)-->Stale file handle`	

If one client removes a file and then creates a new file that re-uses the freed inode, other filehandles (on other clients) that point to the re-used inode must be marked stale. Inode generation numbers were added to the basic Unix filesystem to add a time history to an inode. In addition to the inode number, the filehandle must match the current generation number of the inode, or it is marked stale. When the inode is re-used for a new file, its generation number is incremented. Stale filehandles become a problem when one user's work tramples on an area in use by another, or when a filesystem on a server is rebuilt from a backup tape. When restoring from a dump tape onto a fresh filesystem, all of the inode generation numbers in the filesystem are set to random numbers. This causes every filehandle in use for that filesystem to become stale—every inode pointed to by a pre-restore filehandle now probably points to a completely different file on the disk.

Therefore, a quick way to cripple an NFS network is to restore a fileserver from a dump tape without rebooting the NFS clients. When you rebuild the server's filesystems, all of the inode generation numbers are reset; when you load the tape, files end up with different inode numbers and different inode generation numbers than they had on the original filesystem. All NFS client filehandles are now invalid because of the new generation numbers and the (random) renumbering of each file's inode. Any attempt to use an open filehandle results in stale filehandle errors. If you are going to restore an NFS-exported filesystem from tape, unmount it from its clients or reboot the clients.

NFS Version 3

There are four versions of the NFS protocol: Versions 2, 3, and 4. Version 1 did exist, but it was only a prototype, and neither an implementation nor specification was ever released. Version 4 has been specified, but at the time this book was written, there were no commercial implementatons. Version 3 has three major differences from Version 2:

Large file support

Version 2 supported files up to four gigabytes in length, though most implementations are limited to up to two-gigabyte files. Version 3 supports files up to and including $2^{64} - 1$ bytes in length. Large file support was the primary driver for a protocol revision.

Writes to unstable storage

Version 2 of the NFS protocol specified that NFS servers could not reply successfully to a *write* request until the data had been committed to stable storage, usually magnetic disk, but non-volatile RAM was permissible as well. This limited the write throughput of NFS clients, and so Version 3 of the protocol permits the client to indicate that the *write* need not be committed to stable storage. This allows NFS servers to respond quickly to *write* requests. Of course, clients are still interested in committing their data to stable storage, and so Version 3 has a new procedure called *commit*, which tells the NFS server to write the uncommitted data to stable storage before returning success.

The theory behind this, supported by experimental measurement, is that faster throughput is gained by the NFS server committing data to stable storage in parallel with the client doing something else (such as generating more NFS requests), before the client issues the *commit*. Typically, the NFS Version 3 client will issue a *commit* when it is about to close a file, or when buffer space is tight.

Large transfer sizes

NFS Version 2 had a limit of 8192 bytes per NFS read and write request. NFS Version 3 lets the client and server negotiate a mutually acceptable limit.

Recall from "Datagrams and packets" in Chapter 1 that packets larger than the medium's MTU must be fragmented. Fragmentation of output packets is easy, but the other direction, reassembly of input fragments, is harder if the fragments arrive out of order, or if a fragment is dropped or delayed. With larger NFS transfer sizes, the risk of a reassembly problem is higher, and if there is a problem, the entire datagram must be retransmitted, including all the fragments. NFS Version 2 was designed to be gentler to the network during the days when operating systems, routers, and network hardware were less capable. Nowadays, these components are much more effective, and so NFS Version 3 removes the artificial limits to transfer size.

NFS over TCP

Both NFS Version 2 and Version 3 operate over UDP and TCP. Since TCP is stateful, and NFS is stateless, it would seem to be a contradiction, if not an impossibility for NFS to operate over TCP. However, the layer between NFS and TCP is RPC, and RPC is implemented to hide state issues of TCP from NFS.

The first time an NFS client contacts a server over TCP, the RPC layer takes care of establishing a connection. If a server crashes, the client won't know that immediately, but the next time it sends a request over the connection, the connection will break due to a connection reset from the server, or a connection timeout. In either case, the RPC layer simply re-establishes a connection.

Some NFS/TCP implementations, such as that in Solaris, maintain a single connection between the NFS client and server, such that all traffic—for all users and mount points—is multiplexed between the client and server. Other implementations, such as those in the BSD releases, have one connection per mountpoint. Aside from a user-level NFS client like a web browser, or a Java application linked to NFS classes, you are not likely to encounter an NFS client that creates a connection per user.

If the client crashes, the server will periodically close connections that haven't been used in a while. On a Solaris NFS server, this connection idle timer defaults to six minutes.

NFS components

NFS is similar to other RPC services in its use of a server-side daemon (*nfsd*) to process incoming requests. It differs from the typical client-server model in that processes on NFS clients make some RPC calls themselves, and other RPC calls are made by the clients' async threads. All of the NFS client and server code is contained in the kernel, instead of in the server daemon executable—a decision also driven by performance requirements.

nfsd and NFS server threads

With all of the NFS code in the kernel, why bother with user processes for the server? Why not make NFS a purely kernel-to-kernel service, without any user processes? On systems that have an *nfsd* daemon, *nfsd* does the following:

- Initializes a transport endpoint to be used by the kernel to process NFS requests from. This involves allocating a transport endpoint on which to listen for requests, and then registering the endpoint with the portmapper (*rpcbind*). It is much more convenient to do this from a user-level program than in the kernel.

- Invokes a system call to start in-kernel processing of NFS requests on the transport endpoint.

What the aforementioned system call does varies among implementations. Two common variations are:

- The *nfsd* daemon makes *one* system call that *never* returns, and that system call executes the appropriate NFS code in the system's kernel. The process container in which this system call executes is necessary for scheduling, multi-threading, and providing a user context for the kernel. Multithreading in this case means running multiple (forked) copies of the same daemon, so that multiple NFS requests may be handled in parallel on the client and server hosts. For these systems, the most pressing need for NFS daemons to exist as processes centers around the need for multithreading NFS RPC requests. Making NFS a purely kernel resident service would require the kernel to support multiple threads of execution.

- On systems with kernel thread support, such as Solaris 2.2 and higher, the NFS server daemon (*nfsd*) takes care of some initialization before making a system call that causes the kernel to create kernel threads for processing NFS requests in parallel. The system call *does* return to *nfsd* in this case. Since the kernel creates the multiple threads for parallel processing, there is no need for *nfsd* to fork copies of itself; only one copy of *nfsd* is running.

The alternative to multiple daemons or kernel thread support is that an NFS server is forced to handle one NFS request at a time. Running multiple daemons or kernel threads allows the server to have multiple, independent threads of execution, so the server can handle several NFS requests at once. Daemons or threads service requests in a pseudo-round robin fashion—whenever a daemon or thread is done with a request it goes to the end of the queue waiting for a new request. Using this scheduling algorithm, a server is always able to accept a new NFS request as long as at least one daemon or thread is waiting in queue. Running multiple daemons or threads lets a server start multiple disk operations at the same time and handle quick turnaround requests such as *getattr* and *lookup* while disk-bound requests are in progress.

Still, why do systems that have kernel server thread support need a running *nfsd* daemon process? With an NFS server that supported just UDP, it would be possible for it to simply exit once the endpoint was sent to the kernel. With the introduction of NFS/TCP implementations, transport endpoints get created and closed down continuously. Thus *nfsd* is needed to listen for, accept, and tell the kernel about new connections. Similarly, when the connections are broken, *nfsd* takes care of telling the kernel that the endpoint is about to be closed, and then closes it.

Client I/O system

On the client side, each process accessing an NFS-mounted filesystem makes its own RPC calls to NFS servers. A single process will be a client of many NFS servers if it is accessing several filesystems on the client. For operations that do not involve block I/O, such as getting the attributes of a file or performing a name lookup, having each process make its own RPC calls provides adequate performance. However, when file blocks are moved between client and server, NFS needs to use the Unix file buffer cache mechanism to provide throughput similar to that achieved with a local disk. On many implementations, the client-side async threads are the parts of NFS that interact with the buffer cache.

Before looking at async threads in detail, some explanation of buffer cache and file cache management is required. The traditional Unix buffer cache is a portion of the system's memory that is reserved for file blocks that have been recently referenced. When a process is reading from a file, the operating system performs read-ahead on the file and fills the buffer cache with blocks that the process will need in future operations. The result of this "pre-fetch" activity is that not all *read( )* system calls require a disk operation: some can be satisfied with data in the buffer cache. Similarly, data that is written to disk is written into the cache first; when the cache fills up, file blocks are flushed out to disk. Again, the buffer cache allows the operating system to bunch up disk requests, instead of making every system call wait for a disk transfer.

SunOS 4.x, System V Release 4, and Solaris replace the buffer cache with a page mapping system. Instead of transferring files into and out of the buffer cache, the virtual memory management system directly maps files into a process's address space, and treats file accesses as page faults. Any page that is not being used by the system can be taken to cache file pages. The net effect is the same as that of a buffer cache, but the size of the cache is not fixed. The file page cache could be a large percentage of the system's memory if only one or two processes are doing file I/O operations. For this discussion, we'll refer to the in-memory copies of file blocks as the "buffer cache," whether it is implemented as a cache of file pages or as a traditional Unix buffer cache.

The client-side async threads improve NFS performance by filling and draining the buffer cache on behalf of NFS clients. When a process reads from an NFS-mounted file, it performs the *read* RPC itself. To pre-fetch data for the buffer cache, the kernel has the async threads send more *read* RPC requests to the server, *as if* the reading process had requested this data. NFS functions properly without any async threads on a client—but no read-ahead is done without them, limiting the throughput of the NFS filesystem. When the async threads are running, the client's kernel can initiate several RPC calls at the same time. If restricted to a single RPC call per process, NFS client performance suffers—sometimes dramatically.

When a client writes to a file, the data is put into the buffer cache. After a complete buffer is filled, the operating system writes out the data in the cache to the filesystem. If the data needs to be written to an NFS server, the kernel makes an RPC call to perform the write operation. If there are async threads available, they make the *write* RPC requests for the client, draining the buffer cache when the cache management system dictates. If no async threads can make the RPC call, the process calling *write()* performs the RPC call itself. Again, without any async threads, the kernel can still write to NFS files, but it must do so by forcing each client process to make its own RPC calls. The async threads allow the client to execute multiple RPC requests at the same time, performing write-behind on behalf of the processes using NFS files.

NFS read and write requests are performed in NFS buffer sizes. The buffer size used for disk I/O requests is independent of the network's MTU and the server or client filesystem block size. It is chosen based on the most efficient size handled by the network transport protocol, and is usually 8 kilobytes for NFS Version 2, and 32 kilobytes for NFS Version 3. The NFS client implements this buffering scheme, so that all disk operations are done in larger (and usually more efficient) chunks. When reading from a file, an NFS Version 2 *read* RPC requests an entire 8 kilobyte NFS buffer. The client process may only request a small portion of the buffer, but the buffer cache saves the entire buffer to satisfy future references.

For write requests, the buffer cache batches them until a full NFS buffer has been written. Once a full buffer is ready to be sent to the server, an async thread picks up the buffer and performs the *write* RPC request. The size of a buffer in the cache and the size of an NFS buffer may not be the same; if the machine has 2 kilobyte buffers then four buffers are needed to make up a complete 8 kilobyte NFS Version 2 buffer. The async thread attempts to combine buffers from consecutive parts of a file in a single RPC call. It groups smaller buffers together to form a single NFS buffer, if it can. If a process is performing sequential write operations on a file, then the async threads will be able to group buffers together and perform *write* operations with NFS buffer-sized requests. If the process is writing random data, it is likely that NFS writes will occur in buffer cache-sized pieces.

On systems that use page mapping (SunOS 4.x, System V Release 4, and Solaris), there is no buffer cache, so the notion of "filling a buffer" isn't quite as clear. Instead, the async threads are given file pages whenever a write operation crosses a page boundary. The async threads group consecutive pages together to form a single NFS buffer. This process is called *dirty page clustering*.

If no async threads are running, or if all of them are busy handling other RPC requests, then the client process performing the *write()* system call executes the RPC itself (as if there were no async threads at all). A process that is writing large numbers of file blocks enjoys the benefits of having multiple *write* RPC requests performed in parallel: one by each of the async threads and one that it does itself.

As shown in Figure 7-2, some of the advantages of asynchronous Unix *write()* operations are retained by this approach. Smaller write requests that do not force an RPC call return to the client right away.

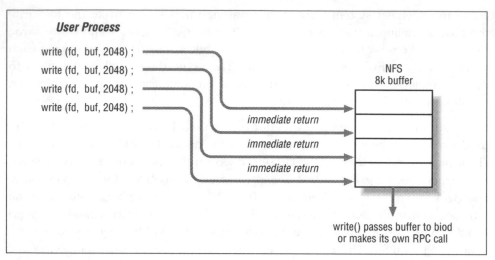

Figure 7-2. NFS buffer writing

Doing the read-ahead and write-behind in NFS buffer-sized chunks imposes a logical block size on the NFS server, but again, the logical block size has nothing to do with the actual filesystem implementation on either the NFS client or server. We'll look at the buffering done by NFS clients when we discuss data caching and NFS write errors. The next section discusses the interaction of the async threads and Unix system calls in more detail.

 The async threads exist in Solaris. Other NFS implementations use multiple block I/O daemons (*biod* daemons) to achieve the same result as async threads.

NFS kernel code

The functions performed by the parallel async threads and kernel server threads provide only part of the boost required to make NFS performance acceptable. The *nfsd* is a user-level process, but contains no code to process NFS requests. The *nfsd* issues a system call that gives the kernel a transport endpoint. All the code that sends NFS requests from the client and processes NFS requests on the server is in the kernel.

It is possible to put the NFS client and server code entirely in user processes. Unfortunately, making system calls is relatively expensive in terms of operating system overhead, and moving data to and from user space is also a drain on the system. Implementing NFS code outside the kernel, at the user level, would require every NFS RPC to go through a very convoluted sequence of kernel and user process transitions, moving data into and out of the kernel whenever it was received or sent by a machine.

The kernel implementation of the NFS RPC client and server code eliminates most copying except for the final move of data from the client's kernel back to the user process requesting it, and it eliminates extra transitions out of and into the kernel. To see how the NFS daemons, buffer (or page) cache, and system calls fit together, we'll trace a *read()* system call through the client and server kernels:

- A user process calls *read()* on an NFS mounted file. The process has no way of determining where the file is, since its only pointer to the file is a Unix file descriptor.

- The VFS maps the file descriptor to a vnode and calls the read operation for the vnode type. Since the VFS type is NFS, the system call invokes the NFS client read routine. In the process of mapping the type to NFS, the file descriptor is also mapped into a filehandle for use by NFS. Locally, the client has a virtual node (vnode) that locates this file in its filesystem. The vnode contains a pointer to more specific filesystem information: for a local file, it points to an inode, and for an NFS file, it points to a structure containing an NFS filehandle.

- The client read routine checks the local buffer (or page) cache for the data. If it is present, the data is returned right away. It's possible that the data requested in this operation was loaded into the cache by a previous NFS read operation. To make the example interesting, we'll assume that the requested data is not in the client's cache.

- The client process performs an NFS *read* RPC. If the client and server are using NFS Version 3, the read request asks for a complete 32 kilobyte NFS buffer (otherwise it will ask for an 8 kilobyte buffer). The client process goes to sleep waiting for the RPC request to complete. Note that the client process itself makes the RPC, not the async thread: the client can't continue execution until the data is returned, so there is nothing gained by having another process perform its RPC. However, the operating system will schedule async threads to perform read-ahead for this process, getting the next buffer from the remote file.

- The server receives the RPC packet and schedules a kernel server thread to handle it. The server thread picks up the packet, determines the RPC call to be made, and initiates the disk operation. All of these are kernel functions, so the server thread never leaves the kernel. The server thread that was scheduled goes to sleep waiting for the disk read to complete, and when it does, the kernel schedules it again to send the data and RPC acknowledgment back to the client.

- The reading process on the client wakes up, and takes its data out of the buffer returned by the NFS *read* RPC request. The data is left in the buffer cache so that future read operations do not have to go over the network. The process's *read()* system call returns, and the process continues execution. At the same time, the read-ahead RPC requests sent by the async threads are pre-fetching additional buffers of the file. If the process is reading the file sequentially, it will be able to perform many *read()* system calls before it looks for data that is not in the buffer cache.

Obviously, changing the numbers of async threads and server threads, and the NFS buffer sizes impacts the behavior of the read-ahead (and write-behind) algorithms. Effects of varying the number of daemons and the NFS buffer sizes will be explored as part of the performance discussion in Chapter 17.

Caching

Caching involves keeping frequently used data "close" to where it is needed, or preloading data in anticipation of future operations. Data read from disks may be cached until a subsequent write makes it invalid, and data written to disk is usually cached so that many consecutive changes to the same file may be written out in a single operation. In NFS, data caching means not having to send an RPC request over the network to a server: the data is cached on the NFS client and can be read out of local memory instead of from a remote disk. Depending upon the filesystem structure and usage, some cache schemes may be prohibited for certain operations to guarantee data integrity or consistency with multiple processes reading or writing the same file. Cache policies in NFS ensure that performance is acceptable while also preventing the introduction of state into the client-server relationship.

File attribute caching

Not all filesystem operations touch the data in files; many of them either get or set the attributes of the file such as its length, owner, modification time, and inode number. Because these attribute-only operations are frequent and do not affect the data in a file, they are prime candidates for using cached data. Think of *ls -l* as a classic example of an attribute-only operation: it gets information about directories and files, but doesn't look at the contents of the files.

NFS caches file attributes on the client side so that every *getattr* operation does not have to go all the way to the NFS server. When a file's attributes are read, they remain valid on the client for some minimum period of time, typically three seconds. If the file's attributes remain static for some maximum period, normally 60 seconds, they are flushed from the cache. When an application on the NFS client modifies an NFS attribute, the attribute is immediately written back to the server. The only exceptions are implicit changes to the file's size as a result of writing to the file. As we will see in the next section, data written by the application is not immediately written to the server, so neither is the file's size attribute.

The same mechanism is used for directory attributes, although they are given a longer minimum lifespan. The usual defaults for directory attributes are a minimum cache time of 30 seconds and a maximum of 60 seconds. The longer minimum cache period reflects the typical behavior of periods of intense filesystem activity—files themselves are modified almost continuously but directory updates (adding or removing files) happen much less frequently.

The attribute cache can get updated by NFS operations that include attributes in the results. Nearly all of NFS Version 3's RPC procedures include attributes in the results.

Attribute caching allows a client to make a steady stream of access to a file without having to constantly get attributes from the server. Furthermore, frequently accessed files and directories, such as the current working directory, have their attributes cached on the client so that some NFS operations can be performed without having to make an RPC call.

In the previous section, we saw how the async thread fills and drains the NFS client's buffer or page cache. This presents a cache consistency problem: if an async thread performs read-ahead on a file, and the client accesses that information at some later time, how does the client know that the cached copy of the data is valid? What guarantees are there that another client hasn't changed the file, making the copy of the file's data in the buffer cache invalid?

An NFS client needs to maintain cache consistency with the copy of the file on the NFS server. It uses file attributes to perform the consistency check. The file's modification time is used as a cache validity check; if the cached data is newer than the modification time then it remains valid. As soon as the file's modification time is newer than the time at which the async thread read data, the cached data must be flushed. In page-mapped systems, the modification time becomes a "valid bit" for cached pages. If a client reads a file that never gets modified, it can cache the file's pages for as long as needed.

This feature explains the "accelerated make" phenomenon seen on NFS clients when compiling code. The second and successive times that a software module (located on an NFS fileserver) is compiled, the *make* process is faster than the first build. The reason is that the first make reads in header files and causes them to be cached. Subsequent builds of the same modules or other files using the same headers pick up the cached pages instead of having to read them from the NFS server. As long as the header files are not modified, the client's cached pages remain valid. The first compilation requires many more RPC requests to be sent to the server; the second and successive compilations only send RPC requests to read those files that have changed.

The cache consistency checks themselves are by the file attribute cache. When a cache validity check is done, the kernel compares the modification time of the file to the timestamp on its cached pages; normally this would require reading the file's attributes from the NFS server. Since file attributes are kept in the file's inode (which is itself cached on the NFS server), reading file attributes is much less "expensive" than going to disk to read part of the file. However, if the file attributes are not changing frequently, there is no reason to re-read them from the server on every cache validity check. The data cache algorithms use the file attribute cache to speed modification time comparisons.

Keeping previously read data blocks cached on the client does not introduce state into the NFS system, since nothing is being modified on the client caching the data. Long-lived cache data introduces consistency problems if one or more other clients have the file open for writing, which is one of the motivations for limiting the attribute cache validity period. If the attribute cache data never expired, clients that opened files for reading only would never have reason to check the server for possible modifications by other clients. Stateless NFS operation requires each client to be oblivious to all others and to rely on its attribute cache only for ensuring consistency. Of course, if clients are using different attribute cache aging schemes, then machines with longer cache attribute lifetimes will have stale data. Attribute caching and its effects on NFS performance is revisited in "Attribute caching" in Chapter 18.

Client data caching

In the previous section, we looked at the async thread's management of an NFS client's buffer cache. The async threads perform read-ahead and write-behind for the NFS client processes. We also saw how NFS moves data in NFS buffers, rather than in page- or buffer cache-sized chunks. The use of NFS buffers allows NFS operations to utilize some of the sequential disk I/O optimizations of Unix disk device drivers.

Reading in buffers that are multiples of the local filesystem block size allows NFS to reduce the cost of getting file blocks from a server. The overhead of performing an RPC call to read just a few bytes from a file is significant compared to the cost of reading that data from the server's disk, so it is to the client's and server's advantage to spread the RPC cost over as many data bytes as possible. If an application sequentially reads data from a file in 128-byte buffers, the first read operation brings over a full (8 kilobytes for NFS Version 2, usually more for NFS Version 3) buffer from the filesystem. If the file is less than the buffer size, the entire file is read from the NFS server. The next *read( )* picks up data that is in the buffer (or page) cache, and following reads walk through the entire buffer. When the application reads data that is not cached, another full NFS buffer is read from the server. If there are async threads performing read-ahead on the client, the next buffer may already be present on the NFS client by the time the process needs data from it. Performing reads in NFS buffer-sized operations improves NFS performance significantly by decoupling the client application's system call buffer size and the VFS implementation's buffer size.

Going the other way, small write operations to the same file are buffered until they fill a complete page or buffer. When a full buffer is written, the operating system gives it to an async thread, and async threads try to cluster write buffers together so they can be sent in NFS buffer-sized requests. The eventual *write* RPC call is performed synchronous to the async thread; that is, the async thread does not continue execution (and start another write or read operation) until the RPC call completes. What happens on the server depends on what version of NFS is being used.

- For NFS Version 2, the write RPC operation does not return to the client's *async thread* until the file block has been committed to stable, nonvolatile storage. All write operations are performed synchronously on the server to ensure that no state information is left in volatile storage, where it would be lost if the server crashed.

- For NFS Version 3, the write RPC operation typically is done with the *stable* flag set to off. The server will return as soon as the write is stored in volatile or nonvolatile storage. Recall from the section, "NFS Version 3," that the client can later force the server to synchronously write the data to stable storage via the *commit* operation.

There are elements of a write-back cache in the async threads. Queueing small write operations until they can be done in buffer-sized RPC calls leaves the client with data that is not present on a disk, and a client failure before the data is written to the server would leave the server with an old copy of the file. This behavior is similar to that of the Unix buffer cache or the page cache in memory-mapped systems. If a client is writing to a local file, blocks of the file are cached in memory and are not flushed to disk until the *operating system* schedules them. If the machine crashes between the time the data is updated in a file cache page and the time that page is flushed to disk, the file on disk is not changed by the write. This is also expected of systems with local disks—applications running at the time of the crash may not leave disk files in well-known states.

Having file blocks cached on the server during writes poses a problem if the server crashes. The client cannot determine which RPC write operations completed before the crash, violating the stateless nature of NFS. Writes cannot be cached on the server side, as this would allow the client to think that the data was properly written when the server is still exposed to losing the cached request during a reboot.

Ensuring that writes are completed before they are acknowledged introduces a major bottleneck for NFS write operations, especially for NFS Version 2. A single Version 2 file write operation may require up to three disk writes on the server to update the file's inode, an indirect block pointer, and the data block being written. Each of these server write operations must complete before the NFS *write* RPC returns to the client. Some vendors eliminate most of this bottleneck by committing the data to nonvolatile, nondisk storage at memory speeds, and then moving data from the NFS write buffer memory to disk in large (64 kilobyte) buffers. Even when using NFS Version 3, the introduction of nonvolatile, nondisk storage can improve performance, though much less dramatically than with NFS Version 2.

Using the buffer cache and allowing async threads to cluster multiple buffers introduces some problems when several machines are reading from and writing to the same file. To prevent file inconsistency with multiple readers and writers of the same file, NFS institutes a flush-on-close policy:

- All partially filled NFS buffers are written to the NFS server when a file is closed.

- For NFS Version 3 clients, any writes that were done with the stable flag set to off are forced onto the server's stable storage via the *commit* operation.

This ensures that a process on another NFS client sees all changes to a file that it is opening for reading:

Client A	Client B
open( )	
write( )	
NFS Version 3 only: commit	
close( )	
	open( )
	read( )

The *read( )* system call on Client B will see all of the data in a file just written by Client A, because Client A flushed out all of its buffers for that file when the *close( )* system call was made. Note that file consistency is less certain if Client B opens the file before Client A has closed it. If overlapping read and write operations will be performed on a single file, file locking must be used to prevent cache consistency problems. When a file has been locked, the use of the buffer cache is disabled for that file, making it more of a write-through than a write-back cache. Instead of bundling small NFS requests together, each NFS write request for a locked file is sent to the NFS server immediately.

Server-side caching

The client-side caching mechanisms—file attribute and buffer caching—reduce the number of requests that need to be sent to an NFS server. On the server, additional cache policies reduce the time required to service these requests. NFS servers have three caches:

- The inode cache, containing file attributes. Inode entries read from disk are kept in-core for as long as possible. Being able to read and write these attributes in memory, instead of having to go to disk, make the get- and set-attribute NFS requests much faster.

- The directory name lookup cache, or DNLC, containing recently read directory entries. Caching directory entries means that the server does not have to open and re-read directories on every pathname resolution. Directory searching is a fairly expensive operation, since it involves going to disk and searching linearly for a particular name in the directory. The DNLC cache works at the VFS layer, not at the local filesystem layer, so it caches directory entries for all types of filesystems. If you have a CD-ROM drive on your NFS server, and mount it on NFS clients, the DNLC becomes even more important because reading directory entries from the CD-ROM is much slower than reading them from a local hard disk. Server configuration effects that affect both the inode and DNLC cache systems are discussed in "Kernel configuration" in Chapter 16.

- The server's buffer cache, used for data read from files. As mentioned before, file blocks that are written to NFS servers cannot be cached, and must be written to disk before the client's RPC *write* call can complete. However, the server's buffer or page cache acts as an efficient read cache for NFS clients. The effects of this caching are more pronounced in page-mapped systems, since nearly all of the server's memory can be used as a read cache for file blocks.

  For NFS Version 3 servers, the buffer cache is used also for data written to files whenever the *write* RPC has the stable flag set to off. Thus, NFS Version 3 servers that do not use nondisk, nonvolatile memory to store writes can perform almost as fast as NFS Version 2 servers that do.

Cache mechanisms on NFS clients and servers provide acceptable NFS performance while preserving many—but not all—of the semantics of a local filesystem. If you need finer consistency control when multiple clients are accessing the same files, you need to use file locking.

File locking

File locking allows one process to gain exclusive access to a file or part of a file, and forces other processes requiring access to the file to wait for the lock to be released. Locking is a stateful operation and does not mesh well with the stateless design of NFS. One of NFS's design goals is to maintain Unix filesystem semantics on all files, which includes supporting record locks on files.

Unix locks come in two flavors: BSD-style file locks and System V-style record locks. The BSD locking mechanism implemented in the *flock()* system call exists for whole file locking only, and on Solaris is implemented in terms of the more general System V-style locks. The System V-style locks are implemented through the *fcntl()* system call and the *lockf()* library routine, which uses *fcntl()*. System V locking operations are separated from the NFS protocol and handled by an RPC lock daemon and a status monitoring daemon that recreate and verify state information when either a client or server reboot.

Lock and status daemons

The RPC lock daemon, *lockd*, runs on both the client and server. When a lock request is made for an NFS-mounted file, *lockd* forwards the request to the server's *lockd*. The lock daemon asks the status monitor daemon, *statd*, to note that the client has requested a lock and to begin monitoring the client.

The file locking daemon and status monitor daemon keep two directories with lock "reminders" in them: */var/statmon/sm* and */var/statmon/sm.bak*. (On some systems, these directories are */etc/sm* and */etc/sm.bak*.) The first directory is used by the status monitor on an NFS server to track the names of hosts that have locked one or more of its files. The files in */var/statmon/sm* are empty and are used primarily as pointers for lock renegotiation after a server or client crash. When *statd* is asked to monitor a system, it creates a file with that system's name in */etc/statmon/sm*.

If the system making the lock request must be notified of a server reboot, then an entry is made in */var/statmon/sm.bak* as well. When the status monitor daemon starts up, it calls the status daemon on all of the systems whose names appear in */var/statmon/sm.bak* to notify them that the NFS server has rebooted. Each client's status daemon tells its lock daemon that locks may have been lost due to a server crash. The client-side lock daemons resubmit all outstanding lock requests, recreating the file lock state (on the server) that existed before the server crashed.

Client lock recovery

If the server's *statd* cannot reach a client's status daemon to inform it of the crash recovery, it begins printing annoying messages on the server's console:

```
statd: cannot talk to statd at client, RPC: Timed out(5)
```

These messages indicate that the local *statd* process could not find the port-mapper on the client to make an RPC call to its status daemon. If the client has also rebooted and is not quite back on the air, the server's status monitor should eventually find the client and update the file lock state. However, if the client was taken down, had its named changed, or was removed from the network altogether, these messages continue until *statd* is told to stop looking for the missing client.

To silence *statd*, kill the status daemon process, remove the appropriate file in */var/statmon/sm.bak*, and restart *statd*. For example, if server *onaga* cannot find the *statd* daemon on client *noreaster*, remove that client's entry in */var/statmon/sm.bak* :

```
onaga# ps -eaf | fgrep statd
root    133     1  0   Jan 16 ?        0:00 /usr/lib/nfs/statd
root   8364  6300  0 06:10:27 pts/13   0:00 fgrep statd
onaga# kill -9 133
onaga# cd /var/statmon/sm.bak
onaga# ls
noreaster
onaga# rm noreaster
onaga# cd /
onaga# /usr/lib/nfs/statd
```

Error messages from *statd* should be expected whenever an NFS client is removed from the network, or when clients and servers boot at the same time.

Recreating state information

Because permanent state (state that survives crashes) is maintained on the server host owning the locked file, the server is given the job of asking clients to re-establish their locks when state is lost. Only a server crash removes state from the system, and it is missing state that is impossible to regenerate without some external help.

When a client reboots, it by definition has given up all of its locks, but there is no state *lost*. Some state information may remain on the server and be out-of-date, but this "excess" state is flushed by the server's status monitor. After a client reboot, the server's status daemon notices the inconsistency between the locks held by the server and those the client thinks it holds. It informs the server *lockd* that locks from the rebooted client need reclaiming. The server's *lockd* sets a grace period—

45 seconds by default—during which the locks must be reclaimed or be lost. When a client reboots, it will not reclaim any locks, because there is no record of the locks in its local *lockd*. The server releases all of them, removing the old state from the client-server system.

Think of this server-side responsibility as dealing with your checkbook and your local bank branch. You keep one set of records, tracking what your balance is, and the bank maintains its own information about your account. The bank's information is the "truth," no matter how good or bad your recording keeping is. If you vanish from the earth or stop contacting the bank, then the bank tries to contact you for some finite grace period. After that, the bank releases its records and your money. On the other hand, if the bank were to lose its computer records in a disaster, it could ask you to submit checks and deposit slips to recreate the records of your account.

NFS futures

NFS Version 4

In 1998, Sun Microsystems and the Internet Society completed an agreement giving the Internet Society control over future versions of NFS, starting with NFS Version 4. The Internet Society is the umbrella body for the Internet Engineering Task Force (IETF). IETF now has a working group chartered to define NFS Version 4. The goals of the working group include:

Better access and performance on the Internet
> NFS can be used on the Internet, but it isn't designed to work through firewalls (although, in Chapter 12 we'll discuss a way to use NFS through a firewall). Even if a firewall isn't in the way, certain aspects of NFS, such as pathname parsing, can be expensive on high-latency links. For example, if you want to look at */a/b/c/d/e* on a server, your NFS Version 2 or 3 client will need to make five lookup requests before it can start reading the file. This is hardly noticeable on an ethernet, but very annoying on a modem link.

Mandatory security
> Most NFS implementations have a default form of authentication that relies on a trust between the client and server. With more people on the Internet, trust is insufficient. While there are security flavors for NFS that require strong authentication based on cryptography, these flavors aren't universally implemented. To claim conformance to NFS Version 4, implementations will have to offer a common set of security flavors.

Better heterogeneity

NFS has been implemented on a wide array of platforms, including Unix, PCs, Macintoshes, Java, MVS, and web browsers, but many aspects of it are very Unix-centric, which prevents it from being the file-sharing system of choice for non-Unix systems.

For example, the set of attributes that NFS Versions 2 and 3 use is derived completely from Unix without thought about useful attributes that Windows 98, for example, might need. The other side of the problem is that some existing NFS attributes are hard to implement by some non-Unix systems.

Internationalization and localization

This refers to pathname strings and not the contents of files. Technically, filenames in NFS Versions 2 and 3 can only be 7-bit ASCII, which is very limiting. Even if one uses the eighth bit, that still doesn't help the Asian users.

There are no plans to add explicit internationalization and localization hooks to file content. The NFS protocol's model has always been to treat the content of files as an opaque stream of bytes that the application must interpret, and Version 4 will not vary from that.

There has been talk of adding an optional attribute that describes the MIME type of contents of the file.

Extensibility

After NFS Version 2 was released, it took nine years for the first NFS Version 3 implementations to appear on the market. It will take at least seven years from the time NFS Version 3 was first available for Version 4 implementations to be marketed. The gap between Version 2 and Version 3 was especially painful because of the write performance issue. Had NFS Version 2 included a method for adding procedures, the pain could have been reduced.

At the time this book was written, the NFS Version 4 working group published the initial NFS Version 4 specification in the form of RFC 3010, which you can peruse from IETF's web site at *http://www.ietf.org*. Several of the participants in the working group have prototype implementations that interoperate with each other. Early versions of the Linux implementation are available from *http://www.citi. umich.edu/projects/nfsv4/*. Some of the characteristics of NFS Version 4 that are not in Version 3 include:

No sideband protocols

The separate protocols for mounting and locking have been incorporated into the NFS protocol.

Statefulness

NFS Version 4 has an OPEN operation that tells the server the client has opened the file, and a corresponding CLOSE operation. Recall earlier in this chapter, in the section "Statelessness and crash recovery," that the point was made that crash recovery in NFS Versions 2 and 3 is simple because the server retains very little state. By adding such state, recovery is more complicated. When a server crashes, clients have a grace period to reestablish the OPEN state. When a client crashes, because the OPEN state is leased (i.e., has a time limit that expires if not renewed), a dead client will eventually have its leases timed out, allowing the server to delete any state. Another point in the "Statelessness and crash recovery" section is that the operations in NFS Versions 2 and 3 are nonidempotent where possible, and the idempotent operations results are cached in a duplicate request cache. For the most part, this is still the case with NFS Version 4. The only exceptions are the OPEN, CLOSE, and locking operations. Operations like RENAME continue to rely on the duplicate request cache, a solution with theoretical holes, but in practice has proven to be quite sufficient. Thus NFS Version 4 retains much of the character of NFS Versions 2 and 3.

Aggressive caching

Because there is an OPEN operation, the client can be much more lazy about writing data to the server. Indeed, for temporary files, the server may never see any data written before the client closes and removes the file.

Security

Aside from lack of multivendor support, the other problem with NFS security flavors is that they become obsolete rather quickly. To mitigate this, IETF specified the RPCSEC_GSS security flavor that NFS and other RPC-based protocols could use to normalize access to different security mechanisms. RPCSEC_GSS accomplishes this using another IETF specification called the Generic Security Services Application Programming Interface (GSS-API). GSS-API is an abstract layer for generating messages that are encrypted or signed in a form that can be sent to a peer on the network for decryption or verification. GSS-API has been specified to work over Kerberos V5, the Simple Public Key Mechanism, and the Low Infrastructure Public Key system (LIPKEY). We will discuss NFS security, RPCSEC_GSS, and Kerberos V5 in more detail in Chapter 12.

The Secure Socket Layer (SSL) and IPSec were considered as candidates to provide NFS security. SSL wasn't feasible because it was confined to connection-oriented protocols like TCP, and NFS and RPC work over TCP and UDP. IPSec wasn't feasible because, as noted in the section "NFS over TCP," NFS clients typically don't have a TCP connection per user; whereas, it is hard, if not impossible, for an IPSec implementation to authenticate multiple users over a single TCP/IP connection.

8

Diskless Clients

This chapter is devoted to diskless clients running Solaris. Diskless Solaris clients need not be served by Solaris machines, since many vendors have adopted Sun's diskless boot protocols. The current Solaris diskless client support relies entirely on NFS for root and swap filesystem service and uses NIS maps for host configuration information. Diskless clients are probably the most troublesome part of NFS. It is a nontrivial matter to get a machine with no local resources to come up as a fully functioning member of the network, and the interactions between NIS servers, boot servers, and diskless clients create many ways for the boot procedure to fail.

There are many motivations for using diskless clients:

- They are quieter than machines with disks.

- They are easier to administer, since there is no local copy of the operating system that requires updates.

- When using fast network media, like 100Mb ethernet, diskless clients can perform faster if the server is storing the client's data in a disk array. The reason is that client workstations typically have one or two disk spindles, whereas if the client data can be striped across many, usually faster spindles, on the server, the server can provide better response.

In Solaris 8, support for the unbundled tools (*AdminSuite*) necessary to configure a server for diskless client support was dropped. As the Solaris 8 release notes stated:

> Solstice AdminSuite 2.3 software is no longer supported with the Solaris 8 operating environment. Any attempt to run Solstice AdminSuite 2.3 to configure Solstice AutoClients or diskless clients will result in a failure for which no patch is available or planned. While it may be possible to manually edit configuration files to enable diskless clients, such an operation is not recommended or supported.

Setting up a diskless client from scratch without tools is very impractical. Fortunately, Solaris 8, 1/01 Update has been released, which replaces the unbundled AdminSuite with bundled tools for administering diskless support on the Solaris 8, 1/01 Update servers. Unfortunately, Solaris 8, 1/01 Update was not available in time to write about its new diskless tools in this book. Thus, the discussion in the remainder of this chapter focuses on diskless support in Solaris through and including Solaris 7.

NFS support for diskless clients

Prior to SunOS 4.0, diskless clients were supported through a separate distributed filesystem protocol called Network Disk, or ND. A single raw disk partition was divided into several logical partitions, each of which had a root or swap filesystem on it. Once an ND partition was created, changing a client's partition size entailed rebuilding the diskless client's partition from backup or distribution tapes. ND also used a smaller buffer size than NFS, employing 1024-byte buffers for filesystem read and write operations.

In SunOS 4.0 and Solaris, diskless clients are supported entirely through NFS. Two features in the operating system and NFS protocols allowed ND to be replaced: swapping to a file and mounting an NFS filesystem as the root directory. The page-oriented virtual memory management system in SunOS 4.0 and Solaris treats the swap device like an array of pages, so that files can be used as swap space. Instead of copying memory pages to blocks of a raw partition, the VM system copies them to blocks allocated for the swap file. Swap space added in the filesystem is addressed through a vnode, so it can either be a local Unix filesystem (UFS) file or an NFS-mounted file. Diskless clients now swap directly to a file on their boot servers, accessed via NFS.

The second change supporting diskless clients is the VFS_MOUNTROOT() VFS operation. On the client, it makes the named filesystem the root device of the machine. Once the root filesystem exists, other filesystems can be mounted on any of its vnodes, so an NFS-mounted root partition is a necessary bootstrap for any filesystem mount operations on a diskless client. With the root filesystem NFS-mounted, there was no longer a need for a separate protocol to map root and swap filesystem logical disk blocks into server filesystem blocks, so the ND protocol was removed from SunOS.

Setting up a diskless client

To set up a diskless client, you must have the appropriate operating system software loaded on its boot server. If the client and server are of the same architecture, then they can share the */usr* filesystem, including the same */usr/platform/ <platform>* directory. However, if the client has a different processor or platform architecture, the server must contain the relevant */usr* filesystem and/or */usr/platform/<platform>* directory for the client. The */usr* filesystem contains the operating system itself, and will be different for each diskless client processor architecture. The */usr/platform* directory contains subdirectories that in turn contain executable files that depend on both the machine's hardware implementation (platform) and CPU architecture. Often several different hardware implementations share the same set of platform specific executables. Thus, you will find that */usr/platform* contains lots of symbolic links to directories that contain the common machine architecture.

Platform architecture and processor architecture are not the same thing; processor architecture guarantees that binaries are compatible, while platform architecture compatibility means that page sizes, kernel data structures, and supported devices are the same. You can determine the platform architecture of a running machine using *uname -i*:

```
% uname -i
SUNW,Ultra-5 10
```

You can also determine the machine architecture the platform directory in */usr/ platform* is likely symbolically linked to:

```
% uname -m
sun4u
```

If clients and their server have the same processor architecture but different platform architectures, then they can share */usr* but */usr/platform* needs to include subdirectories for both the client and server platform architectures. Platform specific binaries for each client are normally placed in */export* on the server.

In Solaris, an unbundled product called *AdminSuite* is used to set up servers for diskless NFS clients. This product is currently available as part of the *Solaris Easy Access Server* (*SEAS*) 2.0 product and works on Solaris up to Solaris 7.

For each new diskless client, the AdminSuite software can be used to perform the following steps:

* Give the client a name and an IP address, and add them both to the NIS *hosts* map or */etc/hosts* file if desired.

- Set up the boot parameters for the client, including its name and the paths to its root and swap filesystems on the server. The boot server keeps these values in its */etc/bootparams* file or in the NIS *bootparams* map. A typical *bootparams* file entry looks like this:

```
buonanotte      root=sunne:/export/root/buonanotte \
                swap=sunne:/export/swap/buonanotte
```

The first line indicates the name of the diskless client and the location of its root filesystem, and the second line gives the location of the client's swap filesystem. Note that:

— The swap "filesystem" is really just a single file exported from the server.

— Solaris diskless clients do not actually use *bootparams* to locate the swap area; this is done by the diskless administration utlities setting up the appropriate entry in the client's *vfstab* file.

- The client system's MAC address and hostname must be added to the NIS *ethers* map (or the */etc/ethers* file) so that it can determine its IP address using the Reverse ARP (RARP) protocol. To find the client's MAC address, power it on without the network cable attached, and look for its MAC address in the power-on diagnostic messages.

- Add an entry for the client to the server's */tftpboot* directory, so the server knows how to locate a boot block for the client. Diskless client servers use this information to locate the appropriate boot code and to determine if they should answer queries about booting the client.

- Create root and swap filesystems for the client on the boot server. These filesystems must be listed in the server's */etc/dfs/dfstab* file so they can be NFS-mounted. After the AdminSuite software updates */etc/dfs/dfstab*, it will run *shareall* to have the changes take effect. Most systems restrict access to a diskless client root filesystem to that client. In addition, the filesystem export must allow *root* to operate on the NFS-mounted filesystem for normal system operation. A typical */etc/dfs/dfstab* entry for a diskless client's root filesystem is:

```
share -F nfs -o rw=vineyard,root=vineyard /export/root/vineyard
share -F nfs -o rw=vineyard,root=vineyard /export/swap/vineyard
```

The *rw* option prevents other diskless clients from accessing this filesystem, while the *root* option ensures that the superuser on the client will be given normal *root* privileges on this filesystem.

Most of these steps could be performed by hand, and if moving a client's diskless configuration from one server to another, you may find yourself doing just that. However, creating a root filesystem for a client from scratch is not feasible, and it is easiest and safest to use software like AdminSuite to add new diskless clients to the network.

The AdminSuite software comes in two forms:

* A GUI that is launched from the *solstice* command:

  `# `**`solstice &`**

  You then double click on the Host Manager icon. Host Manager comes up as simple screen with an Edit menu item that lets you add new diskless clients, modify existing ones, and delete existing ones. When you add a new diskless client, you have to tell it that you want it to be diskless. One reason for this is that Host Manager is intended to be what its name implies: a general means for managing hosts, whether they be diskless, servers, standalone or other types. The other reason is that "other types" includes another kind of NFS client: cache-only clients (referred to as AutoClient hosts in Sun's product documentation). There is another type of "diskless" client, which Host Manager doesn't support: a disk-full client that is installed over the network. A client with disks can have the operating system installed onto those disks, via a network install (*netinstall*). Such *netinstall* clients are configured on the server in a manner very similar to how diskless clients are, except that unique root and swap filesystems are not created, and when the client boots over the network, it is presented with a set of screens for installation. We will discuss *netinstall* later in this chapter, in the section "Brief introduction to JumpStart administration."

* A set of command line tools. The command *admhostadd*, which will typically live in */opt/SUNWadm/bin*, is used to add a diskless client.

It is beyond the scope of this book to describe the details of Host Manager, or its command-line equivalents, including how to install them. You should refer to the AdminSuite documentation, and the online manpages, typically kept under */opt/ SUNWadm/man*.

Regardless of what form of the AdminSuite software is used, the default server filesystem naming conventions for diskless client files are shown in Table 8-1.

Table 8-1. Diskless client filesystem locations

Filesystem	Contents
/export/root	Root filesystems
/export/swap	Swap filesystems
/export/exec	*/usr* executables, libraries, etc.

The */export/exec* directory contains a set of directories specific to a release of the operating system, and processor architecture. For example, a Solaris 7 SPARC client would look for a directory called */export/exec/Solaris_2.7_sparc.all/usr*. If all clients have the same processor architecture as the server, then */export/exec/<os-release-name>_<processor_name>.all* will contain symbolic links to the server's */usr* filesystem.

To configure a server with many disks and many clients, create several directories for root and swap filesystems and distribute them over several disks. For example, on a server with two disks, split the */export/root* and */export/swap* filesystems, as shown in Table 8-2.

Table 8-2. Diskless client filesystems on two disks

Disk	Root Filesystems	Swap Filesystems
0	/export/root1	/export/swap1
1	/export/root2	/export/swap2

Some implementations (not the AdminSuite software) of the client installation tools do not allow you to specify a root or swap filesystem directory other than */export/ root* or */export/swap*. Perform the installation using the tools' defaults, and after the client has been installed, move its root and swap filesystems. After moving the client's filesystems, be sure to update the *bootparams* file and NIS map with the new filesystem locations.

As an alternative to performing an installation and then juggling directories, use symbolic links to point the */export* subdirectories to the desired disk for this client. To force an installation on */export/root2* and */export/swap2*, for example, create the following symbolic links on the diskless client server:

```
server# cd /export
server# ln -s root2 root
server# ln -s swap2 swap
```

Verify that the *bootparams* entries for the client reflect the actual location of its root and swap filesystems, and also check the client's */etc/vfstab* file to be sure it mounts its filesystems from */export/root2* and */export/swap2*. If the client's */etc/ vfstab* file contains the generic */export/root* or */export/swap* pathnames, the client won't be able to boot if these symbolic links point to the wrong subdirectories.

Diskless client boot process

Debugging any sort of diskless client problems requires some knowledge of the boot process. When a diskless client is powered on, it knows almost nothing about its configuration. It doesn't know its hostname, since that's established in the boot scripts that it hasn't run yet. It has no concept of IP addresses, because it has no hosts file or hosts NIS map to read. The only piece of information it knows for certain is its 48-bit Ethernet address, which is in the hardware on the CPU (or Ethernet interface) board. To be able to boot, a diskless client must convert the 48-bit Ethernet address into more useful information such as a boot server name, a hostname, an IP address, and the location of its root and swap filesystems.

Reverse ARP requests

The heart of the boot process is mapping 48-bit Ethernet addresses to IP
addresses. The Address Resolution Protocol (ARP) is used to locate a 48-bit
Ethernet address for a known IP address. Its inverse, Reverse ARP (or RARP), is
used by diskless clients to find their IP addresses given their Ethernet addresses.
Servers run the *rarpd* daemon to accept and process RARP requests, which are
broadcast on the network by diskless clients attempting to boot.

IP addresses are calculated in two steps. The 48-bit Ethernet address received in
the RARP is used as a key in the */etc/ethers* file or *ethers* NIS map. *rarpd* locates
the hostname associated with the Ethernet address from the *ethers* database and
uses that name as a key into the *hosts* map to find the appropriate IP address.

For the *rarpd* daemon to operate correctly, it must be able to get packets from
the raw network interface. RARP packets are not passed up through the TCP or
UDP layers of the protocol stack, so *rarpd* listens directly on each network interface (e.g., *hme0*) device node for RARP requests. Make sure that all boot servers
are running *rarpd* before examining other possible points of failure. The best way
to check is with *ps*, which should show the *rarpd* process:

```
% ps -eaf | grep rarpd
    root   274    1  0   Apr 16 ?        0:00 /usr/sbin/in.rarpd -a
```

Some implementations of *rarpd* are multithreaded, and some will fork child processes. Solaris *rarpd* implementations will create a process or thread for each network interface the server has, plus one extra process or thread. The purpose of
the extra thread or child process is to act as a delayed responder. Sometimes,
rarpd gets a request but decides to delay its response by passing the request to
the delayed responder, which waits a few seconds before sending the response. A
per-interface *rarpd* thread/process chooses to send a delayed response if it
decides it is not the best candidate to answer the request. To understand how this
decision is made, we need to look at the process of converting Ethernet addresses
into IP addresses in more detail.

The client broadcasts a RARP request containing its 48-bit Ethernet address and
waits for a reply. Using the *ethers* and *hosts* maps, any *RARP* server receiving the
request attempts to match it to an IP address for the client. Before sending the
reply to the client, the server verifies that it is the best candidate to boot the client
by checking the */tftpboot* directory (more on this soon). If the server has the
client's boot parameters but might not be able to boot the client, it delays sending
a reply (by giving the request to the delayed responder daemon) so that the correct server replies first. Because RARP requests are broadcast, they are received
and processed in somewhat random order by all boot servers on the network. The
reply delay compensates for the time skew in reply generation. The server that

thinks it can boot the diskless client immediately sends its reply to the client; other machines may also send their replies a short time later.

You may ask "Why should a host other than the client's boot server answer its RARP request?" After all, if the boot server is down, the diskless client won't be able to boot even if it does have a hostname and IP address. The primary reason is that the "real" boot server may be very loaded, and it may not respond to the RARP request before the diskless client times out. Allowing other hosts to answer the broadcast prevents the client from getting locked into a cycle of sending a RARP request, timing out, and sending the request again. A related reason for having multiple RARP replies is that the RARP packet may be missed by the client's boot server. This is functionally equivalent to the server not replying to the RARP request promptly: if some host does not provide the correct answer, the client continues to broadcast RARP packets until its boot server is less heavily loaded. Finally, RARP is used for other network services as well as for booting diskless clients, so RARP servers must be able to reply to RARP requests whether they are diskless client boot servers or not.

After receiving any one of the RARP replies, the client knows its IP address, as well as the IP address of a boot server (found by looking in the packet returned by the server). In some implementations, a diskless client announces its IP addresses with a message of the form:

```
Using IP address 192.9.200.1 = C009C801
```

A valid IP address is only the first step in booting; the client needs to be able to load the boot code if it wants to eventually get a Unix kernel running.

Getting a boot block

A local and remote IP address are all that are needed to download the boot block using a simple file transfer program called *tftp* (for trivial *ftp*). This minimal file transfer utility does no user or password checking and is small enough to fit in the boot PROM. Downloading a boot block to the client is done from the server's */tftpboot* directory.

The server has no specific knowledge of the architecture of the client issuing a RARP or *tftp* request. It also needs a mechanism for determining if it can boot the client, using only its IP address—the first piece of information the client can discern. The server's */tftpboot* directory contains boot blocks for each architecture of client support, and a set of symbolic links that point to these boot blocks:

```
[wahoo]% ls -l /tftpboot
total 282
lrwxrwxrwx  1 root  root    26 Feb 17 12:43 828D0E09 -> inetboot.sun4u.Solaris_2.7
```

```
lrwxrwxrwx  1 root  root     26 Feb 17 12:43 828D0E09.SUN4U -> inetboot.sun4u.
Solaris_2.7
lrwxrwxrwx  1 root  root     26 Apr 27 18:14 828D0E0A -> inetboot.sun4u.Solaris_2.7
lrwxrwxrwx  1 root  root     26 Apr 27 18:14 828D0E0A.SUN4U -> inetboot.sun4u.
Solaris_2.7
-rw-r--r--  1 root root 129632 Feb 17 12:21 inetboot.sun4u.Solaris_2.7
lrwxrwxrwx  1 root root      1 Feb 17 12:17 tftpboot -> .
```

The link names are the IP addresses of the clients in hexadecimal. The first client link—*828D0E09*—corresponds to IP address 130.141.14.9:

```
828D0E09
```
Insert dots to put in IP address format:
```
82.8D.0E.09
```
Convert back to decimal:
```
130.141.14.9
```

Two links exist for each client—one with the IP address in hexadecimal, and one with the IP address and the machine architecture. The second link is used by some versions of *tftpboot* that specify their architecture when asking for a boot block. It doesn't hurt to have both, as long as they point to the correct boot block for the client.

The previous section stated that a server delays its response to a RARP request if it doesn't think it's the best candidate to boot the requesting client. The server makes this determination by matching the client IP address to a link in */tftpboot*. If the link exists, the server is the best candidate to boot the client; if the link is missing, the server delays its response to allow another server to reply first.

The client gets its boot block via *tftp*, sending its request to the server that answered its RARP request. When the *inetd* daemon on the server receives the *tftp* request, it starts an *in.tftpd* daemon that locates the right boot file by following the symbolic link representing the client's IP address. The *tftpd* daemon downloads the boot file to the client. In some implementations, when the client gets a valid boot file, it reports the address of its boot server:

```
Booting from tftp server at 130.141.14.2 = 828D0E02
```

It's possible that the first host to reply to the client's RARP request can't boot it—it may have had valid *ethers* and *hosts* map entries for the machine but not a boot file. If the first server chosen by the diskless client does not answer the *tftp* request, the client broadcasts this same request. If no server responds, the machine complains that it cannot find a *tftp* server.

The *tftpd* daemon should be run in secure mode using the *-s* option. This is usually the default configuration in its */etc/inetd.conf* entry:

```
tftp dgram udp wait root /usr/sbin/in.tftpd in.tftpd -s /tftpboot
```

The argument after the *-s* is the directory that *tftp* uses as its root—it does a *chdir( )* into this directory and then a *chroot( )* to make it the root of the filesystem visible to the *tftp* process. This measure prevents *tftp* from being used to take any file other than a boot block in *tftpboot*.

The last directory entry in */tftpboot* is a symbolic link to itself, using the current directory entry (.) instead of its full pathname. This symbolic link is used for compatibility with older systems that passed a full pathname to *tftp*, such as */tftpboot/ C009C801.SUN4U*. Following the symbolic link effectively removes the */tftpboot* component and allows a secure *tftp* to find the request file in its root directory. Do not remove this symbolic link, or older diskless clients will not be able to download their boot files.

Booting a kernel

Once the boot file is loaded, the diskless client jumps out of its PROM monitor and into the boot code. To do anything useful, *boot* needs a root and swap filesystem, preferably with a bootable kernel on the root device. To get this information, *boot* broadcasts a request for boot parameters. The *bootparamd* RPC server listens for these requests and returns a gift pack filled with the location of the root filesystem, the client's hostname, and the name of the boot server. The filesystem information is kept in */etc/bootparams* or in the NIS *bootparams* map.

The diskless client mounts its root filesystem from the named boot server and boots the kernel image found there. After configuring root and swap devices, the client begins single user startup and sets its hostname, IP addresses, and NIS domain name from information in its */etc* files. It is imperative that the names and addresses returned by *bootparamd* match those in the client's configuration files, which must also match the contents of the NIS maps.

As part of the single user boot, the client mounts its */usr* filesystem from the server listed in its */etc/vfstab* file. At this point, the client has root and swap filesystems, and looks (to the Unix kernel) no different than a system booting from a local disk. The diskless client executes its boot script files, and eventually enters multiuser mode and displays a login prompt. Any breakdowns that occur after the */usr* filesystem is mounted are caused by problems in the boot scripts, not in the diskless client boot process itself.

Managing boot parameters

Every diskless client boot server has an */etc/bootparams* file and/or uses a *bootparams* NIS map. On Solaris, the */etc/nsswitch.conf* file's bootparams entry controls whether the information is read from */etc/bootparams*, NIS, or both, and in what order.

Here are some suggestions for managing diskless client boot parameters:

- Keep the boot parameters in the *bootparams* map if you are using NIS. Obviously, if your NIS master server is also a diskless client server, it will contain a complete */etc/bootparams* file.

- If you have diskless clients in more than one NIS domain, make sure you have a separate NIS *bootparams* map for each domain.

- On networks with diskless clients from different vendors, make sure that the format of the boot parameter information used by each vendor is the same. If one system's *bootparamd* daemon returns a boot parameter packet that cannot be understood by another system, you will not be able to use the NIS *bootparams* map. We'll look at the problems caused by differing boot parameter packet formats in "Boot parameter confusion" in Chapter 15.

Eliminating copies of the boot parameter information on the other servers reduces the chances that you'll have out-of-date information on boot servers after you've made a configuration change.

Managing client swap space

Once a client is running, it may need more swap space. Generally, allocating swap space equal to the physical memory on the client is a good start. Power users, or those who open many windows, run many processes in the background, or execute large compute-intensive jobs, may need to have their initial swap allocation increased.

You can increase the swap space on a diskless client, without shutting down the client, provided you have sufficient space on the server to hold both the client's old swap file, the server's new swap file, and a temporary swap file equal in size to the old swap file. Here is the procedure:

1. Create a temporary swap file on the boot server, using *mkfile*:

   ```
   wahoo# cd /export/swap
   wahoo# mkfile 64M honeymoon.tmp
   wahoo# ls -l honeymoon.tmp
   -rw------T  1 root root      67108864 Jan  9 00:38 honeymoon.tmp
   wahoo# share -o root=honeymoon /export/swap/honeymoon.tmp
   ```

   Make sure you do not use the *-n* option to *mkfile*, since this causes the swap file to be incompletely allocated. If the client tries to find a swap block that should have been pre-allocated by *mkfile*, but doesn't exist, the client usually panics and reboots.

2. On the client, mount the temporary swap file:

   ```
   honeymoon# mkdir /tmp/swap.tmp
   honeymoon# mount wahoo:/export/swap/honeymoon.tmp /tmp/swap.tmp
   honeymoon# swap -a /tmp/swap.tmp
   ```

What is interesting about this is that a regular file, and not a directory, is exported, and yet it is mounted on top of a directory mount point. Even more interesting is what happens when you do an *ls -l* on it:

```
honeymoon# ls -l /tmp/swap.tmp
-rw------T  1 root root     67108864 Jan  9 00:38 swap.tmp
```

The */tmp/swap.tmp* directory point has become a regular file after the mount.

3. On the client, add the new swap file to the swap system:

```
honeymoon# swap -a /tmp/swap.tmp
```

4. Now remove the old swap file from the swap system:

```
honeymoon# swap -d /dev/swap
```

5. Unmount the old swap file:

```
honeymoon# umount /dev/swap
```

At this point the diskless client is swapping to *wahoo:/export/swap/honeymoon. tmp*. It is now safe to construct a bigger *wahoo:/export/swap/honeymoon*.

6. Remove the old swap file from the server and create a bigger one to replace it:

```
wahoo# cd /export/swap
wahoo# unshare /export/swap/honeymoon
wahoo# rm /export/swap/honeymoon
wahoo# mkfile 256M honeymoon
wahoo# share -o root=honeymoon /export/swap/honeymoon
```

7. On the client, remount the expanded swap file, add it to the swap system, remove the temporary swap file from the swap system, unmount the temporary swap file, and remove its mount point:

```
honeymoon# mount wahoo:/export/swap/honeymoon /dev/swap
honeymoon# swap -a /dev/swap
honeymoon# swap -d /tmp/swap.tmp
honeymoon# umount /tmp/swap.tmp
honeymoon# rmdir /tmp/swap.tmp
```

8. Remove the temporary swap file from the server:

```
wahoo# unshare /export/swap/honeymoon
wahoo# rm /export/swap/honeymoon
```

Of course, that is a lot of steps. If you don't mind rebooting the client, it is far simpler to do:

```
Shutdown client honeymoon
wahoo# cd /export/swap
wahoo# rm honeymoon
wahoo# mkfile 256M honeymoon
wahoo# shareall
Boot client honeymoon
```

Note that the last bit in the world permission field of a swap file is *T*, indicating that "sticky-bit" access is set even though the file has no execute permissions. The *mkfile* utility sets these permissions by default. Enabling the sticky bit on a non-executable file has two effects:

- The virtual memory system does not perform read-ahead of this file's data blocks.

- The filesystem code does not write out inode information or indirect blocks each time the file is modified.

Unlike regular files, no read-ahead should be done for swap files. The virtual memory management system brings in exactly those pages it needs to satisfy page fault conditions, and performing read-ahead for swap files only consumes disk bandwidth on the server.

Eliminating the write operations needed to maintain inode and indirect block information does not present a problem because the diskless client cannot extend its swap filesystem. Only the file modification time field in the inode will change, so this approach trades off an incorrect modification time (on the swap file) for fewer write operations.

Changing a client's name

If you have not changed the default diskless client configuration, it's easiest to shut down the client, remove its root and swap filesystems, and then create a new client, with the new name, using the AdminSuite software. However, if you have made a large number of local changes—modifying configuration files, setting up a name service, and creating mount points—then it may be easier to change the client's name using the existing root and swap filesystems.

Before making any changes, shut down the client system so that you can work on its root filesystem and change NIS maps that affect it. On the NIS master server, you need to make several changes:

1. Update */etc/bootparams* to reflect the new client's name and root and swap filesystem pathnames.

2. Add the new hostname to the hosts map in place of the old client name. If any mail aliases include the old hostname, or if the host is embedded in a list of local hostnames, update these files as well.

3. Modify the *ethers* NIS map if all hosts are listed in it.

4. Rebuild the *bootparams*, *ethers*, and *hosts* maps.

On the client's boot server, complete the renaming process:

1. Rename the root and swap filesystems for the client:

```
# cd /export/root
# mv oldname newname
```

```
# cd /export/swap
# mv oldname newname
```

2. Update the server's list of exported NFS filesystems with the new root and swap pathnames. Also change the *rw=* and *root* options in */etc/dfs/dfstab*. After modifying the file, *share* the newly named filesystems, or *shareall* filesystems, so that the client will be able to find them when it reboots.

3. In the client's root filesystem, modify its *hosts* file and boot scripts to reflect the new hostname:

```
# cd /export/root/newname/etc
# vi hosts
# vi hostname.*[0-9]*
# vi nodename
# vi /etc/net/*/hosts
```

In Solaris, the hostname is set in a configuration file with the network interface as an extension; for example: *hostname.hme0*. It is essential that the host's name and IP address in its own *hosts* file agree with its entries in the NIS map, or the machine either boots with the wrong IP address or doesn't boot at all.

Aside from shutting the client down, the remainder of this operation could be automated using a script that takes the old and new client names as arguments. The number of changes that were made to NIS maps should indicate a clear benefit of using NIS: without the centralized administration, you would have had to change the */etc/ethers* and */etc/bootparams* files on every server, and update */etc/hosts* on *every* machine on the network.

Troubleshooting

When diskless clients refuse to boot, they do so rather emphatically. Shuffling machines and hostnames to accommodate changes in personnel increases the likelihood that a diskless machine will refuse to boot. Start debugging by verifying that hostnames, IP addresses, and Ethernet addresses are all properly registered on boot and NIS servers. The point at which the boot fails usually indicates where to look next for the problem: machines that cannot even locate a boot block may be getting the wrong boot information, while machines that boot but cannot enter single-user mode may be missing their */usr* filesystems.

Missing and inconsistent client information

There are a few pieces of missing host information that are easily tracked down. If a client tries to boot but gets no RARP response, check that the NIS *ethers* map or the */etc/ethers* files on the boot servers contain an entry for the client with the proper MAC address. A client reports RARP failures by complaining that it cannot get its IP address.

Diskless clients that boot part-way but hang after mounting their root filesystems may have */etc/hosts* files that do not agree with the NIS *ethers* or *hosts* maps. It's also possible that the client booted using one name and IP address combination, but chose to use a different name while going through the single-user boot process. Check the boot scripts to be sure that the client is using the proper hostname, and also check that its local */etc/hosts* file agrees with the NIS maps.

Other less obvious failures may be due to confusion with the *bootparams* map and the *bootparamd* daemon. Since the diskless client broadcasts a request for boot parameters, any host running *bootparamd* can answer it, and that server may have an incorrect */etc/bootparams* file, or it may have bound to an NIS server with an out-of-date map.

Sometimes when you correct information, things still do not work. The culprit could be caching. Solaris has a name service cached daemon, */usr/sbin/nscd*, which, if running, acts as a frontend for some databases maintained in */etc* or NIS. The *nscd* daemon could return stale information and also stale negative information, such as a failed lookup of an IP address in the *hosts* file or map. You can re-invoke *nscd* with the *-i* option to invalidate the cache. See the manpage for more details.

Checking boot parameters

The *bootparamd* daemon returns a fairly large bundle of values to a diskless client. In addition to the pathnames used for root and swap filesystems, the diskless client gets the name of its boot server and a default route. Depending on how the */etc/nsswitch.conf* is set up, the boot server takes values from a local */etc/bootparams*, so ensure that local file copies match NIS maps if they are used. Changing the map on the NIS master server will not help a diskless client if its boot server uses only a local copy of the boot parameters file.

Debugging rarpd and bootparamd

You can debug boot parameter problems by enabling debugging on the boot server. Both *rarpd* and *bootparamd* accept a debug option.

By enabling debugging in *rarpd* on the server, you can see what requests for what Ethernet address the client is making, and if *rarpd* can map it to an IP address. You can turn on *rarpd* debugging by killing it on the server and starting it again with the *-d* option:

```
# ps -eaf | grep rarpd
    root   274    1  0   Apr 16 ?        0:00 /usr/sbin/in.rarpd -a
    root  5890 5825  0 01:02:18 pts/0    0:00 grep rarpd
# kill 274
```

```
# /usr/sbin/in.rarpd -d -a
/usr/sbin/in.rarpd:[1]    device hme0 ethernetaddress 8:0:20:a0:16:63
/usr/sbin/in.rarpd:[1]    device hme0 address 130.141.14.8
/usr/sbin/in.rarpd:[1]    device hme0 subnet mask 255.255.255.0
/usr/sbin/in.rarpd:[5]    starting rarp service on device hme0 address 8:0:20:a0:16:63
/usr/sbin/in.rarpd:[5]    RARP_REQUEST for 8:0:20:a0:65:8f
/usr/sbin/in.rarpd:[5]    trying physical netnum 130.141.14.0 mask ffffff00
/usr/sbin/in.rarpd:[5]    good lookup, maps to 130.141.14.9
/usr/sbin/in.rarpd:[5]    immediate reply sent
```

Keep in mind that when starting a daemon with the *-d* option, it usually stays in the foreground, so you won't get a shell prompt unless you explicitly place it in the background by appending an ampersand (&) to command invocation.

The two things to look out for when debugging *rarpd* are:

- Does *rarpd* register a RARP_REQUEST? If it doesn't, this could indicate a physical network problem, or the server is not on the same physical network as the client.

- Can *rarpd* map the client's Ethernet address back to an IP address? If not, this could indicate a bad *ethers* map, a bad */etc/ethers* file, or an */etc/nsswitch.conf* file that is not pointing at the right place.

By enabling debug mode in *bootparamd* on the server, you can see the hostname, addresses, and pathnames given to the diskless client. You can turn on *bootparamd* debugging by killing it on the server and starting it again with the *-d* option:

```
# ps -eaf | grep bootparamd
    root    276    1  0    Apr 16 ?          0:00 /usr/sbin/rpc.bootparamd
    root   5878  5825  0 00:33:27 pts/0      0:00 grep bootparamd

# kill 276
# rpc.bootparamd -d
in debug mode.
msg 1:  group =  260   mib_id =      0   length = 128
msg 2:  group =  261   mib_id =      0   length = 132
msg 3:  group = 1025   mib_id =      0   length = 36
msg 4:  group = 1026   mib_id =      0   length = 64
msg 5:  group =  260   mib_id =     20   length = 144
msg 6:  group =  260   mib_id =    100   length = 88
msg 7:  group = 1026   mib_id =      1   length = 0
msg 8:  group = 1026   mib_id =      2   length = 0
msg 9:  group =  260   mib_id =     21   length = 2464
msg 10: group =  260   mib_id =     22   length = 360
mibget getmsg() 11 returned EOD (level 0, name 0)
interface_addr = 130.141.14.8.
interface_mask = 255.255.255.0
22 records for ipRouteEntryTable
Whoami returning name = honeymoon, router address = 130.141.14.253
getfile_1: file is "honeymoon" 130.141.14.8 "/export/root/honeymoon"
```

The messages that start with *msg* are the results of asking the IP layer for Simple Network Management Protocol (SNMP) Management Information Base (MIB) information. The *bootparamd* daemon makes this inquiry to find the IP address of the best router for the diskless client. The messages that say *group = 260* are the ones of interest for this purpose. Of those messages, the ones with a *mib_id* of 0 or 20 are of interest. Normally both kinds of messages will appear. If not, that may indicate a problem with the server's network configuration. But if there are no problems, we can expect the debug output to show a router address for the client.

The *getfile_1* message is simply reporting that it knows where the client's root filesystem is. Note the IP address is the same as the server's interface, which means that the NFS server for the client is the same as the *bootparamd* server.

If the server shows strange boot parameters passed to the client, check that the server's */etc/bootparams* file is correct, and that the boot server's NIS server has up-to-date maps.

If the boot parameters received by the client are incorrect, check that the server answering the request for them has current information. Because requests are broadcast to *bootparamd*, the server that can reply in the shortest time supplies the information. If the client refuses to boot at all, complaining of:

```
null domain name
invalid domain name
invalid boot parameters
```

or similar problems, verify that the host answering its broadcasts is using the same boot protocol and configuration files. See "Boot parameter confusion" in Chapter 15 for an example of invalid boot parameters.

Also ensure that the boot server exports the client's root and swap filesystems with the proper *root* mapping and access restrictions. In */etc/dfs/dfstab*, both the root and swap filesystems should have the options:

```
rw=client,root=client
```

to limit access to the diskless client and to allow the superuser to write to the filesystems. If the swap filesystem is not exported so that *root* can write to it, the diskless client will not be able to start the *init* process to begin the single-user boot.

Missing /usr

After setting the host and domain names and configuring network interfaces in the boot process, a machine mounts its */usr* filesystem. If there are problems with */usr*, the boot process either hangs or fails at the first reference to the */usr* filesystem. The two most common problems are not being able to locate the NFS server for */usr* and attempting to mount the wrong */usr*.

NIS cannot be started until after */usr* is mounted, since client-side daemons like *ypbind* live in */usr*. Generally, */usr* is mounted from the boot server, so a diskless client needs its own name and its server's hostname in its */etc/hosts*. If */usr* is not mounted from the root/swap filesystem server, the */usr* server's hostname must appear in the local hosts file as well. You may need as many as four different entries in the "runt" */etc/hosts* file on a diskless client: its hostname, a localhost entry, the boot server's name, and the name of the */usr* server.

Heterogeneous client/server environments create another set of problems. Clients of different architectures need their own */usr* filesystems with executables built for the client's CPU, not the server's. The most obvious problem is when the client mounts the wrong */usr*. If the executables on it were built for a different CPU, then the first attempt to invoke one of them produces a fairly descriptive error. However, if the */usr/platform* directory is for the correct CPU architecture but doesn't contain the right kernel architecture (for example, Sun's *sun4u* and *sun4m* variants), then the client boots, but certain Unix utilities will not work. Processes that read the kernel or user address spaces, such as *crash*, are the most likely to break.

If you suspect that you're mounting the wrong */usr*, first check the client's */etc/ vfstab* file to see where it gets */usr*:

```
wahoo:/export/root/honeymoon                        - /        nfs - - rw
wahoo:/export/swap/honeymoon                        - /dev/swap nfs - - -
wahoo:/export/exec/Solaris_2.7_sparc.all/usr - /usr      nfs - - ro
```

In this example, we would check */export/exec/Solaris_2.7_sparc.all/usr* on the server *wahoo*. The directories in */export/exec* have names with this format: *Solaris_ <release>_<architecture>*. If the client and the server are of the same CPU architecture and are running the same release of the operating system, the *usr* subdirectory in */export/exec/Solaris_<release>_<architecture>* is a symbolic link to the server's */usr* directory.

If the client and server do not have the same release and CPU architectures, the directories in */export/exec* contain complete operating system releases.

Three things can go wrong with this link-and-directory scheme:

- The links */export/exec/*/usr* point to the wrong place. This is possible if you changed the architecture of the server but restored */export* from a backup tape. Make sure that *Solaris_2.7_sparc.all/usr* links point to */usr* only if the server is a SPARC running Solaris 7. You'll get "exec format" errors if you mount a */usr* of the wrong architecture on the client.

- The */export/exec/** directories referenced by the clients don't exist. This is possible if you added a client of a new, different CPU architecture but did not install the appropriate operating system software for it. If you try to mount a directory that doesn't exist, you should see "cannot mount root" errors on the client.

- The client may have the wrong mount point listed in its */etc/vfstab* file. If you did not specify the architecture of the client correctly when using the Admin-Suite software, the client's *vfstab* file is likely to contain the wrong mount information.

If you are unsure of how a mount and link combination will work, experiment on another diskless client having the same architecture. For example, mount */export/exec/Solaris_2.7_sparc.all/usr* on */mnt*, and then try a sample command to be sure you've mounted the right one:

```
client# mount wahoo:/export/exec/Solaris_2.7_sparc.all/usr /mnt
client# cd /var
client# /mnt/bin/ls
4lib        dict        krb5        oasys       sbin        ucblib
5bin        dist.       kvm         old         share       vmsys
X           dt          lib         openwin     snadm       xpg4
adm         games       lost+found  platform    spool
aset        include     mail        preserve    src
bin         java        man         proc        tmp
ccs         java1.1     net         pub         ucb
demo        kernel      news        sadm        ucbinclude
```

If commands are executed properly, then you should be able to mount */usr* safely on the diskless client in question.

Configuration options

Adding disks to local clients opens two configuration options. You can use the local disk for swap space, or you can build an entire bootable system on it and put the root and swap filesystems on the local disk. This latter configuration is called a *dataless* client, and makes sense if the client does not need most of the local disk for a very large swap space. If the client has a large swap partition and uses it frequently, adding a local disk may improve performance by reducing the client's traffic to its boot server. In other instances, the local disk provides private storage for sensitive files.

Dataless clients contain no user or data files on their local disks. Everything on the local disk can be reconstructed from operating system release tapes or from system installation scripts. The local disks are used for the root and swap filesystems, while */usr* and all other filesystems are NFS-mounted. The dataless architecture provides some performance advantages from both the client and server perspective, particularly when the client has a large swap space.

A significant portion—usually more than 50% and sometimes 90%—of a diskless client's network traffic is caused by reading and writing the root and swap filesystems. Clients with local disks place less of a load on the network and on the boot server by sending their swap traffic to this disk.

Dataless clients

You may choose to use the dataless client configuration if you have to support a few machines of a new client architecture and would have to carve the disk space out of the server's */export* partition. Adding a local disk keeps the server configuration simple and puts all files specific to the new client architecture on the local disks.

The best network architecture for dataless clients is one in which desktop machines run application sets with large, randomly accessed virtual address spaces. If the machine has a reasonably high level of paging activity, depending on the speed of the network and capacity of the NFS servers, using a local disk improves performance. Dataless clients may appear to be more expensive per seat than diskless clients, since the diskless machines get root and swap space at "bulk" prices from the server. On the other hand, in a pure diskless client environment, you must purchase additional disk space to hold the clients' root and swap filesystems. If you allocate some portion of the server's cost as the cost of replacing local disks, the dataless and diskless architectures have much less of a price differential. Be careful when analyzing client/server cost projections. You'll get the fairest numbers when you compare the total cost of the desktop workstation, any local disk, and the desktop's share of the cost of servers providing root, swap, and user filesystems.

When you do add local disks, it's important to choose your disk size carefully. If larger local disks are attached to dataless clients, they become inviting homes for user files that may not be backed up regularly. If you plan to configure dataless clients, use the smallest disk possible to contain the root and swap filesystems, with enough room on the local disk's root partition to contain a very large */var* directory. Applications that use enough virtual memory to justify a local disk probably create huge temporary files on */var/tmp* as well.

Management of dataless nodes is slightly more complex than that of diskless nodes. Even though the local disks contain no user files or tools, they may still have host-specific configuration information in the */etc* directory, such as software password files. Use care when modifying the private parts of a dataless node so that the entire node can be recreated from a boot tape or archive tape if the local disk must be replaced. You will probably want to create a script that creates spool directories, copies printer configuration files, and creates NFS mount points on the client; you can use this script on dataless or new diskless clients as well. If possible, mount the dataless client spool directories from an NFS server so that the dataless client's disk contains no host-specific information. Ideally, you should not have to do backups of a dataless client.

After Solaris 2.5.1, the AdminSuite product stopped supporting the dataless configuration option. This is a bit of an inconvenience to you, but it is surmountable.

Consider that a dataless client is like a disk-full client except that */usr* is mounted from an NFS server instead of from a local disk. The steps for doing this are:

1. Install the operating system on a disk-full client. If possible (depending on how many disks you have and how big they are), install all the software without specify a */usr* partition. If you have to, specify a separate */var* partition if that is what it takes to prevent a */usr* partition from being created. It's OK to have the */usr* partition created, but once you mount */usr* from the NFS server, the question then is what do you do with the redundant local disk space? You can always mount it as another partition, say */spare*, and have it around for future additional needs such as more *swap*, or more */var* space.

2. Edit */etc/vfstab* on the client to mount */usr* from an NFS server that has been set up for diskless client support. If there was an entry for */usr* in */etc/vfstab*, comment it out. For example you might comment out */usr*'s *vfstab*:

   ```
   # /dev/dsk/c0t0d0s6 /dev/rdsk/c0t0d0s6     /usr      ufs  1  no   -
   ```

   and add:

   ```
   wahoo:/export/exec/Solaris_2.7_sparc.all/usr - /usr      nfs  -  -      ro
   ```

3. Edit */etc/hosts* and add the IP address of the NFS server. Both dataless and diskless clients require this, because while the system is booting, without */usr* available, the software needed to access NIS or DNS won't be around, so */etc/hosts* is needed to resolve the name of the NFS server to an IP address:

   ```
   130.141.14.2          wahoo
   ```

4. Test this by rebooting the client. If you run into any problems, you can always shut the system down, and boot the system as single user.

There is a drawback to this scheme. Applying some patches and packages will be less straightforward, because patches and packages can contain both */usr* and *root* files, but the dataless client's */usr* partition won't be writable by the utilities used to add patches and packages. The workaround for this is very dependent on the patch and packaging scheme used by the operating system. In case of Solaris, the *patchadd* utility has a *-R pathname* option, which is normally used to apply patches to a diskless client's root partitions. In that case, *patchadd* is run on the NFS server. In the case of a dataless client, you would invoke *patchadd* as:

```
client # patchadd -R / -M . 107460-03
```

For a package that contains both root and */usr* files, you could invoke the Solaris *pkgadd* command to install the package in a temporary place, and then copy the non-*usr* files to the dataless client's root:

```
client # mkdir /tmp/scratch
client # pkgadd -d . -R /tmp/scratch SUNWxxxx
client # cd /tmp/scratch
client # rm -rf usr
client # find . -print | cpio -dump /
```

Swapping on a local disk

In this configuration option, the client's root and */usr* filesystems are NFS-mounted, but swap is from a local disk. The AdminSuite software doesn't provide an option for diskless client accessing local swap, but again it is surmountable. The steps are:

1. If not already done, add the diskless client to the boot server via the Admin-Suite software. Go ahead and define a swap partition on the server so that you don't run the risk of confusing the AdminSuite software.

2. Boot the client from the boot server.

3. Identify and create the swap partition from the local disk. In Solaris, the easiest way to this is via the *format* command. When you invoke the *format* command, it will display the list of disks attached to the client. You then select one of the local disks and then use the "partition" command from inside *format* to find an existing partition and resize it, or create a partition with the desired size.

4. Edit */etc/vfstab* on the client to mount *swap* from the partition you identified in the previous step. For example you might change the two NFS-related *swap vfstab* entries from:

```
wahoo:/export/swap/honeymoon  -        /dev/swap nfs   -    -   -
/dev/swap                     -        -         swap  -    -   -
```

to:

```
/dev/dsk/c0t0d0s7             -        -         swap  -    no  -
```

5. Reboot the client via diskless boot.

In general, the swap partition should cover most, if not all, of the local disk.

Of course, if you followed the example in "Managing client swap space," then you know you ought to be able to switch from NFS swap to local swap without a client reboot. This is only possible if the local swap partition is at least as big as the NFS-mounted swap file. Instead of rebooting the client in step 5, you would do:

```
honeymoon# swap -a /dev/dsk/c0t0d0s7
honeymoon# swap -d /dev/swap
```

Brief introduction to JumpStart administration

Diskless NFS was conceived in the mid-1980s during a time when disks for desktops were bulky, small in capacity, and expensive. Much has changed since then. Because so much disk space comes with desktop systems today, you may want to utilize it, despite most of the advantages of diskless operation. One advantage of diskless—ease of administration—is still quite critical. If you decide that aside from ease of administration, you'd prefer to have your clients be disk-full or even data-less, you can still leverage the inherent diskless support in your desktops to centralize many administration tasks, including:

- Upgrading and patching the desktop operating systems
- Modifying configuration files

Consider that you can install the operating system on your desktop's local disk by booting from the network interface instead of a disk, i.e., a *netinstall*. On a SPARC system, at the boot prompt you would do:

```
ok boot net - install
```

Solaris NFS servers have a feature known as *JumpStart* installation that lets you customize the configuration of your desktops. The difference between JumpStart-driven configuration and diskless driver configuration is that with the former, the onus is on the user to shut down and boot the desktop over the network to let JumpStart configuration take effect. With diskless configuration, the system administrator can make changes on the server and have the changes take immediate effect. However, as discussed earlier in this chapter, often such changes on the NFS server have to be coordinated with the desktop user. Thus, you can argue that in terms of ease of administration, there's no qualitative difference between Jump-Start and diskless operation.

It is beyond the scope of this book to describe the JumpStart feature in detail. The Solaris documentation and the book *Automating Solaris Installations*, by Paul Anthony Kasper and Alan L. McClellan (Prentice Hall PTR/Sun Microsystems Press, 1995), are extensive treatments of the subject. Once you've grasped the theory of JumpStart installation, of particular interest will be the section "Bypassing the Installation Software" in Chapter 10 of Kasper's and McClellan's book. This section describes how you can use "begin" and "finish" scripts to modify the state of a system, without being forced to reinstall the operating system. Thus configuration tasks can be done quickly and efficiently, with no unnecessary user interaction.

Client/server ratios

The number of clients that can be supported from a single server depends on many variables: the type of work done on each client, the type of disks and network interfaces on the server, the number of clients on the network, and the configuration of the clients. Diskless clients used in a software engineering shop do not have the same server requirements as diskless machines used to run the documentation group. Similarly, when dozens of diskless clients are put onto the same physical network, the network itself becomes a bottleneck before the server does. Instead of adopting a somewhat arbitrary client-server ratio, use the following steps to calculate a rough client-server distribution:

1. Set up a diskless or dataless client on a network with its own server. Put home directories, applications, tools, and other NFS-mounted filesystems on another server, so that the server under test does nothing but handle root and swap filesystem requests from the client. Use only one client for this test so that the server does not become a bottleneck: you want to measure the load imposed by a single client in an unconstrained environment.

2. Run a normal workload on the client, using scripts or a live user to produce a typical traffic pattern. On the server, measure the average traffic generated (over the course of several hours) and also try to measure the peak request rates produced by the client. Use the *nfsstat* utility on the server to determine the number of NFS requests per second that the server handles. *nfsstat* is described in more detail in Chapter 14.

3. Repeat the first two steps for each "type" of client or user: diskless client, dataless client, development engineer, testing/quality assurance lab, documentation writer, and so on. Blend these figures together based on the percentage of each client type to determine the average NFS load imposed by all of the clients.

4. Tune and benchmark the server using the methodologies described in Chapter 17. The benchmarks should produce an expected upper bound on the number of NFS operations that the server can provide.

5. Divide the server's capacity by the weighted average of the client request rates to determine a coarse client-server ratio. Conversely, you can multiply the weighted number of NFS operations performed by each client by the number of clients to set a goal for the server tuning process.

The ratio produced in this manner should be used as a coarse estimate only. The client-server ratio will be overstated because each diskless client server may handle other responsibilities, such as serving other NFS filesystems or driving printers. It may also be understated, because it is rare to find an environment in which the average load produced by N hosts is N times the load produced by a single host. Desktop users simply aren't that synchronized. We'll take closer looks at server and client tuning, NFS benchmarking, and performance optimization in later chapters.

9

The Automounter

The *automounter* is a tool that automatically mounts NFS filesystems when they are referenced and unmounts them when they are no longer needed. It applies NIS management to NFS configuration files so that you can edit a single NIS map and have it affect client mount information throughout the network. Using the automounter, you don't have to keep */etc/vfstab* files up-to-date by hand.[*] Mount information, including the server's name, filesystem pathname on the server, local mount point and mount options, is contained in automounter *maps*, which are usually maintained in NIS maps.

Why would you want to bother with another administrative tool? What's wrong with putting all of the remote filesystem information in each hosts' */etc/vfstab* file? There are many motivations for using the automounter:

- */etc/vfstab* files on every host become much less complex as the automounter handles the common entries in this file.

- The automounter maps may be maintained using NIS, streamlining the administration of mount tables for all hosts in the network the same way NIS streamlines user account information.

- Your exposure to hanging a process when an NFS server crashes is greatly reduced. The automounter unmounts all filesystems that are not in use, removing dependencies on fileservers that are not currently referenced by the client.

---

[*] The automounter is included in Solaris, Compaq's Tru64 Unix, SGI's IRIX, IBM's AIX, and other commercial Unix operating systems. A public domain version called *amd* is available on *http://www.cs. columbia.edu/~ezk/am-utils/* and *amd* runs on almost any Unix system. Because it is kernel- and server-independent, the *amd* automounter is easily migrated to other NFS client platforms.

- The automounter extends the basic NFS mount protocol to find the "nearest server" for replicated, read-only filesystems. The NFS server that is closest to the client—going through the fewest number of bridges and routers—will handle the mount request. Distributing client load in this manner reduces the load on the more heavily used network hardware.

In a large and dynamic NFS environment, it is difficult to keep the *vfstab* file on each machine up-to-date. Doing so requires creating mount points and usually hand-editing configuration files; automatic distribution of *vfstab* files is made difficult by the large number of host-specific entries in each. As you add new software packages or filesystems on the network, you usually have to edit every *vfstab* file. Using the automounter, you change one NIS map and allow the automounter to provide the new mount point information on all NIS clients.

Adding NFS servers is usually accompanied by a juggling of directories. It is likely that every client will be required to mount filesystems from the new server. As new NFS servers add filesystems to the network, the clients develop new dependencies on these servers, and their *vfstab* files grow in complexity.

Users cannot simply mount filesystems at their whim without *root* privileges. The automounter handles this problem by performing the mount as the filesystems are referenced, which is usually the point at which users decide they need to perform the mount themselves. Some users request that their machines mount only those filesystems of interest to them to eliminate the possibility that their machines will hang if a server containing "uninteresting" files hangs. The automounter eliminates dependencies on these unrelated NFS servers by imposing a working-set notion on the set of mounted filesystems. When a filesystem is first referenced, the automounter mounts it at the appropriate place in the local filesystem. After several minutes (ten by default), the automounter attempts to unmount all filesystems that it previously mounted. If the filesystem is quiescent, and therefore probably uninteresting to the client, then the automounter's *umount()* system call succeeds, and the client is relieved of the server dependency. If the filesystem is busy, the automounter ignores the error returned by *umount()*.

Using the automounter also adds another level of transparency to the network. Once a client's */etc/vfstab* file is created, the client has a static idea of *where* each remote filesystem is located. It becomes difficult for the system administrator to move tools, users, or any other directory without going to each host and changing the */etc/vfstab* files to reflect the change. The automounter makes the location of NFS filesystems even more transparent to NFS clients by removing hardcoded server names and pathnames from the clients' */etc/vfstab* files.

Placing NFS filesystems in automounter maps greatly simplifies the administrative overhead of adding or reconfiguring NFS servers. Because the maps may be maintained using NIS, a single file is propagated to all NFS clients. Editing the individual */etc/vfstab* files is not required. The automounter is also conducive to simpler mounting schemes. For example, mounting 50 directories of tools and utilities under */tools* produces an unwieldy *vfstab* file. In addition, the *tools* mount point becomes a bottleneck, since any directory *stat( )* or *getwd( )* call that touches it also touches all NFS servers with filesystems mounted in */tools*. More frequently, tools and utilities are mounted haphazardly, creating administrative problems. Simply remembering where things are is difficult, as users become confused by irregular naming schemes.

Managing */tools* with the automounter offers several advantages. All of the individual mount points are replaced by a single map that creates the appropriate mount points as needed. The automounter mount point contains only the handful of entries corresponding to the working set of tools that the user employs at any one time. It's also much simpler to add a new tool: instead of having to create the mount point and edit */etc/vfstab* on every host in the network, you simply update the NIS-managed automounter map.

Finally, the automounter looks for a filesystem on one of several servers. Manual pages, read-only libraries, and other replicated filesystems will be mounted from the first server in a set to respond to the mount request. In addition to providing a simple load-balancing scheme similar to that of NIS, the automounter removes single-host dependencies that would make a diskless or dataless workstation unusable in the event of a server crash.

Automounter maps

The behavior of the automounter is governed by its maps. An *indirect map* is useful when you are mounting several filesystems with common pathname prefixes (as seen on the clients, not necessarily on the servers). A good example is the */tools* directory described previously, although home directories also fit the indirect map model well. A *direct map* is used for irregularly named filesystems, where each mount point does not have a common prefix with other mount points. Some good examples of mounts requiring direct maps are */usr/local* and */usr/man*.

Direct and indirect maps vary in how the automounter emulates the underlying mount point. For a direct map, the automounter looks like a symbolic link at each mount point in the map. With an indirect map, the automounter emulates a directory of symbolic links, where the directory is the common pathname prefix shared by all of the automounter-managed mount points. This is confusing and is best explained by the examples that follow.

The *master map* is a meta-map (a map describing other maps). It contains a list of indirect maps and direct mount points and tells the automounter where to look for all of its map information. We'll look at a typical master map after seeing how the indirect and direct maps are used to mount NFS filesystems.

Indirect maps

Indirect maps are the simplest and most useful automounter convention. They correspond directly to regularly named filesystems, such as home directories, desktop tools, and system utility software. While tools directories may not be consistently named across fileservers, for example, you can use NFS mounts to make them appear consistent on a client machine. The automounter replaces all of the */etc/vfstab* entries that would be required to effect this naming scheme on the clients.

Each indirect map has a directory associated with it that is specified on the command line or in the master map (see "The master map" later in this chapter). The map itself contains a *key*, which is the name of the mount point in the directory, optional NFS mount options, and the *server:pathname* pair identifying the source of the filesystem. Automounter maps are usually named *auto_contents*, where *contents* describes the map. The map name does not have to correspond to its mount point—it can be anything that indicates the map's function. Maps are placed in */etc* or maintained via NIS.

The best way to understand how an indirect map works is to look at an example. We'll look at an automounter map and equivalent *vfstab* file for a directory structure like this:

```
/tools/deskset
/tools/sting
/tools/news
/tools/bugview
```

Here is an indirect automounter map for the */tools* directory, called *auto_tools*:

```
deskset          -ro       mahimahi:/tools2/deskset
sting                      mahimahi:/tools2/sting
news                       thud:/tools3/news
bugview                    jetstar:/usr/bugview
```

The first field is called the *map key* and is the final component of the mount point. The map name suffix and the mount point do not have to share the same name, but adopting this convention makes it easy to associate map names and mount points. This four-entry map is functionally equivalent to the */etc/vfstab* excerpt:

```
mahimahi:/tools2/desket  - /tools/deskset  nfs - - ro
mahimahi:/tools2/string  - /tools/sting    nfs - -
thud:/tools3/news        - /tools/news     nfs - -
jetstar:/usr/bugview     - /tools/bugview  nfs - -
```

Notice that the server-side mount points have no common pathname prefixes, but that the client's *vfstab* and automounter map establish a regularly named view of filesystems.

There are basically two kinds of automounters: older ones that use symbolic links and newer ones that don't. Using the *auto_tools* map, older implementations of the automounter emulate *tools* in a directory of symbolic links. When any process on the client makes a reference to something in */tools*, the automounter completes the appropriate NFS mount and makes a symbolic link in */tools* pointing to the actual mount point for the filesystem. Suppose you go to execute */tools/news/bin/ rn*. Using the automounter effectively breaks this pathname up into three components:

- The prefix */tools* picks an automounter map. (We will see in the section "The master map" just how */tools* refers to the *auto_tools* map.) In this case, the map for the */tools* directory is the *auto_tools* map.

- The next pathname component is the key within this map. *news* selects the server filesystem *thud:/tools3/news*; the automounter mounts this filesystem and makes a link to it in */tools* on the client.

- The remainder of the path, *bin/rn*, is passed to the NFS server *thud* since it is relative to the directory from which the *news* toolset is mounted.

Keep in mind that this list applies to older automounters that use symbolic link map entries to NFS mount points. There are problems with using symbolic links, and newer automounters solve them. The newer automounters don't use symbolic links and effectively put the NFS mounts "in place." The next section will explain in more detail.

Note that the automounter map doesn't contain any information about the */tools* directory itself, only about the subdirectories in it that are used for mount points. This makes it extremely easy to relocate a set of mount points—you simply change the master map that associates the directory */tools* with the map *auto_tools*. We'll come back to the master map later on.

Inside the automounter

At this point, it's useful to take a look under the hood of the automounter. This background makes the operation of indirect maps a little clearer and will make direct maps much easier to understand.

As mentioned before, automounter implementations come in two designs. The first one is a purely user-level approach that relies heavily on symbolic links. The second is a hybrid user-level and kernel-level approach called the *autofs* automounter, which eschews symbolic links.

User-level automounters

The original automounters were strictly user-level daemons that required no support in the kernel. SunOS 4.x automounters were all user-level, as were the automounters in Solaris 2.0 through Solaris 2.3. As many automounters were derived from SunOS 4.x or Solaris code, you'll find that several non-Solaris implementations are still user-level.

Before walking through the sequence of automounter operations in detail, some knowledge of mount information is necessary. The *mount()* system call takes the filesystem type (*ufs, nfs, hsfs,* etc.) and mount point from the */etc/vfstab* table, and a packet of parameters that are type-specific. For NFS mounts, the argument vector passed to *mount()* includes the server's hostname and a socket address (IP host address and port number pair) to be used for sending requests to that server. For normal NFS mounts, the remote server's hostname and IP address are used, and the IP port number is the well-known NFS port number 2049. The kernel uses this information to put together an RPC client handle for calling the remote NFS server.

User-level automounters capitalize on this architecture by creating a set of mount arguments that points to itself, a process on the local host, with a different port number than 2049. In effect, a system running the automounter has mounted a *daemon* on each mount point, instead of a remote filesystem. NFS requests for these mount points are intercepted by the automounter, since it appears to be a regular, remote NFS server to the kernel. No kernel modifications are necessary to run the automounter, and the automounter's functions are transparent to user processes.

We'll take a look at how the user-level automounter works using the indirect *auto_tools* map discussed earlier. The NFS client host is named *wahoo*. From boot time, the complete sequence of events is:

1. The user-level automounter advertises the */tools* mount point in */etc/mnttab*, making it look like any other NFS-mounted filesystem except for the more verbose information about the server's IP address and port:

   /etc/mnttab excerpt
   ```
   thud:/export/home/thud /tmp_mnt/home/thud nfs rw,dev=218980f 929944999
   wahoo:(pid161)     /tools     nfs      ro,ignore,map=/etc/auto_
   tools,indirect,dev=2180009 920935886
   ```

   The first *mnttab* entry is for a normal NFS mount point listed in the *vfstab* file. The second is for an indirect map and was added when the automounter was started. Instead of a *server:directory* pair, the automounter entry contains its process ID and the local host's name. The device numbers for NFS-mounted filesystems are simply unique values assigned by the kernel on each *mount* operation. This entry is added to *mnttab* when the automounter starts up and reads its maps.

2. A user goes to execute */tools/news/bin/rn*. The kernel performs a lookup of the executable's pathname and finds that the *tools* component is a mount point. An NFS *lookup* request for the next component, *news*, is sent to the listed process—the automounter—via a loopback RPC mechanism.

3. The user-level automounter emulates a directory of symbolic links under the indirect map mount point. The *lookup* request on the *news* component is received by the automounter daemon, and it returns information identical to that received when performing a *lookup* on a symbolic link on a remote NFS server. The automounter looks up the appropriate filesystem in */etc/auto_tools* and mounts it in its staging area, */tmp_mnt*. This operation uses the *mount()* system call, which places a new entry in the *mnttab* file.

4. Now that the automounted filesystem has been referenced, the user-level automounter adds a symbolic link to its emulated directory. The new link in */tools* points to the newly mounted filesystem. The equivalent command-line operations are:

```
# mount thud:/tools3/news /tmp_mnt/tools/news
# ln -s /tmp_mnt/tools/news /tools/news
```

5. The client-side process receives the reply from its *lookup* request and goes to read the link. This time, the automounter returns the contents of the symbolic link, which points to the automounter staging area. Note that the automounter fabricates a response to the client's *readlink* request; it looks like there's a symbolic link on the disk but it's really an artifact of the automounter. The client process follows the link's target pathname to the appropriate subdirectory of */tmp_mnt*.

6. The client process can now trace every pathname in */tools/news* to a subdirectory of */tmp_mnt/tools/news*, through the new entry in */etc/mnttab* and the symbolic link emulation provided by the automounter. A client process pathname lookup finds */tools* in the mount table and sends its query to the automounter. The automounter's link points to */tmp_mnt/news*, which is also listed in the mount table. To the client, the automounter looks exactly like a directory and a symbolic link.

If this seems to be a convoluted mechanism for mounting a single filesystem, it is. However, this approach is taken to minimize the number of NFS mounts performed and to thereby improve performance by keeping */etc/mnttab* as small as possible. When you mount several subdirectories of the same remote filesystem, only one NFS mount is required. The various subdirectories of this common mount point are referenced by symbolic links, not by individual mounts. In the sample indirect map earlier, *mahimahi:/tools2* contains several utilities. */tools2* will be mounted on the NFS client when the first utility in it is referenced, and references to other subdirectories of */tools2* simply contain links back to the existing mount in */tmp_mnt*.

The staging area */tmp_mnt* is a key to the indirect map mechanism. If the staging area concept is eliminated, then the indirect map mount point becomes another directory filled with direct mounts. The primary advantage of indirect maps is that they allow the mount points in a directory to be managed independently—the mounts occur when a process references the mount point, and not the parent directory itself. We'll look at some problems with direct mounts shortly.

As a result of linking */tools* to the actual NFS mount point, a user would encounter the following:

```
% cd /tools/bin
% /usr/bin/pwd
/tmp_mnt/tools/bin
```

In other words, instead of *pwd* displaying */tools/bin*, it gets */tmp_mnt/tools/bin*. This behavior breaks lots of software. For example, a program might record the current working directory, and cache it in a file. A subsequent invocation of the program might read the cache, and attempt to access */tmp_mnt/tools/bin*, and find that it isn't there. This is because a user-level automounter responds to attempts to access */tools*, not */tmp_mnt/tools*. For the remainder of this chapter, we will refer to this issue as the "*pwd* problem."

There are other side-effects of the user-level automounter that may catch the user off-guard. The automounter creates and controls the indirect map mount point. It emulates the entire directory, so that no user, even the superuser, can create entries in it. This has an important implication for creating indirect maps: they cannot be mounted over an existing directory, because the automounter hides the underlying files. If a directory must contain a mixture of automounter mount points and "normal" directory entries, a direct map must be used.

This is an important but subtle point: when you poke at a user-level automounter mount point with *ls*, it appears that there is a directory filled with symbolic links. In reality, this directory and the links in it do not exist on any disk. If this hurts to think about, it's really no different than the way NFS itself works: there may be no filesystem called */tools/news* on your local disk, but NFS makes it *look* like it's there. The user-level automounter speaks to the NFS protocol, allowing it to fabricate replies to NFS RPC calls that are indistinguishable from the real thing.

Because the user-level automounter controls the contents of a *readdir* NFS RPC reply, *ls* behaves strangely. The user-level automounter displays only currently mounted links in the directory it emulates. If no reference is made to a subdirectory of the indirect map directory, it appears empty:

```
% cd /tools
% ls
% ls /tools/news
bin lib spool
```

```
% cd /tools
% ls -l
total 1
lrwxrwxrwx  1 root           19 Aug 31 12:59 news -> /tmp_mnt/tools/news
```

Why not display potential mounts as well? Doing so could result in a great deal of unintended mounting activity—a *mount storm*—when *ls -l* is executed in this directory. A newer automounter described in the next section allows you to browse potential mounts, as well as fix the *pwd* problem described earlier. Another approach is to use *hierarchical mounts*, as described later in this chapter.

The autofs automounter

The *pwd* problem described in the previous section was solved in Solaris 2.4 with the introduction of a hybrid user-level and kernel-level automounter, which retained a user-level automounter daemon, but introduced a new filesystem known as *autofs*. The *autofs* filesystem is a pseudo-filesystem that allows you to mount automounter points like */tools/news* as directory objects directly underneath */tools*, instead of as symbolic links. The automounter daemon is no longer an NFS server, but instead responds to requests from the in-kernel *autofs* filesystem to mount NFS filesystems on the mount points that *autofs* creates.

Let's take a look at how adding *autofs* changes how the automounter works using the example of the indirect *auto_tools* map. The NFS client host is still named *wahoo*. From boot time, the complete sequence of events is:

1. The *autofs* automounter advertises the */tools* mount point in */etc/mnttab*, making it look like any other NFS-mounted filesystem except for the more verbose information about the server's IP address and port:

   ```
   /etc/mnttab excerpt
   thud:/export/home/thud /home/thud nfs nosuid,dev=218980f 929944999
   auto_tools /tools    autofs ignore,indirect,nosuid,dev=2b40002 922482272
   ```

   The first *mnttab* entry is for a normal NFS mount point listed in the *vfstab* file. Note that the mount point is */home/thud* and not */tmp_mnt/home/thud*. The second is for an indirect map and was added when the automounter was started. Instead of a process ID and the local host's name, the entry simply has the map name and a filesystem type of *autofs*. The device numbers for *autofs*-mounted filesystems are assigned by the kernel on each *mount* operation. This entry is added to *mnttab* when the automounter starts up and reads its maps.

2. A user goes to execute */tools/news/bin/rn*. The kernel performs a lookup of the executable's pathname, and finds that the *tools* component is a mount point. The kernel invokes the *lookup* entry point of the *autofs* filesystem request for *tools*. The kernel then proceeds to the next component in the pathname, *news*, and again invokes the lookup entry point of *autofs*. The *autofs*

filesystem sends a request to the automounter daemon (*automountd*)—via a loopback RPC mechanism—to mount *news*.

3. The automounter daemon receives the request from *autofs*. The request includes the name of the map (*auto_tools*), the entry in the map *autofs* is interested in (*news*), and the mount point the client wants to mount *news* onto (*/tools/news*). The automounter daemon examines the *tools* indirect map looking for the entry:

```
news        thud:/tools3/news
```

The automounter daemon checks if */tools/news* exists, and if not, creates the *news* directory under */tools*. Because */tools* is an *autofs* filesystem, the result of the *mkdir()* system call from the daemon is a call to the *mkdir* entry point in the *autofs* filesystem.

The automounter daemon then determines that the *news* map entry is to be satisfied by NFS, and so does the equivalent of:

```
# mount -F nfs thud:/tools3 /tools/news
```

The results of the mount are returned—again, via a loopback RPC mechanism —to *autofs*.

4. The *autofs* filesystem receives the reply from the automounter daemon, and now the kernel can proceed with the next components in the pathname, *bin* and *rn*. Because the automounter daemon mounted an NFS filesystem onto */tools/news*, the automounter is not involved in the processing of *bin* and *rn*.

As with the user-level automounter, the original *autofs* automounter didn't display potential mounts of indirect maps like *auto_tools*. The next section describes an enhanced *autofs* automounter that supports the ability to browse the potential mounts under a mount point such as */tools*.

The enhanced autofs automounter: Browsing indirect maps

In Solaris 2.6, the *autofs* automounter was modified so that displaying directories of the mount points of indirect maps shows every entry; in other words, it allows a user to *browse* the map:

```
% cd /tools
% ls -l
total 4
dr-xr-xr-x  1 root   root     19 Aug 31 12:59 bugview
dr-xr-xr-x  1 root   root     19 Aug 31 12:59 deskset
dr-xr-xr-x  1 root   root     19 Aug 31 12:59 news
dr-xr-xr-x  1 root   root     19 Aug 31 12:59 sting
```

When the *readdir* entry point in the *autofs* filesystem is called on */tools* for the first time, there are no *autofs* directories underneath it, and so, *autofs* makes an RPC call to the automounter daemon to read the *auto_tools* map to return the list of map entries. The map entries are used to construct a directory listing for the *ls* command. Note that the attributes of the directories are faked. This is because we want to avoid mount storms, as described in the earlier section "User-level automounters."

Now see what happens we start to populate */tools* with real entries:

```
% ls /tools/news
bin lib spool
% cd /tools
% ls -l
total 1
dr-xr-xr-x  1 root   root   19 Aug 31 12:59 bugview
dr-xr-xr-x  1 root   root   19 Aug 31 12:59 deskset
drwxrwxr-x  5 root   other 512 Jun 10 17:03 news
dr-xr-xr-x  1 root   root   19 Aug 31 12:59 sting
```

Invoking the *ls* command on */tools/news* causes */tools/news* to be NFS-mounted from *thud:/tools3/news*. When the *readdir* entry point in the *autofs* filesystem is called on */tools* for the second time, there is now an NFS directory, *news*, underneath it. Thus, *autofs* combines the list of map entries with the list of NFS-mounted directories.

By default, indirect maps can be browsed, but browsing can be turned off with the -*nobrowse* option to an indirect map.

Direct maps

Direct maps define point-specific, nonuniform mount points. The best example of the need for a direct map entry is */usr/man*. The */usr* directory contains numerous other entries, so it cannot be an indirect mount point. Building an indirect map for */usr/man* that uses */usr* as a mount point will "cover up" */usr/bin* and */usr/etc*. A direct map allows the automounter to complete mounts on a single directory entry.

The key in a direct map is a full pathname, instead of the last component found in the indirect map. Direct maps also follow the */etc/auto_contents* naming scheme. Here is a sample */etc/auto_direct*:

```
/usr/man        wahoo:/usr/share/man
/usr/local/bin  mahimahi:/usr/local/bin.sun4
```

The automounter registers the entire direct mount point pathname in the *mnttab* file, instead of the parent directory of all of the mount points:

```
auto_direct /usr/local/bin autofs ignore,direct,intr,ro,dev=2cc000a  933723158
```

The *mnttab* entry's map type is listed as *direct*. Operation of the automounter on a direct mount point is similar to the handling of an indirect mount. The *autofs* automounter is passed the entire direct mount point pathname in the RPC from *autofs*, since the mount point is the key in the map. See Table 9-1 for automounter map entry formats.

A major difference in behavior is that the real direct mount points are always visible to *ls* and other tools that read directory structures. The automounter treats direct mounts as individual directory entries, not as a complete directory, so the automounter gets queried whenever the directory containing the mount point is read. Client performance is affected in a marked fashion if direct mount points are used in several well-traveled directories. When a user reads a directory containing a number of direct mounts, the automounter initiates a flurry of mounting activity in response to the directory read requests. The section, "Conversion of direct maps" describes a trick that lets you use indirect maps instead of direct maps. By using this trick, you can avoid mount storms caused by multiple direct mount points.

Table 9-1. Automounter map entry formats

Key	Mount options	Server:directory pair
indirect map: `deskset`		`mahimahi:/tools2/deskset`
direct map: `/usr/man`	`-ro`	`thud:/usr/man`

Invocation and the master map

Now that we've seen how the automounter manages NFS mount information in various maps, we'll look at how it chooses which maps to use and how it gets started. The key file that tells the automounter about map files and mount points is the master map, which is the default map read by the automounter if no other command-line options are specified. This covers the format and use of the master map, some command-line options, and some timeout tuning techniques.

The master map

The master map is the map of maps. When the automounter is started, it reads the master map from where the */etc/nsswitch.conf* configuration file says to read it, as determined by the *nsswitch.conf* entry named *automount:*. The default *nsswitch. conf*—whether files, or NIS is used—has *files* listed first. The master map file, */etc/ auto_master*, lists all direct and indirect maps and their associated directories. It consists of triplets of directory name, map name, and mount options to be used with that map. Suppose your */etc/auto_master* file contains:

```
# Directory     Map                NFS Mount Options
/tools          /etc/auto_tools    -ro
/-              /etc/auto_direct
```

The first entry is for the indirect map */etc/auto_tools*; entries in this map are mounted read-only (due to the *-ro* option) under the */tools* directory. The second line of the master file is for a direct map; because there is no directory for the automounter to manage, the place holder */-* is used. Note that the master map format is different from other automounter maps in the following ways:

- With the master maps, the mount options are in the third column, whereas regular automounter maps place the options in the second column.

- The first column in a master map is always an absolute pathname that starts with a leading slash (/) and can have one or more additional slashes, whereas with indirect maps the first column is a map key that must not contain a slash.

The earlier example is somewhat limiting in that changes to the *auto_tools* or *auto_direct* map must be made by editing each */etc/auto_tools* or */etc/auto_direct* file on each NFS client. Instead, if we drop the */etc/* prefix, we can allow the maps to be maintained in NIS or files:

```
# Directory     Map              NFS Mount Options
/tools          auto_tools       -ro
/-              auto_direct
```

In this example, we observe three things:

- Two map names—*auto_direct* and *auto_tools*—are used in place of the files pulled from */etc* in the previous example.

- The system decides to use NIS or files for *auto_direct* and *auto_tools* based on whether *files* or *nis* (or both) are specified in *nsswitch.conf*.

- Even though the corresponding map names in NIS are *auto_direct* and *auto_tools*, the *auto master* file uses a canonical name form, which uses underscores and not periods to separate the prefix *auto* from the unique suffix (*direct* or *tools*). The reason is that in some directory systems, such as NIS+, a period is a reserved character.

There is no requirement that the master map be maintained as a local file. Indeed you might find it easier if you configure your network's clients' *nfsswitch.conf* file to read all the maps, including the master map from NIS by setting *automount:* line in *nsswitch.conf* as:

```
automount: nis
```

This way you can exercise control over each client's namespace without having to reconfigure every client each time you want to add or delete a map from the master map. We will cover how the automounter maps are integrated into NIS later, in the section "Integration with NIS."

The default master map is not going to appear as in the examples presented so far. The default Solaris */etc/auto_master* file looks something like this:

```
+auto_master
/net            -hosts          -nosuid,nobrowse
/home           auto_home       -nobrowse
/xfn            -xfn
```

We will discuss the first entry, +*auto_master* in the section "Mixing NIS and files in the same map." The second entry, */net*, will be covered in "The -hosts map." The third entry, */home*, will be covered in "Key substitutions."

The last entry, */xfn*, is for the X/Open Federated Naming Standard (XFN), which is a now-deprecated standard for federating directory systems. Recall from "Brief survey of common directory services" in Chapter 2 that there are lots of directory services. XFN represented an attempt to allow them all to seamlessly co-exist in a global namespace. The idea was to allow users in one DNS domain to browse or access information (such as files, printers, or calendars) from another domain, even if the naming system that organized the information did not easily support cross-domain operations (as is the case with NIS). Because it appears that the world will be unifying under LDAP, and because *nsswitch.conf* meets most of the requirements for directory service switching, XFN has been deprecated. While the */xfn* entry persists to allow you to browse any NIS or files data represented in XFN, expect XFN and */xfn* to disappear from future Solaris releases.

Command-line options

The *autofs* automounter is started during the boot sequence from the */etc/init.d/ autofs* script. The automounter consists of two programs:

automount

Used to initialize the automounter's mount points after it reads the master map.

automountd

A daemon that handles requests from the in-kernel *autofs* filesystem to mount and unmount filesystems.

Each program has several command-line options.

Automount command-line options

-t time

This is the time, in seconds, to wait before attempting to unmount a quiescent filesystem. The default is 600 seconds, but this value may need to be adjusted to accommodate various client usage patterns as described in the section "Tuning timeout values."

-v

If set, this option prints out any new *autofs* mounts or unmounts. The automount command will perform a mount for each new direct and indirect map, and will perform an unmount for each map no longer listed in the master map or any of its submaps.

Automountd command-line options

-T

Turns on NFS call tracing, so the user sees the expansion of NFS calls handled by the automounter. If this option is used for debugging, then the standard output and standard error of the automounter daemon should be redirected to a file from its invocation in */etc/init/autofs*:

```
/usr/lib/autofs/automountd -T > /tmp/auto_nfscalls 2&1
Excerpt from /tmp/auto_nfscalls
t8      LOOKUP REQUEST: Tue Sep 28 10:39:36 1999
t8          name=news[] map=auto.tools opts=intr,nosuid path=/tools direct=0
t8      LOOKUP REPLY    : status=0
t1      MOUNT REQUEST:   Tue Sep 28 10:39:36 1999
t1          name=news[] map=auto.tools opts=intr,nosuid path=/tools direct=0
t1      MOUNT REPLY     : status=0, AUTOFS_DONE
```

In this example, the automounter daemon was asked by *autofs* to look up the directory *news*. It returned a status structure indicating that the daemon is requesting an NFS mount. The *autofs* filesystem then asked the daemon to perform the NFS mount, and the automounter returned a successful status. The prefixes *t8* and *t1* indicate the thread in the automounter daemon that did the operation.

-v

Turns on a verbose mode that logs status messages to the console.

-n

Turns off browsing of indirect maps.

-D var=value

Assigns the *value* to the variable *var* within the automounter's environment. The "Variable substitutions" section contains more information on variable substitutions within automounter maps.

The null map

The automounter also has a map "white-out" feature, via the *-null* special map. It is used after a directory to effectively delete any map entry affecting that directory from the automounter's set of maps. It must precede the map entry being deleted. For example:

```
/tools -null
```

This feature is used to override *auto_master* or direct map entries that may have been inherited from an NIS map. If you need to make per-machine changes to the automounter maps, or if you need local control over a mount point managed by the automounter, white-out the conflicting map entry with the *-null* map.

Tuning timeout values

When a filesystem has remained quiescent for some time, it is a candidate for unmounting. If the filesystem is busy, the attempts to unmount it will fail until the last open files and directories are closed. If an unmount attempt fails, the automounter tries it again later. However, it is difficult for the automounter to know if the filesystem is in fact in use. The simplest way to find out is to attempt to unmount it. So every ten minutes (or the period specified with the *-t* flag to *automount*) the automounter attempts to unmount every mounted filesystem.

There are two situations in which increasing the default unmount timeout period improves performance of the automounter:

- When client processes keep files open for more than ten minutes
- When one or more processes requiring automounted filesystems run regularly, with periods greater than the default timeout

When the automounter attempts to unmount a filesystem, it either succeeds, or the one or more open files from one or more processes cause the *umount()* call to return EBUSY. If there are several filesystems used by processes that behave in this fashion, then the automounter wastes numerous *umount()* system calls. The cost isn't just the overhead of checking to see if a filesystem is in use. There are several caches that hold references on the filesystem that must be flushed. All this activity consumes CPU time, which can impact the performance of a system that is already under high load. Increasing the default unmount timeout period (using the *-t* option) to match the average filehandle lifetime reduces the overhead of using the automounter:

```
automount -t 3600
```

The timeout period is specified in seconds. The reduced number of mount operations comes at a cost of a longer binding to the NFS server. If the filesystem is mounted when the NFS server crashes, you will have lost the "working set" advantage of using the automounter—your system hangs until the server recovers.

As mentioned earlier, regularly scheduled processes may require longer automounter timeout periods. Regularly scheduled processes include those run by *cron* and repetitive operations performed by interactive users, such as *make* runs done several times an hour during bug-fixing cycles. Each regularly scheduled process begins by causing a filesystem mount; a corresponding unmount is done sometime before its next invocation if the default timeout period is shorter than the time between invocations.

If the time between process instances is long, the overhead of these repetitive mount operations is negligible. However, a job that is run every ten minutes initiates a sequence of mount and unmount operations, adding to the overhead incurred by running the automounter. For interactive processes that run to completion in a minute or less, the time to complete the mount increases the response time of the system, and it is sure to elicit complaints. In both cases, system performance is improved by reducing the overhead of the automounter through a longer default unmount timeout period.

You may not want to use the automounter for filesystems that are mounted or accessed nearly constantly through the day. The mail spool, for example, might be better placed in each client's */etc/vfstab* file because it will be in near-constant use on the client. Most other filesystems benefit from the streamlined NFS administration provided by the automounter. Using the automounter is simplified even further by managing the maps themselves with NIS.

Integration with NIS

If maps are maintained on each client machine, then the administrative benefits of using the automounter are lost; the burden of maintenance is shifted away from the *vfstab* file and onto the new map files. To solve the administrative problem, all three types of maps may be distributed using NIS.

To add an automounter map to the NIS database, insert a set of clauses for it in the NIS master server's *Makefile in /var/yp*:

```
In definition of target all:
all:    passwd hosts ..... auto.tools

auto.tools:    auto.tools.time

auto.tools.time: $(DIR)/auto_tools
        -@if [ -f $(DIR)/auto_tools ]; then \
            sed -e "/^#/d" -e s/#.*$$// $(DIR)/auto_tools | \
                $(MAKEDBM) - /var/yp/$(DOM)/auto.tools;\
            touch auto.tools.time; \
            echo "updated auto.tools"; \
            if [ ! $(NOPUSH) ]; then \
                $(YPPUSH) auto.tools; \
                echo "pushed auto.tools"; \
            fi \
        else \
            echo "couldn't find $(DIR)/auto_tools"; \
        fi
```

The new map name must be added to the list of targets built by default when *make* is issued with no arguments. A dependency linking the map name *auto.tools* to the timestamp file *auto.tools.time* is added, and the large section defines how to rebuild the map and the timestamp file from the map source file. The *makefile* actions strip out all lines beginning with a comment (*#*) marker, and strip comments from the ends of lines. The *makedbm* program builds an NIS map from the input file. The input file should not have blank lines in it.

The key in an automounter map becomes the NIS map key, and the mount options and server and directory names are the data values. Dumping a map with *ypcat* requires the *-k* option to match up map keys and server information:

```
% ypcat auto.tools
-ro,intr thud:/epubs/deskset
jetstar:/usr/Bugview
-ro,intr mahimahi:/tools2/deskset1.0

% ypcat -k auto.tools
sundesk -ro,intr thud:/epubs/deskset
bugview jetstar:/usr/Bugview
deskset -ro,intr mahimahi:/tools2/deskset1.0
```

NIS-managed maps are specified by map name rather than by absolute pathname:

```
Master map
/tools          auto_tools       -ro
/source         auto_source      -rw
```

Mixing NIS and files in the same map

As with the password NIS map, it is sometimes necessary to have variations in the configuration on a per-machine basis. Using the notation +*mapname,* it is possible to include an NIS map in a local automounter map. For example, as mentioned earlier in this chapter, */etc/auto_master* file can have an entry in it like:

```
+auto_master
```

This is useful if you want more control over the order with which map information from the */etc/auto_master* file versus the name service gets processed. The appearance of this entry causes map information from the NIS *auto.master* map to read in as if it were where the +*auto_master* entry was. For example, let's say *nsswtch.conf* has an *automount:* entry that specifies *files* to be processed before *nis.* The *auto.master* map in NIS might contain:

```
/docs           auto_temporary          -ro
```

The */etc/auto_master* file might contain:

```
/tools          auto_tools          -ro
+auto_master
/docs           auto_docs
```

```
/src            auto_source
/-              auto_direct
```

The effect is that the accesses to */docs/XXX* are satisfied from the *auto_temporary* map and not from the *auto_docs* map.

The use of entries with leading plus signs is not limited to *auto_master* entries. Any of the maps that *auto_master* refers to can contain +*mapname* entries if they are local files. Suppose, for example, that client machines on your network share a common set of source trees, but some clients are allowed to access operating system source code as well. On those machines without source code rights, the */etc/auto_source* map contains a single reference to the NIS map:

```
+auto_source
```

However, on clients that have more privileges, the operating system source code mount points can be included with the NIS map:

```
sunos5.7        -ro     srcserv:/source/sunos5.7
sunos5.8        -ro     srcserv:/source/sunos5.8
nfs             -ro     bigguy:/source/nfs_internals
+auto_source
```

Updating NIS-managed automount maps

The automounter reads indirect NIS maps for each mount request it must handle. A change in one of these maps is reflected as soon as the map is built and pushed to the NIS servers. New tools get installed in */tools* by inserting a new map entry in *auto_tools* rather than editing the */etc/vfstab* files on each client machine. The automounter sees map updates the next time it has to perform a mount.

The only way to change the mount parameters for a currently mounted filesystem is to unmount the filesystem manually. Some automounters will also require that you send the automounter daemon a SIGHUP (kill -1). When the automounter receives this signal, it parses the *mnttab* file and notices that some of its mounted filesystems were unmounted by someone else. It invalidates the links for those mount points; the next reference through the same entry remounts the filesystem with the new parameters.

Direct maps are subject to an update restriction. While the maps may be updated with the automounter running, changes are not made visible through the automounter until it is restarted. Under Solaris, re-running the *automount* command suffices. The automounter creates a mount table entry for each direct mount point, so they cannot be added or removed without the automounter's intervention. If a direct mount point is removed from a direct map maintained by NIS, attempts to reference the mount point return "file not found" errors: the mount point is still listed in the *mnttab* file but the automounter's direct map no longer has a corresponding entry for it.

Using NIS to manage the automounter maps makes administration of a large number of NFS clients much simpler: all of the work that formerly went into */etc/vfstab* file maintenance is eliminated. In a large environment with hundreds of users, the task of map management can become quite complex as well. If new users are added to the system, or filesystems are shuffled to meet performance goals, then the automounter maps must be modified to reflect the new configurations. The benefits of using the automounter are significantly increased when the maps are simplified using key and variable substitutions.

Key and variable substitutions

There are two forms of substitutions that are performed in automounter maps: *variable substitution* and *key substitution*. Variables are useful for hiding architecture or operating system dependencies when maintaining a uniform naming scheme, while key substitutions impress a degree of regularity on the automounter maps.

Key substitutions

The ampersand (&) expands to the matched key value in a map; it is used in the server:directory path pair to copy key values into directory path component names. Let's say you have a map that lists all the exported directories on your network that exist for the purpose storing users' home directories. Let's call this map *auto_home_exports*. Initially, this map looks like:

```
thud            -rw     thud:/export/home/thud
wahoo           -rw     wahoo:/export/home/wahoo
mahimahi        -rw     mahimahi:/export/home/mahimahi
```

We can rewrite it using key substitution:

```
thud            -rw     &:/export/home/&
wahoo           -rw     &:/export/home/&
mahimahi        -rw     &:/export/home/&
```

With the right-hand side rewritten, the map's regular form can be further condensed using the asterisk (*) wildcard:

```
*       -rw     &:/export/home/&
```

The asterisk is a default case. Nothing after it will ever be matched, so it should be the last (or only) entry in the map. It matches all keys, providing a value for the & substitutions that fill in the right-hand side of the map information.

For example, assume that the clients are using the *auto_home_exports* map for the */home_exports* mount point. Every reference through */home_exports* matches the wildcard map entry. When a lookup of */home_exports/thud/jan* is performed, the automounter gets an RPC request to look up *thud* in the */home_exports* directory. Referring to the indirect map, the automounter finds the wildcard, which matches the key *thud*. The automounter makes *thud* the default key, and expands the *server:directory* component as:

```
thud:/export/home/thud
```

This entry is equivalent to a *thud*-specific entry:

```
thud -rw thud:/export/home/thud
```

Special case mappings may be added ahead of the wildcard map entry:

```
mahimahi2      -rw     mahimahi:/export/home/mahimahi2
*              -rw     &:/export/home/&
```

Of course, wildcards can get you into trouble as well. Assume that you are using the following simple indirect map for *auto_home_exports*:

```
*       -rw     &:/export/home/&
```

and a user tries to access */home_exports/foo*. The automounter then tries to mount *foo:/export/home/foo*, but it's probable that no host named *foo* exists. In this case, the user will get a somewhat puzzling "No such host" error message when the automounter cannot find the server's name in the NIS *hosts* map.

The concise wildcard-based naming scheme is useful for machines exporting a single home directory, but when multiple home directories are exported from several disks on a server, the one-to-one mapping of home directory names to server names breaks down. If naming conventions permit, you can create hostname aliases in the NIS *hosts* map that match the additional home directory names, allowing the wildcard map to be used.

To see how this works, let's simplify the following *auto_home_exports map* for the three servers *mahimahi, thud,* and *wahoo*:

```
mahimahi       -rw     mahimahi:/export/home/mahimahi
mahimahi2      -rw     mahimahi:/export/home/mahimahi2
thud           -rw     thud:/export/home/thud
thud2          -rw     thud:/export/home/thud2
thud3          -rw     thud:/export/home/thud3
wahoo          -rw     wahoo:/export/home/wahoo
```

Applying wildcard key matching substitution to the regularly named directories shortens the *auto_home_exports* map so that only the secondary and tertiary home directories are listed:

```
mahimahi2      -rw     mahimahi:/export/home/mahimahi2
thud2          -rw     thud:/export/home/thud2
```

```
thud3              -rw     thud:/export/home/thud3
*                  -rw     &:/export/home/&
```

Adding hostname aliases for *mahimahi* and *thud* to the hosts map condenses the *auto_home_servers* map even further:

NIS hosts map
```
192.9.201.5      mahimahi mahimahi2
192.9.201.6      thud thud2 thud3
192.9.201.7      wahoo
```

auto_home_servers map
```
*         -rw     &:/export/home/&
```

When a reference to */home_exports/thud2/jan* is seen by the automounter, the wildcard map turns it into the *server:directory* pair:

```
thud2:/export/home/thud2
```

Because *thud2* is a *hosts* database alias for *thud*, the mount request is sent to the right server.

This trick simply perpetuates the existing naming scheme but it does not help subsume all home directories under a single mount point. Users tend to like the C shell's tilde expansion mechanism, which locates a user's home directory from the NIS or local password files. Using a tilde reference such as *~jan* causes the correct mount to be completed as long as the */etc/passwd* file or *passwd* NIS map contains an entry like:

```
jan:K8pLWWc.J4XIY:999:99:Jan Smith:/home_servers/thud2/jan:/bin/csh:
```

But there is no obvious, consistent absolute path to every user's home directory, because the paths contain a hostname-specific component.

To make a completely uniform naming scheme, you need to build a fairly verbose map that hides the hostname dependencies in the home directory paths. Given the set of home directories:

```
/export/home/thud/stern
/export/home/thud2/jan
/export/home/mahimahi/johnc
/export/home/wahoo/kenney
```

an indirect *auto_home* map that mounts all users' home directories under */home* looks like this:

```
stern    -rw     thud:/export/home/thud/stern
jan      -rw     thud:/export/home/thud2/jan
johnc    -rw     mahimahi:/export/home/mahimahi/johnc
kenney   -rw     wahoo:/export/home/wahoo/kenney
```

Users can find any user through the */home* switchboard, without having to know their home directory server. This scheme is useful where hard coded, absolute pathnames are required. You can juggle user's home directories to distribute free disk space without having to search for all occurrences of absolute pathnames; changing the automounter map effects the change.

To make this switchboard available, the following would appear in the *auto_master* map:

```
/home          auto_home   -nobrowse
```

The *nobrowse* option is there because there is one entry in *auto_home* for every home directory, and unless your organization is quite small, you'll find that users that do the following:

```
% ls /home
```

generate lots of unnecessary network traffic.

Variable substitutions

If you are managing automounter maps through NIS, you may end up using the same map on machines running different releases of the operation system or having different CPU architectures. Directories with utilities or source code frequently need to be distinguished based on operating system release and machine architecture. Presenting these directories with a uniform naming scheme eliminates ugly pathnames, user confusion, and potentially dangerous actions, for example, a user building an object tree in the wrong subdirectory for that operating system release.

The automounter allows variables to be substituted into the right-hand components of map entries. The following example shows how to mount */usr/local/bin* from a set of architecture-specific directories:

```
Automounter daemon invocation
/usr/lib/autofs/automountd -D MACHTYPE=`/usr/bin/uname -m'

auto_direct map
/usr/local/bin  -ro    mahimahi:/local/bin.$MACHTYPE
```

Variable substitutions apply equally well to indirect maps. The following example shows how source code for a project is mapped out based on operating system release:

```
/usr/lib/autofs/automountd -D OPSYS="SunOS5.6"

notes    -rw    srcserv:/source/notes.$OPSYS
news     -rw    srcserv:/source/news.$OPSYS
chem     -rw    srcserv:/source/chem.$OPSYS
```

Variable and key substitution combine to collapse the map in the previous example to another one-liner:

```
*        -rw    srcserv:/source/&.$OPSYS
```

A source code automounter map is useful when there are one or more levels of dependencies in the source tree, or when the source trees themselves live on several different servers. The automounter ensures that the developers mount only those servers containing source code that they are currently using.

Builtin variables

Some automounters have builtin variables. The builtin variables for Solaris are shown in Table 9-2.

Table 9-2. Solaris automounter variables

Variable	Meaning
ARCH	output of `uname -m`
CPU	output of `uname -p`
HOST	output of `uname -n`
OSNAME	output of `uname -s`
OSREL	output of `uname -r`
OSVERS	output of `uname -v`
NATISA	output of `isainfo -n`

If you can use builtin variables, then you should use them instead of specifying the value of variables with the *-D* option to *automountd*. The reason is that editing the script that starts the automountd process is going to be very tedious as your site grows. So in the previous section, we had the example:

```
Automounter daemon invocation
/usr/lib/autofs/automountd -D MACHTYPE=`/usr/bin/uname -m'
```

Don't do that! Leave the *automountd* parameters alone, and instead have the map use the *$ARCH* builtin, instead of the custom *$MACHTYPE* variable:

```
auto_direct map
/usr/local/bin  -ro     mahimahi:/local/bin.$ARCH
```

Advanced map tricks

The automounter has several features that complement the "normal" NFS mount options. It can mount replicated filesystems from one of several potential servers, and it can perform hierarchical mounts of all of a server's directories when any one of them is referenced. This section starts with a discussion of these advanced automounter features, then explains how to get better performance out of the automounter by converting direct map entries into indirect maps and by using the automounter's subdirectory mount feature.

Replicated servers

Multiple location support in the automounter implements a simple network load-balancing scheme for replicated filesystems. At first glance, this seems to be a bit of overkill; after all, you don't need or want replication for read-write filesystems. However, serving large, read-only filesystems such as the manpages may add to an NFS server's request load. Having multiple servers share this load improves performance by reducing the total load placed on the most heavily used servers. Ideally, you want clients that are "close" to each server to mount its filesystems, reducing the amount of traffic that must go through bridges or routers.

For example, if you have four NFS servers that each export the manpages, the best client mounting scheme is probably not to have one-quarter of the clients mount */usr/man* from each server. Instead, clients should mount the manpages from the server that is closest to them. Replicated filesystems are included in automounter maps simply by listing all possible servers in the map:

```
/usr/man        -ro     wahoo:/usr/man mahimahi:/usr/man \
                        thud:/usr/man onaga:/usr/man
```

The backslash at the end of the first line continues this indirect map entry onto the next line. If more than one *server:directory* pair is listed in an automounter map, the automounter pings all servers by sending a request to the *null* procedure of all NFS servers. From the set that responds, the automounter picks one that is "closest" by comparing the address of the servers with that of the clients. Ties are broken by using the server that responded to the ping first. The selected server is used by the automounter to serve the mount point.

There is also an element of load balancing at work here: if one of the */usr/man* servers is so heavily loaded with other NFS traffic that it cannot reply to the ping before another server on the same net, then the client will choose the other server to handle its mount request. Solaris 2.6 introduced the feature of client-side failover, which was discussed in the section "Replication" in Chapter 6. While it doesn't explicitly implement load balancing, if, after the mount, one server becomes overloaded enough, a client will find the server to be unresponsive and will dynamically switch to another server. Keep in mind the following:

- If the *ro* mount option is not present, or if the *soft* option is present, client-side failover is not enabled, and in that situation, once a client performs a mount from a server, it continues to use that server until it unmounts the filesystem.

- If the list of servers providing the filesystem changes, once the filesystem is mounted, with or without failover, the client cannot choose a different server before unmounting its first choice.

You can use the first-answer feature of replicated map entries to solve the multihomed host problem presented in "Multihomed servers" in Chapter 16. Let's say that you have an NFS server on four networks, with hostnames *boris, boris-bb2, boris-bb3,* and *boris-bb4* on those networks. Mounting all filesystems from *boris* makes the multihomed host perform loopback packet routing, but using the "right" hostname requires knowing which name is on your network. Building an auto-mounter map with replicated entries solves this problem by letting the auto-mounter find the fastest route to *boris*:

```
natasha    -rw,hard       boris:/export/home/boris \
                          boris-bb2:/export/home/boris \
                          boris-bb3:/export/home/boris \
                          boris-bb4:/export/home/boris
```

This would be an entry in the *auto_home* map. Since the server pathnames are the same, you can use a shorter form of the replicated map entry, putting all of the server names in a comma-separated list:

```
natasha    -rw,hard    boris,boris-bb2,boris-bb3,boris-bb4:/home/boris
```

The network interface on *boris* that is closest to the client will respond first, and each NFS client of *boris* will mount */home/natasha* from the best network inter-face. Note that the replicated mount points don't refer to multiple filesystems, but rather multiple names for the same filesystem. The automounter just provides a neat way of managing all of them in a single place. Because */export/home/natasha* is mounted read-write, client-side failover is not enabled. This is somewhat unfor-tunate since this is the one situation where client-side failover of a writable file-system is safe: the filesystem is the same, because the physical host is the same. But the client has no way of knowing that.

When the automounter pings the remote servers, it's performing the equivalent of:

```
rpcinfo -u hostname nfs
```

for each listed server. If you see a larger number of *null* procedure calls than usual in the output of *nfsstat* on the NFS server, it might indicate that your auto-mounter mounts of replicated filesystems are being performed repeatedly. The *null* calls do not require any disk accesses to service, but they can consume net-work bandwidth on the server; if the number of *null* calls becomes excessive it may be due to client machines continually mounting and unmounting replicated filesystems. Changing the value of the *-t* option to *automount* (as discussed previ-ously in "Tuning timeout values") reduces the frequency of mounting and unmounting.

You can also examine the */etc/rmtab* file on the server to see how frequently its clients are mounting and unmounting automounted filesystems. When a file-system is mounted, an entry is added to the */etc/rmtab* file. When it gets unmounted, the entry isn't deleted from the file—it is commented out by making the first character in the line a pound sign (*#*):

```
#epeche:/usr/share/man
#haos:/usr/share/man
#epeche:/usr/share/man
depeche:/usr/share/man
chaos:/usr/share/man
```

In this example, client *depeche* has mounted */usr/share/man* three times, and client *chaos* has mounted that filesystem twice. This gives you client information to go along with the *null* NFS RPC counts provided by *nfsstat*—you can tell which clients have been repeatedly mounting and unmounting a filesystem. Watch the size of the */etc/rmtab* file over time; if it grows regularly and contains multiple entries for the same clients and filesystems, then you may want to change the automounter timeout value on those clients.

Hierarchical mounts

In addition to handling multiple servers for the same filesystem, the automounter can mount multiple trees from the same server in a hierarchy of mount points. Hierarchical mounts are simply a special form of indirect maps.

The -hosts map

The most widely used hierarchical mount is the builtin *-hosts* map, which mounts all exported filesystems from a named host.

The *-hosts* map references only the hosts database; the map semantics are built into the automounter. It is usually mounted on */net* indicating that it contains filesystems from the entire network. The following line would appear in the master map:

```
/net -hosts -nobrowse
```

Except when using the enhanced *autofs* automounter, a user can then force mounts of all filesystems from a server by referencing the server's name as a sub-directory of */net*:

```
% showmount -e wahoo
/export1     (everyone)
/export2   honeymoon
/export3   honeymoon
% cd /net/wahoo
% ls -l
total 3
drwxrwxr-x  22 root     staff       512 Aug 12 16:02 export1
drwxrwxr-x   8 root     staff       512 Feb 18  1999 export2
drwxrwxr-x   9 root     staff       512 Sep  8 16:19 export3
```

When the automounter has to mount a filesystem on */net*, it sends a request to the server asking for all exported filesystems. The automounter sorts the filesystems by pathname length, ensuring that subdirectories of exported filesystems appear later in the list than their parents.[*] The original automounter would then mount each item in the sorted list.

The enhanced *autofs* automounter will lazily mount each exported filesystem as soon as a process does something significant such as changing its current working directory to an exported filesystem:

```
% cd /net/wahoo
% ls -l
total 3
dr-xr-xr-x   1 root     root           1 Sep 28 14:54 export1
dr-xr-xr-x   1 root     root           1 Sep 28 14:54 export2
dr-xr-xr-x   1 root     root           1 Sep 28 14:54 export3
% cd export1
% cd ..
% ls -l
total 3
drwxrwxr-x  22 root     root         512 Aug 12 16:02 export1
dr-xr-xr-x   1 root     root           1 Sep 28 14:54 export2
dr-xr-xr-x   1 root     root           1 Sep 28 14:54 export3
```

The act of doing the *cd export1* causes the automounter to perform an NFS mount over the */net/wahoo/export1 autofs* vnode. Thus, users cannot casually force the client to mount each filesystem unless they do something like:

```
% ls /net/wahoo/*
```

This command invocation tells *ls* to read each directory of each exported file-system of *wahoo*. The *autofs* filesystem considers an invocation of its *readdir* entry point to be a significant operation worthy of triggering an NFS mount.

There are a number of caveats for using the *-hosts* map with automounters that don't support lazy mounting of hierarchies:

- By including the entire *hosts* database, the *hosts* map references servers that are both local and on remote networks; a casual reference to a remote server causes an NFS mount to occur through a router or gateway.

- If the server itself is slow, or has a large number of filesystems (diskless client servers), then the *-hosts* map has a definite performance impact.

- Unmounts of the filesystems are done from the bottom up, in the reverse order of the mounts. If a higher-level mount point is busy, then an unmount

---

[*] If a directory pathname has a length of x characters, then any of its subdirectory's pathnames have length $> x$. Sorting by pathname length puts a parent directory ahead of all paths to its subdirectories.

of the entire hierarchy fails. When the automounter fails to unmount a higher-level mount point, it must remount the filesystems it just unmounted. It walks back down the hierarchy from the busy mount point, mounting each filesystem. The remote server's filesystems are mounted on an all-or-nothing basis.

- Earlier in this section, we said that the "most widely used hierarchical mount is the builtin *-hosts* map." If you are not careful, it can be the most widely used map, period. The reason why this is not good is that *-hosts* is location-dependent. Once your users get used to accessing resources like */net/wahoo/tools,* instead of accessing */tools,* it becomes difficult to move the resource to a different physical location. It is best to discourage use of */net.* One way to do so is to respond rapidly to requests to modify existing maps, or add new maps, and also, bury the physical location several directories deep on the server that holds the resource. Users will prefer pathnames like */tools/debugger* over */net/wahoo/export/software/tools/debugger.*

These caveats don't apply to the enhanced *autofs* automounter. However, by default it does support browsing. Thus a new caveat is that if a network has lots of hosts, then users that do:

```
% ls /net
```

will trigger lots of network traffic as the automounter gets the list of hosts from NIS. Thus, you should use the *-nobrowse* option on the *-hosts* map.

Users sometimes complain that they cannot see a new filesystem exported from a server. This is because a */net* mount from the server was in effect before the filesystem was exported, and the automounter has to timeout the mount before unmounting and remounting. Rather than waiting for that to happen, a simple workaround is to tell your users to access the server under */net* with a name that differs by capitalizing one letter of the hostname. This works because hostnames are case-insensitive, yet Unix pathnames are case-sensitive. So, for example, if */net/wahoo* was in effect before *wahoo:/export4* was exported, then simply accessing */net/Wahoo* will allow you to access *export4* as well as the pre-existing *export1,* *export2,* and *export3.*

Hierarchical mounts in non -hosts maps

Let's return to our */tools* example. Recall that */tools* has:

```
/tools/deskset
/tools/sting
```

```
/tools/news
/tools/bugview
```

and is an indirect automounter map for the */tools* directory, called *auto_tools*:

```
deskset          -ro,intr mahimahi:/tools2/deskset
sting                     mahimahi:/tools2/sting
news                      thud:/tools3/news
bugview                   jetstar:/usr/bugview
```

/tools/deskset contains several subdirectories, one of which is *wonderworks-v1.0*. You recently get a Version 2.0 of Wonderworks, and you find that it requires more disk space than what *mahimahi:/tools2/deskset* has available. You have several choices here:

- Create a new map entry into *auto_tools* called *deskset2* for the new version of wonderworks. The problem with this is that your users expect to look in */tools/deskset*, and not */tools/deskset2* for the desktop productivity tools.

- Move the *deskset* directory from *mahimahi* to a server with a large partition. The problem is that this will impact existing users that have *mahimahi:/tools2/ deskset* mounted.

- Create a hierarchical mount for the *deskset* map entry such that */tools/deskset/ wonderworks-v2.0* is mounted from somewhere else. This solution has none of the disadvantages of the previous choices.

To do the last choice requires the following steps:

1. Create a mount point for *wonderworks-v2.0* on server *mahimahi*:

    On mahimahi:
    # mkdir /tools/deskset/wonderworks-v2.0

2. Create a directory on another server (e.g., *wahoo:/export/tools/deskset/wonderworks-v2.0*) with sufficient disk space, and copy the *wonderworks-v2.0* package to it. If necessary, export the directory via a new entry in */etc/dfs/ dfstab* and the *shareall* command.

3. Change the deskset entry in the *auto_tools* map to:

    ```
    deskset          / -ro,intr mahimahi:/tools2/deskset \
                     /wonderworks-v2.0 -ro,intr mahimahi:/tools2/deskset
    ```

Now when the user accesses */tools/deskset*, he or she will be able reference both */tools/wonderworks-v1.0* and */tools/wonderworks-v1.0*.

As the example suggests, the syntax of a hierarchical mount's map entry is:

key-name subdirectory1 [*−mount-options*] *server-filesystem-1* [*subdirectory2* [*−mount-options*] *server-filesystem-2*] . . .

where a *server-filesystem* is one of:

- *server_name:pathname*

- *server_name-i:pathname-i,server_name-ii:pathname-ii*[,...]

- *server_name-i,server_name-ii*[,...]:*pathname*

Conversion of direct maps

Direct mounts are useful for handling nonuniform naming schemes, but they may cause a number of performance problems if several direct mount points are included in a directory that is frequently searched. You can usually get better performance out of the automounter by converting direct maps into indirect maps. Instead of putting direct map mount points in the client filesystem, create symbolic links that point to a staging area managed by an indirect map.

Again, an example helps to explain the conversion process. Consider replacing a direct map for */usr/local* with an indirect map *auto_stage*. To convert the direct map into an indirect map, we first create a symbolic link */usr/local* that points to a staging area that we'll let the automounter manage:

```
Original direct map
/usr/local      mahimahi:/local/$ARCH
# ln -s /stage/local /usr/local

New entry in auto_master map
/stage          auto_stage      -ro

New indirect map auto_stage containing
local    -ro    mahimahi:/local/$ARCH
```

Note that */usr/local* didn't exist before we made the link, since it was managed by the automounter. Also, we don't have to create the */stage* staging directory, since it is an indirect map mount point.

The symbolic link points to a subdirectory of the mount point managed by the indirect map *auto_stage*. With the direct map, any reference to */usr/local* is directed to the */stage* mount point, which causes the automounter to mount the appropriate architecture-specific directory. This makes */usr/local* look like a link to the mount.

Let's say a user now accesses */usr/local/bin/emacs*. The client kernel follows */usr/local* down to the symbolic link, which points to the */stage/local* automounter mount point. The automounter picks up the reference to */stage* as a reference to the *auto_stage* map, and it uses the next component—*local*—as a key in the map. This causes *mahimahi:/local/$ARCH* to be automounted. If you have several direct mount points, they can all be converted into links sharing a single *auto_stage* map.

Multiple indirection

So far the only map we've seen that refers to other maps is the *auto_master* map. Let's collect all of the indirect maps we've added to *auto_master* in this chapter:

```
# Directory    Map             Mount Options
/home          auto_home       -nobrowse
/net           -hosts          -nobrowse
/tools         auto_tools      -ro
/source        auto_source     -rw
/stage         auto_stage      -ro
```

One problem with this approach is that the top-level root (/) directory is beginning to get cluttered. Of course, one could simply add another component to the mount directory. If we want to put everything under */auto*, then we could change indirect map entries of the master map to:

```
# Directory    Map             Mount Options
/auto/home     auto_home       -nobrowse
/auto/net      -hosts          -nobrowse
/auto/tools    auto_tools      -ro
/auto/source   auto_source     -rw
/auto/stage    auto_stage      -ro
```

If you are using the *autofs* automounter, then there is a more elegant approach: simply treat each indirect map as a map entry in new indirect map called *auto_auto*. To do this, the master map would look like:

```
# Directory    Map             Mount Options
/auto          auto_auto
/-             auto_direct
```

The *auto_auto* map is an indirect map. Like all other indirect maps, its first field has to be a directory relative to */auto*, its second field has to be a set of mount options, and its third field has to be the name of the thing we are mounting. Here is what *auto_auto* looks like:

```
# Directory    Options                       Map being mounted
home           -fstype=autofs,nobrowse        auto_home
net            -fstype=autofs,nobrowse        -hosts
tools          -fstype=autofs,ro              auto_tools
source         -fstype=autofs,rw              auto_source
stage          -fstype=autofs,ro              auto_stage
```

The second and third fields in *auto_auto* are basically swapped from what they would be in *auto_master*. The difference is the presence of the *fstype* option. This option is needed to unambiguously tell the *autofs* automounter that this is not map entry referring to an NFS-mounted filesystem.

There is no limit on multiple indirection. This fact allows you to create sensible hierarchies that can be extended ad infinitum. Let's return to the *auto_source* example, which contains:

```
sunos5.6        -ro     srcserv:/source/sunos5.6
sunos5.7        -ro     srcserv:/source/sunos5.7
nfs             -ro     bigguy:/source/nfs_internals
```

You've decided to add Linux, BSD, FreeBSD, and System V sources to this map, and you have multiple versions of each. Rather than having a map of contain entries called *sunos5.6, sunos5.7, linux1.0, linux2.0, bsd4.3, bsd4.4, sysVr3, sysVr4*, etc., you decide that you want a hierarchy that branches first on the name of the operating system and then on the release. So you change *auto_source* to:

```
bsd             -fstype=autofs          auto_bsd
linux           -fstype=autofs          auto_linux
nfs             -ro                     bigguy:/source/nfs_internals
sunos           -fstype=atofs           auto_sunos
sysv            -fstype=atofs           auto_sysv
```

The *auto_bsd* map might contain:

```
4.1c        -ro     ancient:/export/source/bsd4.1c
4.2         -ro     ancient:/export/source/bsd4.2
4.3         -ro     ancient:/export/source/bsd4.3
4.4         -ro     srcsrv:/source/bsd4.4
```

This should be enough to get the idea; for brevity, we won't expand on what the other maps might look like.

Note that the *auto_source* map example contains both entries with *fstype=autofs*, and an *nfs* entry referring to *bigguy:/source/nfs internals*.

By the way, you probably will want to leave the *-hosts* and *auto_home* maps at */net* and */home*. The reason is that lots of software assumes these mount points exist. So you would want *auto_master* to look like:

```
# Directory     Map             Mount Options
/auto           auto_auto
/home           auto_home       -nobrowse
/net            -hosts          -nobrowse
/-              auto_direct
```

Executable indirect maps

The *autofs* automounter contains another feature known as executable maps. If permissions on an indirect map file are marked as executable, then the *autofs* automounter assumes it is an executable program or shell script, and executes it, passing the key as the first and only argument to the program or script. The program or script must then display an indirect map entry, which can be hierarchal. For example, suppose */etc/auto_master* has:

```
# Directory     Map             Mount Options
/auto           auto_auto
/home           auto_home       -nobrowse
/net            -hosts          -nobrowse
```

```
/net2            /etc/auto_exec
/-               auto_direct
```

Examine */etc/auto_exec*:

```
% ls -l /etc/auto_exec
-rwxr-xr-x   1 root      sys           76 Oct 26 09:58 /etc/auto_exec
% cat /etc/auto_exec
#!/bin/sh
/usr/sbin/showmount -e $1 | \
awk 'NR > 1 {print $1        "'$1'":"$1 " \\"}' | sort
```

This script takes the key value as if it is a hostname, and asks the NFS server, via the *showmount* command, which filesystems are exported. The output of *showmount* is then formatted by the *awk* command to produce a hierarchical map entry. You can test the script manually by doing:

```
% /etc/auto_exec foo
/export1         foo:/export1 \
/export2         foo:/export2 \
```

Thus, the script implements functionality similar to */net*, with one difference. Note that the *-nobrowse* mount option isn't included in the */net2* entry of *auto_master*. This is because executable maps can't be browsed. There doesn't seem to be any reason why the enhanced *autofs* automounter couldn't have been implemented to support it, perhaps by having a *browse=* option that referred to yet another program or script to do the browsing.

If, for some reason, the executable program or script cannot resolve the key to a map entry, then it should display zero bytes of output to standard output. Any output displayed to standard error will be logged by the automounter onto the system console.

 Make sure that if you have an automounter map file with the executable permission bit set that you actually want it to be executed.

Side effects

The automounter has several side effects that cause confusion in both processes and users that encounter its emulated directories. This section uncovers some utilities that are disturbed by the automounter.

Long search paths

If you have many directories listed in your search path, logging into a system using the automounter for some of these directories increases your login time significantly. Instead of listing the directories in your search path, create "wrappers" for the utilities of interest and put them in */usr/local/bin*. The wrappers can set environment variables and execute the appropriate utility, causing the automounter to mount the necessary filesystem when you use it instead of when you log in.

For example, you can include Frame 6.0 in your search path in your *.cshrc* file:

```
set path = ( /tools/deskset/frame6.0/bin $path )
```

If */tools* is managed by the automounter, your shell causes */tools/deskset* to be mounted when it builds the command hash table after setting your search path. Instead of listing all directories in */tools*, create a wrapper in */usr/local/bin* for the *maker* utility in */tools/deskset/frame6.0/bin* so that you don't have to list any subdirectory of */tools* in your search path:

```
Wrapper for maker
#!/bin/sh
PATH=/tools/deskset/frame6.0/bin:$PATH
exec /tools/deskset/frame6.0/bin/maker
```

This wrapper sets the search path as well, so that any executables invoked by *maker* will be able to find related utilities in its executable directory. By putting this wrapper in */usr/local/bin*, you avoid having to automount */tools/frame6.0* when you log in. For just a few directories, the automounter overhead isn't that large, but with ten or more software packages loaded, logging in becomes a slow process. Furthermore, not mounting all of these filesystems when you log in shields you from server crashes: your workstation will only hang if one of the servers you're using crashes.

Avoiding automounted filesystems

Utilities run out of *cron*, such as nightly *find* jobs, are easily overworked by the automounter. The solution is to modify *cron* jobs to avoid remote filesystems:

- Confine *cron* jobs to run *find* on local filesystems.

- Use an option to *find* like *-xdev* or *-mount* to force *find* to not cross mount points.

This uses the above constraints to implement a script to search for core files:

```
mount | grep -v remote | awk ' { print $1 } ' | xargs -i find {} -name 'core*' -
mount | /usr/bin/mailx -s"core file report" joe@eng
```

The *mount* invocation shows what is currently mounted, *grep* filters out anything that isn't local, *awk* prints the first argument (the mount points), *xargs* passes each mount point to a separate invocation of *find*, and *find* searches for files starting with the name *core* within the mount point's filesystem.

10

In this chapter:
- *PC/NFS today*
- *Limitations of PC/NFS*
- *Configuring PC/NFS*
- *Common PC/NFS usage issues*
- *Printer services*

PC/NFS Clients

PC/NFS refers to an implementation of the NFS protocol for IBM-compatible personal computers running the Windows or NT operating systems. Originally, NFS implementations for the IBM-compatible PC were confined to the client-side of NFS. Today, most vendors of PC/NFS offer both a client and server, though they are often packaged and sold separately. This chapter is confined to PC/NFS clients, and where it uses the term "PC/NFS" the term "PC/NFS client" is meant.

Using PC/NFS, PC machines can mount NFS filesystems as logical disks and use them as large virtual disks. Note that a client-only implementation does not limit the direction or types of file transfer operations that are possible within PC/NFS. It simply means that the PC is always the active entity in the Windows-NFS server relationship; the user must mount an NFS filesystem on the PC and then copy files between it and the local disk. In this chapter, we'll look at why you would want to use PC/NFS, alternatives to PC/NFS, setting up PC/NFS, and PC/NFS usage issues.

PC/NFS today

The first NFS client for Microsoft DOS or Windows operating systems was developed by Sun Microsystems in the mid-1980s and was called "PC/NFS." The PC/NFS brand name has become a generic term to refer to any product that provides an NFS client feature on Microsoft operating systems. Today, Sun Microsystems has abandoned the PC/NFS business, leaving a fairly competitive field of several vendors of commercial PC/NFS products. There are also some freeware or shareware clients if you look hard enough, but there does not appear to be much development activity around them.

It is beyond the scope of this book to provide a detailed survey of PC/NFS implementations, since they each have unique features, and new releases for each arrive all the time. You can use Internet search engines, Usenet archives from sources like *google.com*, and as a last resort, queries to Usenet's *comp.protocols.nfs* news-group to get feedback on what products people prefer. You can also look at *www. connectathon.org* to see which companies test products at the annual Connecta-thon interoperability testing event. While the Connnectathon web site won't tell you which companies test NFS and which of those have PC/NFS clients, the list of companies is not too long, so you could go to the web site of each and see which have PC/NFS implementations.

When selecting a PC/NFS implementation, your minimum set of required features should include all of the following:

* NFS Versions 2 and 3
* NFS over UDP and TCP
* Some integration with Unix authorization

The last feature amounts to allowing users of PC/NFS clients to use the same pass-word to access the NFS server as they would if they were logging into the system the NFS server resides on. Some PC/NFS clients accomplish this by acting as an NIS client to access the password database from NIS. Most will also integrate by the use of the PCNFSD protocol. This was a protocol invented by Sun Microsys-tems to facilitate access to Unix password database authorization, as well as printers connected to Unix systems. Note that while support for this protocol is common among PC/NFS implementations, finding a PCNFSD server is not always easy. Ironically, even as of Solaris 8, Solaris doesn't include one. You should expect that the vendor of your selected PC/NFS client can provide a PCNFSD server for the Unix server platform you have deployed. If you have trouble, you might poke around the PC/NFS vendors websites. For example, Hummingbird's *ftp.hcl.com* FTP server has source and binaries for its HCLNFSD protocol. Note that the HCLNFSD protocol is similar in functionality to the PCNFSD protocol, but has been enhanced to work better with the Hummingbird PC/NFS product. HCLNFSD is *not* compatible with the PCNFSD protocol. While several non-Hummingbird PC/NFS implementations support HCLNFSD in addition to Hummingbird, if you have a PC/NFS client that supports only the PCNFSD protocol, Hummingbird's HCLNFSD implementation will be of no use. If you are in this predicament, try using a search engine to find PCNFSD source code or binaries. For example, typing this query into *www.google.com*:

```
source code for pcnfsd
```

turned up this URL:

http://www.sunfreeware.com/programlist.html

which had both source and binaries (Solaris 2.6, SPARC) for PCNFSD. Obviously, URLs come and go, so don't be surprised if you find PCNFSD somewhere else.

Advanced and interesting features of some PC/NFS implementations include:

- Kerberos V5 security for NFS mounts. This allows clients to access NFS servers that share filesystems via Kerberos V5 security only.

- RPC/DH security for NFS mounts. This allows clients to access NFS servers that share filesystems via RPC/DH security only.

- Integration with NIS+.

You should expect that future PC/NFS implementations will add features like NFS Version 4 and integration with LDAP (so that the Unix authentication database in LDAP can be accessed).

Limitations of PC/NFS

The NFS protocol is the *lingua franca* of file-sharing protocols in that it is implemented on the widest variety of operating system environments, both client and server. These environments include Unix (nearly all of them), Windows, NT, MacOS, MVS, OS/400, OS/2, VMS, many real-time operating systems, and systems designed for network-attached storage, such as the ONTAP system for Network Appliance's hardware. One reason why NFS has been so successful is that it is very simple. This simplicity has a price; NFS does not take the approach of supporting every arcane, operating-specific file semantic for all the environments it supports. Using NFS on non-Unix platforms, especially as a client, can limit you. This is very noticeable with PC/NFS. For example, the Windows and NT worlds have notions of enforced locking, which NFS, even via the NFS Lock Manager, does not provide. While PC/NFS implementations do their best to emulate this semantic and others, you will find that some applications work in unexpected ways over NFS.

These limitations apply to NFS Versions 2 and 3. NFS Version 4 goes a long way toward supporting Windows and NT file semantics. At the time of this writing, there were no known generally available NFS Version 4 implementations.

NFS versus SMB (CIFS)

SMB stands for Server Message Block and is the file access protocol that is native to Windows and NT. In 1996, Microsoft, the owner of the SMB protocol, renamed SMB to CIFS: the Common Internet File System. However, at the time of this writing, CIFS was not as common as NFS when it came to came to the variety of client implementations. CIFS is, however, growing in the number of server implementations. When you consider the plethora of low-end, network-attached storage boxes aimed at consumers and small office environments, that often support CIFS but not NFS, it is arguable that CIFS has surpassed NFS in the number of unique server implementations. The installed base of Windows and NT desktop computers as compared to non-Windows, non-NT desktops is a big reason for this trend.

Unix is becoming a popular platform for CIFS servers. This is likely due to the popularity of the open source package called Samba, which is a CIFS server for Unix platforms. Samba is developed and maintained by a world-wide community of programmers dedicated to producing a server as compatible with Microsoft's clients as possible. This is no mean task; at the time of this writing, the shared opinion of many in the CIFS server industry was that published CIFS specifications were inadequate to build a compatible server. The Samba developers, and no doubt other non-Microsoft implementors, have often resorted to using packet sniffers between existing Windows and NT clients and servers to deduce the protocol formats and semantics.

The emergence of Samba has led to a massive shift from deploying PC/NFS to deploying Samba instead. This is for at least three reasons:

- Samba is free of charge under Free Software Foundation's GNU Public License.

- It is easier for system administrators to install and maintain Samba on a few server hosts than to install and maintain PC/NFS on many client hosts.

- It is perceived that SMB has better security than NFS. This is false. Nor is it quite true to say that NFS has better security. You can have Kerberos V5 (see "Kerberos V5" in Chapter 12) security for your collection of PC/SMB clients if all your SMB servers run Windows 2000.* You can have Kerberos V5 security for certain PC/NFS clients if all your servers support NFS secured with Kerberos V5.†

  However, when comparing a situation where you cannot run Windows on all your SMB servers with a situation where you cannot run NFS servers that support Kerberos V5 or NFS/dh, (see "AUTH_DH: Diffie-Hellman authentication" in Chapter 12), then the SMB environment is more secure.

---

* At the time this book was written, only SMB servers on Windows 2000 supported Kerberos V5 security, partly because the Windows 2000 Kerberos V5 is incompatible with Kerberos V5 specification in RFC 1510. See the article, "Microsoft "embraces and extends" Kerberos V5," by Theodore Ts'o (USENIX *;login*, November, 1997).

† See "How secure is RPC/DH?" in Chapter 12 for the set of known NFS servers and PC/NFS clients that support Kerberos V5.

Why PC/NFS?

With the ubiquity of CIFS servers on Unix platforms, it begs the question, why run NFS on a Windows or NT client? This question was asked of the *comp.protocols. smb* and *comp.protocols.nfs* Usenet newsgroups in the summer of 2000. The responses can be summarized as follows:

Speed

Some respondents claimed that NFS was faster. An article by Jeff Ballard for *Network Computing* magazine's web site ("Increasing File Access Through SMB," March 6, 2000, *www.nwc.com*) compared three Unix-based SMB servers. An interesting quotation from the article is:

> If it's speed you want, NFS is probably a better solution [than SMB] for you.

Some direct research was done to investigate such claims. A 256 MB file was created in the */tmp* directory of a Solaris 8 file server. The server was an Ultra 10, with a 440 Mhz Ultra Sparc II processor and 512 MB of primary memory. A Windows 98 client (a Sony Vaio Z505HS, with a 500 Mhz Pentium III processor and 128 MB of primary memory) was used to copy (via Windows Explorer) the file between the file server and client. Using Samba as the SMB server, and native SMB client in the client, copying the file from the server to the client's *My Documents* folder took about one minute. However copying the file from the *My Documents* folder to the SMB server took about ten minutes. When using a free evaluation copy of an NFS client on the client, and the native NFS server on the Solaris 8 system, the respective file transfer times were about 45 seconds each. The quoted times are qualified with "about," because Windows Explorer did not display file transfer times, leaving the tester timing the results with the second hand of a timepiece.

The informal results were obtained without any tuning of the Solaris NFS server or the Samba server. It is quite possible that tuning the Samba server would have improved performance. Also, single stream file transfer speed is only one part of performance. About the only conclusion you should make is that you need to consider performance when making the decision to use NFS or SMB on Windows or NT clients.

Administrative complexity

Administering an SMB server is much different than administering an NFS server. Even if you are primarily a Unix shop with some Windows or NT clients, running an SMB server is still going to require at least as much expertise as running an NFS server.

One respondent said if you have few (ten or less) potential SMB clients, then you should strongly consider the trade-off of purchasing and installing commercial PC/NFS products on Windows and NT systems, versus devoting administration resources to SMB.

It required most of a day to install and configure the precompiled Samba binaries on the Solaris 8 server, plus lots of fiddling on the Windows 98 client, before the Network Neighborhood folder would recognize the Solaris 8 server. One unexpected result was that the passwords for SMB users apparently have to be managed separately from the corresponding Unix passwords, due to absence of an NTLM server on the network. This is because the Windows 98 client in the testbed was apparently sending encrypted passwords. Since the password database in NIS or files encrypts the passwords with a different scheme than Windows 98, Samba provides the option to maintain a separate database.

Software compatibility

One respondent claimed that there are Windows- or NT-based applications that work only over NFS. Rational's Clearcase, a software configuration management (source code control) system, was found to be an example.

There is one more consideration: reliability. The SMB protocol is based on TCP/IP and is very stateful, like the NFS lock manager. State recovery is very simplistic; when the TCP connection between an SMB client and server is lost, the SMB server removes all state that belongs to the SMB client. There is no mechanism to allow a client to reestablish state. In contrast to the NFS environment, the filing protocol has no state to recover. The NFS environment's locking protocol is stateful, but there is a state recovery mechanism: clients are given a grace period to re-establish state. The consequence of the SMB approach is that a client has a higher opportunity to lose its locks and other valuable state after a server restart than with the NFS environment. Andy Watson and Paul Benn, in a white paper from Network Appliance ("Multiprotocol Data Access: NFS, CIFS, and HTTP," TR3014, Revision 3, May 1999, *www.netapp.com*), wrote:

> If a CIFS client attempts file access on an established connection while the server is unavailable (down or not yet finished rebooting), this is effectively the equivalent of a failed disk from the perspective of the application software. In many cases, the application will report an error and allow the user to retry, but some applications will simply hang or exit.

At the time this book was written, this statement was true for both Windows ME and Windows 2000. However, there are rumors that future versions of Windows will address this recovery issue.

Configuring PC/NFS

The steps for installing and using a PC/NFS client will vary from vendor to vendor. You can expect that they will offer simple GUI-based installation that is compatible with Windows and NT norms, such as Installshield installation technology.

The installer will walk you through most, if not all, of the necessary configuration. At install time or connect time, you should be asked to state how you will be authenticated, via NIS or PCNFSD, and you might be asked if you want to cache your username and password.

Server-side PC/NFS configuration

There should not be any additional configuration for a PC/NFS client other than that needed for a Unix-based NFS client, unless the client requires the use of the PCNFSD protocol (either because you do not run NIS, or because you want to give your PCs access to Unix-connected printers). You may find that the PC/NFS client does not use reserved source ports (IP address port values less than 1024), and if so, you may have to disable "port monitoring" on the server as we'll discuss in "Port monitoring" in Chapter 12.

If you need to run a PCNFSD daemon on the server, you will want to add it to the *rc* scripts that get started when the Unix server boots up. For Solaris, you would add a script to */etc/init.d*:

```
#!/bin/sh
PCNFSD_NAME=hclnfsd # in /opt/pcnfs/bin
PATH=/opt/pcnfsd/bin:$PATH
export PATH

case "$1" in
start )

    # The named directory is used as a temporary area for print spool files.

        $PCNFSD -A /var/run
   ;;
stop )
   pkill $PCNFSD
   ;;
esac
exit 0
```

and then link this script to a hard or soft link in */etc/rc3.d* to start it before the NFS server.

Common PC/NFS usage issues

We'll conclude this chapter with a look at a few practical issues that come up in PC/NFS installations.

Mounting filesystems

Some PC/NFS clients will require an explicit step to connect to an NFS server. This step will be performed by a GUI application, where the user identifies the NFS server host and the server's filesystem to mount. The mount occurs on a drive letter rather than an arbitrary mount point.

Other PC/NFS clients will be tightly integrated with the Windows Network Neighborhood. You would then click on the Network Neighborhood icon on the desktop screen, and see a list of hosts advertising filesystems available to NFS or SMB clients.

In either case, to complete the connection to the server, you may be prompted with a password, unless you decide to connect as *nobody*. As *nobody*, you'll have access only to files with world read, write, or execute permissions.

If using AUTH_SYS, the client takes your password and sends it to the PCNFSD daemon server, or checks with the NIS or NIS+ server's *passwd* map to see if you are authorized to assume that AUTH_SYS identity. Thus, it is the client, and not the NFS server, that is performing the authentication.* However, if the connection uses NFS/dh (see "AUTH_DH: Diffie Hellman authentication" in Chapter 12) or Kerberized NFS (see "Enabling Kerberized NFS" in Chapter 12), then the server performs the authentication without sending a password to the server, encrypted or not.

Checking file permissions

Windows/NT and Unix have different file permissions conventions. By default, users on PCs are given the permissions of the anonymous user *nobody*, which generally means that PC users can access files with the appropriate world permissions. As we'll discuss in "Superuser mapping" in Chapter 12, being mapped to *nobody* is very restrictive and may prevent users from accessing their home directories on Unix file servers.

With NFS Version 2, there is no mechanism for Windows or NT to perform Unix file permission checking. File permissions exist only on the Unix server side, not on the PC/NFS side. This problem is solved by calling on the PCNFSD server. The first time the PC/NFS user accesses the server, the PC/NFS client mounts the filesystem and contacts the PCNFSD server to get user identifiers, group identifiers, and supplementary group identifiers for the authenticated user. The PC/NFS client can then compare the identifiers with the attributes (user and group ownership and permissions) of files accessed to see if the user should have access or not.

---

* The same is true when using a Unix NFS client with AUTH_SYS.

If the NFS mount uses NFS Version 3, which has an ACCESS procedure, contacting the PCNFSD server for the user's identifiers for the purpose of permission is
not necessary. Of course, if AUTH_SYS is being used, the user's identifiers are still
necessary.

Unix to Windows/NT text file conversion

Windows/NT and Unix differ in their end-of-line and end-of-file conventions on
text files. PC/NFS includes the *dos2unix* and *unix2dos* utilities to convert between
the two formats (the text editor you use on Windows might have the capability to
convert between the two text formats as well). When converting to Windows
format, Unix end-of-line characters (\n) are converted to newlines and carriage
returns, and an end-of-file character (CTRL-Z) is added. Going the other way, extra
carriage returns and the end-of-file marker are stripped out of the file.

If you look at a Unix text file on a PC without doing the end-of-line conversion,
you'll find that consecutive lines of text fall into a stepped arrangement instead of
starting on the left margin:

```
C> type h:\test.txt
This is a line
                of text without carriage returns
```

In this example, you need to convert file *test* to Windows format before reading it
on the PC/NFS client. The conversion entails the addition of carriage returns
(CTRL-M characters) to the end of each line and adding an end-of-file marker
(CTRL-Z) to the end of the file.

You can put Windows files of any sort—executable, binary, or text—on a Unix
fileserver and access them using normal Windows mechanisms. PC/NFS doesn't
care about the content of the files. The file format conversion problem exists only
for text files that were created on one system that must be read on another. If you
put a Windows binary on a Unix NFS server, it will not require any format conversion to be read and executed by the PC/NFS client.

Text file conversion utilities are available on Unix as well. Solaris has *unix2dos*
and *dos2unix*. Linux has *mcopy*.

Printer services

PC/NFS lets you access a printer attached to a Unix host by redirecting printer
output to a file on the PC/NFS print host. It's up to the server to spool the file to
the printer, using the standard Unix *lpr* or *lp* mechanism. There's no requirement
that the Unix printer be directly attached to the print host; if the server has to print
remotely, it does so transparently to the PC/NFS client.

The PC/NFS print and authentication functions are performed by the same machine: both services are handled by the PCNFSD daemon that runs on the authentication server. You may choose to run PCNFSD daemons on several NFS servers to separate the authentication and printing services. PC/NFS clients will send requests to PCNFSD daemons used for printing if the PC printer definitions explicitly name the print host.

Note that some PC/NFS implementations support printing via the LPR protocol, thus obviating the need to run the PCNFSD daemon if it is not needed for authentication and permissions checking purposes.

11

In this chapter:
• What is file locking?
• NFS and file locking
• Troubleshooting
  locking problems

File Locking

In "File locking" in Chapter 7, we introduced the concept of file locking and the two primary components: the RPC lock daemon and the status monitor. This chapter will delve more deeply into file locking and will examine the administrative aspects.

What is file locking?

File locking is the act of ensuring that when you access a file, usually via a software application, no one can change the file until you are done examining it. If you want to modify the file, then file locking ensures that no one else can examine or modify the file until you are done modifying it.

The earliest versions of Unix had no way to lock files except to create lock files. The idea is that two or more processes would more or less simultaneously try to create a lock file in exclusive mode, via the O_EXCL flag of the *open()* system call. The operating system would return success to the process that won the race, and a "file exists" error to losing processes. One problem with this scheme is that it relies on the winning process to remove the lock file before it exits. If the process is running buggy software, this might not happen. Some applications mitigate this problem by recording the process ID of the winner into the contents of the lock file. A process that finds that it gets a "file exists" error can then read the lock file to see if the owning process is still running.

Still, lock files can be clumsy. In the 1980s, Unix versions were released with file locking support built into the operating system. The System V branch of Unix offered file locking via the *fcntl()* system call, whereas the BSD branch provided the *flock()* system call. In both cases, when the process that creates the lock dies, the lock will be automatically released.

Exclusive and shared locks

Both *fcntl* and *flock* give the choice of either an exclusive lock, where only one process could hold the lock, or a shared lock, where multiple holders could simultaneously exist, to the exclusion of holders of the exclusive lock. The exclusive lock is sometimes called a "single writer" lock, because its exclusive nature lends itself to allowing safe writes to a file. The shared lock is sometimes called a "multiple readers" lock because its shared nature lends itself to allowing multiple safe reads of a file.

Record locks

The *fcntl* system call also has the feature of byte range record locking. This means that the application can partition a file into as many arbitrarily sized segments or records that it wants, and by specifying a file offset and length, lock them. Thus, it is possible to have both an exclusive lock and a shared lock on a file, provided the file offsets and lengths of each record lock do not overlap.

Mandatory versus advisory locking

Both *fcntl* and *flock* offer *advisory* locking. Advisory locking is locking that requires the cooperation of participating processes. Suppose process A acquires an exclusive lock on the file, with the intent to write it. Suppose process B opens the file with the intent to write it. If process B fails to acquire a lock, there is nothing to prevent it from issuing a write system call and corrupting the process that A is writing. For this reason, advisory locking is sometimes called *unenforced* locking.

System V (and therefore Solaris) offers *mandatory* or *enforced* locking as an option. This option is enabled if mandatory lock permissions are set on a file. Mandatory lock permissions are an overload of the set group ID execution bit (02000 in octal). If the set group ID execution bit is set, and if the group execution bit is not set, then all reads and writes to the file will use enforced locking. So, for example:

```
% chmod 2644 example
% ls -l example
-rw-r-lr--   1 mre       staff          9 Dec 28 10:52 example
```

This makes file *example* readable and writable by the file's owner, and readable by everyone else. The appearance of the *l* in the first field of the output of the *ls* command tells you that mandatory locking is enabled. Of course, you can use any combination of read or write permissions for the file's owner, group, and world.

If the mandatory lock permissions are set on a file, then every *write()* or *read()* system call results in an implicit sequence of:

```
fcntl(...); /* lock the file at the range we are reading or writing */
read(...); /* or */ write(...);
fcntl(...); /* unlock the file at the range locked above */
```

What if the process has already acquired a lock by an explicit *fcntl* call? If the range locked is equal to or encompasses the range the read or write is done on, then no implicit pair of *fcntl* calls are done. If the range explicitly locked partly overlaps the range read or write will do, then implicit *fcntl* calls are done on the unlocked portion of the range.

Mandatory locking seems very useful, but it is open to denial of service attacks. Suppose mandatory lock permissions are set on a file. An attacker named Mallet decides to issue an *fcntl* call to get an exclusive lock on the entire file. Bob now tries to read the file and finds that his application hangs. A proponent of mandatory locking might point out that the mistake was in allowing the file to be accessible by Mallet (if Mallet can't open the file, he can't lock it). The counter argument is that if you are going to rely on permissions to avoid a denial of service (and restricted permissions are a good thing to have for critical applications), then the set of users who can access the file is limited to those with a vested interest in avoiding denial of service. In that case, mandatory locking is no more useful than advisory locking.

Windows/NT locking scheme

The discussion so far has been about Unix locking paradigms. The Windows world has a different paradigm. There are two major differences between Unix and Windows locking:

- The first difference is that the Windows world supports a share reservation programming interface. Share reservations apply to the entire file and are specified at the time a file is created or opened. A share reservation consists of a pair of modes. The first is the access mode, which is how the application will access the file: read, write, or read/write. The second is the access that the application will deny to other applications: none, read, write, or read/write. When the application attempts to open a file, the operating system checks to see if there are any other open requests on the file. If so, it first compares the application's access mode with the deny mode of the other openers. If there is a match, then the open is denied. If not, then the operating system compares the application's deny mode with the access mode of the other openers. Again, if there is a match, the open is denied.

- The second difference is that there is no advisory locking. Whole file locking, byte range locking, and share reservation locking are all mandatory or enforced.*

 Share reservations in the Windows world do not interact at all with Windows byte range or whole file locking.

NFS and file locking

The NFS (Versions 2 and 3) protocol does not support file locking, but the NFS environment supports an ancillary protocol called NLM, which originally stood for "Network Lock Manager." When an NFS filesystem on an NFS client gets a request to lock a file, instead of an NFS remote procedure call, it generates an NLM remote procedure call.

The NLM protocol

The NLM protocol consists of remote procedure calls that pattern *fcntl* arguments and results. Because blocking locks are supported (a process blocks waiting for a lock that conflicts with another holder), the NLM protocol has the notion of callbacks, from the file server to the NLM client to notify that a lock is available. In this way, the NLM client sometimes acts as an RPC server in order to receive delayed results from lock calls.

NLM recovery

The NFS protocol is stateless, but because file locking is inherently stateful, NLM is stateful. This results in a more complex scheme to recover from failures. There are three types of recovery scenarios to consider:

- Server crash
- Client crash
- Network partition

Server crash

When the NLM server crashes, NLM clients that are holding locks must reestablish them on the server when it restarts. The NLM protocol deals with this by having

---

* As it turns out, very few Windows programs rely on byte range mandatory locking.

the status monitor on the server send a notification message to the status monitor of each NLM client that was holding locks. The initial period after a server restart is called the grace period. During the grace period, only requests to reestablish locks are granted. Thus, clients that reestablish locks during the grace period are guaranteed to not lose their locks.

Client crash

When an NLM client crashes, it is desirable that any locks it was holding at the time be removed from all the NLM servers it had locks on. The NLM protocol deals with this by having the status monitor on the client send a message to each server's status monitor once the client reboots. The client reboot indication tells the server that the client no longer needs its locks.

Of course, if the client crashes and never comes back to life, the client's locks will persist indefinitely. This is not good for two reasons:

- Resources are indefinitely leaked.

- Eventually another client will want to get a conflicting lock on at least one of the files the crashed client had locked. Thus the other client is postponed indefinitely.

This is one of the administrative issues you will need to deal with, which we will cover later in this chapter.

Network partition

Suppose an NLM client is holding a lock, but the network route between it and the NLM server goes down: a network partition. At this point, from the perspective of the server, the situation is indistinguishable from a client that crashes but never comes back. Again, this is a situation you will need to handle.

Mandatory locking and NFS

NLM supports only advisory whole file and byte range locking, and until NFS Version 4 is deployed, this means that the NFS environment cannot support mandatory whole file and byte range locking. The reason goes back to how mandatory locking interacts with advisory *fcntl* calls.

Let's suppose a process with ID 1867 issues an *fcntl* exclusive lock call on the entire range of a local file that has mandatory lock permissions set. This *fcntl* call is an advisory lock. Now the process attempts to write the file. The operating system can tell that process 1867 holds an advisory lock, and so, it allows the write to proceed, rather than attempting to acquire the advisory lock on behalf of the process 1867 for the duration of the write. Now suppose process 1867 does the same sequence on another file with mandatory lock permissions, but this file is on an NFS filesystem. Process 1867 issues an *fcntl* exclusive lock call on the entire range of a file that has mandatory lock permissions set. Now process 1867 attempts to write the file. While the NLM protocol has fields in its lock requests to uniquely identify the process on the client that locked the file, the NFS protocol has no fields to identify the processes that are doing writes or reads. The file is advisory locked, and it has the mandatory lock permissions set, yet the NFS server has no way of knowing if the process that sent the write request is the same one that obtained the lock. Thus, the NFS server cannot lock the file on behalf of the NFS client. For this reason, some NFS servers, including Solaris servers, refuse any read or write to a file with the mandatory lock permissions set.

NFS and Windows lock semantics

The NLM protocol supports byte range locking and share reservations.

While Windows byte range locking is mandatory, on Unix servers it will be advisory. To the dismay of Windows software developers, this means that non-PC/NFS clients might step on PC/NFS clients, because the non-PC/NFS client does not try to acquire a lock. It also means that servers that support both NFS/NLM and SMB might not correctly handle cases where an NFS client is doing a read or write to a file that an SMB client has established a mandatory lock on.

PC/NFS clients will emulate share reservation semantics by issuing the share reservation remote procedure calls to the NLM server. However, most non-PC/NFS clients, or even local processes on Unix NLM servers will not honor the deny semantics of the share reservation of the PC/NFS client. Another problem with the emulation is that Windows semantics expect the share reservation and exclusive file creation to be atomic. The share reservation and file creation go out as separate operations, hence no atomicity, allowing a window of vulnerability, where a client can succeed in its exclusive create, but not get the share reservation.

Troubleshooting locking problems

Lock problems will be evident when an NFS client tries to lock a file, and it fails because someone has it locked. For applications that share access to files, the expectation is that locks will be short-lived. Thus, the pattern your users will notice when something is awry is that yesterday an application started up quite quickly, but today it hangs. Usually it is because an NFS/NLM client holds a lock on a file that your application needs to lock, and the holding client has crashed.

Diagnosing NFS lock hangs

On Solaris, you can use tools like *pstack* and *truss* to verify that processes are hanging in a lock request:

```
client1% ps -eaf | grep SuperApp
    mre 23796 10031  0 11:13:22 pts/6     0:00 SuperApp
client1% pstack 23796
23796:  SuperApp
 ff313134 fcntl    (1, 7, ffbef9dc)
 ff30de48 fcntl    (1, 7, ffbef9dc, 0, 0, 0) + 1c8
 ff30e254 lockf    (1, 1, 0, 2, ff332584, ff2a0140) + 98
 0001086c main     (1, ffbefac4, ffbefacc, 20800, 0, 0) + 1c
 00010824 _start   (0, 0, 0, 0, 0, 0) + dc
client1% truss -p 23796
fcntl(1, F_SETLKW, 0xFFBEF9DC)  (sleeping...)
```

This verifies that the application is stuck in a lock request. We can use *pfiles* to see what is going on with the files of process 23796:

```
client1% pfiles 23796
pfiles 23796
23796:  SuperApp
  Current rlimit: 256 file descriptors
   0: S_IFCHR mode:0620 dev:136,0 ino:37990 uid:466 gid:7 rdev:24,37
      O_RDWR
   1: S_IFREG mode:0644 dev:208,1823 ino:5516985 uid:466 gid:300 size:0
      O_WRONLY|O_LARGEFILE
      advisory write lock set by process 3242
   2: S_IFCHR mode:0620 dev:136,0 ino:37990 uid:466 gid:7 rdev:24,37
      O_RDWR
```

That we are told that there is an advisory lock set on file descriptor 1 that is set by another process, process ID 3242, is useful, but unfortunately it doesn't tell us if 3242 is a local process or a process on another NFS client or NFS server. We also aren't told if the file mapped to file descriptor 1 is a local file, or an NFS file. We are, however, told that the major and minor device numbers of the filesystem are 208 and 1823 respectively. If you run the *mount* command without any arguments, this dumps the list of mounted file systems. You should see a display similar to:

```
/ on /dev/dsk/c0t0d0s0 read/write/setuid/intr/largefiles/onerror=panic/dev=2200000
on Thu Dec 21 11:13:33 2000
/usr on /dev/dsk/c0t0d0s6 read/write/setuid/intr/largefiles/onerror=panic/
dev=2200006 on Thu Dec 21 11:13:34 2000
/proc on /proc read/write/setuid/dev=31c0000 on Thu Dec 21 11:13:29 2000
/dev/fd on fd read/write/setuid/dev=32c0000 on Thu Dec 21 11:13:34 2000
/etc/mnttab on mnttab read/write/setuid/dev=3380000 on Thu Dec 21 11:13:35 2000
/var on /dev/dsk/c0t0d0s7 read/write/setuid/intr/largefiles/onerror=panic/
dev=2200007 on Thu Dec 21 11:13:40 2000
/home/mre on spike:/export/home/mre remote/read/write/setuid/intr/dev=340071f on
Thu Dec 28 08:51:30 2000
```

The numbers after *dev=* are in hexadecimal. Device numbers are constructed by taking the major number, shifting it left several bits, and then adding the minor number. Convert the minor number 1823 to hexadecimal, and look for it in the mount table:

```
client1% printf "%x\n" 1823
71f
client1% mount | grep 'dev=.*71f'
/home/mre on spike:/export/home/mre remote/read/write/setuid/intr/dev=340071f on
Thu Dec 28 08:51:30 2000
```

We now know four things:

- This is an NFS file we are blocking on.
- The NFS server name is *spike*.
- The filesystem on the server is */export/home/mre*.
- The inode number of the file is 5516985.

One obvious cause you should first eliminate is whether the NFS server *spike* has crashed or not. If it hasn't crashed, then the next step is to examine the server.

Examining lock state on NFS/NLM servers

Solaris and other System V-derived systems have a useful tool called *crash* for analyzing system state. Crash actually reads the Unix kernel's memory and formats its data structures in a more human readable form. Continuing with the example from "Diagnosing NFS lock hangs," assuming */export/home/mre* is a directory on a UFS filesystem, which can be verified by doing:

```
spike# df -F ufs | grep /export
/export                 (/dev/dsk/c0t0d0s7 ):  503804 blocks   436848 files
```

then you can use *crash* to get more lock state.

The *crash* command is like a shell, but with internal commands for examining kernel state. The internal command we will be using is *lck*:

```
spike# crash
dumpfile = /dev/mem, namelist = /dev/ksyms, outfile = stdout
> lck
Active and Sleep Locks:
INO         TYP START END      PROC PID  FLAGS STATE  PREV     NEXT    LOCK
30000c3ee18 w   0     0        13   136  0021  3      48bf0f8  ae9008  6878d00
30000dd8710 w   0     MAXEND   17   212  0001  3      8f1a48   8f02d8  8f0e18
30001cce1c0 w   193   MAXEND   -1   3242 2021  3      6878850  c43a08  2338a38

Summary From List:
  TOTAL    ACTIVE   SLEEP
    3        3        0
>
```

An important field is PROC. PROC is the "slot" number of the process. If it is -1, that indicates that the lock is being held by a nonlocal (i.e., an NFS client) process, and the PID field thus indicates the process ID, relative to the NFS client. In the sample display, we see one such entry:

```
30001cce1c0  w   193    MAXEND  -1   3242  2021 3      6878850   c43a08   2338a38
```

Note that the process id, 3242, is equal to that which the *pfiles* command displayed earlier in this example. We can confirm that this lock is for the file in question via *crash*'s *uinode* command:

```
> uinode 30001cce1c0
UFS INODE MAX TABLE SIZE = 34020
ADDR          MAJ/MIN   INUMB  RCNT LINK   UID   GID    SIZE   MODE   FLAGS
30001cce1c0  136,  7   5516985  2    1    466   300    403  f---644  mt rf
>
```

The inode numbers match what *pfiles* earlier displayed on the NFS client. However, inode numbers are unique per local filesystem. We can make doubly sure this is the file by comparing the major and minor device numbers from the *uinode* command, 136 and 7, with that of the filesystem that is mounted on */export*:

```
spike# ls -lL /dev/dsk/c0t0d0s7
brw-------  1 root    sys     136,  7 May  6  2000 /dev/dsk/c0t0d0s7
spike#
```

Clearing lock state

Continuing with our example from "Examining lock state on NFS/NLM servers," at this point we know that the file is locked by another NFS client. Unfortunately, we don't know which client it is, as *crash* won't give us that information. We do however have a potential list of clients in the server's */var/statmon/sm* directory:

```
spike# cd /var/statmon/sm
spike# ls
client1      ipv4.10.1.0.25  ipv4.10.1.0.26  gonzo     java
```

The entries prefixed with *ipv4* are just symbolic links to other entries. The non-symbolic link entries identify the hosts we want to check for.

The most likely cause of the lock not getting released is that the holding NFS client has crashed. You can take the list of hosts from the */var/statmon/sm* directory and check if any are dead, or not responding due to a network partition. Once you determine which are dead, you can use Solaris's *clear_locks* command to clear lock state. Let's suppose you determine that *gonzo* is dead. Then you would do:

```
spike# clear_locks gonzo
```

If clearing the lock state of dead clients doesn't fix the problem, then perhaps a now-live client crashed, but for some reason after it rebooted, its status monitor did not send a notification to the NLM server's status monitor. You can log onto the live clients and check if they are currently mounting the filesystem from the server (in our example, *spike:/export*). If they are not, then you should consider using *clear_locks* to clear any residual lock state those clients might have had.

Ultimately, you may be forced to reboot your server. Short of that there are other things you could do. Since you know the inode number and filesystem of file in question, you can determine the file's name:

```
spike# cd /export
find . -inum 5516985 -print
./home/mre/database
```

You could rename file *database* to something else, and copy it back to a file named *database*. Then kill and restart the *SuperApp* application on *client1*. Of course, such an approach requires intimate knowledge or experience with the application to know if this will be safe.

12

Network Security

The simplicity and transparency provided by NFS and NIS must be weighed against security concerns. Providing access to all files to all users may not be in the best interests of security, particularly if the files contain sensitive or proprietary data. Not all hosts may be considered equally secure or "open," so access may be restricted to certain users. Transparency must be limited when dealing with secured hosts: if you have taken precautions to prevent unauthorized access to a machine, you don't want someone to be able to sit down and use an open window or logged-in terminal to access the secured machine. To enforce access restrictions, you always want password verification for users, which means eliminating some of the network transparency provided by NIS.

This chapter describes mechanisms for tightening access restrictions to machines and filesystems. It is not intended to be a complete list of security loopholes and their fixes. The facilities and administrative techniques covered are meant to complement the network transparency provided by NFS and NIS while still enforcing local security measures. For a more detailed treatment of security issues, refer to *Practical Unix Security*, by Garfinkel and Spafford (O'Reilly & Associates, 1996).

User-oriented network security

One area of concern is user access to hosts on the network. Figure 12-1 shows several classes of permissions to consider, reflecting the ways in which a user might access a host from another host on the network.

Remote logins are not the only concern; remote execution of commands using *rsh* should be considered in the same context. This section covers only login restrictions; we'll look at protecting data in NFS filesystems later in this chapter. Local login restrictions are defined by the local host's password file, NIS password maps,

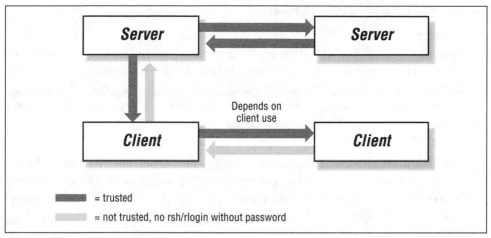

Figure 12-1. Client-server remote logins

and the use of netgroups. Across the network, access is determined by the notion of trusted hosts and trusted users.

Trusted hosts and trusted users

Defining a *trusted host* requires two machines: one that will be trusted and one that is extending the trust to it. The local host *lh* trusts remote host *rh* if users can log into *lh* from *rh* without supplying their passwords. Similarly, a user is trusted if he or she can log into a host from some remote machine without supplying a password. Trust is defined only for the local host; users and machines may be trusted on some systems but not on others.

The relationships between hosts often define the realm of trusted users and trusted hosts. Two NIS or NFS clients, for example, may trust all users and all other client hosts. On the NFS server, only other servers may be trusted hosts and only the system administration staff may be trusted users.

The following trusted user and trusted host descriptions apply in an environment in which you do not have to be wary of users or outsiders who will attempt to compromise security. These are basic security measures that fit in with the other network management strategies discussed in this book. If you need to secure your systems against all attacks, then you must consider the effects of having security compromised on any machine in your network. Again, these extensive security mechanisms are discussed in *Practical Unix Security*.

Some of the common patterns of trusting hosts and users are:

Server-Server

Generally, servers trust each other. A few users can be trusted in server-to-server relationships if each server has a password file that contains a subset of the NIS password map, or a password file with no NIS references. To emphasize the previous warning, extending trust between servers means that if one server is compromised, then they all are.

Server-Client

Most clients should trust the servers and users on the servers. A system administrator may need to run performance monitoring daemons on the client from the server and require transparent access to the client. Similarly, the server may be used to distribute files to the clients on a regular basis.

Client-Server

This is probably the most restrictive relationship. Only users with a need to use a service are generally given transparent access to the servers. Remote access to the server for access to a server's printer can be controlled via the *-u* option to the *lpadmin* command, instead of by trusting client machines on the server.

Client-Client

Client-client relationships depend upon how you have centralized your disk resources. If all files live on one or more fileservers, then client-to-client relationships are generally relaxed. However, if you are using the clients as isolated systems, with some per-client storage containing private data, then client-client relationships look more like those between clients and servers. The scope of the client-client relationships depends upon the sensitivity of the data on the clients: if you don't want other users to see the private data, then you must treat the client machine like a server.

The */etc/hosts.equiv* and *.rhosts* files (in each user's home directory) define the set of trusted hosts, users, and user-host pairs for each system. Again, trust and transparent access are granted by the machine being accessed remotely, so these configuration files vary from host to host. The *.rhosts* file is maintained by each user and specifies a list of hosts or user-host pairs that are also parsed for determining if a host or user is trusted.

Enabling transparent access

Both *rlogin* and *rsh* use the *ruserok()* library routine to bypass the normal login and password security mechanism. The *ruserok()* routine is invoked on the server side of a connection to see if the remote user gets transparent (i.e., no password prompt) access. To understand the semantics, let's look at its function prototype:

```
int ruserok(const char *rhost, int suser, const char *ruser,
    const char *luser);
```

The *rhost* parameter is the name of the remote host from where the remote user is. The *ruser* parameter is the login name of the remote user. The *luser* parameter is the name of local login name that the remote user wants transparent access to. Often *luser* and *ruser* are the same, but not always. The *suser* parameter is set to 1 if the UID of *luser* is 0, i.e., superuser. Otherwise, *suser* is set to 0.

ruserok() checks first if *luser* exists; i.e., does *getpwnam()* return success for *luser* ? It then determines if the remote user and hostname given are trusted on the *local* host; it is usually called by the remote daemon for these utilities during its startup. If the user or host are not trusted, then the user must supply a password to log in or get "Permission denied" errors when attempting to use *rsh*. If the remote host trusts the user and host, execution (or login) proceeds without any other verification of the user's identity.

The *hosts.equiv* file contains either hostnames or host-user pairs:

```
hostname [username]
```

If a username follows the hostname, only that combination of user and hostnames is trusted. Netgroup names, in the form *+@group*, may be substituted for either hostnames or usernames. As with the password file, using a plus sign (+) for an entry includes the appropriate NIS map: in the first column, the hosts map is included, and in the second column, the password map is included. Entries that grant permission contain the hostname, a host and username, or a netgroup inclusion.

The following is */etc/hosts.equiv* on host *mahimahi*:

```
wahoo
bitatron +
corvette johnc
+@source-hosts
+@sysadm-hosts +@sysadm-users
```

The first example trusts all users on host *wahoo*. Users on *wahoo* can *rlogin* to *mahimahi* without a password, but only if the *ruser* and *luser* strings are equal. The second example is similar to the first, except that any remote user from *bitatron* can claim to be any local user and get access as the local user; i.e., *luser* and *ruser* do not have to be equal. This is certainly useful to the users who have access to *bitatron*, but it is very relaxed (or lax) security on *mahimahi*. The third example is the most restrictive. Only user *johnc* is trusted on host *corvette*, and of course *luser* and *ruser* (both "johnc") must be the same. Other users on host *corvette* are not trusted and must supply a password when logging in to *mahimahi*.

The last two entries use netgroups to define lists of hosts and users. The *+@source-hosts* entry trusts all hosts whose names appear in the *source-hosts* netgroup. If usernames are given as part of the netgroup triples, they are ignored. This means that hostname wildcards grant overly generous permissions. If the *source-hosts* netgroup contained *(,stern,)*, then using this netgroup in the first column of *hosts.equiv* effectively opens up the machine to all hosts on the network. If you need to restrict logins to specific users from specific machines, you must use either explicit names or netgroups in both the first and second column of *hosts.equiv*.

The last example does exactly this. Instead of trusting one host-username combination, it trusts all combinations of hostnames in *sysadm-hosts* and the usernames in *sysadm-users*. Note that the *usernames* in the *sysadm-hosts* netgroup and the *hostnames* in the *sysadm-users* netgroup are completely ignored.

Permission may be revoked by preceding the host or user specification with a minus sign (–):

```
-wahoo
+ -@dangerous-users
```

The first entry denies permission to all users on host *wahoo*. The second example negates all users in the netgroup *dangerous-users* regardless of what machine they originate from (the plus sign (+) makes the remote machine irrelevant in this entry).

If you want to deny permission to everything in both the hosts and password NIS maps, leave *hosts.equiv* empty.

The *.rhosts* file uses the same syntax as the *hosts.equiv* file, but it is parsed *after* *hosts.equiv*. The sole exception to this rule is when granting remote permission to *root*. When the superuser attempts to access a remote host, the *hosts.equiv* file is ignored and only the */.rhosts* file is read. For all other users, the *ruserok( )* routine first reads *hosts.equiv*. If it finds a positive match, then transparent access is granted. If it finds a negative match, and there is no *.rhosts* file for *luser*, then transparent access is denied. Otherwise, the *luser*'s *.rhosts* file is parsed until a match, either positive or negative, is found. If an entry in either file denies permission to a remote user, the file parsing stops at that point, even if an entry further down in the file grants permission to that user and host combination.

Usernames that are not the same on all systems are handled through the user's *.rhosts* file. If you are user *julie* on your desktop machine *vacation*, but have username *juliec* on host *starter*, you can still get to that remote host transparently by adding a line to your *.rhosts* file on *starter*. Assuming a standard home directory scheme, your *.rhosts* file would be */home/juliec/.rhosts* and should contain the name of the machine you are logging in from and your username on the originating machine:

```
vacation julie
```

From *vacation*, you can execute commands on *starter* using:

```
% rsh starter -l juliec "ls -l"
```

or:

```
% rlogin starter -l juliec
```

On *starter*, the *ruserok()* routine looks for a *.rhosts* file for user *juliec*, your username on that system. If no entry in *hosts.equiv* grants you permission (probably the case because you have a different username on that system), then your *.rhosts* file entry maps your local username into its remote equivalent. You can also use netgroups in *.rhosts* files, with the same warnings that apply to using them in */etc/hosts.equiv*.

As a network manager, watch for overly permissive *.rhosts* files. Users may accidentally grant password-free access to any user on the network, or map a foreign username to their own Unix username. If you have many password files with private, non NIS managed entries, watch the use of *.rhosts* files. Merging password files to eliminate non-uniform usernames may be easier than maintaining a constant lookout for unrestricted access granted through a *.rhosts* file.

Using netgroups

Netgroups have been used in several examples already to show how triples of host, user, and domain names are used in granting access across the network. The best use of netgroups is for the definition of splinter groups of a large NIS domain, where creating a separate NIS domain would not justify the administrative effort required to keep the two domains synchronized.

Because of the variety of ways in which netgroups are applied, their use and administration are sometimes counterintuitive. Perhaps the most common mistake is defining a netgroup with host or usernames not present in the NIS maps or local host and password files. Consider a netgroup that includes a hostname in another NIS domain:

```
remote-hosts   (poi,-,-), (muban,-,-)
```

When a user attempts to *rlogin* from host *poi*, the local server-side daemon attempts to find the hostname corresponding to the IP address of the originating host. If *poi* cannot be found in the NIS *hosts.byaddr* map, then an IP address, instead of a hostname, is passed to *ruserok()*. The verification process fails to match the hostname, even though it appears in the netgroup. Any time information is shared between NIS domains, the appropriate entries must appear in both NIS maps for the netgroup construction to function as expected.

Even though netgroups are specified as host and user pairs, no utility uses both names together. There is no difference between the following two netgroups:

```
group-a        (los, mikel,) (bitatron, stern, )
group-b        (los, -,) (bitatron, -,) (-, mikel, ) (-, stern, )
```

Things that need hostnames—the first column of *hosts.equiv* or NFS export lists—produce the set of hosts {*los, bitatron*} from both netgroups. Similarly, anything that takes a username, such as the password file or the second column of *hosts. equiv*, always finds the set {*mikel, stern*}. You can even mix-and-match these two groups in *hosts.equiv*. All four of the combinations of the two netgroups, when used in both columns of *hosts.equiv*, produce the same net effect: users *stern* and *mikel* are trusted on hosts *bitatron* and *los*.

The triple-based format of the netgroups map clouds the real function of the netgroups. Because all utilities parse either host or usernames, you will find it helpful to define netgroups that contain only host or usernames. It's easier to remember what each group is supposed to do, and the time required to administer a few extra netgroups will be more than made up by time not wasted chasing down strange permission problems that arise from the way the *netgroups* map is used.

An example here helps to show how the *netgroup* map can produce unexpected results. We'll build a netgroup containing a list of users and hosts that we trust on a server named *gate*. Users in the netgroup will be able to log in to *gate*, and hosts in the netgroup will be able to mount filesystems from it. The netgroup definition looks like this:

```
gate-group    (,stern,), (,johnc,), (bitatron, -,), (corvette, -,)
```

In the */etc/dfs/dfstab* file on *gate*, we'll add a host access restriction:

```
share -o rw=gate-group /export/home/gate
```

No at-sign (@) is needed to include the netgroup name in the */etc/dfs/dfstab* file. The *netgroup* map is searched first for the names in the *rw=* list, followed by the *hosts* map.

In */etc/hosts.equiv* on *gate*, we'll include the *gate-group* netgroup:

```
+ +@gate-group
```

To test our access controls, we go to a machine not in the netgroup—NFS client *vacation*—and attempt to mount */export/home/gate*. We expect that the *mount* will fail with a "Permission denied" error:

```
vacation# mount gate:/home/gate/home/gate /mnt
vacation#
```

The mount completes without any errors. Why doesn't this netgroup work as expected?

The answer is in the wildcards left in the host fields in the netgroup entries for users *stern* and *johnc*. Because a wildcard was used in the host field of the netgroup, *all* hosts in the NIS map became part of *gate-group* and were added to the access list for */export/home/gate*. When creating this netgroup, our intention was probably to allow users *stern* and *johnc* to log in to *gate* from any host on the network, but instead we gave away access rights.

A better way to manage this problem is to define two netgroups, one for the users and one for the hosts, so that wildcards in one definition do not have strange effects on the other. The modified */etc/netgroup* file looks like this:

```
gate-users:    (,stern,), (,johnc,)
gate-hosts:    (bitatron,,), (corvette,,)
```

In the */etc/dfs/dfstab* file on *gate*, we use the *gate-hosts* netgroup:

```
share -o rw=gate-hosts /export/home/gate
```

and in */etc/hosts.equiv*, we use the netgroup *gate-users*. When host information is used, the *gate-hosts* group explicitly defines those hosts in the group; when user names are needed, the *gate-users* map lists just those users. Even though there are wildcards in each group, those wildcards are in fields that are not referenced when the maps are used in these function-specific ways.

How secure are NIS and NFS?

NFS and NIS have bad reputations for security. NFS earned its reputation because of its default RPC security flavor AUTH_SYS (see "RPC security" later in this chapter) is very weak. There are better security flavors available for NFS on Solaris and other systems. However, the better security flavors are not available for all, or even most NFS implementations, resulting in a practical dilemma for you. The stronger the NFS security you insist on, the more homogenous your computing environment will become. Assuming that secure file access across the network is a requirement, another option to consider is to not run NFS and switch to another file access system. Today there are but two practical choices:

SMB (also known as CIFS)
This limits your desktop environment to Windows. However, as discussed in "NFS versus SMB (CIFS)" in Chapter 10, if you want strong security, you'll have to have systems capable of it, which means running Windows clients and servers throughout.

DCE/DFS
At the time this book was written, DCE/DFS was available as an add-on product developed by IBM's Pittsburgh Laboratory (also known as Transarc) unit for Solaris, IBM's AIX, and Windows. Other vendors offer DCE/DFS for

their own operating systems (for example, HP offers DCE/DFS). So DCE/DFS offers the file access solution that is both heterogeneous and very secure.

NIS has earned its reputation because it has no authentication at all. The risk of this is that a successful attacker could provide a bogus NIS map to your users by having a host he controls masquerade as an NIS server. So the attacker could use a bogus host map to redirect the user to a host he controls (of course DNS has the same issue).* Even more insidious, the attacker could gain root access when logging into a system, simply by providing a bogus *passwd* map. Another risk is that the encrypted password field from the *passwd* map in NIS is available to everyone, thus permitting attackers to perform faster password guessing than if they manually tried passwords via login attempts.

These issues are corrected by NIS+. If you are uncomfortable with NIS security then you ought to consider NIS+. In addition to Solaris, NIS+ is supported by AIX and HP/UX, and a client implementation is available for Linux. By default NIS+ uses the RPC/dh security discussed in "AUTH_DH: Diffie-Hellman authentication." As discussed in "How secure is RPC/DH?," RPC/dh security is not state of the art. Solaris offers an enhanced Diffie-Hellman security for NIS+, but so far, other systems have not added it to their NIS+ implementations.

Ultimately, the future of directory services is LDAP, but at the time this book was written, the common security story for LDAP on Solaris, AIX, HP/UX, and Linux was not as strong as that of NIS+. You can get very secure LDAP out of Windows 2000, but then your clients and servers will be limited to running Windows 2000.

Password and NIS security

Several volumes could be written about password aging, password guessing programs, and the usual poor choices made for passwords. Again, this book won't describe a complete password security strategy, but here are some common-sense guidelines for password security:

- Watch out for easily guessed passwords. Some obvious bad password choices are: your first name, your last name, your spouse or a sibling's name, the name of your favorite sport, and the kind of car you drive. Unfortunately, enforcing any sort of password approval requires modifying or replacing the standard NIS password management tools.

- Define and repeatedly stress local password requirements to the user community. This is a good first-line defense against someone guessing passwords, or using a password cracking program (a program that tries to guess user

---

* An enhancement to DNS, DNSSEC has been standardized but it is not widely deployed.

passwords using a long list of words). For example, you could state that all passwords had to contain at least six letters, one capital and one non-alphabetic character.

- Remind users that almost any word in the dictionary can be found by a thorough password cracker.

- Use any available password guessing programs that you find, such as Alec Muffet's *crack*. Having the same weapons as a potential intruder at least levels the playing field.

In this section, we'll look at ways to manage the root password using NIS and to enforce some simple workstation security.

Managing the root password with NIS

NIS can be used to solve a common dilemma at sites with advanced, semi-trusted users. Many companies allow users of desktop machines to have the root password on their local hosts to install software, make small modifications, and power down/boot the system without the presence of a system administrator. With a different, user-specific root password on every system, the job of the system administrator quickly becomes a nightmare. Similarly, using the same root password on all systems defeats the purpose of having one.

Root privileges on servers should be guarded much more carefully, since too many hands touching host configurations inevitably creates untraceable problems. It is important to stress to semi-trusted users that their lack of root privileges on servers does not reflect a lack of expertise or trust, but merely a desire to exert full control over those machines for which you have full and total responsibility. Any change to a server that impacts the entire network becomes your immediate problem, so you should have jurisdiction over those hosts. One way to discourage would-be part-time superusers is to require anyone with a server root password to carry the 24-hour emergency beeper at least part of each month.

Some approach is required that allows users to gain superuser access to their own hosts, but not to servers. At the same time, the system administrator must be able to become *root* on any system at any time to perform day-to-day maintenance. To solve the second problem, a common superuser password can be managed by NIS. Add an entry to the NIS password maps that has a UID of 0, but login name that is something other than *root*. For example, you might use a login name of *netroot*. Make sure the */etc/nsswitch.conf* file on each host lists *nis* on the *passwd:* entry:

```
passwd: files nis
```

Users are granted access to their own host via the *root* entry in the */etc/passwd* file.

Instead of creating an additional root user, some sites use a modified version of *su* that consults a "personal" password file. The additional password file has one entry for each user that is allowed to become root, and each user has a unique root password.* With either system, users are able to manage their own systems but will not know the root passwords on any other hosts. The NIS-managed *netroot* password ensures that the system administration staff can still gain super-user access to every host.

Making NIS more secure

Aside from the caveats about trivial passwords, there are a few precautions that can be taken to make NIS more secure:

- If you are trying to keep your NIS maps private to hide hostnames or user-names within your network, do not make any host that is on two or more net-works an NIS server. Users on the external networks can forcibly bind to your NIS domain and dump the NIS maps from a server that is also performing routing duties. While the same trick may be performed if the NIS server is inside the router, it can be defeated by disabling IP packet forwarding on the router. Appendix A covers this material in more detail.

- On the master NIS server, separate the server's password file and the NIS pass-word file so that all users in the NIS password file do not automatically gain access to the NIS master server. A set of changes for building a distinct pass-word file was presented in "Using alternate map source files" in Chapter 4.

- Periodically check for null passwords using the following *awk* script:

    ```
    #! /bin/sh
    # ( cat /etc/shadow; ypcat passwd ) | awk -F':' '{if ($2 == "") print $1 ;}'
    ```

    The subshell concatenates the local password file and the NIS *passwd* map; the *awk* script prints any username that does not have an entry in the pass-word field of the password map.

- Consider configuring the system so that it cannot be booted single-user without supplying the root password. On Solaris 8, this is the default behavior, and can be overridden by adding this entry to */etc/default/sulogin*:

    ```
    PASSREQ=NO
    ```

    When the system is booted in single-user mode, the single-user shell will not be started until the user supplies the root password.

---

* An *su*-like utility is contained in *Unix System Administration Handbook*, by Evi Nemeth, Scott Seebass, and Garth Snyder (Prentice-Hall, 1990).

- Configure the system so that superuser can only log into the console, i.e., superuser cannot *rlogin* into the system. On Solaris 8, you do this by setting the *CONSOLE* variable in */etc/default/login*:

  ```
  CONSOLE=/dev/console
  ```

- On Sun systems, the boot PROM itself can be used to enforce security. To enforce PROM security, change the *security-mode* parameter in the PROM to *full*:

  ```
  # eeprom security-mode=full
  ```

  No PROM commands can be entered without supplying the PROM password; when you change from *security-mode=none* to *security-mode=full* you will be prompted for the new PROM password. This is not the same as the root password, and serves as a redundant security check for systems that can be halted and booted by any user with access to the break or reset switches.

 There is *no* mechanism for removing the PROM security without supplying the PROM password. If you forget the PROM password after installing it, there is no software method for recovery, and you'll have to rely on Sun's customer service organization to recover!

The secure nets file

If the file */var/yp/securenets* is present, then *ypserv* and *ypxfrd* will respond only to requests from hosts listed in the file. Hosts can be listed individually by IP address or by a combination of network mask and network. Consult your system's manual pages for details.

The point of this feature is to keep your NIS domain secure from access outside the domain. The more information an attacker knows about your domain, the more effective he or she can be at engineering an attack. The *securenets* file makes it harder to gather information.

Because *ypserv* and *ypxfrd* only read the *securenets* file at startup time, in order for changes to take effect, you must restart NIS services via:

```
# /usr/lib/netsvc/yp/ypstop
# /usr/lib/netsvc/yp/ypstart
```

Unknown password entries

If a user's UID changes while he or she is logged in, many utilities break in esoteric ways. Simple editing mistakes, such as deleting a digit in the UID field of the password file and then distributing the "broken" map file, are the most common source of this problem. Another error that causes a UID mismatch is the replacement of an NIS password file entry with a local password file entry where the two UIDs are not identical. The next time the password file is searched by UID, the user's password file entry will not be found if it no longer contains the correct UID. Similarly, a search by username may turn up a UID that is different than the real or effective user ID of the process performing the search.

The *whoami* command replies with "no login associated with uid" if the effective UID of its process cannot be found in the password file. Other utilities that check the validity of UIDs are *rcp*, *rlogin*, and *rsh*, all of which generate "can not find password entry for user id" messages if the user's UID cannot be found in the password map. These messages appear on the terminal or window in which the command was typed.

NFS security

Filesystem security has two aspects: controlling access to and operations on files, and limiting exposure of the contents of the files. Controlling access to remote files involves mapping Unix file operation semantics into the NFS system, so that certain operations are disallowed if the remote user fails to provide the proper credentials. To avoid giving superuser permissions across the network, additional constraints are put in place for access to files by *root*. Even more stringent NFS security requires proving that the Unix-style credentials contained in each NFS request are valid; that is, the server must know that the NFS client's request was made by a valid user and not an imposter on the network.

Limiting disclosure of data in a file is more difficult, as it usually involves encrypting the contents of the file. The client application may choose to enforce its own data encryption and store the file on the server in encrypted form. In this case, the client's NFS requests going over the network contain blocks of encrypted data. However, if the file is stored and used in clear text form, NFS requests to read or write the file will contain clear text as well. Sending parts of files over a network is subject to some data exposure concerns. In general, if security would be compromised by any part of a file being disclosed, then either the file should not be placed on an NFS-mounted filesystem, or you should use a security mechanism for RPC that encrypts NFS remote procedure calls and responses over the network. We will cover one such mechanism later in this section.

You can prevent damage to files by restricting write permissions and enforcing user authentication. With NFS you have the choice of deploying some simple security mechanisms and more complex, but stronger RPC security mechanisms. The latter will ensure that user authentication is made secure as well, and will be described later in this section. This section presents ways of restricting access based on the user credentials presented in NFS requests, and then looks at validating the credentials themselves using stronger RPC security.

RPC security

Under the default RPC security mechanism, AUTH_SYS, every NFS request, including mount requests, contains a set of user credentials with a UID and a list of group IDs (GIDs) to which the UID belongs. NFS credentials are the same as those used for accessing local files, that is, if you belong to five groups, your NFS credentials contain your UID and five GIDs. On the NFS server, these credentials are used to perform the permission checks that are part of Unix file accesses—verifying write permission to remove a file, or execute permission to search directories. There are three areas in which NFS credentials may not match the user's local credential structure: the user is the superuser, the user is in too many groups, or no credentials were supplied (an "anonymous" request). Mapping of root and anonymous users is covered in the next section.

Problems with too many groups depend upon the implementation of NFS used by the client and the server, and may be an issue only if they are different (including different revisions of the same operating system). Every NFS implementation has a limit on the number of groups that can be passed in a credentials structure for an NFS RPC. This number usually agrees with the maximum number of groups to which a user may belong, but it may be smaller. On Solaris 8 the default and maximum number of groups is 16 and 32, respectively. However, under the AUTH_SYS RPC security mechanism, the maximum is 16. If the client's group limit is larger than the server's, and a user is in more groups than the server allows, then the server's attempt to parse and verify the credential structure will fail, yielding error messages like:

```
RPC: Authentication error
```

Authentication errors may occur when trying to mount a filesystem, in which case the superuser is in too many groups. Errors may also occur when a particular user tries to access files on the NFS server; these errors result from any NFS RPC operation. Pay particular attention to the *group* file in a heterogeneous environment, where the NIS-managed *group* map may be appended to a local file with several entries for common users like *root* and *bin*. The only solution is to restrict the number of groups to the smallest value allowed by all systems that are running NFS.

Superuser mapping

The superuser is not given normal file access permissions to NFS-mounted files. The motivation behind this restriction is that root access should be granted on a per-machine basis. A user who is capable of becoming root on one machine should not necessarily have permission to modify files on a file server. Similarly, a *setuid* program that assumes root privileges may not function properly or as expected if it is allowed to operate on remote files.

To enforce restrictions on superuser access, the root's UID is mapped to the anonymous user *nobody* in the NFS RPC credential structure. The superuser frequently has fewer permissions than a nonprivileged user for NFS-mounted filesystems, since *nobody*'s group usually includes no other users. In the password file, *nobody* has a UID of 60001, and the group *nobody* also has a GID of 60001. When an executable, that is owned by root with the *setuid* bit set on the permissions, runs, its effective user ID is root, which gets mapped to *nobody*. The executable still has permissions on the local system, but it cannot get to remote files unless they have been explicitly exported with root access enabled.

Most implementations of NFS allow the root UID mapping to be defeated. Some do this by letting you change the UID used for *nobody* in the server's kernel. Others do this by letting you specify the UID for the anonymous user at the time you export the filesystem. For example, in this line in */etc/dfs/dfstab*:

```
share -o ro,anon=0 /export/home/stuff
```

Changing the UID for *nobody* from 60001 to 0 allows the superuser to access all files exported from the server, which may be less restrictive than desired.

Most NFS servers let you grant root permission on an exported filesystem on a per-host basis using the *root=* export option. The server exporting a filesystem grants root access to a host or list of hosts by including them in the */etc/dfs/dfstab* file:

```
share -o rw,root=bitatron:corvette /export/home/work
```

The superuser on hosts *bitatron* and *corvette* is given normal root filesystem privileges on the server's */export/home/work* directory. The name of a netgroup may be substituted for a hostname; all of the hosts in the netgroup are granted root access.

Root permissions on a remote filesystem should be extended only when absolutely necessary. While privileged users may find it annoying to have to log into the server owning a filesystem in order to modify something owned by *root*, this restriction also eliminates many common mistakes. If a system administrator wants to purge */usr/local* on one host (to rebuild it, for example), executing *rm -rf ** will have disastrous consequences if there is an NFS-mounted filesystem with root permission under */usr/local*. If */usr/local/bin* is NFS-mounted, then it is possible to wipe out the server's copy of this directory from a client when root permissions are extended over the network.

One clear-cut case where root permissions should be extended on an NFS filesystem is for the root and swap partitions of a diskless client, where they are mandatory. One other possible scenario in which root permissions are useful is for cross-server mounted filesystems. Assuming that only the system administration staff is given superuser privileges on the file servers, extending these permissions across NFS mounts may make software distribution and maintenance a little easier. Again, the pitfalls await, but hopefully the community with networked root permissions is small and experienced enough to use these sharp instruments safely.

On the client side, you may want to protect the NFS client from foreign *setuid* executables of unknown origin. NFS-mounted *setuid* executables should not be trusted unless you control superuser access to the server from which they are mounted. If security on the NFS server is compromised, it's possible for the attacker to create *setuid* executables which will be found—and executed—by users who NFS mount the filesystem. The *setuid* process will have root permission on the host on which it is running, which means it can damage files on the local host. Execution of NFS-mounted *setuid* executables can be disabled with the *nosuid* mount option. This option may be specified as a suboption to the *-o* command-line flag, the automounter map entry, or in the */etc/vfstab* entry:

```
automounter auto_local entry:
bin                      -ro,nosuid            toolbox:/usr/local/bin
vfstab entry:
toolbox:/usr/local/bin - /usr/local/bin nfs - no ro,nosuid
```

A bonus is that on many systems, such as Solaris, the *nosuid* option also disables access to block and character device nodes (if not, check your system's documentation for a *nodev* option). NFS is a file access protocol and it doesn't allow remote device access. However it allows device nodes to be stored on file servers, and they are interpreted by the NFS client's operating system. So here is another problem with mounting without *nosuid*. Suppose under your NFS client's */dev* directory you have a device node with permissions restricted to *root* or a select group of users. The device node might be protecting a sensitive resource, like an unmounted disk partition containing, say, personal information of every employee. Let's say the major device number is 100, and the minor is 0. If you mount an NFS filesystem without *nosuid*, and if that filesystem has a device node with wide open permissions, a major number of 100, and a minor number of 0, then there is nothing stopping unauthorized users from using the remote device node to access your sensitive local device.

The only clear-cut case where NFS filesystems should be mounted without the *nosuid* option is when the filesystem is a root partition of a diskless client. Here you have no choice, since diskless operation requires *setuid* execution and device access.

We've discussed problems with *setuid* and device nodes from the NFS client's perspective. There is also a server perspective. Solaris and other NFS server implementations have a *nosuid* option that applies to the exported filesystem:

```
share -o rw,nosuid /export/home/stuff
```

This option is highly recommended. Otherwise, malicious or careless users on your NFS clients could create *setuid* executables and device nodes that would allow a careless or cooperating user logged into the server to commit a security breach, such as gaining superuser access. Once again, the only clear-cut case where NFS filesystems should be exported without the *nosuid* (and *nodev* if your system supports it, and decouples *nosuid* from *nodev* semantics) option is when the filesystem is a root partition of a diskless client, because there is no choice if diskless operation is desired. You should ensure that any users logged into the diskless NFS server can't access the root partitions, lest the superuser on the diskless client is careless. Let's say the root partitions are all under */export/root*. Then you should change the permissions of directory */export/root* so that no one but superuser can access:

```
# chown root /export/root
# chmod 700 /export/root
```

Unknown user mapping

NFS handles requests that do not have valid credentials in them by mapping them to the *anonymous* user. There are several cases in which an NFS request has no valid credential structure in it:

- The NFS client and server are using a more secure form of RPC like RPC/DH, but the user on the client has not provided the proper authentication information. RPC/DH will be discussed later in this chapter.

- The client is a PC running PC/NFS, but the PC user has not supplied a valid username and password. The PC/NFS mechanisms used to establish user credentials are described in "Configuring PC/NFS" in Chapter 10.

- The client is not a Unix machine and cannot produce Unix-style credentials.

- The request was fabricated (not sent by a real NFS client), and is simply missing the credentials structure.

Note that this is somewhat different behavior from Solaris 8 NFS servers. In Solaris 8 the default is that invalid credentials are rejected. The philosophy is that allowing an NFS user with an invalid credential is no different then allowing a user to log in as user *nobody* if he has forgotten his password. However, there is a way to override the default behavior:

```
share -o sec=sys:none,rw  /export/home/engin
```

This says to export the filesystem, permitting AUTH_SYS credentials. However if a user's NFS request comes in with invalid credentials or non-AUTH_SYS security, treat and accept the user as anonymous. You can also map all users to anonymous, whether they have valid credentials or not:

```
share -o sec=none,rw  /export/home/engin
```

By default, the anonymous user is *nobody*, so unknown users (making the credential-less requests) and superuser can access only files with world permissions set. The *anon* export option allows a server to change the mapping of anonymous requests. By setting the anonymous user ID in */etc/dfs/dfstab*, the unknown user in an anonymous request is mapped to a well-known local user:

```
share -o rw,anon=100 /export/home/engin
```

In this example, any request that arrives without user credentials will be executed with UID 100. If */export/home/engin* is owned by UID 100, this ensures that unknown users can access the directory once it is mounted. The user ID mapping does not affect the real or effective user ID of the process accessing the NFS-mounted file. The anonymous user mapping just changes the user credentials used by the NFS server for determining file access permissions.

The anonymous user mapping is valid only for the filesystem that is exported with the *anon* option. It is possible to set up different mappings for each filesystem exported by specifying a different anonymous user ID value in each line of the */etc/dfs/dfstab* file:

```
share -o rw,anon=100 /export/home/engin
share -o rw,anon=200 /export/home/admin
share -o rw,anon=300 /export/home/marketing
```

Anonymous users should almost *never* be mapped to *root*, as this would grant superuser access to filesystems to any user without a valid password file entry on the server. An exception would be when you are exporting read-only, and the data is not sensitive. One application of this is exporting directories containing the operating system installation. Since operating systems like Solaris are often installed over the network, and superuser on the client drives the installation, it would be tedious to list every possible client that you want to install the operating system on.

Anonymous users should be thought of as transient or even unwanted users, and should be given as few file access permissions as possible. RPC calls with missing UIDs in the credential structures are rejected out of hand on the server if the server exports its filesystems with *anon=-1*. Rather than mapping anonymous users to *nobody*, filesystems that specify *anon=-1* return authentication errors for RPC calls with no credentials in them.

Normally, with the anonymous user mapped to *nobody*, anonymous requests are accepted but have few, if any, permissions to access files on the server. Mapping unknown users is a risky venture. Requests that are missing UIDs in their credentials may be appearing from outside the local network, or they may originate from machines on which security has been compromised. Thus, if you must export filesystems with the anonymous user mapped to a UID other than *nobody*, you should limit it to a smaller set of hosts:

```
share -o rw=engineering,anon=100 /export/home/engin # a nergroup
share -o rw=admin1:admin2,anon=200 /export/home/admin # a pair of hosts
share -o rw=.marketing.widget.com,anon=300 /export/home/marketing # a domain
```

We discuss limiting exports to certain hosts in the next section.

Access to filesystems

In addition to being protected from root access, some filesystems require protection from certain hosts. A machine containing source code is a good example; the source code may be made available only to a selected set of machines and not to the network at large. The list of hosts to which access is restricted is included in the server's */etc/dfs/dfstab* file with the *rw=* option:

```
share -o rw=noreast,root=noreast /export/root/noreast
```

This specification is typical of that for the root filesystem of a diskless client. The client machine is given root access to the filesystem, and access is further restricted to host *noreast* only. No user can look at *noreast*'s root filesystem unless he or she can log into *noreast* and look locally. The hosts listed in a *rw=* list can be individual hostnames or netgroup names, separated by colons. On Solaris 8, the hosts can also be DNS domain names, if prefixed by a leading dot (.), or a network number if preceded by a leading at sign (@). Solaris 8 also has the capability to deny specific hosts (individual hostnames, netgroups, domains, or network numbers) access. For example:

```
share -o rw=-marketing /source
```

Restricting host access ensures that NFS is not used to circumvent login restrictions. If a user cannot log into a host to restrict access to one or more filesystems, the user should not be able to recreate that host's environment by mounting all of its NFS-mounted filesystems on another system.

Read-only access

By default, NFS filesystems are exported with write access enabled for any host that mounts them. Using the *ro* or *ro=* option in the */etc/dfs/dfstab* file, you can specify whether the filesystem is exported read-only, and to what hosts:

```
share -o ro=system-engineering /source
```

In this example, the machines in *system-engineering* netgroup are authorized to only browse the source code; they get read-only access. Of course, this prevents users on machines authorized to modify the source from doing their job. So you might instead use:

```
share -o rw=source-group,ro=system-engineering /source
```

In this example, the machines in *source-group* are authorized to modify the source code get read and write access, whereas the machines in the *system-engineering* netgroup, which are authorized to only browse the source code, get read-only access.

Port monitoring

Port monitoring is used to frustrate "spoofing"—hand-crafted imitations of valid NFS requests that are sent from unauthorized user processes. A clever user could build an NFS request and send it to the *nfsd* daemon port on a server, hoping to grab all or part of a file on the server. If the request came from a valid NFS client kernel, it would originate from a privileged UDP or TCP port (a port less than 1024) on the client. Because all UDP and TCP packets contain both source and destination port numbers, the NFS server can check the originating port number to be sure it came from a privileged port.

NFS port monitoring may or may not be enabled by default. It is usually governed by a kernel variable that is modified at boot time. Solaris 8 lets you modify this via the */etc/system* file, which is read-only at boot time. You would add this entry to */etc/system* to enable port monitoring:

```
set nfssrv:nfs_portmon = 1
```

In addition, if you don't want to reboot your server for this to take effect, then, you can change it on the fly by doing:

```
echo "nfs_portmon/W1" | adb -k -w
```

This script sets the value of *nfs_portmon* to 1 in the kernel's memory image, enabling port monitoring. Any request that is received from a nonprivileged port is rejected.

By default, some *mountd* daemons perform port checking, to be sure that mount requests are coming from processes running with root privileges. It rejects requests that are received from nonprivileged ports. To turn off port monitoring in the mount daemon, add the *-n* flag to its invocation in the boot script:

```
mountd -n
```

Not all NFS clients send requests from privileged ports; in particular, some PC implementations of the NFS client code will not work with port monitoring enabled. In addition, some older NFS implementations on Unix workstations use nonprivileged ports and require port monitoring to be disabled. This is one reason why, by default, the Solaris 8 *nfs_portmon* tunable is set to zero. Another reason is that on operating systems like Windows, with no concept of privileged users, anyone can write a program that binds to a port less than 1024. The Solaris 8 *mountd* also does not monitor ports, nor is there any way to turn on mount request port monitoring. The reason is that as of Solaris 2.6 and onward, each NFS request is checked against the *rw=*, *ro=*, and *root=* lists. With that much checking, filehandles given out a mount time are longer magic keys granting access to an exported filesystem as they were in previous versions of Solaris and in other, current and past, NFS server implementations.

Check your system's documentation and boot scripts to determine under what conditions, if any, port monitoring is enabled.

Using NFS through firewalls

If you are behind a firewall that has the purpose of keeping intruders out of your network, you may find your firewall also prevents you from accessing services on the greater Internet. One of these services is NFS. It is true there aren't nearly as many public NFS servers on the Internet as FTP or HTTP servers. This is a pity, because for downloading large files over wide area networks, NFS is the best of the three protocols, since it copes with dropped connections. It is very annoying to have an FTP or HTTP connection time-out halfway into a 10 MB download. From a security risk perspective, there is no difference between surfing NFS servers and surfing Web servers.

You, or an organization that is collaborating with you, might have an NFS server outside your firewall that you wish to access. Configuring a firewall to allow this can be daunting if you consider what an NFS client does to access an NFS server:

- The NFS client first contacts the NFS server's portmapper or *rpcbind* daemon to find the port of the *mount* daemon. While the portmapper and *rpcbind* daemons listen on a well-known port, *mountd* typically does not. Since:

  — Firewalls typically filter based on ports.

  — Firewalls typically block all incoming UDP traffic except for some DNS traffic to specific DNS servers.

  — Portmapper requests and responses often use UDP.

  mountd alone can frustrate your aim.

- The NFS client then contacts the *mountd* daemon to get the root filehandle for the mounted filesystem.

- The NFS client then contacts the portmapper or *rpcbind* daemon to find the port that the NFS server typically listens on. The NFS server is all but certainly listening on port 2049, so changing the firewall filters to allow requests to 2049 is not hard to do. But again we have the issue of the portmapper requests themselves going over UDP.

- After the NFS client mounts the filesystem, if it does any file or record locking, the lock requests will require a consultation with the portmapper or *rpcbind* daemon to find the lock manager's port. Some lock managers listen on a fixed port, so this would seem to be a surmountable issue. However, the lock manager makes callbacks to the client's lock manager, and the source port of the callbacks is not fixed.

- Then there is the status monitor, which is also not on a fixed port. The status monitor is needed every time a client makes first contact with a lock manager, and also for recovery.

To deal with this, you can pass the following options to the *mount* command, the automounter map entry, or the *vfstab:*

mount commmand:
```
mount -o proto=tcp,public nfs.eisler.com:/export/home/mre /mre
```

automounter auto_home entry:
```
mre -proto=tcp,public nfs.eisler.com:/export/home/&
```

vfstab entry:
```
nfs.eisler.com:/export/home/mre - /mre nfs - no proto=tcp,public
```

The *proto=tcp* option forces the mount to use the TCP/IP protocol. Firewalls prefer to deal with TCP because it establishes state that the firewall can use to know if a TCP segment from the outside is a response from an external server, or a call from an external client. The former is not usually deemed risky, whereas the latter usually is.

The *public* option does the following:

- Bypasses the portmapper entirely and always contacts the NFS server on port 2049 (or a different port if the *port=* option is specified to the *mount* command). It sends a NULL ping to the NFS Version 3 server first, and if that fails, tries the NFS Version 2 server next.

- Makes the NFS client contact the NFS server directory to get the initial filehandle. How is this possible? The NFS client sends a LOOKUP request using a null filehandle (the *public filehandle*) and a pathname to the server (in the preceding example, the pathname would be */export/home*). Null filehandles are extremely unlikely to map to a real file or directory, so this tells the server that understands public filehandles that this is really a mount request. The name is interpreted as a multicomponent place-name, with each component separated by slashes (/). A filehandle is returned from LOOKUP.

- Marks the NFS mounts with the *llock* option. This is an undocumented mount option that says to handle all locking requests for file on the NFS filesystem locally. This is somewhat dangerous in that if there is real contention for the filesystem from multiple NFS clients, file corruption can result. But as long as you know what you are doing (and you can share the filesystem to a single host, or share it read-only to be sure), this is safe to do.

If your firewall uses Network Address Translation, which translates private IP addresses behind the firewall to public IP addresses in front of the firewall, you shouldn't have problems. However, if you are using any of the security schemes discussed in the section "Stronger security for NFS," be advised that they are designed for Intranets, and require collateral network services like a directory service (NIS for example), or a key service (a Kerberos Key Distribution Center for example). So it is not likely you'll be able to use these schemes through a firewall until the LIPKEY scheme, discussed in "NFS security futures," becomes available.

Some NFS servers require the *public* option in the *dfstab* or the equivalent when exporting the filesystem in order for the server to accept the public filehandle. This is not the case for Solaris 8 NFS servers.

What about allowing NFS clients from the greater Internet to access NFS servers located behind your firewall? This a reasonable thing to do as well, provided you take some care. The NFS clients will be required to mount the servers' filesystems with the *public* option. You will then configure your firewall to allow TCP connections to originate from outside your Intranet to a specific list of NFS servers behind the firewall. Unless Network Address Translation gets in the way, you'll want to use the *rw=* or *ro=* options to export the filesystems only to specific NFS clients outside your Intranet. Of course, you should export with the *nosuid* option, too.

If you are going to use NFS firewalls to access critical data, be sure to read the section "NFS and IPSec" later in this chapter.

Access control lists

Some NFS servers exist in an operating environment that supports Access Control Lists (ACLs). An ACL extends the basic set of read, write, execute permissions beyond those of file owner, group owner, and other. Let's say we have a set of users called *linus*, *charlie*, *lucy*, and *sally*, and these users comprise the group *peanuts*. Suppose *lucy* owns a file called *blockhead*, with group ownership assigned to *peanuts*. The permissions of this file are 0660 (in octal). Thus *lucy* can read and write to the file, as can all the members of her group. However, *lucy* decides she doesn't want *charlie* to read the file, but still wants to allow the other *peanuts* group members to access the file. What *lucy* can do is change the permissions to 0600, and then create an ACL that explicitly lists only *linus* and *sally* as being authorized to read and write the file, in addition to herself. Most Unix systems, including Solaris 2.5 and higher, support a draft standard of ACLs from the POSIX standards body. Under Solaris, *lucy* would prevent *charlie* from accessing her file by doing:

```
% chmod 0600 blockhead
% setfacl -m mask:rw-,user:linus:rw-,user:sally:rw- blockhead
```

To understand what *setfacl* did, let's read back the ACL for *blockhead*:

```
% getfacl blockhead

# file: blockhead
# owner: lucy
# group: peanuts
user::rw-
user:linus:rw-              #effective:rw-
user:sally:rw-              #effective:rw-
group::---                  #effective:---
mask:rw-
other:---
```

The *user:* entries for *sally* and *linus* correspond to the *rw* permissions *lucy* requested. The *user::* entry simply points out that the owner of the file, *lucy* has *rw* permissions. The *group::* entry simply says that the group owner, *peanuts*, has no access. The *mask:* entry says what the maximum permissions are for any users (other than the file owner) and groups. If *lucy* had not included mask permissions in the *setfacl* command, then *linus* and *sally* would be denied access. The *getfacl* command would instead have shown:

```
% getfacl blockhead

# file: blockhead
# owner: lucy
# group: peanuts
user::rw-
user:linus:rw-              #effective:---
user:sally:rw-              #effective:---
group::---                  #effective:---
mask:---
other:---
```

Note the difference from the two sets of *getfacl* output: the effective permissions granted to *linus* and *sally*.

Once you have the ACL on a file the way you want it, you can take the output of *getfacl* on one file and apply it to another file:

```
% touch patty
% getfacl blockhead | setfacl -f /dev/stdin patty
% getfacl patty
```

```
# file: patty
# owner: lucy
# group: peanuts
user::rw-
user:linus:rw-          #effective:rw-
user:sally:rw-          #effective:rw-
group::---              #effective:---
mask:rw-
other:---
```

It would be hard to disagree if you think this is a pretty arcane way to accomplish something that should be fairly simple. Nonetheless, ACLs can be leveraged to solve the "too many groups" problem described earlier in this chapter in the section "RPC security." Rather than put users into lots of groups, you can put lots of users into ACLs. The previous example showed how to copy an ACL from one file to another. You can also set a default ACL on a directory, such that any files or directories created under the top-level directory are inherited. Any files or directories created in a subdirectory inherit the default ACL. It is easier to hand edit a file containing the ACL description than to create one on the command line. User *lucy* creates the following file:

```
user::rwx
user:linus:rwx
user:sally:rwx
group::---
mask:rwx
other:---
default:user::rwx
default:user:linus:rwx
default:user:sally:rwx
default:group::---
default:mask:rwx
default:other:---
```

It is the *default:* entries that result in inherited ACLs. The reason why we add execution permissions is so that directories have search permissions, i.e., so *lucy* and her cohorts can change their current working directories to her protected directories.

Once you've got default ACLs set up for various groups of users, you then apply it to each top-level directory that you create:

```
% mkdir lucystuff
% setfacl -f /home/lucy/acl.default lucystuff
```

Note that you cannot apply an ACL file with *default:* entries in it to nondirectories. You'll have to create another file without the *default:* entries to use *setfacl -f* on nondirectories:

```
% grep -v '^default:' | /home/lucy/acl.default > /home/lucy/acl.files
```

The preceding example strips out the *default:* entries. However it leaves the executable bit on in the entries:

```
% cat /home/lucy/acl.files
user::rwx
user:linus:rwx
user:sally:rwx
group::---
mask:rwx
other:---
```

This might not be desirable for setting an ACL on existing regular files that don't have the executable bit. So we create a third ACL file:

```
% sed 's/x$/-/' /home/lucy/acl.files | sed 's/^mask.*$/mask:rwx/' \
    > /home/lucy/acl.noxfiles
```

This first turns off every execute permission bit, but then sets the mask to allow execute permission should we later decide to enable execute permission on a file:

```
% cat /home/lucy/acl.noxfiles
user::rw-
user:linus:rw-
user:sally:rw-
group::---
mask:rwx
other:---
```

With an ACL file with *default:* entries, and the two ACL files without *default:* entries, *lucy* can add protection to existing trees of files. In the following example, *oldstuff* is an existing directory containing a hierarchy of files and subdirectories:

fix the directories:
```
% find oldstuff -type d -exec setfacl -f /home/lucy/acl.default {} \;
```

fix the nonexecutable files:
```
% find oldstuff ! -type d ! ( -perm -u=x -o -perm -g=x -o -perm -o=x ) \
   -exec setfacl f /home/lucy/acl.noxfiles {} \;
```

fix the executable files:
```
% find oldstuff ! -type d ( -perm -u=x -o -perm -g=x -o -perm -o=x ) \
   -exec setfacl -f /home/lucy/acl.noxfiles {} \;
```

In addition to solving the "too many groups in NFS" problem, another advantage of ACLs versus groups is potential decentralization. As the system administrator, you are called on constantly to add groups, or to modify existing groups (add or delete users from groups). With ACLs, users can effectively administer their own groups. It is a shame that constructing ACLs is so arcane, because it effectively eliminates a way to decentralize a security access control for logical groups of users. You might want to create template ACL files and scripts for setting them to make it easier for your users to use them as a way to wean them off of groups. If you succeed, you'll reduce your workload and deal with fewer issues of "too many groups in NFS."

In Solaris, ACLs are not preserved when copying a file from the local *ufs* filesystem to a file in the *tmpfs* (*/tmp*) filesystem. This can be a problem if you later copy the file back from */tmp* to a *ufs* filesystem. Also, in Solaris, ACLs are not, by default, preserved when generating *tar* or *cpio* archives. You need to use the *-p* option to *tar* to preserve ACLs when creating and restoring a *tar* archive. You need to use the *-P* option to *cpio* when creating and restoring *cpio* archives. Be aware that non-Solaris systems probably will not be able to read archives with ACLs in them.

ACLs that deny access

We showed how we can prevent *charlie* from getting access to *lucy's* files by creating an ACL that included only *linus* and *sally*. Another way *lucy* could have denied *charlie* files is to set a deny entry for *charlie*:

```
% setfacl -m user:charlie:--- blockhead
```

No matter what the group ownership of *blockhead* is, and no matter what the other permissions on *blockhead* are, *charlie* will not be able read or write the file.

ACLs and NFS

ACLs are ultimately enforced by the local filesystem on the NFS server. However, the NFS protocol has no way to pass ACLs back to the client. This is a problem for NFS Version 2 clients, because they use the nine basic permissions bits (read, write, execute for user, group, and other) and the file owner and group to decide if a user should have access to the file. For this reason, the Solaris NFS Version 2 server reports the minimum possible permissions in the nine permission bits whenever an ACL is set on a file. For example, let's suppose the permissions on a file are 0666 or *rw-rw-rw-*. Now let's say an ACL is added for user *charlie* that gives him permissions of ---, i.e., he is denied access. When an ACL is set on a file, the Solaris NFS Version 2 server will see that there is a user that has no access to the file. As a result, it will report to most NFS Version 2 clients permissions of 0600, thereby denying nearly everyone (those accessing from NFS clients) but *lucy* access to the file. If it did not, then what would happen is that the NFS client would see permissions of 0666 and allow *charlie* to access the file. Usually *charlie's* application would succeed in opening the file, but attempts to read or write the file would fail in odd ways. This isn't desirable. Even less desirable is that if the file were cached on the NFS client, *charlie* would be allowed to read the file.[*]

---

[*] A similar security issue occurs when the superuser accesses a file owned by a user with permissions 0600. If the superuser is mapped to *nobody* on the server, then the superuser shouldn't be allowed to access the file. But if the file is cached, the superuser can read it. This is an issue only with NFS Version 2, not Version 3.

This is not the case for the NFS Version 3 server though. With the NFS Version 3 protocol, there is an *ACCESS* operation that the client sends to the server to see if the indicated user has access to the file. Thus the exact, unmapped permissions are rendered back to the NFS Version 3 client.

We said that the Solaris NFS server will report to most NFS Version 2 clients permissions of 0600. However, starting with Solaris 2.5 and higher, a side band protocol to NFS was added, such that if the protocol exists, the client can not only get the exact permissions, but also use the sideband protocol's ACCESS procedure for allowing the server to permissions the access checks. This then prevents *charlie* or the superuser from gaining unauthorized access to files.

What if you have NFS clients that are not running Solaris 2.5 or higher, or are not running Solaris at all? In that situation you have two choices: live with the fact that some users will be denied access due to the minimal permissions behavior, or you can use the *aclok* option of the Solaris *share* command to allow maximal access. If the filesystem is shared with *aclok*, then if anyone has read access to the files, then everyone does. So, *charlie* would then be allowed to access file *blockhead*.

Another issue with NFS and ACLs is that the NFS protocol has no way to set or retrieve ACLs, i.e., there is no protocol support for the *setfacl* or *getfacl* command. Once again, the sideband protocol in Solaris 2.5 and higher comes to the rescue. The sideband protocol allows ACLs to be set and retrieved, so *setfacl* and *getfacl* work across NFS.

IBM's AIX and Compaq's Tru64 Unix have sideband ACL protocols for manipulating ACLs over NFS. Unfortunately, none of the three protocols are compatible with each other.

Are ACLs worth it?

With all the arcane details, caveats, and limitations we've seen, you as the system administrator may decide that ACLs are more pain than benefit. Nonetheless, ACLs are a feature that are available to users. Even if you don't want to actively support them, your users might attempt to use them, so it is a good idea to become familiar with ACLs.

Stronger security for NFS

The security mechanisms described so far in this chapter are essentially refinements of the standard Unix login/password and file permission constraints, extended to handle distributed environments. Some additional care is taken to restrict superuser access over the network, but nothing in RPC's AUTH_SYS authentication protocol ensures that the user specified by the UID in the credential structure is permitted to use the RPC service, and nothing verifies that the user (or user running the application sending RPC requests) is really who the UID professes to be.

Simply checking user credentials is like giving out employee badges: the badge holder is given certain access rights. Someone who is not an employee could steal a badge and gain those same rights. Validating the user credentials in an NFS request is similar to making employees wear badges with their photographs on them: the badge grants certain access rights to its holder, and the photograph on the badge ensures that the badge holder is the "right" person. Stronger RPC security mechanisms than AUTH_SYS exist, which add credential validation to the standard RPC system. These stronger mechanisms can be used with NFS. We will discuss two of the stronger RPC security mechanisms available with Solaris 8, AUTH_DH, and RPCSEC_GSS. Both mechanisms rely on cryptographic techniques to achieve stronger security.

Security services

Before we describe AUTH_DH and RPCSEC_GSS, we will explain the notion of security services, and which services RPC provides. Security isn't a monolithic concept, but among others, includes notions like authorization, auditing, and compartmentalization. RPC security is concerned with four services: identification, authentication, integrity, and privacy. Identification is merely the name RPC gives to the client and the server. The client's name usually corresponds to the UID. The server's name usually corresponds to the hostname. Authentication is the service that proves that the client and server are who they identify themselves to be. Integrity is the service that ensures the messages are not tampered with, or at least ensures that the receiver knows they have been tampered with. Privacy is the service that prevents eavesdropping.

Brief introduction to cryptography

Before we describe how the AUTH_DH and RPCSEC_GSS mechanisms work, we will explain some of the general principles of cryptography that apply to both mechanisms. A complete treatment of the topic can be found in the book *Applied Cryptography*, by Bruce Schneier (John Wiley and Sons, Inc., 1996).

There are four general cryptographic techniques that are pertinent: symmetric key encryption, asymmetric key encryption, public key exchange, and one way hash functions.

Symmetric key encryption

In a symmetric encryption scheme, the user knows some secret value (such as a password), which is used to encrypt a value such as a timestamp. The secret value is known as a *secret key*. The problem with symmetric encryption is that to get another host to validate your encrypted timestamp, you need to get your secret key (password) onto that host. Think of this problem as a password checking exercise: normally your password is verified on the local machine. If you were required to get your password validated on an NFS server, you or the system administrator would somehow have to get your password on that machine for it to perform the validation. An example of a symmetric key encryption scheme is the *Data Encryption Standard* (*DES*).

Asymmetric key encryption

Asymmetric key encryption involves the use of a public key to encrypt a secret value, such as a symmetric key, and, a private key to decrypt the same value. A public key and private key are associated as a pair. One half of the pair gets generated from the other via a series of arithmetic operations. The private key is never equal to the public key, hence the term *asymmetric*. As the names suggest, the public key is well-known to everyone, whereas the private key is known only to its owner. This helps solve the problem of getting a secret key on both hosts. You choose a symmetric secret key, encrypt it with the server's public key, send the result to the server and the server decrypts the secret key with its own private key. The secret key can then be used to encrypt a value like a timestamp, which the server validates by decrypting with the shared secret key. Alternatively, we could have encrypted the timestamp value with the server's public key, sent it to the server, and let the server decrypt it with the server's private key. However, asymmetric key encryption is usually much slower than symmetric key encryption. So, typically software that uses asymmetric key encryption uses symmetric key encryption once the shared secret key is established

The public key is published so that it is available for authentication services. The encryption mechanism used for asymmetric schemes typically uses a variety of exponentiation and other arithmetic operators that have nice commutative properties. The encryption algorithm is complex enough, and the keys themselves should be big enough (at least 1024 bits), to guarantee that a public key can't be decoded to discover its corresponding private key. Asymmetric key encryption is also called public key encryption. An example of an asymmetric key encryption is RSA.

Public key exchange

Public key exchange is similar to asymmetric key encryption in all ways but one: it does not encrypt a shared secret key with either public or private key. Instead, two agents, say a user and a server, generate a shared symmetric secret key that uniquely identifies one to the other but cannot be reproduced by a third agent, even if the initial agents' public keys are grabbed and analyzed by some attacker.

Here is how the shared secret key, also called a *common key*, is computed. The user sends to the server the user's public key, and the server sends to the user the server's public key. The user creates a common key by applying a set of arithmetic operations onto the server's public key and the user's private key. The server generates the *same* key by applying the same arithmetic onto the user's public key and the server's private key. Because the algorithm uses commutative operations, the operation order does not matter—both schemes generate the same key, but *only* those two agents can recreate the key because it requires knowing at least one private key. An example of a public key exchange algorithm is Diffie-Hellman or DH for short.

One-way hash functions and MACs

A *one-way hash function* takes a string of octets of any length and produces a fixed width value called the *hash*. The function is designed such that given the hash, it is hard to find the string used as input to the one-way hash function, or for that matter, any string that produces the same hash result.

Let's say you and the server have established a common symmetric secret key using one of the three previously mentioned techniques. You now want to send a message to the server, but want to make sure an attacker in the middle cannot tamper with the message without the server knowing. What you can do is first combine your message with the secret key (you don't have to encrypt your message with the secret key), and then take this combination and apply the one way hash function to it.* This computation is called a *message authentication code* or *MAC*. Then send both the MAC and the message (not the combination with the secret key) to the server. The server can then verify that you sent the message, and not someone who intercepted it by taking the message, combining it with the shared secret key in the same way you did, and computing the MAC. If the server's computed MAC is the same as the MAC you sent, the server has verified that you sent it.

Even though your message and MAC are sent in the clear to the server, an attacker in the middle cannot change the message without the server knowing it because this would change the result of the MAC computation on the server. The attacker can't change the MAC to match a tampered message because he doesn't know the

---

* For brevity, we don't describe how a secret key and a message are combined, nor how the one-way hash function is applied. Unless you are a skilled cryptographer, you should not attempt to invent your own scheme. Instead, use the algorithm described in RFC2104.

secret key that only the server and you know. An example of a one-way hash function is MD5. An example of a MAC algorithm is HMAC-MD5.

Note that when you add a MAC to a message you are enabling the security service of integrity.

NFS and IPSec

IPSec is the standard protocol for security at the IP network level. With IPSec you can beef up your trusted host relationships with strong cryptography. IPSec was invented by the Internet Engineering Task Force (IETF) to deal with three issues:

- Attackers are becoming quite adept at spoofing IP addresses. The attacker targets a host to victimize. The victim shares some resources (such as NFS exports) to only a specific set of clients and uses the source IP address of the client to check access rights. The attacker selects the IP address of one of these clients to masquerade as. Sometimes the attacker is lucky, and the client is down, so this is not too difficult. Or the attacker has to take some steps such as disabling a router or loading the targeted client. If the attacker fails, you might see messages like:

    ```
    IP: Hardware address '%s' trying to be our address %s!
    ```
    or:
    ```
    IP: Proxy ARP problem? Hardware address '%s' thinks it is %s
    ```
    on the legitimate client's console.

    Once the legitimate client is disabled, the attacker then changes the IP address on a machine that he controls to that of the legitimate client and can then access the victim.

- An attacker that controls a gateway can easily engineer attacks where he tampers with the IP packets.

- Finally, if the Internet is to be a tool enabling more collaboration between organizations, then there needs to be a way to add privacy protections to sensitive traffic.

Here is what IPSec can do:

- Via per-host keys, allows hosts to authenticate each other. This frustrates IP spoofing attacks.

- Using a session key derived from per-host keys as input to a MAC, protects the integrity of IP traffic to frustrate packet tampering.

- Using a session key, encrypts all the data in the IP packet to frustrate eavesdropping.

The first two capabilities are provided by the *AH* (*Authentication Header*) feature of IPSec. The all three capabilities are provided by the *ESP* (*Encapsulating Security Payload*) feature of IPSec.

Many systems, including Solaris 8, have IPSec support. We won't go into the details of how to set up IPSec. However, we will point out that IPSec can be a useful tool to improve the security of your NFS environment:

- If you use the AH feature, then all NIS lookups are safe from tampering on the NIS server, or the NIS traffic. So the attacker cannot fool your NFS server into believing that client *gonzo* has IP address 192.4.5.6, instead of 10.1.2.3.

- Enabling AH on NFS clients and servers prevents attackers from spoofing the clients you list on servers' *rw=, ro=,* and *root=* lists.

- ESP used on the NFS client and server makes operating through firewalls safer when accessing sensitive data.

While IPSec is useful for securing NFS, because its security is host based, it does not protect your network from attackers that log onto your IPSec-protected hosts and assume the identity of other users. The discussions of AUTH_DH and RPCSEC_GSS that follow address this issue.

AUTH_DH: Diffie-Hellman authentication

AUTH_DH is an RPC security flavor that uses encryption techniques to improve on AUTH_SYS.

Old terms: AUTH_DES, secure RPC, and, secure NFS

AUTH_DH was originally called AUTH_DES, and indeed, you'll find that most documentation of AUTH_DH still calls it AUTH_DES. However, the _DES part of the name is a misnomer. While the DES algorithm is used in AUTH_DH, as we will see later, it is the Diffie-Hellman algorithm that is central to the workings of the AUTH_DH. We will not refer to AUTH_DES again.

When AUTH_DH is combined with RPC, the combination is often referred to as "Secure RPC." When RPC, and AUTH_DH are combined with NFS, the result is often referred to as "Secure NFS." However, in the 13 years since AUTH_DH was invented, two things have occurred:

- AUTH_DH is no longer considered secure by many security experts. After you read the material on AUTH_DH, you might concur.

- RPCSEC_GSS, a stronger, more secure security flavor for RPC is now available with Solaris 8 and other NFS implementations.

We will not use the terms "Secure RPC" or "Secure NFS" again, since they are confusing. Instead, we will use RPC/DH and NFS/dh to refer to RPC secured with AUTH_DH, and NFS secured with RPC/DH, respectively.

Diffie-Hellman key exchange

AUTH_DH uses Diffie-Hellman public key exchange. Using this encryption scheme, RPC can be made more secure by requiring each client to establish a valid common key before making RPC requests to the server. Diffie-Hellman key exchange relies on each agent that wants to establish a common key to agree on two pieces of information beforehand. For AUTH_DH these pieces are:

- A base for the exponentiation part of the calculation. AUTH_DH uses a base of 3.

- A modulus used for the remainder part of the calculation. AUTH_DH uses a modulus of 0xd4a0ba0250b6fd2ec626e7efd637df76c716e22d0944b88b. Let's label this constant as AUTH_DH_MOD.

Let PRIV_C be the private key of the client. Then the public key of the client is:

(1) PUBLIC_C = (3 $^{PRIV\_C}$) mod AUTH_DH_MOD

Let PRIV_S be the private key of the server. Then the public key of the server is:

(2) PUBLIC_S = (3 $^{PRIV\_S}$) mod AUTH_DH_MOD

The client computes a common key between the client and server as:

(3) COMMON_C_S = (PUBLIC_S $^{PRIV\_C}$) mod AUTH_DH_MOD

The server computes the common key between the server and client as:

(4) COMMON_S_C = (PUBLIC_C $^{PRIV\_S}$) mod AUTH_DH_MOD

To prove that COMMON_C_S equals COMMON_S_C, we replace PUBLIC_S in statement (3) with the expression it was derived from in statement (2) and drop the MOD part of the expression. We do the same for PUBLIC_C in statement (4) with the expression from statement (2):

(3.1) COMMON_C_S_PRIME = (3 $^{PRIV\_S}$)$^{PRIV\_C}$ = 3 $^{PRIV\_S\ *\ PRIV\_C}$
(4.1) COMMON_S_C_PRIME = (3 $^{PRIV\_C}$)$^{PRIV\_S}$ = 3 $^{PRIV\_C\ *\ PRIV\_S}$

Because multiplication is a commutative operation, it is obvious that COMMON_C_S_PRIME equals COMMON_S_C_PRIME. Therefore, COMMON_C_S equals COMMON_S_C.

How RPC/DH works

RPC/DH uses a combination of Diffie-Hellman key exchange and DES encryption. User validation is performed by the server, based on information in the RPC request.

The client and server decide on the common key via the Diffie-Hellman algorithm discussed previously in "Diffie-Hellman key exchange." The common key will be used to construct a shared secret DES key. Note that because AUTH_DH_MOD is 192 bits, the common key will be 192 bits. However, DES uses 64 bit keys, such that the low order bit of each octet is a parity bit, making DES effectively a 56-bit symmetric key algorithm. AUTH_DH deals with this by selecting the middle 64 bits of the common key. These 64 bits are split into eight octets. Parity is added to the low order bit of each octet. In addition the high order bit of each octet is unused, making this effectively a 48-bit shared secret key.

The first time the client contacts the server, it generates a random session key, and encrypts it with the shared secret DES key. The session key is also a DES key. The client also generates a time-to-live value (in seconds) called the *window*, and a window value that is one second less than the first window value. The two window values are encrypted with the session key. The encrypted session key and the encrypted window values are sent to the server. The server can decrypt the encrypted session key because it knows the common key, and therefore the shared secret DES key. With the session key, it can decrypt the window values. If the second window value is not one less than the first, the server knows something odd is going on, and it rejects the client's request.

The first time, and on every subsequent contact to the server, the client encrypts the current time using the session key. It sends its RPC request to the server.

The server decrypts the timestamp, using the same session key, and verifies that it is accurate. If the decrypted timestamp falls outside of the time to live window, the server rejects the request.

So far we've described how RPC/DH does authentication. We will now look at how identity works in RPC/DH. Recall that AUTH_SYS sends a UID, GID, and a list of supplementary GIDs. The first time RPC/DH contacts the server to establish the session key, it sends no UIDs or GIDs. Instead it sends a string, called a *netname*, which identifies two items:

- The user (albeit, the username is a UID expressed in ASCII-decimal)

- The domain name of the user (usually this is an NIS domain name)

The server does three things with the netname:

- Locates an NIS server serving the specified domain that knows about the user.

- Looks up the user's netname in the NIS *netid* map for the user's UID, GID, and list of supplementary groups.

- Looks up the user's netname in the NIS *publickey* map for the user's Diffie-Hellman public key. With that, and the server's private key, the server can determine the common key, then the shared secret key, then decrypt the session key, and use that to verify that the request came from a user corresponding to the netname.

By the way, notice that AUTH_DH doesn't have the "too many groups" problem of AUTH_SYS that was discussed in "RPC security," since no GID list is sent on the wire.

RPC/DH state and NFS statelessness

The title of the section says it all. How can we reconcile the fact that NFS is stateless, and yet RPC/DH clearly establishes state in the form of a session key, with a time to live? This state has to be kept on the server. The answer is that this is not state that has to be recovered in the event of a server crash, which is in stark contrast to file locking state. If the server reboots, or if it even decides to throw away an RPC/DH session, it is not a disaster. The client simply gets an error indicating that the server has no knowledge of the session, and the client establishes a new session key as if it was the first contact between the client and server.

We'll now look at how NFS/dh works by first seeing how to add the security features to NFS, and then seeing how the public and private keys are managed within this system

Enabling NFS/dh

Enabling NFS/dh on a filesystem is quite simple: export and mount the filesystem with the *sec=dh* option. On the NFS server, the */etc/dfs/dfstab* entry looks like this:

```
share -o sec=dh,rw /export/home/thud
```

When a filesystem is exported with the *sec=dh* option, clients using NFS Version 2 must mount it with the *sec-dh* option if they are to enjoy normal user access privileges in the filesystem. On the NFS client, add the *sec=dh* option in the automounter map entry, or the */etc/vfstab* entry for the filesystem:

```
automounter auto_home entry:
thud                          -sec=dh              bonk:/export/home/thud

vfstab entry:
bonk:/export/home/thud - /thud nfs  - no  sec=dh,rw
```

If the client is using NFS Version 3, it will use Version 3 of the MOUNT protocol. MOUNT Version 3 will return the RPC security flavor that the directory is exported with, along with the filehandle of the directory. Thus, with NFS Version 3, the *sec=dh* mount option is not necessary.

If a user accessing the filesystem can generate a session key with the NFS server, it is used to encrypt the timestamps sent with that user's NFS requests. If the server decrypts the timestamps successfully, the netname presented by the user is trusted and is used to derive normal Unix-style credentials for the purpose of file access.

It's possible, though, that the user can't exchange a session key with the server. This will be the case if the user doesn't have a public key defined, or if the user cannot supply the proper private key to generate a common key using Diffie-Hellman key exchange. When there is no valid common key, some NFS servers remap the user to *nobody*. However, by default, Solaris 8 rejects such users. If you want to give such users anonymous access you can export the filesystem with the following line in */etc/dfs/dfstab*:

```
share -o sec=dh:none,rw /export/home/thud
```

Within the NFS/dh system, a user without a valid public/private key pair becomes an anonymous user on the NFS server and is subject to the same access restrictions (discussed earlier in this chapter) that apply to the anonymous user *nobody*. To utilize NFS/dh without impairing a user's ability to do work, you must define public and private key pairs for trusted users and trusted hosts.

Public and private keys

Public and private keys are maintained in the *publickey.byname* NIS map, which is built from */etc/publickey* on the master NIS server.* The only key that is defined by default is one for *nobody*, which is required for the anonymous user mapping. Public and encrypted secrets keys are contained in the */etc/publickey* file, along with a unique identifier for the machine or user owning these keys.

```
unix.10461@nesales publickey:privatekey
```

The keys are long strings of hexadecimal digits, representing the encrypted key values. Obviously, the NIS map cannot contain the actual private keys, or the entire encryption mechanism would be baseless. Instead, the */etc/publickey* file's *private key* field contains the user's private key, encrypted with the user's login password. For host entries, the private key is encrypted using the root password. The private keys themselves are large random numbers, just like the session key that is used by RPC/DH.

Identifiers in */etc/publickey* are called *netnames* and take one of two forms:

```
unix.uid@NISdomain
unix.host@NISdomain
```

---

* If you are not running NIS or NIS+, you can still create keys, and use NFS/dh with the *publickey* entry in *nsswitch.conf* set to *files*. You will need to set up an NIS domain name on each NFS client and server (see "Enabling NIS on client hosts" in Chapter 3 for how to set up a domain name on a host). You will also have to devise a means for keeping all the */etc/publickey* files on each client and server synchronized, since the encrypted private key field must change every time the user's password changes.

The first form is used for user keys; it defines a key valid in the current NIS domain. The host key is used to create a RPC/DH key for the superuser on the named host. No user key is required for *root*—only a host key.

The */etc/publickey* file is changed by the RPC/DH utilities that create and manage key values. Because it contains encrypted key strings, it is not easily edited by the superuser, just as the password fields in */etc/passwd* cannot be hand-edited. The *publickey* file should exist *only* on the NIS master server, or else users' private keys will become out of date when they change their passwords (and therefore change the encryption key used to store their private keys).

Creating keys

The superuser can add user keys (on the NIS master server) using *newkey -u user*. As *root*, run *newkey* with the user's login name:

```
nismaster# newkey -u stern
Adding new key for unix.1461@nesales.East.Sun.COM.
Enter stern's login password:
```

The password is used to encrypt the private key so that it can be safely placed in the *publickey* maps. Unfortunately, the user's existing password in the NIS *passwd* maps must be supplied, requiring you to know the user's password. This is fine if you are adding the user to *passwd* map anyway; he is therefore a new user. However, it is very inconvenient if you are adding NFS/dh security and have a large pool of existing users because:

- You could change every user's login password to the same value. The problem with that is that for a period of time every user has the same password, and you can expect that some of your users will take malicious advantage of that.

- You could change every user's login password to a unique value. The problem with that is you have to somehow securely get the new passwords to each user. Unless you have a secure email system like PGP or S/MIME installed that pretty much leaves you to walk to every user's office or telephone them. That you are considering NFS/dh suggests that you have a large user base. This is simply not practical.

Hopefully, a future version of Solaris will fix this so that you can supply any password to *newkey*. The way it would work is that you'd use the same RPC/DH password to encrypt every private key via newkey. You'd tell your users what the RPC/DH password is, and they would each use c*hkey -p* (more on *chkey* later) to change the RPC/DH password to match their login password. Once all the users had done the *chkey*, you'd then start exporting NFS filesystems with NFS/dh.

You cannot achieve the ideal, but you can come close. What you can do is create a *template* user login, with a unique UID (let's use *66666* for this example) and GID, and assign it a password that you intend to publish to all your users. Make sure that *template* has a shell of */dev/null* in the *passwd* map, so that no one can log in as *template*. Now create keys for *template*:

```
nismaster# newkey -u template
Adding new key for unix.66666@nesales.East.Sun.COM.
Enter template's login password:
```

If you look at the */etc/publickey* on host *nismaster* you should see something like:

```
unix.66666@nesales.East.Sun.COM 74365f4e03701cf96de938a59baa39f1039ada407b4ab3a3:
9b7130a3f38c6e86f431f81ce1cf64b5e59991d3d5d1ce0596fd5167cb878b51
```

The netname of *template* is *unix.66666@nesales.East.Sun.COM.* Each of your users will have a similar netname, except for the number between the *unix* prefix, and the *@nesale.East.Sun.COM* suffix. The last long hexadecimal number after the colon (:) is user *template*'s private key, encrypted with *template*'s login password.

Now for each user, make a copy of *template*'s entry in the */etc/publickey* file, but change the netname to match the user. Let's say that your set of users is *stern*, *labiaga*, and *mre,* with UIDs of 1461, 15124, and 23154, respectively. You then edit the */etc/publickey* file to look like:

```
unix.66666@nesales.East.Sun.COM 74365f4e03701cf96de938a59baa39f1039ada407b4ab3a3:
9b7130a3f38c6e86f431f81ce1cf64b5e59991d3d5d1ce0596fd5167cb878b51
unix.1461@nesales.East.Sun.COM 74365f4e03701cf96de938a59baa39f1039ada407b4ab3a3:
9b7130a3f38c6e86f431f81ce1cf64b5e59991d3d5d1ce0596fd5167cb878b51
unix.15124@nesales.East.Sun.COM 74365f4e03701cf96de938a59baa39f1039ada407b4ab3a3:
9b7130a3f38c6e86f431f81ce1cf64b5e59991d3d5d1ce0596fd5167cb878b51
unix.23514@nesales.East.Sun.COM 74365f4e03701cf96de938a59baa39f1039ada407b4ab3a3:
9b7130a3f38c6e86f431f81ce1cf64b5e59991d3d5d1ce0596fd5167cb878b51
```

You now want to push the *publickey* file changes into the *publickey* NIS maps:

```
nismaster# cd /var/yp
nismaster# make publickey
updated publickey
pushed publickey
```

You have now almost effortlessly fully populated the *publickey* maps, but each entry has the same public key, same private key, and the same password. This is not what you want for the long term. So now you tell your users to expend some effort. Each user should be told to:

- Change his or her RPC/DH password that the private key is encrypted with (changing the password to the user's login password is recommended).

- Change his or her public and private key.

Here are the instructions we give to each user:

```
client% chkey -p
Updating nis publickey database.
Reencrypting key for 'unix.1461@nesales.East.Sun.COM'.
Please enter the Secure-RPC password for stern:
Please enter the login password for stern:
Sending key change request to nismaster ...

client% chkey
Updating nis publickey database.
Generating new key for 'unix.1461@nesales.East.Sun.COM'.
Please enter the Secure-RPC password for stern:
Sending key change request to nismaster ...
```

The first *chkey* command invocation reencrypts his private key with his login password. The second *chkey* invocation generates a brand new and unique private key and public key pair.

If the user supplies an invalid password, no password or key will be created. If the user's password is valid, and the NIS master server is receiving key updates, the key will be added to, or modified in, the NIS *publickey* maps. Both the *chkey* and *newkey* utilities update the */etc/publickey* file on the NIS master server.

To ensure that your users are following the *chkey* instructions, you can check the *publickey.byname* map to see if both the private key and the public key fields of each user have changed, by comparing them to that of the user *template*.

The only way to create host keys (for superuser verification) is to use *newkey -h* as *root*:

```
# newkey -h bitatron
Adding new key for unix.bitatron@nesales.East.Sun.COM.
New password:
```

You must create a host key for every NFS client (so that the client can mount filesystems shared with *sec=dh*) and NFS server (so that the server can generate the common key).

To receive NIS map updates from *newkey* or *chkey*, the master NIS server must be able to run *rpc.ypupdated*. On Solaris 8, this daemon is started as part of the */usr/lib/netsvc/yp/ypstart* script, which in turn is started by the */etc/init.d/rpc* boot script.

On every machine that will be using NFS/dh, make sure you are running the *keyserv* daemon. This process is used to cache private and common keys, and is also started out of */etc/init.d/rpc* with lines of the form:

```
if [ -x /usr/sbin/keyserv -a \
    -n "'/usr/bin/domainname 2>/dev/null'" ]; then
     /usr/sbin/keyserv >/dev/msglog 2>&1
     echo " keyserv\c"
 fi
```

As you can see, *keyserv* will not start if there is no domain name established. Make sure *keyserv* can start, or you will not be able to create session keys, even if you have a valid public and private key pair in the *publickey* NIS maps.

Establishing a session key

When you log into a machine that is running NFS/dh, the password you supply to *login* is used to attempt to decrypt your encrypted private key (in the *publickey* map). If the login and RPC/DH passwords do not match you get errors like:

```
Password does not decrypt secret key (type = 192-0) for 'unix.23514@nesales.East.
Sun.COM'.
Password does not decrypt any secret keys for unix.23514@nesales.East.Sun.COM.
```

The private key is given to the *keyserv* daemon, which caches it for generating common keys. The common keys are used to exchange session keys with NFS servers, as described earlier in this section. Therefore, the entire session key generation procedure goes like this:

1. You define a public and private key pair, using *newkey* or *chkey*. The private key is a large, random number; it is stored in the *publickey* map by encrypting it with your password.

2. When you log into a machine, your password is used to decrypt your private key. The private key is given to the *keyserv* daemon, where it is cached until you log out.

3. To access an NFS filesystem mounted with the *sec=dh* option, you must establish a common key with the NFS server. You form a common key using your private key and the public key for the NFS server. This is done automatically by the RPC/DH system.

4. From the common key, you derive a shared secret key by taking a subset of the bits of the common key. This secret key is used to encrypt a randomly generated session key, which is passed to the NFS server. All of your NFS requests to that server contain a timestamp encrypted with the session key. The server decrypts this timestamp to validate your NFS requests.

Note that you must supply your login password for the *keyserv* daemon to be given your private key. If you don't supply a password when you log into a machine—for example, you *rlogin* to another machine—then there is no way for the *keyserv* daemon to automatically receive your decrypted private key. To establish a session key in this situation, use the *keylogin* utility, which accepts your login password and uses it to decrypt your private key:

```
remote% keylogin
Password:
```

Note that if your login and RPC/DH passwords are different, whether you use *rlogin* or not, you must use *keylogin* to allow *keyserv* to see your private key. Or else you can use *chkey -p* to change your RPC/DH password to your login password.

Keys that are decrypted via *keylogin* are also passed to *keyserv*, where they remain until the user executes a *keylogout*. If you are going to be logging into nontrusted hosts, use *keylogin* to decrypt your key, and add *keylogout* to your *.logout* file (in your home directory) so that your key is destroyed when you log out.

You must reference the NIS *passwd* map in order for the automatic private key caching to occur. For proper operation of NFS/dh, do not put users in the local file */etc/passwd*, or their encrypted private keys may become out-of-date when they change their local passwords but do not change the NIS-managed password used to encrypt the private key in the *publickey* map. On the NIS master server, make sure you use an alternate password source file, instead of the default */etc/passwd*.

There's one thing missing: how does the root, or host, private key get decrypted? You establish a session key using the *host* key for the NFS server. In order for the server to exchange keys with you, it must be able to decrypt the host's private key, and this requires the root password or a "hidden" copy of the root key. One obvious approach is to force someone to supply the root password when the machine boots, so that the host private key in the *publickey* map can be decrypted and given to the *keyserv* daemon. However, this is often too restrictive: if an NFS server boots and no system administrator is present to supply the root password, no NFS/dh services will be available.

You can solve this dilemma by using the *-r* option to *keylogin* to store the host's private key in the protected */etc/.rootkey* file of the NFS server. Note that this is *not* the root password; it's the large, random number used as the host's private key. When the *keyserv* daemon starts up, it reads the host's key out of this file so that clients of the host can establish session keys with it.

A similar issue applies to the NFS client when you are using the automounter to access NFS mounted filesystems. Unless the superuser has logged into the system, and thus manually established his private key into keyserv, users will not be able use the automounter to access filesystems exported with *sec=dh*. Once again, you use *keylogin -r*, this time running it on the NFS client. When the *keyserv* daemon starts up, it reads the host's key out of this file so that the automounter can establish session keys on NFS servers.

NFS/dh checklist

This list summarizes what you need to do to create the various daemons and files that must be in place for proper operation of NFS/dh:

1. Create keys for users with *chkey* or *newkey -u*. Create a host key for each machine on which you need secure *root* access using *newkey -h*.

2. Make sure the NIS master server is running *rpc.ypupdated*.

3. Push the *publickey* map to all NIS slaves after making any changes to it, so that NFS/dh is operating before the next NIS map transfer.

4. Establish a */etc/.rootkey* file on every NFS server and client via *keylogin -r*.

5. If you are using NFS/dh on trusted hosts, make sure that users perform a *keylogin* to produce a temporary private key. If users do not supply a password when they log into a host, the local *keyserv* process on that host must be given the user's private key explicitly. Also, have users add *keylogout* to their . *logout* files to remove the temporary keys given to *keyserv*.

6. Ensure that each client that is using NFS/dh is running the *keyserv* daemon.

7. To export a filesystem using NFS/dh, add the *sec=dh* option to its entry in */etc/ dfs/dfstab*. On NFS Version 2 clients, mount the filesystem with the *sec=dh* option in the mount options field of the automounter map or */etc/vfstab*.

Finally, make sure that your client and server clocks remain well-synchronized (see "Time synchronization" in Chapter 14 for a simple scheme). Since NFS/dh uses encrypted timestamps for validation, drifting client clocks may cause the server to reject otherwise valid NFS/dh requests because they appear to be replays of out-of-date requests. The NFS server code has a small window for checking client timestamps, and if the clock drift falls within this window, the RPC call is executed.

On Solaris 8, the default window size is five minutes (300 seconds). If you are serious about using NFS/dh, you will probably want to leave this window unchanged. However, you can change it to a different value, by modifying the *authdes_win* tunable parameter in the */etc/system* file:

```
* 10 minutes
set rpcsec:authdes_win = 600
```

You can also set it on a live system without rebooting by:

```
# echo authdes_win/W 0t600 | adb -k -w
authdes_win:    0x12c  =  0x258
```

The shorter the window, the less time a would-be network spoofer has to attempt to replay any request, but on the other hand, the less clock drift you can tolerate.

How secure is RPC/DH?

RPC/DH is flawed for several reasons:

- It uses a 192-bit modulus for its public and private keys. In 1987, 192 bits was appropriate because for larger sizes, it was found that common key generation took several minutes to complete on Motorola 68010 processors, which were still used in a significant number of Sun's installed base of systems. However, by 1990, advances in RISC processors produced workstation machines that could, by brute force, derive the private key from any public key in under a day.

- It uses only a 48-bit shared secret key for encrypting the session key. This can be brute forced in less than a day as well.

- Recall the discussion about requiring users to do a *keylogin* if they are using *rlogin* between trusted hosts. The point of *rlogin* with trusted hosts is to avoid constant password challenges. Also, the more times the same password is entered, the more opportunity for someone to look over your shoulder (or to eavesdrop on the network) to see it.

- RPC/DH does a better job of authentication than AUTH_SYS, but there is no support for integrity or privacy. It is obvious why privacy is desirable, but why is integrity so important to NFS? Say we are using NFS/dh, and our attacker in the middle intercepts a request to read a particular file. He prevents the read from proceeding. However, he takes the RPC/DH header, and concatenates it with a new NFS request to write the same file (this is known as a *splicing attack*). As we discussed earlier in "One-way hash functions and MACs," this would not be possible if RPC/DH had integrity services.

- It's impossible to extend RPC/DH to fix the above issues.

For these reasons, many security experts will tell you that NFS/dh is waste of time to deploy, even though the successful attacks on NFS/dh require the attacker to have much more sophistication than that needed to attack NFS over AUTH_SYS. If you understand the risks and you are comfortable with the security offered by one more of:

- NIS

- DNS (that is, DNS without DNSSEC)

- NFS over AUTH_SYS

- Transparent security discussed earlier in "User-oriented network security"

- Password-based security such as what *imap*, *telnet*, and *ftp* offer

then you ought to be comfortable with RPC/DH. If you aren't comfortable with any of the above, including RPC/DH, then you should be running a very secure combination of directory service and file service. One combination would be NIS+ with enhanced DH security, as mentioned in "How secure are NIS and NFS?" earlier in this chapter, and Kerberized NFS as described in the next section.

RPCSEC_GSS: Generic security services for RPC

The previous section described a complete security system for NFS and RPC, and the subsection "How secure is RPC/DH?" discusses its flaws. Sun decided to develop a new RPC security flavor that would address the problems, with one added feature: it would be infinitely extendable, so that key size limitations, and problems with cryptographic algorithms (cryptographers are constantly finding problems with various algorithms) would not slow development of new security mechanisms.

The new security flavor is called RPCSEC_GSS. Note that it does not have the AUTH_ prefix like AUTH_SYS and AUTH_DH. This is because it provides integrity and privacy services in addition to authentication.

RPCSEC_GSS is based on the Generic Security Services API (GSS-API). GSS-API provides the ability to write applications that can authenticate clients and servers, integrity protect the messages they exchange, and also privacy protect the messages they exchange. GSS-API also permits one to "plug in" different security mechanisms or providers without changing the application that uses GSS-API. Figure 12-2 depicts the GSS-API multiplex applications that are consumers of GSS-API, and mechanisms that are providers for GSS-API.

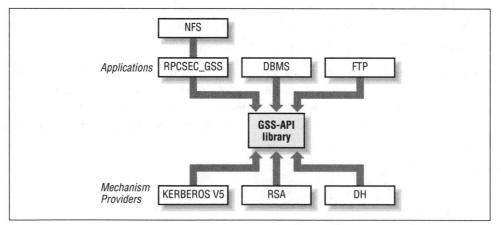

Figure 12-2. GSS-API architecture

RPCSEC_GSS leverages GSS-API capabilities to provide authentication, integrity, and privacy if the security mechanism provider supports those services. Currently Kerberos V5 is the mostly widely deployed GSS-API security provider, and it does support all three services. NFS over RPCSEC_GSS can use Kerberos V5's capabilities. At the time this book was written:

- Solaris (2.6, 7, and 8) was the only known Unix operating system offering an NFS implementation that supported Kerberos V5 security.

- At least two PC/NFS implementations—Hummingbird's Maestro, and Netmanage's Interdrive—supported Kerberos V5 security.

Kerberos V5

The Kerberos V5 system was developed at the Massachusetts Institute of Technology. It is another mechanism for enforcing security within a service, but it differs from RPC/DH in several ways:

- Kerberos uses multiple levels of DES encryption to exchange keys and passwords. No public key encryption is used.

- A *Key Distribution Center* (*KDC*) is required to maintain Kerberos V5 service passwords; this server must be kept safe from attack to preserve the integrity of the Kerberos system. RPC/DH uses the *publickey* map, which is available to all NIS clients. The data in the *publickey* map is encrypted using user's login passwords, not an additional RPC/DH password.

- Kerberos V5 authentication is built into the entire service, or application, not just into the session layer. For example, you can use Kerberos to make the line printer spooling daemon secure. Doing so, however, requires the source code to the line printer software.

- Kerberos V5 has the notion of *forwardable* credentials. Think back to earlier in this chapter (see "Establishing a session key") when we talked about *rlogin*, transparent access, and the fact that when using NFS/dh, you still had to provide a password to *keylogin* even though (or rather, because) *rlogin* didn't prompt for one. Kerberos V5 has replacements for programs like *rlogin* and *telnet* that work like that which they replace, but also support some extra features:

  — Kerberos V5 is used to authenticate the user, not passwords.

  — Traffic between the client and server is optionally encrypted as a way to provide privacy protection.

  — Credentials can be forwarded from the client to the server. This feature, known as a *forwardable ticket granting ticket*, allows the following sequence of events:

  a. The user logs into his desktop machine. He is prompted for his Unix login password, which also happens to be his Kerberos V5 password. This results in a *ticket granting ticket* (TGT) being sent from the KDC to his desktop. His home directory is NFS-mounted but exported with Kerberos V5 security (*sec=krb5*).

b. The NFS filesystem uses the TGT to get an NFS *service ticket* from the KDC, which allows the user to be authenticated to the NFS server. The service ticket is encrypted with the NFS server's key, which both the KDC and the NFS server know about. The NFS server can decrypt the service ticket from the client because the server stores the server's key in its */etc/krb5/krb5.keytab* file, which is analogous to RPC/DH's */etc/.rootkey* file.

c. The user now wishes to log onto a remote system. He uses a Kerberized version of *rlogin* to do so, passing a command-line option that indicates that he wants his TGT to be forwarded.

d. The NFS filesystem on the remote system must do an NFS mount of the user's home directory, which is still exported with *sec=krb5*. It needs an NFS service ticket to authenticate the user to the NFS server. Because the TGT has been forwarded, no password prompt to the user is necessary.

Thus the user, having authenticated himself once when he logged into his desktop, can roam freely and securely among the network, as he did in the days when the network was using simple host-based trust for *rlogin* and NFS.

SEAM: Kerberos V5 for Solaris

Sun's Kerberos V5 implementation is called *Sun Enterprise Authentication Mechanism* (SEAM).

For this chapter to completely explain how to set up SEAM for running Kerberos V5 and NFS secured with Kerberos V5, it would have to include as much material as was written in this chapter about NIS and NFS/dh, and all the chapters leading up to it. In other words, the title of this book would be *Managing NIS, Kerberos V5, and NFS*. Fortunately, the SEAM documentation is well-written, and the installation fairly turnkey.* Thus it is not clear that much value could be added in this book to explain minutiae of SEAM.

However, the rest of this section collects some practical overview information on SEAM that you might find useful as you approach the issue of deploying Kerberos V5.

SEAM 1.0 is available for Solaris 2.6 and Solaris 7, and is packaged with the *Solaris Easy Access Server* (SEAS) 3.0 product, which is unbundled from Solaris 2.6 and Solaris 7. If you bought a server from Sun, you might find SEAS 3.0 preinstalled. At

---

* This appraisal is the opinion of one of the co-authors of this book, Mike Eisler, who was the project lead for SEAM while employed by Sun Microsystems, Inc.

the time this book was written, SEAM 1.0.1 was available for Solaris 8 as a free download from Sun's website. Look for the product called *Solaris 8 Admin Pack*. Do not attempt to run SEAM 1.0 on Solaris 8. If you upgrade to Solaris 8 from a Solaris 2.6 or Solaris 7 system that has SEAM 1.0 installed, then you should immediately install SEAM 1.0.1.

SEAM 1.0 and SEAM 1.0.1 rely on a GUI-based installation technology that is similar to Installshield for Windows systems. What you do not want to do is go ahead and install SEAM without reading the documentation. A couple of notes:

- SEAM 1.0 comes on the SEAS 3.0 CD-ROM. Install the SEAS 3.0 documentation first, and read through the SEAM 1.0 documentation.

- SEAM 1.0.1 is part of the Solaris 8 Admin Pack, and at the time this book was written, the only way to get SEAM 1.0.1 was to download it. You can download SEAM 1.0.1 separately from the rest of the Admin Pack. However, be warned that it comes in a self-extracting shell script, otherwise known as a *shar* file; the term *shar* stands for *shell archive*. The *shar* file proceeds to run the GUI installer, and the installer does not let you install the documentation first, because it doesn't have the documentation. Instead, you first need to download the documentation separately (which includes all the documentation of the Admin Pack, so it is a large download). Once you've downloaded the documentation, start reading it.

  There is also documentation on SEAM in the Solaris 8 administration documents. It is worth reading this as well.

Note that the SEAS 3.0 and Admin Pack documentation are packaged in the form of web pages.

As you read the SEAM documentation, it should be clear that SEAM and NIS plus RPC/DH share some parallels, including:

- Both have master servers (SEAM has a master KDC, and NIS has a master NIS server).

- Both recommend one or more slave servers.

- Both have a distinct client component.

- Both have a client-side daemon for managing session keys (SEAM has *gssd*, RPC/DH has *keyserv*).

If you read the SEAM 1.0 documentation from the SEAS 3.0 product, the SEAM 1.0.1 documentation from the Admin Pack, and the SEAM documentation in Solaris 8, you see that progressive releases of Solaris, from 2.6 onward, integrate more and more components of SEAM. Table 12-1 describes the progression so far.

Table 12-1. SEAM progression

Solaris Release	Unbundled Product	SEAM Version	Features Integrated with Solaris	Features Integrated in Unbundled Product
Solaris 2.6	SEAS 3.0	SEAM 1.0	RPCSEC_GSS hooks	KDC, Remote KDC administration, Kerberized networking utilities, Kerberos client utilities, RPCSEC_GSS, GSS-API, Kerberos V5 GSS provider, Kerberos V5 PAM module
Solaris 7	SEAS 3.0	SEAM 1.0	RPCSEC_GSS, GSS-API	KDC, Remote KDC administration, Kerberized networking utilities, Kerberos client utilities, Kerberos V5 GSS provider, Kerberos V5 PAM module
Solaris 8	Solaris 8 Admin Pack	SEAM 1.0.1	RPCSEC_GSS, GSS-API, Kerberos client utilities, Kerberos V5 GSS provider, Kerberos V5 PAM module	KDC, Remote KDC administration, Kerberized networking utilities

Presumably the progression in Table 12-1 will continue with future versions of Solaris and other operating systems.

The fifth column of Table 12-1 consistently lists "Kerberized networking utilities." These are utilities like *rlogin*, *rsh*, *rcp*, *ftp*, and *telnet* (and their server daemons) that have been modified to understand Kerberos V5 security. The reason they are there is that they facilitate the deployment of an Intranet that sends no passwords in the clear over the wire, and indeed, via forwardable TGTs, enables you to send no passwords at all. Without these utilities, there would be less point in having strong NFS security, since passwords would often appear on your network. This is another drawback of RPC/DH: it does not add strong security to the basic networking utilities.

By now, we've mentioned PAM several times without explaining it. Recall that your RPC/DH password is used to decrypt your private key. If your RPC/DH password is the same as your Unix login password, then you don't need to provide your RPC/DH password separately. How does this happen? The Solaris *login* command has code in it to try to decrypt the user's private key with the Unix login password. Now suppose you've installed Kerberos V5 and would like the system to attempt to use the Unix login password as the key that decrypts your TGT from the KDC. One way would be for your operating system vendor to change the *login* command to do so. But then, you decide you'd like the *su* command and the desktop lock screen feature to do the same. After a while, it gets to be a lot of utilities to maintain. A better way is to have pluggable framework that calls security mechanism specific code in shared objects and has them take care of acquiring credentials. This is what PAM does. SEAM provides a Kerberos V5 PAM module. Check out your system's documentation for information on PAM; PAM is common to many Unix systems.

Here are some final recommendations for and observations about SEAM installation:

- SEAM allows you to use it without DNS running. Don't do that. If you ever change your mind, you'll have to repopulate the entire principal (analogous to an RPC/DH *netname*) database in the KDC.

- It is better to install SEAM clients (which can be NFS clients or NFS servers) by utilizing the preconfiguration steps that the documentation talks about, and the GUI installer tries to walk you through. Keep in mind that the preconfiguration information need only, and should only, be established once, on an NFS server. You then run the SEAM installer on each host, pointing it at the preconfigured information on an NFS mounted or automounted filesystem (usually same filesystem where the installer lives). This reduces per-host installation tedium.

- The SEAM documentation is very task-oriented, and hence very practical. Even if you ultimately want to do things differently, practice first, and follow the documentation examples as close to verbatim as possible before you try something complex or a little bit different.

- Do not skip any steps. SEAM is rather unforgiving if a small, but critical step is missed. You'll find that you can cut and paste from the web-based documentation into your command shell, and if you make that a habit, you'll stay out of trouble.

Enabling Kerberized NFS

This section assumes that you've gone through the installation and configuration that the SEAM documentation describes.

Enabling Kerberized NFS on a filesystem is quite simple: export and mount the filesystem with the *sec=krb5* option. On the NFS server, the */etc/dfs/dfstab* entry looks like this:

```
share -o sec=krb5,rw /export/home/thud
```

When a filesystem is exported with the *sec=krb5* option, clients using NFS Version 2 must mount it with the *sec=krb5* option if they are to enjoy normal user access privileges in the filesystem. On the NFS client, add the *sec=krb5* option in the automounter map entry or the */etc/vfstab* entry for the filesystem:

automounter auto_home entry:
```
thud                          -sec=krb5        bonk:/export/home/thud
```

vfstab entry:
```
bonk:/export/home/thud - /thud nfs  - no  sec=krb5
```

As was the case for enabling NFS/dh (see "Enabling NFS/dh") with NFS Version 3, the *sec=krb5* option is not necessary in the automounter map or *vfstab* entries.

The *krb5* option uses a combination of DES symmetric key encryption and the MD5 one-way hash function to produce the RPC credentials that are sent to, and authenticated by, the NFS server.

Not only is there a *krb5* option to *sec=*, but there are *krbi* and *krbp* as well.

Like the *krb5* option, *krb5i* uses Kerberos V5 to authenticate users to NFS servers when the filesystem is exported with *sec=krb5i*. Unlike *krb5*, it also computes an MD5-based MAC on every remote procedure call request to the server, and every response to the client. The MAC is computed on an entire message: RPC header, plus NFS arguments or results. Thus *krb5i* provides *i*ntegrity protection, hence the trailing *i* in *krb5i*.

Like *krb5* and *krb5i*, *krb5p* uses Kerberos V5 to authenticate. Like *krb5i* it uses Kerberos V5 to provide integrity. Unlike *krb5* and *krb5i*, *krb5p* uses Kerberos V5's DES encryption to provide privacy. Note that only the NFS arguments and results are encrypted; the RPC headers go in the clear. So an attacker could deduce which NFS operation is being performed, but not on what file, nor what the file or directory content is.

Security and performance

So, why wouldn't a client want to always mount with *krb5p*? It is, after all, the most secure of *sec=* options we've seen in this book. The reason is that as soon as you involve cryptography in data processing, you slow down the processing. This is because cryptography tends to be a highly CPU-bound function. Consider the performance results in Table 12-2. The NFS client and server were each running Solaris 8 with SEAM. Both the systems were Sun Ultra 5 systems, each with 128 megabytes of RAM, and one 270 Mhz CPU. A 200 megabyte file was written from the client to the server to the server's */tmp* file system, via the *mkfile* utility. NFS Version 3 over TCP was used. As we can see from Table 12-2, the *krb5* option does not cost much to use relative to *sys*. But *krb5i* and *krb5p* added increasingly significant overhead. Some people have the reasonable perspective that drop off in throughput is not as important as the increased CPU utilization.

Table 12-2. Kerberized NFS performance

sec= value	Throughput in MB/sec	Throughput Degradation Relative to *sec=sys*	Percent CPU Utilization on Server
sys	5.40	N/A	69%
krb5	5.26	2.6%	70%
krb5i	4.44	17.7%	77%
krb5p	1.45	73.1%	99%

Combining krb5, krb5i, krb5p

You can combine the *krb5** options with each other.

Let's suppose */export/home* on server *labrador* contains the home directories of security conscious folks, though some are less paranoid than others. You can accommodate everyone by adding the following to */etc/dfs/dfstab*:

```
share  o sec=krb5p:krb5i:krb5,rw /export/home
```

This means the clients pick any of the three flavors of *krb5* when they mount the NFS filesystem. Note that this is one instance where even if the client is using NFS Version 3, that the administrator on the client may want to specify a *sec=* option in their automounter maps or *vfstab* or on their *mount* command line. The reason is that the client (at least the Solaris 8 client) will pick from the array of security flavors that *mountd* returns the first security flavor that the client supports. So if a client prefers *krb5* but *krb5p* is first, *sec=* is needed for the *mount* command to override the automatic choice.

Given the results in Table 12-2, you might want to be careful about exporting filesystems with *krb5i* or *krb5p* security enabled. If you have data that can go in the clear on the network, then never export it with *krb5p*. If your users are writing data over the network, and very bad things could happen if an attacker spliced the RPC header from a *sec=krb5* NFS request onto a forged set of destructive arguments, then enable *krb5i*. Otherwise *krb5* should be sufficient. Indeed, for certain kinds of read-only data, *sec=sys* or *sec=none* are fine.

IPSec versus krb5i and krb5p

As discussed earlier in "NFS and IPSec," IPSec can provide integrity (AH) and privacy (ESP) services. If you are enabling AH and ESP then do you need to use *krb5i* or *krb5p*? Note that the session keys for AH and ESP are derived from per-host keys, whereas the session keys for *krb5i* and *krb5p* are derived from per user keys. If you are paranoid about attacks on hosts to find the IPSec keys, then you'll want to run *krb5i* and *krb5p* in addition to AH and ESP. However, it will cost you double in CPU utilization to do so. In general, it is not necessary to use *krb5i* if

AH is used, and not necessary to use *krb5p* is ESP is used. However, even if AH or ESP is used to protect NFS traffic, it still makes sense to use *krb5* protection on your NFS traffic if you want strong authentication.

Planning a transition from NFS/sys to stronger NFS security

Perhaps you've been exporting filesystems with *sec=sys* (the default if *sec=* is not specified) for some time, and now decide to start using better NFS security, such as NFS/dh or Kerberized NFS. One issue is that it takes less time to reconfigure servers to use stronger NFS security than to reconfigure clients, because there are more client machines, and more user ids than host ids to add to the various tables that RPC/DH and Kerberos V5 require. Also, some NFS client implementations may not be running Solaris 8, and may support the stronger NFS security that you decide to switch to. So even after you get your servers reconfigured to use Kerberos V5 security, it won't be practical to simply change:

```
share -o rw /export/home
```

to:

```
share -o sec=krb5,rw /export/home
```

and not expect some chaos. That you can combine any two or more *sec=* options on the same *dfstab* entry allows you to stage some graceful transitions.

For example, suppose you've decided to use NFS/dh. You may have some legacy software running on some NFS clients that is stuck on older systems. Thus you can't upgrade the client systems to an operating system that can support stronger NFS security. You can do the following:

```
share -o sec=sys,rw=legacy-group,sec=dh,rw=upgrade-group /export/home
```

such that the legacy machines and upgrade machines are each placed in their own netgroup.

NFS security futures

In a previous section, "Asymmetric key encryption," we mentioned the RSA public key algorithm, but did not talk about any NFS security that uses RSA. RSA is arguably the best asymmetric key encryption algorithm known to us. It is the foundation of most Public Key Infrastructure (PKI) products, as well as networking protocols like SSL/TLS and S/MIME. So why doesn't NFS use it? The main issue with RSA is that it was patented and so royalties were due to its rights holders. Now that the patent has expired, expect to see the following features in the future:

- Asymmetric key technology integrated with Kerberos V5. Without asymmetric key technology, a physical compromise of the KDC effectively compromises all of the principals listed in KDC, as it stores each user's symmetric key. With asymmetric key technology, only the public key needs to be stored in the KDC.

- The NFS Version 4 protocol specifies an SSL-like GSS-API mechanism provider called LIPKEY as one of the two required security providers to RPCSEC_ GSS (Kerberos V5 being the other). LIPKEY uses asymmetric key algorithms. So when NFS Version 4 is deployed widely, expect to see RSA used to secure it. Like SSL, LIPKEY can be easily used through a firewall.

The poor performance of *krb5p* (Table 12-2) is due largely to the fact that DES is a very slow algorithm. There are faster, not to mention more secure, algorithms, but many of them are proprietary, subject to royalties. The royalty free *Advanced Encryption Standard* (*AES*) has been selected to replace DES. AES is faster and more secure than DES. Expect to see future versions of NFS run over Kerberos V5 and LIPKEY using AES as the encryption algorithm.

Viruses

A computer virus is a piece of code that modifies the operating system or system utilities with harmful or annoying side effects. Like human viruses, a computer virus reproduces itself and spreads through a vector, or carrier. Once one computer is infected, the virus attempts to copy itself onto floppies or other removable media that will be taken to other systems. When an infected disk is inserted into a healthy system, the virus loads itself into the uninfected system. Entire networks of computers may be infected from a single disk that infects a system that later infects a file server, for example.

Effects of viruses vary greatly. Some simply render the machine useless, echoing annoying messages back to the user but preventing any "real" command execution. Others are destructive in nature, scribbling on critical filesystem information on hard disks or removing key files.

Viruses are virtually unknown in time-sharing operating systems such as Unix that enforce kernel protection. The operating system cannot be modified without superuser permission, so random user applications cannot inject viruses into the system. The Windows operating system, on the other hand, does not protect its kernel code or disk files, so an executable can overwrite parts of the kernel, the DOS image on disk, or various system utilities. Once the disk image is infected, the system remains infected, even through reboots or power cycles. Note that viruses are not the same as worms, rabbits, or other user-level processes that consume resources or reproduce rapidly enough to bring a system to a halt. A computer virus specifically damages the operating system.

Enforcing basic security around the root password and superuser access to machines should be sufficient to deter deliberate planting of viruses in the Unix kernel. In addition to securing access from the local area network, verify that your systems are safe from attacks from external networks such as the Internet. If you can prevent unauthorized superuser access, then you must only worry about things that you or your system administrators do as *root*.

Watch what you put into *cron* entries. Any script that gets run by *cron* should be owned by *root* and either not writable or writable only by *root*. If a user asks for a shell script to be added to *root*'s *crontab*, install the script so that the user cannot modify it once it has been added to the *crontab* file.

Similarly, avoid any package that requires an executable to be run as *root* as part of its installation process, unless you can vouch for the integrity of the package's provider. In general, vendors stand behind the safety of their software, and you should not worry about "branding" utilities that write serial number information into executable images or packages. It is becoming the norm for vendors to include a strong cryptographic checksum like MD5, or a verifiable digital signature with software on removable media or web sites. Such practices are a good sign that your vendor is taking care to secure its software from viruses, but such practices do you the most good when you take the time to verify the checksum or signature before installing the software.

The same guidelines that apply to Windows users also apply to Unix system administrators: if you don't know where an executable came from, don't run it as *root*. This is especially true for executables taken from public domain sources. If you can't get the source code, don't experiment with it unless you are willing to perform a post-installation check for damage. Above all else, use common sense. If you feel uncomfortable loaning your car keys to a complete stranger, you should feel equally queasy about installing strange software on your system as *root*.

13

Network Diagnostic and Administrative Tools

Distributed computing architectures rely on a well-conditioned network and properly configured servers for their adequate performance and operation. NFS and NIS client performance degrades if your network is congested or your servers are unreliable. Retransmitted requests add to the noise level on the network or to the request backlog on the server, generally exacerbating any performance problems.

Whenever you make a change, you run the risk of affecting more than just one machine. If you add a new NFS client, for example, you should consider all possible impacts on the computing environment: network bandwidth consumed by traffic to and from this node, or the incremental workload imposed on any servers used by the client. Similarly, when upgrading server resources you must identify those areas that are the tightest constraints: CPU speed, disk speed, or aggregate disk space. Adding another server to a network may not be as economical or beneficial as upgrading to faster disks, adding CPUs to an expandable server or offloading other tasks, such as web service to another host.

This portion of the book focuses on network analysis, debugging, and performance tuning. Its goal is to present the tools, procedures, and evaluation criteria used for analyzing network, NFS, or NIS problems. In addition to tuning and administration, these techniques can be used to evaluate proposals for expanding an existing network with additional clients or servers. Symptoms and causes of common problems will be examined in detail, but the overall focus is on developing techniques to be used on complex problems peculiar to your specific combination of hardware and software.

In this chapter, we present tools for examining the configuration and performance of individual network components, starting at the lowest level of basic point-to-point connectivity and working up to the RPC layer where the NFS- and NIS-specific issues come into play. The chapter includes examples relevant to problem diagnosis to define the methods for collecting and interpreting data about the network and its components. A healthy network is essential to the proper behavior of NFS and NIS. Developing network diagnostic skills is necessary for resolving problems that may only be apparent at the application level. NFS may behave poorly because of a saturated network or due to an overloaded server; a thorough examination of the problem requires checking each component involved. If you fail to understand the low-level operation of a facility, you are more likely to misinterpret performance or usage statistics provided for that facility. We cover the lower layers of the network protocols in detail so that you can see how they affect the performance and behavior of the application layer protocols like NFS and NIS.

As explained in "Name service switch" in Chapter 2, NIS and DNS can be used concurrently to resolve hostnames on the same system, although throughout the remainder of this book, we assume that NIS is the only name service running. In some cases, we refer to local files that are used without NIS. However, examples and discussions refer to the most common NIS maps, as shown in Table 13-1.

Table 13-1. Common NIS maps and their nicknames

Map Name	Nickname	Local File
passwd.byname	*passwd*	*/etc/passwd*
group.byname	*group*	*/etc/group*
hosts.byname	*hosts*	*/etc/inet/hosts*
ipnodes.byname	*ipnodes*	*/etc/inet/ipnodes*
rpc.bynumber	*rpc*	*/etc/rpc*
services.byname	*services*	*/etc/inet/services*
netmasks.byaddr	*netmasks*	*/etc/inet/netmasks*

The */etc/inet/ipnodes* file and *ipnodes* NIS map form a database that associates the names of nodes with their IP addresses. The IP addresses can be either IPv4 or IPv6 addresses. The *ipnodes* database was introduced in Solaris 8 to support IPv6-aware[*] and IPv6-enabled[†] applications that need to obtain IPv6 addresses. When these applications need IPv4 addresses, they first consult the *ipnodes* database. If the address is not found, they then consult the traditional *hosts* database. IPv6-unaware[‡] applications simply consult the *hosts* database, as they are unaware of IPv6 extensions. Although not a requirement, IPv4 addresses defined in the *hosts*

---

[*] IPv6-aware applications can communicate with nodes that do not have an IPv4 address. This means that the application can handle the larger IPv6 addresses.

[†] IPv6-enabled applications take advantage of some IPv6-specific feature. The enabled applications can still operate over IPv4, though in a degraded mode. IPv6-enabled applications are also IPv6-aware.

[‡] IPv6-unaware applications cannot handle IPv6 addresses; therefore, they cannot communicate with nodes that do not have an IPv4 address.

database should be copied to the *ipnodes* database in order to prevent delays in name resolution, and to keep the *ipnodes* and *hosts* database in sync.

Throughout this chapter we assume that your system is capable of using both IPv4 and IPv6, and uses the *ipnodes* database to obtain IP address mappings. If your system does not support IPv6 yet, then replace references to the *ipnodes* database with the *hosts* database. To reiterate, an unsuccessful lookup of an IPv4 address in the *ipnodes* database implies a subsequent lookup of the same address in the *hosts* database.

Broadcast addresses

Many network problems stem from confusion or inconsistency in the way hosts form their IP broadcast addresses. Broadcast addresses are used when a packet must be sent to all machines on the local area network. For example, if your host needs to send a packet to another machine, it must know the remote machine's IP address and Ethernet address. It can determine the remote IP address by looking up the remote hostname in the NIS *ipnodes* map, but it may not have the corresponding Ethernet address. If this is the first time your machine is talking to this particular remote host, it won't have had an opportunity to locate or save the remote Ethernet address. The way to determine the remote machine's Ethernet address is to ask all of the hosts on the network if they have the information, using the Address Resolution Protocol (ARP). To broadcast this request to all hosts on the network, your host uses a special kind of destination address called a broadcast address. A normal (or unicast) address identifies only one host; a broadcast address identifies all hosts on the network.

To be an effective broadcast, the packet must reach all nodes on the local area network and be recognized as a broadcast packet by them. An improperly formed broadcast address, or one that other systems do not recognize as such, can be responsible for failures ranging from NIS clients that cannot find servers to storms of broadcast packets initiated by a single packet sent with the wrong broadcast address.

Like host addresses, broadcast addresses exist in both the MAC and IPv4 layers of the protocol stack. There are no broadcast addresses in IPv6; their function is superseded by multicast addresses.* An IPv4 broadcast address is converted into a MAC broadcast address, just as a host-specific IP address is converted into a 48-bit

---

* Multicast addresses are used to define subgroups of recipients of data. If a sender needs to contact a large number of hosts simultaneously, the sender can multicast a single message to all hosts listening on the given multicast address, instead of issuing multiple copies of the same message to every single host. The hosts listening on the multicast address do not need to be part of the same subnetwork as the sender.

Ethernet address. At the MAC layer, there is exactly one broadcast address; for Ethernet it is:

```
ff:ff:ff:ff:ff:ff
```

Every node on the local network receives a packet having this destination MAC address. A host may ignore a broadcast if the request is for a service that it does not provide. A host processes every broadcast packet, at the very least deciding to discard it. Therefore, a high level of broadcast traffic hurts the performance of each host on the network.

While the MAC layer broadcast address is very clearly defined, there is some variation in the form of IPv4 broadcast addresses. There are two distinct popular forms, mostly due to evolution of the networking code in Berkeley-based Unix systems.* Examples of broadcast addresses of each form are shown for each IPv4 address class in Table 13-2. IPv4 address classes are described in the section "IPv4 address classes" in Chapter 1.

Table 13-2. Broadcast address forms

Address Class	Example	Ones Form	Zeros Form
Class A	89.	89.255.255.255	89.0.0.0
Class B	129.7.	129.7.255.255	129.7.0.0
Class C	192.6.4.	192.6.4.255	192.6.4.0
Classless	192.1.2. /23	192.1.3.255	192.1.3.0

The ones form is the most widely accepted and is used in all examples in this book. Octets of the IPv4 address that specify the host number are filled in with 1-valued bits. A variation on the ones form is the zeros form, in which the host number is expressed as zero-valued octets. The all-ones form:

```
255.255.255.255
```

is a variation of the proper ones form address where the 255-valued octets occupy only the host number portion of the address.

Confusion regarding the "proper" broadcast address stems from the interpretation of octet values 0 and 255 in IPv4 addresses. Zero-valued octets should be used as place holders when specifying a network number and imply "this" network, without any real implication for host numbers. For example, 129.7.0.0 means *network number* 129.7., but it does not necessarily name any hosts on the network.

---

* The 4.2 BSD release of Unix introduced TCP/IP and required use of the zeros form of broadcast addresses. All derivatives of 4.2 BSD, including SunOS 3.x and early versions of Ultrix, retained this broadcast address requirement. In 4.3 BSD, the ones form of broadcast addresses was adopted, although the zeros form was still supported. Unix operating systems that are descendants of 4.3 BSD—SunOS 4.x included—support both one- and zero-filled broadcast addresses. Solaris supports only the ones form.

Conversely, the one-filled octets are treated like wildcards and imply "any" host on the network. The network number is specified but the host number matches all hosts on that network. Using these connotations for octet values 0 and 255, the ones form of the broadcast address is "correct." There are cases in which the zeros form must be used for backwards compatibility with older operating system releases. Many systems were built using the zeros form of broadcast addresses.

The sole requirement in adopting a broadcast address form is to make the choice consistent across all machines on the network and compatible with your vendor's supported convention. Machines that expect a zeros-form broadcast address interpret a one-filled octet as part of a host number rather than a wildcard. Mixing broadcast address forms on the same network is the most common cause of broadcast storms, in which every confused node on the network transmits and retransmits replies to a broadcast address of a form complementary to the one it is using.

Broadcast addresses, muticast addresses, IP addresses, and other characteristics of the Ethernet interface are set with the *ifconfig* utility. Because *ifconfig* governs the lowest level interface of a node to the network, it is the logical place to begin the discussion of network tools.

MAC and IP layer tools

The tools covered in this section operate at the MAC and IP layers of the network protocol stack. Problems that manifest themselves as NFS or NIS failures may be due to an improper host or network configuration problem. The tools described in this section are used to ascertain that the basic network connectivity is sound. Issues that will be covered include setting network addresses, testing connectivity, and burst traffic handling.

ifconfig: interface configuration

ifconfig sets or examines the characteristics of a network interface, such as its IP address or availability. At boot time, *ifconfig* is used to initialize network interfaces, possibly doing this in stages since some information may be available on the network itself through NIS. You can also use *ifconfig* to examine the current state of an interface and compare its address assignments with NIS map information. Interfaces may be physical devices, logical devices associated with a physical network interface, IP tunnels, or pseudo-devices such as the loopback device. Examples of physical devices include Ethernet interfaces or packet drivers stacked on top of low-level synchronous line drivers. IP tunnels are point-to-point interfaces that enable an IP packet to be encapsulated within another IP packet, appearing as a physical interface. For example, an IPv6-in-IPv4 tunnel allows IPv6 packets to be encapsulated within IPv4 packets, allowing IPv6 traffic to cross routers that understand only IPv4.

Examining interfaces

To list all available network interfaces, invoke *ifconfig* with the *-a* option:[*]

```
% ifconfig -a
lo0: flags=1000849<UP,LOOPBACK,RUNNING,MULTICAST,IPv4> mtu 8232 index 1
          inet 127.0.0.1 netmask ff000000
hme0: flags=1000843<UP,BROADCAST,RUNNING,MULTICAST,IPv4> mtu 1500 index 2
          inet 131.40.52.126 netmask ffffff00 broadcast 131.40.52.255
lo0: flags=2000849<UP,LOOPBACK,RUNNING,MULTICAST,IPv6> mtu 8252 index 1
          inet6 ::1/128
hme0: flags=2000841<UP,RUNNING,MULTICAST,IPv6> mtu 1500 index 2
          inet6 fe80::a00:20ff:fe81:23f1/10
hme0:1: flags=2080841<UP,RUNNING,MULTICAST,ADDRCONF,IPv6> mtu 1500 index 2
          inet6 fec0::56:a00:20ff:fe81:23f1/64
hme0:2: flags=2080841<UP,RUNNING,MULTICAST,ADDRCONF,IPv6> mtu 1500 index 2
          inet6 2100::56:a00:20ff:fe81:23f1/64
```

In this example, *ifconfig* lists four different interfaces, *lo0*, *hme0*, *hme0:1*, and *hme0:2*. *lo0* is the loopback pseudo-device used by IP to communicate between network applications that specify the local host on both end-points. *hme0* is the actual physical Ethernet device configured on the host. Note that *lo0* is listed in two different lines: the first line reports the loopback configuration in use by IPv4, and the third line reports the loopback configuration in use by IPv6. IPv4 specifies 127.0.0.1 as the loopback address; IPv6 specifies ::1/128. Similarly, the second line reports the IPv4 address used by the *hme0* device (131.40.52.126), and the fourth line reports the device's IPv6 link-local address (fe80::a00:20ff:fe81:23f1/10).

Solaris supports multiple logical interfaces associated with a single physical network interface. This allows a host to be assigned multiple IP addresses (even if the host only has a single network interface). This is particularly useful when a host communicates over various IPv6 addresses. In this example, *hme0:1* and *hme0:2* are logical interfaces associated with the physical network interface *hme0*. *hme0:1* uses the site-local IPv6 address fec0::56:a00:20ff:fe81:23f1/64, and *hme0:2* uses the global IPv6 address 2100::56:a00:20ff:fe81:23f1/64.

To examine a particular network interface, invoke *ifconfig* with its name as an argument. By default, the IPv4 interface configuration is reported, unless you specify the address family you are interested in, as in the third example:

---

[*] The protocols listed will depend on the contents of *inet_type(4)*. Both IPv6 and IPv4 will be listed if */etc/default/inet_type* does not exist, or if it defines DEFAULT_IP=BOTH. Only IPv4 will be listed if DEFAULT_IP=IP_VERSION4. The network interface Ethernet address will also be reported when *ifconfig* is invoked as *root*.

```
% ifconfig hme0
hme0: flags=1000843<UP,BROADCAST,RUNNING,MULTICAST,IPv4> mtu 1500 index 2
        inet 131.40.52.126 netmask ffffff00 broadcast 131.40.52.255

% ifconfig lo0
lo0: flags=1000849<UP,LOOPBACK,RUNNING,MULTICAST,IPv4> mtu 8232 index 1
        inet 127.0.0.1 netmask ff000000

% ifconfig hme0 inet6
hme0: flags=2000841<UP,RUNNING,MULTICAST,IPv6> mtu 1500 index 2
        inet6 fe80::a00:20ff:fe81:23f1/10
```

If the specified interface does not exist on the system or is not configured into the kernel, *ifconfig* reports the error "No such device."

The *flags* field is a bitmap that describes the state of the interface. Values for the flags may be found in */usr/include/net/if.h*. The most common settings are:

UP

The network interface has been marked up and is enabled to send or receive packets.

RUNNING

Kernel resources, such as device driver buffers, have been allocated to the interface to allow it to handle packets. An interface can be marked UP but not be running if the kernel is having trouble getting resources assigned to the interface. This is usually never a problem for Ethernet interfaces, but may surface when synchronous serial lines or fiber optic links are used. Note that Solaris hosts always have this flag set, regardless of the state of the interface.

BROADCAST

A valid broadcast address has been assigned to this interface. The interface reports its broadcast address when queried, and broadcast packets can be sent from the interface. There are no broadcast addresses in IPv6—their function is superseded by multicast addresses

LOOPBACK

The interface is a loopback device: packets sent out on the device are immediately placed on a receive queue for other processes on the local host. Although the loopback device is implemented entirely in software, you must configure it as though it were a physical network interface.

MULTICAST

A valid multicast address has been assigned to this interface. Listening on a multicast address is analogous to listening to a particular band of the radio dial. The packet is not addressed to a particular interface, instead, it is addressed to all interfaces listening on that multicast address.

IPV4 / IPV6

> Indicates the version of the Internet Protocol in use. The same interface can be configured to use both versions, although *ifconfig* prints the respective configuration on separate lines.

The *mtu* specifies the maximum transmission unit of the interface. IP uses path MTU discovery to determine the maximum transmission unit size across the link. On point-to-point links, the MTU is negotiated by the applications setting up the connection on both sides.

Every configured physical device is assigned a unique index number. The kernel associates the configuration values (IP address, MTU, etc.) with the index number for internal bookkeeping. It provides a useful means for network programming APIs to identify network interfaces.

The second line of *ifconfig*'s output shows the Internet (IP) address assigned to this interface, the broadcast (IPv4 only) address, and the network mask that is applied to the IPv4 address to derive the broadcast address. The previous example shows the ones form of the broadcast address. When invoked by *root*, *ifconfig* also displays the interface's Ethernet address where applicable.

The output of *ifconfig* resembles the first example for almost all Ethernet interfaces configured to use IPv4, and the third example for almost all Ethernet interfaces configured to use IPv6. *ifconfig* reports different state information if the interface is for a synchronous serial line, the underlying data link for point-to-point IP networks. Point-to-point links are one foundation of a wide-area network, since they allow IP packets to be run over long-haul serial lines. When configuring a point-to-point link, the broadcast address is replaced with a destination address for the other end of the point-to-point link, and the BROADCAST flag is replaced by the POINTTOPOINT flag:

```
this-side% ifconfig ipdptp0
ipdptp0: flags=10088d1<UP,POINTOPOINT,RUNNING,NOARP,MULTICAST,PRIVATE,IPv4> mtu
8232 index 3
        inet 131.40.46.1 --> 131.40.1.12 netmask ffffff00
```

This interface is a serial line that connects networks 131.40.46.0 and 131.40.1.0; the machine on the other end of the line has a similar point-to-point interface configuration with the local and destination IP addresses reversed:

```
that-side% ifconfig ipdptp0
ipdptp0: flags=10088d1<UP,POINTOPOINT,RUNNING,NOARP,MULTICAST,PRIVATE,IPv4> mtu
8232 index 5
        inet 131.40.1.12 --> 131.40.46.1 netmask ffffff00
```

Marking the line PRIVATE means that the host-to-host connection will not be advertised to routers on the network. Note also that the Address Resolution Protocol (ARP) is not used over point-to-point links.

Initializing an interface

In addition to displaying the status of a network interface, *ifconfig* is used to configure the interface. During the boot process, Solaris identifies the network interfaces to be configured by searching for */etc/hostname.*[0-9] and */etc/hostname6.*[0-9] files. For example the presence of */etc/hostname.hme0* and */etc/hostname.hme1* indicate that the two network interfaces *hme0* and *hme1* need to be assigned an IPv4 address at boot time. Similarly, the presence of */etc/hostname6.hme0* indicates that *hme0* needs to be configured to use IPv6. You can statically assign an IP address to the interface by specifying the corresponding hostname in the */etc/hostname.*[0-9] or */etc/hostname6.*[0-9] file. Hostnames and their corresponding IP addresses may be managed through NIS, which requires a functioning network to retrieve map values. This chicken-and-egg problem is solved by invoking *ifconfig* twice during the four steps required to bring a host up on the network:

1. Early in the boot sequence, */etc/init.d/network* executes *ifconfig* to set the IP address of the interface. *ypbind* has not yet been started, so NIS is not running at this point. *ifconfig* matches the hostname in the local */etc/inet/ipnodes* file, and assigns the IP address found there to the interface. The network mask is obtained by matching the longest possible mask in */etc/inet/netmasks*. If it is not specified, then it is based on the class of the IPv4 address, as shown in Table 13-3 later in this chapter. The default broadcast address is the address with a host part of all ones. *ifconfig* also sets up the streams plumbing and the link-local IPv6 addresses.

2. IP routing is started by */etc/init.d/inetinit* when the machine comes up to multiuser mode. The host obtains its site-local, global, and multicast addresses from the network IPv6 routers that advertise prefix information. Critical network daemons, such as *ypbind* and the portmapper, are started next by */etc/init.d/rpc*.

3. *ifconfig* is invoked again, out of */etc/init.d/inetsvc*, to reset the broadcast address and network mask of the IPv4 interfaces. Now that NIS is running, maps that override the default values may be referenced. If you must override the NIS network masks, it is recommended to use the */etc/inet/netmasks* file with the appropriate mask instead of hand-tailoring the values directly onto the *ifconfig* command in the boot script.

   For example, add the desired netmask entry to */etc/inet/netmasks*:

   ```
   131.40.0.0      255.255.255.0
   ```

   The boot script updates all IPv4 up and configured network devices by invoking:

   ```
   /usr/sbin/ifconfig -au4 netmask + broadcast +
   ```

The *netmask* argument tells *ifconfig* which parts of the IP address form the network number, and which form the host number. Any bit represented by a one in the *netmask* becomes part of the network number. The *broadcast* argument specifies the broadcast address to be used by this host. The plus signs in the example cause *ifconfig* to read the appropriate NIS map for the required information. For the netmask, *ifconfig* reads the *netmasks* map, and for the broadcast address, it performs a logical *and* of the netmask and host IP address read from the NIS *ipnodes* map.

4. *inetd*-based services and RPC services such as NFS, the automounter and the lock manager are started once the network interface has been fully configured. Applications that require a fully functional network interface, such as network database servers, should be started after the last *ifconfig* is issued in the boot sequence.

Do not specify the hostname in */etc/hostname*.[0-9]* if you plan to use DHCP to obtain your IPv4 addresses. DHCP enables your host to dynamically obtain IPv4 addresses, as well as other client configuration information over the network. By default, IPv6 address configuration is performed automatically as well. Hosts obtain their addresses and configuration information from IPv6 routers which advertise the prefix information used by the hosts to generate site-local and global addresses. Note that the host still invokes *ifconfig* to plumb the device and establish its link-local IPv6 address (in */etc/init.d/network*), the router discovery daemon *in.ndpd* is later invoked in */etc/init.d/inetinit* to acquire the additional site-local and global addresses.

Multiple interfaces

You can place a system on more than one network by either installing multiple physical network interfaces, or by configuring multiple logical interfaces associated with a physical network interface. In the first case, each network uses separate physical media, in the second case the networks are on the same physical media. A host that acts as a gateway between two networks is a good example of a system connected to physically separate networks. A host configured to run over both IPv4 and IPv6 is an example of a system with multiple logical interfaces and a single physical network.

ifconfig can configure the interfaces one at a time, or in groups. For example, if a host has several interfaces, they can be enabled individually by using *ifconfig*:

```
...
ifconfig hme0 acadia up netmask + broadcast +
...
ifconfig hme1 acadia-gw up broadcast 192.254.1.255 netmask +
```

As in the previous example, the plus signs (+) make *ifconfig* read the *netmasks* database for its data. In both examples, the interfaces are marked *up* and configured with a single command.

ifconfig can also configure multiple interfaces at once using the *-a* option:

```
ifconfig -auD4 netmask + broadcast +
```

The *-auD4* set of options instructs *ifconfig* to update the netmask and broadcast configuration for all IPv4 *up* devices that are not under DHCP control.

Each network interface has a distinct hostname and IP address. One convention for two-network systems is to append *-gw* to the "primary" hostname. In this configuration, each network interface is on a separate IP network. Host *acadia* from the previous example appears in the NIS *ipnodes* map on network 192.254.1.0 and 131.40.52.0:

```
192.254.1.1     acadia
131.40.52.20    acadia-gw
```

To hosts on the 131.40.52 network, the machine is *acadia-gw*, but on the 192.254.1 network, the same host is called *acadia*.

Systems with more than two network interfaces can use any convenient host naming scheme. For example, in a campus with four backbone Ethernet segments, machine names can reflect both the "given" name and the network name. A host sitting on all four IP networks is given four hostnames and four IP addresses:

```
ipnodes file:
128.44.1.1      boris-bb1
128.44.2.1      boris-bb2
128.44.3.1      boris-bb3
128.44.4.1      boris-bb4
```

If the additional interfaces are configured after NIS is started, then the NIS *ipnodes* map is relied upon to provide the IP address for each interface. To configure an interface early in the boot process—before NIS is started—the appropriate hostname and IP address must be in */etc/inet/ipnodes* on the local machine.

Note that you can configure the multiple physical network interfaces to be on separate IP networks. You can turn on IP interface groups on the host, such that it can have more than one IP address on the same subnet, and use the outbound networks for multiplexing traffic. You can also enable interface trunking on the host to use the multiple physical network interfaces as a single IP address. Trunking offers a measure of fault tolerance, since the trunked interface keeps working even if one of the network interfaces fails. It also scales as you add more network interfaces to the host, providing additional network bandwidth. We revisit IP interface groups and trunking in "Network infrastructure" in Chapter 17.

Mismatched host information

If you have inconsistent hostname and IP address information in the NIS *hosts* map and the local *hosts* file, or the NIS *ipnodes* map and the local *ipnodes* file, major confusion will result. The host may not be able to start all of its services if its host IP address changes during the boot process, and other machines will not know how to map the host's name to an IP address that is represented on the network.

You will find that some network activity works fine, where others fail. For example, you will be able to telnet into other systems from your misconfigured host, but the other systems will not be able to telnet into your misconfigured host. This is because the other hosts are using a different IP address than the one *ifconfig* used to configure your network interface. You will be able to mount NFS filesystems exported without restrictions, but will not be able to mount filesystems that are exported to your specific host (either explicitly or via netgroups) since the NFS server sees your request as coming from a different host.

This kind of failure indicates that the local host's IP address has changed between the early boot phase and the last *ifconfig*. You may find that the local */etc/inet/ hosts* file disagrees with the NIS *hosts* map or the local */etc/inet/ipnodes* file disagrees with the NIS *ipnodes* map.

Mismatched IPv4 addresses between the *hosts* and *ipnodes* maps will lead to inconsistent behavior between IPv6-aware or -enabled applications and IPv6-unaware applications, because they obtain their address information from different sources. If the *hosts* database contains the correct information but the *ipnodes* database is corrupted, then IPv6-unaware applications will work correctly, while the IPv6-aware and -enabled applications will experience problems. The reverse is true when the corrupted information is in the *hosts* database.

Subnetwork masks

The second *ifconfig* in the boot process installs proper masks and broadcast addresses if subnetting is used to divide a larger IP address space. Default subnetwork masks and broadcast addresses are assigned based on IP address class, as shown in Table 13-3.

Table 13-3. Default broadcast addresses

Address Class	Network Address	Network Mask	Broadcast Address
Class A	x.0.0.0	255.0.0.0	x.255.255.255
Class B	x.y.0.0	255.255.0.0	x.y.255.255
Class C	x.y.z.0	255.255.255.0	x.y.z.255

The NIS *netmasks* map contains an association of network numbers and subnetwork masks and is used to override the default network masks corresponding to each class of IP address. A simple example is the division of a Class B network into Class C-like subnetworks, so that each subnetwork number can be assigned to a distinct physical network. To effect such a scheme, the *netmasks* NIS map contains a single entry for the Class B address:

```
131.40.0.0     255.255.255.0
```

Broadcast addresses are derived from the network mask and host IP address by performing a logical *and* of the two. Any bits that are *not* masked out by the netmask become part of the broadcast address, while those that are masked out are set to all ones in Solaris (other systems may set them to all zeros).

Network numbers are matched based on the number of octets normally used for an address of that class. IP address 131.40.52.28 has a Class B network number, so the first two octets in the IP address are used as an index into the *netmasks* map. Similarly, IP address 89.4.1.3 is a Class A address; therefore, only the first octet is used as a key into *netmasks*. This scheme simplifies the management of *netmasks*. By listing the network number to be partitioned, you do not have to itemize all subnetworks in the *netmasks* file.

Continuing the previous example, consider this *ifconfig*:

```
ipnodes excerpt:
131.40.52.28    mahimahi

netmasks map:
131.40.0.0      255.255.255.0

ifconfig line:
ifconfig hme0 mahimahi netmask +

Resulting interface configuration:
% ifconfig hme0
hme0: flags=1000843<UP,BROADCAST,RUNNING,MULTICAST,IPv4> mtu 1500 index 2
        inet 131.40.52.28 netmask ffffff00 broadcast 131.40.52.255
```

Using a plus sign (+) as the netmask instead of an explicit network mask forces the second *ifconfig* to read the NIS *netmasks* map for the correct mask. The four-octet mask is logically *and*-ed with the IP address, producing the broadcast network number. In the preceding example, the broadcast address is in the ones form. Note that the *network* mask is actually displayed as a hexadecimal mask value, and not as an IP address.

A more complex example involves dividing the Class C network 192.6.4 into four subnetworks. To get four subnetworks, we need an additional two bits of network number, which are taken from the two most significant bits of the host number. The netmask is therefore extended into the next two bits, making it 26 bits instead of the default 24-bit Class C netmask:

```
Partitioning requires:
24 bits of Class C network number
2 additional bits of subnetwork number
6 bits left for host number

Last octet has 2 bits of netmask, 6 of host number:
11000000 binary = 192 decimal

Resulting netmasks file entry:
192.6.4.0         255.255.255.192
```

Again, only one entry in *netmasks* is needed, and the key for the entry matches the Class C network number that is being divided.

You use variable length subnetting when using Classless IP addressing. You specify how many bits of the IP address to use for the network, and how many to use for the host by setting the appropriate netmask entry. The format of the netmask entry is the same as before, however, there should be an entry for each subnet defined. *ifconfig* uses the longest possible matching mask. Say your engineering organization has been given control of the 131.40.86.0 network (addresses 131.40.86.0 -> 131.40.86.255). You decide to partition it into four separate subnetworks that map the four groups in your organization: Systems Engineering, Applications Engineering, Graphics Engineering, and Customer Support. You plan to use a single system to serve as your gateway between the four separate subnets and the enterprise network. Your enterprise network address is 131.40.7.22, and is therefore connected to the 131.40.7.0 enterprise network. In order to partition the 131.40.86 address space into four separate subnets, you need to use the two upper bits of the last octet to identify the network. Table 13-4 shows the distribution of the IP addresses to the different networks.

Table 13-4. Network assignment

Organization	Address Range	Subnetwork
Systems Eng	131.40.86.0 -> 131.40.86.63	131.40.86.0
Applications Eng	131.40.86.64 -> 131.40.86.127	131.40.86.64
Graphics Eng	131.40.86.128 -> 131.40.86.191	131.40.86.128
Customer Support	131.40.86.192 -> 131.40.86.255	131.40.86.192

The last octet of the address will have two bits of netmask and six of host number:

```
11000000 binary = 192 decimal
The resulting netmask: 255.255.255.192
```

The resulting netmasks file is:

```
131.40.0.0      255.255.255.0
131.40.86.0     255.255.255.192
131.40.86.64    255.255.255.192
131.40.86.128   255.255.255.192
131.40.86.192   255.255.255.192
```

The first entry indicates that the Class B network 131.40.0.0 is subnetted. The next four entries represent the four variable-length subnets for the classless addresses for the different groups. Addresses 131.40.86.0 through 131.40.86.255 have a subnet mask with 26 bits in the subnet fields and 6 bits in the host field. All other addresses in the range 131.40.0.0 through 131.40.255.255 have a 24 bit subnet field. The IP address assignments for the five network interfaces are shown in Table 13-5.

Table 13-5. Assigning addresses to interfaces

Interface	Subnetwork Range	Broadcast	Sample IP Address
hme0	131.40.7.0 Backbone	131.40.7.255	131.40.7.22
hme1	131.40.86.0 -> 131.40.86.63	131.40.86.63	131.40.86.1
hme2	131.40.86.64 -> 131.40.86.127	131.40.86.63	131.40.86.65
hmc3	131.40.86.128 -> 131.40.86.191	131.40.86.63	131.40.86.129
hme4	131.40.86.192 -> 131.40.86.255	131.40.86.63	131.40.86.193

For example, the server would direct network traffic to the *hme0* interface when communicating with IP address 131.40.7.78, since it is part of the 131.40.7.0 subnet; *hme1* when communicating with 131.40.86.32, since it is part of the 131.40.86.0 subnet; *hme2* when communicating with 131.40.7.78, and so on.

ifconfig only governs the local machine's interface to the network. If a host cannot exchange packets with a peer host on the same network, then it is necessary to verify that a datagram circuit to the remote host exists and that the remote node is properly advertising itself on the network. Tools that perform these tests are *arp* and *ping*.

IP to MAC address mappings

Applications use IP addresses and hostnames to identify remote nodes, but packets sent on the Ethernet identify their destinations via a 48-bit MAC-layer address. The Ethernet interface on each host only receives packets that have its MAC address of a broadcast address in the destination field. IP addresses are completely independent of the 48-bit MAC-level address; several disjoint networks may use the same sets of IP addresses although the 48-bit addresses to which they map are unique worldwide.

You can tell who makes an Ethernet interface by looking at the first three octets of its address. Some of the most popular prefixes are shown in Table 13-6. Fortunately, newer diagnostic tools such as *ethereal* know how to map the prefix number to the vendor of the interface. *ethereal* is introduced later in this chapter in the "ethereal / tethereal" section.

Table 13-6. Ethernet address prefixes

Prefix	Vendor	Prefix	Vendor	Prefix	Vendor
00:00:0c	Cisco	00:20:85	3Com	00:e0:34	Cisco
00:00:3c	Auspex	00:20:af	3Com	00:e0:4f	Cisco
00:00:63	Hewlett-Packard	00:60:08	3Com	00:e0:a3	Cisco
00:00:65	Network General	00:60:09	Cisco	00:e0:f7	Cisco
00:00:69	Silicon Graphics	00:60:2f	Cisco	00:e0:f9	Cisco
00:00:f8	DEC	00:60:3e	Cisco	00:e0:fe	Cisco
00:01:fa	Compaq	00:60:47	Cisco	02:60:60	3Com
00:04:ac	IBM	00:60:5c	Cisco	02:60:8c	3Com
00:06:0d	Hewlett-Packard	00:60:70	Cisco	08:00:02	3Com
00:06:29	IBM	00:60:83	Cisco	08:00:09	Hewlett-Packard
00:06:7c	Cisco	00:60:8c	3Com	08:00:1a	Data General
00:06:c1	Cisco	00:60:97	3Com	08:00:1b	Data General
00:07:01	Cisco	00:60:b0	Hewlett-Packard	08:00:20	Sun Micro-systems
00:07:0d	Cisco	00:80:1c	Cisco	08:00:2b	DEC
00:08:c7	Compaq	00:80:5f	Compaq	08:00:5a	IBM
00:10:11	Cisco	00:90:27	Intel	08:00:69	Silicon Graphics
00:10:1f	Cisco	00:90:b1	Cisco	08:00:79	Silicon Graphics
00:10:2f	Cisco	00:a0:24	3Com	10:00:5a	IBM
00:10:4b	3Com	00:aa:00	Intel	10:00:90	Hewlett-Packard
00:10:79	Cisco	00:c0:4f	Dell	10:00:d4	DEC
00:10:7b	Cisco	00:c0:95	Network Appliance	3C:00:00	3Com
00:10:f6	Cisco	00:e0:14	Cisco	aa:00:03	DEC
00:20:35	IBM	00:e0:1e	Cisco	aa:00:04	DEC

ARP, the Address Resolution Protocol, is used to maintain tables of 32- to 48-bit address translations. The *ARP table* is a dynamic collection of MAC-to-IPv4 address mappings. To fill in the MAC-level Ethernet packet headers, the sending host must resolve the destination IPv4 address into a 48-bit address. The host first checks its ARP table for an entry keyed by the IPv4 address, and if none is found, the host broadcasts an ARP request containing the recipient's IPv4 address. Any machine supporting ARP address resolution responds to an ARP request with a packet containing its MAC address. The requester updates its ARP table, fills in the MAC address in the Ethernet packet header, and transmits the packet.

If no reply is received for the ARP request, the transmitting host sends the request again. Typically, a delay of a second or more is inserted between consecutive ARP requests to prevent a series of ARP packets from saturating the network. Flurries of ARP requests sometimes occur when a malformed packet is sent on the network; some hosts interpret it as a broadcast packet and attempt to get the Ethernet address of the sender via an ARP request. If many machines are affected, the ensuing flood of network activity can consume a considerable amount of the available bandwidth. This behavior is referred to as an *ARP storm*, and is most frequently caused by an electrical problem in a transceiver that damages packets after the host has cleanly written them over its network interface.

To examine the current ARP table entries, use *arp -a*:

```
% arp -a
Net to Media Table: IPv4
Device   IP Address             Mask            Flags  Phys Addr
------   --------------------   ---------------  -----  ---------------
hme0     caramba                255.255.255.255         08:00:20:b9:2b:t6
hme1     socks                  255.255.255.255         08:00:20:e7:91:5d
hme0     copper                 255.255.255.255         00:20:af:9d:7c:92
hme0     roger                  255.255.255.255  SP     08:00:20:a0:33:90
hme0     universo               255.255.255.255  U
hme0     peggy                  255.255.255.255  SP     08:00:20:81:23:f1
hme1     duke                   255.255.255.255         00:04:00:20:56:d7
hme0     224.0.0.0              240.0.0.0        SM     01:00:5e:00:00:00
hme1     224.0.0.0              240.0.0.0        SM     01:00:5e:00:00:00
hme1     daisy                  255.255.255.255         08:00:20:b5:3d:d7
```

The *arp -a* output listing reports the interface over which the ARP notification arrived, the IP address (or hostname) and its Ethernet address mapping. The unresolved entry (denoted by the *U* flag) is for a host that did not respond to an ARP request; after several minutes the entry is removed from the table. Complete entries in the ARP table may be *static* or *dynamic*, indicating how the address mappings were added and the length of their expected lifetimes.

Solaris identifies static entries with the *S* flag. The host's own Ethernet address as well as all multicast address entries (identified by the *M* flag) will always be static. The previous example was run on the host *roger*, therefore the static nature of the entry for its own Ethernet address and multicast entries. The absence of the *S* flag identifies a dynamic or learned entry.

Dynamic entries are added on demand during the course of normal IP traffic handling. Infrequently used mappings added in this fashion have a short lifetime; after five minutes without a reference to the entry, the ARP table management routines remove it. This ongoing table pruning is necessary to minimize the overhead of ARP table lookups. The ARP table is accessed using a hash table; a smaller, sparser table has fewer hash key collisions. A host that communicates regularly with many other hosts may have an ARP table that is fairly large, while a host that is quiescent or exchanging packets with only a few peers has a small ARP table.

The difference between dynamic and permanent entries is how they are added to the ARP table. Dynamic entries are added on the fly, as a result of replies to ARP requests. Permanent entries are loaded into the ARP table once at boot time, and are useful if a host must communicate with a node that cannot respond to an ARP request during some part of its startup procedure. For example, a diskless client may not have ARP support embedded in the boot PROM, requiring its boot server to have a permanent ARP table entry for it. Once the diskless node is running the Unix kernel, it should be able to respond to ARP requests to complete dynamic ARP table entries on other hosts.

The *arp -a* output reports a mask for every entry. This mask is used during lookup of an entry in the ARP table. The lookup function in the kernel applies the mask to the address being queried and compares it with the one in the table. If the resulting addresses match, the lookup is successful. A mask of 255.255.255.255 (all ones) means that the two addresses need to be exactly the same in order to be considered equivalent. A mask of 240.0.0.0 means that only the upper four bits of the address are used to find a matching address. In the previous example, all multicast addresses use the Ethernet address corresponding to the 240.0.0.0 entry. The ARP mask does not provide much useful information to the regular user. Be sure not to confuse this ARP mask with the netmask specified by the *ifconfig* command. The ARP mask is generated and used only by the internal kernel routines to reduce the number of entries that need to be stored in the table. The netmask specified by the *ifconfig* command is used for IP routing.

A variation of the permanent ARP table entry is a *published* mapping. Published mappings are denoted by the *P* flag. Published entries include the IP address for the current host, and the addresses that have been explicitly added by the *-s* or *-f* options (explained later in this chapter).

Publishing ARP table entries turns a host into an ARP server. Normally, a host replies only to requests for its own IP address, but if it has published entries then it replies for multiple IP addresses. If an ARP request is broadcast requesting the IP address of a published entry, the host publishing that entry returns an ARP reply to the sender, even though the IP address in the ARP request does not match its own.

This mechanism is used to cope with machines that cannot respond to ARP requests due to lack of ARP support or because they are isolated from broadcast packets by a piece of network partitioning hardware that filters out broadcast packets. This mechanism is also useful in SLIP or PPP configurations. When any of these situations exist, a machine is designated as an ARP server and is loaded with ARP entries from a file containing hostnames, Ethernet addresses, and the *pub* qualifier. For example, to publish the ARP entries for hosts *relax* and *stress* on server *irie*, we put the ARP information into a configuration file */etc/arptable* and then load it using *arp -f*:

```
irie# cat /etc/arptable
relax   08:00:20:73:3e:ec          pub
stress  08:00:20:b9:18:3d  pub
irie# arp -f /etc/arptable
```

The *-f* option forces *arp* to read the named file for entries, alternatively the *-s* option can be used to add a single mapping from the command line:

```
irie# arp -s relax 08:00:20:73:3e:ec pub
```

As a diagnostic tool, *arp* is useful for resolving esoteric point-to-point connectivity problems. If a host's ARP table contains an incorrect entry, the machine using it will not be reachable, since outgoing packets will contain the wrong Ethernet address. ARP table entries may contain incorrect Ethernet addresses for several reasons:

- Another host on the network is answering ARP requests for the same IP address, or all IP addresses, emulating a duplicate IP address on the network.

- A host with a published ARP entry contains the wrong Ethernet address in its ARP table.

- Either of the above situations exist, and the incorrect ARP reply arrives at the requesting host after the correct reply. When ARP table entries are updated dynamically, the last response received is the one that "wins." If the correct ARP response is received from a host that is physically close to the requester, and a duplicate ARP response arrives from a host that is located across several Ethernet bridges, then the later—and probably incorrect—response is the one that the machine uses for future packet transmissions.

Inspection of the ARP table can reveal some obvious problems; for example, the three-octet prefix of the machine's Ethernet address does not agree with the vendor's label on the front of the machine. If you believe you are suffering from intermittent ARP failures, you can delete specific ARP table entries and monitor the table as it is repopulated dynamically. ARP table entries are deleted with *arp -d*, and only the superuser can delete entries. In the following example, we delete the ARP table entry for *fenwick*, then force the local host to send an ARP request for *fenwick* by attempting to connect to it using *telnet*. By examining the ARP table after the connection attempt, we can see if some other host has responded incorrectly to the ARP request:

```
# arp -d fenwick
fenwick (131.40.52.44) deleted
# telnet fenwick
...Telnet times out...
# arp -a | grep fenwick
hme0   fenwick           255.255.255.255     08:00:20:79:61:eb
```

An example involving intermittent ARP failures is presented in Chapter 15.

IPv6 nodes use the neighbor discovery mechanism to learn the link layer address (MAC in the case of Ethernet) of the other nodes connected to the link. The IPv6 neighbor discovery mechanism delivers the functionality previously provided by the combination of ARP, ICMP router discovery, and ICMP redirect mechanisms. This is done by defining special ICMP6 message types: neighbor solicitation and neighbor advertisement. A node issues neighbor solicitations when it needs to request the link-layer (MAC) address of a neighbor. Nodes will also issue neighbor advertisement messages in response to neighbor solicitation messages, as well as when their link-layer address changes.

Using ping to check network connectivity

ping is similar to *arp* in that it provides information about hosts on a network rather than information about data that is sent on the network. *arp* provides a low-level look at the MAC addressing used by a host, but it is not that powerful for diagnosing connectivity problems. *ping* is a more general purpose tool for investigating point-to-point connectivity problems and areas of questionable physical network topology.

ping uses the Internetwork Control Message Protocol (ICMP) echo facility to ask a remote machine for a reply. ICMP is another component of the network protocol stack that is a peer of IP and ARP. The returned packet contains a timestamp added by the remote host which is used to compute the round trip packet transit time. In its simplest form, *ping* is given a hostname or IP address and returns a verdict on connectivity to that host:

```
% ping shamrock
shamrock is alive
% ping 131.40.1.15
131.40.1.15 is alive
```

The -*s* option puts *ping* into continuous-send mode, and displays the sequence numbers and transit times for packets as they are returned. Optionally, the packet size and packet count may be specified on the command line:

```
ping [-s] host [packet-size] [packet-count]
```

For example:

```
% ping -s mahimahi
PING mahimahi: 56 data bytes
64 bytes from mahimahi (131.40.52.28): icmp_seq=0. time=3. ms
64 bytes from mahimahi (131.40.52.28): icmp_seq=1. time=2. ms
64 bytes from mahimahi (131.40.52.28): icmp_seq=2. time=2. ms
64 bytes from mahimahi (131.40.52.28): icmp_seq=3. time=3. ms
64 bytes from mahimahi (131.40.52.28): icmp_seq=4. time=2. ms
^C
----mahimahi PING Statistics----
5 packets transmitted, 5 packets received, 0% packet loss
round-trip (ms)  min/avg/max = 2/2/3
```

and:

```
% ping -s mahimahi 100 3
PING mahimahi: 100 data bytes
108 bytes from mahimahi (131.40.52.28): icmp_seq=0. time=3. ms
108 bytes from mahimahi (131.40.52.28): icmp_seq=1. time=3. ms
108 bytes from mahimahi (131.40.52.28): icmp_seq=2. time=3. ms

----mahimahi PING Statistics----
3 packets transmitted, 3 packets received, 0% packet loss
round-trip (ms)  min/avg/max = 3/3/3
```

The eight bytes added to each ICMP echo request in the corresponding reply are the timestamp information added by the remote host. If no explicit count on the number of packets is specified, then *ping* continues transmitting until interrupted. By default, *ping* uses a 56-byte packet, which is the smallest IP packet, complete with headers and checksums, that will be transmitted on the Ethernet.

The *ping* utility is good for answering questions about whether the remote host is attached to the network and whether the network between the hosts is reliable. Additionally, *ping* can indicate that a hostname and IP address are not consistent across several machines. The replies received when the host is specified by name may contain an incorrect IP address. Conversely, if *ping*ing the remote host by name does not produce a reply, try the IP address of the host. If a reply is received when the host is specified by address, but not by name, then the local machine has an incorrect view of the remote host's IP address. These kinds of problems are generally machine specific, so intermittent *ping* failures can be a hint of IP address confusion: machines that do not agree on the IP addresses they have been assigned.

If NIS is used, this could indicate that the NIS *ipnodes* map was corrupted or changed (incorrectly) since the remote host last booted. The NIS *ipnodes* map supersedes the local */etc/inet/ipnodes* file,[*] so a disparity between the two values

---

* You can change the search order for *hosts* and *ipnodes* in */etc/nsswitch.conf* in order to reverse the precedence order.

for a remote machine is ignored; the NIS *ipnodes* map takes precedence. However, in the absence of NIS, the failure of a remote node to answer a *ping* to its hostname indicates the */etc/inet/ipnodes* files are out of synchronization.

Larger packet sizes may be used to test connectivity through network components that are suspected of damaging large packets or trains of packets. *ping* only sends one packet at a time, so it won't test the capacity of a network interface. However, it tells you whether packets close to the network's MTU can make it from point to point intact, through all of the network hardware between the two hosts.

Using the packet count indicators and transit times, *ping* can be used to examine connectivity, network segment length, and potential termination problems. Electrical problems, including poor or missing cable termination, are among the most difficult problems to diagnose and pinpoint without repeatedly splitting the network in half and testing the smaller segments. If *ping* shows that packets are dropped out of sequence, or that return packets are received in bursts, it is likely that either a network cable segment has an electrical fault or that the network is not terminated properly. These problems are more common in older 10Base-5 and 10Base-2 networks than in newer CAT5 twisted pair networks.

For example, the following output from *ping* indicates that the network is intermittently dropping packets; this behavior is usually caused by improper termination and is quite random in nature:

```
% ping -s mahimahi
PING mahimahi: 56 data bytes
64 bytes from mahimahi (131.40.52.28): icmp_seq=0. time=3. ms
64 bytes from mahimahi (131.40.52.28): icmp_seq=1. time=2. ms
64 bytes from mahimahi (131.40.52.28): icmp_seq=16. time=1295. ms
64 bytes from mahimahi (131.40.52.28): icmp_seq=17. time=3. ms
64 bytes from mahimahi (131.40.52.28): icmp_seq=18. time=2. ms
```

The gap between packets 1 and 16, along with the exceptionally long packet delay, indicates that a low-level network problem is consuming packets.

Gauging Ethernet interface capacity

Even with a well-conditioned network and proper host configuration information, a server may have trouble communicating with its clients because its network interface is overloaded. If an NFS server is hit with more packets than it can receive through its network interface, some client requests will be lost and eventually retransmitted. To the NFS clients, the server appears painfully slow, when it's really the server's network interface that is the problem.

The *spray* utility provides a very coarse estimate of network interface capacity, both on individual hosts and through network hardware between hosts. *spray* showers a target host with consecutive packets of a fixed length by making remote procedure calls to the *rpc.sprayd* daemon on the remote host. After the last packet is sent, the *rpc.sprayd* daemon is queried for a count of the packets received; this value is compared to the number of packets sent to determine the percentage dropped between client and server.

On its own, *spray* is of limited usefulness as a measure of the packet handling capability of a machine. The packet containing the RPC call may be lost by the client, due to other activity on its network interface; it may be consumed by a collision on the network; or it may be incident to the server but not copied from the network by the server's network interface due to a lack of buffer space or excessive server CPU loading. Many packets are lost on the sending host, and *spray* has no knowledge of where the packets vanish once they get pass the application layer. Due to these factors, *spray* is best used to gauge the relative packet-handling speeds of two or more machines.

Here are some examples of using *spray* to test various network constraints. *spray* requires a hostname and takes a packet count, delay value, and packet length as optional arguments:

```
spray [-c count] [-d delay] [-1 length] host
```

For example:

```
% spray wahoo
sending 1162 packets of length 86 to wahoo ...
        675 packets (58.090%) dropped by wahoo
        1197 packets/sec, 103007 bytes/sec
```

spray reports the number of packets received, as well as the transfer rate. The packet drop rates are only meaningful when used to compare the relative network input and output rates of the two machines under test.

It's important to note that network interface speed depends upon much more than CPU speed. A faster CPU helps a host process network protocols faster, but the network interface and bus hardware usually determine how quickly the host can pull packets from the network. A fast network interface may be separated from the CPU by a bus that has a high latency. Even a high-throughput I/O system may exhibit poor network performance if there is a large time overhead required to set up each packet transfer from the network interface to the CPU. Similar hosts stress each other fairly, since their network interfaces have the same input capacity.

Even on a well-conditioned, little-used network, a client machine that has a significantly faster CPU than its server may perform worse under the stress of *spray* than the same two machines with the client and server roles reversed. With increased CPU speed comes increased packet handling speed, so a faster machine can transmit packets quickly enough to outpace a slower server. If the disparity between client and server is great, then the client is forced to retransmit requests and the server is additionally burdened with the duplicate requests. Use *spray* to exercise combinations of client and server with varying packet sizes to identify cases in which a client may race ahead of its server. When a fast NFS client is teamed with a slower server, the NFS mount parameters require tuning as described in "Slow server compensation" in Chapter 18.

Send various sized packets to an NFS server to see how it handles "large" and "small" NFS requests. Disk write operations are "large," usually filling several full-size IP packets. Other operations, such as getting the attributes of a file, fit into a packet of 150 bytes or less. Small packets are more easily handled by all hosts, since there is less data to move around, but NFS servers may be subject to bursts of large packets during intense periods of client write operations. If no explicit arguments are given, *spray* sends 1162 packets of 86 bytes. In most implementations of *spray*, if either a packet count or packet length are given, the other argument is chosen so that 100 kbytes of data are transferred between client and server. Try using *spray* with packet sizes of 1500 bytes to judge how well an NFS server or the network handle write requests.

Normally, no delay is inserted between packets sent by *spray*, although the *-d* option may be used to specify a delay in microseconds. Insert delays between the packets to simulate realistic packet arrival rates, under "normal" conditions. Client requests may be separated by several tens of microseconds, so including a delay between packets may give you a more accurate picture of packet handling rates.

In Figure 13-1, *baxter* and *arches* are identical machines and *acadia* is a faster machine with a faster network interface. *spray* produces the following output:

```
Fast machine to slow machine:
[acadia]% spray baxter -c 100 -l 1160
sending 100 packets of length 1162 to baxter ...
        39 packets (39.000%) dropped by baxter
        520 packets/sec, 605037 bytes/sec

Fast machine to slow machine, with delay:
[acadia]% spray baxter -c 100 -l 1160 -d 1
sending 100 packets of length 1162 to baxter ...
        no packets dropped by baxter
        99 packets/sec, 115680 bytes/sec

Slow machine to fast machine:
[baxter]% spray acadia -c 100 -l 1160
sending 100 packets of length 1162 to acadia ...
        no packets dropped by acadia
        769 packets/sec, 893846 bytes/sec

Slow machine to identical machine:
[baxter]% spray arches -c 100 -l 1160
sending 100 packets of length 1162 to arches ...
        no packets dropped by arches
        769 packets/sec, 893846 bytes/sec
```

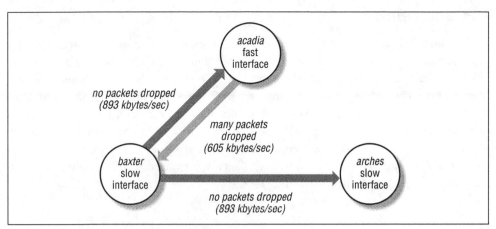

Figure 13-1. Testing relative packet handling rates

When the fast machine sprays the slower one, a significant number of packets are dropped; but adding a one-microsecond delay between the packets allows the slow machine to keep pace and receive all incident packets. The slow machine to fast machine test produces the same packet handling rate as the slow machine showering an identical peer; if the slow machine sprays the fast one, the network bandwidth used is more than 30% greater than when the fast machine hammers the slow one. Note that you couldn't get NFS to insert delays like this, but performing the test with delays may indicate the location of a bottleneck. Knowing your constraints, you can change other configuration parameters, such as NFS client behavior, to avoid the bottleneck. We'll look at these tuning procedures more in Chapter 18.

The four tools discussed to this point—*ifconfig, arp, ping,* and *spray*—focus on the issues of packet addressing and routing. If they indicate a problem, all network services, such as *telnet* and *rlogin,* will be affected. We now move up through the network and transport layers in the network protocol stack, leaving the MAC and IP layers for the session and application layers.

Remote procedure call tools

Network failures on a grand scale are generally caused by problems at the MAC or IP level, and are immediately noticed by users. Problems involving higher layers of the network protocol stack manifest themselves in more subtle ways, affecting only a few machines or particular pairs of clients and servers. The utilities discussed in the following sections analyze functionality from the remote procedure call (RPC) layer up through the NFS or NIS application layer. The next section contains a detailed examination of the RPC mechanism at the heart of NFS and NIS.

RPC mechanics

The Remote Procedure Call (RPC) mechanism imposes a client/server relationship on machines in a network. A server is a host that physically owns some shared resource, such as a disk exported for NFS service or an NIS map. Clients operate on resources owned by servers by making RPC requests; these operations appear (to the client) to have been executed locally. For example, when performing a read RPC on an NFS-mounted disk, the reading application has no knowledge of where the read is actually executed. Many client-server relationships may be defined for each machine on a network; a server for one resource is often a client for many others in the same network.

Identifying RPC services

Services available through RPC are identified by four values:

- Program number
- Version number
- Procedure number
- Protocol (UDP or TCP)

The program number uniquely identifies the RPC service. Each RPC service, such as the *mountd* or NIS server daemons, is assigned a program number. The file */etc/rpc* and the *rpc* NIS map contain an enumeration of RPC program numbers, formal names, and nicknames for each service:

```
Excerpt from /etc/rpc:
nfs           100003  nfsprog
ypserv        100004  ypprog
mountd        100005  mount showmount
ypbind        100007
```

Note that program 100005, *mountd*, has two names, reflecting the fact that the *mountd* daemon services both *mount* requests and the *showmount* utility.

Program numbers can also be expressed in hexadecimal. Well-known RPC services such as NFS and NIS are assigned reserved program numbers in the range 0x0 to 0x199999. Numbers above this range may be assigned to local applications such as license servers. The well-known programs are commonly expressed in decimal, though.

A version number is used to differentiate between various flavors of the same service, and is mostly utilized to evolve the service over time, while providing backwards compatibility if so desired. For example, there are two versions of the NFS service: Versions 2 and 3 (there is no Version 1). Each version of the program may be composed of many procedures. Each version of the NFS service, program number 100003, consists of several procedures, each of which is assigned a procedure number. These procedures perform client requests on the NFS server. For example: read a directory, create a file, read a block from a file, write to a file, get the file's attributes, or get statistics about a filesystem. The procedure number is passed in an RPC request as an "op code" for the RPC server. Procedure numbers start with 1; procedure 0 is reserved for a "null" function. While RPC program numbers are well-advertised, version and procedure numbers are particular to the service and often are contained in a header file that gets compiled into the client program. NFS procedure numbers, for example, are defined in the header files */usr/include/nfs/nfs.h*.

RPC clients and servers deal exclusively with RPC program numbers. At the session layer in the protocol stack, the code doesn't really care what protocols are used to provide the session services. The UDP and TCP transport protocols need port numbers to identify the local and remote ends of a connection. The portmapper is used to perform translation between the RPC program number-based view of the world and the TCP/UDP port numbers.

RPC portmapper — rpcbind

The *rpcbind* daemon (also known as the portmapper),* exists to register RPC services and to provide their IP port numbers when given an RPC program number. *rpcbind* itself is an RPC service, but it resides at a well-known IP port (port 111) so that it may be contacted directly by remote hosts. For example, if host *fred* needs to mount a filesystem from host *barney*, it must send an RPC request to the *mountd* daemon on *barney*. The mechanics of making the RPC request are as follows:

* *fred* gets the IP address for *barney*, using the *ipnodes* NIS map. *fred* also looks up the RPC program number for *mountd* in the *rpc* NIS map. The RPC program number for *mountd* is 100005.

* Knowing that the portmapper lives at port 111, *fred* sends an RPC request to the portmapper on *barney*, asking for the IP port (on *barney*) of RPC program 100005. *fred* also specifies the particular protocol and version number for the RPC service. *barney*'s portmapper responds to the request with port 704, the IP port at which *mountd* is listening for incoming mount RPC requests over the specified protocol. Note that it is possible for the portmapper to return an error, if the specified program does not exist or if it hasn't

---

* The *rpcbind* daemon and the old portmapper provide the same RPC service. The portmapper implements Version 2 of the portmap protocol (RPC program number 100000), where the *rpcbind* daemon implements Versions 3 and 4 of the protocol, in addition to Version 2. This means that the *rpcbind* daemon already implements the functionality provided by the old portmapper. Due to this overlap in functionality and to add to the confusion, many people refer to the *rpcbind* daemon as the portmapper.

been registered on the remote host. *barney*, for example, might not be an NFS server and would therefore have no reason to run the *mountd* daemon.

- *fred* sends a *mount* RPC request to *barney*, using the IP port number returned by the portmapper. This RPC request contains an RPC procedure number, which tells the *mountd* daemon what to do with the request. The RPC request also contains the parameters for the procedure, in this case, the name of the filesystem *fred* needs to mount.

The portmapper is also used to handle an *RPC broadcast*. Recall that a network broadcast is a packet that is sent to all hosts on the network; an RPC broadcast is a request that is sent to all servers for a particular RPC service. For example, the NIS client *ypbind* daemon uses an RPC broadcast to locate an NIS server for its domain. There's one small problem with RPC broadcasts: to send a broadcast packet, a host must fill in the remote port number, so all hosts receiving the packet know where to deliver the broadcast packet. RPC doesn't have any knowl- edge of port numbers, and the RPC server daemons on some hosts may be regis- tered at different port numbers. This problem is resolved by sending RPC broadcasts to the portmapper, and asking the portmapper to make the RPC call indirectly on behalf of the sender. In the case of the *ypbind* daemon, it sends a broadcast to all *rpcbind* daemons; they in turn call the *ypserv* RPC server on each host.

RPC version numbers

As mentioned before, each new implementation of an RPC server has its own ver- sion number. Different version numbers are used to coordinate multiple imple- mentations of the same service, each of which may have a different interface. As an RPC service matures, the service's author may find it necessary to add new pro- cedures or add arguments to existing procedures. Changing the interface in this way requires incrementing the version number. The first (and earliest) version of an RPC program is version 1; subsequent releases of the server should use consec- utive version numbers. For example, the mount service has several versions, each one supporting more options than its predecessors.

Multiple versions are implemented in a single server process; there doesn't need to be a separate instance of the RPC server daemon for each version supported. Each RPC server daemon registers its RPC program number and all versions it supports with the portmapper. It is helpful to think of dispatching a request through an RPC server as a two-level switch: the first level discriminates on the version number, and chooses a set of procedure routines comprising that version of the RPC ser- vice. The second level dispatch invokes one of the routines in that set based on the program number in the RPC request.

When contacting the portmapper on a remote host, the local and remote sides must agree on the version number of the RPC service that will be used. The rule of thumb is to use the highest-numbered version that both parties understand. In cases where version numbers are not consecutively numbered, or no mutually agreeable version number can be found, the portmapper returns a *version mismatch* error looking like:

```
mount: RPC: Program version mismatch
```

Even though Solaris supports Transport-Independent RPC (TI-RPC), in reality most RPC services use the TCP, UDP and loopback transport protocols. Servers may register themselves for any of the protocols, depending upon the varieties of connections they need to support. UDP packets are unreliable and unsequenced and are often used for broadcast or stateless services. The RPC server for the *spray* utility, which "catches" packets thrown at the remote host, uses the UDP protocol to accept as many requests as it can without requiring retransmission of any missed packets. In contrast to UDP, TCP packets are reliably delivered and are presented in the order in which they were transmitted, making them a requirement when requests must be processed by the server in the order in which they were transmitted by the client. The loopback transports are used for communication within the local host and can be connection-less or connection-oriented. For example, the automounter daemon uses RPC over a connection-oriented loopback transport to communicate with the local kernel.

RPC servers listen on the ports they have registered with the portmapper, and are used repeatedly for short-lived sessions. Connections to an RPC server may exist for the duration of the RPC call only, or may remain across calls. They do not usually fork new processes for each request, since the overhead of doing so would significantly impair the performance of RPC-intensive services such as NFS. Many RPC servers are multithreaded, such as NFS in Solaris, which allows the server to have multiple NFS requests being processed in parallel. A multithreaded NFS server can take advantage of multiple disks and disk controllers, it also allows "fast" NFS requests such as attribute or name lookups to not get trapped behind slower disk requests.

RPC registration

Making RPC calls is a reasonably complex affair because there are several places for the procedure to break down. The *rpcinfo* utility is an analog of *ping* that queries RPC servers and their registration with the portmapper. Like *ping*, *rpcinfo* provides a measure of basic connectivity, albeit at the session layer in the network protocol stack. Pinging a remote machine ensures that the underlying physical network and IP address handling are correct; using *rpcinfo* to perform a similar test verifies that the remote machine is capable of accepting and replying to an RPC request.

rpcinfo can be used to detect and debug a variety of failures:

- "Dead" or hung servers caused by improper configuration or a failed daemon

- RPC program version number mismatches between client and server

- Bogus or renegade RPC servers, such as an NIS server that does not have valid maps for the domain it pretends to serve

- Broadcast-related problems

In its simplest usage, *rpcinfo -p* takes a remote hostname (or uses the local hostname if none is specified) and queries the portmapper on that host for all registered RPC services:

```
% rpcinfo -p corvette
   program vers proto   port  service
    100000    4   tcp    111  portmapper
    100000    3   tcp    111  portmapper
    100000    2   tcp    111  portmapper
    100000    4   udp    111  portmapper
    100000    3   udp    111  portmapper
    100000    2   udp    111  portmapper
    100024    1   udp  32781  status
    100024    1   tcp  32775  status
    100011    1   udp  32787  rquotad
    100002    2   udp  32789  rusersd
    100002    3   udp  32789  rusersd
    100002    2   tcp  32777  rusersd
    100002    3   tcp  32777  rusersd
    100021    1   udp   4045  nlockmgr
    100021    2   udp   4045  nlockmgr
    100021    3   udp   4045  nlockmgr
    100021    4   udp   4045  nlockmgr
    100021    1   tcp   4045  nlockmgr
    100021    2   tcp   4045  nlockmgr
    100021    3   tcp   4045  nlockmgr
    100021    4   tcp   4045  nlockmgr
    100012    1   udp  32791  sprayd
    100008    1   udp  32793  walld
    100001    2   udp  32795  rstatd
    100001    3   udp  32795  rstatd
    100001    4   udp  32795  rstatd
    100068    2   udp  32796  cmsd
    100068    3   udp  32796  cmsd
    100068    4   udp  32796  cmsd
    100068    5   udp  32796  cmsd
    100005    1   udp  32810  mountd
    100005    2   udp  32810  mountd
    100005    3   udp  32810  mountd
    100005    1   tcp  32795  mountd
```

```
100005   2   tcp   32795   mountd
100005   3   tcp   32795   mountd
100003   2   udp   2049    nfs
100003   3   udp   2049    nfs
100227   2   udp   2049
100227   3   udp   2049
100003   2   tcp   2049    nfs
100003   3   tcp   2049    nfs
100227   2   tcp   2049
100227   3   tcp   2049
```

The output from *rpcinfo* shows the RPC program and version numbers, the protocols supported, the IP port used by the RPC server, and the name of the RPC service. Service names come from the *rpc.bynumber* NIS map; if no name is printed next to the registration information then the RPC program number does not appear in the map. This may be expected for third-party packages that run RPC server daemons, since the hardware vendor creating the */etc/rpc* file doesn't necessarily list all of the software vendors' RPC numbers. However, a well-known RPC service should be listed properly. Missing RPC service names could indicate a corrupted or incomplete *rpc.bynumber* NIS map. One exception is the NFS ACL service, defined as RPC program 100227. Solaris does not list it in */etc/rpc*, and therefore its name is not printed in the previous output. The NFS ACL service implements the protocol used between Solaris hosts to exchange ACL (Access Control List) information, though it is currently only interoperable between Solaris hosts. If the client or server do not implement the service, then traditional Unix file access control based on permission bits is used.

If the portmapper on the remote machine has died or is not accepting connections for some reason, *rpcinfo* times out attempting to reach it and reports the error. This is a good first step toward diagnosing any RPC-related problem: verify that the remote portmapper is alive and returning valid RPC service registrations.

rpcinfo can also be used like *ping* for a particular RPC server:

```
rpcinfo -u host program version       UDP-based services
rpcinfo -t host program version       TCP-based services
```

The *-u* or *-t* parameter specifies the transport protocol to be used—UDP or TCP, respectively. The hostname must be specified, even if the local host is being queried. Finally, the RPC program and version number are given; the program may be supplied by name (one reported by *rpcinfo -p*) or by explicit numerical value.

As a practical example, consider trying to mount an NFS filesystem from server *mahimahi*. You can mount it successfully, but attempts to operate on its files hang the client. You can use *rpcinfo* to check on the status of the NFS RPC daemons on *mahimahi*:

```
% rpcinfo -u mahimahi nfs 2
program 100003 version 2 ready and waiting
```

In this example, the NFS v2 RPC service is queried on remote host *mahimahi*. Since the service is specified by name, *rpcinfo* looks it up in the *rpc* NIS map. The *-u* flag tells *rpcinfo* to use the UDP protocol. If the *-t* option had been specified instead, *rpcinfo* would have reported the status of the NFS over TCP service. At the time of this writing, a handful of vendors still do not support NFS over TCP, therefore a *-t* query to one of their servers would report that *rpcinfo* could not find a registration for the service using such a protocol.

rpcinfo -u and *rpcinfo -t* call the null procedure (procedure 0) of the RPC server. The null procedure normally does nothing more than return a zero-length reply. If you cannot contact the null procedure of a server, then the health of the server daemon process is suspect. If the daemon never started running, *rpcinfo* would have reported that it couldn't find the server daemon at all. If *rpcinfo* finds the RPC server daemon but can't get a null procedure reply from it, then the daemon is probably hung.

Debugging RPC problems

In the previous examples, we used *rpcinfo* to see if a particular service was registered or not. If the RPC service is not registered, or if you can't reach the RPC server daemon, it's likely there is a low-level problem in the network. However, sometimes you reach an RPC server, but you find the wrong one or it gives you the wrong answer. If you have a heterogeneous environment and are running multiple versions of each RPC service, it's possible to get RPC version number mismatch errors.

These problems affect NIS and diskless client booting; they are best sorted out by using *rpcinfo* to emulate an RPC call and by observing server responses. Networks with multiple, heterogeneous servers may produce multiple, conflicting responses to the same broadcast request. Debugging problems that arise from this behavior often require knowing the order in which the responses are received.

Here's an example: we'll perform a broadcast and then watch the order in which responses are received. When a diskless client boots, it may receive several replies to a request for boot parameters. The boot fails if the first reply contains incorrect or invalid boot parameter information. *rpcinfo -b* sends a broadcast request to the specified RPC program and version number. The RPC program can either be specified in numeric (100026) form, or in its name equivalent (*bootparam*):

```
% rpcinfo -b bootparam 1
fe80::a00:20ff:feb5:1fba.128.67          unknown
fe80::a00:20ff:feb9:2ad1.128.78          unknown
131.40.52.238.128.67                     mora
131.40.52.81.128.68                      kanawha
131.40.52.221.128.79                     holydev
Next Broadcast
```

```
% rpcinfo -b bootparam 1
131.40.52.81.128.68                          kanawha
fe80::a00:20ff:feb5:1fba.128.67              unknown
131.40.52.238.128.67                         mora
fe80::a00:20ff:feb9:2ad1.128.78              unknown

131.40.52.221.128.79                         holydev
Next Broadcast
```

In this example, a broadcast packet is sent to the boot parameter server (boot-param). *rpcinfo* obtains the RPC program number (100026) from */etc/rpc* or the *rpc.bynumber* NIS map (depending on */etc/nsswitch.conf*). Any host that is running the boot parameter server replies to the broadcast with the standard null procedure "empty" reply. The *universal address* for the RPC service is printed by the requesting host in the order in which replies are received from these hosts (see the sidebar). After a short interval, another broadcast is sent.

Universal addresses

A universal address identifies the location of a transport endpoint. For UDP and TCP, it is composed of the dotted IP address with the port number of the service appended. In this example, the host *kanawha* has a universal address of 131.40.52.81.128.68.

The first four elements in the dotted string form the IP address of the server *kanawha*:

```
% ypmatch 131.40.52.81 hosts.byaddr
131.40.52.81    kanawha
```

The last two elements, "128.68", are the high and low octets of the port on which the service is registered (32836). This number is obtained by multiplying the high octet value by 2^8 and adding it to the low octet value:

```
    128 * 2^8 = 32768    (high octet)
+              68    (low octet)
           -----
            32836    (decimal representation of port)
```

rpcinfo helps us verify that *bootparam* is indeed registered on port 32836:

```
% rpcinfo -p kanawha | grep bootparam
 100026 1 udp 32836 bootparam
```

Server loading may cause the order of replies between successive broadcasts to vary significantly. A busy server takes longer to schedule the RPC server and process the request. Differing reply sequences from RPC servers are not themselves indicative of a problem, if the servers all return the correct information. If one or more servers has incorrect information, though, you will see irregular failures. A machine returning correct information may not always be the first to deliver a response to a client broadcast, so sometimes the client gets the wrong response.

In the last example (diskless client booting), a client that gets the wrong response won't boot. The boot failures may be very intermittent due to variations in server loading: when the server returning an invalid reply is heavily loaded, the client will boot without problem. However, when the servers with the correct information are loaded, then the client gets an invalid set of boot parameters and cannot start booting a kernel.

Binding to the wrong NIS server causes another kind of problem. A renegade NIS server may be the first to answer a *ypbind* broadcast for NIS service, and its lack of information about the domain makes the client machine unusable. Sometimes, just looking at the list of servers that respond to a request may flag a problem, if you notice that one of the servers should not be answering the broadcast:

```
% rpcinfo -b ypserv 1
131.40.52.138.3.255      poi
131.40.52.27.3.166       onaga
131.40.52.28.3.163       mahimahi
```

In this example, all NIS servers on the local network answer the *rpcinfo* broadcast request to the null procedure of the *ypserv* daemon. If *poi* should not be an NIS server, then the network will be prone to periods of intermittent failure if clients bind to it. Failure to fully decommission a host as an NIS server—leaving empty NIS map directories, for example—may cause this problem.

There's another possibility for NIS failure that *rpcinfo* cannot detect: there may be NIS servers on the network, but no servers for the client's NIS domain. In the previous example, *poi* may be a valid NIS server in another domain, in which case it is operating properly by responding to the *rpcinfo* broadcast. You might not be able to get *ypbind* started on an NIS client because all of the servers are in the wrong domain, and therefore the client's broadcasts are not answered. The *rpcinfo* -*b* test is a little misleading because it doesn't ask the NIS RPC daemons what domains they are serving, although the client's requests will be domain-specific. Check the servers that reply to an *rpcinfo* -*b* and ensure that they serve the NIS domain used by the clients experiencing NIS failures.

If a client cannot find an NIS server, *ypbind* hangs the boot sequence with errors of the form:

```
WARNING: Timed out waiting for NIS to come up
```

Using *rpcinfo* as shown helps to determine why a particular client cannot start the NIS service: if no host replies to the *rpcinfo* request, then the broadcast packet is failing to reach any NIS servers. If the NIS domain name and the broadcast address are correct, then it may be necessary to override the broadcast-based search and hand *ypbind* the name and address of a valid NIS server. Tools for examining and altering NIS bindings are the subject of the next section.

NIS tools

Tools discussed to this point help to dissect the session and transport layers under an application such as NIS. The application and the utilities that analyze its behavior and performance all rely on a well-behaved network. Assuming that the lower layers are in place, NIS-oriented tools fine-tune the NIS system and help resolve problems that are caused by information in the NIS maps, rather than the way in which the maps are accessed. The tools described in this section alter client-server bindings, locate NIS servers and information for a particular map, and look up keys in maps.

Key lookup

ypmatch is a *grep*-like command for NIS maps. *ypmatch* finds a single key in an NIS map and prints the data associated with that key:

```
% ypmatch help-request aliases
john.goodman

% ypmatch onaga hosts
131.40.52.27    onaga
```

This procedure differs from using *grep* on the ASCII source file that produced the map in two ways:

- *ypmatch* can be run from any client, while the NIS map source files may only exist on a server with limited user access. Therefore, users who need to parse maps such as the password, ipnodes, or hosts files must use NIS oriented tools to gather their data.

- The client may be bound to an NIS server with a corrupted map set or one that is out-of-date with the NIS master server. In this case, the output of *ypmatch* will not agree with the output of *grep* run on the ASCII source file.

Associated with *ypmatch* is *ypcat*, which is the equivalent of *cat* for NIS files. It writes the entire map file to the standard output:

```
% ypcat hosts
131.40.52.121   vineyard
131.40.52.54    hannah
131.40.52.132   positive
```

NIS maps are stored as DBM databases, indexed files with fast access provided through a hash table. Standard utilities such as *grep* do not produce meaningful results when used on DBM data files. To peek into the contents of an NIS map, you must use *ypmatch* or *ypcat*. Output from NIS tools is colored by the underlying DBM index file organization, and presents several avenues of confusion:

- By default, only the value paired with the key in the map is displayed, and not the key itself. Some maps retain the key as part of the data value because it is needed by applications that retrieve the map entry. Library routines that locate a password file entry based on UID, for example, return the user's login name as part of the password file structure. Other maps such as *aliases* simply store the value associated with the key, when applications (such as mail) that reference the NIS map already have the key value. The following excerpt from *ypcat aliases* is of little value because there are no alias names associated with the alias expansions:

      % **ypcat aliases**
              dan, lauri, paul, harry, bob
              dave, michael
              michael, jan, stewart, tom

  Both *ypcat* and *ypmatch* use the *-k* option to print the data value with its associated key:

      % **ypcat -k aliases**
      south-sales   dan, lauri, paul, harry, bob
      engin-managers dave, michael
      north-engin   michael, jan, stewart, tom

- Some maps do not associate a data value with a key. The most common map of this variety is the *ypservers* map, which simply contains hostnames of NIS servers without any additional information. When using *ypcat* or *ypmatch* with value-less maps, blank lines are produced as output:

      % **ypcat ypservers**

  unless the *-k* option is specified:

      % **ypcat -k ypservers**
      mahimahi
      wahoo
      thud

- An NIS server implements separate procedures to get the "first" and each successive key in a map. *ypcat* uses the "get first key" and "get next key" procedures to locate the first key in the DBM file and to walk through all keys. The ordering of the keys is determined by a linear scan through the DBM index file, rather than the order in which the records appear in the plain text file. Because keys are encountered in the order in which they are hash chained together, *ypcat* produces a seemingly random ordering of the keys. In the hosts file example earlier, the original */etc/inet/hosts* file was sorted by increasing host number in the IP addresses; but the process of hashing the keys into the DBM file produced the ordering seen with *ypcat*.

As a diagnostic tool, *ypmatch* can be used to identify NIS maps that are out of synchronization even after a map transfer has been requested or scheduled. It is often used to see if a change has taken place. After a new map is built, it is generally pushed to other servers using *yppush*. However, NIS map changes may not propagate as quickly as desired. A slave server may be down when a map transfer occurs, in which case it will not get an updated map until the next *ypxfr* transfer.

Displaying and analyzing client bindings

ypwhich provides information about a client's NIS domain binding, and the availability of master servers for various maps in the domain. With no arguments, it returns the name of the NIS server to which the client is currently bound by *ypbind*:

```
% ypwhich
mahimahi
```

If a hostname is passed as a parameter, then *ypwhich* queries the named host for its current binding. If *ypwhich* cannot resolve the hostname into an IP address, it reports an error:

```
% ypwhich gonzo
ypwhich: clnt_create error: RPC: Unknown host
```

An IP address may be used in place of a hostname if you are debugging NIS problems, since NIS itself is used to map the hostname into an IP address. If NIS operation is not reliable, then explicit IP addresses should be used with all of the NIS-oriented debugging tools. For example:

```
% ypwhich 131.40.52.34
wahoo
```

Querying client bindings individually is useful for debugging client problems, but it doesn't provide much useful information about the use of NIS on the network. *ypwhich* is better suited for answering questions about NIS servers: Are there enough servers? Are the clients evenly distributed among the NIS servers? There is no client binding information kept by an NIS server—the binding is something created by the client and known only to the client. The server simply answers requests that are sent to it. To determine the distribution of NIS clients to servers, you must poll the clients.

ypwhich, embedded in a shell script, collects NIS client demographics to perform a "census" of server usage:

```
#! /bin/sh
#       ypcensus - poll for ypservers
( for h in `ypcat hosts | awk '{print $2}'`
  do
        ypwhich $h
  done ) | grep -v 'not running' | sort | uniq -c
```

The *for* expression dumps the *hosts* NIS file, and *awk* extracts the second field—the hostname—from each entry. The loop then queries each host for its NIS server, and then the output from the loop is sorted. The entire loop is executed in a subshell so that its output is treated as a single stream by the next stage of the command pipeline. The *grep* command filters out errors from *ypwhich*, produced when an NIS client has not found a server for its domain. At the end of the pipe, *uniq -c* counts the occurrences of each line, producing the census of NIS servers. Sample output from the script is:

```
% ypcensus
  26 onaga
   7 mahimahi
   8 thud
```

You may find that the total number of bindings recorded is less than the number of clients—some clients may not have formed a server binding when the script was run. Executing *ypwhich* causes the client to bind to a server, so if you "miss" some hosts on the first attempt, execute the script again after all clients have been forced to find servers.

What does the output indicate? With multiple NIS servers, it is possible for the client distribution to load one server more heavily than the others. In the previous example, the large number of clients bound to server *onaga* could be caused by several things:

- The NIS server *onaga* is significantly faster than the other NIS servers, so it always replies to *ypbind* requests before other servers.

- The servers have about the same CPU speed, so the lopsided binding indicates that *onaga* has the lightest CPU load. It generates replies faster than the other servers.

- *onaga* may be "closer" to more NIS clients on the network, counting delays in network hardware. Network topology favors NIS servers that are physically close to the client if bridges or repeaters separate clients and potential NIS servers, adding packet transmission delays that can overshadow CPU scheduling delays on loaded servers.

The few clients bound to *mahimahi* and *thud* may experience NIS timeouts if these NIS servers are heavily loaded. The relatively small number of clients bound to these servers may indicate that they aren't the best candidates for NIS service because they have a higher CPU load.

Results of the binding poll should be compared to desired goals for balancing NIS server usage. If one NIS server is much faster than the others, you may improve the NIS binding distribution by shifting the fast machine's NIS service to one or two machines that are more similar to the other NIS servers.

To see if you have enough NIS servers, or if your choice of servers provides adequate NIS service, watch for broadcasts from NIS clients to the *yserv* port. You can observe network broadcasts using a tool like *snoop* or *ethereal*, both of which watch every packet on the network and print those that meet a defined criteria. *ethereal* and *snoop* are introduced in the "Network analyzers" section. To find all *ypbind* broadcasts, use the following *snoop* command line:

```
# snoop broadcast port sunrpc
        aqua -> 131.40.52.255 NIS C DOMAIN_NONACK mydomain.com
   semaphore -> 131.40.52.255 NIS C DOMAIN_NONACK mydomain.com
```

ypbind sends its RPC broadcast to the portmapper on the *sunrpc* port (port 111), and the portmapper calls the *ypserv* process indirectly. If you see a large number of broadcast calls being made to the portmapper, then your NIS clients are rebinding frequently and you should add more NIS servers or choose servers that have a lighter load.

Other NIS map information

In addition to providing NIS server binding information, *ypwhich* examines the NIS map information: the master server for a map, the list of all maps, and map nickname translations. Map nicknames are more mnemonic forms of map names used in place of the actual DBM filenames in NIS-related utilities; the nickname usually has the *.byaddr* or *.byname* suffix removed. Nicknames exist only within the *ypmatch*, *ypcat*, and *ypwhich* utilities; they are not part of the maps and are not part of the NIS servers. No application will ever perform a key lookup in map *passwd*; it has to use *passwd.byname* or *passwd.byuid*.

ypwhich -x prints the table of nicknames:

```
% ypwhich -x
Use "passwd"           for map "passwd.byname"
Use "group"            for map "group.byname"
Use "networks"         for map "networks.byaddr"
Use "hosts"            for map "hosts.byname"
Use "protocols"        for map "protocols.bynumber"
Use "services"         for map "services.byname"
Use "aliases"          for map "mail.aliases"
Use "ethers"           for map "ethers.byname"
Use "ipnodes"          for map "ipnodes.byname"
Use "project"          for map "project.byname"
```

While map nicknames provide a shorter command-line option for tools that take a map name as a parameter, they can also create name conflicts with non-standard maps that share commonly used map names. For example, a daemon that maps popular internal resource server names to IP ports might create an NIS map called *services* advertising its default mappings. This map name will not conflict with the NIS map created from */etc/inet/services* because the latter is converted into the map *services.byname*. Users of *ypcat* and *ypmatch* may be surprised by output that appears to confuse the map names.

The following example doesn't work at first because the *ypmatch* utility turns the map name *services* into *services.byname*, using the standard nickname translation. NIS completely ignores the map you want. If you use *ypmatch -t*, nickname translation is suppressed and you locate the desired map:

```
% ypmatch cullinet services
Can't match key cullinet in map services.byname.  Reason: no such key in map.
% ypmatch -t cullinet services
cullinet        6667
```

If you create your own maps, it's best to pick names that do not conflict with the standard map nicknames. Finally, *ypwhich* finds the master server for a map, or prints the list of all known maps if passed the *-m* option:

```
% ypwhich -m passwd
mahimahi
% ypwhich -m
```
excerpt follows
```
protocols.byname mahimahi
passwd.byuid mahimahi
passwd.byname mahimahi
hosts.byname mahimahi
rpc.bynumber mahimahi
group.bygid mahimahi
netmasks.byaddr mahimahi
hosts.byaddr mahimahi
netgroup mahimahi
group.byname mahimahi
mail.aliases mahimahi
services.byname mahimahi
netgroup.byhost mahimahi
protocols.bynumber mahimahi
ethers.byname mahimahi
bootparams mahimahi
ypservers mahimahi
```

ypwhich -m examines the NIS master server name embedded in the NIS map DBM file.

You can also explode an NIS map using *makedbm -u*, which "undoes" a DBM file. You see the data records as well as the two additional records added by DBM containing the NIS master name and the map's timestamp. If you have concerns about data disappearing from NIS maps, dump the entire map (including keys) using *makedbm -u*:

```
[wahoo]% cd /var/yp/nesales
[wahoo]% /usr/etc/yp/makedbm -u  ypservers
YP_LAST_MODIFIED 0649548751
YP_MASTER_NAME wahoo
```

```
wahoo wahoo
redsox redsox
thud thud
```

The map master information is useful if you have changed NIS master servers and need to verify that client maps are built correctly and synchronized with the new master server.

Setting initial client bindings

The *ypinit* command is used to preconfigure a list of NIS servers to contact at startup time. *ypinit* stores the list of NIS servers in the file */var/yp/binding/domain-name/ypservers*, where *domainname* resolves to your NIS domain name. Normally, *ypinit* is run only once after installing the system, though it may also be run whenever a new NIS server is added to the network or an existing one is decommissioned:

```
# ypinit -c

In order for NIS to operate sucessfully, we have to construct a list of the
NIS servers.  Please continue to add the names for YP servers in order of
preference, one per line.  When you are done with the list, type a <control D>
or a return on a line by itself.
    next host to add:  onaga
    next host to add:  mahimahi
    next host to add:  131.40.52.126
    next host to add:  ^D
The current list of yp servers looks like this:

onaga
mahimahi
131.40.52.126

Is this correct?  [y/n: y]  y
```

Make sure to include the necessary hostname to IP address mappings in */etc/inet/ipnodes* or */etc/inet/hosts* before running the *ypinit* command, otherwise *ypinit* will fail. The resulting *ypservers* file:

```
% cat ypservers
onaga
mahimahi
131.40.52.126
```

Note that it is not necessary to preconfigure an initial list of NIS servers, since *ypbind* will broadcast a request on the network to find the available servers if the initial list does not exist. *ypbind* is started by */usr/lib/netsvc/yp/ypstart* which in turn is invoked by the */etc/init.d/rpc* startup script:

Excerpt from /usr/lib/netsvc/yp/ypstart:
```
if [ -d /var/yp/binding/$domain -a -f /var/yp/binding/$domain/ypservers ]; then
```

```
        /usr/lib/netsvc/yp/ypbind > /dev/null 2>&1
        echo " ypbind\c"
elif [ -d /var/yp/binding/$domain ]; then
        /usr/lib/netsvc/yp/ypbind -broadcast > /dev/null 2>&1
        echo " ypbind\c"
fi
```

The next section will explain in more detail when and why you may want to bind to specific NIS servers, and how you can modify the binding once *ypbind* has been started.

Modifying client bindings

The *ypset* utility forcefully changes the server binding. It is mostly used to dissect tangles of intertwined NIS servers and to point a client at a server that is not hearing its broadcasts. The normal NIS server search is conducted by *ypbind* through a broadcast request. The first server answering the request is bound to the domain, and is probably the most lightly loaded or closest server to the requesting host. As shown in the previous *rpcinfo* examples, a server's response time, relative to other NIS servers, varies over time as its load fluctuates.

If the server's load increases so that NIS requests are not serviced before the RPC call times out on the client machine, then the client's *ypbind* daemon dissolves the current binding and rebroadcasts a request for NIS service. With varying server loads and local network traffic conditions, the timeout/rebroadcast system effects a dynamic load balancing scheme between NIS clients and servers.

Neither *ypset* nor *ypinit* should be used to implement a static load balancing scheme for two reasons:

- The initial *ypinit* or *ypset* may implement your chosen server allocation, but poor response time from this server causes the client to break the binding and perform a broadcast-based search. This dynamic rebinding will undo the attempts to effect a preferred binding.

- Extreme disparity in NIS server usage is indicative of other network problems or of excessive server loading imposed by NFS service, interactive use, or print spooling.

There are four valid uses of *ypinit* and *ypset*:

- Point a client at an NIS server that is isolated from it by a router or gateway that does not forward broadcast packets.

- Test the services provided by a particular server, if you have recently installed or rebuilt the maps on that server.

- Force servers to rebind to themselves instead of cross-binding.

- Point a client to use a known and trusted server for security reasons, instead of using any NIS server on the network.

Again, *ypinit* is used to set the initial static binding at boot time, *ypset* is used to change this binding after boot time. It is recommended to use an IP address as the argument to *ypset* to avoid using the very same NIS service that *ypbind* is having trouble starting.

```
# ypset 131.40.52.28
# ypwhich
mahimahi
```

Alternatively, you can verify that the */etc/inet/ipnodes* or */etc/inet/hosts* file lists the IP address for the new NIS server, and that */etc/nsswitch.conf* is configured to use *files* before it uses NIS.

In some NIS implementations (Solaris and others), *ypbind* no longer allows *ypset* to change its binding unless this functionality is explicitly enabled. If the *ypset* option is used when *ypbind* is started, then *ypbind* accepts requests from any remote machine to rebind to a specified server:

```
ypbind -ypset
```

The use of *-ypset* is a security risk as it allows a third party to change the binding to a potentially hostile server. Without the *-ypset* parameter, attempts to change the server binding will fail:

```
wahoo# ypset thud
ypset: Sorry, ypbind on host localhost has rejected your request.
```

A more restrictive form is:

```
ypbind -ypsetme
```

which only allows *root* on the local machine to invoke *ypset* to alter the binding. To discourage manually changing the binding, the startup script does not specify either of these options when it invokes *ypbind*.

Network analyzers

Network analyzers are ultimately the most useful tools available when it comes to debugging network problems. They are powerful tools that allow you to inspect network traffic at every level of the network stack in various degrees of detail. Good network analyzers provide powerful filters that reduce the amount of information to what is relevant for the task at hand. *Snoop*, *ethereal*, and *tcpdump* are three of the most popular network analyzers available today. *Snoop* and *ethereal* provide excellent support for RPC protocols and we use them throughout the rest of this book. The *snoop* network analyzer is bundled with Solaris, it provides powerful filters for analysis of problems related to NFS, RPC and NIS. *ethereal* is a

GUI-based network analyzer program available free of charge. It is available for various types of operating systems, including many flavors of Unix. These utilities require *superuser* privileges in order to open the network interface device.

snoop

The *snoop* network analyzer bundled with Solaris captures packets from the network and displays them in various forms according to the set of filters specified. *Snoop* can capture network traffic and display it on the fly, or save it into a file for future analysis. Being able to save the network traffic into a file allows you to display the same data set under various filters, presenting different views of the same information.

In its simplest form, *snoop* captures and displays all packets present on the network interface:

```
# snoop
Using device /dev/hme (promiscuous mode)
      narwhal -> 192.32.99.10  UDP D=7204 S=32823 LEN=252
2100::56:a00:20ff:fe8f:ba43 -> ff02::1:ffb6:12ac ICMPv6 Neighbor solicitation
      caramba -> schooner      NFS C GETATTR3 FH=0CAE
     schooner -> caramba       NFS R GETATTR3 OK
      caramba -> schooner      TCP D=2049 S=1023    Ack=341433529 Seq=2752257980
Len=0 Win=24820
      caramba -> schooner      NFS C GETATTR3 FH=B083
     schooner -> caramba       NFS R GETATTR3 OK
 mp-broadcast -> 224.12.23.34  UDP D=7204 S=32852 LEN=177
      caramba -> schooner      TCP D=2049 S=1023    Ack=341433645 Seq=2752258092
Len=0 Win=24820
  . . .
```

By default *snoop* displays only a summary of the data pertaining to the highest level protocol. The first column displays the source and destination of the network packet in the form "source -> destination". *Snoop* maps the IP address to the hostname when possible, otherwise it displays the IP address. The second column lists the highest level protocol type. The first line of the example shows the host *narwhal* sending a request to the address 192.32.99.10 over UDP. The second line shows a neighbor solicitation request initiated by the host with global IPv6 address 2100::56:a00:20ff:fe8f:ba43. The destination is a link-local multicast address (prefix FF02:). The contents of the third column depend on the protocol. For example, the 252 byte-long UDP packet in the first line has a destination port = 7204 and a source port= 32823. NFS packets use a *C* to denote a call, and an *R* to denote a reply, listing the procedure being invoked.

The fourth packet in the example is the reply from the NFS server *schooner* to the client *caramba*. It reports that the NFS GETATTR (get attributes) call returned success, but it doesn't display the contents of the attributes. *Snoop* simply displays the summary of the packet before disposing of it. You can not obtain more details about this particular packet since the packet was not saved. To avoid this limitation, *snoop* should be instructed to save the captured network packets in a file for later processing and display by using the *-o* option:

```
# snoop -o /tmp/capture -c 100
Using device /dev/hme (promiscuous mode)
100 100 packets captured
```

The *-o* option instructs *snoop* to save the captured packets in the */tmp/capture* file. The capture file mode bits are set using *root*'s file mode creation mask. Non-privileged users may be able to invoke *snoop* and process the captured file if given *read* access to the capture file. The *-c* option instructs *snoop* to capture only 100 packets. Alternatively, you can interrupt *snoop* when you believe you have captured enough packets.

The captured packets can then be analyzed as many times as necessary under different filters, each presenting a different view of data. Use the *-i* option to instruct *snoop* where to read the captured packets from:

```
# snoop -i /tmp/capture -c 5
  1   0.00000    caramba -> mickey     PORTMAP C GETPORT prog=100003 (NFS)
                                       vers=3 proto=UDP
  2   0.00072    mickey -> caramba     PORTMAP R GETPORT port=2049
  3   0.00077    caramba -> mickey     NFS C NULL3
  4   0.00041    mickey -> caramba     NFS R NULL3
  5   0.00195    caramba -> mickey     PORTMAP C GETPORT prog=100003 (NFS)
                                       vers=3 proto=UDP
5 packets captured
```

The *-i* option instructs *snoop* to read the packets from the */tmp/capture* capture file instead of capturing new packets from the network device. Note that two new columns are added to the display. The first column displays the packet number, and the second column displays the time delta between one packet and the next in seconds. For example, the second packet's time delta indicates that the host *caramba* received a reply to its original portmap request 720 microseconds after the request was first sent.

By default, *snoop* displays summary information for the top-most protocol in the network stack for every packet. Use the *-V* option to instruct snoop to display information about every level in the network stack. You can also specify packets or a range of them with the *-p* option:

```
# snoop -i /tmp/capture -V -p 3,4
```

3	0.00000	caramba -> mickey	ETHER Type=0800 (IP), size = 82 bytes
3	0.00000	caramba -> mickey	IP D=131.40.52.27 S=131.40.52.223 LEN=68, ID=35462
3	0.00000	caramba -> mickey	UDP D=2049 S=55559 LEN=48
3	0.00000	caramba -> mickey	RPC C XID=969440111 PROG=100003 (NFS) VERS=3 PROC=0

```
3   0.00000     caramba -> mickey      NFS C NULL3

4   0.00041     mickey -> caramba      ETHER Type=0800 (IP), size = 66 bytes
4   0.00041     mickey -> caramba      IP  D=131.40.52.223 S=131.40.52.27 LEN=52,
                                          ID=26344
4   0.00041     mickey -> caramba      UDP D=55559 S=2049 LEN=32
4   0.00041     mickey -> caramba      RPC R (#3) XID=969440111 Success
4   0.00041     mickey -> caramba      NFS R NULL3
```

The *-V* option instructs *snoop* to display a summary line for each protocol layer in the packet. In the previous example, packet 3 shows the Ethernet, IP, UDP, and RPC summary information, in addition to the NFS NULL request. The *-p* option is used to specify what packets are to be displayed, in this case *snoop* displays packets 3 and 4.

Every layer of the network stack contains a wealth of information that is not displayed with the *-V* option. Use the *-v* option when you're interested in analyzing the full details of any of the network layers:

```
# snoop -i /tmp/capture -v -p 3
ETHER:  ----- Ether Header -----
ETHER:
ETHER:  Packet 3 arrived at 15:08:43.35
ETHER:  Packet size = 82 bytes
ETHER:  Destination = 0:0:c:7:ac:56, Cisco
ETHER:  Source      = 8:0:20:b9:2b:f6, Sun
ETHER:  Ethertype = 0800 (IP)
ETHER:
IP:   ----- IP Header -----
IP:
IP:   Version = 4
IP:   Header length = 20 bytes
IP:   Type of service = 0x00
IP:         xxx. .... = 0 (precedence)
IP:         ...0 .... = normal delay
IP:         .... 0... = normal throughput
IP:         .... .0.. = normal reliability
IP:   Total length = 68 bytes
IP:   Identification = 35462
IP:   Flags = 0x4
IP:         .1.. .... = do not fragment
IP:         ..0. .... = last fragment
IP:   Fragment offset = 0 bytes
IP:   Time to live = 255 seconds/hops
IP:   Protocol = 17 (UDP)
IP:   Header checksum = 4503
IP:   Source address = 131.40.52.223, caramba
IP:   Destination address = 131.40.52.27, mickey
IP:   No options
IP:
UDP:  ----- UDP Header -----
UDP:
UDP:  Source port = 55559
```

```
UDP:    Destination port = 2049 (Sun RPC)
UDP:    Length = 48
UDP:    Checksum = 3685
UDP:
RPC:    ----- SUN RPC Header -----
RPC:
RPC:    Transaction id = 969440111
RPC:    Type = 0 (Call)
RPC:    RPC version = 2
RPC:    Program = 100003 (NFS), version = 3, procedure = 0
RPC:    Credentials: Flavor = 0 (None), len = 0 bytes
RPC:    Verifier   : Flavor = 0 (None), len = 0 bytes
RPC:
NFS:    ----- Sun NFS -----
NFS:
NFS:    Proc = 0 (Null procedure)
NFS:
```

The Ethernet header displays the source and destination addresses as well as the type of information embedded in the packet. The IP layer displays the IP version number, flags, options, and address of the sender and recipient of the packet. The UDP header displays the source and destination ports, along with the length and checksum of the UDP portion of the packet. Embedded in the UDP frame is the RPC data. Every RPC packet has a transaction ID used by the sender to identify replies to its requests, and by the server to identify duplicate calls. The previous example shows a request from the host *caramba* to the server *mickey*. The *RPC version = 2* refers to the version of the RPC protocol itself, the program number 100003 and Version 3 apply to the NFS service. NFS procedure 0 is always the NULL procedure, and is most commonly invoked with no authentication information. The NFS NULL procedure does not take any arguments, therefore none are listed in the NFS portion of the packet.

The amount of traffic on a busy network can be overwhelming, containing many irrelevant packets to the problem at hand. The use of filters reduces the amount of noise captured and displayed, allowing you to focus on relevant data. A filter can be applied at the time the data is captured, or at the time the data is displayed. Applying the filter at capture time reduces the amount of data that needs to be stored and processed during display. Applying the filter at display time allows you to further refine the previously captured information. You will find yourself applying different display filters to the same data set as you narrow the problem down, and isolate the network packets of interest.

Snoop uses the same syntax for capture and display filters. For example, the *host* filter instructs *snoop* to only capture packets with source or destination address matching the specified host:

```
# snoop host caramba
Using device /dev/hme (promiscuous mode)
```

```
     caramba -> schooner      NFS C GETATTR3 FH=B083
    schooner -> caramba       NFS R GETATTR3 OK
     caramba -> schooner      TCP D=2049 S=1023     Ack=3647506101 Seq=2611574902
Len=0 Win=24820
```

In this example the *host* filter instructs *snoop* to capture packets originating at or addressed to the host *caramba*. You can specify the IP address or the hostname, and *snoop* will use the name service switch to do the conversion. *Snoop* assumes that the hostname specified is an IPv4 address. You can specify an IPv6 address by using the *inet6* qualifier in front of the *host* filter:

```
# snoop inet6 host caramba
Using device /dev/hme (promiscuous mode)
     caramba -> 2100::56:a00:20ff:fea0:3390     ICMPv6 Neighbor advertisement
2100::56:a00:20ff:fea0:3390 -> caramba          ICMPv6 Echo request (ID: 1294
Sequence number: 0)
     caramba -> 2100::56:a00:20ff:fea0:3390     ICMPv6 Echo reply (ID: 1294
Sequence number: 0)
```

You can restrict capture of traffic addressed to the specified host by using the *to* or *dst* qualifier in front of the host filter:

```
# snoop to host caramba
Using device /dev/hme (promiscuous mode)
    schooner -> caramba       RPC R XID=1493500696 Success
    schooner -> caramba       RPC R XID=1493500697 Success
    schooner -> caramba       RPC R XID=1493500698 Success
```

Similarly you can restrict captured traffic to only packets originating from the specified host by using the *from* or *src* qualifier:

```
# snoop from host caramba
Using device /dev/hme (promiscuous mode)
     caramba -> schooner      NFS C GETATTR3 FH=B083
     caramba -> schooner      TCP D=2049 S=1023     Ack=3647527137 Seq=2611841034
Len=0 Win=24820
```

Note that the *host* keyword is not required when the specified hostname does not conflict with the name of another *snoop* primitive. The previous *snoop from host caramba* command could have been invoked without the *host* keyword and it would have generated the same output:

```
 # snoop from caramba
Using device /dev/hme (promiscuous mode)
     caramba -> schooner      NFS C GETATTR3 FH=B083
     caramba -> schooner      TCP D=2049 S=1023     Ack=3647527137 Seq=2611841034
Len=0 Win=24820
```

For clarity, we use the *host* keyword throughout this book. Two or more filters can be combined by using the logical operators *and* and *or*:

```
# snoop -o /tmp/capture -c 20 from host caramba and rpc nfs 3
Using device /dev/hme (promiscuous mode)
20 20 packets captured
```

Snoop captures all NFS Version 3 packets originating at the host *caramba*. Here, *snoop* is invoked with the *-c* and *-o* options to save 20 filtered packets into the */tmp/capture* file. We can later apply other filters during display time to further analyze the captured information. For example, you may want to narrow the previous search even further by only listing TCP traffic by using the *proto* filter:

```
# snoop -i /tmp/capture proto tcp
Using device /dev/hme (promiscuous mode)
    1   0.00000     caramba -> schooner    NFS C GETATTR3 FH=B083
    2   2.91969     caramba -> schooner    NFS C GETATTR3 FH=0CAE
    9   0.37944     caramba -> rea         NFS C FSINFO3 FH=0156
   10   0.00430     caramba -> rea         NFS C GETATTR3 FH=0156
   11   0.00365     caramba -> rea         NFS C ACCESS3 FH=0156 (lookup)
   14   0.00256     caramba -> rea         NFS C LOOKUP3 FH=F244 libc.so.1
   15   0.00411     caramba -> rea         NFS C ACCESS3 FH=772D (lookup)
```

Snoop reads the previously filtered data from */tmp/capture*, and applies the new filter to only display TCP traffic. The resulting output is NFS traffic originating at the host *caramba* over the TCP protocol. We can apply a UDP filter to the same NFS traffic in the */tmp/capture* file and obtain the NFS Version 3 traffic over UDP from host *caramba* without affecting the information in the */tmp/capture* file:

```
# snoop -i /tmp/capture proto udp
Using device /dev/hme (promiscuous mode)
    1   0.00000     caramba -> rea         NFS C NULL3
```

So far, we've presented filters that let you specify the information you are interested in. Use the *not* operator to specify the criteria of packets that you wish to have excluded during capture. For example, you can use the *not* operator to capture all network traffic, except that generated by the remote shell:

```
# snoop not port login
Using device /dev/hme (promiscuous mode)
        rt 086 > BROADCAST       RIP R (25 destinations)
       rt-086 -> BROADCAST       RIP R (10 destinations)
     caramba -> schooner         NFS C GETATTR3 FH=B083
     schooner -> caramba         NFS R GETATTR3 OK
     caramba -> donald           NFS C GETATTR3 FH=00BD
     jamboree -> donald          NFS R GETATTR3 OK
     caramba -> donald           TCP D=2049 S=657    Ack=3855205229
Seq=2331839250 Len=0 Win=24820
     caramba -> schooner         TCP D=2049 S=1023   Ack=3647569565
Seq=2612134974 Len=0 Win=24820
      narwhal -> 224.2.127.254   UDP D=9875 S=32825 LEN=368
```

On multihomed hosts (systems with more than one network interface device), use the *-d* option to specify the particular network interface to *snoop* on:

```
snoop -d hme2
```

You can *snoop* on multiple network interfaces concurrently by invoking separate instances of *snoop* on each device. This is particularly useful when you don't know what interface the host will use to generate or receive the requests. The *-d* option can be used in conjunction with any of the other options and filters previously described:

```
# snoop -o /tmp/capture-hme0 -d hme0 not port login &
# snoop -o /tmp/capture-hme1 -d hme1 not port login &
```

Filters help refine the search for relevant packets. Once the packets of interest have been found, use the *-V* or *-v* options to display the packets in more detail. You will see how this top-down technique is used to debug NFS-related problems in Chapter 14. Often you can use more than one filter to achieve the same result. Refer to the documentation shipped with your OS for a complete list of available filters.

ethereal / tethereal

ethereal is an open source free network analyzer for Unix and Windows. It allows you to examine data from a live network or from a capture file on disk. You can interactively browse the capture data, viewing summary and detail information for each packet. It is very similar in functionality to *snoop*, although perhaps providing more powerful and diversified filters. At the time of this writing, *ethereal* is beta software and its developers indicate that it is far from complete. Although new features are continuously being added, it already has enough functionality to be useful. We use version 0.8.4 of *ethereal* in this book. Some of the functionality, as well as look-and-feel may have changed by the time you read these pages.

In addition to providing powerful display filters, *ethereal* provides a very nice Graphical User Interface (GUI) which allows you to interactively browse the captured data, viewing summary and detailed information for each packet. The official home of the *ethereal* software is *http://www.zing.org*. You can download the source and documentation from this site and build it yourself, or follow the links to download precompiled binary packages for your environment. You can download precompiled Solaris packages from *http://www.sunfreeware.com*. In either case, you will need to install the *GTK+* Open Source Free Software GUI Toolkit as well as the *libpcap* packet capture library. Both are available on the *ethereal* website.

tethereal is the text-only functional equivalent of *ethereal*. They both share a large amount of the source code in order to provide the same level of data capture, filtering, and packet decoding. The main difference is the user interface: *tethereal* does not provide the nice GUI provided by *ethereal*. Due to its textual output, *tethereal* is used throughout this book.* Examples and discussions concerning

---

* In our examples, we reformat the output that *tethereal* generates by adding or removing white spaces to make it easier to read.

tethereal also apply to *ethereal*. Many of the concepts will overlap those presented in the *snoop* discussion, though the syntax will be different.

In its simplest form, *tethereal* captures and displays all packets present on the network interface:

```
# tethereal
Capturing on hme0
      caramba -> schooner    NFS V3 GETATTR Call XID 0x59048f4a
      schooner -> caramba    NFS V3 GETATTR Reply XID 0x59048f4a
      caramba -> schooner    TCP 1023 > nfsd [ACK] Seq=2139539358 Ack=1772042332
                             Win=24820 Len=0
      concam -> 224.12.23.34 UDP Source port: 32939  Destination port: 7204
mp-broadcast -> 224.12.23.34 UDP Source port: 32852  Destination port: 7204
      narwhal -> 224.12.23.34 UDP Source port: 32823  Destination port: 7204
       vm-086 -> 224.0.0.2    HSRP Hello (state Active)
      caramba -> mickey      YPSERV V2 MATCH Call XID 0x39c4533d
       mickey -> caramba     YPSERV V2 MATCH Reply XID 0x39c4533d
```

By default *tethereal* displays only a summary of the highest level protocol. The first column displays the source and destination of the network packet. *tethereal* maps the IP address to the hostname when possible, otherwise it displays the IP address. You can use the *-n* option to disable network object name resolution and have the IP addresses displayed instead. Each line displays the packet type, and the protocol-specific parameters. For example, the first line displays an NFS Version 3 GETATTR (get attributes) request from client *caramba* to server *schooner* with RPC transaction ID 0x59048f4a. The second line reports *schooner*'s reply to the GETATTR request. You know that this is a reply to the previous request because of the matching transaction IDs.

Use the *-w* option to have *tethereal* write the packets to a data file for later display. As with *snoop*, this allows you to apply powerful filters to the data set to reduce the amount of noise reported. Use the *-c* option to set the number of packets to read when capturing data:

```
# tethereal -w /tmp/capture -c 5
Capturing on hme0
10
```

Use the *-r* option to read packets from a capture file:

```
# tethereal -r /tmp/capture -t d
  1  0.000000  caramba -> mickey    PORTMAP V2 GETPORT Call XID 0x39c87b6e
  2  0.000728   mickey -> caramba   PORTMAP V2 GETPORT Reply XID 0x39c87b6e
  3  0.00077   caramba -> mickey    NFS V3 NULL Call XID 0x39c87b6f
  4  0.000416   mickey -> caramba   NFS V3 NULL Reply XID 0x39c87b6f
  5  0.001957  caramba -> mickey    PORTMAP V2 GETPORT Call XID 0x39c848db
```

tethereal reads the packets from the */tmp/capture* file specified by the *-r* option. Note that two new columns are added to the display. The first column displays the packet number, and the second column displays the time delta between one packet and the next in seconds. The *-t d* option instructs *tethereal* to use delta timestamps, if not specified, *tethereal* reports timestamps relative to the time elapsed between the first packet and the current packet. Use the *-t a* option to display the actual date and time the packet was captured. *tethereal* can also read capture files generated by other network analyzers, including *snoop*'s capture files.

As mentioned in the *snoop* discussion, network analyzers are most useful when you have the ability to filter the information you need. One of *tethereal*'s strongest attributes is its rich filter set. Unlike *snoop*, *tethereal* uses different syntax for capture and display filters. Display filters are called read filters in *tethereal*, therefore we will use the *tethereal* terminology during this discussion. Note that a read filter can also be specified during packet capturing, causing only packets that pass the read filter to be displayed or saved to the output file. Capture filters are much more efficient than read filters. It may be more difficult for *tethereal* to keep up with a busy network if a read filter is specified during a live capture.

Capture filters

Packet capture and filtering is performed by the Packet Capture Library (*libpcap*). Use the *-f* option to set the capture filter expression:

```
# tethereal -f "dst host donald"
Capturing on hme0
     schooner -> donald     TCP nfsd > 1023 [PSH, ACK] Seq=1773285388 Ack=2152316770
                            Win=49640 Len=116
      mickey -> donald      UDP Source port: 934  Destination port: 61638
      mickey -> donald      UDP Source port: 934  Destination port: 61638
      mickey -> donald      UDP Source port: 934  Destination port: 61638
     schooner -> donald     TCP nfsd > 1023 [PSH, ACK] Seq=1773285504 Ack=2152316882
                            Win=49640 Len=116
```

The *dst host* filter instructs *tethereal* to only capture packets with a destination address equal to *donald*. You can specify the IP address or the hostname, and *tethereal* will use the name service switch to do the conversion. Substitute *dst* with *src* and *tethereal* captures packets with a source address equal to *donald*. Simply specifying *host donald* captures packets with either source or destination addresses equal to *donald*.

Use protocol capture filters to instruct *tethereal* to capture all network packets using the specified protocol, regardless of origin, destination, packet length, etc:

```
# tethereal -f "arp"
Sun_a0:33:90 -> ff:ff:ff:ff:ff:ff          ARP   Who has 131.40.51.7?      Tell
131.40.51.125
Sun_b9:2b:f6 -> Sun_a0:33:90               ARP   131.40.51.223 is at 08:00:20:b9:2b:
f6
00:90:2b:71:e0:00 -> ff:ff:ff:ff:ff:ff     ARP   Who has 131.40.51.77?    Tell 131.
40.51.17
```

The *arp* filter instructs *tethereal* to capture all of the ARP packets on the network. Notice that *tethereal* replaces the Ethernet address prefix with the *Sun_* identifier (08:00:20). The list of prefixes known to *tethereal* can be found in */etc/ manuf* file located in the *tethereal* installation directory.

Use the *and, or,* and *not* logical operators to build complex and powerful filters:

```
# tethereal -w /tmp/capture -f "host 131.40.51.7 and arp"
# tethereal -r /tmp/capture
Sun_a0:33:90 -> ff:ff:ff:ff:ff:ff         ARP Who has 131.40.51.7?        Tell
131.40.51.125
Sun_b9:2b:f6 -> Sun_a0:33:90              ARP 131.40.51.7 is at 08:00:20:b9:2b:f6
```

tethereal captures all ARP requests for the 131.40.51.7 address and writes the packets to the */tmp/capture* file. We should point out that the source address of the first packet is not 131.40.51.7, and highlight the fact that the destination address is the Ethernet broadcast address. You may ask then, why is this packet captured by *tethereal* if neither the source nor destination address match the requested host? You can use the *-V* option to analyze the contents of the captured packet to answer this question:

```
# tethereal -r /tmp/ether -V
Frame 1 (60 on wire, 60 captured)
    Arrival Time: Sep 25, 2000 13:34:08.2305
    Time delta from previous packet: 0.000000 seconds
    Frame Number: 1
    Packet Length: 60 bytes
    Capture Length: 60 bytes
Ethernet II
    Destination: ff:ff:ff:ff:ff:ff (ff:ff:ff:ff:ff:ff)
    Source: 08:00:20:a0:33:90 (Sun_a0:33:90)
    Type: ARP (0x0806)
Address Resolution Protocol (request)
    Hardware type: Ethernet (0x0001)
    Protocol type: IP (0x0800)
    Hardware size: 6
    Protocol size: 4
    Opcode: request (0x0001)
    Sender hardware address: 08:00:20:a0:33:90
    Sender protocol address: 131.40.51.125
    Target hardware address: ff:ff:ff:ff:ff:ff
    Target protocol address: 131.40.51.7
...
(Contents of second packet have been omitted)
```

The *-V* option displays the full protocol tree. Each layer of the packet is printed in detail (for clarity, we omit printing the contents of the second packet). The frame information is added by *tethereal* to identify the network packet. Note that the frame information is not part of the actual network packet, and is therefore not transmitted over the wire.

The Ethernet frame displays the broadcast destination address, and the source MAC address. Notice how the 08:00:20 prefix is replaced by the *Sun_* identifier.

The Address Resolution Protocol (ARP) part of the frame, indicates that this is a request asking for the hardware address of 131.40.51.7. This explains why *tethereal* captures the packet when the *host 131.40.51.7 and arp* filter is specified.

Use the *not* operator to specify the criteria of packets that you wish to have excluded during capture. For example, use the *not* operator to capture all network packets, except ARP related network traffic:

```
# tethereal -f "not arp"
Capturing on hme0
    concam -> 224.12.23.34 UDP Source port: 32939  Destination port: 7204
    donald -> schooner     TCP 1023 > nfsd [ACK] Seq=2153618946 Ack=1773368360
Win=24820 Len=0
  narwhal -> 224.12.23.34 UDP Source port: 32823  Destination port: 7204
    donald -> schooner     NFS V3 GETATTR Call XID 0x5904b03e
  schooner -> caramba      NFS V3 GETATTR Reply XID 0x5904b03e
```

This section discussed how to restrict the amount of information captured by *tethereal.* In the next section, you see how to apply the more powerful read filters to find the exact information you need. Refer to *tethereal*'s documentation for a complete set of capture filters.

Read filters

Capture filters provide limited means of refining the amount of information gathered. To complement them, *tethereal* provides a rich read (display) filter language used to build powerful filters. Read filters further remove the noise from a packet trace to let you see packets of interest. A packet is displayed if it meets the requirements expressed in the filter. Read filters let you compare the fields within a protocol against a specific value, compare fields against fields, or simply check the existence of specified fields and protocols.

Use the *-R* option to specify a read filter. The simplest read filter allows you to check for the existence of a protocol or field:

```
# tethereal -r /tmp/capture -R "nfs"
 3  0.001500    caramba -> mickey    NFS V3 NULL Call XID 0x39c87b6f
 4  0.001916     mickey -> caramba   NFS V3 NULL Reply XID 0x39c87b6f
54  2.307132    caramba -> schooner  NFS V3 GETATTR Call XID 0x590289e7
55  2.308824   schooner -> caramba   NFS V3 GETATTR Reply XID 0x590289e7
56  2.309622    caramba -> mickey    NFS V3 LOOKUP Call XID 0x590289e8
57  2.310400     mickey -> caramba   NFS V3 LOOKUP Reply XID 0x590289e8
```

tethereal reads the capture file */tmp/capture* and displays all packets that contain the NFS protocol.

You can specify a filter that matches the existence of a given field in the network packet. For example, use the *nfs.name* filter to instruct *tethereal* to display all packets containing the NFS *name* field in either requests or replies:

```
# tethereal -r /tmp/capture -R "nfs.name"
 56  2.309622    caramba -> mickey    NFS V3 LOOKUP Call XID 0x590289e8
 57  2.310400    mickey -> caramba    NFS V3 LOOKUP Reply XID 0x590289e8
```

You can also specify the value of the field. For example use the *frame.number* ==
56 filter, to display packet number 56:

```
# tethereal -r /tmp/capture -R "frame.number == 56"
 56  2.309622    caramba -> mickey    NFS V3 LOOKUP Call XID 0x590289e8
```

This is equivalent to *snoop*'s *-p* option. You can also specify ranges of values of a
field. For example, you can print the first three packets in the capture file by
specifying a range for *frame.number*.

```
# tethereal -r /tmp/capture -R "frame.number <= 3"
  1  0.000000    caramba -> mickey    PORTMAP V2 GETPORT Call XID 0x39c87b6e
  2  0.000728    mickey -> caramba    PORTMAP V2 GETPORT Reply XID 0x39c87b6e
  3  0.001500    caramba -> mickey    NFS V3 NULL Call XID 0x39c87b6f
```

You can combine basic filter expressions and field values by using logical operators to build more powerful filters. For example, say you want to list all NFS Version 3 *Lookup* and *Getattr* operations. You know that NFS is an RPC program,
therefore you first need to determine the procedure number for the NFS operations by finding their definition in the *nfs.h* include file:

```
$ grep NFSPROC3_LOOKUP /usr/include/nfs/nfs.h
#define       NFSPROC3_LOOKUP ((rpcproc_t)3)
$ grep NFSPROC3_GETATTR /usr/include/nfs/nfs.h
#define       NFSPROC3_GETATTR ((rpcproc_t)1)
```

The two *grep* operations help you determine that the NFS *Lookup* operation is RPC
procedure number 3 of the NFS Version 3 protocol, and the NFS *Getattr* operation
is procedure number 1. You can then use this information to build a filter that
specifies your interest in protocol NFS with RPC program Version 3, and RPC procedures 1 or 3. You can represent this with the filter expression:

```
nfs and rpc.programversion == 3 and(rpc.procedure == 1 or rpc.procedure == 3)
```

The *tethereal* invocation follows:

```
# tethereal -r /tmp/capture -R "nfs and rpc.programversion == 3 and \
 (rpc.procedure == 1 or rpc.procedure == 3)"
 54  2.307132    caramba -> schooner   NFS V3 GETATTR Call XID 0x590289e7
 55  2.308824    schooner -> caramba   NFS V3 GETATTR Reply XID 0x590289e7
 56  2.309622    caramba -> mickey     NFS V3 LOOKUP Call XID 0x590289e8
 57  2.310400    mickey -> caramba     NFS V3 LOOKUP Reply XID 0x590289e8
```

The filter displays all NFS Version 3 *Getattr* and all NFS Version 3 *Lookup* operations. Refer to *tethereal*'s documentation for a complete description of the rich
filters provided. In Chapter 14, you will see how to use *tethereal* to debug NFS-
related problems.

14

NFS Diagnostic Tools

The previous chapter described diagnostic tools used to trace and resolve network and name service problems. In this chapter, we present tools for examining the configuration and performance of NFS, tools that monitor NFS network traffic, and tools that provide various statistics on the NFS client and server.

NFS administration tools

NFS administration problems can be of different types. You can experience problems mounting a filesystem from a server due to export misconfiguration, problems with file permissions, missing information, out-of-date information, or severe performance constraints. The output of the NFS tools described in this chapter will serve as input for the performance analysis and tuning procedures in Chapter 17.

Mount information is maintained in three files, as shown in Table 14-1.

Table 14-1. Mount information files

File	Host	Contents
/etc/dfs/sharetab	server	Currently exported filesystems
/etc/rmtab	server	*host:directory* name pairs for clients of this server
/etc/mnttab	client	Currently mounted filesystems

An NFS server is interested in the filesystems (and directories within those filesystem) it has exported and what clients have mounted filesystems from it. The */etc/dfs/sharetab* file contains a list of the current exported filesystems and under normal conditions, it reflects the contents of the */etc/dfs/dfstab* file line-for-line.

The existence of */etc/dfs/dfstab* usually determines whether a machine becomes an NFS server and runs the *mountd* and *nfsd* daemons. During the boot process, the server checks for this file and executes the *shareall* script which, in turn, exports all filesystems specified in */etc/dfs/dfstab*. The *mountd* and *nfsd* daemons will be started if at least one filesystem was successfully exported via NFS. An excerpt of the */etc/init.d/nfs.server* boot script is shown here:

```
startnfsd=0
if [ -f /etc/dfs/dfstab ]; then
      /usr/sbin/shareall -F nfs
      if /usr/bin/grep -s nfs /etc/dfs/sharetab >/dev/null; then
            startnfsd=1
      fi
fi

if [ $startnfsd -ne 0 ]; then
      /usr/lib/nfs/mountd
      /usr/lib/nfs/nfsd -a 16
fi
```

The dynamically managed file of exported filesystems, */etc/dfs/sharetab*, is truncated to zero length during the boot process. This takes place in the *nfs.server* boot script, although the truncation code is not shown in this example. Once *mountd* is running, the contents of */etc/dfs/sharetab* determine the mount operations that will be permitted by *mountd*.

/etc/dfs/sharetab is maintained by the *share* utility, so the modification time of */etc/dfs/sharetab* indicates the last time filesystem export information was updated. If a client is unable to mount a filesystem even though the filesystem is named in the server's */etc/dfs/dfstab* file, verify that the filesystem appears in the server's */etc/dfs/sharetab* file by using *share* with no arguments:

```
server% share
-                   /export/home1   rw    "Cool folks"
-                   /export/home2   root=mahimahi:thud    ""
```

If the *sharetab* file is out-of-date, then re running *share* on the server should make the filesystem available. Note that there's really no difference between *cat /etc/dfs/sharetab* and *share* with no arguments. Except for formatting differences, the output is the same.

When *mountd* accepts a mount request from a client, it notes the directory name passed in the mount request and the client hostname in */etc/rmtab*. Entries in *rmtab* are long-lived; they remain in the file until the client performs an explicit *umount* of the filesystem. This file is not purged when a server reboots because the NFS mounts themselves are persistent across server failures.

Before an NFS client shuts down, it should try to unmount its remote filesystems. Clients that mount NFS filesystems, but never unmount them before shutting down, leave stale information in the server's *rmtab* file.

In an extreme case, changing a hostname without performing a *umountall* before taking the host down makes permanent entries in the server's *rmtab* file. Old information in */etc/rmtab* has an annoying effect on *shutdown*, which uses the remote mount table to warn clients of the host that it is about to be rebooted. *shutdown* actually asks the *mountd* daemon for the current version of the remote mount table, but *mountd* loads its initial version of the table from the */etc/rmtab* file. If the *rmtab* file is not accurate, then uninterested clients may be notified, or *shutdown* may attempt to find hosts that are no longer on the network. The out-of-date *rmtab* file won't cause the shutdown procedure to hang, but it will produce confusing messages. The contents of the *rmtab* file should only be used as a hint; mission-critical processing should never depend on its contents. For instance, it would be a very bad idea for a server to skip backups of filesystems listed in *rmtab* on the simple assumption that they are currently in use by NFS clients. There are multiple reasons why this file can be out-of-date.

The *showmount* command is used to review server-side mount information. It has three invocations:

showmount -a [server]	*Prints client:directory pairs for server's clients.*
showmount -d [server]	*Simply prints directory names mounted by server's clients.*
showmount -e [server]	*Prints the list of shared filesystems.*

For example:

```
% showmount -a
bears:/export/home1
bears:/export/home2/wahoo
honeymoon:/export/home2/wahoo
131.40.52.44:/export/home1
131.40.52.44:/export/home2

% showmount -d mahimahi
/export/home1
/export/home2

% showmount -e mahimahi
/export/home1        (everyone)
/export/home2        (everyone)
```

In the first example, an unknown host, indicated by the presence of an IP address instead of a hostname, has mounted filesystems from the local host. If the IP address is valid on the local network, then the host's name and IP address are mismatched in the name service hosts file or in the client's */etc/hosts* file. However, this could also indicate a breach of security, particularly if the host is on another network or the host number is known to be unallocated.

Finally, the client can review its currently mounted filesystems using *df*, getting a brief look at the mount points and corresponding remote filesystem information:

df		*Shows current mount information.*
df -F *fstype*		*Looks at filesystems of type fstype only.*
df *directory*		*Locates mount point for directory.*

For example:

```
% df -k -F nfs
filesystem              kbytes    used    avail  capacity  Mounted on
onaga:/export/onaga     585325   483295   43497    92%     /home/onaga
thud:/export/thu        427520   364635   20133    95%     /home/thud
mahimahi:/export/mahimahi
                        371967   265490   69280    79%     /home/mahimahi
```

The *-k* option is used to report the total space allocated in the filesystem in kilobytes. When *df* is used to locate the mount point for a directory, it resolves symbolic links and determines the filesystem mounted at the link's target:

```
% ls -l /usr/local/bin
lrwxrwxrwx  1 root          16 Jun  8 14:51 /usr/local/bin -> /tools/local/bin
% df -k /usr/local/bin
filesystem               kbytes    used    avail  capacity  Mounted on
mahimahi:/tools/local    217871   153022   43061    78%     /tools/local
```

df may produce confusing or conflicting results in heterogeneous environments. Not all systems agree on what the bytes used and bytes available fields should represent; in most cases they are the number of usable bytes available to the user left on the filesystem. Other systems may include the 10% space buffer included in the filesystem and overstate the amount of free space on the filesystem.

Detailed mount information is maintained in the */etc/mnttab* file on the local host. Along with host (or device) names and mount points, *mnttab* lists the mount options used on the filesystem. *mnttab* shows the current state of the system, while */etc/vfstab* only shows the filesystems to be mounted "by default." Invoking *mount* with no options prints the contents of *mnttab*; supplying the *-p* option produces a listing that is suitable for inclusion in the */etc/vfstab* file:

```
% mount
/proc on /proc read/write/setuid on Wed Jul 26 01:33:02 2000
/ on /dev/dsk/c0t0d0s0 read/write/setuid/largefiles on Wed Jul 26 01:33:02 2000
/usr on /dev/dsk/c0t0d0s6 read/write/setuid/largefiles on Wed Jul 26 01:33:02 2000
/dev/fd on fd read/write/setuid on Wed Jul 26 01:33:02 2000
/export/home on /dev/dsk/c0t0d0s7 setuid/read/write/largefiles on Wed Jul 26 01:
33:04 2000
/tmp on swap read/write on Wed Jul 26 01:33:04 2000
/home/labiaga on berlin:/export/home11/labiaga intr/nosuid/noquota/remote on Thu
Jul 27 17:39:59 2000
/mnt on paris:/export/home/rome read/write/remote on Thu Jul 27 17:41:07 2000

% mount -p
/proc - /proc proc - no rw,suid
/dev/dsk/c0t0d0s0 - / ufs - no rw,suid,largefiles
/dev/dsk/c0t0d0s6 - /usr ufs - no rw,suid,largefiles
```

```
fd - /dev/fd fd - no rw,suid
/dev/dsk/c0t0d0s7 - /export/home ufs - no suid,rw,largefiles
swap - /tmp tmpfs - no rw
berlin:/export/home11/labiaga - /home/labiaga nfs - no intr,nosuid,noquota
paris:/export/home/rome - /mnt nfs - no rw
```

Although you can take the output of the *mount -p* command and include the NFS mounts in the client's */etc/vfstab* file, it is not recommended. Chapter 9 describes the many reasons why dynamic mounts are preferred. However, if static cross-mounting is required, use the background (*bg*) option to avoid deadlock during server reboots when two servers cross-mount filesystems from each other and reboot at the same time.

NFS statistics

The client- and server-side implementations of NFS compile per-call statistics of NFS service usage at both the RPC and application layers. *nfsstat -c* displays the client-side statistics while *nfsstat -s* shows the server tallies. With no arguments, *nfsstat* prints out both sets of statistics:

```
% nfsstat -s
Server rpc:
Connection oriented:
calls        badcalls    nullrecv    badlen      xdrcall     dupchecks
10733943     0           0           0           0           1935861
dupreqs
0
Connectionless:
calls        badcalls    nullrecv    badlen      xdrcall     dupchecks
136499       0           0           0           0           0
dupreqs
0

Server nfs:
calls        badcalls
10870161     14
Version 2: (1716 calls)
null         getattr     setattr     root        lookup      readlink
48 2%        0 0%        0 0%        0 0%        1537 89%    13 0%
read         wrcache     write       create      remove      rename
0 0%         0 0%        0 0%        0 0%        0 0%        0 0%
link         symlink     mkdir       rmdir       readdir     statfs
0 0%         0 0%        0 0%        0 0%        111 6%      7 0%
Version 3: (10856042 calls)
null         getattr     setattr     lookup      access      readlink
136447 1%    4245200 39% 95412 0%    1430880 13% 2436623 22% 74093 0%
read         write       create      mkdir       symlink     mknod
376522 3%    277812 2%   165838 1%   25497 0%    24480 0%    0 0%
remove       rmdir       rename      link        readdir     readdirplus
359460 3%    33293 0%    8211 0%     69484 0%    69898 0%    876367 8%
fsstat       fsinfo      pathconf    commit
1579 0%      7698 0%     4253 0%     136995 1%
```

```
Server nfs_acl:
Version 2: (2357 calls)
null        getacl      setacl      getattr     access
0 0%        5 0%        0 0%        2170 92%    182 7%
Version 3: (10046 calls)
null        getacl      setacl
0 0%        10039 99%   7 0%
```

The server-side RPC fields indicate if there are problems removing the packets from the NFS service end point. The kernel reports statistics on connection-oriented RPC and connectionless RPC separately. The fields detail each kind of problem:

calls

The NFS calls value represents the total number of NFS Version 2, NFS Version 3, NFS ACL Version 2 and NFS ACL Version 3 RPC calls made to this server from all clients. The RPC calls value represents the total number of NFS, NFS ACL, and NLM RPC calls made to this server from all clients. RPC calls made for other services, such as NIS, are not included in this count.

badcalls

These are RPC requests that were rejected out of hand by the server's RPC mechanism, before the request was passed to the NFS service routines in the kernel. An RPC call will be rejected if there is an authentication failure, where the calling client does not present valid credentials.

nullrecv

Not used in Solaris. Its value is always 0.

badlen/xdrcall

The RPC request received by the server was too short (*badlen*) or the XDR headers in the packet are malformed (*xdrcall*). Most likely this is due to a malfunctioning client. It is rare, but possible, that the packet could have been truncated or damaged by a network problem. On a local area network, it's rare to have XDR headers damaged, but running NFS over a wide-area network could result in malformed requests. We'll look at ways of detecting and correcting packet damage on wide-area networks in "NFS over wide-area networks" in Chapter 18.

dupchecks/dupreqs

The *dupchecks* field indicates the number of RPC calls that were looked up in the duplicate request cache. The *dupreqs* field indicates the number of RPC calls that were actually found to be duplicates. Duplicate requests occur as a result of client retransmissions. A large number of *dupreqs* usually indicates that the server is not replying fast enough to its clients. Idempotent requests can be replayed without ill effects, therefore not all RPCs have to be looked up on the duplicate request cache. This explains why the *dupchecks* field does not match the calls field.

The statistics for each NFS version are reported independently, showing the total number of NFS calls made to this server using each version of the protocol. A version-specific breakdown by procedure of the calls handled is also provided. Each of the call types corresponds to a procedure within the NFS RPC and NFS_ACL RPC services.

The null procedure is included in every RPC program for *ping*ing the RPC server. The null procedure returns no value, but a successful return from a call to *null* ensures that the network is operational and that the server host is alive. *rpcinfo* calls the null procedure to check RPC server health. The automounter (see Chapter 9) calls the null procedure of all NFS servers in parallel when multiple machines are listed for a single mount point. The automounter and *rpcinfo* should account for the total *null* calls reported by *nfsstat*.

Client-side RPC statistics include the number of calls of each type made to all servers, while the client NFS statistics indicate how successful the client machine is in reaching NFS servers:

```
% nfsstat -c
Client rpc:
Connection oriented:
calls       badcalls    badxids     timeouts    newcreds    badverfs
1753584     1412        18          64          0           0
timers      cantconn    nomem       interrupts
0           1317        0           18
Connectionless:
calls       badcalls    retrans     badxids     timeouts    newcreds
12443       41          334         80          166         0
badverfs    timers      nomem       cantsend
0           4321        0           206


Client nfs:
calls       badcalls    clgets      cltoomany
1661217     23          1661217     3521
Version 2:  (234258 calls)
null        getattr     setattr     root        lookup      readlink
0 0%        37 0%       0 0%        0 0%        184504 78%  811 0%
read        wrcache     write       create      remove      rename
49 0%       0 0%        24301 10%   3 0%        2 0%        0 0%
link        symlink     mkdir       rmdir       readdir     statfs
0 0%        0 0%        12 0%       12 0%       24500 10%   27 0%
Version 3:  (1011525 calls)
null        getattr     setattr     lookup      access      readlink
0 0%        417691 41%  14598 1%    223609 22%  47438 4%    695 0%
read        write       create      mkdir       symlink     mknod
56347 5%    221334 21%  1565 0%     106 0%      48 0%       0 0%
remove      rmdir       rename      link        readdir     readdirplus
807 0%      14 0%       676 0%      24 0%       475 0%      5204 0%
fsstat      fsinfo      pathconf    commit
8 0%        10612 1%    95 0%       10179 1%
```

```
Client nfs_acl:
Version 2: (411477 calls)
null          getacl        setacl        getattr       access
0 0%          181399 44%    0 0%          185858 45%    44220 10%
Version 3: (3957 calls)
null          getacl        setacl
0 0%          3957 100%     0 0%
```

In addition to the total number of NFS calls made and the number of rejected NFS calls (*badcalls*), the client-side statistics indicate if NFS calls are being delayed due to a lack of client RPC handles. Client RPC handles are opaque pointers used by the kernel to hold server connection information. In SunOS 4.x, the number of client handles was fixed, causing the NFS call to block until client handles became available. In Solaris, client handles are allocated dynamically. The kernel maintains a cache of up to 16 client handles, which are reused to speed up communication with the server. The *clgets* count indicates the number of times a client handle has been requested. If the NFS call cannot find an unused client handle in the cache, it will not block until one frees up. Instead, it will create a brand new client handle and proceed. This count is reflected by *cltoomany*. The client handle is destroyed when the reply to the NFS call arrives. This count is of little use to system administrators since nothing can be done to increase the cache size and reduce the number of misses.

Included in the client RPC statistics are counts for various failures experienced while trying to send NFS requests to a server:

calls

   Total number of calls made to all NFS servers.

badcalls

   Number of RPC calls that returned an error. The two most common RPC failures are timeouts and interruptions, both of which increment the *badcalls* counter. The connection-oriented RPC statistics also increment the *interrupts* counter. There is no equivalent counter for connectionless RPC statistics. If a server reply is not received within the RPC timeout period, an RPC error occurs. If the RPC call is interrupted, as it may be if a filesystem is mounted with the *intr* option, then an RPC interrupt code is returned to the caller. *nfsstat* also reports the *badcalls* count in the NFS statistics. NFS call failures do not include RPC timeouts or interruptions, but do include other RPC failures such as authentication errors (which will be counted in both the NFS and RPC level statistics).

badxids

   The number of bad XIDs. The XID in an NFS request is a serial number that uniquely identifies the request. When a request is retransmitted, it retains the same XID through the entire timeout and retransmission cycle. With the Solaris multithreaded kernel, it is possible for the NFS client to have several RPC requests outstanding at any time, to any number of NFS servers. When a response is received from an NFS server, the client matches the XID in the response to an RPC call in progress. If an XID is seen for which there is no active RPC call—because the client already received a response for that XID—then the client increments *badxid*. A high *badxid* count, therefore, indicates that the server is receiving some retransmitted requests, but is taking a long time to reply to all NFS requests. This scenario is explored in "Slow server compensation" in Chapter 18.

timeouts

Number of calls that timed out waiting for a server's response. For hard-mounted filesystems, calls that time out are retransmitted, with a new timeout period that may be longer than the previous one. However, calls made on soft-mounted filesystems may eventually fail if the retransmission count is exceeded, so that the call counts obey the relationship:

```
timeout + badcalls >= retrans
```

The final retransmission of a request on a soft-mounted filesystem increments *badcalls* (as previously explained). For example, if a filesystem is mounted with *retrans=5*, the client reissues the same request five times before noting an RPC failure. All five requests are counted in *timeout*, since no replies are received. Of the failed attempts, four are counted in the *retrans* statistic and the last shows up in *badcalls*.

newcreds

Number of times client authentication information had to be refreshed. This statistic only applies if a secure RPC mechanism has been integrated with the NFS service.

badverfs

Number of times server replies could not be authenticated. The number of times the client could not guarantee that the server was who it says it was. These are likely due to packet retransmissions more than security breaches, as explained later in this section.

timers

Number of times the starting RPC call timeout value was greater than or equal to the minimum specified timeout value for the call. Solaris attempts to dynamically tune the initial timeout based on the history of calls to the specific server. If the server has been sluggish in its reponse to this type of RPC call, the timeout will be greater than if the server had been replying normally. It makes sense to wait longer before retransmitting for the first time, since history indicates that this server is slow to reply. Most client implementations use an exponential back-off strategy that doubles or quadruples the timeout after each retransmission up to an implementation-specific limit.

cantconn

Number of times a connection-oriented RPC call failed due to a failure to establish a connection to the server. The reasons why connections cannot be created are varied; one example is the server may not be running the *nfsd* daemon.

nomem

Number of times a call failed due to lack of resources. The host is low in memory and cannot allocate enough temporary memory to handle the request.

interrupts

Number of times a connection-oriented RPC call was interrupted by a signal before completing. This counter applies to connection-oriented RPC calls only. Interrupted connection and connectionless RPC calls also increment *badcalls*.

retrans

Number of calls that were retransmitted because no response was received from the NFS server within the timeout period. This is only reported for RPC over connectionless transports. An NFS client that is experiencing poor server response will have a large number of retransmitted calls.

cantsend

Number of times a request could not be sent. This counter is incremented when network plumbing problems occur. This will mostly occur when no memory is available to allocate buffers in the various network layer modules, or the request is interrupted while the client is waiting to queue the request downstream. The *nomem* and *interrupts* counters report statistics encountered in the RPC software layer, while the *cantsend* counter reports statistics gathered in the kernel TLI layer.

The statistics shown by *nfsstat* are cumulative from the time the machine was booted, or the last time they were zeroed using *nfsstat -z*:

```
nfsstat -z      Resets all counters.
nfsstat -sz     Zeros server-side RPC and NFS statistics.
nfsstat -cz     Zeros client-side RPC and NFS statistics.
nfsstat -crz    Zeros client-side RPC statistics only.
```

Only the superuser can reset the counters.

nfsstat provides a very coarse look at NFS activity and is limited in its usefulness for resolving performance problems. Server statistics are collected for all clients, while in many cases it is important to know the distribution of calls from each client. Similarly, client-side statistics are aggregated for all NFS servers.

However, you can still glean useful information from *nfsstat*. Consider the case where a client reports a high number of bad verifiers. The high *badverfs* count is most likely an indication that the client is having to retransmit its secure RPC requests. As explained in Chapter 12, every secure RPC call has a unique credential and verifier with a unique timestamp (in the case of AUTH_DES) or a unique sequence number (in the case of RPCSEC_GSS). The client expects the server to include this verifier (or some form of it) in its reply, so that the client can verify that it is indeed obtaining the reply from the server it called.

Consider the scenario where the client makes a secure RPC call using AUTH_DES, using timestamp T1 to generate its verifier. If no reply is received within the timeout period, the client retransmits the request, using timestamp T1+delta to generate its verifier (bumping up the *retrans* count). In the meantime, the server replies to the original request using timestamp T1 to generate its verifier:

```
RPC call (T1)                  --->
                        ** time out **
RPC call (retry: T1+delta)  --->
                           <--- Server reply to first RPC call (T1 verifier)
```

The reply to the client's original request will cause the verifier check to fail because the client now expects T1+delta in the verifier, not T1. This consequently bumps up the *badverf* count. Fortunately, the Solaris client will wait for more replies to its retransmissions and, if the reply passes the verifier test, an NFS authentication error will be avoided. Bad verifiers are not a big problem, unless the count gets too high, especially when the system starts experiencing NFS authentication errors. Increasing the NFS *timeo* on the mount or automounter map may help alleviate this problem. Note also that this is less of a problem with TCP than UDP. Analysis of situations such as this will be the focus of Chapter 16, Chapter 17, and Chapter 18.

For completeness, we should mention that verifier failures can also be caused when the security content expires before the response is received. This is rare but possible. It usually occurs when you have a network partition that is longer than the lifetime of the security context. Another cause might be a significant time skew between the client and server, as well as a router with a ghost packet stored, that fires after being delayed for a very long time. Note that this is not a problem with TCP.

I/O statistics

Solaris' *iostat* utility has been extended to report I/O statistics on NFS mounted filesystems, in addition to its traditional reports on disk, tape I/O, terminal activity, and CPU utilization. The *iostat* utility helps you measure and monitor performance by providing disk and network I/O throughput, utilization, queue lengths and response time.

The *-xn* directives instruct *iostat* to report extended disk statistics in tabular form, as well as display the names of the devices in descriptive format (for example, *server:/export/path*). The following example shows the output of *iostat -xn 20* during NFS activity on the client, while it concurrently reads from two separate NFS filesystems. The server *assisi* is connected to the same hub to which the client is connected, while the test server *paris* is on the other side of the hub and other side of the building network switches. The two servers are identical; they have the same memory, CPU, and OS configuration:

```
% iostat -xn 20
...
                    extended device statistics
    r/s    w/s    kr/s    kw/s wait actv wsvc_t asvc_t  %w  %b device
    0.0    0.1    0.0     0.4  0.0  0.0    0.0    3.6   0   0 c0t0d0
    0.0    0.0    0.0     0.0  0.0  0.0    0.0    0.0   0   0 fd0
    0.0    0.0    0.0     0.0  0.0  0.0    0.0    0.0   0   0 rome:vold(pid239)
    9.7    0.0  310.4     0.0  0.0  3.3    0.2  336.7   0 100 paris:/export
   34.1    0.0 1092.4     0.0  0.0  3.2    0.2   93.2   0  99 assisi:/export
```

The *iostat* utility iteratively reports the disk statistics every 20 seconds and calculates its statistics based on a delta from the previous values. The first set of statistics is usually uninteresting, since it reports the cumulative values since boot time. You should focus your attention on the following set of values reporting the current disk and network activity. Note that the previous example does not show the cumulative statistics. The output shown represents the second set of values, which report the I/O statistics within the last 20 seconds. The first two lines represent the header, then every disk and NFS filesystem on the system is presented in separate lines. The first line reports statistics for the local hard disk *c0t0d0*. The second line reports statistics for the local floppy disk *fd0*. The third line reports statistics for the volume manager *vold*. In Solaris, the volume manager is implemented as an NFS user-level server. The fourth and fifth lines report statistics for the NFS filesystems mounted on this host. Included in the statistics are various values that will help you analyze the performance of the NFS activity:

r/s

Represents the number of read operations per second during the time interval specified. For NFS filesystems, this value represents the number of times the remote server was called to read data from a file, or read the contents of a directory. This quantity accounts for the number of *read*, *readdir*, and *readdir+* RPCs performed during this interval. In the previous example, the client contacted the server *assisi* an average of 34.1 times per second to either read the contents of a file, or list the contents of directories.

w/s

Represents the number of write operations per second during the time interval specified. For NFS filesystems, this value represents the number of times the remote server was called to write data to a file. It does not include directory operations such as *mkdir*, *rmdir*, etc. This quantity accounts for the number of write RPCs performed during this interval.

kr/s

Represents the number of kilobytes per second read during this interval. In the preceding example, the client is reading data at an average of 1,092.4 KB/s from the NFS server *assisi*. The optional *-M* directive would instruct *iostat* to display data throughput in MB/sec instead of KB/sec.

kw/s

Represents the number of kilobytes written per second during this interval. The optional *-M* directive would instruct *iostat* to display data throughput in MB/sec.

wait

Reports the average number of requests waiting to be processed. For NFS filesystems, this value gets incremented when a request is placed on the asynchronous request queue, and gets decreased when the request is taken off the queue and handed off to an NFS async thread to perform the RPC call. The length of the wait queue indicates the number of requests waiting to be sent to the NFS server.

actv

Reports the number of requests actively being processed (i.e., the length of the run queue). For NFS filesystems, this number represents the number of active NFS async threads waiting for the NFS server to respond (i.e., the number of outstanding requests being serviced by the NFS server). In the preceding example, the client has on average 3.2 outstanding RPCs pending for a reply by the server *assisi* at all times during the interval specified. This number is controlled by the maximum number of NFS async threads configured on the system. Chapter 18 will explain this in more detail.

wsvc_t

Reports the time spent in the wait queue in milliseconds. For NFS filesystems, this is the time the request waited before it could be sent out to the server.

asvc_t

Reports the time spent in the run queue in milliseconds. For NFS filesystems, this represents the average amount of time the client waits for the reply to its RPC requests, after they have been sent to the NFS server. In the preceding example, the server *assisi* takes on average 93.2 milliseconds to reply to the client's requests, where the server *paris* takes 336.7 milliseconds. Recall that the server *assisi* and the client are physically connected to the same hub, whereas packets to and from the server *paris* have to traverse multiple switches to communicate with the client. Analysis of *nfsstat -s* on *paris* indicated a large amount of NFS traffic directed at this server at the same time. This, added to server load, accounts for the slow response time.

%w

Reports the percentage of time that transactions are present in the wait queue ready to be processed. A large number for an NFS filesytem does not necessarily indicate a problem, given that there are multiple NFS async threads that perform the work.

%b

Reports the percentage of time that *actv* is non-zero (at least one request is being processsed). For NFS filesystems, it represents the activity level of the server mount point. 100% busy does not indicate a problem since the NFS server has multiple *nfsd* threads that can handle concurrent RPC requests. It simply indicates that the client has had requests continuously processed by the server during the measurement time.

snoop

Network analyzers are ultimately the most useful tools available when it comes to debugging NFS problems. The *snoop* network analyzer bundled with Solaris was introduced in "Network analyzers" in Chapter 13. This section presents an example of how to use *snoop* to resolve NFS-related problems.

Consider the case where the NFS client *rome* attempts to access the contents of the filesystems exported by the server *zeus* through the */net* automounter path:

```
rome% ls -la /net/zeus/export
total 5
dr-xr-xr-x  3 root     root          3 Jul 31 22:51 .
dr-xr-xr-x  2 root     root          2 Jul 31 22:40 ..
drwxr-xr-x  3 root     other       512 Jul 28 16:48 eng
dr-xr-xr-x  1 root     root          1 Jul 31 22:51 home
rome% ls /net/zeus/export/home
/net/zeus/export/home: Permission denied
```

The client is not able to open the contents of the directory */net/zeus/export/home*, although the directory gives read and execute permissions to all users:

```
rome% df -k /net/zeus/export/home
filesystem           kbytes   used   avail capacity  Mounted on
-hosts                    0      0       0     0%     /net/zeus/export/home
```

The *df* command shows the *-hosts* automap mounted on the path of interest. This means that the NFS filesystem *rome:/export/home* has not yet been mounted. To investigate the problem further, *snoop* is invoked while the problematic *ls* command is rerun:

```
rome# snoop -i /tmp/snoop.cap rome zeus
    1   0.00000      rome -> zeus      PORTMAP C GETPORT prog=100003 (NFS) vers=3
proto=UDP
    2   0.00314      zeus -> rome      PORTMAP R GETPORT port=2049
```

```
 3    0.00019      rome -> zeus      NFS C NULL3
 4    0.00110      zeus -> rome      NFS R NULL3
 5    0.00124      rome -> zeus      PORTMAP C GETPORT prog=100005 (MOUNT) vers=1
proto=TCP
 6    0.00283      zeus -> rome      PORTMAP R GETPORT port=33168
 7    0.00094      rome -> zeus      TCP D=33168 S=49659 Syn Seq=1331963017 Len=0
Win=24820 Options=<nop,nop,sackOK,mss 1460>
 8    0.00142      zeus -> rome      TCP D=49659 S=33168 Syn Ack=1331963018
Seq=4025012052 Len=0 Win=24820 Options=<nop,nop,sackOK,mss 1460>
 9    0.00003      rome -> zeus      TCP D=33168 S=49659      Ack=4025012053
Seq=1331963018 Len=0 Win=24820
10    0.00024      rome -> zeus      MOUNT1 C Get export list
11    0.00073      zeus -> rome      TCP D=49659 S=33168      Ack=1331963062
Seq=4025012053 Len=0 Win=24776
12    0.00602      zeus -> rome      MOUNT1 R Get export list 2 entries
13    0.00003      rome -> zeus      TCP D=33168 S=49659      Ack=4025012173
Seq=1331963062 Len=0 Win=24820
14    0.00026      rome -> zeus      TCP D=33168 S=49659 Fin Ack=4025012173
Seq=1331963062 Len=0 Win=24820
15    0.00065      zeus -> rome      TCP D=49659 S=33168      Ack=1331963063
Seq=4025012173 Len=0 Win=24820
16    0.00079      zeus -> rome      TCP D=49659 S=33168 Fin Ack=1331963063
Seq=4025012173 Len=0 Win=24820
17    0.00004      rome -> zeus      TCP D=33168 S=49659      Ack=4025012174
Seq=1331963063 Len=0 Win=24820
18    0.00058      rome -> zeus      PORTMAP C GETPORT prog=100005 (MOUNT) vers=3
proto=UDP
19    0.00412      zeus -> rome      PORTMAP R GETPORT port=34582
20    0.00018      rome -> zeus      MOUNT3 C Null
21    0.00134      zeus -> rome      MOUNT3 R Null
22    0.00056      rome -> zeus      MOUNT3 C Mount /export/home
23    0.23112      zeus -> rome      MOUNT3 R Mount Permission denied
```

Packet 1 shows the client *rome* requesting the port number of the NFS service (RPC program number 100003, Version 3, over the UDP protocol) from the server's *rpcbind* (portmapper). Packet 2 shows the server's reply indicating *nfsd* is running on port 2049. Packet 3 shows the automounter's call to the server's *nfsd* daemon to verify that it is indeed running. The server's successful reply is shown in packet 4. Packet 5 shows the client's request for the port number for RPC program number 100005, Version 1, over TCP (the RPC MOUNT program). The server replies with packet 6 with port=33168. Packets 7 through 9 are TCP hand shaking between our NFS client and the server's *mountd*. Packet 10 shows the client's call to the server's *mountd* daemon (which implements the MOUNT program) currently running on port 33168. The client is requesting the list of exported entries. The server replies with packet 12 including the names of the two entries exported. Packets 18 and 19 are similar to packets 5 and 6, except that this time the client is asking for the port number of the MOUNT program version 3 running over UDP. Packet 20 and 21 show the client verifying that version 3 of the MOUNT service is up and running on the server. Finally, the client issues the Mount */export/home* request to the server in packet 22, requesting the filehandle of the */export/home* path. The server's *mountd* daemon checks its export list, and determines that the host *rome* is not present in it and replies to the client with a "Permission Denied" error in packet 23.

The analysis indicates that the "Permission Denied" error returned to the *ls* command came from the MOUNT request made to the server, not from problems with directory mode bits on the client. Having gathered this information, we study the exported list on the server and quickly notice that the filesystem */export/home* is exported only to the host *verona*:

```
rome$ showmount -e zeus
export list for zeus:
/export/eng  (everyone)
/export/home verona
```

We could have obtained the same information by inspecting the contents of packet 12, which contains the export list requested during the transaction:

```
rome# snoop -i /tmp/cap -v -p 10,12
...
         Packet 10 arrived at 3:32:47.73
RPC:  ----- SUN RPC Header -----
RPC:
RPC:  Record Mark: last fragment, length = 40
RPC:  Transaction id = 965581102
RPC:  Type = 0 (Call)
RPC:  RPC version = 2
RPC:  Program = 100005 (MOUNT), version = 1, procedure = 5
RPC:  Credentials: Flavor = 0 (None), len = 0 bytes
RPC:  Verifier   : Flavor = 0 (None), len = 0 bytes
RPC:
MOUNT:----- NFS MOUNT -----
MOUNT:
MOUNT:Proc = 5 (Return export list)
MOUNT:
...
         Packet 12 arrived at 3:32:47.74
RPC:  ----- SUN RPC Header -----
RPC:
RPC:  Record Mark: last fragment, length = 92
RPC:  Transaction id = 965581102
RPC:  Type = 1 (Reply)
RPC:  This is a reply to frame 10
RPC:  Status = 0 (Accepted)
RPC:  Verifier   : Flavor = 0 (None), len = 0 bytes
RPC:  Accept status = 0 (Success)
RPC:
MOUNT:----- NFS MOUNT -----
MOUNT:
MOUNT:Proc = 5 (Return export list)
MOUNT:Directory = /export/eng
MOUNT:Directory = /export/home
MOUNT: Group = verona
MOUNT:
```

For simplicity, only the RPC and NFS Mount portions of the packets are shown. Packet 10 is the request for the export list, packet 12 is the reply. Notice that every RPC packet contains the transaction ID (XID), the message type (call or reply), the status of the call, and the credentials. Notice that the RPC header includes the string *"This is a reply to frame 10"*. This is not part of the network packet. *Snoop* keeps track of the XIDs it has processed and attempts to match calls with replies and retransmissions. This feature comes in very handy during debugging. The Mount portion of packet 12 shows the list of directories exported and the group of hosts to which they are exported. In this case, we can see that */export/home* was only exported with access rights to the host *verona*. The problem can be fixed by adding the host *rome* to the export list on the server.

Useful filters

Information is most useful when it can be organized into categories and noise can be filtered and ignored. *snoop* provides powerful capture filters that allow you to collect only the kind of information you are interested in. The following list of *snoop* filters is useful when capturing NFS-related traffic. *snoop* provides very nice NFS and RPC level debugging features. The logical *and*, *or*, and *not* operators can be used on filters to build more powerful composite filters. You are encouraged to review the *snoop* documentation to learn more about the multiple filters available.

host

> Captures all traffic directed to or originating from the host specified. The following example captures all traffic destined to or coming from the host *rome*:

>> `# snoop host rome`

> Note that the *host* keyword is not required when the specified hostname does not conflict with the name of another *snoop* primitive. The previous *snoop host rome* command could have been invoked without the *host* keyword, and it would have generated the same output.

port nfs

> Captures NFS traffic regardless of the version. Note that MOUNT, NLM and Portmapper traffic is not captured. Useful once the mount has already occurred. The following two examples capture all NFS protocol traffic involving the host *rome*. A logical AND operation is implied by the juxtaposition of two boolean expressions. The two filters are equivalent:

>> `# snoop host rome port nfs`
>> `# snoop host rome and port nfs`

port 111

> Captures rpcbind and portmapper traffic. Useful during filesystem mount negotiation. This example captures all rpcbind traffic on the network:

>> `# snoop port 111`

rpc prog [,vers [,proc]]

Use *rpc 100005* to capture MOUNT protocol related traffic. Useful during the mount process. The following example displays all MOUNT protocol traffic between the hosts *zeus* and *rome*:

```
# snoop rpc 100005 host zeus rome
```

Use *rpc 100021* to capture NLM traffic. Useful for tracking lock manager related traffic. The following example captures all NFS Version 3 Network Lock Manager traffic between hosts *zeus* and *rome*. Note that NLM v4 is used for NFS Version 3:

```
# snoop host zeus host rome rpc 100021,4
```

Publicly available diagnostics

Only a handful of publicly available NFS diagnostic tools exist at the time of this writing. The *ethereal/tethereal* network analyzer introduced in Chapter 13 provides detailed information for diagnosis of NFS problems at the protocol level. The *NFS-WATCH* utility is mainly used to monitor NFS traffic over the network. The *nfsbug* and *SATAN* utilities are used to report potential security problems on NFS servers.

ethereal / tethereal

As described in Chapter 13, *ethereal/tethereal* can be used to capture network traffic and decode it to a great level of detail. Since *ethereal/tethereal* can decode NFS Version 2 and NFS Version 3 packets, it can be used to debug NFS communication, permissions, performance, and data corruption problems. It is very similar in functionality to *snoop*. It provides powerful filtering and is available for a diverse set of platforms where *snoop* is not.

Consider the example presented in the previous *snoop* section, where the NFS client *rome* attempts to access the contents of the filesystems exported by the server *zeus* through the */net* automounter path:

```
rome% ls -la /net/zeus/export
total 5
dr-xr-xr-x   3 root     root          3 Jul 31 22:51 .
dr-xr-xr-x   2 root     root          2 Jul 31 22:40 ..
drwxr-xr-x   3 root     other       512 Jul 28 16:48 eng
dr-xr-xr-x   1 root     root          1 Jul 31 22:51 home
rome% ls /net/zeus/export/home
/net/zeus/export/home: Permission denied
```

The network traffic is captured into the */tmp/ethereal.cap* file concurrently with the operation. Note that only traffic between *rome* and *zeus* is captured:

```
rome# tethereal -w /tmp/ethereal.cap host rome and host zeus
46 ^C
```

```
rome# tethereal -r /tmp/ethereal.cap
    1   0.000000       rome -> zeus        PORTMAP V2 GETPORT Call XID 0x398fd3ea
    2   0.003138       zeus -> rome        PORTMAP V2 GETPORT Reply XID 0x398fd3ea
    3   0.003328       rome -> zeus        NFS V3 NULL Call XID 0x398fd3eb
    4   0.004613       zeus -> rome        NFS V3 NULL Reply XID 0x398fd3eb
    5   0.005823       rome -> zeus        PORTMAP V2 GETPORT Call XID 0x398fca35
    6   0.008871       zeus -> rome        PORTMAP V2 GETPORT Reply XID 0x398fca35
    7   0.009823       rome -> zeus        TCP 49699 > 33168 [SYN] Seq=1251769928 Ack=0
Win=24820 Len=0
    8   0.011067       zeus -> rome        TCP 33168 > 49699 [SYN, ACK] Seq=3939269366
Ack=1251769929 Win=24820 Len=0
    9   0.011100       rome -> zeus        TCP 49699 > 33168 [ACK] Seq=1251769929
Ack=3939269367 Win=24820 Len=0
   10   0.011339       rome -> zeus        MOUNT V1 EXPORT Call XID 0x398f20d9
   11   0.012102       zeus -> rome        TCP 33168 > 49699 [ACK] Seq=3939269367
Ack=1251769973 Win=24776 Len=0
   12   0.018302       zeus -> rome        MOUNT V1 EXPORT Reply XID 0x398f20d9
   13   0.018332       rome -> zeus        TCP 49699 > 33168 [ACK] Seq=1251769973
Ack=3939269463 Win=24820 Len=0
   14   0.018588       rome -> zeus        TCP 49699 > 33168 [FIN, ACK] Seq=1251769973
Ack=3939269463 Win=24820 Len=0
   15   0.019245       zeus -> rome        TCP 33168 > 49699 [ACK] Seq=3939269463
Ack=1251769974 Win=24820 Len=0
   16   0.020104       zeus -> rome        TCP 33168 > 49699 [FIN, ACK] Seq=3939269463
Ack=1251769974 Win=24820 Len=0
   17   0.020143       rome -> zeus        TCP 49699 > 33168 [ACK] Seq=1251769974
Ack=3939269464 Win=24820 Len=0
   18   0.020661       rome -> zeus        PORTMAP V2 GETPORT Call XID 0x398f0440
   19   0.024550       zeus -> rome        PORTMAP V2 GETPORT Reply XID 0x398f0440
   20   0.024731       rome -> zeus        MOUNT V3 NULL Call XID 0x398f0441
   21   0.026323       zeus -> rome        MOUNT V3 NULL Reply XID 0x398f0441
   22   0.026881       rome -> zeus        MOUNT V3 MNT Call XID 0x398f0442
   23   0.179757       zeus -> rome        MOUNT V3 MNT Reply XID 0x398f0442
```

The explanation given in the *snoop* section describing each packet applies to the *tethereal* capture file as well. The main difference is that listing the XID next to the operation type is less intuitive than expanding the arguments to the call as performed by *snoop*. We suspect this will be addressed in the future. You can see that the reason for failure is not obvious by just looking at this output format.

Fortunately, *tethereal* has extensive filtering capabilities and we can request all mount operations that failed. Using the *mount.status* filter, we determine that packet 23 returned a failure. We can then print the protocol tree for packet 23 alone and verify that indeed it failed with ERR_ACCESS:

```
rome# tethereal -r /tmp/ethereal.cap -R "mount.status != 0"
   23   0.179757       zeus -> rome        MOUNT V3 MNT Reply XID 0x398f0442
rome# tethereal -r /tmp/ethereal.cap -V -R "frame.number == 23"
...
Remote Procedure Call
    XID: 0x398f0442 (965674050)
    Message Type: Reply (1)
    Program: MOUNT (100005)
```

```
        Program Version: 3
        Procedure: MNT (1)
        Reply State: accepted (0)
        Verifier
            Flavor: AUTH_NULL (0)
            Length: 0
        Accept State: RPC executed successfully (0)
    Mount Service
        Program Version: 3
        Procedure: MNT (1)
        Status: ERR_ACCESS (13)
```

For simplicity, only the RPC and Mount portions of the packet are shown. The RPC header decodes the transaction ID, message type indicating this to be a reply, program, and version number as well as the procedure invoked. The credential verifier is also decoded indicating that the server used no verifier in its reply (since the call did not specify it to begin with). A nice feature of *snoop*, that *tethereal* does not yet have, is the ability to indicate the frame for which this is a reply.

As expected, the status field of the mount service reply reports an error. Packet 12 contains the results of the export information request:

```
rome# tethereal -r /tmp/ethereal.cap -V -R "frame.number == 12"
    ...
Remote Procedure Call
    Last Fragment: Yes
    Fragment Length: 92
    XID: 0x398f20d9 (965681369)
    Message Type: Reply (1)
    Program: MOUNT (100005)
    Program Version: 1
    Procedure: EXPORT (5)
    Reply State: accepted (0)
    Verifier
        Flavor: AUTH_NULL (0)
        Length: 0
    Accept State: RPC executed successfully (0)
Mount Service
    Program Version: 1
    Procedure: EXPORT (5)
    Data (68 bytes)

 0  0000 0001 0000 000b 2f65 7870 6f72 742f    ......../export/
10  656e 6700 0000 0000 0000 0001 0000 000c    eng.............
20  2f65 7870 6f72 742f 686f 6d65 0000 0001    /export/home....
30  0000 0006 7665 726f 6e61 0000 0000 0000    ....verona......
40  0000 0000                                   ....
```

The Data field of the Mount packet shows a hex dump of the export list. The interpreted text value is in the far right column. We can see how the export list is encoded into the packet as a set of exported directories, each followed by the list of hosts (or group of hosts) that they give access to.

Useful filters

Read filters help you remove the noise from a packet trace and let you see only the packets that interest you. If a packet meets the requirements expressed in the read filter, then it is printed. Read filters let you compare the fields within a protocol against a specific value, compare fields against other fields, and check the existence of specified fields or protocols altogether. One of the main strengths of *tethereal* is its powerful filters. You are encouraged to learn more about them from the *tethereal* documentation. The following list includes some of the read filters you are most likely to use when analyzing NFS-related traffic:

nfs

> Displays NFS traffic regardless of the version. Note that MOUNT, NLM, and Portmapper traffic is not captured. Useful once the mount has already occurred. The following example displays all NFS protocol traffic involving the host *rome*:
>
> ```
> # tethereal -R "nfs and ip.addr == rome"
> ```

nfs.status

> Displays all replies to successful NFS calls when *nfs.status* == *0* or the replies to unsuccessful NFS calls otherwise. The originating call can be obtained using the *rpc.xid* filter. The following example displays all NFS failures:
>
> ```
> # tethereal -R "nfs.status != 0"
> ```

rpc

> Displays all RPC traffic regardless of the program number. The following example displays all RPC traffic on the wire:
>
> ```
> # tethereal -R "rpc"
> ```

rpc.xid

> Displays the RPC call or reply matching a given Transaction ID. This is useful when the call packet is available and the matching reply is needed, or vice-versa. The following example finds the RPC call and reply with transaction ID equal to 0x398f0441:
>
> ```
> # tethereal -R "rpc.xid == 0x398f0441"
> ```

tcp.port == 111 or udp.port == 111

> Displays rpcbind and portmapper traffic. Useful during filesystem mount negotiation. The following example displays all rpcbind traffic on the network:
>
> ```
> # tethereal -R "tcp.port == 111 or udp.port == 111"
> ```

rpc.program, rpc.programversion, rpc.procedure

> Use *rpc.program* == *100005* to capture MOUNT protocol related traffic. Useful during the mount process. The following example displays all MOUNT protocol traffic between the hosts *zeus* and *rome*:
>
> ```
> # tethereal -R "rpc.program == 100005 and ip.addr == zeus \
> and ip.addr == rome"
> ```

Use *rpc.program == 100021* to capture NLM traffic. Useful for tracking lock manager-related traffic. The following example displays all NFS Version 3 Network Lock Manager traffic between hosts *zeus* and *rome*. Note that NLM v4 is used for NFS Version 3:

```
# tethereal -R "rpc.program == 100021 and rpc.programversion == 4 \
and ip.addr == rome and ip.addr == zeus"
```

NFSWATCH

NFSWATCH was developed by David Curry of Purdue University in the late 1980s, with some improvements to the basic framework provided by Jeff Mogul of Digital Equipment Corporation (now Compaq). It is mainly used to monitor NFS activity on a given server, or NFS activity on the local network. NFSWATCH gathers its data by monitoring the network interface of the system where it is invoked.

NFSWATCH 4.3 is the most recent version at the time of this writing, and only supports NFS Version 2 over UDP. You should be aware that at the time of this writing, a bug in the tool causes NFS Version 3 traffic to the server to incorrectly increment the NFS Version 2 counters. This is due to the fact that the tool does not check the NFS version number of the packet received.

Regardless of its current limitations, NFSWATCH is still a very useful tool whose main features are worth mentioning:

1. The tool categorizes the incoming network traffic and continuously updates the statistics on the display. You can also instruct the tool to create a more detailed log file of the network traffic.

2. It allows you to log statistics for every NFS operation, for every exported filesystem, for files for which you specify particular interest, or for NFS clients that access your server.

3. It reports usage of NFS clients and users of the filesystems.

4. It can be run interactively or remotely (via *rsh*), or it can be scheduled to run from *cron*.

5. Total runtime can be specified for unsupervised traffic monitoring.

NFSWATCH is available at *ftp://gatekeeper.dec.com/pub/net/ip/nfs/nfswatch4.3.tar.gz*. The following example shows a sample log file of an NFSWATCH run on server *zeus* for a period of five seconds:

```
# NFSwatch log file
#    Packets from: all hosts
#    Packets to:   zeus
#
# begin
```

```
#
Date: Tue Aug  1 16:31:22 2000
Cycle Time: 5
Elapsed Time:
#
# total packets       network  to host  dropped
#
Interval Packets:       2371     2371       0
Total Packets:          2371     2371       0
#
# packet counters              int     pct    total
#
ND Read:                         0      0%       0
ND Write:                        0      0%       0
NFS Read:                      166      7%     166
NFS Write:                     346     15%     346
NFS Mount:                       0      0%       0
YP/NIS/NIS+:                     0      0%       0
RPC Authorization:               0      0%       0
Other RPC Packets:            1844     78%    1844
TCP Packets:                     2      0%       2
UDP Packets:                  2358     99%    2358
ICMP Packets:                    1      0%       1
Routing Control:                 2      0%       2
Address Resolution:             10      0%      10
Reverse Addr Resol:              0      0%       0
Ethernet/FDDI Bdcst:            13      1%      13
Other Packets:                   0      0%       0
#
# nfs counters                 int     pct    total
#
/export/home:                  512    100%     512       (0/0/5/0/12/0/154/0/
335/2/0/0/0/0/3/1/0/0)
#
# file counters                int     pct    total
#
#
# nfs procs
#
  Procedure       int   pct    total  completed  ave.resp  var.resp  max.resp
   CREATE           2    0%        2
   GETATTR          0    0%        0
   GETROOT          0    0%        0
   LINK             0    0%        0
   LOOKUP          12    2%       12
   MKDIR            3    1%        3
   NULLPROC         0    0%        0
   READ           154   30%      154
   READDIR          0    0%        0
   READLINK         0    0%        0
   REMOVE           0    0%        0
   RENAME           0    0%        0
   RMDIR            1    0%        1
   SETATTR          5    1%        5
```

```
STATFS        0    0%       0
SYMLINK       0    0%       0
WCACHE        0    0%       0
WRITE       335   65%     335
```

The NFSWATCH log shows the distribution of NFS READ, NFS WRITE, NFS MOUNT, NIS, and RPC AUTHORIZATION packets among others. The NFS counters section indicates the total number NFS operations per filesystem exported (one in this case) during the interval. The operation distribution denoted by *(0/0/ 5/0/12/0/154/0/335/2/0/0/0/0/3/1/0/0)* indicates that the majority of the operations occurred in the middle of the interval. The *packet counters* and *nfs procs* indicate that there were close to twice as many writes as reads. The low lookup count leads us to believe that most writes occurred to the same file.

nfsbug

The *nfsbug* utility was written by Leendert van Doorn in the mid-1990s to test hosts for well-known NFS problems and bugs. *nfsbug* is available at *http://www.cs. vu.nl/~leendert*. Use it to identify (and consequently correct) the following problems:

- Find worldwide exportable filesystems. This is a common occurrence in large organizations with hundreds or thousands of NFS clients. System administrators choose to export filesystems to all clients instead of grouping the hosts into netgroups and exporting the filesystems only to the netgroups that really need access to the filesystems.

- Determine the effectiveness of the export list.

- Determine if filesystems can be mounted through the portmapper.

- Attempt to guess filehandles and obtain access to filesystems not exported to the test client.

- Exercise the system for well-known bugs.*

SATAN

SATAN is a tool used to find well-known security holes in Unix systems. SATAN stands for Security Administrator's Tool for Analyzing Networks. At the time of this writing, none of the problems SATAN probes for are new. Each one has already been discussed in CERT bulletins and each can be countered either by installing the appropriate patch or fixing a system configuration flaw. SATAN is available at *http://www.fish.com/satan*.

---

* According to Leendert's web page, the tool has not been updated in recent years, although he still plans to get to it at some point.

SATAN was written by Dan Farmer and Wietse Venema and first released for general availability in April of 1995. The tool is intended to help system administrators identify several common network-related security problems, hopefully before someone else has a chance to exploit them. The tool provides a description of the problem, explains the consequences if no action is taken, and indicates how to correct the problem. Note that the tool itself will not exploit the security hole. At the time of this writing, SATAN can identify and fix the following problems related to NFS and NIS:

- NFS filesystems exported to arbitrary hosts
- NFS filesystems exported to unprivileged programs
- NFS filesystems exported via the portmapper
- NIS password file access from arbitrary hosts

An extensive discussion of SATAN and its features can be found in Martin Freiss' book titled *Protecting Networks with SATAN* (O'Reilly & Associates).

Version 2 and Version 3 differences

NFS Version 2 and NFS Version 3 are entirely separate protocols and should be treated as such. The two protocols define different over-the-wire operations. For example, a single over-the-wire NFS Version 3 operation may correspond to several over-the-wire NFS Version 2 operations. Consider the case of a long list (*ls -l*) of an NFS-mounted directory that generates a series of *readdir/lookup/getattr* NFS Version 2 calls. The same operation generates one or more *readdir+* NFS Version 3 calls instead.

In general, NFS Version 3 attempts to reduce the number of over-the-wire requests by placing more information into each RPC. This makes NFS Version 3 more efficient under certain circumstances but less under others. The important point here is to understand that it is not possible to compare many of the NFS operations between the two protocols.

For example, writing a several megabyte file over NFS Version 3 will generate far fewer RPC write operations than the same file written over NFS Version 2. This is because NFS Version 3 writes generated by current Solaris clients are 32 KB in length.* In contrast, NFS Version 2 writes can only be up to 8 KB. You should be careful not to assume that NFS Version 2 writes are faster only because *nfsstat -c* reports that the server handles more of them.

---

* The NFS Version 3 protocol does not impose a size limit on the write request. The fact that many NFS-Version 3 clients use 32 KB is an implementation detail.

You may also notice that NFS Version 3 generates fewer *lookup* and *getattr* operations than NFS Version 2. The reduction in lookups in NFS Version 3 is partly due to the use of *readdir+,* which includes the filehandle of the directory entries along with the directory names. The reduction of *getattrs* is mostly due to the fact that NFS Version 3 operations include post-operation attributes in all replies.

NFS server logging

Solaris 8 introduces the new NFS Server Logging utility. This utility enables the system to log file transfer operations between an NFS server and any of its clients. This utility was created to provide logging facilities to sites that publish their archives via NFS within the intranet, and via WebNFS over the Internet.

The NFS Server Logging utility provides the system administrator with the tools to track file downloads and uploads, as well as directory modification operations on NFS exported filesystems. Be careful not to confuse this functionality with UFS Logging.*

The NFS Server Logging utility is not intended to serve as a debugging tool that can be turned on to peek at filesystem traffic during a short period of time and then be turned back off. NFS Server Logging is most useful when it is enabled before the filesystem is shared for the first time, and remains enabled the entire time the filesystem is exported. It needs to run continuously in order to monitor all NFS filesystem activity on the server, otherwise, important path mapping information may not be obtained. This is discussed in more detail in the "Filehandle to path mapping" section.

This utility provides functionality different from that provided by the public domain tools previously discussed. These tools generate records of individual RPC transactions, whereas NFS Server Logging generates records of conceptual file operations. Network sniffer tools like *Ethereal* and *snoop* report a file copy as a sequence of distinct NFS read operations of certain length and offset performed by the client. In contrast, the NFS Server Logging utility generates a single record specifying the total transfer size and the duration of the transfer. The NFS Server Logging utility reports accesses at the conceptual level (file uploads or downloads), where network sniffers report the details of the RPC and NFS operations. Consequently, the logs generated by the NFS Server Logging utility are orders of magnitude smaller and more manageable than sniffer output. The NFS Server logs can be useful to determine the frequency with which files in the archives are

---

* UFS logging is the process of storing transactions (changes that make up a complete UFS operation) in a log before the transactions are applied to the filesystem. Once a transaction is stored, it can be later applied to the filesystem. This prevents filesystems from becoming inconsistent, eliminating the need to run *fsck.*

accessed or to determine what NFS clients have accessed the files. These logs can be used to manually or programmatically track access to objects within the exported filesystem in the same way that FTP logs are used. As previously pointed out, the information recorded in the NFS log is not intended to serve as a debugging tool. The network sniffer tools previously described are a better choice for that.

Consider the case where the server *zeus* exports a filesystem with NFS logging enabled. The client *rome* then copies the file */net/zeus/export/foo.tar.Z* to its local disk. The NFS Server Logging utility records the access with a single record of the form:

```
Fri Jul 28 09:27:12 2000 0 rome 136663 /export/foo.tar.Z b _ o r 32721 nfs 0 *
```

This entry indicates that on Fri Jul 28 2000 at 09:27:12 in the morning, a file was downloaded by the host *rome*. The file was 136663 bytes in length and was located on the server at */export/foo.tar.Z*. The file was downloaded by userID *32721* using *nfs*. The meaning of each field is explained in detail later in this section.

In contrast, the *snoop* utility generates multiple transactions:

```
 1   0.00000      rome -> zeus     NFS C LOOKUP3 FH=0222 foo.tar.Z
 2   0.00176      zeus -> rome     NFS R LOOKUP3 OK FH=EEAB
 3   0.00026      rome -> zeus     NFS C ACCESS3 FH=0222 (lookup)
 4   0.00125      zeus -> rome     NFS R ACCESS3 OK (lookup)
 5   0.00018      rome -> zeus     NFS_ACL C GETACL3 FH=EEAB mask=10
 6   0.00139      zeus -> rome     NFS_ACL R GETACL3 OK
 7   0.00026      rome -> zeus     NFS C ACCESS3 FH=EEAB (read)
 8   0.00119      zeus -> rome     NFS R ACCESS3 OK (read)
 9   0.00091      rome -> zeus     NFS C READ3 FH=EEAB at 0 for 32768
10   0.00020      rome -> zeus     NFS C READ3 FH=EEAB at 32768 for 32768
11   0.00399      zeus -> rome     UDP IP fragment ID=56047 Offset=0    MF=1
12   0.02736      zeus -> rome     UDP IP fragment ID=56048 Offset=0    MF=1
13   0.00009      rome -> zeus     NFS C READ3 FH=EEAB at 65536 for 32768
14   0.00020      rome -> zeus     NFS C READ3 FH=EEAB at 98304 for 32768
15   0.00017      rome -> zeus     NFS C READ3 FH=EEAB at 131072 for 8192
16   0.03482      zeus -> rome     UDP IP fragment ID=56049 Offset=0    MF=1
17   0.02740      zeus -> rome     UDP IP fragment ID=56050 Offset=0    MF=1
18   0.02739      zeus -> rome     UDP IP fragment ID=56051 Offset=0    MF=1
```

A single user-level copy command translates into multiple NFS operations. The NFS client must first find the object via the LOOKUP3 operation, determine access rights to the object via the ACCESS3 and GETACL3 operations and then finally read the information from the server via multiple READ3 operations.

The NFS Server Logging mechanism was designed to emulate the FTP logging mechanism found in many FTP public domain implementations. The log generated is specifically compatible with the log format generated by the popular Washington University's FTP daemon (WU-ftpd). WU-ftpd log format was chosen because of the popularity of this particular FTP service, as well as the availability of a number of public domain and home-grown utilities that already consume WU-ftpd logs.

Each NFS log record contains the following space-separated fields:

Date

The timestamp from the start of the operation. It is represented in local time in the form of a 26-character string. The fields are constant width. The time-stamp is formatted with *ctime(3C)*. In the previous example, this was Fri Jul 28 09:27:12 2000.

ElapsedTime

For reads and writes, this is the approximate elapsed time from the first to last operation. It is truncated to whole seconds. In the previous example it is *0*, meaning it took less than one second.

ClientName

Name of the system accessing the object. The name service switch is used on the server to generate the client name. This means that hostnames will be printed for those machines known within the name service. IP addresses will be printed for hostnames that are outside the name service control. In the previous example, this is *rome*.

TransferSize

Total number of bytes read or written. It is always 0 for operations other than read or write (*mkdir, rmdir*, etc). In the previous example, this is 136663.

PathName

Absolute pathname of the object accessed on the server. This pathname is always reported from the server's namespace point of view. It is possible for the server to be unable to map NFS filehandles to pathnames. In such a case, the NFS filehandle is printed instead of the component name. See "Filehandle to path mapping" for details. In the previous example, the *PathName* is */export/foo*. The client may have mounted the pathname on */mnt* or */net/zeus*, but the pathname reported is always the server's absolute pathname.

DataType

Indicates the type of data transfer, ASCII transfers are denoted with *a* and binary transfers are denoted with *b*. NFS transfers are always binary; there-fore, this field will always have a value of *b*.

TransferOption

Indicates any special processing performed by the service. For FTP logs, it indicates if the WU-ftpd daemon performed any kind of compression (denoted with *C*), or if the file was tarred (denoted by *T*), or if the file was uncom-pressed (denoted with *U*). For NFS transfers this field will always have a value of '_', since no special action is performed by the NFS server.

Operation

> The operation performed by the server, by default this is either *i* for incoming (upload) or *o* for outgoing (download). Note that this is always relative to the server. If the extended log format is in use, the operation is reported in extended format (i.e., *read, write, create, setattr, mkdir*, etc.). Note that this is incompatible with the WU-ftpd log format and existing unmodified tools that process these type of logs will not be able to process the extended NFS log. In the previous example the client read the file, which means it was down-loaded from the server, therefore the log denotes this with an *o*.

AccessMode

> Indicates the type of the user accessing the file. For FTP transfers, a guest user is denoted as *g*, an anonymous user is denoted as *a* and the real user is denoted as *r*. All NFS transfers report the real user identifier contained in the RPC; therefore, this field will alway be *r*.

UserID

> User identifier (UID) used for the NFS operations. Note that the logging utility makes no attempt to map the uid to the user name. Doing this could lead to incorrect mappings when the request arrives from a different name service domain than the one the server belongs to. Different name service domains do not necessarily share the same user name space. UID 32721 on the Eng domain may map to a very different user on the Corp domain. In the previous example it is 32721.

Service

> Type of service accessed by the client. The basic log format entry reports *nfs*. The extended log format entry reports the NFS version and protocol as well. NFS Version 3 over TCP is reported as *nfs3-tcp* in the extended log format, and as *nfs* in the basic log format.

Authenticated

> Indicates whether the user is authenticated or not. A value of 0 indicates that the user is not authenticated, or using the AUTH_SYS RPC authentication. A value of 1 means that the user is authenticated via extended methods (such as AUTH_DES) and the next field will include the user's principle name. In the previous example the client is using AUTH_SYS, therefore the field is 0.

PrincipleName

> The user's principle name if authenticated; otherwise, the field will be '*'.

NFS server logging mechanics

There are three main components involved in the logging process. First, the *share* command is used to enable NFS Logging on the filesystem. Second, the kernel stores enough information about each RPC operation in a temporary work buffer file. Third, the *nfslogd* daemon processes the RPC information stored in the tempo-rary work buffer file, consolidates the operations into file transfer operations and generates the final NFS log file.

Table 14-2 lists the various files involved in the logging process, the information contained in them, who or what program creates and modifies them and who con-sumes their contents. The */var/nfs/nfslog* file contains the actual NFS transaction log records. The */etc/nfs/nfslog.conf* and */etc/default/nfslogd* files specify various logging configuration values. The */var/nfs/fhpath* file contains the path mapping information. The remaining two files are temporary and only needed to help con-struct the NFS transaction log records. Each file will be discussed in more detail throughout this chapter.

Table 14-2. NFS server logging files

File	Contents	Creator/ Modifier	Consumer
/etc/nfs/nfslog.conf	Logging configuration	Administrator	*share, nfslogd*
/etc/default/nfslogd	*nfslogd*-specific configuration	Administrator	*nfslogd*
/etc/nfs/nfslogtab	Information on location of the work buffer files	*share, unshare nfs-logd*	*nfslogd*
/var/nfs/nfslog	NFS transaction log records	*nfslogd*	Administrator
/var/nfs/nfslog_work-buffer	RPC operations recorded by the kernel and consumed by the nfslogd daemon	Unix kernel	*nfslogd*
/var/nfs/fhpath	filehandle to path mapping	*nfslogd*	*nfslogd*

Enabling NFS server logging

Before enabling logging on a filesystem, make sure to first define the default direc-tory where the NFS log and working files are to be created. Solaris ships with the default directory set to */var/nfs*. Make sure you have enough disk space available in */var/nfs* or set the default directory to a different partition. Instructions on how to change the default directory and how to spread the logs and files across mul-tiple partitions are provided in "NFS server logging configuration."

Once the location of the files has been specified, logging NFS traffic on a file-system is simple. First, export the filesystem using the *-o log* directive. Second, start the *nfslogd* daemon if it is not yet running. The NFS log file will be created a few minutes later in the directory previously specified, after the kernel has gath-ered enough information to generate the NFS transaction records. Note that set-ting the *-o log* directive in the */etc/dfs/dfstab* file will cause the *nfslogd* daemon to be started automatically the next time the machine is booted. The daemon will automatically detect when other filesystems are shared with logging enabled.

The rest of the chapter explains the specifics of how the NFS Server Logging mechanism works, its main components, and configuration parameters. Enabling logging is straightforward, unfortunately cleaning up working files after logging has been disabled requires some manual work. We will explain this in "Disabling NFS server logging."

To enable NFS Server Logging on a filesystem, the filesystem must first be exported with the *-o log [=<tag>]* directive:

```
# share -o log /export
```

When no *tag* is specified, the kernel will record the temporary RPC information in the default work buffer file */var/nfs/nfslog_workbuffer_in_process*. Again, this temporary file does not contain any information useful to the user, instead it's used by the NFS Logging mechanism as a temporary buffer. It is the *nfslogd* daemon that reads this work buffer, processes its information, and generates the NFS log file. By default, the NFS log file is stored in */var/nfs/nfslog*.

The *nfslogd* daemon must be running in order to generate the NFS log file. Note that the daemon is started at boot time only when one or more filesystems in */etc/ dfs/dfstab* have the *-o log* directive specified. If you share a filesystem manually with logging enabled and the *nfslogd* daemon had not previously been started, you must invoke it manually:

```
# /usr/lib/nfs/nfslogd
```

To assure that the *nfslogd* daemon is started after a reboot, make sure to specify the *-o log* directive in */etc/dfs/dfstab*.

NFS server logging configuration

By default, the NFS log file, the temporary work buffer files, and the filehandle mapping tables are created in the */var/nfs* directory. These defaults can be over-ridden by sharing the filesystem with specific logging parameters associated with a logging tag. Logging tags are defined in the */etc/nfs/nfslog.conf* file. Each entry in the file consists of a mandatory tag identifier and one or more logging parameters.

The following is a sample */etc/nfs/nfslog.conf* configuration file:

```
# NFS server log configuration file.
#
# <tag> [ defaultdir=<dir_path> ] \
#              [ log=<logfile_path> ] [ fhtable=<table_path> ] \
#              [ buffer=<bufferfile_path> ] [ logformat=basic|extended ]

global          defaultdir=/var/nfs \
                  log=logs/nfslog \
              fhtable=workfiles/fhtable buffer=workfiles/nfslog_workbuffer
eng          log=/export/eng/logs/nfslog
```

```
corp           defaultdir=/export/corp/logging
extended    logformat=extended log=extended_logs/nfslog
```

The *global* tag specifies the default set of values to be used when no tag is specified in the *share* command. Note that the *eng, corp,* and *extended* tags do not specify all possible parameters. The *global* values are used, unless they are specifically replaced in the tag. Take for example:

```
# share -o log=eng /export/eng
```

where the NFS log file will be named *nfslog* and located in the */export/eng/logs* directory. The work buffer file and filehandle table (explained later) remain under */var/nfs/workfiles*. Any of the *global* values can be overridden by specific tags.

The following describes each parameter in the configuration file:

defaultdir=<path>

Specifies the default directory where all logging files are placed. Every tag can specify its *defaultdir* and override the value specified by the *global* tag. This path is prepended to all relative paths specified by the other parameters. *defaultdir* must be an absolute path, or an error is reported by the *share* command. In the previous sample configuration, filesystems shared with the *global* tag will place their work files and NFS log file in */var/nfs*. Filesystems shared with the *corp* tag place their work files in */export/corp/logging*.

log=<path><file>

Specifies the name and location of the NFS log file. This is the file that actually contains the log of file transfers and the file that the system administrator will be most interested in. *defaultdir* is prepended to *log* to determine the full path, except in the case when *log* already identifies an absolute path. Using the previous sample configuration, filesystems shared with the *global* tag place the NFS log file in */var/nfs/logs/nfslog*.

fhtable=<path><file>

Specifies the name and location of the filehandle to path mapping database. NFS operations use filehandles and not filenames to identify the file being worked on. The *nfslogd* daemon builds a mapping of filehandles and stores it in the location specified by *fhtable*. This is explained in detail in "Filehandle to path mapping." The path concatenation rules described earlier apply.

buffer=<path><file>

Specifies the name and location of the temporary work buffer file, where the kernel will store the raw RPC information to later be consumed by the *nfslogd* daemon. This file is intended for internal consumption of the *nfslogd* daemon. The *nfslogd* daemon wakes up periodically to consume the information stored in this file. The file is backed by permanent storage, to prevent loss of RPC operation information on reboot. The *nfslogd* daemon will remove the work buffer file once it has processed the information. The path concatenation rules described earlier apply.

logformat=basic | extended

Specifies the format of the NFS log file. Two values are valid: basic and extended. The basic format is compatible with the log format generated by the Washington University's FTPd utility. The extended format provides more detailed information. Under basic format, only reads and writes are recorded. Under extended format, reads, writes, and directory modification operations (*mkdir, rmdir,* and *remove*) are reported, as well as the NFS version and protocol used in the operation. The basic format is assumed when no *logformat* is specified. Note that the extended format is not compatible with Washington University's FTPd log format. Using the previous sample configuration, filesystems shared with the *extended* tag will log extended filesystem activity in the */var/nfs/extended_logs/nfslog* file.

Table 14-3 defines the values for the logging files when filesystems are shared with the various tags.

Table 14-3. Logging files under different tags

Tag	Log	fhtable	Buffer
global	*/var/nfs/logs/nfslog*	*/var/nfs/workfiles/ fhtable*	*/var/nfs/workfiles/nfslog_ workbuffer*
eng	*/export/eng/logs/nfs- log*	*/var/nfs/workfiles/ fhtable*	*/var/nfs/workfiles/nfslog_ workbuffer*
corp	*/export/corp/logging/ logs/nfslog*	*/export/corp/logging/ workfiles/fhtable*	*/export/corp/logging/work- files/nfslog_workbuffer*
extended	*/var/nfs/extended_ logs/nfslog*	*/var/nfs/workfiles/ fhtable*	*/var/nfs/workfiles/nfslog_ workbfuffer*

The temporary work buffers can grow large in a hurry, therefore it may not be a good idea to keep them in the default directory */var/nfs*, especially when */var* is fairly small. It is recommended to either spread them out among the filesystems they monitor, or place them in a dedicated partition. This will allow space in your */var* partition to be used for other administration tasks, such as storing core files, printer spool directories, and other system logs.

Basic versus extended log format

Logging using the basic format only reports file uploads and downloads. On the other hand, logging using the extended format provides more detailed information of filesystem activity, but may be incompatible with existing tools that process WU-Ftpd logs. Tools that expect a single character identifier in the *operation* field will not understand the multicharacter description of the extended format.

Home-grown scripts can be easily modified to understand the richer format. Logging using the extended format reports directory creation, directory removal, and file removal, as well as file reads (downloads) and file writes (uploads). Each record indicates the NFS version and protocol used during access.

Let us explore the differences between the two logs by comparing the logged information that results from executing the same sequence of commands against the NFS server *zeus*. First, the server exports the filesystem using the *extended* tag previously defined in the */etc/nfs/nfslog.conf* file:

```
zeus# share -o log=extended /export/home
```

Next, the client executes the following sequence of commands:

```
rome% cd /net/zeus/export/home
rome% mkdir test
rome% mkfile 64k 64k-file
rome% mv 64k-file test
rome% rm test/64k-file
rome% rmdir test
rome% dd if=128k-file of=/dev/null
256+0 records in
256+0 records out
```

The resulting extended format log on the server reflects corresponding NFS operations:

```
zeus# cat /var/nfs/extended_logs/nfslog
Mon Jul 31 11:00:05 2000 0 rome 0 /export/home/test b _ mkdir r 19069 nfs3-tcp 0 *
Mon Jul 31 11:00:33 2000 0 rome 0 /export/home/64k-file b _ create r 19069 nfs3-
tcp 0 *
Mon Jul 31 11:00:33 2000 0 rome 65536 /export/home/64k-file b _ write r 19069
nfs3-tcp 0 *
Mon Jul 31 11:00:49 2000 0 rome 0 /export/home/64k-file->/export/home/test/64k-
file b _ rename r 19069 nfs3-tcp 0 *
Mon Jul 31 11:00:59 2000 0 rome 0 /export/home/test/64k-file b _ remove r 19069
nfs3-tcp 0 *
Mon Jul 31 11:01:01 2000 0 rome 0 /export/home/test b   rmdir r 19069 nfs3-tcp 0 *
Mon Jul 31 11:01:47 2000 0 rome 131072 /export/home/128k-file b _ read r 19069
nfs3-tcp 0 *
```

Notice that the *mkfile* operation generated two log entries, a 0-byte file, *create*, followed by a 64K *write*. The rename operation lists the original name followed by an arrow pointing to the new name. File and directory deletions are also logged. The *nfs3-tcp* field indicates the protocol and version used: NFS Version 3 over TCP.

Now let us compare against the basic log generated by the same sequence of client commands. First, let us reshare the filesystem with the basic log format. It is highly recommended to never mix extended and basic log records in the same file. This will make post-processing of the log file much easier. Our example places extended logs in */var/nfs/extended_logs/nfslog* and basic logs in */var/nfs/ logs/nfslog*:

```
zeus# share -o log /export/home
```

Next, the client executes the same sequence of commands listed earlier. The resulting basic format log on the server only shows the file upload (incoming operation denoted by *i*) and the file download (outgoing operation denoted by *o*). The directory creation, directory removal, and file rename are not logged in the basic format. Notice that the NFS version and protocol type are not specified either:

```
zeus# cat /var/nfs/logs/nfslog
 Mon Jul 31 11:35:08 2000 0 rome 65536 /export/home/64k-file b _ i r 19069 nfs 0 *
 Mon Jul 31 11:35:25 2000 0 rome 131072 /export/home/128k-file b _ o r 19069 nfs 0 *
```

The nfslogd daemon

It is the *nfslogd* daemon that generates the ultimate NFS log file. The daemon periodically wakes up to process the contents of the work buffer file created by the kernel, performs hostname and pathname mappings, and generates the file transfer log record. Since the filesystem can be reshared with logging disabled, or simply be unshared, the *nfslogd* daemon cannot rely on the list of exported filesystems to locate the work buffer files. So how exactly does the *nfslogd* daemon locate the work buffer files?

When a filesystem is exported with logging enabled, the *share* command adds a record to the */etc/nfs/nfslogtab* file indicating the location of the work buffer file, the filesystem shared, the tag used to share the filesystem, and a 1 to indicate that the filesystem is currently exported with logging enabled. This system table is used to keep track of the location of the work buffer files so they can be processed at a later time, even after the filesystem is unshared, or the server is rebooted. The *nfslogd* daemon uses this system file to find the location of the next work buffer file that needs to be processed. The daemon removes the */etc/nfs/nfslogtab* entry for the work buffer file after processing if the corresponding filesystem is no longer exported. The entry will not be removed if the filesystem remains exported.

The *nfslogd* daemon removes the work buffer file once it has processed the information. The kernel creates a new work buffer file when more RPC requests arrive. To be exact, the work buffer file currently accessed by the kernel has the *_in_process* string appended to its name (name specified by the *buffer* parameter in */etc/nfs/nfslog.conf*). The daemon, asks the kernel to rename the buffer to the name specified in the configuration file once it is ready to process it. At this point the kernel will again create a new buffer file with the string appended and start writing to the new file. This means that the kernel and the *nfslogd* daemon are always working on their own work buffer file, without stepping on each others' toes. The *nfslogd* daemon will remove the work buffer file once it has processed the information.

You will notice that log records do not show up immediately on the log after a client accesses the file or directory on the server. This occurs because the *nfslogd* daemon waits for enough RPC information to gather in the work buffer before it can process it. By default it will wait five minutes. This time can be shortened or lengthened by tuning the value of IDLE_TIME in */etc/default/nfslogd*.

Consolidating file transfer information

The NFS protocol was not designed to be a file transfer protocol, instead it was designed to be a file access protocol. NFS file operations map nicely to Unix file-system calls and as such, its file data access and modification mechanisms operate on regions of files. This enables NFS to minimize the amount of data transfer required between server and client, when only small portions of the file are needed. The NFS protocol enables reads and writes of arbitrary number of bytes at any given offset, in any given order. NFS clients are not required to read a file on an NFS server in any given order, they may start in the middle and read an arbitrary number of bytes at any given offset.

The random byte access, added to the fact that NFS Versions 2 and 3 do not define an open or close operation, make it hard to determine when an NFS client is done reading or writing a file. Despite this limitation, the *nfslogd* daemon does a decent job identifying file transfers by using various heuristics to determine when to generate the file transfer record.

Filehandle to path mapping

Most NFS operations take a filehandle as an argument, or return a filehandle as a result of the operation. In the NFS protocol, a filehandle serves to identify a file or a directory. Filehandles contain all the information the server needs to distinguish an individual file or directory. To the client, the filehandle is opaque. The client stores the filehandles for use in a later request. It is the server that generates the filehandle:

```
    1   0.00000      rome -> zeus      NFS C LOOKUP3 FH=0222 foo.tar.Z
    2   0.00176      zeus -> rome      NFS R LOOKUP3 OK FH=EEAB
...
    9   0.00091      rome -> zeus      NFS C READ3 FH=EEAB at 0 for 32768
...
```

Consider packets 1, 2, and 9 from the *snoop* trace presented earlier in this chapter. The client must first obtain the filehandle for the file *foo.tar.Z*, before it can request to read its contents. This is because the NFS READ procedure takes the filehandle as an argument and not the filename. The client obtains the filehandle by first invoking the LOOKUP procedure, which takes as arguments the name of the file requested and the filehandle of the directory where it is located. Note that the directory filehandle must itself first be obtained by a previous LOOKUP or MOUNT operation.

Unfortunately, NFS server implementations today do not provide a mechanism to obtain a filename given a filehandle. This would require the kernel to be able to obtain a path given a vnode, which is not possible today in Solaris. To overcome this limitation, the *nfslogd* daemon builds a mapping table of filehandle to pathnames by monitoring all NFS operations that generate or modify filehandles. It is from this table that it obtains the pathname for the file transfer log record. This filehandle to pathname mapping table is by default stored in the file */var/nfs/fhtable*. This can be overridden by specifying a new value for *fhtable* in */etc/nfs/nfslog.conf.*

In order to successfully resolve all filehandles, the filesystem must be shared with logging enabled from the start. The *nfslogd* daemon will not be able to resolve all mappings when logging is enabled on a previously shared filesystem for which clients have already obtained filehandles. The filehandle mapping information can only be built from the RPC information captured while logging is enabled on the filesystem. This means that if logging is temporarily disabled, a potentially large number of filehandle transactions will not be captured and the *nfslogd* daemon will not be able to reconstruct the pathname for all filehandles. If a filehandle can not be resolved, it will be printed on the NFS log transaction record instead of printing the corresponding (but unknown) pathname.

The filehandle mapping table needs to be backed by permanent storage since it has to survive server reboots. There is no limit for the amount of time that NFS clients hold on to filehandles. A client may obtain a filehandle for a file, read it today and read it again five days from now without having to reacquire the filehandle (not encountered often in practice). Filehandles are even valid across server reboots.

Ideally the filehandle mapping table would only go away when the filesystem is destroyed. The problem is that the table can get pretty large since it could potentially contain a mapping for every entry in the filesystem. Not all installations can afford reserving this much storage space for a utility table. Therefore, in order to preserve disk space, the *nfslogd* daemon will periodically prune the oldest contents of the mapping table. It removes filehandle entries that have not been accessed since the last time the pruning process was performed. This process is automatic, the *nfslogd* daemon will prune the table every seven days by default. This can be overridden by setting PRUNE_TIMEOUT in */etc/default/nfslogd*. This value specifies the number of hours between prunings. Making this value too small can increase the risk that a client may have held on to a filehandle longer than the PRUNE_TIMEOUT and perform an NFS operation after the filehandle has been removed from the table. In such a case, the *nfslogd* daemon will not be able to resolve the pathname and the NFS log will include the filehandle instead of the pathname. Pruning of the table can effectively be disabled by setting the PRUNE_ TIMEOUT to INT_MAX. Be aware that this may lead to very large tables, potentially causing problems exceeding the database maximum values. This is therefore highly discouraged, since in practice the chance of NFS clients holding on to filehandles for more than a few days without using them is extremely small. The *nfslogd* daemon uses *ndbm** to manage the filehandle mapping table.

NFS log cycling

The *nfslogd* daemon periodically cycles the logs to prevent an individual file from becoming extremely large. By default, the ten most current NFS log files are located in */var/nfs* and named *nfslog, nfslog.0,* through *nfslog.9.* The file *nfslog* being the most recent, followed by *nfslog.1* and *nfslog.9* being the oldest. The log files are cycled every 24 hours, saving up to 10 days worth of logs. The number of logs saved can be increased by setting MAX_LOGS_PRESERVE in */etc/default/nfslogd.* The cycle frequency can be modified by setting CYCLE_FREQUENCY in the same file.

Manipulating NFS log files

Sometimes it may be desirable to have the *nfslogd* daemon close the current file, and log to a fresh new file. The daemon holds an open file descriptor to the log file, so renaming it or copying it somewhere else may not achieve the desired effect. Make sure to first shut down the daemon before manipulating the log files. To shut down the daemon, send it a SIGHUP signal. This will give the daemon enough time to flush pending transactions to the log file. You can use the Solaris *pkill* command to send the signal to the daemon. Note that the daemon can take a few seconds to flush the information:

```
# pkill -HUP -x -u 0 nfslogd
```

Sending it a SIGTERM signal will simply close the buffer files, but pending transactions will not be logged to the file and will be discarded.

Other configuration parameters

The configuration parameters in the */etc/default/nfslogd* tune the behavior of the *nfslogd* daemon. The *nfslogd* daemon reads the configuration parameters when it

---

* See *dbm_clearerr(3C).*

starts, therefore any changes to the parameters will take effect the next time the daemon is started. Here is a list of the parameters:

UMASK

Used to set the file mode used to create the log files, work buffer files, and filehandle mapping tables. Needless to say one has to be extremely careful setting this value, as it could open the doors for unathorized access to the log and work files. The default is 0x137, which gives read/write access to root, read access to the group that started the *nfslogd* daemon, and no access to other.

MIN_PROCESSING_SIZE

The *nfslogd* daemon waits until MIN_PROCESSING_SIZE bytes are gathered in the work buffer file before it starts processing any information. The idea is to wait long enough for information to gather to make the processing worth while. Note that the *nfslogd* daemon will process the work buffer regardless of the size after an implementation timer fires indicating that the work buffer has been ignored for too long. The default value is 512 Kb.

IDLE_TIME

The *nfslogd* daemon sleeps up to IDLE_TIME seconds waiting for information to be gathered in the work buffer files. This value indirectly affects the frequency with which the *nfslogd* daemon checks updates of the file */etc/nfs/ nfslog.conf.* Increasing this value too much will cause the temporary work buffer files to become large, potentially using more disk space than desired. Making this value too short will cause the *nfslogd* daemon to wake up frequently and potentially have nothing to do since the MIN_PROCESSING_SIZE of its buffers may not have been reached.

MAX_LOGS_PRESERVE

The *nfslogd* daemon periodically cycles the logs in order to keep their size manageable. This value specifies the maximum number of logs to save in the log directory. When this value is reached, the oldest log is discarded to make room for a new log. The logs are saved with a numbered extension, beginning with .0 through .MAX_LOGS_PRESERVE-1. The oldest log will be the one with the highest numbered extension.

Consider the following three tags:

```
Excerpt from /etc/nfs/nfslog.conf:
sales      log=/export/logs/nfslog fhtable=sales-table
corp       log=/export/logs/nfslog fhtable=corp-table
eng        log=/export/logs/eng/englog

Excerpt from /etc/default/nfslogd:
MAX_LOGS_PRESERVE=10
```

Both the *sales* and *corp* tags send the final log records to */export/logs/nfslog*. The *eng* tag sends the log records to */export/logs/eng/nfslog*. You will have a total of up to 10 log files named *nfslog, nfslog.0, ..., nfslog.9* in */export/logs*. Similarly, you will have a total of up to ten log files named *englog, englog.0, ..., englog.9* in */export/logs/eng*. Notice that the fact that two tags use the same log file does not affect the total number of logs preserved.

CYCLE_FREQUENCY

Specifies the frequency with which log files are cycled (see MAX_LOGS_ PRESERVE). The value is specified in hours. This helps keep the log file size manageable. The default is to cycle every 24 hours.

MAPPING_UPDATE_INTERVAL

Specifies the time interval, in seconds, between updates of the records in the filehandle mapping table. Ideally the access time of entries queried in the mapping table should be updated on every access. In practice, updates of this table are much more expensive than queries. Instead of updating the access time of a record each time the record is accessed, the access time is updated only when the last update is older than MAPPING_UPDATE_INTERVAL seconds. By default updates are performed once per day. Make sure this value is always less than the value specified by PRUNE_TIMEOUT, otherwise all of the entries in the filehandle mapping tables will be considered timed out.

PRUNE_TIMEOUT

Specifies how frequent the pruning of the filehandle mapping tables is invoked. This value represents the minimum number of hours that a record is guaranteed to remain in the mapping table. The default value of seven days (168 hours) instructs the *nfslogd* daemon to perform the database pruning every seven days and remove the records that are older than seven days. Note that filehandles can remain in the database for up to 14 days. This can occur when a record is created immediately after the pruning process has finished. Seven days later the record will not be pruned because it is only six days and hours old. The record will be removed until the next pruning cycle, assuming no client accesses the filehandle within that time. The MAPPING_UPDATE_ INTERVAL may need to be updated accordingly.

Disabling NFS server logging

Unfortunately, disabling logging requires some manual cleanup. Unsharing or resharing a filesystem without the *-o log* directive stops the kernel from storing information into the work buffer file. You must allow the *nfslogd* daemon enough time to process the work buffer file before shutting it down. The daemon will notice that it needs to process the work buffer file once it wakes up after its IDLE_ TIME has been exceeded.

Once the work buffer file has been processed and removed by the *nfslogd* daemon, the *nfslogd* daemon can manually be shutdown by sending it a SIGHUP signal. This allows the daemon to flush the pending NFS log information before it is stopped. Sending any other type of signal may cause the daemon to be unable to flush the last few records to the log.

There is no way to distinguish between a graceful server shutdown and the case when logging is being completely disabled. For this reason, the mapping tables are not removed when the filesystem is unshared, or the daemon is stopped. The system administrator needs to remove the filehandle mapping tables manually when he/she wants to reclaim the filesystem space and knows that logging is being permanently disabled for this filesystem.*

Time synchronization

Distributing files across several servers introduces a dependency on synchronized time of day clocks on these machines and their clients. Consider the following sequence of events:

```
caramba % date
Mon Sep 25 18:11:24 PDT 2000
caramba % pwd
/home/labiaga
caramba % touch foo
caramba % ls -l foo
-rw-r--r--   1 labiaga  staff           0 Sep 25 18:18 foo

aqua % date
Mon Sep 25 17:00:01 PDT 2000
aqua % pwd
/home/labiaga
aqua % ls -l foo
-rw-r--r--   1 labiaga  staff           0 Sep 25  2000 foo
aqua % su
aqua # rdate caramba
Mon Sep 25 18:16:51 2000
aqua % ls -l foo
-rw-r--r--   1 labiaga  staff           0 Sep 25 18:18 foo
```

On host *caramba*, a file is created that is stamped with the current time. Over on host *aqua*, the time of day clock is over an hour behind, and file *foo* is listed with the month-day-year date format normally reserved for files that are more than six months old. The problem stems from the time skew between *caramba* and *aqua*: when the *ls* process on *aqua* tries to determine the age of file *foo*, it subtracts the

---

* Keep in mind that if logging is later reenabled, there will be some filehandles that the *nfslogd* daemon will not be able to resolve since they were obtained by clients while logging was not enabled. If the filehandle mapping table is removed, then the problem is aggravated.

file modification time from the current time. Under normal circumstances, this produces a positive integer, but with *caramba*'s clock an hour ahead of the local clock, the difference between modification time and current time is a negative number. This makes file *foo* a veritable Unix artifact, created before the dawn of Unix time. As such, its modification time is shown with the "old file" format.*

Time of day clock drift can be caused by repeated bursts of high priority interrupts that interfere with the system's hardware clock or by powering off (and subsequently booting) a system that does not have a battery-operated time of day clock.†

In addition to confusing users, time skew wreaks havoc with the timestamps used by *make*, jobs run out of *cron* that depend on *cron*-started processes on other hosts, and the transfer of NIS maps to slave servers, which fail if the slave server's time is far enough ahead of the master server. It is essential to keep all hosts sharing filesystems or NIS maps synchronized to within a few seconds.

rdate synchronizes the time of day clocks on two hosts to within a one-second granularity. Because it changes the local time and date, *rdate* can only be used by the superuser, just as the *date* utility can only be used by *root* to explicitly set the local time. *rdate* takes the name of the remote time source as an argument:

```
% rdate mahimahi
couldn't set time of day: Not owner
% su
# rdate mahimahi
Mon Sep 25 18:16:51 2000
```

One host is usually selected as the master timekeeper, and all other hosts synchronize to its time at regular intervals. The ideal choice for a timekeeping host is one that has the minimum amount of time drift, or that is connected to a network providing time services. If the time host's clock loses a few seconds each day, the entire network will fall behind the real wall clock time. All hosts agree on the current time, but this time slowly drifts further and further behind the real time.

---

* Some Unix utilities have been modified to handle small time skews in a graceful manner. For example, *ls* tolerates clock drifts of a few minutes and correctly displays file modification times that are slightly in the future.

† The hardware clock, or "hardclock" is a regular, crystal-driven timer that provides the system heartbeat. In kernel parlance, the hardclock timer interval is a "tick," a basic unit of time-slicing that governs CPU scheduling, process priority calculation, and software timers. The software time of day clock is driven by the hardclock. If the hardclock interrupts at 100 Hz, then every 100 hardclock interrupts bump the current time of day clock by one second. When a hardclock interrupt is missed, the software clock begins to lose time. If there is a hardware time of day clock available, the kernel can compensate for missed hardclock interrupts by checking the system time against the hardware time of day clock and adjusting for any drift. If there is no time of day clock, missed hardware clock interrupts translate into a tardy system clock.

While the remote host may be explicitly specified, it is more convenient to create the hostname alias *timehost* in the NIS hosts file and to use the alias in all invocations of *rdate*:

```
131.40.52.28    mahimahi timehost
131.40.52.26    wahoo
131.40.52.150   kfir
```

Some systems check for the existence of the hostname *timehost* during the boot sequence, and perform an *rdate timehost* if *timehost* is found.

This convention is particularly useful if you are establishing a new timekeeping host and you need to change its definition if your initial choice proves to be a poor time standard. It is far simpler to change the definition of *timehost* in the NIS hosts map than it is to modify the invocations of *rdate* on all hosts.

Time synchronization may be performed during the boot sequence, and at regular intervals using *cron*. The interval chosen for time synchronization depends on how badly each system's clock drifts: once-a-day updates may be sufficient if the drift is only a few seconds a day, but hourly synchronization is required if a system loses time each hour. To run *rdate* from *cron*, add a line like the following to each host's *crontab* file:

```
Hourly update:
52 * * * * rdate timehost > /dev/null 2>&1

Daily update:
52 1 * * * rdate timehost > /dev/null 2>&1
```

The redirection of the standard output and standard error forces *rdate*'s output to */dev/null*, suppressing the normal echo of the updated time. If a *cron*-driven command writes to standard output or standard error, *cron* will mail the output to *root*.

To avoid swamping the *timehost* with dozens of simultaneous *rdate* requests, the previous example performs its *rdate* at a random offset into the hour. A common convention is to use the last octet of the machine's IP address (mod 60) as the offset into the hour, effectively scattering the *rdate* requests throughout each hour.

The use of *rdate* ensures a gross synchronization accurate to within a second or two on the network. The resolution of this approach is limited by the *rdate* and *cron* utilities, both of which are accurate to one second. This is sufficient for many activities, but finer synchronization with a higher resolution may be needed. The Network Time Protocol (NTP) provides fine-grain time synchronization and also keeps wide-area networks in lock step. NTP is outside the scope of this book.

In this chapter:
- *Duplicate ARP replies*
- *Renegade NIS server*
- *Boot parameter confusion*
- *Incorrect directory content caching*
- *Incorrect mount point permissions*
- *Asynchronous NFS error messages*

Debugging Network Problems

This chapter consists of case studies in network problem analysis and debugging, ranging from Ethernet addressing problems to a machine posing as an NIS server in the wrong domain. This chapter is a bridge between the formal discussion of NFS and NIS tools and their use in performance analysis and tuning. The case studies presented here walk through debugging scenarios, but they should also give you an idea of how the various tools work together.

When debugging a network problem, it's important to think about the potential cause of a problem, and then use that to start ruling out other factors. For example, if your attempts to bind to an NIS server are failing, you should know that you could try testing the network using *ping*, the health of *ypserv* processes using *rpcinfo*, and finally the binding itself with *ypset*. Working your way through the protocol layers ensures that you don't miss a low-level problem that is posing as a higher-level failure. Keeping with that advice, we'll start by looking at a network layer problem.

Duplicate ARP replies

ARP misinformation was briefly mentioned in "IP to MAC address mappings" in Chapter 13, and this story showcases some of the baffling effects it creates. A network of two servers and ten clients suddenly began to run very slowly, with the following symptoms:

- Some users attempting to start a document-processing application were waiting ten to 30 *minutes* for the application's window to appear, while those on well-behaved machines waited a few seconds. The executables resided on a fileserver and were NFS mounted on each client. Every machine in the group experienced these delays over a period of a few days, although not all at the same time.

- Machines would suddenly "go away" for several minutes. Clients would stop seeing their NFS and NIS servers, producing streams of messages like:

  ```
  NFS server muskrat not responding still trying
  ```

  or:

  ```
  ypbind: NIS server not responding for domain "techpubs"; still trying
  ```

The local area network with the problems was joined to the campus-wide backbone via a bridge. An identical network of machines, running the same applications with nearly the same configuration, was operating without problems on the far side of the bridge. We were assured of the health of the physical network by two engineers who had verified physical connections and cable routing.

The very sporadic nature of the problem—and the fact that it resolved itself over time—pointed toward a problem with ARP request and reply mismatches. This hypothesis neatly explained the extraordinarily slow loading of the application: a client machine trying to read the application executable would do so by issuing NFS Version 2 requests over UDP. To send the UDP packets, the client would ARP the server, randomly get the wrong reply, and then be unable to use that entry for several minutes. When the ARP table entry had aged and was deleted, the client would again ARP the server; if the correct ARP response was received then the client could continue reading pages of the executable. Every wrong reply received by the client would add a few minutes to the loading time.

There were several possible sources of the ARP confusion, so to isolate the problem, we forced a client to ARP the server and watched what happened to the ARP table:

```
# arp -d muskrat
muskrat (139.50.2.1) deleted
# ping -s muskrat
PING muskrat: 56 data bytes
No further output from ping
```

By deleting the ARP table entry and then directing the client to send packets to *muskrat*, we forced an ARP of *muskrat* from the client. *ping* timed out without receiving any ICMP echo replies, so we examined the ARP table and found a surprise:

```
# arp -a | fgrep muskrat
le0    muskrat              255.255.255.255      08:00:49:05:02:a9
```

Since *muskrat* was a Sun workstation, we expected its Ethernet address to begin with 08:00:20 (the prefix assigned to Sun Microsystems), not the 08:00:49 prefix used by Kinetics gateway boxes. The next step was to figure out how the wrong Ethernet address was ending up in the ARP table: was *muskrat* lying in its ARP replies, or had we found a network imposter?

Using a network analyzer, we repeated the ARP experiment and watched ARP replies returned. We saw two distinct replies: the correct one from *muskrat*, followed by an invalid reply from the Kinetics FastPath gateway. The root of this problem was that the Kinetics box had been configured using the IP broadcast address 0.0.0.0, allowing it to answer all ARP requests. Reconfiguring the Kinetics box with a non-broadcast IP address solved the problem.

The last update to the ARP table is the one that "sticks," so the wrong Ethernet address was overwriting the correct ARP table entry. The Kinetics FastPath was located on the other side of the bridge, virtually guaranteeing that its replies would be the last to arrive, delayed by their transit over the bridge. When *muskrat* was heavily loaded, it was slow to reply to the ARP request and its ARP response would be the last to arrive. Reconfiguring the Kinetics FastPath to use a proper IP address and network mask cured the problem.

ARP servers that have out-of-date information create similar problems. This situation arises if an IP address is changed without a corresponding update of the server's published ARP table initialization, or if the IP address in question is re-assigned to a machine that implements the ARP protocol. If an ARP server was employed because *muskrat* could not answer ARP requests, then we should have seen exactly one ARP reply, coming from the ARP server. However, an ARP server with a published ARP table entry for a machine capable of answering its own ARP requests produces exactly the same duplicate response symptoms described above. With both machines on the same local network, the failures tend to be more intermittent, since there is no obvious time-ordering of the replies.

There's a moral to this story: you should rarely need to know the Ethernet address of a workstation, but it does help to have them recorded in a file or NIS map. This problem was solved with a bit of luck, because the machine generating incorrect replies had a different manufacturer, and therefore a different Ethernet address prefix. If the incorrectly configured machine had been from the same vendor, we would have had to compare the Ethernet addresses in the ARP table with what we believed to be the correct addresses for the machine in question.

Renegade NIS server

A user on our network reported that he could not log into his workstation. He supplied his username and the same password he'd been using for the past six months, and he consistently was told "Login incorrect." Out of frustration, he rebooted his machine. When attempting to mount NFS filesystems, the workstation was not able to find any of the NFS server hosts in the *hosts* NIS map, producing errors of the form:

```
nfs mount: wahoo: : RPC: Unknown host
```

There were no error messages from *ypbind*, so it appeared that the workstation
had found an NIS server. The culprit looked like the NIS server itself: our guess
was that it was a machine masquerading as a valid NIS server, or that it was an
NIS server whose maps had been destroyed. Because nobody could log into the
machine, we rebooted it in single-user mode, and manually started NIS to see
where it bound:

```
Single-user boot
# /etc/init.d/inetinit start
NIS domainname is nesales
Starting IPv4 router discovery.
Starting IPv6 neighbor discovery.
Setting default IPv6 interface for multicast: add net ff00::/8: gateway fe80::a00:
20ff:fea0:3390
# /etc/init.d/rpc start
starting rpc services: rpcbind keyserv ypbind done.
# ypwhich
131.40.52.25
```

We manually invoked the */etc/init.d/inetinit* startup script to initialize the domain
name and configure the routing. We then invoked the */etc/init.d/rpc* script to start
ypbind. Notice that *ypwhich* was not able to match the IP address of the NIS
server in the *hosts* NIS map, so it printed the IP address. The IP address belonged
to a gateway machine that was not supposed to be a NIS server. It made sense
that clients were binding to it, if it was posing as an NIS server, since the gateway
was very lightly loaded and was probably the first NIS server to respond to *ypbind*
requests.

We logged into that machine, and verified that it was running *ypserv*. The domain
name used by the gateway was *nesales*—it had been brought up in the wrong
domain. Removing the */var/yp/nesales* subdirectory containing the NIS maps and
restarting the NIS daemons took the machine out of service:

```
# cd /var/yp
# rm -rf nesales
# /usr/lib/netsvc/yp/ypstop
# /usr/lib/netsvc/yp/ypstart
```

We contacted the person responsible for the gateway and had him put the
gateway in its own NIS domain (his original intention). Machines in *nesales* that
had bound to the renegade server eventually noticed that their NIS server had
gone away, and they rebound to valid servers.

As a variation on this problem, consider an NIS server that has damaged or incomplete maps. Symptoms of this problem are nearly identical to those previously
described, but the IP address printed by *ypwhich* will be that of a familiar NIS
server. There may be just a few maps that are damaged, possibly corrupted during
an NIS transfer operation, or all of the server's maps may be corrupted or lost. The
latter is most probable when someone accidentally removes directories in */var/yp*.

To check the consistency of various maps, use *ypcat* to dump all of the keys known to the server. A few damaged maps can be replaced with explicit *yppush* operations on the master server. If all of the server's maps are damaged, it is easiest to reinitialize the server. Slave servers are easily rebuilt from a valid master server, but if the master server has lost the DBM files containing the maps, initializing the machine as an NIS master server regenerates only the default set of maps. Before rebuilding the NIS master, save the NIS *Makefile*, in */var/yp* or */etc/yp*, if you have made local changes to it. The initialization process builds the default maps, after which you can replace your hand-crafted *Makefile* and build all site-specific NIS maps.

Boot parameter confusion

Different vendors do not always agree on the format of responses to various broadcast requests. Great variation exists in the *bootparam* RPC service, which supplies diskless nodes with the name of their boot server, and pathname for their root partition. If a diskless client's request for boot parameters returns a packet that it cannot understand, the client produces a rather cryptic error message and then aborts the boot process.

As an example, we saw the following strange behavior when a diskless Sun workstation attempted to boot. The machine would request its Internet address using RARP, and receive the correct reply from its boot server. It then downloaded the boot code using *tftp*, and sent out a request for boot parameters. At this point, the boot sequence would abort with one of the errors:

```
null domain name
invalid reply
```

Emulating the request for boot parameters using *rpcinfo* located the source of the invalid reply quickly. Using a machine close to the diskless node, we sent out a request similar to that broadcast during the boot sequence, looking for *bootparam* servers:

```
% rpcinfo -b bootparam 1
192.9.200.14.128.67    clover
192.9.200.1.128.68     lucy
192.9.200.4.128.79     bugs
```

lucy and *bugs* were boot and root/swap servers for diskless clients, but *clover* was a machine from a different vendor. It should not have been interested in the request for boot parameters. However, *clover* was running *rpc.bootparamd*, which made it listen for boot parameter requests, and it used the NIS *bootparams* map to glean the boot information. Unfortunately, the format of its reply was not digestible by the diskless Sun node, but its reply was the first to arrive. In this case, the solution merely involved turning off *rpc.bootparamd* by commenting it out of the startup script on *clover*.

If *clover* supported diskless clients of its own, turning off *rpc.bootparamd* would not have been an acceptable solution. To continue running *rpc.bootparamd* on *clover*, we would have had to ensure that it never sent a reply to diskless clients other than its own. The easiest way to do this is to give *clover* a short list of clients to serve, and to keep *clover* from using the *bootparams* NIS map.*

Incorrect directory content caching

A user of a Solaris NFS client reported having intermittent problems accessing files mounted from a non-Unix NFS server. The Solaris NFS client *tarsus* was apparently able to list files that had previously been removed by another NFS client, but was unable to access the contents of the files. The files would eventually disappear. The NFS client that initially removed the files did not experience any problems and the user reported that the files had indeed been removed from the server's directory. He verified this by logging into the NFS server and listing the contents of the exported directory.

We suspected the client *tarsus* was not invalidating its cached information, and proceeded to try to reproduce the problem while capturing the NFS packets to analyze the network traffic:

```
[1] tarsus$ ls -l /net/inchun/export/folder
total 8
-rw-rw-rw-   1 labiaga   staff        2883 Apr 10 20:03 data1
-rw-rw-rw-   1 root      other          12 Apr 10 20:01 data2


[1] protium$ rm /net/inchun/export/folder/data2


[2] tarsus$ ls /net/inchun/export/folder
data1    data2
[3] tarsus$ ls -l /net/inchun/export/folder
/net/inchun/export/folder/data2: Stale NFS file handle
total 6
-rw-rw-rw-   1 labiaga   staff        2883 Apr 10 20:03 data1
```

The first directory listing on *tarsus* correctly displayed the contents of the NFS directory */net/inchun/export/folder* before anything was removed. The problems began after the NFS client *protium* removed the file *data2*. The second directory listing on *tarsus* continued showing the recently removed *data2* file as part of the directory, although the extended directory listing reported a "Stale NFS filehandle" for *data2*.

---

* Solaris uses the name switch to specify the name service used by *rpc.bootparamd*. Remove NIS from the *bootparams* entry in */etc/nsswitch.conf* and remove the "+" entry from */etc/bootparams* to avoid using NIS. Once *bootparamd* is restarted, it will no longer use the *bootparams* NIS map.

This was a typical case of inconsistent caching of information by an NFS client. Solaris NFS clients cache the directory content and attribute information in memory at the time the directory contents are first read from the NFS server. Subsequent client accesses to the directory first validate the cached information, comparing the directory's cached modification time to the modification time reported by the server. A match in modification times indicates that the directory has not been modified since the last time the client read it, therefore it can safely use the cached data. On the other hand, if the modification times are different, the NFS client purges its cache, and issues a new NFS *Readdir* request to the server to obtain the updated directory contents and attributes. Some non-Unix NFS servers are known for not updating the modification time of directories when files are removed, leading to directory caching problems. We used *snoop* to capture the NFS packets between our client and server while the problem was being reproduced. The analysis of the snoop output should help us determine if we're running into this caching problem.

To facilitate the discussion, we list the *snoop* packets preceded by the commands that generated them. This shows the correlation between the NFS traffic and the Unix commands that generate the traffic:

```
[1] tarsus $ ls -l /net/inchun/export/folder
total 8
-rw-rw-rw-   1 labiaga   staff       2883 Apr 10 20:03 data1
-rw-rw-rw-   1 root      other         12 Apr 10 20:01 data2

    7    0.00039    tarsus -> inchun    NFS C GETATTR2 FH=FA14
    8    0.00198    inchun -> tarsus    NFS R GETATTR2 OK
    9    0.00031    tarsus -> inchun    NFS C READDIR2 FH=FA14 Cookie=0
   10    0.00220    inchun -> tarsus    NFS R READDIR2 OK 4 entries (No more)
   11    0.00033    tarsus -> inchun    NFS C LOOKUP2 FH=FA14 data2
   12    0.00000    inchun -> tarsus    NFS R LOOKUP2 OK FH=F8CD
   13    0.00000    tarsus -> inchun    NFS C GETATTR2 FH=F8CD
   14    0.00000    inchun -> tarsus    NFS R GETATTR2 OK
   15    0.00035    tarsus -> inchun    NFS C LOOKUP2 FH=FA14 data1
   16    0.00211    inchun -> tarsus    NFS R LOOKUP2 OK FH=F66F
   17    0.00032    tarsus -> inchun    NFS C GETATTR2 FH=F66F
   18    0.00191    inchun -> tarsus    NFS R GETATTR2 OK
```

Packets 7 and 8 contain the request and reply for attributes for the */net/inchun/export/folder* directory. The attributes can be displayed by using the *-v* directive:

```
Excerpt from: snoop -i /tmp/capture -p 7,8 -v
ETHER:  ----- Ether Header -----
ETHER:
ETHER:  Packet 8 arrived at 20:45:9.75
...
NFS:  ----- Sun NFS -----
NFS:
NFS:  Proc = 1 (Get file attributes)
NFS:  Status = 0 (OK)
```

```
NFS:   File type = 2 (Directory)
NFS:   Mode = 040777
NFS:    Type = Directory
NFS:    Setuid = 0, Setgid = 0, Sticky = 0
NFS:    Owner's permissions = rwx
NFS:    Group's permissions = rwx
NFS:    Other's permissions = rwx
NFS:   Link count = 2, UID = 0, GID = -2, Rdev = 0x0
NFS:   File size = 512, Block size = 512, No. of blocks = 1
NFS:   File system id = 7111, File id = 161
NFS:   Access time       = 11-Apr-00 12:50:18.000000 GMT
NFS:   Modification time = 11-Apr-00 12:50:18.000000 GMT
NFS:   Inode change time = 31-Jul-96 09:40:56.000000 GMT
```

Packet 8 shows the */net/inchun/export/folder* directory was last modified on April 11, 2000 at 12:50:18.000000 GMT. *tarsus* caches this timestamp to later determine when the cached directory contents need to be updated. Packet 9 contains the request made by *tarsus* for the directory listing from *inchun*. Packet 10 contains *inchun*'s reply with four entries in the directory. A detailed view of the packets shows the four directory entries: ".", "..", "*data1*", and "*data2*". The EOF indicator notifies the client that all existing directory entries have been listed, and there is no need to make another NFS *Readdir* call:

```
Excerpt from: snoop -i /tmp/capture -p 9,10 -v
ETHER:   ----- Ether Header -----
ETHER:
ETHER:   Packet 10 arrived at 20:45:9.74
...
NFS:   ----- Sun NFS -----
NFS:
NFS:   Proc = 16 (Read from directory)
NFS:   Status = 0 (OK)
NFS:    File id  Cookie Name
NFS:        137    50171 .
NFS:         95    50496 ..
NFS:        199    51032 data1
NFS:        201    51706 data2
NFS:     4 entries
NFS:   EOF = 1
NFS:
```

The directory contents are cached by *tarsus*, so that they may be reused in a future directory listing. The NFS *Lookup* and NFS *Getattr* requests, along with their corresponding replies in packets 11 thru 18, result from the long listing of the directory requested by *ls -l*. An NFS *Lookup* obtains the filehandle of a directory component. The NFS *Getattr* requests the file attributes of the file identified by the previously obtained filehandle.

NFS Version 2 filehandles are 32 bytes long. Instead of displaying a long and cryptic 32-byte number, *snoop* generates a shorthand version of the filehandle and displays it when invoked in summary mode. This helps you associate filehandles

with file objects more easily. You can obtain the exact filehandle by displaying the
network packet in verbose mode by using the *-v* option. The packet 7 filehandle
FH=FA14 is really:

```
Excerpt from: snoop -i /tmp/capture -p 7 -v
NFS: ----- Sun NFS -----
NFS:
NFS:  Proc = 1 (Get file attributes)
NFS:  File handle = [FA14]
NFS:   0204564F4C32000000000000000000000000A10000001C4DFF20A00000000000
```

Next, *protium*, a different NFS client comes into the picture, and removes one file
from the directory previously cached by *tarsus*:

```
[1] protium $ rm /net/inchun/export/folder/data2

22   0.00000   protium -> inchun    NFS C GETATTR2 FH=FA14
23   0.00000   inchun -> protium    NFS R GETATTR2 OK
24   0.00000   protium -> inchun    NFS C REMOVE2 FH=FA14 data2
25   0.00182   inchun -> protium    NFS R REMOVE2 OK
```

Packets 22 and 23 update the cached attributes of the */net/inchun/export/folder*
directory on *protium*. Packet 24 contains the actual NFS *Remove* request sent to
inchun, which in turn acknowledges the successful removal of the file in packet 25.

tarsus then lists the directory in question, but fails to detect that the contents of
the directory have changed:

```
[2] tarsus $ ls /net/inchun/export/folder
data1   data2

39   0.00000   tarsus -> inchun    NFS C GETATTR2 FH=FA14
40   0.00101   inchun -> tarsus    NFS R GETATTR2 OK
```

This is where the problem begins. Notice that two NFS *Getattr* network packets
are generated as a result of the directory listing but no *Readdir* request. In this
case, the client issues the NFS *Getattr* operation to request the directory's modification time:

```
Excerpt from: snoop -i /tmp/capture -p 39,40 -v
ETHER: ----- Ether Header -----
ETHER:
ETHER:  Packet 40 arrived at 20:45:10.88
...
NFS: ----- Sun NFS -----
NFS:
NFS:  Proc = 1 (Get file attributes)
NFS:  Status = 0 (OK)
NFS:  File type = 2 (Directory)
NFS:  Mode = 040777
NFS:   Type = Directory
NFS:   Setuid = 0, Setgid = 0, Sticky = 0
NFS:   Owner's permissions = rwx
```

```
NFS:   Group's permissions = rwx
NFS:    Other's permissions = rwx
NFS:   Link count = 2, UID = 0, GID = -2, Rdev = 0x0
NFS:   File size = 512, Block size = 512, No. of blocks = 1
NFS:   File system id = 7111, File id = 161
NFS:   Access time        = 11-Apr-00 12:50:18.000000 GMT
NFS:   Modification time = 11-Apr-00 12:50:18.000000 GMT
NFS:   Inode change time = 31-Jul-96 09:40:56.000000 GMT
```

The modification time of the directory is the same as the modification time before the removal of the file! *tarsus* compares the cached modification time of the directory with the modification time just obtained from the server, and determines that the cached directory contents are still valid since the modification times are the same. The directory listing is therefore satisfied from the cache instead of forcing the NFS client to read the updated directory contents from the server. This explains why the removed file continues to show up in the directory listing:

```
[3] tarsus $ ls -l /net/inchun/export/folder
/net/inchun/export/folder/data2: Stale NFS file handle
total 6
-rw-rw-rw-   1 labiaga  staff        2883 Apr 10 20:03 data1

  44   0.00000    tarsus -> inchun    NFS C GETATTR2 FH=FA14
  45   0.00101    inchun -> tarsus    NFS R GETATTR2 OK
  46   0.00032    tarsus -> inchun    NFS C GETATTR2 FH=F66F
  47   0.00191    inchun -> tarsus    NFS R GETATTR2 OK
  48   0.00032    tarsus -> inchun    NFS C GETATTR2 FH=F8CD
  49   0.00214    inchun -> tarsus    NFS R GETATTR2 Stale NFS file handle
```

The directory attributes reported in packet 45 are the same as those seen in packet 40, therefore *tarsus* assumes that it can safely use the cached filehandles associated with the cached entries of this directory. In packet 46, *tarsus* requests the attributes of filehandle F66F, corresponding to the *data1* file. The server replies with the attributes in packet 47. *tarsus* then proceeds to request the attributes of filehandle F8CD, which corresponds to the *data2* file. The server replies with a "Stale NFS filehandle" error because there is no file on the server associated with the given filehandle. This problem would never have occurred had the server updated the modification time after removing the file causing *tarsus* to detect that the directory had been changed.

Directory caching works nicely when the NFS server obeys Unix directory semantics. Many non-Unix NFS servers provide such semantics even if they have to submit themselves to interesting contortions. Having said this, there is nothing in the NFS protocol specification that requires the modification time of a directory to be updated when a file is removed. You may therefore need to disable Solaris NFS directory caching if you're running into problems interacting with non-Unix servers. To permanently disable NFS directory caching, add this line to */etc/system*:

```
set nfs:nfs_disable_rddir_cache = 0x1
```

The Solaris kernel reads */etc/system* at startup and sets the value of *nfs_disable_rddir_cache* to 0x1 in the *nfs* kernel module. The change takes effect only after reboot. Use *adb* to disable caching during the current session, postponing the need to reboot. You still need to set the tunable in */etc/system* to make the change permanent through reboots:

```
aqua# adb -w -k /dev/ksyms /dev/mem
physmem     3ac8
nfs_disable_rddir_cache/W1
nfs_disable_rddir_cache:    0x0       =    0x1
```

adb is an interactive assembly level debugger that enables you to consult and modify the kernel's memory contents. The *-k* directive instructs *adb* to perform kernel memory mapping accessing the kernel's memory via */dev/mem*, and obtaining the kernel's symbol table from */dev/ksyms*. The *-w* directive allows you to modify the kernel memory contents. A word of caution: *adb* is a power tool that will cause serious data corruption and potential system panics when misused.

Incorrect mount point permissions

Not all problems involving NFS filesystems originate on the network or other fileservers. NFS filesystems closely resemble local filesystems, consequently common local system administration concepts and problem solving techniques apply to NFS mounted filesystems as well. A user reported problems resolving the "current directory" when inside an NFS mounted filesystem. The filesystem was automounted using the following direct map:

```
Excerpt from /etc/auto_direct:
/packages        -ro              aqua:/export
```

The user was able to *cd* into the directory and list the directory contents except for the ".." entry. He was not able to execute the *pwd* command when inside the NFS directory either:

```
$ cd /packages
$ ls -la
./..: Permission denied
total 6
drwxr-xr-x   4 root     sys         512 Oct  1 12:16 ./
drwxr-xr-x   2 root     other       512 Oct  1 12:16 pkg1/
drwxr-xr-x   2 root     other       512 Oct  1 12:16 pkg2/
$ pwd
pwd: cannot determine current directory!
```

He performed the same procedure as *superuser* and noticed that it worked correctly:

```
# cd /packages
# ls -la
```

```
total 8
drwxr-xr-x    4 root      sys          512 Oct  1 12:16 .
drwxr-xr-x   38 root      root        1024 Oct  1 12:14 ..
drwxr-xr-x    2 root      other        512 Oct  1 12:16 pkg1
drwxr-xr-x    2 root      other        512 Oct  1 12:16 pkg2
# pwd
/packages
# ls -ld /packages
drwxr-xr-x    4 root      sys          512 Oct  1 12:16 /packages
```

Note that the directory permission bits for */packages* are *0755*, giving *read* and *execute* permission to everyone, in addition to write permission to root, its owner. Since the filesystem permissions were not the problem, he proceeded to analyze the network traffic, suspecting that the NFS server could be returning the "Permission denied" error. *snoop* reported two network packets when a regular user executed the *pwd* command:

```
1   0.00000      caramba -> aqua         NFS C GETATTR3 FH=0222
2   0.00050         aqua -> caramba      NFS R GETATTR3 OK
```

Packet 1 contains *caramba*'s request for attributes for the current directory having filehandle *FH=0222*. Packet 2 contains the reply from the NFS server *aqua*:

```
Excerpt of packet 2:
IP:   Source address = 131.40.52.125, aqua
IP:   Destination address = 131.40.52.223, caramba
IP:   No options
IP:

...

NFS:  ----- Sun NFS -----
NFS:
NFS:  Proc = 1 (Get file attributes)
NFS:  Status = 0 (OK)
NFS:    File type = 2 (Directory)
NFS:    Mode = 0755
NFS:      Setuid = 0, Setgid = 0, Sticky = 0
NFS:      Owner's permissions = rwx
NFS:      Group's permissions = r-x
NFS:      Other's permissions = r-x
NFS:    Link count = 4, User ID = 0, Group ID = 3
NFS:    File size = 512, Used = 1024
NFS:    Special: Major = 0, Minor = 0
NFS:    File system id = 584115552256, File id = 74979
NFS:    Last access time       = 03-Oct-00 00:41:55.160003000 GMT
NFS:    Modification time      = 01-Oct-00 19:16:32.399997000 GMT
NFS:    Attribute change time = 01-Oct-00 19:16:32.399997000 GMT
NFS:
NFS:
```

Along with other file attributes, the NFS portion of the packet contains the mode bits for *owner, group* and *other.* These mode bits were the same as those reported by the *ls -la* command, so the problem was not caused by the NFS server either.

Because this was an automounted filesystem, we suggested rebooting *caramba* in single-user mode to look at the mount point itself, before the automounter had a chance to cover it with an *autofs* filesystem. At this point, we were able to uncover the source of the problem:

```
Single-user boot:
# ls -ld /packages
drwx------   2 root      staff           512 Oct  1 12:14 /packages
```

The mount point had been created with *0700* permissions, refusing access to anyone but the *superuser.* The *0755* directory permission bits previously reported in multi-user mode were those of the NFS filesystem mounted on the */packages* mount point. The NFS filesystem mount was literally covering up the problem.

In Solaris, a lookup of ".." in the root of a filesystem results in a lookup of ".." in the mount point sitting under the filesystem. This explains why users other than the *superuser* were unable to access the ".." directory—they did not have permission to open the directory to read and traverse it. The *pwd* command failed as well when it tried to open the ".." directory in order to read the contents of the parent directory on its way to the top of the root filesystem. The misconstrued permissions of the mount point were the cause of the problem, not the permissions of the NFS filesystem covering the mount point. Changing the permissions of the mount point to *0755* fixed the problem.

Asynchronous NFS error messages

This final section provides an in-depth look at how an NFS client does write-behind, and what happens if one of the write operations fails on the remote server. It is intended as an introduction to the more complex issues of performance analysis and tuning, many of which revolve around similar subtleties in the implementation of NFS.

When an application calls *read( )* or *write( )* on a local or Unix filesystem (UFS) file, the kernel uses inode and indirect block pointers to translate the offset in the file into a physical block number on the disk. A low-level physical I/O operation, such as "write this buffer of 1024 bytes to physical blocks 5678 and 5679" is then passed to the disk device driver. The actual disk operation is scheduled, and when the disk interrupts, the driver interrupt routine notes the completion of the current operation and schedules the next. The block device driver queues the requests for the disk, possibly reordering them to minimize disk head movement.

Once the disk device driver has a read or write request, only a media failure causes the operation to return an error status. Any other failures, such as a permission problem, or the filesystem running out of space, are detected by the filesystem management routines before the disk driver gets the request. From the point of view of the *read()* and *write()* system calls, everything from the filesystem write routine down is a black box: the application isn't necessarily concerned with how the data makes it to or from the disk, as long as it does so reliably. The actual write operation occurs asynchronously to the application calling *write()*. If a media error occurs—for example, the disk has a bad sector brewing—then the media-level error will be reported back to the application during the next *write()* call or during the *close()* of the file containing the bad block. When the driver notices the error returned by the disk controller, it prints a media failure message on the console.

A similar mechanism is used by NFS to report errors on the "virtual media" of the remote fileserver. When *write()* is called on an NFS-mounted file, the data buffer and offset into the file are handed to the NFS write routine, just as a UFS write calls the lower-level disk driver write routine. Like the disk device driver, NFS has a driver routine for scheduling write requests: each new request is put into the page cache. When a full page has been written, it is handed to an NFS async thread that performs the RPC call to the remote server and returns a result code. Once the request has been written into the local page cache, the *write()* system call returns to the application—just as if the application was writing to a local disk. The actual NFS write is synchronous to the NFS async thread, allowing these threads to perform write-behind. A similar process occurs for reads, where the NFS async thread performs some read-ahead by fetching NFS buffers in anticipation of future *read()* system calls. See "Client I/O system" in Chapter 7 for details on the operation of the NFS async threads.

Occasionally, an NFS async thread detects an error when attempting to write to a remote server, and the error is printed (by the NFS async thread) on the client's console. The scenario is identical to that of a failing disk: the *write()* system call has already returned, so the error must be reported on the console in the next similar system call.

The format of these error messages is:

```
NFS write error on host mahimahi: No space left on device.
(file handle: 800006 2 a0000 3ef 12e09b14 a0000 2 4beac395)
```

The number of potential failures when writing to an NFS-mounted disk exceeds the few media-related errors that would cause a UFS write to fail. Table 15-1 gives some examples.

Table 15-1. NFS-related errors

Error	Typical Cause
Permission denied	Superuser cannot write to remote filesystem.
No space left on device	Remote disk is full.
Stale filehandle	File or directory has been removed on the server without the client's knowledge.

Both the "Permission denied" and the "No space left on device" errors would have been detected on a local filesystem, but the NFS client has no way to determine if a write operation will succeed at some future time (when the NFS async thread eventually sends it to the server). For example, if a client writes out 1KB buffers, then its NFS async threads write out 8KB buffers to the server on every 8th call to *write()*. Several seconds may go by between the time the first *write()* system call returns to the application and the time that the eighth call forces the NFS async thread to perform an RPC to the NFS server. In this interval, another process may have filled up the server's disk with some huge write requests, so the NFS async thread's attempt to write its 8-KB buffer will fail.

If you are consistently seeing NFS writes fail due to full filesystems or permission problems, you can usually chase down the user or process that is performing the writes by identifying the file being written. Unfortunately, Solaris does not provide any utility to correlate the filehandles printed in the error messages with the path-name of the file on the remote server. Filehandles are generated by the NFS server and handed opaquely to the NFS client. The NFS client cannot make any assumptions as to the structure or contents of the filehandle, enabling servers to change the way they generate the filehandle at any time. In practice, the structure of a Solaris NFS filehandle has changed little over time. The following script takes as input the filehandle printed by the NFS client and generates the corresponding server filename:*

```
 1 #!/bin/sh
 2
 3  if [ $# -ne 8 ]; then
 4            echo "Usage: fhfind <filehandle> e.g."
 5            echo
 6            echo "fhfind 1540002 2 a0000 4d 48df4455 a0000 2 25d1121d"
 7            exit 1
 8 fi
 9
10 FSID=$1
11 INUMHEX=`echo $4 | tr [a-z] [A-Z]`
12
13 ENTRY=`grep ${FSID} /etc/mnttab | grep -v lofs`
14 if [ "${ENTRY}" = "" ] ; then
15            echo "Cannot find filesystem for devid ${FSID}"
```

* Thanks to Brent Callaghan for providing the basis for this script.

```
16                exit 1
17 fi
18 set - ${ENTRY}
19  MNTPNT=$2
20
21 INUM='echo "ibase=16;${INUMHEX}" | bc'
22
23 echo "Searching ${MNTPNT} for inode number ${INUM} ..."
24 echo
25
26 find ${MNTPNT} -mount -inum ${INUM} -print 2>/dev/null
```

The script takes the expanded filehandle string from the NFS write error and maps it to the full pathname of the file on the server. The script is to be executed on the NFS server:

```
mahimahi# fhfind 800006 2 a0000 3ef 12e09b14 a0000 2 4beac395
Searching /spare for inode number 1007 ...

/spare/test/info/data
```

The eight values on the command line are the eight hex digits in the filehandle reported in the NFS error message. The script makes strict assumptions about the contents of the Solaris server filehandle. As mentioned before, the OS vendor is free to change the structure of the filehandle at any time, so there's no guarantee this script will work on your particular configuration. The script takes advantage of the fact that the filehandle contains the inode number of the file in question, as well as the device id of the filesystem in which the file resides. The script uses the device id in the filehandle (*FSID* in line 10) to obtain the filesystem entry from */etc/mnttab* (line 13). In line 11, the script obtains the inode number of the file (in hex) from the filehandle, and applies the *tr* utility to convert all lowercase characters into uppercase characters for use with the *bc* calculator. Line 18 and 19 extract the mount point from the filesystem entry, to later use it as the starting point of the search. Line 21 takes the hexadecimal inode number obtained from the filehandle, and converts it to its decimal equivalent for use by *find*. In line 26, we finally begin the search for the file matching the inode number. Although *find* uses the mount point as the starting point of the search, a scan of a large filesystem may take a long time. Since there's no way to terminate the *find* upon finding the file, you may want to kill the process after it prints the path.

Throughout this chapter, we used tools presented in previous chapters to debug network and local problems. Once you determine the source of the problem, you should be able to take steps to correct and avoid it. For example, you can avoid delayed client write problems by having a good idea of what your clients are doing and how heavily loaded your NFS servers are. Determining your NFS workload and optimizing your clients and servers to make the best use of available resources requires tuning the network, the clients, and the servers. The next few chapters present NFS tuning and benchmarking techniques.

16

Server-Side Performance Tuning

Performance analysis and tuning, particularly when it involves NFS and NIS, is a topic subject to heated debate. The focus of the next three chapters is on the analysis techniques and configuration options used to identify performance bottlenecks and improve overall system response time. Tuning a network and its servers is similar to optimizing a piece of user-written code. Finding the obvious flaws and correcting poor programming habits generally leads to marked improvements in performance. Similarly, there is a definite and noticeable difference between networked systems with abysmal performance and those that run reasonably well; those with poor response generally suffer from "poor habits" in network resource use or configuration. It's easy to justify spending the time to eliminate major flaws when the return on your time investment is so large.

However, all tuning processes are subject to a law of diminishing returns. Getting the last 5–10% out of an application usually means hand-rolling loops or reading assembly language listings. Fine-tuning a network server to an "optimum" configuration may yield that last bit of performance, but the next network change or new client added to the system may make performance of the finely tuned system worse than that of an untuned system. If other aspects of the computing environment are neglected as a result of the incremental server tuning, then the benefits of fine-tuning certainly do not justify its costs.

Our approach will be to make things "close enough for jazz." Folklore has it that jazz musicians take their instruments from their cases, and if all of the keys, strings, and valves look functional, they start playing music. Fine-tuning instruments is frowned upon, especially when the ambient street noise masks its effects. Simply ensuring that network and server performance are acceptable—and remain consistently acceptable in the face of network changes—is often a realistic goal for the tuning process.

As a network manager, you are also faced with the task of balancing the demands of individual users against the global constraints of the network and its resources. Users have a local view: they always want their machines to run faster, but the global view of the system administrator must be to tune the network to meet the aggregate demands of all users. There are no constraints in NFS or NIS that keep a client from using more than its fair share of network resources, so NFS and NIS tuning requires that you optimize both the servers and the ways in which the clients use these servers.[*]

Characterization of NFS behavior

You must be able to characterize the demands placed on your servers as well as available configuration options before starting the tuning process. You'll need to know the quantities that you can adjust, and the mechanisms used to measure the success of any particular change. Above all else, it helps to understand the general behavior of a facility before you begin to measure it. In the first part of this book, we have examined individual NFS and NIS requests, but haven't really looked at how they are generated in "live" environments.

NFS requests exhibit randomness in two ways: they are typically generated in bursts, and the types of requests in each burst usually don't have anything to do with each other. It is very rare to have a steady, equally spaced stream of requests arriving at any server. The typical NFS request generation pattern involves a burst of requests as a user loads an application from an NFS server into memory or when the application reads or writes a file. These bursts are followed by quiet periods when the user is editing, thinking, or eating lunch. In addition, the requests from one client are rarely coordinated with those from another; one user may be reading mail while another is building software. Consecutive NFS requests received by a server are likely to perform different functions on different parts of one or more disks.

NFS traffic volumes also vary somewhat predictably over the course of a day. In the early morning, many users read their mail, placing a heavier load on a central mail server; at the end of the day most file servers will be loaded as users wrap up their work for the day and write out modified files. Perhaps the most obvious case of time-dependent server usage is a student lab. The hours after class and after dinner are likely to be the busiest for the lab servers, since that's when most people gravitate toward the lab.

---

[*] Add-on products such as the Solaris Bandwidth Manager allow you to specify the amount of network bandwidth on specified ports, allowing you to restrict the amount of network resources used by NFS. The *Sun BluePrints Resource Management* book published by Sun Microsystems Press provides good information on the Solaris Bandwidth Manager.

Simply knowing the sheer volume of requests won't help you characterize your NFS work load. It's easy to provide "tremendous" NFS performance if only a few requests require disk accesses. Requests vary greatly in the server resources they need to be completed. "Big" RPC requests force the server to read or write from disk. In addition to the obvious NFS read and write requests, some symbolic link resolutions require reading information from disk. "Small" NFS RPC requests simply touch file attribute information, or the directory name look-up cache, and can usually be satisfied without a disk access if the server has previously cached the attribute information.

The average percentage of all RPC calls of each type is the "NFS RPC mixture," and it defines the *kind* of work the server is being asked to do, as opposed to simply the volume of work presented to it. The RPC mixture indicates possible areas of improvement, or flags obvious bottlenecks. It is important to determine if your environment is data- or attribute-intensive, since this will likely dictate the network utilization and the type of tuning required on the client and server.

A data-intensive environment is one in which large file transfers dominate the NFS traffic. Transfers are considered large if the size of the files is over 100 MB. Examples of these environments include computer aided design and image processing. An attribute-intensive environment, on the other hand, is dominated by small file and meta-data access. The NFS clients mostly generate traffic to obtain directory contents, file attributes, and the data contents of small files. For example, in a software development environment, engineers edit relatively small source files, header files, and makefiles. The compilation and linkage process involves a large number of attribute checks that verify the modification time of the files to decide when new object files need to be rebuilt, resulting in multiple frequent small file reads and writes. Because of their nature, attribute-intensive environments will benefit greatly from aggressive caching of name-lookup information on the server, and a reduced network collision rate. On the other hand, a high-bandwidth network and a fast server with fast disks will most benefit data-intensive applications due to their dependence on data access. Studies have shown that most environments are attribute intensive. Once you have characterized your NFS workload, you will need to know how to measure server performance as seen by NFS clients.

Measuring performance

The NFS RPC mixture is useful for tuning the server to handle the load placed on it, but the real measure of success is whether the clients see a faster server or not. Users may still get "server not responding" messages after some bottlenecks are eliminated because you haven't removed all of the constraints, or because something other than the server is causing performance problems.

Measuring the success of a tuning effort requires you to measure the average response time as seen by an average client. There are two schools of thought on how to determine this threshold for this value:

- Use an absolute value for the "threshold of pain" in average server response time. The system begins to appear sluggish as response time approaches 40 milliseconds. As of this writing, typical NFS servers are capable of providing response times well below this threshold, in the range of one to ten milliseconds, and they keep getting faster.

- Base the threshold on the performance of the server with a minimal load, such as only one client. When the server's performance exceeds twice this "ideal" response time, the server has become loaded.

It's easy to measure the average server response time on a client by dividing the number of NFS RPC calls made by the time in which they were completed. Use the *nfsstat* utility to track the number of NFS calls, and a clock or the Unix *time* command to measure the elapsed time in a benchmark or network observation. Obviously, this must be done over a short, well-monitored period of time when the client is generating NFS requests nearly continuously. Any gap in the NFS requests will increase the average server response time. You can also use NFS benchmark traffic generators such as the *SPEC* SFS97* RPC-generating benchmark, or review the smoothed response times recorded by some versions of *nfsstat -m*.

You'll get different average response times for different RPC mixtures, since disk-intensive client activity is likely to raise the average response time. However, it is the *average* response that matters most. The first request may always take a little longer, as caches get flushed and the server begins fetching data from a new part of the disk. Over time, these initial bumps may be smoothed out, although applications with very poor locality of reference may suffer more of them. You must take the average over the full range of RPC operations, and measure response over a long enough period of time to iron out any short-term fluctuations.

Users are most sensitive to the sum of response times for all requests in an operation. One or two slow responses may not be noticed in the sequence of an operation with several hundred NFS requests, but a train of requests with long response times will produce complaints of system sluggishness.

An NFS server must be able to handle the traffic bursts without a prolonged increase in response time. The randomness of the NFS requests modulates the server's response time curve, subject to various constraints on the server. Disk

---

* The Standard Performance Evaluation Corporation (*http://www.spec.org*) mission is to "establish, maintain, and endorse a standardized set of relevant benchmarks and metrics for performance evaluation of modern computer systems."

bandwidth and CPU scheduling constraints can increase the time required for the server's response time to return to its average value.

Ideally, the average response time curve should remain relatively "flat" as the number of NFS requests increases. During bursts of NFS activity, the server's response time may increase, but it should return to the average level quickly. If a server requires a relatively long time to recover from the burst, then its average response time will remain inflated even when the level of activity subsides. During this period of increased response time, some clients may experience RPC time-outs, and retransmit their requests. This additional load increases the server's response time again, increasing the total burst recovery time.

NFS performance does not scale linearly above the point at which a system constraint is hit. The NFS retransmission algorithm introduces positive feedback when the server just can't keep up with the request arrival rate. As the average response time increases, the server becomes even more loaded from retransmitted requests. A slow server removes some of the random elements from the network: the server's clients that are retransmitting requests generate them with a fairly uniform distribution; the clients fall into lock step waiting for the server, and the server itself becomes saturated. Tuning a server and its clients should move the "knee" of the performance curve out as far as possible, as shown in Figure 16-1.

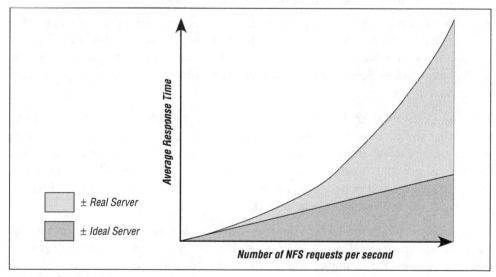

Figure 16-1. Ideal versus actual server response

Knowing what to measure and how to measure it lets you evaluate the relative success of your tuning efforts, and provides valuable data for evaluating NFS server benchmarks.

Benchmarking

Benchmarks of NFS performance should be judged in terms of their realistic repro-
duction of the NFS call arrival rates and RPC distribution. A benchmark that sends
out a steady, regularly spaced stream of NFS requests tests only how well a server
operates under ideal conditions. If you can't run actual client workloads on a network, there are a few conditions to be aware of:

- Ensure that the RPC mixture of the benchmark matches that of your NFS clients. Running a benchmark that does a large percentage of write operations
  tells you little about how NFS servers perform if your clients mostly read files.
  Conversely, if you have a large percentage of write operations, the wrong
  benchmark RPC mixture overstates expected server performance. Use the
  nfsstat tool to determine accurate RPC mixtures for your servers. You may
  want to run several benchmarks, testing performance with client loads simu-
  lating normal and heavy conditions. The SPEC website, *http://www.spec.org,*
  contains information about the *SFS97* RPC-generating benchmark, which is
  widely used by NFS vendors to compare their servers to one another.

- Watch out for cache effects. Clients cache parts of files that have been recently
  read and not modified. Repeatedly reading the same file may only generate a
  fraction of the desired number of *read* RPC requests.

- When gauging a particular limit, such as the maximum number of short RPCs
  or the maximum NFS disk transfer rate, try to isolate the quantity under test as
  much as possible. Stress testing is often useful for determining a server's
  behavior under severe loads, but it helps to stress only one component at a
  time.

The last point rings of Heisenberg's Uncertainty Principle. In short, Heisenberg
stated that the process of observing something changes it. A goal of NFS performance measurement should be to change the actual performance being measured
as little as possible. Using networked measurement tools that add to the traffic
level on a congested network, or running suites of utilities that drain the server's
CPU, color the results of any benchmarks.

When benchmarking a network router or gateway, ensure that you are measuring
the desired capacity and not another constraint. To determine maximum IP packet
forwarding rates, for example, you should put a packet generator on one side of
the router and a packet counting device such as a LAN analyzer on the other.
Timing *rpc* transfers of large files through the router gives a fair indication of maximum disk transfer rates or maximum network data transfer rates, but tells you
little about the router's network interface because the packets forwarded are not
"typical" in size.

The goal of the next section is to indicate the common areas in which performance bottlenecks are created. The remainder of this chapter covers techniques for relaxing these constraints on the server as much as possible. The majority of the following discussion concerns NFS, although NIS-specific topics will be introduced where applicable.

Identifying NFS performance bottlenecks

The stateless design of NFS makes crash recovery simple, but it also makes it impossible for a client to distinguish between a server that is slow and one that has crashed. In either case, the client does not receive an RPC reply before the RPC timeout period expires. Clients can't tell why a server appears slow, either: packets could be dropped by the network and never reach the server, or the server could simply be overloaded. Using NFS performance figures alone, it is hard to distinguish a slow server from an unreliable network. Users complain that "the system is slow," but there are several areas that contribute to system sluggishness.

An overloaded server responds to all packets that it enqueues for its *nfsd* daemons, perhaps dropping some incoming packets due to the high load. Those requests that are received generate a response, albeit a response that arrives sometime after the client has retransmitted the request. If the network itself is to blame, then packets may not make it from the client or server onto the wire, or they may vanish in transit between the two hosts.

Problem areas

The potential bottlenecks in the client-server relationship are:

Client network interface
> The client may not be able to transmit or receive packets due to hardware or configuration problems at its network interface. We will explore client-side bottlenecks in Chapter 18.

Network bandwidth
> An overly congested network slows down both client transmissions and server replies. Network partitioning hardware installed to reduce network saturation adds delays to roundtrip times, increasing the effective time required to complete an RPC call. If the delays caused by network congestion are serious, they contribute to RPC timeouts. We explore network bottlenecks in detail in Chapter 17.

Server network interface
> A busy server may be so flooded with packets that it cannot receive all of them, or it cannot queue the incoming requests in a protocol-specific structure

once the network interface receives the packet. Interrupt handling limitations can also impact the ability of the server to pull packets in from the network.

Server CPU loading

NFS is rarely CPU-constrained. Once a server has an NFS request, it has to schedule an *nfsd* thread to have the appropriate operation performed. If the server has adequate CPU cycles, then the CPU does not affect server performance. However, if the server has few free CPU cycles, then scheduling latencies may limit NFS performance; conversely a system that is providing its maximum NFS service will not make a good CPU server. CPU loading also affects NIS performance, since a heavily loaded system is slower to perform NIS map lookups in response to client requests.

Server memory usage

NFS performance is somewhat related to the size of the server's memory, if the server is doing nothing but NFS. NFS will use either the local disk buffer cache (in systems that do not have a page-mapped VM system) or free memory to cache disk pages that have recently been read from disk. Running large processes on an NFS server hurts NFS performance. As a server runs out of memory and begins paging, its performance as either an NIS or NFS server suffers. Disk bandwidth is wasted in a system that is paging local applications, consumed by page fault handling rather than NFS requests.

Server disk bandwidth

This area is the most common bottleneck: the server simply cannot get data to or from the disks quickly enough. NFS requests tend to be random in nature, exhibiting little locality of reference for a particular disk. Many clients mounting filesystems from a server increase the degree of randomness in the system. Furthermore, NFS is stateless, so NFS Version 2 write operations on the server must be committed to disk before the client is notified that the RPC call completed. This synchronous nature of NFS write operations further impairs performance, since caching and disk controller ordering will not be utilized to their fullest extent. NFS Version 3 eases this constraint with the use of safe asynchronous writes, which are described in detail in the next section.

Configuration effects

Loosely grouped in this category are constrictive server kernel configurations, poor disk balancing, and inefficient mount point naming schemes. With poor configurations, all services operate properly but inefficiently.

Throughput

The next two sections summarize NFS throughput issues.

NFS writes (NFS Version 2 versus NFS Version 3)

Write operations over NFS Version 2 are synchronous, forcing servers to flush data to disk* before a reply to the NFS client can be generated. This severely limits the speed at which synchronous write requests can be generated by the NFS client, since it has to wait for acknowledgment from the server before it can generate the next request. NFS Version 3 overcomes this limitation by introducing a two-phased commit write operation. The NFS Version 3 client generates asynchronous write requests, allowing the server to acknowledge the requests without requiring it to flush the data to disk. This results in a reduction of the round-trip time between the client and server, allowing requests to be sent more quickly. Since the server no longer flushes the data to disk before it replies, the data may be lost if the server crashes or reboots unexpectedly. The NFS Version 3 client assumes the responsibility of recovering from these conditions by caching a copy of the data. The client must first issue a commit operation for the data to the server before it can flush its cached copy of the data. In response to the commit request, the server either ensures the data has been written to disk and responds affirmatively, or in the case of a crash, responds with an error causing the client to synchronously retransmit the cached copy of the data to the server. In short, the client is still responsible for holding on to the data until it receives acknowledgment from the server indicating that the data has been flushed to disk.

For all practical purposes, the NFS Version 3 protocol removes any limitations on the size of the data block that can be transmitted, although the data block size may still be limited by the underlying transport. Most NFS Version 3 implementations use a 32 KB data block size. The larger NFS writes reduce protocol overhead and disk seek time, resulting in much higher sequential file access.

NFS/TCP versus NFS/UDP

TCP handles retransmissions and flow control for NFS, requiring only individual packets to be retransmitted in case of loss, and making NFS practical over lossy and wide area network practical. In contrast, UDP requires the whole NFS operation to be retransmitted if one or more packets is lost, making it impractical over lossy networks. TCP allows read and write operations to be increased from 8 KB to 32 KB. By default, Solaris clients will attempt to mount NFS filesystems using NFS Version 3 over TCP when supported by the server. Note that workloads that mainly access attributes or consist of short reads will benefit less from the larger transfer size, and as such you may want to reduce the default read size block by using the *rsize=n* option of the *mount* command. This is explored in more detail in Chapter 18.

---

* The effect of NVRAM is discussed in "Disk array caching and Prestoserve" later in this chapter.

Locating bottlenecks

Given all of the areas in which NFS can break down, it is hard to pick a starting point for performance analysis. Inspecting server behavior, for example, may not tell you anything if the network is overly congested or dropping packets. One approach is to start with a typical NFS client, and evaluate its view of the network's services. Tools that examine the local network interface, the network load perceived by the client, and NFS timeout and retransmission statistics indicate whether the bulk of your performance problems are due to the network or the NFS servers.

In this and the next two chapters, we look at performance problems from excessive server loading to network congestion, and offer suggestions for easing constraints at each of the problem areas outlined above. However, you may want to get a rough idea of whether your NFS servers or your network is the biggest contributor to performance problems before walking through all diagnostic steps. On a typical NFS client, use the *nfsstat* tool to compare the retransmission and duplicate reply rates:

```
% nfsstat -rc
Client rpc:
Connection oriented:
calls       badcalls    badxids     timeouts    newcreds    badverfs
1753584     1412        18          64          0           0
timers      cantconn    nomem       interrupts
0           1317        0           18
Connectionless:
calls       badcalls    retrans     badxids     timeouts    newcreds
12443       41          334         80          166         0
badverfs    timers      nomem       cantsend
0           4321        0           206
```

The *timeout* value indicates the number of NFS RPC calls that did not complete within the RPC timeout period. Divide *timeout* by *calls* to determine the *retransmission rate* for this client. We'll look at an equation for calculating the maximum allowable retransmission rate on each client in "Retransmission rate thresholds" in Chapter 18.

If the client-side RPC counts for *timeout* and *badxid* are close in value, the network is healthy. Requests are making it to the server but the server cannot handle them and generate replies before the client's RPC call times out. The server eventually works its way through the backlog of requests, generating duplicate replies that increment the *badxid* count. In this case, the emphasis should be on improving server response time.

Alternatively, *nfsstat* may show that *timeout* is large while *badxid* is zero or negligible. In this case, packets are never making it to the server, and the network interfaces of client and server, as well as the network itself, should be examined. NFS does not query the lower protocol layers to determine where packets are being consumed; to NFS the entire RPC and transport mechanisms are a black box. Note that NFS is like *spray* in this regard—it doesn't matter whether it's the local host's interface, network congestion, or the remote host's interface that dropped the packet—the packets are simply lost. To eliminate all network-related effects, you must examine each of these areas.

Server tuning

If the server is not able to field new requests or efficiently schedule and handle those that it does receive, then overall performance suffers. In some cases, the only way to rectify the problem is to add a new server or upgrade existing hardware. However, identification of the problem areas should be a prerequisite for any hardware changes, and some analyses may point to software configuration changes that provide sufficient relief. The first area to examine is the server's CPU utilization.

CPU loading

The CPU speed of a pure NFS server is rarely a constraining factor. Once the *nfsd* thread gets scheduled, and has read and decoded an RPC request, it doesn't do much more within the NFS protocol that requires CPU cycles. Other parts of the system, such as the Unix filesystem and cache management code, may use CPU cycles to perform work given to them by NFS requests. NFS usually poses a light load on a server that is providing pure NFS service. However, very few servers are used solely for NFS service. More common is a central server that performs mail spool and delivery functions, serves telnet, and provides NFS file service.

There are two aspects to CPU loading: increased *nfsd* thread scheduling latency, and decreased performance of server-resident, CPU-bound processes. Normally, the *nfsd* threads will run as soon as a request arrives, because they are running with a kernel process priority that is higher than that of all user processes. However, if there are other processes doing I/O, or running in the kernel (doing system calls) the latency to schedule the *nfsd* threads is increased. Instead of getting the CPU as soon as a request arrives, the *nfsd* thread must wait until the next context switch, when the process with the CPU uses up its time slice or goes to sleep. Running an excessive number of interactive processes on an NFS server will generate enough I/O activity to impact NFS performance. These loads affect a server's ability to schedule its *nfsd* threads; latency in scheduling the threads translates into decreased NFS request handling capacity since the *nfsd* threads cannot accept incoming requests as quickly. Systems with more than one CPU have additional horse-power to schedule and run its applications and *nfsd* threads. Many

SMP NFS servers scale very well as CPUs are added to the configuration. In many cases doubling the number of CPUs nearly doubles the maximum throughput provided by the NFS server.

The other aspect of CPU loading is the effect of *nfsd* threads on other user-level processes. The *nfsd* threads run entirely in the kernel, and therefore they run at a higher priority than other user-level processes. *nfsd* threads take priority over other user-level processes, so CPU cycles spent on NFS activity are taken away from user processes. If you are running CPU-bound (computational) processes on your NFS servers, they will not impact NFS performance. Instead, handling NFS requests cripples the performance of the CPU-bound processes, since the *nfsd* threads always get the CPU before they do.

CPU loading is easy to gauge using any number of utilities that read the CPU utilization figures from the kernel. *vmstat* is one of the simplest tools that breaks CPU usage into user, system, and idle time components:

```
% vmstat 10
 procs     memory            page            disk          faults      cpu
 r b w   swap  free  re  mf pi po fr de sr dd f0 s0 --   in   sy   cs us sy id
...Ignore first line of output
 0 0 34 667928 295816 0   0  0  0  0  0  0  1  0  0  0  174  126   73  0  1 99
```

The last three columns show where the CPU cycles are expended. If the server is CPU bound, the *idle* time decreases to zero. When *nfsd* threads are waiting for disk operations to complete, and there is no other system activity, the CPU is idle, not accumulating cycles in *system* mode. The *system* column shows the amount of time spent executing system code, exclusive of time waiting for disks or other devices. If the NFS server has very little (less than 10%) CPU idle time, consider adding CPUs, upgrading to a faster server, or moving some CPU-bound processes off of the NFS server.

The "pureness" of NFS service provided by a machine and the type of other work done by the CPU determines how much of an impact CPU loading has on its NFS response time. A machine used for print spooling, hardwire terminal server, or modem line connections, for example, is forced to handle large numbers of high-priority interrupts from the serial line controllers. If there is a sufficient level of high-priority activity, the server may miss incoming network traffic. Use *iostat*, *vmstat*, or similar tools to watch for large numbers of interrupts. Every interrupt requires CPU time to service it, and takes away from the CPU availability for NFS.

If an NFS server must be used as a home for terminals, consider using a networked terminal server instead of hardwired terminals.* The largest advantage of

---

* A terminal server has RS-232 ports for terminal connections and runs a simple ROM monitor that connects terminal ports to servers over *telnet* sessions. Terminal servers vary significantly: some use RS-232 DB-25 connectors, while others have RJ-11 phone jacks with a variable number of ports.

terminal servers is that they can accept terminal output in large buffers. Instead of writing a screenful of output a character at a time over a serial line, a host writing to a terminal on a terminal server sends it one or two packets containing all of the output. Streamlining the terminal and NFS input and output sources places an additional load on the server's network interface and on the network itself. These factors must be considered when planning or expanding the base of terminal service.

Along these lines, NFS servers do not necessarily make the best gateway hosts. Each fraction of its network bandwidth that is devoted to forwarding packets or converting protocols is taken away from NFS service. If an NFS server is used as a router between two or more networks, it is possible that the non-NFS traffic occludes the NFS packets. The actual performance effects, if any, will be determined by the bandwidth of the server's network interfaces and other CPU loading factors.

NFS server threads

The default number of *nfsd* threads is chosen empirically by the system vendor, and provides average performance under average conditions. The number of threads is specified as an argument to the *nfsd* daemon when it is started from the boot scripts:

```
/usr/lib/nfs/nfsd -a 16
```

This example starts 16 kernel *nfsd* threads.

In Solaris, the *nfsd* daemon creates multiple kernel threads that perform the actual filesystem operations. It exists as a user-level process in order to establish new connections to clients, allowing a server to accept more NFS requests while other *nfsd* threads are waiting for a disk operation to complete. Increasing the number of server-side threads improves NFS performance by allowing the server to grab incoming requests more quickly. Increasing *nfsd* threads without bound can adversely affect other system resources by dedicating excessive compute resources to NFS, making the optimal choice an exercise in observation and tuning.

Context switching overhead

All *nfsd* threads run in the kernel and do not context switch in the same way as user-level processes do. The two major costs associated with a context switch are loading the address translation cache and resuming the newly scheduled task on the CPU. In the case of NFS server threads, both of these costs are near zero. All of the NFS server code lives in the kernel, and therefore has no user-level address translations loaded in the memory management unit. In addition, the task-to-task switch code in most kernels is on the order of a few hundred instructions. Systems can context switch much faster than the network can deliver NFS requests.

NFS server threads don't impose the "usual" context switching load on a system because all of the NFS server code is in the kernel. Instead of using a per-process context descriptor or a user-level process "slot" in the memory management unit, the *nfsd* threads use the kernel's address space mappings. This eliminates the address translation loading cost of a context switch.

Choosing the number of server threads

The maximum number of server threads can be specified as a parameter to the *nfsd* daemon:

```
# /usr/lib/nfs/nfsd -a 16
```

The *-a* directive indicates that the daemon should listen on all available transports. In this example the daemon allows a maximum of 16 NFS requests to be serviced concurrently. The *nfsd* threads are created on demand, so you are only setting a high water mark, not the actual number of threads. If you configure too many threads, the unused threads will not be created. You can throttle NFS server usage by limiting the maximum number of *nfsd* threads, allowing the NFS server to concentrate on performing other tasks.

It is hard to come up with a magic formula to compute the ideal number of *nfsd* threads, since hardware and NFS implementations vary considerably between vendors. For example, at the time of this writing, Sun servers are recommended[*] to use the maximum of:

- 2 *nfsd* threads for each active client process
- 16 to 32 *nfsd* threads for each CPU
- 16 *nfsd* threads per 10Mb network or 160 per 100Mb network

Memory usage

NFS uses the server's page cache (in SunOS 4.x, Solaris and System V Release 4) for file blocks read in NFS *read* requests. Because these systems implement page mapping, the NFS server will use available page frames to cache file pages, and use the buffer cache[†] to store UFS inode and file metadata (direct and indirect blocks).

---

[*] Refer to the *Solaris 8 NFS Server Performance and Tuning Guide for Sun Hardware* (February 2000).

[†] In Solaris, SunOS 4.x, and SVR4, the buffer cache stores only UFS metadata. This in contrast to the "traditional" buffer cache used by other Unix systems, where file data is also stored in the buffer cache. The Solaris buffer cache consists of disk blocks full of inodes, indirect blocks, and cylinder group information only.

In Solaris, you can view the buffer cache statistics by using *sar -b*. This will show you the number of data transfers per second between system buffers and disk (*bread/s* & *bwrite/s*), the number of accesses to the system buffers (logical reads and writes identified by *lread/s* & *lwrit/s*), the cache hit ratios (*%rcache* & *%wcache*), and the number of physical reads and writes using the raw device mechanism (*pread/s* & *pwrit/s*):

```
# sar -b 20 5
SunOS bunker 5.8 Generic sun4u    12/06/2000

10:39:01 bread/s lread/s %rcache bwrit/s lwrit/s %wcache pread/s pwrit/s
10:39:22      19     252      93      34     103      67       0       0
10:39:43      21     612      97      46     314      85       0       0
10:40:03      20     430      95      35     219      84       0       0
10:40:24      35     737      95      49     323      85       0       0
10:40:45      21     701      97      60     389      85       0       0

Average       23     546      96      45     270      83       0       0
```

In practice, a cache hit ratio of 100% is hard to achieve due to lack of access locality by the NFS clients, consequently a cache hit ratio of around 90% is considered acceptable. By default, Solaris grows the dynamically sized buffer cache, as needed, until it reaches a high watermark specified by the *bufhwm* kernel parameter. By default, Solaris limits this value to 2% of physical memory in the system. In most cases, this 2%[*] ceiling is more than enough since the buffer cache is only used to cache inode and metadata information. You can use the *sysdef* command to view its value:

```
# sysdef
...
*
* Tunable Parameters
*
41385984   maximum memory allowed in buffer cache (bufhwm)
...
```

If you need to modify the default value of *bufhwm*, set its new value in */etc/ system*, or use *adb* as described in Chapter 15.

The actual file contents are cached in the page cache, and by default the filesystem will cache as many pages as possible. There is no high watermark, potentially causing the page cache to grow and consume all available memory. This means that all process memory that has not been used recently by local applications may be reclaimed for use by the filesystem page cache, possibly causing local processes to page excessively.

---

[*] 2% of total memory can be too much buffer cache for some systems, such as the Sun Sparc Center 2000 with very large memory configurations. You may need to reduce the size of the buffer cache to avoid starving the kernel of memory resources, since the kernel address space is limited on Super Sparc-based systems. The newer Ultra Sparc-based systems do not suffer from this limitation.

If the server is used for non-NFS purposes, enable priority paging to ensure that it has enough memory to run all of its processes without paging. Priority paging prevents the filesystem from consuming excessive memory by limiting the file cache so that filesystem I/O does not cause unnecessary paging of applications. The filesystem can still grow to use free memory, but cannot take memory from other applications on the system. Enable priority paging by adding the following line to */etc/system* and reboot:

```
*
* Enable Priority Paging
*
set priority_paging=1
```

Priority paging can also be enabled on a live system. Refer to the excellent *Solaris Internals* book written by Mauro and McDougall and published by Sun Microsystems Press for an in-depth explanation of Priority Paging and File System Caching in Solaris. The following procedure for enabling priority paging on a live 64-bit system originally appeared on their book:

```
# adb -kw /dev/ksyms /dev/mem
physmem         3ac8
lotsfree/E
lotsfree:
lotsfree:       234              /* value of lotsfree is printed */
cachefree/Z 0t468                /* set to twice the value of lotsfree */
cachefree:      ea   = 1d4
dyncachefree/Z 0t468             /* set to twice the value of lotsfree */
dyncachefree:   ea   = 1d4
cachefree/E
cachefree:
cachefree:      468
dyncachefree/E
dyncachefree:
dyncachefree:   468
```

Setting *priority_paging=1* in */etc/system* causes a new memory tunable, *cachefree*, to be set to twice the old paging high watermark, *lotsfree*, when the system boots. The previous *adb* procedure does the equivalent work on a live system. *cachefree* scales proportionally to other memory parameters used by the Solaris Virtual Memory System. Again, refer to the *Solaris Internals* book for an in-depth explanation. The same *adb* procedure can be performed on a 32-bit system by replacing the */E* directives with */D* to print the value of a 32-bit quantity and */Z* with */W* to set the value of the 32-bit quantity.

Disk and filesystem throughput

For NFS requests requiring disk access, the constraining performance factor can often be the server's ability to turn around disk requests. A well-conditioned network feels sluggish if the file server is not capable of handling the load placed on it. While there are both network and client-side NFS parameters that may be tuned, optimizing the server's use of its disks and filesystems can deliver large benefit. Efficiency in accessing the disks, adequate kernel table sizes, and an equitable distribution of requests over all disks providing NFS service determine the round-trip filesystem delay.

A basic argument about NFS performance centers on the overhead imposed by the network when reading or writing to a remote disk. If identical disks are available on a remote server and on the local host, total disk throughput will be better with the local disk. This is not grounds for an out-of-hand rejection of NFS for two reasons: NFS provides a measure of transparency and ease of system administration that is lost with multiple local disks, and centralized disk resources on a server take advantage of economies of scale. A large, fast disk or disk array on a server provides better throughput, with the network overhead, than a slower local disk if the decrease in disk access time outweighs the cost of the network data transfer.

Unix filesystem effects

NFS Version 2 write operations are not often able to take advantage of disk controller optimizations or caching when multiple clients write to different areas on the same disk. Many controllers use an elevator-seek algorithm to schedule disk operations according to the disk track number accessed, minimizing seek time. These optimizations are of little value if the disk request queue is never more than one or two operations deep. Read operations suffer from similar problems because read-ahead caching done by the controller is wasted if consecutive read operations are from different clients using different parts of the disk. NFS Version 3 enables the server to take better advantage of controller optimizations through the use of the two-phase commit write.

Writing large files multiplies the number of NFS write operations that must be performed. As a file grows beyond the number of blocks described in its inode, indirect and double indirect blocks are used to point to additional arrays of data blocks. A file that has grown to several megabytes, for example, requires three write operations to update its indirect, double indirect, and data blocks on each write operation. The design of the Unix filesystem is ideal for small files, but imposes a penalty on large files.

Large directories also adversely impact NFS performance. Directories are searched linearly during an NFS *lookup* operation; the time to locate a named directory component is directly proportional to the size of the directory and the position of a name in the directory. Doubling the number of entries in a directory will, on average, double the time required to locate any given entry. Furthermore, reading a large directory from a remote host may require the server to respond with several packets instead of a single packet containing the entire directory structure.

Disk array caching and Prestoserve

As described in "NFS writes (NFS Version 2 versus NFS Version 3)," synchronous NFS Version 2 writes are slow because the server needs to flush the data to disk before an acknowledgment to the client can be generated. One way of speeding up the disk access is by using host-based fast nonvolatile memory. This battery-backed nonvolatile memory serves as temporary cache for the data before it is written to the disk. The server can acknowledge the write request as soon as the request is placed in the cache, since the cache is considered permanent storage (since it's memory-backed and it can survive reboots). Examples of host-based accelerators include the *Sun StorEdge Fast Write Cache* product from Sun Microsystems, Inc., and the *Prestoserve* board from Legato Systems, Inc. They both intercept the synchronous filesystem write operations to later flush the data to the disk drive; significantly improving synchronous filesystem write performance.

Newer disk array systems provide similar benefits by placing the data written in the disk array's NVRAM before the data is written to the actual disk platters. In addition, disk arrays provide extra features that increase data availability through the use of mirroring and parity bits, and increased throughput through the use of striping. There are many good books describing the Berkeley RAID[*] concepts. Refer to Brian Wong's *Configuration and Capacity Planning for Solaris Servers* book, published by Sun Microsystems Press, for a thorough description of disk array caching and *Prestoserve* boards in the Sun architecture.

Disk load balancing

If you have one or more "hot" disks that receive an unequal share of requests, your NFS performance suffers. To keep requests in fairly even queues, you must balance your NFS load across your disks.

Server response time is improved by balancing the load among all disks and minimizing the average waiting time for disk service. Disk balancing entails putting heavily used filesystems on separate disks so that requests for them may be serviced in parallel. This division of labor is particularly important for diskless client servers. If all clients have their root and swap filesystems on a single disk, requests using that disk may far outnumber those using any other on the server. Performance of each diskless client is degraded, as the single path to the target disk is a bottleneck. Dividing client partitions among several disks improves the overall throughput of the client root and swap filesystem requests.

---

[*] RAID stands for Redundant Array of Inexpensive Disks. Researchers at Berkeley defined different types of RAID configurations, where lots of small disks are used in place of a very large disk. The various configurations provide the means of combining disks to distribute data among many disks (striping), provide higher data availability (mirroring), and provide partial data loss recovery (with parity computation).

The average waiting time endured by each request is a function of the random disk transfer rate and of the backlog of requests for that disk. Use the *iostat -D* utility to check the utilization of each disk, and look for imbalance in the disk queues. The *rps* and *wps* values are the number of read and write operations, per second, performed on each disk device, and the *util* column shows the utilization of the disk's bandwidth:

```
% iostat -D 5
      md10            md11            md12            md13
rps wps util   rps wps util   rps wps util   rps wps util
 17  45 33.7     5   4 10.5     3   3  7.5     5   5 11.6
  1   5  6.1    17  20 43.7     1   1  2.0     1   0  1.1
  2   7 10.4    14  22 42.0     0   0  0.7     0   1  2.3
```

If the disk queues are grossly uneven, consider shuffling data on the filesystems to spread the load across more disks. Most medium to large servers take advantage of their disk storage array volume managers to provide some flavor of RAID to stripe data among multiple disks.

If all of your disks are more than 75–80% utilized, you are disk bound and either need faster disks, more disks, or an environment that makes fewer disk requests. Tuning kernel and client configurations usually helps to reduce the number of disk requests made by NFS clients.

Kernel configuration

A significant amount of NFS requests require only information in the underlying inode for a file, rather than access to the data blocks composing the file. A bottleneck can be introduced in the inode table, which serves as a cache for recently opened files. If file references from NFS clients frequently require reloading entries in the inode table, then the file server is forced to perform expensive linear searches through disk-based directory structures for the new file pathname requiring an inode table entry.

Recently read directory entries are cached on the NFS server in the directory name lookup cache, better known as the DNLC. A sufficiently large cache speeds NFS *lookup* operations by eliminating the need to read directories from disk. Taking a directory cache miss is a fairly expensive operation, since the directory must be read from disk and searched linearly for the named component. For simplicity and storage, many implementations only cache pathnames under 30 characters long. Solaris removes this limitation by caching all pathnames regardless of their length. You can check your directory name lookup cache hit rate by running *vmstat -s* on your NFS server:

```
% vmstat -s
...Page and swap info...
 621833654 total name lookups (cache hits 96%)
...CPU info...
```

If you are hitting the cache less than 90% of the time, increase *ncsize* on the NFS server. The *ncsize* kernel tunable specifies the number of entries cached by the DNLC.

In Solaris, every file currently opened holds an inode cache entry active, making the inode readily available without the need to access the disk. To improve performance, inodes for files recently opened are kept in this cache, anticipating that they may be accessed again in the not too distant future. Furthermore, inodes of files recently closed are maintained in an inactive inode cache, in anticipation that the same files may be reopened again soon. Since NFS does not define an open operation, NFS clients accessing files on the server will not hold the file open during access, causing the inodes for these files to only be cached in the inactive inode cache. This caching greatly improves future accesses by NFS clients, allowing them to benefit from the cached inode information instead of having to go to disk to satisfy the operation. The size of the inactive inode table is determined by the *ufs_ninode* kernel tunable and is set to the value of *ncsize* during boot. If you update *ncsize* during runtime, make sure to also update the value of *ufs_ninode* accordingly. The default value for *ncsize* is (*maxusers* * 68) + 360. *Maxusers* can be defined as the number of simultaneous users, plus some margin for daemons, and be set to about one user per megabyte of RAM in the system, with a default limit of 4096 in Solaris.

Cross-mounting filesystems

An NFS client may find many of its processes in a high-priority wait state when an NFS server on which it relies stops responding for any reason. If two servers mount filesystems from each other, and the filesystems are hard-mounted, it is possible for processes on each server to wait on NFS responses from the other. To avoid a deadlock, in which processes on two NFS servers go to sleep waiting on each other, cross-mounting of servers should be avoided. This is particularly important in a network that uses hard-mounted NFS filesystems with fairly large timeout and retransmission count parameters, making it hard to interrupt the processes that are waiting on the NFS server.

If filesystem access requires cross-mounted filesystem, they should be mounted with the background (*bg*) option.* This ensures that servers will not go into a deadly embrace after a power failure or other reboot. During the boot process, a machine attempts to mount its NFS filesystems before it accepts any incoming NFS requests. If two file servers request each other's services, and boot at about the same time, it is likely that they will attempt to cross-mount their filesystems before either server is ready to provide NFS service. With the *bg* option, each NFS mount

---

* There are no adverse effects of using the background option, so you can use it for all your NFS-mounted filesystems.

will time out and be put into the background. Eventually the servers will complete their boot processes, and when the network services are started the back-grounded mounts complete.

This deadlock problem goes away when your NFS clients use the automounter in place of hard-mounts. Most systems today heavily rely on the automounter to administer NFS mounts. Also note that the *bg* mount option is for use by the *mount* command only. It is not needed when the mounts are administered with the automounter.

Multihomed servers

When a server exports NFS filesystems on more than one network interface, it may expend a measurable number of CPU cycles forwarding packets between interfaces. Consider host *boris* on four networks:

```
138.1.148.1     boris-bb4
138.1.147.1     boris-bb3
138.1.146.1     boris-bb2
138.1.145.1     boris-bb1 boris
```

Hosts on network 138.1.148.0 are able to "see" *boris* because *boris* forwards packets from any one of its network interfaces to the other. Hosts on the 138.1.148.0 network may mount filesystems from either hostname:

```
boris:/export/boris
boris-bb4:/export/boris
```

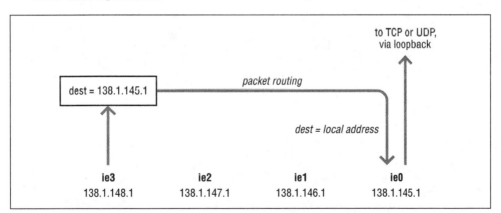

Figure 16-2. A multihomed host

The second form is preferable on network 138.1.148.0 because it does not require *boris* to forward packets to its other interface's input queue. Likewise, on network 138.1.145.0, the *boris:/export/boris* form is preferable. Even though the requests are going to the same physical machine, requests that are addressed to the "wrong" server must be forwarded, as shown in Figure 16-2. This adds to the IP protocol processing overhead. If the packet forwarding must be done for every NFS RPC request, then *boris* uses more CPU cycles to provide NFS service.

Fortunately, the automounter handles this automatically. It is able to determine what addresses are local to its subnetwork and give strong preference to them. If the server reply is not received within a given timeout, the automounter will use an alternate server address, as explained in "Replicated servers" in Chapter 9.

17

Network Performance Analysis

This chapter explores network diagnostics and partitioning schemes aimed at reducing congestion and improving the local host's interface to the network.

Network congestion and network interfaces

A network that was designed to ensure transparent access to filesystems and to provide "plug-and-play" services for new clients is a prime candidate for regular expansion. Joining several independent networks with routers, switches, hubs, bridges, or repeaters may add to the traffic level on one or more of the networks. However, a network cannot grow indefinitely without eventually experiencing congestion problems. Therefore, don't grow a network without planning its physical topology (cable routing and limitations) as well as its logical design. After several spurts of growth, performance on the network may suffer due to excessive loading.

The problems discussed in this section affect NIS as well as NFS service. Adding network partitioning hardware affects the transmission of broadcast packets, and poorly placed bridges, switches, or routers can create new bottlenecks in frequently used network "virtual circuits." Throughout this chapter, the emphasis will be on planning and capacity evaluation, rather than on low-level electrical details.

Local network interface

Ethernet cabling problems, such as incorrect or poorly made Category-5 cabling, affect all of the machines on the network. Conversely, a local interface problem is visible only to the machine suffering from it. An Ethernet interface device driver that cannot handle the packet traffic is an example of such a local interface problem.

The *netstat* tool gives a good indication of the reliability of the local physical network interface:

```
% netstat -in
Name Mtu  Net/Dest     Address      Ipkts   Ierrs  Opkts   Oerrs Collis Queue
lo0  8232 127.0.0.0    127.0.0.1    7188    0      7188    0     0      0
hme0 1500 129.144.8.0  129.144.8.3  139478  11     102155  0     3055   0
```

The first three columns show the network interface, the maximum transmission unit (MTU) for that interface, and the network to which the interface is connected. The *Address* column shows the local IP address (the hostname would have been shown had we not specified -*n*). The last five columns contain counts of the total number of packets sent and received, as well as errors encountered while handling packets. The collision count indicates the number of times a collision occurred when this host was transmitting.

Input errors can be caused by:

*   Malformed or runt packets, damaged on the network by electrical problems.

*   Bad CRC checksums, which may indicate that another host has a network interface problem and is sending corrupted packets. Alternatively, the cable connecting this workstation to the network may be damaged and corrupting frames as they are received.

*   The device driver's inability to receive the packet due to insufficient buffer space.

A high output error rate indicates a fault in the local host's connection to the network or prolonged periods of collisions (a jammed network). Errors included in this count are exclusive of packet collisions.

Ideally, both the input and output error rates should be as close to zero as possible, although some short bursts of errors may occur as cables are unplugged and reconnected, or during periods of intense network traffic. After a power failure, for example, the flood of packets from every diskless client that automatically reboots may generate input errors on the servers that attempt to boot all of them in parallel. During normal operation, an error rate of more than a fraction of 1% deserves investigation. This rate seems incredibly small, but consider the data rates on a Fast Ethernet: at 100 Mb/sec, the maximum bandwidth of a network is about 150,000 minimum-sized packets each second. An error rate of 0.01% means that fifteen of those 150,000 packets get damaged each second. Diagnosis and resolution of low-level electrical problems such as CRC errors is beyond the scope of this book, although such an effort should be undertaken if high error rates are persistent.

Collisions and network saturation

Ethernet is similar to an old party-line telephone: everybody listens at once, everybody talks at once, and sometimes two talkers start at the same time. In a well-conditioned network, with only two hosts on it, it's possible to use close to the maximum network's bandwidth. However, NFS clients and servers live in a burst-filled environment, where many machines try to use the network at the same time. When you remove the well-behaved conditions, usable network bandwidth decreases rapidly.

On the Ethernet, a host first checks for a transmission in progress on the network before attempting one of its own. This process is known as *carrier sense*. When two or more hosts transmit packets at exactly the same time, neither can sense a carrier, and a collision results. Each host recognizes that a collision has occurred, and backs off for a period of time, *t,* before attempting to transmit again. For each successive retransmission attempt that results in a collision, *t* is increased exponentially, with a small random variation. The variation in back off periods ensures that machines generating collisions do not fall into lock step and seize the network.

As machines are added to the network, the probability of a collision increases. Network utilization is measured as a percentage of the ideal bandwidth consumed by the traffic on the cable at the point of measurement. Various levels of utilization are usually compared on a logarithmic scale. The relative decrease in usable bandwidth going from 5% utilization to 10% utilization, is about the same as going from 10% all the way to 30% utilization.

Measuring network utilization requires a LAN analyzer or similar device. Instead of measuring the traffic load directly, you can use the average collision rate as seen by all hosts on the network as a good indication of whether the network is overloaded or not. The collision rate, as a percentage of output packets, is one of the best measures of network utilization. The *Collis* field in the output of *netstat -in* shows the number of collisions:

```
% netstat -in
Name Mtu  Net/Dest    Address     Ipkts   Ierrs  Opkts   Oerrs Collis Queue
lo0  8232 127.0.0.0   127.0.0.1   7188    0      7188    0     0      0
hme0 1500 129.144.8.0 129.144.8.3 139478  11     102155  0     3055   0
```

The collision rate for a host is the number of collisions seen by that host divided by the number of packets it writes, as shown in Figure 17-1.

$$\text{collision rate} = \frac{\text{number of collisions}}{\text{output packets}}$$

Figure 17-1. Collision rate calculation

Collisions are counted only when the local host is transmitting; the collision rate experienced by the host is dependent on its network usage. Because network transmissions are random events, it's possible to see small numbers of collisions even on the most lightly loaded networks. A collision rate upwards of 5% is the first sign of network loading, and it's an indication that partitioning the network may be advisable.

Network partitioning hardware

Network partitioning involves dividing a single backbone into multiple segments, joined by some piece of hardware that forwards packets. There are multiple types of these devices: repeaters, hubs, bridges, switches, routers, and gateways. These terms are sometimes used interchangeably although each device has a specific set of policies regarding packet forwarding, protocol filtering, and transparency on the network:

Repeaters

A repeater joins two segments at the physical layer. It is a purely electrical connection, providing signal amplification and pulse "clean up" functions without regard for the semantics of the signals. Repeaters are primarily used to exceed the single-cable length limitation in networks based on bus topologies, such as 10Base5 and 10Base2. There is a maximum to the number of repeaters that can exist between any two nodes on the same network, keeping the minimum end-to-end transit time for a packet well within the Ethernet specified maximum time-to-live. Because repeaters do not look at the contents of packets (or packet fragments), they pass collisions on one segment through to the other, making them of little use to relieve network congestion.

Hubs

A hub joins multiple hosts by acting as a wiring concentrator in networks based on star topologies, such as 10BaseT. A hub has the same function as a repeater, although in a different kind of network topology. Each computer is connected, typically over copper, to the hub, which is usually located in a wiring closet. The hub is purely a repeater: it regenerates the signal from one set of wires to the others, but does not process or manage the signal in any way. All traffic is forwarded to all machines connected to the hub.

Bridges

Bridges function at the data link layer, and perform selective forwarding of packets based on their destination MAC addresses. Some delay is introduced into the network by the bridge, as it must receive entire packets and decipher their MAC-layer headers. Broadcast packets are always passed through, although some bridge hardware can be configured to forward only ARP broadcasts and to suppress IP broadcasts such as those emanating from *ypbind*.

Intelligent or learning bridges glean the MAC addresses of machines through observation of traffic on each interface. "Dumb" bridges must be loaded with the Ethernet addresses of machines on each network and impose an administrative burden each time the network topology is modified. With either type of bridge, each new segment is likely to be less heavily loaded than the original network, provided that the most popular inter-host virtual circuits do not run through the bridge.

Switches

You can think of a switch as an intelligent hub having the functionality of a bridge. The switch also functions at the data link layer, and performs selective forwarding of packets based on their destination MAC address. The switch forwards packets only to the intended port of the intended recipient. The switch "learns" the location of the various MAC addresses by observing the traffic on each port. When a switch port receives data packets, it forwards those packets only to the appropriate port for the intended recipient. A hub would instead forward the packet to all other ports on the hub, leaving it to the host connected to the port to determine its interest in the packet. Because the switch only forwards the packet to its destination, it helps reduce competition for bandwidth between the hosts connected to each port.

Routers

Repeaters, hubs, bridges, and switches divide the network into multiple distinct physical pieces, but the collection of backbones is still a single *logical* network. That is, the IP network number of all hosts on all segments will be the same. It is often necessary to divide a network logically into multiple IP networks, either due to physical constraints (i.e., two offices that are separated by several miles) or because a single IP network has run out of host numbers for new machines.

Multiple IP networks are joined by routers that forward packets based on their source and destination IP addresses rather than 48-bit Ethernet addresses. One interface of the router is considered "inside" the network, and the router forwards packets to the "outside" interface. A router usually corrals broadcast traffic to the inside network, although some can be configured to forward broadcast packets to the "outside" network. The networks joined by a router need not be of the same type or physical media, and routers are commonly used to join local area networks to point-to-point long-haul internetwork connections. Routers can also help ensure that packets travel the most efficient paths to their destination. If a link between two routers fails, the sending router can determine an alternate route to keep traffic moving. You can install a dedicated router, or install multiple network interfaces in a host and allow it to route packets in addition to its other duties. Appendix A contains a detailed description of how IP packets are forwarded and how routes are defined to Unix systems.

Gateways

> At the top-most level in the network protocol stack, a gateway performs forwarding functions at the application level, and frequently must perform protocol conversion to forward the traffic. A gateway need not be on more than one network; however, gateways are most commonly used to join multiple networks with different sets of native protocols, and to enforce tighter control over access to and from each of the networks.

Replacing an Ethernet hub with a Fast Ethernet hub is like increasing the speed limit of a highway. Replacing a hub with a switch is similar to adding new lanes to the highway. Replacing an Ethernet hub with a Fast Ethernet switch is the equivalent of both improvements, although with a higher cost.

Network infrastructure

Partitioning a low-bandwidth network should ease the constraints imposed by the network on attribute-intensive applications, but may not necessarily address the limitations encountered by data-intensive applications. Data-intensive applications require high bandwidth, and may require the hosts to be migrated onto higher bandwidth networks, such as Fast Ethernet, FDDI, ATM, or Gigabit Ethernet. Recent advances in networking as well as economies of scale have made high bandwidth and switched networks more accessible. We explore their effects on NIS and NFS in the remaining sections of this chapter.

Switched networks

Switched Ethernets have become affordable and extremely popular in the last few years, with configurations ranging from enterprise-class switching networks with hundreds of ports, to the small 8- and 16-port Fast Ethernet switched networks used in small businesses. Switched Ethernets are commonly found in configurations that use a high-bandwidth interface into the server (such as Gigabit Ethernet) and a switching hub that distributes the single fast network into a large number of slower branches (such as Fast Ethernet ports). This topology isolates a client's traffic to the server from the other clients on the network, since each client is on a different branch of the network. This reduces the collision rate, allowing each client to utilize higher bandwidth when communicating to the server.

Although switched networks alleviate the impact of collisions, you still have to watch for "impedance mismatches" between an excessive number of client network segments and only a few server segments. A typical problem in a switched network environment occurs when an excessive number of NFS clients capable of saturating their own network segments overload the server's "narrow" network segment.

Consider the case where 100 NFS clients and a single NFS server are all connected to a switched Fast Ethernet. The server and each of its clients have their own 100 Mbit/sec port on the switch. In this configuration, the server can easily become bandwidth starved when multiple concurrent requests from the NFS clients arrive over its single network segment. To address this problem, you should provide multiple network interfaces to the server, each connected to its own 100 Mb/sec port on the switch. You can either turn on IP interface groups on the server, such that the server can have more than one IP address on the same subnet, or use the outbound networks for multiplexing out the NFS read replies. The clients should use all of the hosts' IP addresses in order for the inbound requests to arrive over the various network interfaces. You can configure BIND round-robin* if you don't want to hardcode the destination addresses. You can alternatively enable interface trunking on the server to use the multiple network interfaces as a single IP address avoiding the need to mess with IP addressing and client naming conventions. Trunking also offers a measure of fault tolerance, since the trunked interface keeps working even if one of the network interfaces fails. Finally, trunking scales as you add more network interfaces to the server, providing additional network bandwidth. Many switches provide a combination of Fast Ethernet and Gigabit Ethernet channels as well. They can also support the aggregation of these channels to provide high bandwidth to either data center servers or to the backbone network.

Heavily used NFS servers will benefit from their own "fast" branch, but try to keep NFS clients and servers logically close in the network topology. Try to minimize the number of switches and routers that traffic must cross. A good rule of thumb is to try to keep 80% of the traffic within the network and only 20% of the traffic from accessing the backbone.

ATM and FDDI networks

ATM (Asynchronous Transfer Mode) and FDDI (Fiber Distributed Data Interface) networks are two other forms of high-bandwidth networks that can sustain multiple high-speed concurrent data exchanges with minimal degradation. ATM and FDDI are somewhat more efficient than Fast Ethernet in data-intensive environments because they use a larger MTU (Maximum Transfer Unit), therefore requiring less packets than Fast Ethernet to transmit the same amount of information. Note that this does not necessarily present an advantage to attribute-intensive environments where the requests are small and always fit in a Fast Ethernet packet.

---

* When BIND's round-robin feature is enabled, the order of the server's addresses returned is shifted on each query to the name server. This allows a different address to be used by each client's request.

Although ATM promises scalable and seamless bandwidth, guaranteed QoS (Quality of Service), integrated services (voice, video, and data), and virtual networking, Ethernet technologies are not likely to be displaced. Today, ATM has not been widely deployed outside backbone networks. Many network administrators prefer to deploy Fast Ethernet and Gigabit Ethernet because of their familiarity with the protocol, and because it requires no changes to the packet format. This means that existing analysis and network management tools and software that operate at the network and transport layers, and higher, continue to work as before. It is unlikely that ATM will experience a significant amount of deployment outside the backbone.

Impact of partitioning

Although partitioning is a solution to many network problems, it's not entirely transparent. When you partition a network, you must think about the effect of partitioning on NIS, and the locations of diskless nodes and their boot servers.

NIS in a partitioned network

NIS is a point-to-point protocol once a server binding has been established. However, when *ypbind* searches for a server, it broadcasts an RPC request. Switches and bridges do not affect *ypbind*, because switches and bridges forward broadcast packets to the other *physical* network. Routers don't forward broadcast packets to other IP networks, so you must make configuration exceptions if you have NIS clients but no NIS server on one side of a router.

It is not uncommon to attach multiple clients to a hub, and multiple hubs to a switch. Each switch branch acts as its own segment in the same way that bridges create separate "collision domains." Unequal distribution of NIS servers on opposite sides of a switch branch (or bridge) can lead to server victimization. The typical bridge adds a small delay to the transit time of each packet, so *ypbind* requests will almost always be answered by a server on the client's side of the switch branch or bridge. The relative delays in NIS server response time are shown in Figure 17-2.

If there is only one server on bridge network A, but several on bridge network B, then the "A" network server handles all NIS requests on its network segment until it becomes so heavily loaded that servers on the "B" network reply to *ypbind* faster, including the bridge-related packet delay. An equitable distribution of NIS servers across switch branch (or bridge) boundaries eliminates this excessive loading problem.

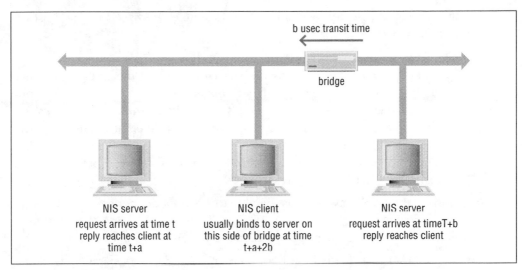

Figure 17-2. Bridge effects on NIS

Routers and gateways present a more serious problem for NIS. NIS servers and clients must be on the same IP network because a router or gateway will not forward the client's *ypbind* broadcast outside the local IP network. If there are no NIS servers on the "inside" of a router, use *ypinit* at configuration time as discussed in "Setting initial client bindings" in Chapter 13.

Effects on diskless nodes

Diskless nodes should be kept on the same logical network as their servers unless tight constraints require their separation. If a router is placed between a diskless client and its server, every disk operation on the client, including swap device operations, has to go through the router. The volume of traffic generated by a diskless client is usually much larger—sometimes twice as much—than that of an NFS client getting user files from a server, so it greatly reduces the load on the router if clients and servers are kept on the same side of the router.[*]

Booting a client through a router is less than ideal, since the diskless client's root and swap partition traffic unnecessarily load the packet forwarding bandwidth of the router. However, if necessary, a diskless client can be booted through a router as follows:

- Some machine on the client's local network must be able to answer Reverse ARP (RARP) requests from the machine. This can be accomplished by

---

[*] Although not directly related to network topology, one of the best things you can do for your diskless clients is to load them with an adequate amount of memory so that they can perform aggressive caching and reduce the number of round trips to the server.

publishing an ARP entry for the client and running *in.rarpd* on some host on the same network:

```
in.rarpd hme 0
```

In Solaris, *in.rarpd* takes the network device name and the instance number as arguments. In this example we start *in.rarpd* on */dev/hme0*, the network interface attached to the diskless client's network. *in.rarpd* uses the *ethers*, *hosts*, and *ipnodes* databases* to map the requested Ethernet address into the corresponding IP address. The IP address is then returned to the diskless client in a RARP reply message. The diskless client must be listed in both databases for *in.rarpd* to locate its IP address.

- A host on the local network must be able to *tftp* the boot code to the client, so that it can start the boot sequence. This usually involves adding client information to */tftpboot* on another diskless client server on the local network.

- Once the client has loaded the boot code, it looks for boot parameters. Some server on the client's network must be able to answer the *bootparams* request for the client. This entails adding the client's root and swap partition information to the local *bootparams* file or NIS map. The machine that supplies the *bootparam* information may not have anything to do with actually booting the system, but it must give the diskless client enough information for it to reach its root and swap filesystem servers through IP routing. Therefore, if the proxy *bootparam* server has a default route defined, that route must point to the network with the client's NFS server on it.

- If the NIS server is located across the router, the diskless client will need to be configured at installation time, or later on with the use of the *ypinit* command, in order to boot from the explicit NIS server. This is necessary because *ypbind* will be unable to find an NIS server in its subnetwork through a broadcast.

Protocol filtering

If you have a large volume of non-IP traffic on your network, isolating it from your NFS and NIS traffic may improve overall system performance by reducing the load on your network and servers. You can determine the relative percentages of IP and non-IP packets on your network using a LAN analyzer or a traffic filtering program. The best way to isolate your NFS and NIS network from non-IP traffic is to install a switch, bridge, or other device that performs selective filtering based on

---

* The *ethers* database is stored in the local file */etc/ethers* or the corresponding NIS map. The *hosts* and *ipnodes* database is located in the local files */etc/inet/hosts* and */etc/inet/ipnodes*, or DNS and NIS maps. The search order depends on the contents of the name switch configuration file */etc/nsswitch.conf*.

protocol. Any packet that does not meet the selection criteria is not forwarded across the device.

Devices that monitor traffic at the IP protocol level, such as routers, filter any non-IP traffic, such as IPX and DECnet packets. If two segments of a local area network must exchange IP and non-IP traffic, a switch, bridge, or router capable of selective forwarding must be installed. The converse is also an important network planning factor: to insulate a network using only TCP/IP-based protocols from volumes of irrelevant traffic—IPX packets generated by a PC network, for example—a routing device filtering at the IP level is the simplest solution.

Partitioning a network and increasing the available bandwidth should ease the constraints imposed by the network, and spur an increase in NFS performance. However, the network itself is not always the sole or primary cause of poor performance. Server- and client-side tuning should be performed in concert with changes in network topology. Chapter 16 has already covered server-side tuning; Chapter 18 will cover the client-side tuning issues.

18

Client-Side Performance Tuning

The performance measurement and tuning techniques we've discussed so far have only dealt with making the NFS server go faster. Part of tuning an NFS network is ensuring that clients are well-behaved so that they do not flood the servers with requests and upset any tuning you may have performed. Server performance is usually limited by disk or network bandwidth, but there is no throttle on the rate at which clients generate requests unless you put one in place. Add-on products, such as the Solaris Bandwidth Manager, allow you to specify the amount of network bandwidth on specified ports, enabling you to restrict the amount of network resources used by NFS on either the server or the client. In addition, if you cannot make your servers or network any faster, you have to tune the clients to handle the network "as is."

Slow server compensation

The RPC retransmission algorithm cannot distinguish between a slow server and a congested network. If a reply is not received from the server within the RPC timeout period, the request is retransmitted subject to the timeout and retransmission parameters for that mount point. It is immaterial to the RPC mechanism whether the original request is still enqueued on the server or if it was lost on the network. Excessive RPC retransmissions place an additional strain on the server, further degrading response time.

Identifying NFS retransmissions

Inspection of the load average and disk activity on the servers may indicate that the servers are heavily loaded and imposing the tightest constraint. The NFS client-side statistics provide the most concrete evidence that one or more slow servers are to blame:

```
% nfsstat -rc
Client rpc:
Connection-oriented:
calls        badcalls     badxids      timeouts     newcreds     badverfs
1753584      1412         18           64           0            0
timers       cantconn     nomem        interrupts
0            1317         0            18
Connectionless:
calls        badcalls     retrans      badxids      timeouts     newcreds
12443        41           334          80           166          0
badverfs     timers       nomem        cantsend
0            4321         0            206
```

The *-rc* option is given to *nfsstat* to look at the RPC statistics only, for client-side NFS operations. The call type demographics contained in the NFS-specific statistics are not of value in this analysis. The test for a slow server is having *badxid* and timeout of the same magnitude. In the previous example, *badxid* is nearly a third the value of *timeout* for connection-oriented RPC, and nearly half the value of *timeout* for connectionless RPC. Connection-oriented transports use a higher timeout than connectionless transports, therefore the number of timeouts will generally be less for connection-oriented transports. The high *badxid* count implies that requests are reaching the various NFS servers, but the servers are too loaded to send replies before the local host's RPC calls time out and are retransmitted. *badxid* is incremented each time a duplicate reply is received for a retransmitted request (an RPC request retains its XID through all retransmission cycles). In this case, the server is replying to all requests, including the retransmitted ones. The client is simply not patient enough to wait for replies from the slow server. If there is more than one NFS server, the client may be outpacing all of them or just one particularly sluggish node.

If the server has a duplicate request cache, retransmitted requests that match a non-idempotent NFS call currently in progress are ignored. Only those requests in progress are recognized and filtered, so it is still possible for a sufficiently loaded server to generate duplicate replies that show up in the *badxid* counts of its clients. Without a duplicate request cache, *badxid* and *timeout* may be nearly equal, while the cache will reduce the number of duplicate replies. With or without a duplicate request cache, if the *badxid* and *timeout* statistics reported by *nfsstat* (on the client) are of the same magnitude, then server performance is an issue deserving further investigation.

A mixture of network and server-related problems can make interpretation of the *nfsstat* figures difficult. A client served by four hosts may find that two of the hosts are particularly slow while a third is located across a network router that is digesting streams of large write packets. One slow server can be masked by other, faster servers: a retransmission rate of 10% (calculated as *timeout/calls*) would indicate short periods of server sluggishness or network congestion if the retransmissions were evenly distributed among all servers. However, if all timeouts occurred while talking to just one server, the retransmission rate *for that server* could be 50% or higher.

A simple method for finding the distribution of retransmitted requests is to perform the same set of disk operations on each server, measuring the incremental number of RPC timeouts that occur when loading each server in turn. This experiment may point to a server that is noticeably slower than its peers, if a large percentage of the RPC timeouts are attributed to that host. Alternatively, you may shift your focus away from server performance if timeouts are fairly evenly distributed or if no timeouts occur during the server loading experiment. Fluctuations in server performance may vary by the time of day, so that more timeouts occur during periods of peak server usage in the morning and after lunch, for example.

Server response time may be clamped at some minimum value due to fixed-cost delays of sending packets through routers, or due to static configurations that cannot be changed for political or historical reasons. If server response cannot be improved, then the clients of that server must adjust their mount parameters to avoid further loading it with retransmitted requests. The relative patience of the client is determined by the timeout, retransmission count, and hard-mount variables.

Timeout period calculation

The timeout period is specified by the mount parameter *timeo* and is expressed in tenths of a second. For NFS over UDP, it specifies the value of a *minor timeout*, which occurs when the client RPC call over UDP does not receive a reply within the *timeo* period. In this case, the timeout period is doubled, and the RPC request is sent again. The process is repeated until the retransmission count specified by the *retrans* mount parameter is reached. A *major timeout* occurs when no reply is received after the retransmission threshold is reached. The default value for the minor timeout is vendor-specific; it can range from 5 to 13 tenths of a second. By default, clients are configured to retransmit from three to five times, although this value is also vendor-specific.

When using NFS over TCP, the *retrans* parameter has no effect, and it is up to the TCP transport to generate the necessary retransmissions on behalf of NFS until the value specified by the *timeo* parameter is reached. In contrast to NFS over UDP, the mount parameter *timeo* in NFS over TCP specifies the value of a major timeout, and is typically in the range of hundreds of a tenth of a second (for example, Solaris has a major timeout of 600 tenths of a second). The *minor timeout* value is internally controlled by the underlying TCP transport, and all you have to worry about is the value of the *major timeout* specified by *timeo*.

After a major timeout, the message:

```
NFS server host not responding still trying
```

is printed on the client's console. If a reply is eventually received, the "not responding" message is followed with the message:

```
NFS server host ok
```

Hard-mounting a filesystem guarantees that the sequence of retransmissions continues until the server replies. After a major timeout on a hard-mounted filesystem, the *initial* timeout period is doubled, beginning a new major cycle. Hard mounts are the default option. For example, a filesystem mounted via:[*]

```
# mount -o proto=udp,retrans=3,timeo=10 wahoo:/export/home/wahoo /mnt
```

has the retransmission sequence shown in Table 18-1.

Table 18-1. NFS timeout sequence for NFS over UDP

Absolute Time	Current Timeout	New Timeout	Event
1.0	1.0	2.0	Minor
3.0	2.0	4.0	Minor
7.0	4.0	2.0	Major, double initial timeout
...NFS server *wahoo* not responding...			
9.0	2.0	4.0	Minor
13.0	4.0	8.0	Minor
21.0	8.0	4.0	Major, double initial timeout

Timeout periods are not increased without bound, for instance, the timeout period never exceeds 20 seconds (*timeo*=200) for Solaris clients using UDP, and 60 seconds for Linux. The system may also impose a minimum timeout period in order to avoid retransmitting too aggressively. Because certain NFS operations take longer to complete than others, Solaris uses three different values for the minimum (and initial) timeout of the various NFS operations. NFS *write* operations typically take the longest, therefore a minimum timeout of 1,250 msecs is used. NFS *read* operations have a minimum timeout of 875 msecs, and operations that act on metadata (such as *getattr, lookup, access,* etc.) usually take the least time, therefore they have the smaller minimum timeout of 750 msecs.

---

[*] We specifically use *proto=udp* to force the Solaris client to use the UDP protocol when communicating with the server, since the client by default will attempt to first communicate over TCP. Linux, on the other hand, uses UDP as the default transport for NFS.

To accommodate slower servers, increase the *timeo* parameter used in the auto-mounter maps or */etc/vfstab*. Increasing *retrans* for UDP increases the length of the major timeout period, but it does so at the expense of sending more requests to the NFS server. These duplicate requests further load the server, particularly when they require repeating disk operations. In many cases, the client receives a reply after sending the second or third retransmission, so doubling the initial timeout period eliminates about half of the NFS calls sent to the slow server. In general, increasing the NFS RPC timeout is more helpful than increasing the retransmission count for hard-mounted filesystems accessed over UDP. If the server does not respond to the first few RPC requests, it is likely it will not respond for a "long" time, compared to the RPC timeout period. It's best to let the client sit back, double its timeout period on major timeouts, and wait for the server to recover. Increasing the retransmission count simply increases the noise level on the network while the client is waiting for the server to respond.

Note that Solaris clients only use the *timeo* mount parameter as a starting value. The Solaris client constantly adjusts the actual timeout according to the smoothed average round-trip time experienced during NFS operations to the server. This allows the client to dynamically adjust the amount of time it is willing to wait for NFS responses given the recent past responsiveness of the NFS server.

Use the *nfsstat -m* command to review the kernel's observed response times over the UDP transport for all NFS mounts:

```
% nfsstat -m
/mnt from mahimahi:/export
  Flags:        vers=3,proto=udp,sec=sys,hard,intr,link,symlink,acl,rsize=32768,
                  wsize=32768,retrans=2,timeo=15
  Attr cache:   acregmin=3,acregmax=60,acdirmin=30,acdirmax=60
  Lookups:      srtt=13 (32ms), dev=6 (30ms), cur=4 (80ms)
  Reads:        srtt=24 (60ms), dev=14 (70ms), cur=10 (200ms)
  Writes:       srtt=46 (115ms), dev=27 (135ms), cur=19 (380ms)
  All:          srtt=20 (50ms), dev=11 (55ms), cur=8 (160ms)
```

The smoothed, average round-trip (*srtt*) times are reported in milliseconds, as well as the average deviation (*dev*) and the current "expected" response time (*cur*). The numbers in parentheses are the actual times in milliseconds; the other values are unscaled values kept by the kernel and can be ignored. Response times are shown for read and write operations, which are "big" RPCs, and for lookups, which typify "small" RPC requests. The response time numbers are only shown for filesystems mounted using the UDP transport. Retransmission handling is the responsibility of the TCP transport when using NFS over TCP.

Without the kernel's values as a baseline, choosing a new timeout value is best done empirically. Doubling the initial value is a good baseline; after changing the timeout value observe the RPC timeout rate and *badxid* rate using *nfsstat*. At first glance, it does not appear that there is any harm in immediately going to *timeo=200*, the maximum initial timeout value used in the retransmission algo-rithm. If server performance is the sole constraint, then this is a fair assumption. However, even a well-tuned network endures bursts of traffic that can cause packets to be lost at congested network hardware interfaces or dropped by the server. In this case, the excessively long timeout will have a dramatic impact on client performance. With *timeo=200*, RPC retransmissions "avoid" network conges-tion by waiting for *minutes* while the actual traffic peak may have been only a few milliseconds in duration.

Retransmission rate thresholds

There is little agreement among system administrators about acceptable retransmis-sion rate thresholds. Some people claim that *any* request retransmission indicates a performance problem, while others chose an arbitrary percentage as a "goal." Determining the retransmission rate threshold for your NFS clients depends upon your choice of the *timeo* mount parameter and your expected response time varia-tions. The equation in Figure 18-1 expresses the expected retransmission rate as a function of the allowable response time variation and the *timeo* parameter.[*]

$$\text{retransmission rate threshold} = \frac{\text{response time variation (millisecond/call)}}{\text{timeo value (millisecond/retransmission)}}$$

$$= X\% \text{ (millisecond/call)}$$

Figure 18-1. NFS retransmission threshold

If you allow a response time fluctuation of five milliseconds, or about 20% of a 25 millisecond average response time, and use a 1.1 second (1100 millisecond) timeout period for metadata operations, then your expected retransmission rate is (5/1100) = .45%.

If you increase your timeout value, this equation dictates that you should *decrease* your retransmission rate threshold. This makes sense: if you make the clients more tolerant of a slow NFS server, they shouldn't be sending as many NFS RPC retrans-missions. Similarly, if you want less variation in NFS client performance, and decide to reduce your allowable response time variation, you also need to reduce your retransmission threshold.

---

[*] This retransmission threshold equation was originally presented in the *Prestoserve User's Manual*, March 1991 edition. The *Manual* and the Prestoserve NFS write accelerator are produced by Legato Systems.

NFS over TCP is your friend

You can alternatively use NFS over TCP to ensure that data is not retransmitted excessively. This, of course, requires that both, the client and server support NFS over TCP. At the time of this writing, many NFS implementations already support NFS over TCP. The added TCP functionality comes at a price: TCP is a heavier weight protocol that uses more CPU cycles to perform extra checks per packet. Because of this, LAN environments have traditionally used NFS over UDP. Improvements in hardware, as well as better TCP implementations have narrowed the performance gap between the two.

A Solaris client by default uses NFS Version 3 over TCP. If the server does not support it, then the client automatically falls back to NFS Version 3 over UDP or NFS Version 2 over one of the supported transports. Use the *proto=tcp* option to force a Solaris client to mount the filesystem using TCP only. In this case, the mount will fail instead of falling back to UDP if the server does not support TCP:

```
# mount -o proto=tcp wahoo:/export /mnt
```

Use the *tcp* option to force a Linux client to mount the filesystem using TCP instead of its default of UDP. Again, if the server does not support TCP, the mount attempt will fail:

```
# mount -o tcp wahoo:/export /mnt
```

TCP partitions the payload into segments equivalent to the size of an Ethernet packet. If one of the segments gets lost, NFS does not need to retransmit the entire operation because TCP itself handles the retransmissions of the segments. In addition to retransmitting only the lost segment when necessary, TCP also controls the transmission rate in order to utilize the network resources more adequately, taking into account the ability of the receiver to consume the packets. This is accomplished through a simple flow control mechanism, where the receiver indicates to the sender how much data it can receive.

TCP is extremely useful in error-prone or lossy networks, such as many WAN environments, which we discuss later in this chapter.

Soft mount issues

Repeated retransmission cycles only occur for hard-mounted filesystems. When the *soft* option is supplied in a mount, the RPC retransmission sequence ends at the first major timeout, producing messages like:

```
NFS write failed for server wahoo: error 5 (RPC: Timed out)
NFS write error on host wahoo: error 145.
(file handle: 800000 2 a0000 114c9 55f29948 a0000 11494 5cf03971)
```

The NFS operation that failed is indicated, the server that failed to respond before the major timeout, and the filehandle of the file affected. RPC timeouts may be caused by extremely slow servers, or they can occur if a server crashes and is down or rebooting while an RPC retransmission cycle is in progress.

With soft-mounted filesystems, you have to worry about damaging data due to incomplete writes, losing access to the text segment of a swapped process, and making soft-mounted filesystems more tolerant of variances in server response time. If a client does not give the server enough latitude in its response time, the first two problems impair both the performance and correct operation of the client. If *write* operations fail, data consistency on the server cannot be guaranteed. The write error is reported to the application during some later call to *write()* or *close()*, which is consistent with the behavior of a local filesystem residing on a failing or overflowing disk. When the actual write to disk is attempted by the kernel device driver, the failure is reported to the application as an error during the next similar or related system call.

A well-conditioned application should exit abnormally after a failed write, or retry the write if possible. If the application ignores the return code from *write()* or *close()*, then it is possible to corrupt data on a soft-mounted filesystem. Some write operations may fail and never be retried, leaving holes in the open file.

To guarantee data integrity, *all* filesystems mounted read-write should be hard-mounted. Server performance as well as server reliability determine whether a request eventually succeeds on a soft-mounted filesystem, and neither can be guaranteed. Furthermore, any operating system that maps executable images directly into memory (such as Solaris) should hard-mount filesystems containing executables. If the filesystem is soft-mounted, and the NFS server crashes while the client is paging in an executable (during the initial load of the text segment or to refill a page frame that was paged out), an RPC timeout will cause the paging to fail. What happens next is system-dependent; the application may be terminated or the system may panic with unrecoverable swap errors.

A common objection to hard-mounting filesystems is that NFS clients remain catatonic until a crashed server recovers, due to the infinite loop of RPC retransmissions and timeouts. By default, Solaris clients allow interrupts to break the retransmission loop. Use the *intr* mount option if your client doesn't specify interrupts by default. Unfortunately, some older implementations of NFS do not process keyboard interrupts until a major timeout has occurred: with even a small timeout period and retransmission count, the time required to recognize an interrupt can be quite large.

If you choose to ignore this advice, and choose to use soft-mounted NFS filesystems, you should at least make NFS clients more tolerant of soft-mounted NFS fileservers by increasing the *retrans* mount option. Increasing the number of attempts to reach the server makes the client less likely to produce an RPC error during brief periods of server loading.

Adjusting for network reliability problems

Even a lightly loaded network can suffer from reliability problems if older bridges or routers joining the network segments routinely drop parts of long packet trains. Older bridges and routers are most likely to affect NFS performance if their network interfaces cannot keep up with the packet arrival rates generated by the NFS clients and servers on each side.

Some NFS experts believe it is a bad idea to micro-manage NFS to compensate for network problems, arguing instead that these problems should be handled by the transport layer. We encourage you to use NFS over TCP, and allow the TCP implementation to dynamically adapt to network glitches and unreliable networks. TCP does a much better job of adjusting transfer sizes, handling congestion, and generating retransmissions to compensate for network problems.

Having said this, there may still be times when you choose to use UDP instead of TCP to handle your NFS traffic.* In such cases, you will need to determine the impact that an old bridge or router is having on your network. This requires another look at the client-side RPC statistics:

```
% nfsstat -rc
Client rpc:
Connection-oriented:
calls      badcalls    badxids     timeouts    newcreds    badverfs
1753569    1412        3           64          0           0
timers     cantconn    nomem       interrupts
0          1317        0           18
Connectionless:
calls      badcalls    retrans     badxids     timeouts    newcreds
12252      41          334         5           166         0
badverfs   timers      nomem       cantsend
0          4321        0           206
```

When *timeouts* is high and *badxid* is close to zero, it implies that the network or one of the network interfaces on the client, server, or any intermediate routing hardware is dropping packets. Some older host Ethernet interfaces are tuned to handle page-sized packets and do not reliably handle larger packets; similarly, many older Ethernet bridges cannot forward long bursts of packets. Older routers or hosts acting as IP routers may have limited forwarding capacity, so reducing the

---

* One example is the lack of NFS over TCP support for your client or server.

number of packets sent for any request reduces the probability that these routers will drop packets that build up behind their network interfaces.

The NFS buffer size determines how many packets are required to send a single, large *read* or *write* request. The Solaris default buffer size is 8KB for NFS Version 2 and 32KB for NFS Version 3. Linux* uses a default buffer size of 1KB. The buffer size can be negotiated down, at mount time, if the client determines that the server prefers a smaller transfer size.

Compensating for unreliable networks involves changing the NFS buffer size, controlled by the *rsize* and *wsize* mount options. *rsize* determines how many bytes are requested in each NFS read, and *wsize* gauges the number of bytes sent in each NFS write operation. Reducing *rsize* and *wsize* eases the peak loads on the network by sending shorter packet trains for each NFS request. By spacing the requests out, and increasing the probability that the entire request reaches the server or client intact on the first transmission, the overall load on the network and server is smoothed out over time.

The read and write buffer sizes are specified in bytes. They are generally made multiples of 512 bytes, based on the size of a disk block. There is no requirement that either size be an integer multiple of 512, although using an arbitrary size can make the disk operations on the remote host less efficient. Write operations performed on non-disk block aligned buffers require the NFS server to read the block, modify the block, and rewrite it. The read-modify-write cycle is invisible to the client, but adds to the overhead of each *write()* performed on the server.

These values are used by the NFS async threads and are completely independent of buffer sizes internal to any client-side processes. An application that writes 400-byte buffers, writing to a filesystem mounted with *wsize=4096*, does not cause an NFS *write* request to be sent to the server until the 11th write is performed.

Here is an example of mounting an NFS filesystem with the read and write buffer sizes reduced to 2048 bytes:

```
# mount -o rsize=2048,wsize=2048 wahoo:/export/home /mnt
```

Decreasing the NFS buffer size has the undesirable effect of increasing the load on the server and sending more packets on the network to read or write a given buffer. The size of the actual packets on the network does not change, but the number of IP packets composing a single NFS buffer decreases as the *rsize* and *wsize* are decreased. For example, an 8KB NFS buffer is divided into five IP packets of about 1500 bytes, and a sixth packet with the remaining data bytes. If the write size is set to 2048 bytes, only two IP packets are needed.

---

* This refers to Version 2.2.14-5 of the Linux kernel.

The problem lies in the number of packets required to transfer the same amount of data. Table 18-2 shows the number of IP packets required to copy a file for various NFS read buffer sizes.

Table 18-2. IP packets, RPC requests as function of NFS buffer size

File Size	IP Packets/RPC Calls			
	rsize	rsize	rsize	rsize
(kbytes)	1024	2048	4096	8192
1	1/1	1/1	1/1	1/1
2	2/2	2/1	2/1	2/1
4	4/4	4/2	3/1	3/1
8	8/8	8/4	6/2	6/1

As the file size increases, transfers with smaller NFS buffer sizes send more IP packets to the server. The number of packets will be the same for 4096- and 8192-byte buffers, but for file sizes over 4K, setting *rsize=4096* always requires twice as many RPC calls to the server. The increased network traffic adds to the very problem for which the buffer size change was compensating, and the additional RPC calls further load the server. Due to the increased server load, it is sometimes necessary to increase the RPC timeout parameter when decreasing NFS buffer sizes. Again, we encourage you to use NFS over TCP when possible and avoid having to worry about the NFS buffer sizes.

NFS over wide-area networks

NFS over wide-area networks (WANs) greatly benefits when it is run over the TCP transport. NFS over TCP is preferred when the traffic runs over error-prone or lossy networks. In addition, the reliable nature of TCP allows NFS to transmit larger packets over this type of network with fewer retransmissions.

Although NFS over TCP is recommended for use over WANs, you may have to run NFS over UDP across the WAN if either your client or server does not support NFS over TCP. When running NFS over UDP across WANs, you must adjust the buffer sizes and timeouts manually to account for the differences between the wide-area and the local-area network. Decrease the *rsize* and *wsize* to match the MTU of the slowest wide-area link you traverse with the mount. While this greatly increases the number of RPC requests that are needed to move a given part of a file, it is the most social approach to running NFS over a WAN.

If you use the default 32KB NFS Version 3 buffer, you send long trains of maximum sized packets over the wide-area link. Your NFS requests will be competing for bandwidth with other, interactive users' packets, and the NFS packet trains are likely to crowd the *rlogin* and *telnet* packets. Sending a 32 KB buffer over a 128 kbps ISDN line takes about two seconds. Writing a small file ties up the WAN link for several seconds, potentially infuriating interactive users who do not get keyboard echo during that time. Reducing the NFS buffer size forces your NFS client to wait for replies after each short burst of packets, giving bandwidth back to other WAN users.

In addition to decreasing the buffer size, increase the RPC timeout values to account for the significant increase in packet transmission time. Over a wide-area network, the network transmission delay will be comparable (if not larger) to the RPC service time on the NFS server. Set your timeout values based on the average time required to send or receive a complete NFS buffer. Increase your NFS RPC timeout to at least several seconds to avoid retransmitting requests and further loading the wide-area network link.

You can also reduce NFS traffic by increasing the attribute timeout (*actimeo*) specified at mount time. As explained in "File attribute caching" in Chapter 7, NFS clients cache file attributes to avoid having to go to the NFS server for information that does not change frequently. These attributes are aged to ensure the client will obtain refreshed attributes from the server in order to detect when files change. These "attribute checks" can cause a significant amount of traffic on a WAN. If you know that your files do not change frequently, or you are the only one accessing them (they are only changed from your side of the WAN), then you can increase the attribute timeout in order to reduce the number of "attribute refreshes."

Over a long-haul network, particularly one that is run over modem or ISDN lines, you will want to make sure that UDP checksums are enabled. Solaris has UDP checksums enabled by default, but not all operating systems use them because they add to the cost of sending and receiving a packet. However, if packets are damaged in transit over the modem line, UDP checksums allow you to reject bad data in NFS requests. NFS requests containing UDP checksum errors are rejected on the server, and will be retransmitted by the client. Without the checksums, it's possible to corrupt data.

You need to enable the checksums on both the client and server, so that the client generates the checksums and the server verifies them. Check your vendor's documentation to be sure that UDP checksums are supported; the checksum generation is not always available in older releases of some operating systems.

NFS async thread tuning

Early NFS client implementations provided *biod* user-level daemons in order to add concurrency to NFS operations. In such implementations, a client process performing an I/O operation on a file hands the request to the *biod* daemon, and proceeds with its work without blocking. The process doesn't have to wait for the I/O request to be sent and acknowledged by the server, because the *biod* daemon is responsible for issuing the appropriate NFS operation request to the server and to wait for its response. When the response is received, the *biod* daemon is free to handle a new I/O request. The idea is to have as many concurrent outstanding NFS operations as the server can handle at once, in order to accelerate I/O handling. Once all *biod* daemons are busy handling I/O requests, the client-side process generating the requests has to directly contact the NFS server and block awaiting its response.

For example, a file read request generated by the client-side process is handed to one *biod* daemon, and the rest of the *biod* daemons are asked to perform read-ahead operations on the same file. The idea is to anticipate the next move of the client-side application, by assuming that it is interested in sequentially reading the file. The NFS client hopes to avoid having to contact the NFS server on the next I/O request by the application, by having the next chunk of data already available.

Solaris, as well as other modern Unix kernels support multiple threads of execution without the need of a user context. Solaris has no *biod* daemons, instead it uses kernel threads to implement read-ahead and write-behind, achieving the same increased read and write throughput.

The number of read-aheads performed once the Solaris client detects a sequential read pattern is specified by the kernel tunable variables *nfs_nra* for NFS Version 2 and *nfs3_nra* for NFS Version 3. Solaris sets both values to four read-aheads by default. Depending on your file access patterns, network bandwidth, and hardware capabilities, you may need to modify the number of read-aheads to achieve optimal use of your resources. For example, you may find that this value needs to be increased on Gigabit Ethernet, but decreased over ISDN. To reduce the number of read-aheads over a low bandwidth connection, you can add the following lines to */etc/system* on the NFS client and reboot the system:

```
set nfs:nfs_nra=2
set nfs:nfs3_nra=1
```

When running over a high bandwidth network, make sure not to set these values too high above their default, not only will sequential read performance not improve, but the increased memory used by the NFS async threads will ultimately degrade overall performance of the system.

If *nfs3_nra* is set to four, and if you have two processes reading two separate files concurrently over NFSVersion 3, the system by default will generate four read-aheads triggered by the read request of the first process, and four more read-aheads triggered by the read request of the second process for a total of eight concurrent read-aheads. The maximum number of concurrent read-aheads for the entire system is limited by the number of NFS async threads available. The kernel tunables *nfs_max_threads* and *nfs3_max_threads* control the maximum number of active NFS async threads active at once per filesystem.

By default, a Solaris client uses eight NFS async threads per NFS filesystem. To drop the number of NFS async threads to two, add the following lines to */etc/ system* on the NFS client and reboot the system:

```
set nfs:nfs_max_threads=2
set nfs:nfs3_max_threads=2
```

After rebooting, you will have reduced the amount of NFS read-ahead and write-behind performed by the client. Note that simply decreasing the number of kernel threads may produce an effect similar to that of eliminating them completely, so be conservative.

Be careful when server performance is a problem, since increasing NFS async threads on the client machines beyond their default usually makes the server performance problems worse. The NFS async threads impose an implicit limit on the number of NFS requests requiring disk I/O that may be outstanding from any client at any time. Each NFS async thread has at most one NFS request outstanding at any time, and if you increase the number of NFS async threads, you allow each client to send more disk-bound requests at once, further loading the network and the servers.

Decreasing the number of NFS async threads doesn't always improve performance either, and usually reduces NFS filesystem throughput. You must have some small degree of NFS request multithreading on the NFS client to maintain the illusion of having filesystem on local disks. Reducing or eliminating the number of NFS async threads effectively throttles the filesystem throughput of the NFS client —diminishing or eliminating the amount of read-ahead and write-behind done.

In some cases, you may want to reduce write-behind client requests because the network interface of the NFS server cannot handle that many NFS write requests at once, such as when you have the NFS client and NFS server on opposite sides of a 56-kbs connection. In these radical cases, adequate performance can be achieved by reducing the number of NFS async threads. Normally, an NFS async thread does write-behind caching to improve NFS performance, and running multiple NFS async threads allows a single process to have several write requests outstanding at once. If you are running eight NFS async threads on an NFS client, then the client will generate eight NFS *write* requests at once when it is performing a sequential write to a large file. The eight requests are handled by the NFS async threads. In contrast to the *biod* mechanism, when a Solaris process issues a new write requests while all the NFS async threads are blocked waiting for a reply from the server, the write request is queued in the kernel and the requesting process returns successfully without blocking. The requesting process does not issue an RPC to the NFS server itself, only the NFS async threads do. When an NFS async thread RPC call completes, it proceeds to grab the next request from the queue and sends a new RPC to the server.

It may be necessary to reduce the number of NFS requests if a server cannot keep pace with the incoming NFS *write* requests. Reducing the number of NFS async threads accomplishes this; the kernel RPC mechanism continues to work without the async threads, albeit less efficiently.

Attribute caching

NFS clients cache file attributes such as the modification time and owner to avoid having to go to the NFS server for information that does not change frequently. The motivations for an attribute caching scheme are explained in "File attribute caching" in Chapter 7. Once a *getattr* for a filehandle has been completed, the information is cached for use by other requests. Cached data is updated in subsequent write operations; the cache is flushed when the lifetime of the data expires. Repeated attribute changes caused by write operations can be handled entirely on the client side, with the net result written back to the server in a single *setattr*. Note that explicit *setattr* operations, generated by a *chmod* command on the client, are not cached at all on the client. Only file size and modification time changes are cached.

The lifetime of the cached data is determined by four mount parameters shown in Table 18-3.

Table 18-3. Attribute cache parameters

Parameter	Default (seconds)	Cache Limit
acregmin	3	Minimum lifetime for file attributes
acregmax	60	Maximum lifetime for file attributes
acdirmin	30	Minimum lifetime for directory attributes
acdirmax	60	Maximum lifetime for directory attributes

The default values again vary by vendor, as does the accessibility of the attribute cache parameters. The minimum lifetimes set the time period for which a size/modification time update will be cached locally on the client. Attribute changes are written out at the end of the maximum period to avoid having the client and server views of the files drift too far apart. In addition, changing the file attributes on the server makes those changes visible to other clients referencing the same file (when their attribute caches time out).

Attribute caching can be turned off with the *noac* mount option:

```
# mount -o noac mahimahi:/export/tools /mnt
```

Without caching enabled, every operation requiring access to the file attributes must make a call to the server. This won't disable read caching (in either NFS async threads or the VM system), but it adds to the cost of maintaining cache consistency. The NFS async threads and the VM system still perform regular cache consistency checks by requesting file attributes, but each consistency check now requires a *getattr* RPC on the NFS server. When many clients have attribute caching disabled, the server's *getattr* count skyrockets:

```
% nfsstat -ns
Server nfs:
calls       badcalls
221628      769
Version 2: (774 calls)
null        getattr     setattr     root        lookup      readlink
8 1%        0 0%        0 0%        0 0%        762 98%     0 0%
read        wrcache     write       create      remove      rename
0 0%        0 0%        0 0%        0 0%        0 0%        0 0%
link        symlink     mkdir       rmdir       readdir     statfs
0 0%        0 0%        0 0%        0 0%        0 0%        4 0%
Version 3: (219984 calls)
null        getattr     setattr     lookup      access      readlink
1173 0%     119692 54%  4283 1%     31493 14%   26622 12%   103 0%
read        write       create      mkdir       symlink     mknod
11606 5%    7618 3%     1892 0%     64 0%       37 0%       0 0%
remove      rmdir       rename      link        readdir     readdirplus
3183 1%     2 0%        458 0%      1295 0%     156 0%      1138 0%
fsstat      fsinfo      pathconf    commit
7076 3%     311 0%      78 0%       1704 0%
```

Upwards of 60% of the NFS calls handled by the server may be requests to return file or directory attributes.

If changes made by one client need to be reflected on other clients with finer granularity, the attribute cache lifetime can be reduced to one second using the *actimeo* option, which sets both the regular file and directory minimum and maximum lifetimes to the same value:

```
# mount -o actimeo=1 mahimahi:/export/tools /mnt
```

This has the same effect as:

```
# mount -o acregmin=1,acregmax=1,acdirmin=1,acdirmax=1 \
    mahimahi:/export/tools /mnt
```

Mount point constructions

The choice of a mount point naming scheme can have a significant impact on NFS server usage. Two common but inefficient constructions are stepping-stone mounts and server-resident symbolic links. In each case, the client must first query the NFS server owning the intermediate mount point (or symbolic link) before directing a request to the correct target server.

A stepping-stone mount exists when you mount one NFS filesystem on top of another directory, which is itself part of an NFS-mounted filesystem from a different server. For example:

```
# mount mahimahi:/usr           /usr
# mount wahoo:/usr/local        /usr/local
# mount poi:/usr/local/bin      /usr/local/bin
```

To perform a name lookup on */usr/local/bin/emacs*, the NFS client performs directory searches and file attribute queries on all three NFS servers, when the only "interesting" server is *poi*. It's best to mount all of the subdirectories of */usr* and */usr/local* from a single fileserver, so that you don't send RPC requests to other fileservers simply because they own the intermediate components in the pathname. Stepping-stone mounts are frequently created for consistent naming schemes, but they add to the load of "small" RPC calls handled by all NFS servers.

Symbolic links are also useful for imposing symmetric naming conventions across multiple filesystems but they impose an unnecessary load on an NFS server that is regularly called upon to resolve the links (if the NFS client does not perform symbolic link caching). NFS pathnames are resolved a component at a time, so any symbolic links encountered in a pathname must be resolved by the host owning them.

For example, consider a */usr/local* that is composed of links to various subdirectories on other servers:

```
# mount wahoo:/usr/local /usr/local
# cd /usr/local
# ls -1
lrwxrwxrwx 1 root 16 May 17 19:12 bin -> /net/poi/bin
lrwxrwxrwx 1 root 16 May 17 19:12 lib -> /net/mahimahi/lib
lrwxrwxrwx 1 root 16 May 17 19:12 man -> /net/irie/man
```

Each reference to any file in */usr/local* must first go through the server *wahoo* to get the appropriate symbolic link resolved. Once the link is read, the client machine can then look up the directory entry in the correct subdirectory of */net*. Every request that requires looking up a pathname now requires two server requests instead of just one. Solaris, as well as other modern NFS implementations reduce this penalty by caching symbolic links. This helps the client avoid unnecessary trips to the intermediate server to resolve readlink requests.

Use *nfsstat -s* to examine the number of symbolic link resolutions performed on each server:

```
% nfsstat -ns
Server nfs:
calls        badcalls
221628       769
Version 2: (774 calls)
null         getattr      setattr       root          lookup        readlink
8 1%         0 0%         0 0%          0 0%          762 98%       0 0%
read         wrcache      write         create        remove        rename
0 0%         0 0%         0 0%          0 0%          0 0%          0 0%
link         symlink      mkdir         rmdir         readdir       statfs
0 0%         0 0%         0 0%          0 0%          0 0%          4 0%
Version 3: (219984 calls)
null         getattr      setattr       lookup        access        readlink
1023 0%      73495 33%    4383 1%       31493 14%     26672 12%     46299 21%
read         write        create        mkdir         symlink       mknod
11606 5%     7618 3%      1892 0%       64 0%         37 0%         0 0%
remove       rmdir        rename        link          readdir       readdirplus
3183 1%      5 0%         308 0%        1145 0%       456 0%        1138 0%
fsstat       fsinfo       pathconf      commit
7076 3%      109 0%       178 0%        1804 0%
```

If the total percentage of *readlink* calls is more than 10% of the total number of *lookup* calls on all NFS servers, there is a symbolic link fairly high up in a frequently traversed path component. You should look at the total number of *lookup* and *readlink* calls on all servers, since the *readlink* is counted by the server that owns the link while the *lookup* is directed to the target of the symbolic link.

If you have one or more symbolic links that are creating a pathname lookup bottleneck on the server, remove the links (on the server) and replace them with a client-side NFS mount of the link's target. In the previous example, mounting the */net* subdirectories directly in */usr/local* would cut the number of */usr/local*-related operations in half. The performance improvement derived from this change may be substantial when symbolic links are not cached, since every *readlink* call requires the server to read the link from disk. Stepping-stone mounts, although far from ideal, are faster than an equivalent configuration built from symbolic links when the clients do not cache symbolic link lookups.

Most filesystem naming problems can be resolved more easily and with far fewer performance penalties by using the automounter, as described in Chapter 9.

Stale filehandles

A filehandle becomes stale whenever the file or directory referenced by the handle is removed by another host, while your client still holds an active reference to the object. A typical example occurs when the current directory of a process, running on your client, is removed on the server (either by a process running on the server

or on another client). For example, the following sequence of operations produces a stale filehandle error for the current directory of the process running on
client1:

```
client1                    client2 or server
% cd /shared/mod1
                           % cd /shared
                           % rm -rf mod1
% ls
.: Stale File Handle
```

It is important to note that recreating the removed directory before *client1* lists the
directory would not have prevented the stale filehandle problem:

```
client1                    client2 or server
% cd /shared/mod1
                           % cd /shared
                           % rm -rf mod1
                           % mkdir mod1
% ls
.: Stale File Handle
```

This occurs because the client filehandle is tied to the inode number and generation count of the file or directory. Removing and recreating the directory *mod1*
results in the creation of a new directory entry with the same name as before but
with a different inode number and generation count (and consequently a different
filehandle). This explains why clients get stale filehandle errors when files or
directories on the server are moved to a different filesystem. Be careful when you
perform filesystem maintenance on the NFS server. Unfortunately you cannot bring
a server down, move files to a new filesystem (perhaps to a larger disk), and
reshare the new filesystem without risking your clients getting stale filehandles.
Moving the files to a new filesystem on the server results in new inode numbers
and generation counts for the files since inode numbers are not preserved across
filesystem moves. If your client gets stale filehandles, then you may need to terminate all processes accessing the filesystem on the client, and unmount the NFS filesystem in order to clear the large number of stale filehandles. Unfortunately,
identifying all the processes that hold a filesystem busy is not always feasible, in
which case you may have to resort to forcibly unmounting the filesystem:

```
# umount -f /shared
```

Specify the *-f* option to the *umount** command to forcibly unmount a filesystem.
This should be done only as a last resort, since using this option can cause data
loss for open files.

---

* The ability to forcibly unmount a filesystem was introduced in Solaris 8. This feature is supported by
  the Linux kernel 2.1.116 or later. Previously, you would have had to reboot the NFS client to clear the
  stale filehandles.

You will also get stale filehandle errors when the server or another client removes a file that your client currently has open:

```
Process A on client1              client2 or server
...
fd = open("/shared/foo", O_RDONLY);
                                  % rm /shared/foo
read(fd, &buffer, buffer_len);
Read fails! Stale File Handle
```

If you consistently suffer from stale filehandle errors, you should look at the way in which users share files using NFS. Even though users see the same set of files, they do not necessarily have to do their work in the same directories. Watch out for users who share directories or copies of code. Use a source code control system that lets them make private copies of source files in their own directories. NFS provides an excellent mechanism for allowing all users to see the common source tree, but nobody should be doing development in it. Similarly, users who share scratch space may decide to clean it out periodically. Any user who had a scratch file open when another user on another NFS client purged the scratch directory will receive stale filehandle errors on the next reference to the (now removed) scratch file.

As with most things, it helps to have an understanding of how your users are using the filesystems presented to them by NFS. In many cases, users want access to a wide variety of filesystems, but they do not want all of them mounted at all times (for fear of server crashes), nor do they want to keep track of where all filesystems are exported from and where they should be mounted. The NFS automounter solves all of these problems by applying NIS management to NFS mount information. As part of your client tuning, consider using the automounter to make client NFS administration easier. Chapter 9 describes the automounter in detail.

A

IP Packet Routing

Routers and gateways join multiple IP networks, forwarding packets between the networks. A single organization may have multiple IP networks because it has multiple buildings, multiple sites, or multiple subgroups that require their own networks. For example, the history and math departments at a university are likely to each have their own IP networks, just as an engineering and manufacturing facility separated by several miles will have independent networks. "Network partitioning hardware" in Chapter 17 discussed network partitioning using routers, and some of the performance considerations when running NFS and NIS in an internetworked environment. This appendix explores the mechanics of IP packet routing in greater detail.

Routers and their routing tables

A router has a unique IP address on each network interface; associated with each IP address is also a unique hostname. A common convention is to add a suffix associated with the network number to the name of the host used on the each network interface as shown in this */etc/hosts* fragment:[*]

```
#
# local network hosts
#
192.9.200.1     fred fred-200
```

---

[*] Of course, identifying a host's interfaces in */etc/hosts* is not sufficient if you are using DNS. An excellent treatment of how to set up multiple interfaces for a host in DNS is discussed on the Web in the document "Frequently Asked Questions about Kerberos" by Ken Hornstein, available (at the time this book was written) at *http://www.nrl.navy.mil/CCS/people/kenh/kerberos-faq.html*. Look for the section entitled "How should I configure my DNS for Kerberos?" Even if you are not using Kerberos, Hornstein's recommendation for "multiple address records per host" is a logical way to configure multiple interfaces in DNS, because his choice associates a single name, such as *fred.widget.com*, with multiple interface specific names, such as *fred-200.widget.com* and *fred-201.widget.com*.

```
192.9.200.2      barney
192.9.200.3      wilma
#
# remote network gateway
192.9.201.1      fred-201
```

Host *fred* is on both the 192.9.200.0 and 192.9.201.0 networks, and has a distinct name and address on each. *netstat -i* shows both interfaces and their associated networks and hostnames:

```
% netstat -i
Name  Mtu   Net/Dest       Address      Ipkts   Ierrs Opkts   Oerrs Collis Queue
hem0  1500  192.9.200.0    fred         349175  104   542039  363   816    0
hme1  1500  192.9.201.0    fred-201     108635  1     4020    22    301    0
lo0   8232  loopback       localhost    74347   0     74347   0     0      0
```

To send a packet to another network, the local host needs some picture of the network and its connections to other networks. Ideally, this picture presents other networks as a "black box" outside of some local gateway, rather than an itemization of a route to every host on every attached network. This paradigm is how we view the U.S. Post Office. Once you drop a letter in the mailbox, the route it takes may involve trucks, planes, or people, and the decisions about routing vehicles are left up to the people doing the delivery.

A host's picture of the local network's connections to other IP networks is contained in the kernel's routing table. This table may be modified in three ways:

- Dynamic routing information is sent periodically by routers that advertise themselves using some well-known protocols, and daemons such as *in.routed* send and interpret route announcements and update the routing table.[*]

- Static routing involves hand-crafting a route table. Static routing is typically used when there is only one router on a network, so a single route suffices for all outbound traffic. Client machines often set up static routing to avoid having to listen to the regular route information broadcasts (see "Static routing" later in this appendix).

- Route redirection requests are sent by routers that are asked to forward packets to networks for which the chosen router is not the best choice. These route table updates are sent in *ICMP redirect* messages.

The routing table determines how to get to foreign IP networks. You can examine the current routing table using *netstat -r*:

```
% netstat -r
Routing tables
```

---

[*] The protocol used by *in.routed* is called RIP, for Routing Information Protocol. There are other routing protocols that send less information or that allow hosts to perform preferential routing when multiple gateways are present, but a discussion of these protocols is beyond the scope of this book.

Destination	Gateway	Flags	Refcnt	Use	Interface
131.40.191.1	gatehost	UGH	0	0	hme0
131.40.56.0	gatehost	UG	0	0	hme0
131.40.208.0	gatehost2	UGD	0	0	hme0
131.40.52.0	wahoo	U	60	80770	hme0
localhost	localhost	UH	4	4767	lo0
default	gatehost	UG	0	0	hme0

The term "gateway" is used somewhat improperly in both *netstat -r* and the following discussion. A gateway performs services at the application layer in the protocol stack, while a router is concerned only with the IP layer. The routing tables show IP routes, and titling the *Gateway* column *Router* instead would be more correct. However, many people associate *Router* with a dedicated IP router, so the less specific term *Gateway* is used.

The information in the routing table determines how to get to a particular remote host or network, and shows the usage statistics for each route. The destination column shows the remote address; if it is a remote network, the address has a .0 suffix to indicate that it is a network number.* Note that you can get to multiple networks through a single gateway. The gateway listed in the routing tables is just the first step that must be taken to reach the remote network; additional routing information on the first gateway directs a packet to another gateway if required.

The *Flags* column describes the gateway:

U

The gateway is up. If this flag appears in *netstat -r*, the gateway is probably up.

G

To get to the destination address, packets must go through a gateway. The gateway's name is in the second column.

H

The gateway is a "host gateway" and is directly connected to the network listed as the destination. In the first line of the routing table in the previous example, destination 131.40.191.1 is the IP address of *gatehost*, the gateway referenced in several other route table entries. Host gateways are always listed with their full IP addresses as the destination and are generally at the far end of a point-to-point link.

D

The route was added after receiving an ICMP redirect message. The local host probably sent a packet to some other router, such as *gatehost*, with a

---

* Of course, if you are using classless IP addressing (see "Classless IP addressing" in Chapter 1), network numbers are likely to not fall in discrete 8-bit widths. Thus in a classless environment, it would be more precise to say that if the destination is a remote network, the last N bits of the address will be zeroes to indicate that the first 32 − N bits of the address are a network number.

destination network of 131.40.208.0. *gatehost* consulted its routing tables and found that the router to this network was *gatehost2*, and to get to *gatehost2* it had to send the packet back out on the same network interface on which it was received. The IP routing algorithm realizes that it should never have been handed a packet for this network in the first place, so it sends an ICMP redirect message to the originator informing it of a better route to network 131.40.208.0. Using static routes in a network with multiple gateways can lead to a steady stream of ICMP redirect requests unless the transmitting hosts update their route tables. Figure A-1 shows the generation of an ICMP redirect message.

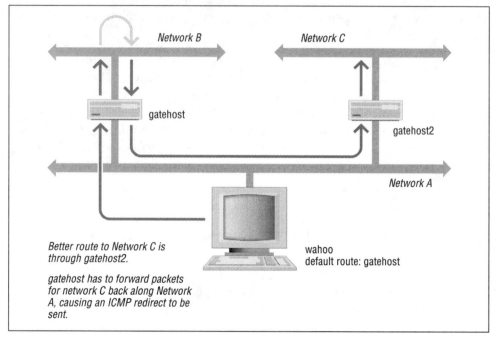

Figure A-1. ICMP redirect generation

The last column in the output of *netstat -r* shows the physical or pseudo device used to reach the gateway. The last three routes deserve some additional explanation. The route with *wahoo* as the gateway describes the local host's connection to the local network. This is known as the interface route of the machine. The next entry shows the loopback device, which is listed as a host gateway. The last line is a *default* routing entry, which is used as a catchall if the destination IP network cannot be matched to any explicit route in the table.

The combination of the flags U, G, and H implies "This host is the gateway to this network": the U flag means the gateway is up, the G flag means the packets must go through a gateway, and the H flag indicates that the remote network is connected to the host listed in the route table. The gateway host has at least one network interface and one or more point-to-point links. A gateway listed with flags U and G has two or more network interfaces and is acting as a routing host. The lack of the H flag means that the remote network isn't attached directly to the gateway; the gateway host listed in the routing table is merely a stepping stone on the way to that remote network.

Armed with the route tables, we can locate the host on our local network that can forward our packets to any destination host. Since we need the MAC address of the destination to send a packet, this presents a problem for the transmitter when the receiver is on another network. How do packets actually get to the remote network?

Let's assume that *wahoo*, at IP address 131.40.52.15, has mounted a filesystem through one or more gateways from the NFS server *bigguy* at IP address 131.40. 208.10. To send a packet to *bigguy*, *wahoo* looks for its IP address in its routing table. It finds it, with *gatehost2* named as the gateway to this network. If the remote IP network was not matched to a destination in the routing tables, the default route, which uses *gatehost*, would be used. *wahoo* sends its packet to *gatehost2*, filling in the MAC address for *gatehost2* but the *IP address* for *bigguy*.

When *gatehost2* receives the packet, it realizes that the IP network in the destination field is not its own. It forwards the packet, using its own routing information to locate a gateway to network 131.40.208.0. *gatehost2* sends the packet to the next gateway, putting in the remote gateway's MAC address but leaving the destination IP address of *bigguy* intact. Eventually, the packet is received by a gateway that is on network 131.40.208.0; this gateway recognizes that its IP network and the destination IP network in the packet are the same, and it sends it along the local area network to *bigguy*. The last gateway to forward the packet is the one that inserts *bigguy*'s MAC address in the packet.

By default, hosts on more than one network are configured as routers in order to forward packets from one interface to another. In some cases, it's desirable to disable automatic IP forwarding, so that the host may communicate on multiple networks but it will not act as a transparent conduit between them. Refer back to the NIS security issues raised in "Making NIS more secure" in Chapter 12. If an NIS client can bind to an NIS server, it can dump the password map from the server. To protect the contents of your password file map, you may want to make it impossible for clients outside the local network to bind to a local NIS server. With IP forwarding enabled, any client can use *ypset* to get to any NIS server, but if IP forwarding is disabled on the host that connects the local network to other networks, *ypset* never makes it beyond this router host. It's also a good idea to disable IP forwarding on machines that join your company network to a larger network such as the Internet. This creates a firewall between your internal networks and the outside world: hosts outside the router cannot get packets into your company networks.

How you disable IP forwarding depends on your system. In Solaris, this is done by creating a special file:

```
# touch /etc/notrouter
```

If the */etc/notrouter file* is present when the system boots, then the system will not perform IP forwarding. If you want to turn off IP forwarding immediately, then do the following:

```
# /usr/sbin/ndd -set /dev/ip ip_forwarding 0
```

Static routing

In an IPv4 network, hosts can dynamically discover the presence of routers by using the ICMP router discovery protocol. Router hosts can run *in.rdisc* in order to advertise themselves through the ICMP router discovery protocol. When a host invokes *in.rdisc* at boot time, it listens on the *224.0.0.1* (ALL_HOSTS) multicast address for router advertisement messages from routers on the network. In turn, router hosts send out advertisement messages to the *224.0.0.1* multicast address advertising all of their IP addresses. Multiple initial advertisement messages are sent out during the first few seconds after the router boots, backing off to transmit advertisement messages approximately once every ten minutes. Optionally, a host can avoid waiting for routers to announce themselves by sending out a few router solicitation messages to the *224.0.0.2* (ALL_ROUTERS) multicast address where routers listen for requests.

If the host does not find a default router, it may choose to start *in.routed* in quiet mode to listen for Router Information Protocol (RIP) advertisements broadcast by router hosts. Router hosts invoke *in.routed* at boot time in order to publish their routing tables using RIP. The route information is broadcast every 30 seconds.

In a small IPv4 network, or one in which there is only one router connecting it to other networks, static routing is preferable to the previously described dynamic routing requiring *rdisc* or *routed*. In a single-outlet network, every route goes through the solitary router, so the entire routing table can be compressed into a default route entry:

```
route add default 131.40.52.14 1
```

The destination is given as *default*, and the gateway address is the IP address or hostname of the router. In Solaris, you can effectively define static routes at boot time by simply creating the */etc/defaultrouter* file on each machine, and putting the name of the default router in this file. If this file exists, the */etc/init.d/inetinit* boot script will read the router name from this file and set up a default route.

Furthermore, if a default route has been established, the */etc/init.d/inetinit* script skips the invocation of *routed* and *rdisc*. You can specify either the IP address or the hostname of the router in */etc/defaultrouter*. If you use the hostname, make sure to also include its IP address mapping in the */etc/hosts* or */etc/inet/ipnodes* file, because no name services are running at the time that the boot script is run.

Note that the IPv6 protocol is designed to be dynamic in nature, therefore IPv6 heavily relies on router discovery. For Solaris hosts, *in.ndpd* is the only mechanism available to discover IPv6 routers. *in.ndpd* sends router solicitation messages and uses the router advertisement messages it receives to autoconfigure the IPv6 host. Although nothing in the IPv6 protocol precludes static routes from being defined, Solaris has chosen not to implement a mechanism to define static routes for IPv6.

B

NFS Problem
Diagnosis

Throughout this book, we've used the output of *nfsstat* on both NFS clients and servers to locate performance bottlenecks or inefficient NFS architectures. The first two sections in this appendix summarize symptoms of problems identified from the output of *nfsstat*. The last list contains typical values for the error variable *errno* that may be returned by file operations on NFS-mounted filesystems.

NFS server problems

Check the output of *nfsstat -s* for the following problems:

badcalls > 0

> RPC requests are being rejected out of hand by the NFS server. This could indicate authentication problems caused by having a user in too many groups, attempts to access exported filesystems as *root*, or an improper Secure RPC configuration.

badlen > 0 or xdrcall > 0

> This indicates a malformed NFS request, detected by RPC or XDR protocol decoding on the server. This can be caused by bugs in the client or server, or by physical network problems.

dupreqs > 0

> The duplicate request cache keeps a record of previously executed NFS requests. The *dupchecks* counter tracks the number of times this cache was consulted, or *checked*. The *dupreqs* counter tracks the number of times a check of the cache had a "hit." In other words, *dupreqs* counts the number of times the NFS server received a previously executed request. For connection-oriented (TCP) requests, a high ratio of *dupreqs* to *dupchecks* is 0.01%. For

connectionless (UDP) requests, a high ratio of *dupreqs* to *dupchecks* is one percent. High ratios indicate one of three problems:

— The timeout set on one or more clients' NFS mounts is too low. Adjust the *timeo* option in the automounter map or the NFS *mount* command upward.

— The server is not responding quickly enough. There could be lots of reasons for this having to do with physical capabilities of the server: processor speed, numbers of processors (if it is a multiprocessor), not enough primary memory (check if the percentage of reads is high, say over 5%; this would indicate lots of reads that would be best served from cache if there was enough memory), numbers of disk drives on the system (spreading more data accesses across more spindles reduces response time; if you've eliminated primary memory as a cause, check if the percentage of writes is high, say over 5%), etc. Other possibilities extend to artificial limits, such as the number of server threads set via *nfsd*.

— There is a routing problem impeding replies from the server to one or more clients.

readlink > 10%
Clients are making excessive use of symbolic links that are on filesystems exported by the server. If the link is to a directory, replace the symbolic link with a directory, and mount both the underlying filesystem and the link's target on the client. If the link is to a file, replace the symbolic link with a hard link.

getattr > 60%
Check for possible non-default attribute cache values on NFS clients. A very high percentage of *getattr* requests may indicate that the attribute cache window has been reduced or set to zero with the *actimeo* or *noac* mount option. It can also indicate that the NFS filesystem implementation is doing a poor job of attribute caching.

null > 1%
The automounter has been configured to mount replicated filesystems, but the timeout values for the mount are too short. The null procedure calls are made by the automounter to locate a server for the filesystem; too many *null* calls indicates that the automounter is retrying the mount frequently. Increase the mount timeout parameter on the automounter command line.

fsinfo > 1%
This is typically used only on mounts. Lots of *fsinfo* calls suggests that the automounter is frequently mounting and unmounting the same filesystems. If

so, tune the automounter to hold mounts longer via the *-t* option to *auto-mount*. This will improve the response time on clients.

Keep in mind that the percentages of each operation type used are only general rules of thumb. Your site may have legitimate reasons for percentages that go outside the rule of thumb.

NFS client problems

Using the output of *nfsstat -c*, look for the following symptoms:

timeout > 5%

The client's RPC requests are timing out before the server can answer them, or the requests are not reaching the server. Check *badxids* to determine the cause of the timeouts.

badxids ~ timeout

RPC requests that have been retransmitted are being handled by the server, and the client is receiving duplicate replies. Increase the *timeo* parameter for this NFS mount to alleviate the request retransmission, or tune the server to reduce the average request service time.

badxids ~ 0

With a large *timeout* count, this indicates that the network is dropping parts of NFS requests or replies in between the NFS client and server. Reduce the NFS buffer size using the *rsize* and *wsize* mount parameters to increase the probability that NFS buffers will transit the network intact.

badcalls > 0

RPC calls on soft-mounted filesystems are timing out. If a server has crashed, then *badcalls* can be expected to increase. But if *badcalls* grows during "normal" operation then soft-mounted filesystems should use a larger *timeo* or *retrans* value to prevent RPC failures. Better yet, mount the filesystem without the *soft* option.

cantconn > 1%

This indicates that the NFS client is having trouble making a TCP connection to the NFS server. Often this is because the NFS server has been or is down. It can also indicate that the connection queue length in the NFS server is too small, or that an attacker is attempting a denial of service attack on the server by clogging the connection queue. If you cannot eliminate connection queue length as a problem, then use the *-l* parameter to *nfsd* to increase the queue length.

NFS errno values

The following system call *errno* values are the result of various NFS call failures:

EINTR

A system call was interrupted when the *intr* option was used on a hard-mounted filesystem.

EACCES

A user attempted to access a file without proper credentials. This error is usually caused by mapping *root* or anonymous users to *nobody*, a user that has almost no permissions on files in the exported filesystem.

EBUSY

The superuser attempted to unmount a filesystem that was in use on the NFS client.

ENOSPC

The fileserver has run out of room on the disk to which the client is attempting an NFS write operation.

ESTALE

An NFS client has asked the server to reference a file that has either been freed or reused by another client.

EREMOTE

An attempt was made to NFS-mount a filesystem that is itself NFS-mounted on the server. Multihop NFS-mounts are not allowed. This error is reported by *mount* on the NFS client.

C

Tunable Parameters

NFS client and server implementations tend to have lots of tunable parameters. This appendix summarizes some of the more important ones. Except as noted, the parameters are tuned by changing a parameter in the kernel, which requires setting a value in a file like */etc/system* on Solaris 8. Note that while many NFS implementations share many of these parameters, the names of the parameters and the methods for setting them will vary between implementations. Table C-1 and Table C-2 summarize client and server tunables.

Table C-1. Client parameters

Parameter	Description	Caveats
clnt_max_conns	This parameter controls the number of connections the client will create between the client and a given server. In Solaris, the default is one. The rationale is that a single TCP connection ought to be sufficient to use the available bandwidth of network channel between the client and server. You may find this to not be the case for network media faster than the traditional 10Base T (10Mb per second). Note that this parameter is not in the Solaris *nfs* module, but it is in the kernel RPC module *rpcmod*.	At the time of this writing, the algorithm used to assign traffic to each connection was a simple round robin approach. You may find diminishing returns if you set this parameter higher than 2. This parameter is highly experimental.

Table C-1. Client parameters (continued)

Parameter	Description	Caveats
clnt_idle_timeout	This parameter sets the number of milliseconds the NFS client will let a connection go idle before closing it. This parameter applies to NFS/TCP connections and is set in the Solaris kernel RPC module called *rpcmod*.	Normally this parameter should be a minute below the lowest server-side idle timeout among all the servers that you connect your client to. Otherwise, you may observe clients sending requests simultaneous with the server tearing down connections. This will result in an unnecessary sequence of connection tear down, followed immediately by connection setup.
nfs_max_threads (NFS Version 2) *nfs3_max_threads* (NFS Version 3)	Sets the number of background read-ahead and write-behind threads on a per NFS-mounted filesystem basis, for NFS Version 2 and Version 3. Read-ahead is a performance win when applications do mostly sequential reads. The NFS filesystem can thus anticipate what the application wants, and so when it performs the next *read()* system call, the required data will already be in the client's cache. Write-behind is a performance win, because the NFS client must synchronize dirty data to the server before the application closes the file. A sequential write pattern is not necessary to leverage the benefits of multiple write-behind threads.	Setting too many of these threads has the following risks: • If there are lots of mounted filesystems, consuming kernel memory for lots of threads could degrade system performance. • If the network link or the NFS server is slow, the network can become saturated.
nfs3_max_transfer_size	Controls the default I/O transfer size for NFS Version 3 mounts.	Given that UDP datagrams are limited to a maximum of 64 KB, adjusting this value beyond its default is dangerous. If you do raise it from its default (32 KB for Solaris, at the time of this writing), make sure that you specify the use of the TCP protocol for all NFS mounts.

Table C-1. Client parameters (continued)

Parameter	Description	Caveats
nfs_nra (NFS Version 2) *nfs3_nra* (NFS Version 3)	Controls the number of blocks the NFS filesystem will read ahead at a time once it detects a sequential read pattern.	This is a parameter that can have diminishing returns if set too high. Not only will sequential read performance not improve, but the increased memory use by the client will ultimately degrade overall performance of the system. If the read pattern is dominated by random and not sequential reads (as might be the case when reading indexed files), setting this tunable to 0 (zero) might be a win.
nfs_shrinkreaddir	This is a parameter that is for enhancing interoperability. Many NFS implementations were based on early source code from Sun Microsystems. This code reads directories in buffers that were much smaller (1038 bytes) than the maximum transfer size. Later, when Sun changed Solaris NFS clients to read directories using maximum transfer sizes, it was found that some servers could not cope. Set this parameter to 1 to force 1038-byte directory read transfers.	
nfs_write_error_ to_cons_only	Controls whether NFS write errors are logged to the system console only, or to the console and *syslog*. By default, errors are logged to both the console and *syslog*.	This is a security issue. The *syslog* setup usually logs errors to a file that is globally readable in */var/adm* directory. Write errors often include the file handle of the file on which the error was encountered. If the file handle can be easily obtained, it is easier for attackers to attack the NFS server, since they can bypass the NFS filesystem to mount such attacks.

Table C-1. Client parameters (continued)

Parameter	Description	Caveats
rsize *wsize*	These are suboptions to the NFS mount command that change read and write transfer block sizes, respectively.	For NFS Version 2 mounts, the maximum is limited to 8KB, per the NFS Version 2 protocol definition.
		For NFS Version 3 mounts, the same caveats for the *nfs3_max_ transfer_size* parameter apply.
-t timeout	This is an option to the *auto-mount* command that sets the number of seconds the auto-mounter will wait before attempting to unmount a file-system. Since unmounting a filesystem often forces the pre-mature flushing of buffers and release of performance enhanc-ing caches, higher values of this parameter can have very benefi-cial effects. If your NFS server performs additional functions, like elec-tronic mail, or it allows users to login to run applications, then it is likely your NFS server will be a heavy client of the auto-mounter, even if the filesystems are local to the NFS server. While you are better off making your NFS servers do only NFS service, if you must allow the NFS server to do non-NFS things, you are strongly encour-aged to increase the auto-mounter timeout.	Lowering the timeout from its default value is almost always a bad idea, except when you have lots of unreliable servers or networks. In that case, more frequent unmounting of auto-mounted filesystems might be a net win.

Table C-2. Server Parameters

Parameter	Description	Caveats
nfs_portmon	This parameter controls whether the NFS server will allow requests with a source port less than 1024. Many operating systems use the nonstandard notion of privileged port numbers, which says that only the superuser can create network endpoints bound to a port less than 1024. Many NFS client implementations will bind to ports less than 1024, and many NFS server implementations will refuse NFS accesses if the port is greater than or equal to 1024. By default, Solaris NFS servers do not care if the client's source port is less than 1024. This is because the security benefits are minimal (given that it is trivial to bind to ports less than 1024 on many non-Unix operating systems).	If you set this parameter to 1 to enable NFS port checking, you may find that some NFS clients cannot access your server.
svc_idle_timeout	This parameter sets the number of milliseconds the NFS server will let a connection go idle before closing it. This parameter applies to NFS/TCP connections and is set in the Solaris kernel RPC module called *rpcmod*.	Normally this parameter should be a minute beyond the highest client-side idle timeout among all the clients that connect to your server. Otherwise, you may observe clients sending requests simultaneous with the server tearing down connections. This will result in an unnecessary sequence of connection teardown, followed immediately by connection setup.

Table C-2. Server Parameters (continued)

Parameter	Description	Caveats
nservers	This is an integer argument to the *nfsd* command. It defines the number of NFS server threads or processes that will be available to service NFS requests.	On some non-Solaris implementations, setting *nservers* too high can result in bad performance due to three effects: • The number of server threads or processes is allocated up front, taking up lots of precious kernel memory that might not be needed if the server load is minimal. This is not a problem on Solaris since threads are allocated on demand and released when demand ebbs. • The thundering herd problem exists, which results when there are lots of threads, and every time a request arrives, all the idle threads, instead of just one idle thread, are dispatched. If the load is moderate, many CPU cycles can be wasted, as the majority of the threads wake up, find there is nothing to do, and then go back to sleep. This is not a problem under Solaris because only one thread at a time is dispatched when a request arrives. • The Robinson Factor[a] is the final effect. Consider the situation when there are threads doing NFS work, but some are idle. By the time an idle thread is dispatched, an active thread has picked up the request, thus wasting a dispatch of the idle thread. This is not a problem with Solaris.

[a] The Robinson Factor is named after David Robinson, the engineer at Sun Microsystems who observed the issue in Sun's NFS server, and fixed it.

Index

We'd like to hear your suggestions for improving our indexes. Send email to *index@oreilly.com*.

About the Authors

Hal Stern is the Chief Technology Officer of iPlanet ecommerce solutions, a Sun/Netscape Alliance. He has previously been the Chief Technologist for the Northeast U.S. at Sun, and worked in various systems engineering and consulting roles. Hal has also developed molecular modeling software for a startup company and was on the research staff at Princeton University. Hal was the system administration columnist for *SunWorld* magazine for five years and was on the editorial and advisory boards of *JavaWorld* magazine. Hal lives in Livingston, NJ with his wife, Toby, and their two children. In addition to the usual work-related golf outings, Hal enjoys ice hockey, 1970s art rock bands, and collecting arcana from Gerry Anderson science fiction TV shows.

Mike Eisler graduated from the University of Central Florida with a Master's degree in Computer Science in 1985. His first exposure to NFS and NIS came while working for Lachman Associates, Inc. He was responsible for porting NFS and NIS to System V platforms. He later joined Sun Microsystems, Inc. as a member of the Solaris Network Technology group, responsible for projects such as NFS server performance, NFS/TCP, WebNFS, NFS secured with Kerberos V5, and NFS Version 4. He later moved to Sun's Java Customer Engineering group, working with JavaCard technology. Mike has authored or co-authored several Requests For Comments documents for the Internet Engineering Task Force, relating to NFS and security. He is currently a Distinguished Software Engineer for Zambeel, Inc., and can be reached at *mike@eisler.com*.

Ricardo Labiaga is a staff engineer at Sun Microsystems, Inc., where he concentrates on networking and wireless technologies. Ricardo spent eight years in the Solaris NFS group at Sun, where he worked on a variety of development projects with a primary focus on automounting and the NFS server. Ricardo is responsible for implementing significant functionality and performance enhancements to the automounter, as well as leading the NFS Server Logging design team. He holds a Master of Science degree in computer engineering from The University of Texas at El Paso.

Colophon

Our look is the result of reader comments, our own experimentation, and feedback from distribution channels. Distinctive covers complement our distinctive approach to technical topics, breathing personality and life into potentially dry subjects.

The animals on the cover of *Managing NFS and NIS,* Second Edition, are tree porcupines, a name meaning "pig with spines." Like the guinea pig, the porcupine is not a pig at all, but a rodent. The tree porcupine is native to the eastern United States and northern Canada. In summer, it feeds on green vegetation and the leaves and twigs of deciduous trees; in winter it eats the bark of evergreens. It will frequently chew away a complete ring of bark from around the tree, thereby killing it. As a result of such behavior, the porcupine does millions of dollars of damage annually to the timber industries.

The spines of the tree porcupine are about two inches long, barbed, and tend to be concealed by the animal's long, coarse fur. Contrary to popular belief, the porcupine does not shoot these spines. The spines are loosely attached to the skin, so when the barb on the spine catches on an attacker, the spine will pull loose from the porcupine. Once embedded, spines will tend to work their way further in and have been known to cause death when they puncture internal organs.

Nicole Arigo was the production editor and the copyeditor for *Managing NFS and NIS,* Second Edition. Clairemarie Fisher O'Leary proofread the book. Ann Schirmer, Mary Brady, and Jane Ellin provided quality control. Johnna VanHoose Dinse wrote the index.

Edie Freedman designed the cover of this book. The cover image is a 19th-century engraving from the Dover Pictorial Archive. Emma Colby produced the cover layout with QuarkXPress 4.1 using Adobe's ITC Garamond font.

Melanie Wang designed the interior layout based on a series design by Nancy Priest. Anne-Marie Vaduva converted the files from Microsoft Word to FrameMaker 5.5.6 using tools created by Mike Sierra. The text and heading fonts are ITC Garamond Light and Garamond Book; the code font is Constant Willison. The illustrations that appear in the book were produced by Robert Romano and Jessamyn Read using Macromedia FreeHand 9 and Adobe Photoshop 6.

Whenever possible, our books use a durable and flexible lay-flat binding. If the page count exceeds this binding's limit, perfect binding is used.

How to stay in touch with O'Reilly

1. Visit Our Award-Winning Web Site

http://www.oreilly.com/

★ "Top 100 Sites on the Web" —*PC Magazine*
★ "Top 5% Web sites" —*Point Communications*
★ "3-Star site" —*The McKinley Group*

Our web site contains a library of comprehensive product information (including book excerpts and tables of contents), downloadable software, background articles, interviews with technology leaders, links to relevant sites, book cover art, and more. File us in your Bookmarks or Hotlist!

2. Join Our Email Mailing Lists

New Product Releases
To receive automatic email with brief descriptions of all new O'Reilly products as they are released, send email to:
ora-news-subscribe@lists.oreilly.com
Put the following information in the first line of your message (*not* in the Subject field):
subscribe ora-news

O'Reilly Events
If you'd also like us to send information about trade show events, special promotions, and other O'Reilly events, send email to:
ora-news-subscribe@lists.oreilly.com
Put the following information in the first line of your message (*not* in the Subject field):
subscribe ora-events

3. Get Examples from Our Books via FTP

There are two ways to access an archive of example files from our books:

Regular FTP
*   ftp to:
    ftp.oreilly.com
    (login: anonymous
    password: your email address)
*   Point your web browser to:
    ftp://ftp.oreilly.com/

FTPMAIL
*   Send an email message to:
    ftpmail@online.oreilly.com
    (Write "help" in the message body)

4. Contact Us via Email

order@oreilly.com
To place a book or software order online. Good for North American and international customers.

subscriptions@oreilly.com
To place an order for any of our newsletters or periodicals.

books@oreilly.com
General questions about any of our books.

software@oreilly.com
For general questions and product information about our software. Check out O'Reilly Software Online at **http://software.oreilly.com/** for software and technical support information. Registered O'Reilly software users send your questions to: **website-support@oreilly.com**

cs@oreilly.com
For answers to problems regarding your order or our products.

booktech@oreilly.com
For book content technical questions or corrections.

proposals@oreilly.com
To submit new book or software proposals to our editors and product managers.

international@oreilly.com
For information about our international distributors or translation queries. For a list of our distributors outside of North America check out:
http://www.oreilly.com/distributors.html

5. Work with Us

Check out our website for current employment opportunites:
http://jobs.oreilly.com/

O'Reilly & Associates, Inc.
101 Morris Street, Sebastopol, CA 95472 USA
TEL   707-829-0515 or 800-998-9938
          (6am to 5pm PST)
FAX   707-829-0104

O'REILLY®

International Distributors

UK, EUROPE, MIDDLE EAST AND AFRICA (EXCEPT FRANCE, GERMANY, AUSTRIA, SWITZERLAND, LUXEMBOURG, AND LIECHTENSTEIN)

INQUIRIES
O'Reilly UK Limited
4 Castle Street
Farnham
Surrey, GU9 7HS
United Kingdom
Telephone: 44-1252-711776
Fax: 44-1252-734211
Email: information@oreilly.co.uk

ORDERS
Wiley Distribution Services Ltd.
1 Oldlands Way
Bognor Regis
West Sussex PO22 9SA
United Kingdom
Telephone: 44-1243-843294
UK Freephone: 0800-243207
Fax: 44-1243-843302 (Europe/EU orders)
or 44-1243-843274 (Middle East/Africa)
Email: cs-books@wiley.co.uk

FRANCE

INQUIRIES & ORDERS
Éditions O'Reilly
18 rue Séguier
75006 Paris, France
Tel: 1-40-51-71-89
Fax: 1-40-51-72-26
Email: france@oreilly.fr

GERMANY, SWITZERLAND, AUSTRIA, LUXEMBOURG, AND LIECHTENSTEIN

INQUIRIES & ORDERS
O'Reilly Verlag
Balthasarstr. 81
D-50670 Köln, Germany
Telephone: 49-221-973160-91
Fax: 49-221-973160-8
Email: anfragen@oreilly.de (inquiries)
Email: order@oreilly.de (orders)

CANADA (FRENCH LANGUAGE BOOKS)
Les Éditions Flammarion ltée
375, Avenue Laurier Ouest
Montréal (Québec) H2V 2K3
Tel: 00-1-514-277-8807
Fax: 00-1-514-278-2085
Email: info@flammarion.qc.ca

HONG KONG
City Discount Subscription Service, Ltd.
Unit A, 6th Floor, Yan's Tower
27 Wong Chuk Hang Road
Aberdeen, Hong Kong
Tel: 852-2580-3539
Fax: 852-2580-6463
Email: citydis@ppn.com.hk

KOREA
Hanbit Media, Inc.
Chungmu Bldg. 210
Yonnam-dong 568-33
Mapo-gu
Seoul, Korea
Tel: 822-325-0397
Fax: 822-325-9697
Email: hant93@chollian.dacom.co.kr

PHILIPPINES
Global Publishing
G/F Benavides Garden
1186 Benavides Street
Manila, Philippines
Tel: 632-254-8949/632-252-2582
Fax: 632-734-5060/632-252-2733
Email: globalp@pacific.net.ph

TAIWAN
O'Reilly Taiwan
1st Floor, No. 21, Lane 295
Section 1, Fu-Shing South Road
Taipei, 106 Taiwan
Tel: 886-2-27099669
Fax: 886-2-27038802
Email: mori@oreilly.com

INDIA
Shroff Publishers & Distributors Pvt. Ltd.
12, "Roseland", 2nd Floor
180, Waterfield Road, Bandra (West)
Mumbai 400 050
Tel: 91-22-641-1800/643-9910
Fax: 91-22-643-2422
Email: spd@vsnl.com

CHINA
O'Reilly Beijing
SIGMA Building, Suite B809
No. 49 Zhichun Road
Haidian District
Beijing, China PR 100080
Tel: 86-10-8809-7475
Fax: 86-10-8809-7463
Email: beijing@oreilly.com

JAPAN
O'Reilly Japan, Inc.
Yotsuya Y's Building
7 Banch 6, Honshio-cho
Shinjuku-ku
Tokyo 160-0003 Japan
Tel: 81-3-3356-5227
Fax: 81-3-3356-5261
Email: japan@oreilly.com

SINGAPORE, INDONESIA, MALAYSIA AND THAILAND
TransQuest Publishers Pte Ltd
30 Old Toh Tuck Road #05-02
Sembawang Kimtrans Logistics Centre
Singapore 597654
Tel: 65-4623112
Fax: 65-4625761
Email: wendiw@transquest.com.sg

ALL OTHER ASIAN COUNTRIES
O'Reilly & Associates, Inc.
101 Morris Street
Sebastopol, CA 95472 USA
Tel: 707-829-0515
Fax: 707-829-0104
Email: order@oreilly.com

AUSTRALIA
Woodslane Pty., Ltd.
7/5 Vuko Place
Warriewood NSW 2102
Australia
Tel: 61-2-9970-5111
Fax: 61-2-9970-5002
Email: info@woodslane.com.au

NEW ZEALAND
Woodslane New Zealand, Ltd.
21 Cooks Street (P.O. Box 575)
Waganui, New Zealand
Tel: 64-6-347-6543
Fax: 64-6-345-4840
Email: info@woodslane.com.au

ARGENTINA
Distribuidora Cuspide
Suipacha 764
1008 Buenos Aires
Argentina
Phone: 5411-4322-8868
Fax: 5411-4322-3456
Email: libros@cuspide.com

O'REILLY®

TO ORDER: **800-998-9938** • **order@oreilly.com** • **http://www.oreilly.com/**
OUR PRODUCTS ARE AVAILABLE AT A BOOKSTORE OR SOFTWARE STORE NEAR YOU.
FOR INFORMATION: **800-998-9938** • **707-829-0515** • **info@oreilly.com**